£60-00
£40-00

PASSIONS AND MORAL PROGRESS IN GRECO-ROMAN THOUGHT

This book contains a collection of essays on the topic of the *pathē* and *prokopē*, or the relationship between the passions and moral advancement in Greek and Roman thought. Recognizing that emotions played a key role in whether individuals lived happily, ancient philosophers extensively discussed the nature of the passions, showing how those who managed their emotions properly made moral progress.

The "passions" refer to those passionate emotions which can turn crucially destructive if left unchecked – for example, unbridled anger, uncontrolled desire, or overwhelming grief. These essays explore the different Greco-Roman perspectives on the passions and moral progress and how they felt best to manage them to preserve and advance their own morality.

More comprehensive and multi-disciplinary than many other books on the subject, this book encompasses philosophy, literature, and religion, containing the efforts of thirteen leading specialists from various fields including classics, ancient philosophy and literature, Hellenistic Judaism, and New Testament scholarship. The contributions are preceded by a full and accessible introduction to the subject by John T. Fitzgerald.

Writers discussed include the Cynics, the Neopythagoreans, Aristotle, Theophrastus, Ovid, Paul, and Clement of Alexandria.

John T. Fitzgerald is Associate Professor of Religious Studies at the University of Miami. His research concentrates on the ways in which Jews and Christians interacted with Greco-Roman culture and appropriated philosophical materials for religious use.

PASSIONS AND MORAL PROGRESS IN GRECO-ROMAN THOUGHT

Edited by

John T. Fitzgerald

LONDON AND NEW YORK

First published 2008
by Routledge
2 Park Square, Milton Park, Abingdon, Oxon OX14 4RN
Simultaneously published in the USA and Canada
by Routledge
270 Madison Ave, New York, NY 10016

*Routledge is an imprint of the Taylor & Francis Group,
an informa business*

© 2008 John T. Fitzgerald for selection and editorial matter;
individual chapters, their contributors

Typeset in Sabon by
Integra Software Services Pvt. Ltd, Pondicherry, India
Printed and bound in Great Britain by
Biddles Ltd, King's Lynn

All rights reserved. No part of this book may be reprinted or
reproduced or utilised in any form or by any electronic,
mechanical, or other means, now known or hereafter
invented, including photocopying and recording, or in any
information storage or retrieval system, without permission in
writing from the publishers.

British Library Cataloguing in Publication Data
A catalogue record for this book is available
from the British Library

Library of Congress Cataloging in Publication Data
Passions and moral progress in Greco-Roman thought / ed[ited
by] John T. Fitzgerald.
   p.   cm.
Includes bibliographical references and index.
1. Philosophy, Ancient. 2. Emotions—History. 3. Ethics—History.
   I. Fitzgerald, John T., 1948–
   B171.P37 2008
   128′.370938—dc22
   2007021588

ISBN10: 0–415–28069–9 (hbk)
ISBN10: 0–203–93612–4 (ebk)

ISBN13: 978–0–415–28069–3 (hbk)
ISBN13: 978–0–203–93612–2 (ebk)

CONTENTS

List of Contributors	vii
Preface	ix
List of Abbreviations	xi

| 1 | The passions and moral progress: an introduction
JOHN T. FITZGERALD | 1 |

PART I
Philosophy — 27

2	Aristotle and Theophrastus on the emotions WILLIAM W. FORTENBAUGH	29
3	The problem of the passions in Cynicism DAVID E. AUNE	48
4	The passions in Neopythagorean writings JOHAN C. THOM	67
5	"Be angry and sin not": Philodemus versus the Stoics on natural bites and natural emotions DAVID ARMSTRONG	79
6	Πάθη and Ἀπάθεια in early Roman empire Stoics EDGAR M. KRENTZ	122
7	Plutarch on moral progress RICHARD A. WRIGHT	136

PART II
Philosophy and literature — 151

| 8 | Passion and progress in Ovid's *Metamorphoses*
S. GEORGIA NUGENT | 153 |

CONTENTS

9   The passions in Galen and the novels of Chariton and Xenophon   175
LOVEDAY C. A. ALEXANDER

PART III
Philosophy and religion   199

10   Philo of Alexandria on the rational and irrational emotions   201
DAVID WINSTON

11   Passions in the Pauline epistles: the current state of research   221
DAVID CHARLES AUNE

12   The logic of action in Paul: how does he differ from the moral philosophers on spiritual and moral progression and regression?   238
TROELS ENGBERG-PEDERSEN

13   Moral progress and divine power in Seneca and Paul   267
JAMES WARE

14   Moral pathology: passions, progress, and protreptic in Clement of Alexandria   284
L. MICHAEL WHITE

Selected Bibliography   322
Index of Ancient Authors and Texts   356
Index of Modern Scholars   386

LIST OF CONTRIBUTORS

Loveday C.A. Alexander is Professor of Biblical Studies at the University of Sheffield, Sheffield, England.

David Armstrong is Professor Emeritus of Classics at The University of Texas at Austin, Austin, Texas.

David Charles Aune is Associate Professor of Religion at Ashland University, Ashland, Ohio.

David E. Aune is Professor of New Testament and Christian Origins at the University of Notre Dame, Notre Dame, Indiana.

Troels Engberg-Pedersen is Professor of New Testament at the Section of Biblical Studies, Faculty of Theology, University of Copenhagen, Copenhagen, Denmark.

John T. Fitzgerald is Associate Professor of Religious Studies at the University of Miami, Coral Gables, Florida.

William W. Fortenbaugh is Professor Emeritus of Classics and Editor of Rutgers University Studies in Classical Humanities at Rutgers University, New Brunswick, New Jersey.

Edgar M. Krentz is Christ Seminary-Seminex Professor of New Testament, Emeritus, at the Lutheran School of Theology at Chicago, Chicago, Illinois.

S. Georgia Nugent is President of Kenyon College, Gambier, Ohio.

Johan C. Thom is Professor of Classics at the University of Stellenbosch, Stellenbosch, South Africa.

James Ware is Associate Professor of Religion at the University of Evansville, Evansville, Indiana.

L. Michael White is R.N. Smith Professor of Classics and Director, Institute

LIST OF CONTRIBUTORS

for the Study of Antiquity and Christian Origins at The University of Texas at Austin, Austin, Texas.

David Winston is Professor Emeritus of Hellenistic and Judaic Studies at the Graduate Theological Union, Berkeley, California.

Richard A. Wright is Assistant Professor of Bible at Oklahoma Christian University, Oklahoma City, Oklahoma.

PREFACE

This volume has its origins in the work of the Hellenistic Moral Philosophy and Early Christianity Section, a program unit of the Society of Biblical Literature. From the outset the group has had an interdisciplinary character, comprising classicists, experts in ancient philosophy, specialists in Hellenistic Judaism, New Testament scholars, and others who are interested in early Christianity and the Greco-Roman world. Over the years we have investigated a number of texts, topics, techniques, and authors, and the results of our research have been published in one translation (Konstan et al. 1998) and in four previous collections of essays (Fitzgerald 1996; 1997; Fitzgerald, Olbricht, and White 2003; Fitzgerald, Obbink, and Holland 2004).

Our interest in the "passions and moral progress" was sparked not only by the widespread current interest in the emotions but also grew out of our work on friendship (*philia*) and frankness of speech (*parrhēsia*). At an early stage in our research we discovered that there was a strong linkage in ancient thought between friendship and frank speech. Whereas the flatterer tended to lavish praise and to avoid criticism in his dealings with his "friends," the true friend was willing to speak frankly to his companion when the latter merited candid criticism and could profit from it. In this regard the passions (*pathē*) were a chief area of concern. Individuals who were given to outbursts of anger, who could not control their desires, or who were paralyzed by grief over the death of a loved one were engaged in conduct that was self-destructive. Genuine friends could not sit idly by and let that happen to a person they cared about (compare the modern American slogan used in efforts to prevent driving while intoxicated: "Friends don't let friends drive drunk"). By speaking candidly to their angry or grieving companions, true friends hoped to persuade such individuals to cease from their ruinous behavior and thereby to improve the quality of their lives. Although those who used frank speech ran the risk of angering their friends and jeopardizing their relationship, their willingness to do so was crucial to their friends fulfilling their potential as people. Without self-control in regard to the passions, there could be no moral or spiritual progress (*prokopē*); indeed, without frank speech, there would only be regress in the moral and spiritual life.

PREFACE

Some of the essays contained in this volume reflect the concerns and insights that led us as a collaborative working group to take up this topic, whereas others are focused on either the passions or moral progress per se. All of the contributors are grateful to Routledge and especially Richard Stoneman for accepting these essays for publication. As the volume's editor, I am also grateful to the contributors for both their patience and their friendly *parrhēsia* while this volume was being prepared. For assistance with the initial copyediting of the manuscript, I am indebted to Robert Maccini.

John T. Fitzgerald

LIST OF ABBREVIATIONS

With some exceptions, the abbreviations used in this volume follow the guidelines of the Society of Biblical Literature as published in *The SBL Handbook of Style* (1999).

Bible Texts And Versions

AV	Authorized Version
HB	Hebrew Bible
JB	Jerusalem Bible
LXX	Septuagint
NAB	New American Bible
NEB	New English Bible
NIV	New International Version
NJPS	*Tanakh: The Holy Scriptures: The New Jewish Publication Society Translation According to the Traditional Hebrew Text*
NT	New Testament
OT	Old Testament
RSV	Revised Standard Version

Primary Sources

Hebrew Bible

Gen	Genesis
Exod	Exodus
Lev	Leviticus
4 Kgdms	4 Kingdoms (LXX) = 2 Kings (HB)
Ps	Psalms
Prov	Proverbs

LIST OF ABBREVIATIONS

Apocryphal/Deuterocanonical Books

4 Macc	4 Maccabees
Wis	Wisdom of Solomon

Old Testament Pseudepigrapha

Ps.-Phocylides	Pseudo-Phocylides, *Sentences*
T. Jos.	Testament of Joseph
T. Reu.	Testament of Reuben

Josephus and Philo

Josephus, *A.J.*	Josephus, *Antiquitates judaicae* (*Jewish Antiquities*)
Philo	
Abr.	*De Abrahamo* (*On the Life of Abraham*)
Agr.	*De agricultura* (*On Agriculture*)
Cher.	*De cherubim* (*On the Cherubim*)
Conf.	*De confusione linguarum* (*On the Confusion of Tongues*)
Congr.	*De congressu eruditionis gratia* (*On the Preliminary Studies*)
Decal.	*De decalogo* (*On the Decalogue*)
Det.	*Quod deterius potiori insidari soleat* (*That the Worse Attacks the Better*)
Deus	*Quod Deus sit immutabilis* (*That God Is Unchangeable*)
Ebr.	*De ebrietate* (*On Drunkenness*)
Fug.	*De fuga et inventione* (*On Flight and Finding*)
Gig.	*De gigantibus* (*On Giants*)
Her.	*Quis rerum divinarum heres sit* (*Who Is the Heir?*)
Leg.	*Legum allegoriae* (*Allegorical Interpretation*)
Migr.	*De migratione Abrahami* (*On the Migration of Abraham*)
Mos.	*De vita Mosis* (*On the Life of Moses*)
Mut.	*De mutatione nominum* (*On the Change of Names*)
Opif.	*De opificio mundi* (*On the Creation of the World*)
Plant.	*De plantatione* (*On Planting*)
Post.	*De posteritate Caini* (*On the Posterity of Cain*)
Praem.	*De praemiis et poenis* (*On Rewards and Punishments*)
Prob.	*Quod omnis probus liber sit* (*That Every Good Person Is Free*)
Prov.	*De providentia* (*On Providence*)
QG	*Quaestiones et solutiones in Genesin* (*Questions and Answers on Genesis*)
Sacr.	*De sacrificiis Abelis et Caini* (*On the Sacrifices of Cain and Abel*)

Sobr.   *De sobrietate* (*On Sobriety*)
Somn.   *De somniis* (*On Dreams*)
Spec.   *De specialibus legibus* (*On the Special Laws*)
Virt.   *De virtutibus* (*On the Virtues*)

New Testament

Matt	The Gospel according to Matthew
Mark	The Gospel according to Mark
Luke	The Gospel according to Luke
John	The Gospel according to John
Acts	The Acts of the Apostles
Rom	Romans
1 Cor	1 Corinthians
2 Cor	2 Corinthians
Gal	Galatians
Eph	Ephesians
Phil	Philippians
Col	Colossians
1 Thess	1 Thessalonians
2 Thess	2 Thessalonians
2 Tim	2 Timothy
Phlm	Philemon
Jas	James
1 Pet	1 Peter
1 John	1 John

Non-Canonical Early Christian Literature

Athenagoras, *Suppl.*	*Supplicatio pro Christianis* (*Plea on Behalf of Christians*)
Augustine	
Civ.	*De civitate Dei* (*City of God*)
Conf.	*Confessiones* (*Confessions*)
Nupt.	*De nuptiis et concupiscentia* (*On Marriage and Concupiscence*)
Clement of Alexandria	
Paed.	*Paedagogus* (*Instructor*)
Protr.	*Protrepticus* (*Exhortation to the Greeks* = *Exhortation to Endurance*)
Quis div.	*Quis dives salvetur* (*Who Is the Rich Man That Will Be Saved?*)
Strom.	*Stromata* (*Miscellanies*)

LIST OF ABBREVIATIONS

Eusebius
Hist. eccl.   *Historia ecclesiastica* (*Ecclesiastical History*)
Praep. ev.   *Praeparatio evangelica* (*Preparation for the Gospel*)
Lactantius, *Inst.*   *Divinae institutiones* (*The Divine Institutes*)
Origen, *Cels.*   *Contra Celsum* (*Against Celsus*)

Classical, Hellenistic, Roman, and Late Antique Works

Achilles Tatius   *Leucippe et Clitophon* (*The Adventures of Leucippe and Clitophon*)
Aelius Aristides, *Or.*   *Orationes* (*Orations*)
Aetius   *Placita* (*Opinions*)
Alcinous [Albinus]
Did.   *Didaskalikos* (*Handbook of Platonism*)
AP   *Anthologia palatina* (*Palatine Anthology*)
Apollonius
Ep. Apoll.   *Epistulae Apollonii* (*Letters of Apollonius*)
Archytas
De educ.   *De educatione* (*On Moral Education*)
De leg.   *De lege et iustitia* (*On Law and Justice*)
Aresas, *De nat. hom.*   *De natura hominis* (*On the Nature of Humanity*)
Aristotle   (See also Ps.-Aristotle)
An. post.   *Analytica posteriora* (*Posterior Analytics*)
De an.   *De anima* (*On the Soul*)
Eth. eud.   *Ethica eudemia* (*Eudemian Ethics*)
Eth. nic. [= *EN*]   *Ethica nichomachea* (*Nicomachean Ethics*)
Gen. an.   *De generatione anamalium* (*On the Generation of Animals*)
Poet.   *Poetica* (*Poetics*)
Pol.   *Politica* (*Politics*)
Rhet.   *Rhetorica* (*Rhetoric*)
Top.   *Topica* (*Topics*)
Arius Didymus   *Liber de philosophorum sectis* (containing his *Epitome of Stoic Ethics* and his *Epitome of Peripatetic Ethics*)
Arrian, *Epict. diss.*   *Epicteti dissertationes* (*The Discourses of Epictetus*) (See also Epictetus, *Diss.*)
Athenaeus, *Deipn.*   *Deipnosophistae* (*Sophists at Dinner*)
Aulus Gellius
Noct. att.   *Noctes atticae* (*Attic Nights*)

LIST OF ABBREVIATIONS

Calcidius
Comm. Tim.   *In Platonis Timaeum commentarius (Commentary on Plato's Timaeus)*

Callicratidas
De dom. felic.   *De domus felicitatis (On the Happiness of the Household)*

Ceb. Tab.   *Cebetis Tabula (Tabula of Cebes)*
Chariton   *De Chaerea et Callirrhoe (Chaereas and Callirhoe)*
Cicero
Acad.   *Academica (On Academic Skepticism)*
Acad. post.   *Academica posteriora (= Acad. 1 =* Book 1 of the second edition of the *Academica) (Posterior Academics)*
Acad. pr.   *Academica priora (= Lucullus = Acad. 2 =* Book 2 of the first edition of the *Academica) (Prior Academics)*
Att.   *Epistulae ad Atticum (Letters to Atticus)*
Brut.   *Brutus*
De or.   *De oratore (On the Orator)*
Fat.   *De fato (On Fate)*
Fin.   *De finibus (On Moral Ends)*
Inv.   *De inventione (On Invention)*
Leg.   *De legibus (On the Laws)*
Off.   *De officiis (On Duties)*
Or. Brut.   *Orator ad M. Brutum (Orator, A Reply to Brutus)*
Quint. fratr.   *Epistulae ad Quintum fratrem (Letters to His Brother Quintus)*
Tim.   *Timaeus*
Tusc.   *Tusculanae disputationes (Tusculan Disputations)*
Clitarchus
Sent. Clit.   *Sententiae Clitarchi (Sentences of Clitarchus)*
Dio Chrysostom, *Or.*   *Orationes (Orations)*
Diodorus of Sicily   *Bibliotheca historica (Library of History)*
Diogenes Laertius   *Vitae philosophorum (Lives of Prominent Philosophers)*
Diotogenes, *De regn.*   *De regni (On Kingship)*
Ep. Pyth.   *Epistulae Pythagoricae (Pythagorean Letters)*
Epictetus
Diss.   *Dissertationes (Discourses)*
Ench.   *Enchiridion (Manual)*

LIST OF ABBREVIATIONS

Epicurus
Ep. Men.   *Epistula ad Menoeceum* (*Epistle to Menoeceus*)
Rat. sent.   *Ratae sententiae* (*Kyriai Doxai*) (*Principal Doctrines*)
SV   *Sententiae Vaticanae* (*Gnomologium vaticanum*) (*Vatican Sayings*)

Galen
De affect. dig.   *De affectuum dignotione* (*On the Diagnosis and Treatment of the Emotions in Each Person's Soul = On the Passions of the Soul*) (see also *Passions*)
De loc. affect.   *De locis affectis* (*On the Affected Parts*)
De nat. facul.   *De naturalibus facultatibus* (*On the Natural Faculties*)
De sanit. tuen.   *De sanitate tuenda* (*On Hygiene*)
Passions   *De affectuum dignotione* (*On the Passions of the Soul*)
PHP   *De placitis Hippocratis et Platonis* (*On the Opinions of Hippocrates and Plato*)
Quod an mor.   *Quod animi mores corporis temperamenta sequantur* (*That the Powers of the Soul Follow the Temperaments of the Body*)

GV   *Carmen aureum* (*The Golden Verses*)
Heraclitus, *All.*   *Allegoriae homericae* (*Quaestiones homericae*) (*Homeric Allegories = Homeric Questions*)
Hesiod, *Op.*   *Opera et dies* (*Works and Days*)
Hippocrates, *Vict.*   *De victus ratione in morbis acutis* (*Regimen in Acute Diseases*)

Homer
Il.   *Ilias* (*Iliad*)
Od.   *Odyssea* (*Odyssey*)

Horace
Carm.   *Carmina* (*Odes*)
Ep.   *Epistulae* (*Letters*)
Sat.   *Satirae* (*Satires*)

Iamblichus
Protr.   *Protrepticus* (*Exhortation to Philosophy*)
VP   *De vita Pythagorica* (*On the Pythagorean Way of Life*)

Isocrates, *Antid.*   *Antidosis*
Julian, *Or.*   *Orationes* (*Orations*)
Juvenal, *Sat.*   *Satirae* (*Satires*)

Longinus, *Subl.*   *De sublimitate* (*On the Sublime*)

Lucian

Bis acc.   *Bis accusatus* (*The Double Indictment*)
Demon.   *Demonax*
Nigr.   *Nigrinus*
Tim.   *Timon*

Lucretius

De rerum nat.   *De rerum natura* (*On the Nature of Things*)

Marcus Aurelius

Med.   *Meditationes* (*Meditations*)

Maximus of Tyre

Diss.   *Dissertationes* (*Discourses*)
Metopus, *De virt.*   *De virtute* (*On Virtue*)

Ovid

Ars   *Ars amatoria* (*The Art of Love*)
Metam.   *Metamorphoses*
P.Herc.   Herculaneum Papyrus
P.Mil.Vogl.   Milan Papyrus Vogliano
Pan. Lat.   XII *Panegyrici Latini* (*Twelve Latin Panegyrics*)

Philodemus

De dis   *On the Gods*
Ira   *De ira* (*On Anger*)
Lib.   *De libertate dicendi* (*On Frank Criticism*)

Philostratus

Vit. Apoll.   *Vita Apollonii* (*Life of Apollonius of Tyana*)
Vit. soph.   *Vita sophistarum* (*Lives of the Sophists*)

Plato

Apol.   *Apologia* (*Apology*)
Ep.   *Epistulae* (*Letters*)
Lach.   *Laches*
Leg.   *Leges* (*Laws*)
Phaed.   *Phaedo*
Phaedr.   *Phaedrus*
Phileb.   *Philebus*
Prot.   *Protagoras*
Resp.   *Respublica* (*Republic*)
Symp.   *Symposium*
Theaet.   *Theaetetus*

LIST OF ABBREVIATIONS

Tim.	*Timaeus*
Pliny the Younger	
Pan.	*Panegyricus (Panegyric to Trajan)*
Plutarch	(See also Ps.-Plutarch)
Adol. poet. aud.	*Quomodo adolescens poetas audire debeat (How the Young Man Should Study Poetry)*
Adul. amic.	*Quomodo adulator ab amico internoscatur (How To Tell a Flatterer from a Friend)*
Alc.	*Alcibiades*
An. corp.	*Animine an corporis affectiones sint peiores (Whether the Affections of the Soul Are Worse Than Those of the Body)*
Ant.	*Antonius*
Caes.	*Caesar*
Comm. not.	*De communibus notitiis contra stoicos (Against the Stoics on Common Conceptions)*
De esu	*De esu carnium (On the Eating of Flesh)*
De gen. Soc.	*De genio Socratis (On the Sign of Socrates)*
Exil.	*De exilio (On Exile)*
Is. Os.	*De Iside et Osiride (On Isis and Osiris)*
Mor.	*Moralia (Moral Essays)*
Praecept. ger. rei publ.	*Praecepta gerendae rei publicae (Precepts of Statecraft)*
Quaest. conv.	*Quaestiones conviviales (Table-Talk)*
Sera	*De sera numinis vindicta (On the Delays of Divine Vengeance)*
Stoic. abs.	*Stoicos absurdiora poetis dicere (The Stoics Talk More Paradoxically Than the Poets)*
Stoic. rep.	*De Stoicorum repugnantis (On Stoic Self-Contradictions)*
Suav. viv.	*Non posse suaviter vivi secundum Epicurum (It is Impossible to Live Pleasantly in the Manner of Epicurus)*
Tranq. an.	*De tranquillitate animi (On Tranquility of Mind)*
Tu. san.	*De tuenda sanitate praecepta (Advice About Keeping Well)*
Virt. mor.	*De virtute morali (On Moral Virtue)*
Virt. prof.	*Quomodo quis suos in virtute sentiat profectus (How Someone May Become Aware of His Progress in Virtue)*

LIST OF ABBREVIATIONS

Virt. vit. — De virtute et vitio (On Virtue and Vice)
Porphyry, VP — Vita Pythagorae (Life of Pythagoras)
Propertius — Elegiae (Elegies)
Ps.-Aristotle, Mund. — De mundo (On the Cosmos)
Ps.-Crates, Ep. — Epistulae (Letters)
Ps.-Demetrius
Typ epist. — Typoi epistolikoi (Epistolary Types)
Ps.-Diogenes, Ep. — Epistulae (Letters)
Ps.-Libanius
Epist. char. — Epistolimaioi charakteres (Epistolary Styles)
Ps.-Plutarch
Apophth. Lac. — Apophthegmata Laconica (Sayings of the Spartans)
Cons. Apoll. — Consolatio ad Apollonium (Letter of Consolation to Apollonius)
De fato — On Fate
De lib. educ. — De liberis educandis (On the Education of Children)
Pyth. Sent. — Sententiae Pythagoricae (Pythagorean Sentences)
Quintilian, Inst. — Institutio oratoria (The Orator's Education)
Seneca
Ben. — De beneficiis (On Benefits)
Constant. — De constantia sapiens (On the Firmness of the Sage)
Ep. — Epistulae morales (Moral Epistles)
Helv. — Ad Helvium matrem, de consolatione (To His Mother Helvia, On Consolation)
Ira — De ira (On Anger)
Marc. — Ad Marciam de consolatione (To Marcia, On Consolation)
Nat. — Naturales quaestiones (Questions About Nature)
Polyb. — Ad Polybium de consolatione (To Polybius, On Consolation)
Prov. — De providentia (On Providence)
Sextus, Sent. Sext. — Sententiae Sexti (Sentences of Sextus)
Sextus Empiricus
Math. — Adversus mathematicos (Against the Mathematicians)
Stobaeus
Ecl. — Eclogae (Selections)
Flor. — Florilegium (Anthology)
Strabo, Geogr. — Geographica (Geography)

Theages, *De virt.*   *De virtute* (*On Virtue*)
Theophrastus
Caus. plant.   *De causis plantarum* (*On the Causes of Plant Growth*)
Hist. plant.   *Historia plantarum* (*Research on Plants*)
Thucydides, *Hist.*   *Historiae* (*History of the Peloponnesian War*)
Timaeus of Locri
De univ. nat.   *De universi natura* (*On the Nature of the Universe*)
Xenophon of Athens
Mem.   *Memorabilia*
Xenophon (Novelist)   *Ephesiaca* (*The Ephesian Story of Anthia and Habrocomes*)

Secondary Sources

ABD   Freedman, D.N. (ed.) (1992) *Anchor Bible Dictionary*, 6 vols, New York: Doubleday
AClass   *Acta Classica*
AFLA   *Annales de la Faculté des Lettres et Sciences humaines d'Aix*, Séries classique
AGP   *Archiv für Geschichte der Philosophie*
AJP   *American Journal of Philology*
AJT   *American Journal of Theology*
ANF   *The Ante-Nicene Fathers*
ANRW   Temporini, H. and Haase, W. (eds) (1972–) *Aufstieg und Niedergang der römischen Welt: Geschichte und Kultur Roms im Spiegel der neueren Forschung*, Berlin: de Gruyter
BDAG   Bauer, W., Danker, F.W., Arndt, W.F., and Gingrich, F.W. (1999) *A Greek-English Lexicon of the New Testament and Other Early Christian Literature*, 3rd edn, Chicago: University of Chicago Press
Bib   *Biblica*
BibInt   *Biblical Interpretation*
BNP   Cancik, H. and Schneider, H. (eds) (2002–) *Brill's New Pauly: Encyclopaedia of the Ancient World*, Leiden: Brill
Bücheler, *Carm.*   Bücheler, F. (ed.) (1894–1926) *Carmina Latina Epigraphica*, 2 vols, with a supplementary third volume by E. Lommatzsch, Leipzig: Teubner. Reprinted (1982) Stuttgart: Teubner

LIST OF ABBREVIATIONS

CAG	Commentaria in Aristotelem graeca
CBQ	Catholic Biblical Quarterly
CBul	The Classical Bulletin
CErc	Cronache Ercolanesi
CIL	Corpus inscriptionum latinarum
CJ	Classical Journal
CMG	Corpus medicorum Graecorum
CP	Classical Philology
CQ	Classical Quarterly
CSHB	Corpus scriptorum historiae byzantinae
DNP	Cancik, H. and Schneider, H. (eds) (1996–) Der neue Pauly: Enzyklopädie der Antike, Stuttgart: Metzler
EkklPhar	Ekklesiastikos Pharos
FHSG	Fortenbaugh, W.W., Huby, P.M., Sharples, R.W., and Gutas, D. (eds) (1992) Theophrastus of Eresus: Sources for His Life, Writings, Thought and Influence, 2 vols, Leiden: Brill
GB	Grazer Beiträge: Zeitschrift für klassische Altertumswissenschaft
GCS	Die griechische christliche Schriftsteller der ersten [drei] Jahrhunderte
GGA	Göttingische Gelehrte Anzeigen
GP	Gow, A.S.F. and Page, D.L. (eds) (1968) The Greek Anthology: The Garland of Philip and Some Contemporary Epigrams, 2 vols, London: Cambridge University Press
GR	Greece and Rome
GRBS	Greek, Roman, and Byzantine Studies
HSCP	Harvard Studies in Classical Philology
HTR	Harvard Theological Review
IBS	Irish Biblical Studies
ICS	Illinois Classical Studies
JAC	Jahrbuch für Antike und Christentum
JBL	Journal of Biblical Literature
JECS	Journal of Early Christian Studies
JETS	Journal of the Evangelical Theological Society
JHI	Journal of the History of Ideas
JP	Journal of Philology
JRE	Journal of Religious Ethics
JRelS	Journal of Religious Studies
JRS	Journal of Roman Studies
JSNT	Journal for the Study of the New Testament
JTS	Journal of Theological Studies
LCL	Loeb Classical Library

LIST OF ABBREVIATIONS

LEC	Les Études classiques
LSJ	Liddell, H.G., Scott, R., and Jones, H.S. (1996) *A Greek-English Lexicon*, 9th edn with rev. supplement, Oxford: Clarendon
MD	Materiali e discussioni per l'analisi de testi classici
MH	Museum helveticum
MP	Museum patavinum: Rivista semestrale della Facoltà di lettere e filosofia
NIB	The New Interpreter's Bible
NovT	Novum Testamentum
NPNF[1]	Nicene and Post-Nicene Fathers, Series 1
NTS	New Testament Studies
OCD	Hornblower, S. and Spawforth, A. (eds) (1996) *Oxford Classical Dictionary*, 3rd edn, Oxford: Clarendon
OLD	Glare, P.G.W. (ed.) (1996) *The Oxford Latin Dictionary*, corrected edn, Oxford: Clarendon
OSAPh	Oxford Studies in Ancient Philosophy
PapLup	Papyrologica Lupiensia
PBACAP	Proceedings of the Boston Area Colloquium in Ancient Philosophy
PL	Patrologia Latina, cited by volume and column number
PW	Pauly, A.F. (1894–1980) *Paulys Realencyclopädie der classischen Altertumwissenschaft*, new edn, G. Wissowa et al., 83 vols, Munich: Druckenmüller
RAC	Klauser, T. et al. (eds) *Reallexikon für Antike und Christentum*, Stuttgart: Hiersemann
REL	Revue des études latines
ResQ	Restoration Quarterly
RevScRel	Revue des sciences religieuses
RPhL	Revue philosophique de Louvain
RTP	Revue de théologie et de philosophie
RTR	Reformed Theological Review
SIFC	Studi italiani di filologia classica
SM	Scripta Minora = Claudii Galeni Pergameni Scripta Minora
SPhilo	Studia philonica
SR	Studies in Religion/Sciences religieuses
StPatr	Studia patristica
SVF	Arnim, H.F.A. von (ed.) (1903–24) *Stoicorum veterum fragmenta*, 4 vols, Leipzig: Teubner (cited by volume and fragment number)
SynPhil	Synthesis Philosophica
TAPA	Transactions of the American Philological Association

LIST OF ABBREVIATIONS

TDNT	Kittel, G. and Friedrich, G. (1964–76) *Theological Dictionary of the New Testament*, trans. G.W. Bromiley, 10 vols, Grand Rapids: Eerdmans
ThTo	*Theology Today*
VC	*Vigiliae christianae*
YCS	*Yale Classical Studies*
ZNW	*Zeitschrift für die neutestamentliche Wissenschaft und die Kunde der älteren Kirche*

1

THE PASSIONS AND MORAL PROGRESS: AN INTRODUCTION

John T. Fitzgerald

This essay is an introduction to the emotions and moral progress in ancient discourse. These two topics were intimately related in Greco-Roman thought, so it is important to consider them together. The essay itself is divided into four unequal parts. Part I is a discussion of terminology for emotions, focusing on the three major English translations of the Greek terms *pathos* and *pathē*. Part II is a survey of ancient works *On Emotions*, with attention also given to treatises on specific emotions, such as anger. Part III is a brief treatment of myth and morality, and Part IV is an introduction to the topic of *prokopē* and the Greco-Roman concern with moral progress, which was deemed possible only if the emotions were properly managed. A brief indication of the arrangement of other essays in the volume concludes this introduction.

Introduction

The current interest in the emotions is as widespread as it is interdisciplinary.[1] From the cognitive and natural sciences to the humanities and social sciences, there is hardly a field of study that is not being invigorated or at least affected by ongoing research into the emotions. The number of new studies published each year in all disciplines is almost mind-boggling, and this research has created renewed interest in how different cultures and previous generations have viewed the emotions and their various manifestations.[2] The reprinting in 1998 of Charles Darwin's pioneering *The Expression of the Emotions in Man and Animals*, first published in 1872, is but one instance of contemporary interest in earlier investigations and theories.[3]

This explosion of interest in the emotions has affected both classics and biblical studies, with scholars from both disciplines making important new contributions to how the emotions were viewed in classical antiquity. To give only one example, M. Nussbaum's highly influential *The Therapy of Desire* (1994b)[4] was not only a response to the growing interest in the emotions[5] but also a powerful catalyst for new research. Since Nussbaum's book appeared, no fewer than ten book-length studies on "ancient emotions" have been published, as well as countless articles in journals, chapters in books, and other forms of publication. Some of these more recent studies have been devoted to the emotions in general, whereas others have focused on specific emotions, such as anger, and still others on particular ancient authors or philosophical schools. The most significant of the book-length treatments include those by C.A. Barton (2001), M. Graver (2002), W.V. Harris (2001), R.A. Kaster (2005), S. Knuuttila (2004), D. Konstan (2001; 2006), R. Sorabji (2000), T. Tieleman (2003), and P. Toohey (2004). Since 1997, at least five significant collections of essays on ancient emotions have appeared: those edited by S.M. Braund and C. Gill (1997), S. Braund and G.W. Most (2003), Konstan and N.K. Rutter (2003), J. Sihvola and T. Engberg-Pedersen (1998), and, in the area of biblical studies, T.H. Olbricht and J.L. Sumney (2001). Collectively, if not individually, these investigations have underscored the importance and demonstrated the veracity of the premise of Konstan's recent book on ancient Greek emotions, namely "that the emotions of the ancient Greeks were in some significant respects different from our own, and that recognizing these differences is important to our understanding of Greek literature and Greek culture generally" (Konstan 2006: ix). The same is true of the Romans and their understanding of the emotions, as Kaster (2005) has convincingly shown. Furthermore, the ancients' "conception of the emotions has something to tell us about our own views, whether about the nature of particular emotions or the category of emotion itself" (Konstan 2006: ix).

The standard Greek terms and their English translations

The differences between the modern and ancient understandings of the emotions are already signaled by the linguistic and conceptual difficulty of translating the standard terms that the Greeks used for "emotion" as a general concept and for the various "emotions" collectively, namely πάθος (*pathos*) and πάθη (*pathē*).[6] Both terms derive from πάσχειν (*paschein*), which fundamentally indicates "to experience something," whether positive or negative (Michaelis 1968: 904; BDAG, s.v. πάσχω, 785; cf. Graver 2002: 79). The latter implication was far more common than the former, so that the verb, especially in early Christian literature, often has the meaning "to suffer." The Greek verb is thus distantly related to the Latin verb for suffering, *patior*, from which the English words "passion" and "passive" derive (Konstan 2006: 3). Precisely how to render the Greek term into English is difficult; indeed, "no translation of the term is adequate, for *pathos* is a technical term whose meaning is determined by the theory in which it functions" (Inwood 1985: 127).

Yet even restricting the translation to how the term was used by one philosophical school, such as the Stoics, does not settle the issue. Cicero already had (or feigned) difficulty translating the Stoic term into Latin when used of grief, fear, pleasure, and anger, and he was tempted to use *morbi*, "diseases,"[7] arguing that it would be a word-for-word translation of *pathē* and that the Greeks also used it not only of pity (*misereri*) and envy (*invidere*) but even of exultation (*gestire*) and joy (*laetari*). He finally settled for *perturbationes animi*, "mental disturbances" (*Tusc.* 3.7; see also 4.10; *Fin.* 3.35), though he does use *morbus* for *pathos* at *Tusc.* 3.20.[8] On occasion, Augustine was to make the same equation: "*perturbatio* is what is called *pathos* in Greek" (*Civ.* 8.17).

There are three translations of *pathos* that are popular in English-language scholarship. Of these, the most popular is "emotion," which has the overwhelming advantage of being the standard term used in the general population and in other academic disciplines. It was the word chosen, for example, by Sorabji (2000: 7, 17), with regard to the Stoic theory of the *pathē*. The least popular of the three translations, on the other hand, is "affection," preferred by M. Frede and Tieleman, though not entirely for the same reasons. Although Frede uses the term "affection" when discussing the Stoics, he employs it primarily for the Platonic–Aristotelian tradition and conjectures that "perhaps the term '*pathos*' originally was restricted to flagrantly irrational emotions, and only later came to refer to the emotions quite generally.... In this tradition the term '*pathos*' takes on the connotation of '*passio*', 'affect', 'purely passive affection.'" The Stoics, by contrast, "think that it is grossly misleading to think of the affections of the soul as *pathē* in the sense of passive affections. They are rather *pathē* in the sense of illnesses, diseases" (Frede 1986: 96–7, 99, italics added). Tieleman, by contrast, chooses "affection" as the term "perhaps best suited to preserve the different shades of meaning of πάθος in its Stoic usage" (Tieleman 2003: 16).

There are, of course, Latin precedents for translating the Greek words by terms belonging to the *affectio* (*adfectio*)/*affectus* (*adfectus*) word group. Aulus Gellius, for example, reports a speech that he heard Herodes Atticus deliver in Greek at Athens about Stoic *apatheia*, which Herodoes attacked as follows: "no one, who felt and thought normally, could be wholly exempt and free from those *adfectionibus* of the mind, which he called πάθη, caused by sorrow, desire, fear, anger, and pleasure" (*Noct. att.* 19.12.3).[9] Similarly, in the context of a discussion of anger, Gellius refers to "all the rest of the emotions, which the Latin philosophers call *affectus* or affections, and the Greeks *pathē*" (*Noct. att.* 1.26.11). Cicero includes joy, desire, and fear as belonging to the category of *affectio* at *Inv.* 1.36, and at 1.41 he calls annoyance, anger, and love "*affectionem animi*" (see also *Tusc.* 4.14). This

3

usage is one of the factors that prompts J. Wisse to say, "*Affectio* is ... roughly equivalent to Greek πάθος in its general sense" (Wisse 1989: 100 n. 102). Indeed, many if not most post-Ciceronian authors preferred to "render *pathos* by *adfectio* or *adfectus*" (Graver 2002: 80). For example, Quintilian, who presents *pathos* and *ēthos* as two emotional modes that can be used by the orator, says that "the Greeks call the one [mode] *pathos*, which we correctly and properly translate as *adfectus*" (*Inst.* 6.2.8). He goes on to link *pathos* with tragedy and says that it is almost entirely concerned with anger, hatred, fear, envy, and pity (6.2.20).[10] M. DiCicco (1995: 147 n. 243) claims that *adfectus* is "coined" here by Quintilian as the Latin equivalent of the Greek *pathos*, but it would be more accurate to say that Quintilian is perhaps the first Latin orator explicitly to equate the two terms in discussing rhetoric. *Adfectus* in Latin was well established as a term for both "emotion" and "strong emotion" or "passion" long before Quintilian was active (*OLD*, s.v. *affectus*) and in equating the two terms he is drawing on a common meaning of *adfectus*.[11]

The third English translation of *pathos* is "passion," which is the term used by B. Inwood (1985: 127–8), A.A. Long and D.N. Sedley (1987: 1.410–23, §65), Braund and Gill (1997) in the title of their volume, and many others. "Passion" is derived from the Latin noun *passio*, which also was a popular ancient term used to render the Greek word *pathos*. Augustine, for instance, says that "the word *passio* for the Greek word *pathos* means a mental agitation (*motus animi*) that is contrary to reason" (*Civ.* 8.17, trans. Wiesen 1968: 79, modified). By Augustine's time, however, Christian usage already had imparted its own negative connotation to the word; as Augustine himself says, "*passio*, the Latin equivalent [of *pathos*], especially in its ecclesiastical use, is usually a term of censure" (*Nupt.* 2.55 = 2.33 PL 44: 469).[12]

In short, there was not one Latin word or word group used to render *pathos* and *pathē*. Augustine refers to this phenomenon in his *City of God*:

> There are two opinions among the philosophers concerning the mental emotions [*animi motibus*], which the Greeks call *pathē*, while certain of our fellow countrymen, like Cicero, describe them as disturbances [*perturbationes*], others as affections [*affectiones*] or affects [*affectus*], and others again, like Apuleius, as passions [*passiones*], which renders the Greek more explicitly.
> (*Civ.* 9.4, trans. Wiesen 1968: 157)[13]

This linguistic situation naturally had implications not only for philosophical debates but also for biblical exegesis. Augustine, for instance, refers to debates about the precise meaning of Paul's words in 1 Thess 4:5 as follows:

> The phrase in the Greek text, ἐν πάθει ἐπιθυμίας [*en pathei epithymias*], is by some rendered in Latin, *in morbo desiderii* or

concupiscentiae, in the disease of desire or of concupiscence; by others, however, *in passione concupiscentiae*, in the passion of concupiscence; or however it is found otherwise in different copies.
(*Nupt.* 2.55 = 2.33 PL 44: 469)[14]

Inasmuch as there is no one English word that corresponds exactly to all of the meanings or nuances of the Greek word *pathos*, many modern scholars eschew the practice of consistently translating the same Greek word with a single English term and use multiple English words. Nussbaum, for instance, uses "emotions" and "passions" "more or less interchangeably" when speaking of the Stoics, and often employs "suffering" when discussing the Epicureans' desire to rid themselves of the painful or disturbing affects of certain *pathē* (Nussbaum 1994b: 319 n. 4, 102 n. 1).

For this volume of essays, no particular translation of *pathos* and *pathē* was imposed on the contributors, who tend to use either "emotions" or "passions" or both terms interchangeably when referring to the *pathē*. Although "emotions" is the more common generic term in modern English, "passions" was selected for the title of the volume as a whole. Three main factors led to this somewhat arbitrary choice. First, "passions" is etymologically closer to the Greek term *pathē* than "emotion" and does not have all the disadvantages of "affections" for modern readers. Second, "passions" has a long and established history in the Western philosophical tradition. Third, and most important, from the outset, members of the Hellenistic Moral Philosophy and Early Christianity Section have referred to this undertaking as the "*pathē* and *prokopē*" project, the "passions and progress" or "P&P" project. Thus, the second term, "progress," proved decisive in choosing the first for the volume's title.

Ancient Greek and Roman works on the emotions

Of the two subjects, "passions" and "progress," the former has been by far the more popular, both in the ancient world and today. Ancient philosophers discussed the emotions in a variety of contexts and genres and even made them the subject of particular works. Individual emotions were also the subject of particular treatments.[15] This attention to – at times, preoccupation with – the emotions was ultimately unavoidable, given ancient philosophy's concern with virtue. Galen spoke for many when he said "the doctrine of the virtues follows necessarily from the doctrine of the emotions" (*PHP* 5.6.1). From both a theoretical and a practical standpoint, to speak of virtue without giving due attention to the emotions was as impossible as it was inconceivable.[16]

It is not entirely clear who wrote the first Περὶ παθῶν (*Peri pathōn*), *On Emotions*, but it is virtually certain that the key impetus for these often heated philosophical discussions and debates came from Plato's Academy.[17] It was while Xenocrates (396/5–314/3 BCE) and Aristotle (384–322 BCE) were students together in the Academy[18] that

> an investigation of emotion was undertaken which was to have profound effects upon the subsequent course of philosophical psychology, rhetoric, poetics, and political and ethical theory. Members of the Academy ... focused upon emotions as distinct from bodily sensations and bodily drives and tried to explain the involvement of cognition in emotional response. A satisfactory explanation was not immediately forthcoming.
> (Fortenbaugh 1975a: 9)

Plato dealt with emotion, especially in the *Philebus*,[19] but he did not devote any of his writings primarily or specifically to this subject. But Plato's concern with emotion was continued by Xenocrates and Aristotle, who, following Plato's death in 347,[20] apparently left Athens together and settled in the town of Assos in the Troad, a region where Erastus and Coriscus, two other former students of Plato, were active and where Hermias, the tyrant of Atarneus, had an interest in philosophy.[21] Even if Assos was not at this time "a colony of the Athenian Academy" (Jaeger 1948: 115), it is highly probable that the Platonists who were there discussed the emotions,[22] and similar discussions doubtless took place in Athens, where Speusippus had succeeded Plato as head of the Academy.[23] In later years,[24] both Xenocrates and Aristotle returned to Athens, though at different times and under different circumstances, with Xenocrates becoming the third head of the Academy in 339/8 after the death of Speusippus,[25] and with Aristotle founding his own school in the Lyceum in 335/4.[26]

It was quite likely during the period when Xenocrates was head of the Academy that he wrote a one-book work *On Emotions* (Diogenes Laertius 4.12), which may have been the first devoted specifically to the passions. Unfortunately, only doxographic reports exist regarding the views of Xenocrates; inasmuch as there are no original fragments or identifiable quotations, nothing specific is known about this work.[27] Since, however, he is generally considered "the most conservative of all Plato's students with regard to alterations of the doctrine" (Jaeger 1948: 111) and "seems, in general, to have attempted to reproduce Plato's thought in a stereotyped and formalized system" (Field and Hornblower 1996), it is likely that his *On Emotions* was essentially a distillation of Plato's views on the emotions, arranged systematically, and with an emphasis on the practical moral implications of Plato's theory.[28]

That Aristotle likewise wrote one or more works specifically on the emotions is also possible, but by no means certain. No such work is extant, but there are two works mentioned in the ancient lists of Aristotle's writings where the term "emotions" appears in the title. As is generally known, there are three such extant lists of Aristotle's works: the earliest is the one that appears in Diogenes Laertius 5.22–7 (Rose 1886: 3–9); the second is the list preserved by Hesychius as an appendix to an anonymous life of Aristotle (Rose 1886: 9–18);[29] and the third (Rose 1886: 19–22) is that given by Ptolemy-al-Garib (Ptolemy the Unknown or Ptolemy the Stranger), who probably was a Peripatetic philosopher (Plezia 1985) rather than a Neoplatonist (Dihle 1957; Plezia 1975). No work on the emotions appears in the third list, so it may be left out of the following discussion; the only evidence that it offers is the argument from silence against a work by Aristotle specifically on the emotions.[30]

The first two lists of Aristotle's works derive from a common Hellenistic source probably compiled in the last quarter of the third century BCE and used by both Diogenes Laertius and the anonymous author whose work is preserved by Hesychius (Moraux 1951: 206–9), yet these lists differ in important ways.[31] Of the two works with "emotions" in the title, one is mentioned by both Diogenes and Hesychius (see below), but only Diogenes Laertius (5.24) gives a Πάθη (*Emotions*) in one book (Rose 1886: 5, #61). What is striking about this title is not only its uniqueness but also its placement, for it is found in the section dealing with dialectic, not in the sections giving Aristotle's rhetorical and ethical works. P. Moraux (1951: 192) tried to explain its odd location in the list of Diogenes Laertius by suggesting that the next entry in the list, διαιρετικόν (*diairetikon*), *Division*, is not the title of a work dealing with logical division, but is rather a note explaining the *genre* of *Emotions*, namely that it was drawn up in divisions. As such, *Emotions* could have been either a rhetorical work giving a compendium of the emotions that an orator could evoke or an ethical work on the emotions. This explanation is more ingenuous than persuasive. It certainly does not explain διαιρετικόν in the list of Diogenes Laertius, where it is followed by ά, indicating that it was a separate one-volume work. For Moraux's explanation to be true, one must presuppose that an early copyist mistook the genre designation "in divisions" for the title of a separate work on logic and added the information that it was a work in one book. Though not impossible, that hardly seems likely.

The other work with "emotions" in the title, as given in the manuscripts of Diogenes Laertius, is περὶ παθῶν ὀργῆς ά (*peri pathōn orgēs a*), literally, *On Emotions of Anger*, one book. That odd title has struck most scholars as erroneous, thus prompting at least four conjectures explaining how it arose. The first is that of I. Düring, who thought that the titles of two separate works had been telescoped together. Thus he proposed περὶ παθῶν <ά περὶ> ὀργῆς ά, *On Emotions*, one book, *On Anger*, one book.[32] The second solution is that of V. Rose (1886: 4, #37), who corrected the reading to περὶ παθῶν <ἢ περὶ> ὀργῆς ά, *On Emotions* or *On Anger*, one book. That is, Rose thought that originally there were two alternative titles for the same work, which he considered a dialogue (Rose 1863: 21, 107–15).[33] The same solution was adopted by R.D. Hicks in his edition of Diogenes Laertius for the Loeb Classical Library (Hicks 1925: 1.466). Only slightly different is the third explanation, which is offered by Moraux (1951: 74), who thought that περὶ παθῶν was the original title and that ὀργῆς was an ancient gloss, indicating that *On Emotions* dealt primarily with anger. In connection with this, he argued that the reading in the list of Hesychius (which he called "the anonymous list") represented an attempt to correct the conflated title and gloss. That is, with ὀργῆς now viewed as part of the original title, a copyist of the list preserved in Hesychius sought to correct the error by changing the plural "emotions" to the singular "emotion": περὶ πάθους ὀργῆς ά, *On the Emotion of Anger*, one book (Moraux 1951: 74 n. 141; 199). Completely different is the fourth solution, that of A.J.P. Kenny (1978: 42), who sought to solve the problem by emending ὀργῆς (*orgēs*) to ὁρμῆς (*hormēs*). The original title was thus *On the Influence of the Emotions*.[34]

Related to these proposals are various attempts to determine the authenticity of the work given in the lists of Diogenes Laertius and Hesychius and to identify it with any extant works or fragments of lost works. Kenny (1978: 42) identified his conjectured *On the Influence of the Emotions* with Book 6 of the *Eudemian Ethics*; if this is correct, it would have been a genuine work of Aristotle. In the collection of fragments that Rose did for the edition produced by the Berlin Academy (Rose 1870),[35] he assigned frgs 94–7 to *On Emotions*, but for his edition of the fragments for the Bibliotheca Teubneriana (Rose 1886) he changed his mind and allotted those four fragments to two other works and assigned nothing to *On Emotions*.[36] For his part, Moraux suggested two possibilities. The first, which he did not consider very likely, is that *On Emotions* could have been a rhetorical work, an extract of the first two books of the *Rhetoric* (Moraux 1951: 76); in that case, it would belong to the authentic works of Aristotle. The second possibility – and the one that Moraux, building upon the insights and observations of Rose (1863: 111) and Heitz (1865: 172–3), endorsed – was that it is a post-Aristotelian work on the emotions, giving the views of later members of the Peripatos, which differed in some key respects from that of Aristotle himself.[37] It was this writing, he suggested, that was used by Cicero, Philodemus, and Seneca. The attribution of this work to Aristotle, however, must have been quite loose, so that what Cicero and Philodemus attributed to the Peripatetics, Seneca attributed directly to Aristotle (Moraux 1951: 76–80). The inclusion of this pseudonymous, post-Aristotelian work in the Hellenistic list of Aristotle's works was thus an error of attribution on the part of the compiler (Moraux 1951: 317).

As the preceding synopsis of views indicates, it is possible that Aristotle devoted one or more works specifically to the emotions. There is, however, no persuasive proof that he ever did so, and there is limited circumstantial evidence to suggest that he did not. Barring the discovery of either new manuscripts or identifiable fragments of the two putative Aristotelian works with "emotions" in the title, no definitive answer is possible.

In any event, it was during the Hellenistic period that philosophical discussion of the emotions began to flourish, with attention given to specific emotions as well as to the emotions collectively. The Epicurean concern with the emotions began with Epicurus himself, who not only made *pathos* a central element in his scientific method (Asmis 1984; Erler 1994: 133–4) but also wrote a περὶ παθῶν δόξαι πρὸς Τιμοκράτην, *Opinions on Emotions, against Timocrates* (Philodemus, *On the Stoics* col. III Dorandi [1982]; Diogenes Laertius 10.28). The work has not survived, but it appears to have been a polemical work aimed at Metrodorus's brother Timocrates, who once belonged to the school of Epicurus "but later defected to become its leading detractor" (Sedley 1997: 342). Epicurus probably depicted him as an example of an individual who was not able to control his emotions (Erler 1994: 91). After Epicurus, attention to the emotions was given throughout the history of the school.[38] Philodemus (first century BCE), for example, wrote treatises on a number of emotions, leading some scholars to conjecture that these works were component parts of a comprehensive *On Emotions* (Dorandi 1990: 2349–51; Erler 1994: 323). Be that as it may, Diogenes of Oenoanda in Lycia (probably second century CE) included a treatment of the emotions and emotional states on the monumental inscription that he had cut on the wall of a stoa in his native city. This discussion constituted a central part of the so-called Ethics Treatise, with the title block giving Περὶ] παθῶν καὶ [πράξεων, *On Emotions and Actions*, as the topic to be dealt with in the treatise (Clay 1990: 2498–509, esp. 2499).[39]

The most famous early work on a particular emotion was produced by Crantor (ca. 336–276/5 BCE), a member of the Old Academy. His *On Grief*, which advocated the moderation of the emotions instead of their eradication (Krämer 1983: 163; Sedley 1996), was highly esteemed (Cicero, *Acad.* 2.135; Diogenes Laertius 4.27) and even recommended for reading by the Stoic philosopher Panaetius (frg. 137 Straaten [1962: 53]).[40] It served as the model for the *Consolation* that Cicero wrote to comfort himself at the death of his daughter Tullia[41] and was used extensively by him in his *Tusculan Disputations*;[42] it was also a chief source for Pseudo-Plutarch's *Consolation to Apollonius* (Hani 2003: 21–3)[43] and had a pervasive impact on the Greco-Roman *consolatio* in general.[44] Even during the heyday of the skeptical Academy, Carneades was concerned with the subject of grief and argued with other philosophical schools about the best methods of assuaging it.[45] Other skeptics were equally concerned with the emotions (Bett 1998).

Among Aristotle's followers, Theophrastus wrote an *On Emotions* in one book (Diogenes Laertius 5.45 = FHSG 436.5; see also FHSG 438), with his treatment covering anger as well as other emotions (FHSG 438–48). In addition, he wrote a work *On Grief* (Περὶ πένθους, *Peri penthous*), also known as *Callisthenes* (Diogenes Laertius 5.44 = FHSG 436.15) because it was a lament for the death of his friend by that name.[46] There is also an *On Emotions* attributed to the first-century BCE Peripatetic philosopher, Andronicus of Rhodes; that work was later translated into Latin by Robert Grosseteste (ca. 1175–1253), but it is now recognized as spurious (Glibert-Thirry 1977a).

9

Needless to say, the early commentators on Aristotle, such as Aspasius (mid-second century CE), gave particular attention to the Stagirite's treatment of the emotions (Sorabji 1999). Aspasius, it should be noted, not only attacked Andronicus's views on emotions (Konstan 2006: 131–2) but also claimed in his *Commentary on the Nicomachean Ethics* (44.20–1 Heylbut [1889]) that Aristotle nowhere offered a definition of *pathos*.[47]

Among the Stoics,[48] Zeno began the tradition of writing a work *On Emotions* (*SVF* 1.41, 211 = Diogenes Laertius 7.4, 110; see also *SVF* 1.205–15).[49] The practice was continued in the Old Stoa by Herillus (*SVF* 1.409 = Diogenes Laertius 7.166), Sphaerus (*SVF* 1.620 = Diogenes Laertius 7.178), and Chrysippus (*SVF* 3.456 = Diogenes Laertius 7.111).[50] No *peri pathōn* is attested for Cleanthes, but he did discuss the passions extensively (*SVF* 1.570–5)[51] and wrote a work *On Envy* (*SVF* 1.481 = Diogenes Laertius 7.175).[52] Similarly, Diogenes of Seleucia (Babylon) did not write a comprehensive work on emotions, but he did discuss them in other writings (Steinmetz 1994: 633), such as his *On Music*, where he adapted "the sophistic and Peripatetic idea that music could be used to train the passions of the young" (Blank 1997: 193). Dionysius of Heraclea on the Pontus wrote a work called Περὶ ἀπαθείας (*Peri apatheias*), *On Freedom from Passion* or *On the Absence of Emotion* (*SVF* 1.422 = Diogenes Laertius 7.167), undoubtedly during his Stoic period.[53] It was apparently the first, but by no means the last, such treatise by a Stoic philosopher,[54] and the same subject was soon thereafter made the subject of a diatribe by Teles the Cynic (frg. 7 Hense [1909: 55–62]).[55]

Of all the Old Stoic works on the emotions, it was that of Chrysippus that proved most important in subsequent periods, especially Book 4 of his *On Emotions*, which was known by its separate title *Therapeutics* (Tieleman 2003: 140–97). During the Middle Stoa, Panaetius discussed the emotions (Steinmetz 1994: 659) and wrote a consolatory *Letter to Tubero* on the endurance of pain, in which he recommended that his student Quintus Aelius Tubero read Crantor's *On Grief* "word for word" (frg. 137 Straaten [1962: 53]).[56] A Stoic version of such a *consolatio* was written by Posidonius and dealt with the alleviation of grief.[57] Comprehensive works on the emotions were written by Hecato (frg. 9 Gomoll [1933]; Diogenes Laertius 7.110) and Posidonius,[58] with the latter's work understood by Plutarch, Galen, and many modern scholars as attacking that of Chrysippus and rivaling if not surpassing it in importance.[59] But it was also the last great comprehensive treatment by a Stoic philosopher. Later Stoics appear not to have written comprehensive treatises on the passions, choosing instead to summarize Stoic teachings – as Arius Didymus did in his *Epitome of Stoic Ethics*[60] – or to focus their energies on particular emotions – as Seneca[61] did in his *On Anger* (*De ira*) and Epictetus did in his "That We Should Not Be Angry" (χαλεπαίνειν, *chalepainein*) with People" (*Diss.* 1.28) and in his "On Freedom from Fear" (*Diss.* 4.7). Another favorite alternative was to focus on particular situations and individuals liable to evoke an emotional response – such as Epictetus's "That We Should Not Be Angry with the Erring" (*Diss.* 1.18).[62]

This concentration on anger within Stoicism may go back to Antipater of Tarsus (second century BCE), who wrote a treatise *On Anger* in at least two books (Athenaeus, *Deipn.* 14.643F = *SVF* 3.65), and Posidonius, who also wrote a work on anger in at least two books,[63] but such treatises had a Cynic precedent in the work of Bion of Borysthenes (ca. 335–245 BCE), whose *On Anger* was mentioned by Philodemus two centuries later (*On Anger*, col. I.16–7 [Indelli 1988: 63]).[64] Yet this focus on anger was hardly restricted to Cynics and Stoics; it spanned all the philosophical schools (Edelstein and Kidd 1988: 1.179) and was a recurring theme in Greek and Roman literature of various kinds (Braund and Most 2003). Philodemus's *On Anger*, for example, gives abundant evidence that anger had been extensively discussed among the Epicureans, who differed among themselves on this emotion.[65] Similarly among the Middle Platonists, Plutarch, in addition to portraying anger in his *Lives* (Alexiou 1999), wrote a περὶ ὀργῆς or *On Anger* (frg. 148 Sandbach [1969: 274–7]), as well as another work that dealt with the control and cure of anger, namely his περὶ ἀοργησίας or *On the Absence of Anger* (*Mor.* 452F–464D).[66] The latter was mentioned by his student Calvenus (Calvisius) Taurus in one of his lectures, as recalled by his own student Aulus Gellius (*Noct. att.* 1.26.7). Anger was also discussed by many other philosophers, including Hieronymus of Rhodes (frgs 21–3 Wehrli [1969]), who began as a member of the Peripatos but may later have founded his own eclectic school of philosophy (Sharples 1996b),[67] and Quintus Sextius (ap. Seneca, *On Anger* 2.36.1), an eclectic who was influenced by both Stoicism and Neopythagoreanism[68] and who founded a short-lived but important philosophical movement at Rome during the period of Augustus (Inwood 1996). Indeed, the philosophical discussions of anger were so numerous that Cicero could say to his brother Quintus, "I won't take it upon myself here to expound to you what philosophers are apt to say on the subject of irascibility, for I don't want to take too long, and you can easily find it in many books" (*Quint. fratr.* 1.1.37, trans. Shackleton Bailey 2002: 39).[69]

The concern with anger is also reflected in more comprehensive treatments of the emotions, such as Galen's *On the Diagnosis and Treatment of the Particular Emotions in Each Person's Soul* (*De affectuum dignotione*), where he adduces his own mother as a negative example of someone who was particularly irascible.[70] In addition to discussing the emotions and their physical manifestations, he relates a number of chilling anecdotes that attest the problem of domestic violence in the ancient world.[71] Consequently, one is almost tempted to translate *pathē* in the title of Galen's work with the word "diseases."[72] For Galen, the problem of the soul's *pathē* was closely related to its *hamartēmata*, "errors" and "wrong acts," as the title of the companion piece to the treatise on the emotions suggests (*On the Diagnosis and*

Treatment of the Errors of Each Person's Soul = De peccatorum dignotione).[73] The recognition that the soul suffered from various *pathē* and diseases prompted many to compare its ills to those of the body.[74] Thus one of Plutarch's works was *Whether the Pathē of the Soul Are Worse than Those of the Body* (*Mor.* 500B–502A), and one of Maximus of Tyre's orations was *Which Diseases (Nosēmata) Are Harsher, Those of the Body or Those of the Soul?* (*Diss.* 7 Trapp [1994]).[75]

As the preceding brief survey indicates, the emotions were a major concern of philosophers in Greco-Roman antiquity.[76] The same was true of Greek and Roman historians, poets, such as Ovid[77] and Virgil,[78] novelists, such as Chariton and Xenophon,[79] and those writers, such as Philo,[80] Paul,[81] and Clement of Alexandria,[82] who were concerned with the role of the emotions in the religious life. Astrologers were by no means exempt from these discussions, as the *Tetrabiblos* of Claudius Ptolemy (second century CE) demonstrates. After covering bodily injuries and diseases (*pathē*) in 3.12, he turns to the soul in 3.13, where he gives its qualities and characteristics and mentions what he later calls "the more moderate diseases (*pathē*)" (3.14). This analysis is accompanied by numerous lists of vices,[83] which are the consequence of baneful planetary influences. Next, he treats the more serious psychic diseases, discussing these under the rubric περὶ παθῶν ψυχικῶν ("On Diseases of the Soul") in 3.14. In making this transition, he calls attention to the greater injurious planetary influences and remarks in good Aristotelian fashion, "One might now with propriety call 'diseases' (*pathē*) those extremes of character which either fall short of or exceed the mean" (3.14).[84] It is in this context, naturally, that Claudius lists the actions – especially the sexual behaviors – that he deemed the most deficient or the most extreme, and thus the most unacceptable.[85]

Myth and morality

Whereas the emotions have been of great interest to both modern scholars and ancient authors, the same is not true of the former as far as *prokopē* in the sense of moral progress is concerned. This relative lack of modern scholarly attention is, of course, not true in regard to the more general idea of historical progress. There have been numerous such studies devoted to progress in civilization, culture, science, technology, and related areas. Along with these studies, there have been fierce debates about the definition of "progress," about whether there was an idea of "progress" in antiquity, and if so, about the range of perspectives on the notions of "progress," "permanence," and "decline," and about the relationship between optimism and pessimism in ancient thought.[86] Such studies have typically given some attention to the issue of moral progression and regression, but this has rarely been the principal concern.[87]

Ancient etiological narratives and Golden Age myths, by contrast, often have a strong moral dimension, even if that is not their major focus. This is particularly true of "decline of civilization narratives," which are intimately connected with ancient primitivism and its view that "human life has degenerated from an ideal primitive past" (Stowers 1994: 85).[88] The most famous of these in Greek literature is Hesiod's myth of the five races of humanity (*Op.* 106–201). As is usually recognized, Hesiod does not invent this myth but takes it over from eastern – perhaps Persian[89] – sources in which there are four metallic races, each of which is more sinful than its predecessor.[90] Hesiod retains this basic sequence, with the transition from the first or "golden" race to the second one shown in the fact that people of the "silver" race are not able to restrain themselves from crimes against each other. That the people of the fifth and final race, those of "iron," are the moral nadir thus comes as no surprise. The only real exception is the fourth race, which Hesiod has inserted into the metallic scheme of his source; the fourth race is that of the heroes of Theban and Trojan fame, who were a more righteous and noble race than either their predecessor or successor.[91]

Other ancient narratives interweave the themes of cultural progress and moral decline. The most famous example of this kind of blended narrative is the primeval history of Genesis 1–11. On the one hand, these chapters give an ancient Israelite account of the origin and growth of human civilization, as evidenced by the advent of clothing (3:21), the beginning of nomadic life (4:20), the domestication of animals (4:20), the invention of musical instruments (4:21), advances in metallurgy (4:22), the inception of agriculture, especially viticulture (9:20), the founding of the first city (4:17), the construction of tall structures made of bricks (11:3–4), the spread of the population (11:2, 9), and the diversification of languages (11:9). On the other hand, this theme of cultural and scientific progress is intertwined with the theme of moral regression. Because of this interweaving, technological advances in the story are accompanied by accounts of the proliferation of sin. Beginning with a simple act of disobedience (3:1–6), humans quickly "progress" to fratricides (4:1–8) and homicides (4:23–4), and to an ever escalating spiral of violence. As a result, the antediluvian earth is filled with violence (6:11). The flood, which constitutes God's ethical response to this moral dilemma, is an utter failure, for it does not solve the problem of human immorality. The story that follows immediately upon the conclusion of the flood narrative makes this point unmistakably clear. Sin and family conflict quickly break out again in the postdiluvian world, doing so in the family of Noah, the most righteous person at the time of the flood (9:20–7). In a similar way, clothes are not a mark of human achievement and an advance from a more primitive state; instead, they are a sign that humans live in a fallen world. In short, for the final redactor of Genesis 1–11, human progress in the arts of "civilization" is not accompanied by more civilized conduct, but by moral regression and greater barbarism. The "poster boy" in this story is Cain, who is not only the first murderer (4:8) but also the founder of the first city (4:17).

Such narratives of primeval times and myths of a Golden Age could be used for vastly different purposes, often political ones. During the imperial period of Rome, for example, one of the main uses of the Golden Age myth and similar tales about earlier ages of human bliss was to praise the reigning emperor, flattering him with the conceit that he had restored the former age of justice (Piccaluga 1996). For instance, Eumenius, one of the panegyricists of the *XII Panegyrici Latini*, prompted by the fact that the two Augusti, Diocletian and Maximian, had assumed the names of *Iovius* and *Herculis*, respectively, praised them by saying, "The Golden Age which existed long ago when Saturn ruled (though not for a very long time) is now reborn under the eternal auspices of Jupiter and Hercules."[92] In vivid contrast to this traditional encomiastic use of the myth, Lactantius employs it in Book 5 of his *Divine Institutes* to castigate the Tetrarchy and Rome itself. Writing in the first decade of the fourth century and at a time of fierce persecution, he not only savaged Jupiter and Hercules as despicable pagan deities but also depicted the Golden Age – the Age of Saturn – as the only time when justice had prevailed and people had lived in peace and harmony. "Jupiter's arrival wrecked this ideal society. Justice was put to flight, true religion was abandoned and *cupiditas* and the institutions to back it were installed."[93] Lactantius, in short, "blames Jupiter for *destroying* the Golden Age. Far from seeking refuge with Jupiter, as the poets would have us believe, justice was a refugee from Jupiter."[94]

"The mythical founder of Rome, the brutal rather than pious Aeneas, encapsulates the values of an unjust society. Jupiter as 'god' demanded human sacrifice, Aeneas performed it."[95] From that point on, the rest of Roman history and its vaunted civilization is nothing other than the sad and sickening tale of increasing moral decline, with Romans "operating as a nation in the way that Jupiter's men behaved at the private level in post-Golden Age society."[96] The Roman institutions that fostered injustice were, above all, religion and law.

> The gap between justice and expediency is well demonstrated by the people of Rome, who got themselves control of the whole world by using Fetials to declare wars and by using forms of law to cover their wrongdoings and to seize and take other people's property.
>
> (*Div. Inst.* 6.9.4)[97]

Furthermore, the Roman jurists are "people who call it law when elderly tyrants turn butcher and go rabid against the innocent" (5.12.1). With the persecution of the Christians, injustice has reached its zenith. Therefore, for Lactantius, the age of Jupiter has indeed returned with Diocletian, but he sees that as no occasion for rejoicing. He condemns it by depicting "the rule of

Diocletian-Jupiter and his colleagues as every bit as evil as the inaugural post-Golden Age regime of Jupiter."[98]

Moral progress

These myths and narratives of progress and decline are not treated in this volume, but it is important to bear them in mind, because they form part of the larger cultural context for the Greco-Roman concern with personal and communal moral progress. Hellenistic and Roman moralists held a variety of views about "primitive times" and how their current situation arose and was to be evaluated in relation to the past, but they were all concerned, in their own historical and existential contexts, with living in such a way that they could fully realize their potential as human beings. They were also concerned with helping their friends, students, and associates to do the same. However the goal of life may have been ultimately defined and understood, success in achieving that goal was typically correlated with success in managing the emotions and with the consistent and skillful use of various spiritual techniques (Hadot 1995; Sorabji 2000: 211–52), such as self-examination, which was "the *sine qua non* for any progress in virtue" (Thom 1995: 163).[99] The most popular term for advancing toward life's goal was *prokopē*, which was a *terminus technicus* for the Stoics.[100] The Old Stoa[101] and Middle Stoa[102] as well as the later Roman Stoics, such as Seneca[103] and Epictetus,[104] were acutely concerned with *prokopē*, which they viewed as an intermediate stage between the polar opposites of vice and virtue.[105] Some Stoics could even distinguish different categories of "progressors," that is, "those who are making moral progress" (*proficientes*).[106] Within this context, both Stoics and their critics paid extraordinary attention to the figure of the sage, the one who had achieved wisdom even though he might not yet be aware of having done so (the so-called διαλεληθὼς σοφός, *dialelēthōs sophos*, "the self-eluding wise man").[107]

Although the Stoics were fond of the word *prokopē*, the term was used by others who were concerned with the moral life, such as Alcinous,[108] Philodemus,[109] Philo,[110] Paul,[111] and especially Plutarch, who wrote a work on *How May One Perceive His Moral Progress Toward Virtue?* (*Mor*. 75A–86A).[112] As with the emotions, the various authors and philosophical schools had their own understanding of what moral progress entailed. And no less an authority than O. Gigon was "convinced that the philosophical notion of '*progressio*,' i.e. *prokopē*, was created by the Peripatos" rather than the Stoics.[113] Be that as it may, other ancient authors discussed and depicted moral progress without using the word *prokopē*. For example, the author of the *Tabula of Cebes*, a work often referred to as an ancient *Pilgrim's Progress*, never uses "to progress" (*prokoptein*) or "progress" in describing the journey to true education and happiness.[114] In using the image of a journey to a desired destination as a schema for the moral life, the *Tabula* of *Cebes* is by no means unique (Harms 1970). Within this schema, stages on the journey mark advances in moral development and thus constitute moral progress. Philo certainly uses this schema (Weiss 1989), and it may well be the case that Lucan, the nephew of Seneca, does the same in his *Civil War* (*Pharsalia*), not only tracing the physical course of the war but simultaneously using it to depict Pompey's moral odyssey as a *proficiens* (Marti 1945: 367–73). As these remarks suggest, the concern of the essays in this volume is with the phenomenon of moral progression and regression, not the specific term used by the various authors.[115]

The organization of essays in this volume

All of the essays in this volume are preceded by abstracts, which provide a basic view of their contents and make any discussion of them here unnecessary. They are divided into three unequal parts. Part I ("Philosophy"), which has contributions from six scholars, is devoted to how the emotions and/or moral progress were treated by different philosophers and schools of philosophy. But ancient philosophy did not exist in an intellectual or social vacuum, strictly isolated and removed from literature and religion. On the contrary, philosophy was linked in crucial ways to both literature (Nussbaum 2003) and religion (Most 2003). The two essays in Part II ("Philosophy and Literature") and the five essays in Part III ("Philosophy and Religion") demonstrate similarities and differences in perspective from those examined in Part I and bring the volume to a close.

Notes

1 A recent example of a highly interdisciplinary study is Gross 2006, which is titled *The Secret History of Emotion: From Aristotle's "Rhetoric" to Modern Brain Science*.
2 See, for instance, the discussion of emotions in Asian thought in Marks and Ames 1995. For the Japanese concept of *amae* or "need-love" as an emotion, see Doi 2005: esp. 185–9, and for an attempt to detect *amae* as a concept in ancient Greece, see Young-Bruehl 2003: 311–28.
3 This was the last of Darwin's four great books to appear. *The Voyage of the Beagle* was first published in 1839 (with the better known second edition published in 1845), *On the Origin of Species* in 1859, and *The Descent of Man* in 1871. All four volumes are now conveniently available in Wilson 2006. The second edition of *The Expression of the Emotions*, edited by his son Francis, appeared posthumously in 1889, seven years after Darwin's death. The third edition of 1998 is accompanied by P. Ekman's helpful introduction and notes. See also Ekman 1973 and Ekman *et al.* 2003. On the more general topic of emotion, evolution, and rationality, see Evans and Cruse 2004.
4 For her pre-1994 work on the topic of the emotions, see Nussbaum 1986; 1987; 1989; 1990; 1993. Her 2001 monograph, subtitled *The Intelligence of Emotions*,

derives from her 1993 Gifford Lectures at the University of Edinburgh; though extremely wide-ranging in scope, it is grounded in her work on ancient emotions.

5 Important studies that appeared just prior to Nussbaum's book include those by Barton 1993 and Cairns 1993 as well as the collection of essays edited by Brunschwig and Nussbaum 1993. J. Annas, who had previously dealt with Epicurean emotions (Annas 1989), discussed both Stoic and Epicurean emotions in her *Hellenistic Philosophy of Mind* (Annas 1992: 103–20, 189–99; see also Annas 1993). Of course, interest in the emotions is not new to classicists; see, for example, Anderson 1964; Milobenski 1964; Fortenbaugh 1975a; Walcot 1978; and Braund 1988.

6 The Greek word πάθη in the authors and works covered in this volume is almost always the neuter plural (τὰ πάθη) of the singular noun τὸ πάθος. But πάθη in Greek is sometimes the feminine singular ἡ πάθη (plural αἱ πάθαι), a word that occurs as early as Herodotus and Plato, and for which LSJ gives *"passive state," "what is done or happens to a person or thing,"* and *"suffering, misfortune"* as the basic meanings. Suffice it here to note that the feminine noun *pathē*, like the neuter plural, occurs in both the singular and the plural in medical writings. For example, *On Head Injuries* in the Hippocratic corpus distinguishes between visible wounds (*trōsiōs*) in the head (*kephalē*) and internal *pathai* in the cranium (*osteon*), with the latter explicitly said to be "not manifest" (13, line 2). Later, in the context of discussing the kind of treatment that a wound (*helkos*) may require, the author makes a similar distinction between the flesh (*sarx*) and the *pathē* of the cranium (13, lines 32–3). References are to the LCL edition of Withington 1927.

7 This sense of the word *pathos* is found in English primarily in medical terms, such as "pathogen" and "pathology," and by extension in certain phrases with negative connotations, such as "pathological liar."

8 Graver (2002: 79) astutely points out Cicero's discussion of how to translate *pathē* is an initial rhetorical ploy that he uses to gain an advantage at the outset of the discussion. Furthermore, "*turbare*-derivatives were already standard in the Latin vocabulary of emotion, and *perturbatio* here and in *Acad.* 1.38–39 is in accordance with Cicero's own regular usage" (Graver 2002: 80). See, e.g., *De or.* 1.214; *Or. Brut.* 128; *Tusc.* 3.15, 18; 4.54; also Quintilian, *Inst.* 6.2.9. For bibliography on Cicero as a translator of Greek terms, see Gawlick and Görler 1994: 1057–8.

9 The translations of Aulus Gellius are those of Rolfe (1946; 1952), slightly modified.

10 On Quintilian, *Inst.* 6.2, see Gill 1984: 158–60; Wisse 1989: 64–5; and esp. Bons and Lane 2003. On Quintilian and his treatment of the emotions in Book 6 of *The Orator's Education*, see also Celentano 2003; Katula 2003, and Rodríguez Martín 2003.

11 On the general topic of rhetoric and emotion, see Konstan 2007.

12 Translations of Augustine's *On Marriage and Concupiscence* are, with slight modifications, those of Holmes (1885), as revised by Warfield, in the *NPNF*[1].

13 For Augustine's use and understanding of *affectus*, *passio*, and *perturbatio*, see O'Daly and Zumkeller 1986.

14 On *concupiscentia* in Augustine, see Bonner 1986.

15 The following discussion of the emotions as dealt with by ancient philosophers is intended to be introductory and representative, not comprehensive. It goes

without saying that various emotions had been portrayed in literature and on stage from the beginning of Greek history, but I omit these in the following discussion.

16 This is especially true of Stoics such as Posidonius, who "believes that the understanding of the nature of emotions is the basis of all ethical philosophy" (Edelstein 1936: 305).

17 See esp. Knuuttila and Sihvola 1998. For Plato on the arousal of emotion, see Blank 1993.

18 See the comparison of the two in Diogenes Laertius 4.6: Xenocrates "was naturally slow and clumsy. Hence Plato, comparing him to Aristotle, said, 'The one needed a spur, the other a bridle'" (trans. Hicks 1925: 1.381).

19 For a brief discussion of Plato's *Philebus*, see the essay in this volume by W.W. Fortenbaugh.

20 For the tradition that Aristotle left the Academy before Plato's death, see Diogenes Laertius 4.2; that tradition is accepted as historical by some scholars, such as Düring (1957: 276, 465). The vast majority of contemporary scholars, however, believes that Aristotle left Athens only after Plato died; see, for example, Tarán 1981: 8–9, and Ostwald and Lynch 1994: 611. On the problem of the "historical Aristotle" and the deficiencies of Diogenes Larterius's biography of Aristotle, see Sollenberger 1992: esp. 3817–18; Fitzgerald 1994.

21 For the tradition that Aristotle and Xenocrates went together to Assos at the invitation of Hermias, see Strabo, *Geogr.* 13.1.57; for Erastus and Corsicus as associates of Hermias, see Plato, *Ep.* 6. Although Flashar (1983a: 231) insists that it is not certain that Xenocrates accompanied Aristotle to Assos, the tradition is accepted by many scholars, including Jaeger (1948: 111), Grant (1980: 45–6), Krämer (1983: 63), Code (1997: 67), Ostwald and Lynch (1994: 611), and Dancy (1997: 568). Others, such as Jaeger (1948: 115) and Wormell (1935; 1996), place Callisthenes and Theophrastus in Assos during this period. Aristotle married Pythias, the niece and adopted daughter of Hermias, but the tyrant's relationship to Plato and the Academy is unclear. According to Strabo, *Geogr.* 13.1.57, Hermias had been a student of both Plato and Aristotle in Athens, whereas *Ep.* 6 in the Platonic corpus, whose authenticity has been disputed, presents Plato and Hermias as personally unacquainted (*Ep.* 6, 322E–323A), though possibly as acquaintances who had not been associated as friends in Athens (Düring 1957: 279). Wormell depicts Hermias as "a former student of the Academy (though he never met Plato)" who, even before Plato's death, was encouraging Erastus and Coriscus "to found a new philosophical school at Assos" (Wormell 1996). For bibliography on the entire Hermias episode, see Sollenberger 1992: 3817 n. 118.

22 Although Düring thinks "we should resist the temptation to speak of an organized school in Assos," he argues "that they went on with their studies and discussions there as a matter of course" (Düring 1957: 276).

23 There is no indication that Speusippus ever wrote a work specifically devoted to the emotions. He did, however, write a work *On Pleasure* as well as one on the Cyrenaic Aristippus (Diogenes Laertius 4.4), so it is likely that he, like Plato, discussed the passions in this context. That is also implicit in the ascription to him of the goal of ἀοχλησία (*aochlēsia*), freedom from disturbance (frg. 77 Tarán [1981: 168] = Clement of Alexandria, *Strom.* 2.22; for discussion of Speusippus's understanding of this term, see Tarán 1981: 435–7). Yet the biographical tradition

THE PASSIONS AND MORAL PROGRESS: AN INTRODUCTION

depicts Speusippus as being particularly prone to anger and illustrates this by the story of him flinging his favorite dog into a well when he was overcome with rage (Diogenes Laertius 4.1).
24 Aristotle stayed in Assos for two to three years, then moved to Mytilene. How long Xenocrates remained in Assos is unknown.
25 According to Diogenes Laertius 4.4, the ailing Speusippus asked Xenocrates to return to Athens to take over the leadership of the Academy. For the pseudonymous correspondence between Speusippus and Xenocrates that deals with this request, see *Socratic Epistles* 30–2 (Malherbe 1977: 296–301).
26 For the problem of the relationship between Xenocrates and Aristotle, see Mulvany 1926: 165; Düring 1957: 58, 314; Gigon 1958: 158–61; 1962: 64; Wehrli 1974: 73–4; and Ostwald and Lynch 1994: 611–12.
27 Krämer 1983: 44; Dancy 1997: 568. *On Emotions* is given by Krämer (1983: 63) as one of the four works by Xenocrates on the basic concepts of ethics.
28 For an interest in practical morality rather than ethical analysis as a characteristic of Xenocrates and his immediate successors, see Field and Hornblower 1996.
29 The *Vita Aristotelis* of Hesychius is also known as the *Vita Menagiana* after its first editor, G. Ménage. Inasmuch as Hesychius is neither the author of the biography nor the compiler of the list of Aristotle's works, Moraux (1951) and other scholars, such as Lord (1986), refer to Hesychius's list as "the anonymous list."
30 Ptolemy also wrote *Life of Aristotle*, and in the preface to that work he mentions that he had read the work of Andronicus of Rhodes (first century BCE) on Aristotle but says that he did not have it at hand when he wrote his biography of Aristotle – though it is clear that Ptolemy did remember it well and presumably used some notes that he had made from it (Plezia 1986; Gottschalk 1987: 1089 n. 48). Andronicus had not only arranged Aristotle's works in a coherent order but also discussed their authenticity and content (Sharples 1996a: 89). Because his list of Aristotle's works thus presumably derives from that of Andronicus, the lack of an *On Emotions* in the list can be used as evidence that Andronicus knew of no such work.
31 The anonymous list preserved by Hesychius contains three major sections, and it is only the first section (nos. 1–139) that goes back to the same source as Diogenes' list. Sollenberger (1992: 3850) argues that the lists of Aristotle's and Strato's works given by Diogenes Laertius derive from the same source. Hermippus of Smyrna, Andronicus of Rhodes, and Ariston of Ceos are the most common suggestions for the ultimate source of Aristotle's list of works as preserved by Diogenes Laertius and Hesychius, with Moraux (1951: 245) favoring Ariston and Düring (1956) arguing that Hermippus found the list in the library at Alexandria and transmitted it. See also Keaney 1963; Lord 1986.
32 In his edition of Diogenes Laertius's list, Düring (1957: 43) prints the titles of these two books on separate lines, giving them as numbers 37a and 37b in the list. For *On Emotions*, he simply cites *Eth. nic.* 2.4 1105b21, whereas he refers to excerpts from Seneca's *De ira* for Aristotle's putative *On Anger* (see Rose 1886: 82, frg. 80). He does not emend the anonymous list preserved by Hesychius, simply indicating in his critical apparatus that the original reference was to two separate works (Düring 1957: 83).

33 Rose's view that the work was a dialogue was contested already by Heitz (1865: 172).
34 It is sometimes argued (for example, by Lord 1986), that the list of Aristotle's works contains some written by Theophrastus, just as the list of the latter's works contains writings by Eudemus of Rhodes. Along these lines, it might be possible to conjecture that the Aristotelian works with "emotions" in the title were really by Theophrastus or another member of the Peripatos, but I know of no scholar who has ventured this hypothesis.
35 Rose did three editions of Aristotelian fragments. The first was published in 1863, and the second (1870) was for the edition produced by the Deutsche Akademie der Wissenschaft zu Berlin, for which Bekker (1831–70) was the chief editor. The third and final edition (1886) was for the Bibliotheca Teubneriana series.
36 Frgs 94–5 became part of frg. 80, which was assigned to *On the Statesman*, and frgs 96–7 became frgs 660–1, which are part of *Letters to Alexander*. For the fragments that he assigned to *On Emotions* in his first edition, see Rose 1863: 112–15, frgs 84–8.
37 For Aristotle and Theophrastus on the emotions, see Fortenbaugh 1975a; 1985; 2002; and his essay in this volume. For Aristotle, see also Rorty 1984; Mills 1985; Gastaldi 1987; Brinton 1988; Leighton 1987; 1996; Nussbaum 1996; Sihvola 1996; Striker 1996a; Cooper 1999: 406–23; Ben-Ze'ev 2003, and Viano 2003.
38 See esp. Annas 1989.
39 On Diogenes of Oenoanda and his evangelical inscription, see esp. Gordon 1996.
40 See Crantor, *On Grief*, frgs 1–6 Mette (1984). Frg. 4 (=Pseudo-Plutarch, *Cons. Apoll.* 104C) indicates that the work was an attempt by Crantor to comfort a certain Hippocles on the death of his children.
41 The fragments of this lost work have been collected by Vitelli (1979). For a discussion, see Kumaniecki 1969; for additional discussion and bibliography, see Gawlick and Görler 1994: 1050, 1083.
42 Graver 2002: 187–94. For Cicero on the emotions, see the bibliography cited by Gawlick and Görler 1994: 1138 and the discussions of Erskine 1997; Graver 2002; and Tieleman 2003: 288–320.
43 The genuineness of the work remains disputed. Hani (2003: 3–12) defends it as a work of Plutarch's youth, but it is more likely a pseudonymous work of the second century CE. For a list of scholars supporting and denying authenticity, see Hani 2003: 3–4 n. 1.
44 See esp. Buresch 1886; Favez 1937; Lattimore 1942; Kassel 1958; Johann 1968; Gregg 1975; and Scourfield 1993.
45 See esp. Cicero, *Tusc.* 3.59–60; also 3.54. Carneades left no writings, but his student Clitomachus preserved many of his arguments on various subjects. See esp. Ioppolo 1980; 1986: 211–14.
46 Cicero, *Tusc.* 3.21. See also Diogenes Laertius 5.1, 39; FHSG 493, 504.
47 I owe this observation to David Konstan, who kindly read a draft of this introduction and offered several helpful suggestions in regard to both substance and bibliography. The errors that remain are, of course, mine alone.
48 For the treatment of the emotions by the Old Stoa, see Rabel 1975; Brennan 1998. For Stoicism and the emotions in general, see Rabel 1977; 1981; Lloyd 1978; Inwood 1985: 127–81; Ledbetter 1993–4; Sorabji 1998; Inwood in Inwood and

THE PASSIONS AND MORAL PROGRESS: AN INTRODUCTION

Donini 1999: 699–714; Brennan 2003; Becker 2004; Strange 2004; Gill 2005; and Sellars 2006: 114–20. For a comparison of the Stoics and John Calvin on the emotions, see Fedler 2002.

49 For Zeno's treatment of the emotions, see esp. Sorabji 2002; see also Steinmetz 1994: 547–48 and the literature he cites.

50 The work is preserved primarily in extensive excerpts given by Galen in his *On the Doctrines of Hippocrates and Plato*. See *SVF* 3.456–90 for the relevant texts and Tieleman 2003 for an attempt to reconstruct Chrysippus's four-book treatise *On Emotions*. See also Bréhier 1951: 48–51, 245–58; Gould 1970: 181–96; Long and Sedley 1987: 1.420–3; Steinmetz 1994: 591, 616–18 (which includes copious bibliography); Graver 2002: 203–14; and Price 2005. For the debate whether Galen understood and thus properly portrayed Stoic views, see the essays by Cooper 1998; Gill 1998; 2006: 207–90; Sorabji 1998. See also Tieleman 1996 and note 59 below.

51 For a brief synopsis of Cleanthes on the emotions, see Steinmetz 1994: 576.

52 For some recent studies on envy, see the volume edited by Konstan and Rutter 2003.

53 See also *SVF* 1.434 = Cicero, *Tusc.* 3.18–21, which von Arnim (1903–24: 1.96) thinks is a lengthy fragment taken from Dionysius's *Peri apatheias*. He is followed in this regard by Steinmetz (1994: 558). In a similar way, Gottschalk (1997: 197) argues from the statement "the sage never gets angry" (*Tusc.* 3.19) that Dionysius is taking a conventional Stoic position. But it is by no means clear that all of this material is to be attributed to Dionysius; indeed, Graver gives only the first two Latin sentences of *Tusc.* 3.19 to Dionysius – not the sentence that has the statement about the sage never feeling anger – and thus can remark that these sentiments could come from either his Stoic or Cyrenaic periods (Graver 2002: 11, 89). On the problem of fragments, including the issue of determining the length of quotation within fragments, see the essays in Most 1997.

54 On *apatheia* in pagan and Christian antiquity, see esp. Spanneut 1994; 2002; on the relation between human emotion and divine *apatheia* in Gregory of Nyssa, see Smith 2004. For the Stoic use of the term *apathēs*, see White 1978: 115–19.

55 For text, translation, and a brief discussion, see O'Neil 1977: 62–71, 92–7; see also the essay by D.E. Aune in this volume.

56 Since Pohlenz 1909, this letter of Panaetius has frequently been suggested as one of the sources for Book 2 of Cicero's *Tusculan Disputations*; see Steinmetz 1994: 649. On Tubero, see Cicero, *Acad. post.* 135; *Brut.* 117; *Fin.* 4.23; *Tusc.* 4.4.

57 Frg. 37 Edelstein and Kidd 1972: 55; for discussion and translation, see Kidd in Edelstein and Kidd 1988: 1.180; 1999: 94.

58 As in the case of Chrysippus, the work of Posidonius on the emotions is preserved chiefly through long excerpts in Galen's *On the Doctrines of Hippocrates and Plato*, so that it is Posidonius's best known ethical work. For text and translation, see Edelstein and Kidd 1972: 49–55, frgs 30–5; 1999: 86–93; for additional Posidonian fragments dealing with the emotions, see Edelstein and Kidd: 1972: 137–62, frgs 150–69; 1999: 204–35. For discussion, see Pohlenz 1898; 1965: 1.140–71; Kidd 1971; Kidd in Edelstein and Kidd 1988: 1.153–79; 2.553–625; Long and Sedley 1987: 1.422–3; Stevens 1993; Steinmetz 1994: 675, 691–2, with copious bibliography; Cooper 1999: 449–84; Graver 2002: 215–23; and Tieleman 2003: 198–287.

59 See Glibert-Thirry 1977b. On the debate whether Posidonius, who is depicted in the ancient sources as taking a heterodox Stoic view of the emotions, was actually more in line with the position of the Old Stoa, see the works cited in note 50 above, esp. the recent contribution by Gill (2006: 207–90).
60 See esp. Arius Didymus, *Epitome of Stoic Ethics* 10–10e Pomeroy (1999), a section that is introduced at the end of 9b with the words, "let us speak next about passions" (*peri pathōn*). Such summaries were not unique to Stoics; for a Middle Platonic example, see Alcinous, *Did.* 32, with the translation and commentary of Dillon 1993: 42–4, 193–8.
61 On Seneca and emotions, see Manning 1974; Inwood 1993; Schiesaro 1997; Wilson 1997. For Seneca and anger, see Fillion-Lahille 1984 and Mattern-Parkes 2001.
62 For Arius Didymus and Epictetus on the emotions, see the essay of E.M. Krentz in this volume, and on Epictetus, see esp. Long 2006d. It is not certain that Arius Didymus was a Stoic, for he also wrote an account of Peripatetic ethics and praised the Platonist philosopher Eudorus. Yet he is included after Posidonius in a generally reliable sequence of Stoic philosophers that appears to have been drawn up in antiquity; this and other considerations make it "likely that he was regarded by his contemporaries as a Stoic" (Pomeroy 1999: 3).
63 Frg. 36 Edelstein and Kidd (1972: 55); see also Kidd in Edelstein and Kidd 1988: 1.178–79; 1999: 93. Among the fragments not assigned to specific works, see frg. 155, which deals with anger. For scholars who believe that Seneca made use of this work in writing his own *On Anger*, see Steinmetz 1994: 675.
64 On the Cynic treatment of the emotions, see the essay by D.E. Aune in this volume.
65 See Erler 1992b; Procopé 1993; Fowler 1997 and the essay in this volume by D. Armstrong.
66 See Pohlenz 1896; Becchi 1990.
67 Hieronymus's treatise on anger apparently carried the title *On Not Being Angry* (Sharples 1996b) and took a position different from that of Theophrastus (Wehrli 1983: 576). In contrast to Sharples, S.A. White argues that "Hieronymus was accused of apostasy for equating happiness with 'absence of disturbance (*aochlêsia*),' but he probably sought to update Aristotelian theory...[and] probably also helped develop the Peripatetic theory of 'moderate passions' from Aristotle's doctrine of the mean" (White 1997).
68 On the treatment of the emotions by Neopythagoreans, see the essay by J.C. Thom in this volume.
69 For the therapy of anger, see esp. Rabbow 1914, with the review by Pohlenz 1916; for anger control, see Schimmel 1979 and esp. Harris 2001.
70 For Galen's treatment of the emotions, see the essays in this volume by L.C.A. Alexander and L.M. White. See also Manuli 1988 and Hankinson 1993.
71 For Galen's anecdotes as evidence of domestic violence against slaves, see Fitzgerald 2007.
72 Stoics generally distinguished between transitory emotions and abiding dispositions, classifying only the latter as diseases (Rabel 1981).
73 Because of the close coherence of these two works, they are almost always treated and translated together; see, for instance, Harkins 1963.
74 For the two kinds of diseases in Galen, see Ballester 1988.

75 For a translation and short discussion of Maximus's oration, see Trapp 1997a: 59–66.
76 In addition to previously cited studies, see Emilsson 1998 (on Plotinus); Engberg-Pedersen 1998 (on Marcus Aurelius); and Kendeffy 2000 (on Lactantius).
77 See the essay in this volume by S.G. Nugent.
78 See Rieks 1989 and Dion 1993. For Virgil and anger, see Wright 1997 and Gill 2003.
79 See the essay in this volume by L.C.A. Alexander.
80 See Völker 1938: 126–54 and the essay in this volume by D. Winston.
81 See the essays in this volume by D.C. Aune, T. Engberg-Pedersen, and J. Ware.
82 For Clement of Alexandria, as well as a number of other ancient moralists, see the essay in this volume by L.M. White.
83 For lists of vices and their use, see Fitzgerald 1992.
84 The translation is that of Robbins 1940: 363, 365.
85 For a discussion of *Tetrabiblos* 3.11–14, see Bouché-Leclercq 1899: 428–36.
86 The literature on the general question of progress is vast. Selected examples include Bury 1924; Teggart 1949; Baillie 1950; Van Doren 1967; Sorel 1969; Nisbet 1980; and Mathiopoulos 1989.
87 Studies dealing specifically with the ancient world include Boughton 1932; Lauffer 1953; Guthrie 1957: 80–94; Luschnat 1959; Edelstein 1967; Thraede 1972; Dodds 1973: 1–25; den Boer 1976; 1977; Blundell 1986; Bracher 1987; Dihle 1988; and Schenkeveld 1998. Whether Xenophanes frg. 18 Diels–Krantz (1951–2) is the earliest expression of a Greek belief in some kind of human progress is debated; contrast the interpretations of Lesher 1991 and Tulin 1993. Lucretius's history of civilization in Book 5 of his *On the Nature of Things* has naturally attracted more commentary than can be given here, but a sampler includes Robin 1916; Taylor 1947; Merlan 1950; Keller 1951; Borle 1962; Beye 1963; Furley 1989: 206–22; and esp. Campbell 2003. Other studies on particular authors include Campbell 1982 (Virgil) and Harder 2003 (Callimachus).
88 On primitivism in the ancient world, see esp. Lovejoy and Boas 1935, and Campbell 2003.
89 So Koch (2005) in his discussion of Daniel 2. In addition to providing a quite extensive discussion of the pertinent Persian materials, he claims that Hesiod and Daniel independently derive the schema of four metals from the same Persian source.
90 The study of Gatz (1967) remains fundamental. For the metallic myth and the idea of a golden age in Virgil and his predecessors, see Johnston 1980. For Juvenal and some ancient attitudes toward the golden age, see Singleton 1972.
91 On the Hesiodic myth, see esp. West 1978: 172–204. For the protest that Hesiod's version of the myth is not a depiction of a gradual but inevitable decline in culture, see Sihvola 1989: 29–31.
92 *Pan. Lat.* 9.18.5 Mynors (1964), trans. Bowen and Garnsey 2003: 44. The speech, "On Restoring the Schools," was delivered in 297 or 298 CE and advocated the rebuilding of a school damaged in the war. On Eumenius, see Hudson-Williams and Winterbottom 1996; on the *XII Panegyrici Latini*, see Maguinness and Winterbottom 1996.
93 Bowen and Garnsey 2003: 10.
94 Bowen and Garnsey 2003: 44.

95 Bowen and Garnsey 2003: 40.
96 Bowen and Garnsey 2003: 41.
97 All translations of Lactantius are those of Bowen and Garnsey 2003.
98 Bowen and Garnsey 2003: 44.
99 A concern with *prokopē* was also central to later monastic life: "The unseen ways to moral progress are to sit and control one's thoughts, ... and [to] observe the canonical hours, not to neglect such hours in private, but to mediate, and, finally, always to observe good moral conversation and to refrain from evil talk" (Martin of Braga, *Sayings of the Egyptian Fathers* 21, trans. Barlow 1969: 22). See also saying 58, where spiritual progress for a monk is defined as humility.
100 See, in general, Kidd 1955: 191–4; Long and Sedley 1987: 1.385, 427; Inwood 1985: 154, 166, 182–215; Annas 1993: 405–6; and Donini in Inwood and Donini 1999: 724–36.
101 The major study of moral progress in the Old Stoa is the massive (xxxvii + 607 pages) but unpublished dissertation of Haber (1972), who examines *prokopē* within the larger context of the Stoics' understanding of psychological development from conception to maturity. She stresses that, inasmuch as the soul was understood in the Old Stoa as a physical organism, *prokopē* was understood by them as both an ethical and a physical phenomenon. See also Görler 1984; Steinmetz 1994: 545 (Zeno) and 616 (Chrysippus); and Blank 1997: 193 (Diogenes of Seleucia).
102 Panaetius was famous as the Stoic whose "ethics were directed towards the man making moral progress, not the sage" (Griffin and Atkins 1991: 168). See, for example, Panaetius, frg. 114 Straaten (1962: 43) = Seneca, *Ep*. 116.5. For Posidonius on the *sapiens* and *proficiens*, see Edelstein and Kidd 1972: 165–7, frgs 174–9; Kidd in Edelstein and Kidd 1988: 2.643–58; 1999: 240–4; Sorabji 2000: 114–15.
103 See Schiesaro 1997: 103, 108, 111; Sorabji 2000: 52, 171, 234–5; and the essay in this volume by J. Ware.
104 See esp. Epictetus, *Diss*. 1.4; Bonhöffer 1894: 144–53 (=1996: 186–99); Dobbin 1998: 88–98; Sorabji 2000: 51–2; and the essay by E.M. Krentz in this volume.
105 The most influential study of the Stoic concept of moral progress remains that of Luschnat 1958, whose contribution has been critically assessed recently by Roskam 2004. A fairly new testimony to the Stoic concept of *prokopē* is P.Mil.Vogl. Inv. 1241, a papyrus fragment that has been discussed by Colombo (1954), who thought it could be a fragment of Chrysippus, Decleva Caizzi and Funghi 1988, and Gigante 1991.
106 On the *sapiens* and *proficiens*, see Fitzgerald 1988: 55–9.
107 The translation of the phrase is that of Sedley 1977: 94. For the Stoics, the transition from folly and vice to wisdom and virtue was so instantaneous that an awareness of its occurrence might even elude the sage. Chrysippus devoted an entire work to this point (Diogenes Laertius 7.198 = *SVF* 2.15), which was typically ridiculed by Stoic critics. That Diogenes Laertius gives Chrysippus's book as one of his works on logic gives support to D. Sedley's contention that Stoic thinking on this matter was influenced by both the sorites (or "heap") argument and the "elusive argument" (διαλελήθως λόγος). See Sedley 1977: 93–5 and Alesse 1997.

108 Alcinous, *Did.* 30.1 As Dillon (1993: 183, 40) points out, Alcinous uses the plural (*prokopai*) to indicate virtues in the process of development, "stages of progress towards virtue."
109 See the essay in this volume by D. Armstrong.
110 See Bonhöffer 1894: 148–9 (=1996: 195–6); Völker 1938; Bréhier 1950: 250–71; Winston 1984: 410–14; Sorabji 2000: 385–6; and the essay by D. Winston in this volume.
111 See the essays in this volume by T. Engberg-Pedersen and J. Ware. For Origen's understanding of moral progress as central for his interpretation of Rom 7: 7–25, see Stowers 1995: 193–97.
112 See the essay by R.A. Wright in this volume.
113 Gigon 1988: 266. In support of this contention, he points to Diogenes Laertius, who says that whereas the Stoics hold that there is nothing intermediate between virtue and vice, the Peripatetics maintain that there is *prokopē*, the state of moral improvement. Gigon also attributes the creation of this concept to Theophrastus rather than Aristotle. The term *prokopē* is indeed attributed in the sources to Theophrastus, but apparently only in regard to *politeia* (FHSG 610). On Aristotle and moral development, see Garver 1994, with the comments of Chaplin 1994.
114 For text, English translation, commentary, and a fairly comprehensive bibliography up to 1981, see Fitzgerald and White 1983. More recent studies and translations in various languages include Pesce 1982; Elsner 1995: 39–46; Ortiz Garcia 1995; Banchich 1997; Ruiz Gito 1997 (also 1993); Trapp 1997b; Ramelli 2003: 56–64; Ramelli in Ramelli and Lucchetta 2004: 359–67; Hirsch-Luipold *et al.* 2005; and Seddon 2005. See also the essay in this volume by L.M. White.
115 For studies dealing with the later patristic concept (found especially in Gregory of Nyssa) of "perpetual progress" or "constant straining" (*epektasis*) toward God – derived from Paul's use of the participle *epekteinomenos* in Phil 3:13 – see Daniélou 1944: 309–26; Mühlenberg 1966; Ferguson 1973; 1976; Heine 1975; and Blowers 1992.

Part I

PHILOSOPHY

2

ARISTOTLE AND THEOPHRASTUS ON THE EMOTIONS

William W. Fortenbaugh

This article begins with the late Platonic Academy, in which Aristotle was active. Emotions were distinguished from passions like hunger and thirst, and the relationship of emotion to thought was explained in terms of efficient causation. Aristotle's definition of emotion in the *Rhetoric* with its emphasis on affecting judgment is said to reflect the rhetorical context. The idea that emotions are followed by pleasure and pain is seen to fit poorly with the subsequent accounts of hate and kindness. It is suggested that Aristotle rejected a general definition of emotion in favor of an analysis that emphasizes similarity. Comparison with Aristotle's analysis of friendship is instructive. The bodily component involved in emotional response is not ignored, nor is the possibility of analysis in terms of the more and the less. Theophrastus' treatment of faultfinding, anger, and rage provides an example. Finally, the relationship of emotion to good character is discussed.

Introduction

Human passions have long been a subject of great interest. Indeed, fascination with the subject can be traced back to the very beginnings of Western literature – more precisely, to Homer's *Iliad*, whose opening line makes reference to the anger of Achilles. In Lattimore's (1951: 59) translation, we read, "Sing, goddess, the anger of Peleus' son Achilleus." In the Greek text, the word translated as "anger," *mēnis*, enjoys pride of place: μῆνιν ἄειδε, θεά, Πηληϊάδεω Ἀχιλῆος. Homer will tell a tale of angry passion whose terrible consequences almost overwhelm the Achaean host. He also will tell how warriors become frightened when confronted by danger, how they respond to appeals for pity, and how they are overcome by laughter.[1] This interest in emotional behavior is not peculiar to Homer. It is clear also in the writings of the lyric poets, tragedians, writers of comedy, historians, rhetoricians, and philosophers.[2] My concern is with the last group, the philosophers, and in particular the early Peripatetics, who not only recognized the importance of emotional response but also subjected it to intense philosophic analysis. I plan to discuss this analysis, beginning with the late Platonic Academy, in which Aristotle played an active part. I will move on to his independent views and take note of those of Theophrastus, Aristotle's pupil and successor as head of the Peripatos. I will not hesitate to restate matters discussed on earlier occasions,[3] for I want to offer an inclusive essay, one that both introduces a topic of great interest and at the same time takes note of its many aspects. However, I also will be modifying earlier views, adding a new analysis as well as illustrative material and replying to recent criticism.[4]

Emotions distinguished from other passions

In Plato's *Philebus*, a late dialogue concerned with pleasure, wisdom, and human happiness,[5] Socrates is made to draw a distinction between three kinds of mixed pleasures and pains. One kind is said to concern the body and to be found in the body itself. By way of illustration, Socrates cites the person who experiences a painful itch and finds pleasant relief in scratching (*Phileb.* 46A8–47C3). A second kind is said to involve body and soul. Socrates' example concerns replenishment. A person who is hungry and expects to be fed feels the pain of an empty stomach and takes pleasure in the thought of being fed (*Phileb.* 47C3–D4). A third kind is assigned to the soul, independent of the body. It is illustrated by a list including anger, fear, longing, lament, love, emulation, and envy and by a lengthy discussion of the mixed feelings of envious individuals (*Phileb.* 47D5–50A9). Each of these three kinds of mixed pleasures and pains can be described as a passion – in Greek, *pathos*[6] – but as Socrates makes clear, they are very different. Bodily disturbances, scabies, and other physiological abnormalities are fundamental to the first kind; normal bodily drives, hunger and thirst, are the basis of the second; and what we call emotions are the stuff of the third. For our purposes, the important point is that Socrates recognizes that emotions such as anger and fear are neither diseased conditions of the body nor natural drives for replenishment. They are, of course, pleasant as well as painful,[7] and for this reason they may be said to resemble the other two kinds of mixed pleasures and pains; but they are significantly different. As Socrates is made to say, they are "that mix which the soul alone often takes to itself" (*Phileb.* 47D8).

What Socrates finds difficult to explain is the relationship between thought and emotion; and as a consequence, he is unable to convince his interlocutor that pleasures and pains, fear and expectation can be correctly called true and false (*Phileb.* 36C6–D2). To be sure, Socrates is able to point out similarities between opinion on the one hand and pleasure and pain on the other, but he runs into trouble when he observes that pleasures often occur together "with" (*meta*) false opinion (*Phileb.* 37E10). The interlocutor construes the preposition "with" as simple concurrence and thinks of opinion as something external to pleasure: the opinion may be false, but no one would call the pleasure false (*Phileb.* 37E12–38A2). Socrates does not give up; he speaks of pleasure and pain "following" (*hepesthai*) true and false opinion (*Phileb.* 38B9), and then he argues that pleasures and pains, including emotions such as fear and anger, sometimes are based on (*epi*) reality and sometimes not (*Phileb.* 40D8–E4). When no objection is raised, Socrates asserts that true and false opinions "fill up" (*anapimplanai*) pleasures and pains with their own affection (*Phileb.* 42A7–9). To speak of "filling up" is to introduce metaphor. It expresses Socrates' belief that opinion and pleasures and pains are intimately connected, but it leaves unclear the precise nature of the connection.

In the *Philebus* Socrates' difficulty is not resolved, but discussion was continued in Plato's Academy. The young Aristotle was a participant, and his early work the *Topics*[8] provides some evidence concerning his contribution. I cite three passages. In Book 4, Aristotle discusses ways to attack an assigned genus. He recommends showing that a more or equally likely candidate is not the genus and illustrates his recommendation by reference to anger. Both pain and the thought of being slighted are parts of the essence of anger; but if the more likely candidate, pain, is not the genus, then neither is the thought of being slighted (*Top.* 4.6 127b26–32).[9] In Book 6, Aristotle takes up definitions in which the preposition "with" occurs. He recommends making clear how the preposition is used and illustrates the recommendation by reference to anger. When anger is defined as "pain with the thought of being slighted," the preposition means "on account of" (*dia*). It does not mean "and" or "made up out of" or "in the same receptacle" or "in the same place" or "in the same time" (*Top.* 6.13 150b27–151a19). As in the preceding example, the thought of being slighted is recognized as essential to anger, but now it is explained as the cause of that emotion. In Book 8, which is generally regarded as later than Books 4 and 6, a causal analysis appears to be accepted without question.[10] Aristotle is discussing the use of coordinate terms in order to establish a premise; and by way of illustration, he introduces anger. If we want to establish that an angry person desires revenge on account of (*dia*) an apparent slight, then we should first win agreement concerning the definition of anger: anger is a desire for revenge on account of (*dia*) an apparent slight (*Top.* 8.1 156a30–3).

Examples advanced in the *Topics* need not represent a view endorsed by Aristotle; but in the case of anger, there seems little reason to doubt that the definition found in Book 8 represents Aristotle's considered opinion. It is in line with his remarks in Book 6 and exhibits striking similarities to the definition of anger set forth in the *Rhetoric*. There, in Book 2, Aristotle defines anger as "a desire for revenge accompanied by pain on account of [*dia*] an apparent slight to oneself or to one's own, the slight being unjustified" (*Rhet.* 2.2 1378a30–2). This definition includes more than the definition of *Top.* 8 – it includes a mention of pain and the qualifier "unjustified"[11] – but in regard to anger being a desire for revenge on account of an apparent slight, it agrees fully with *Top.* 8. Aristotle, it seems, is now entirely clear about the involvement of thought in an emotion such as anger. It is the cause of the emotional response; and as such, it is mentioned in the essential definition of the emotion in question.

Clarity concerning the involvement of thought in emotional response will have been achieved not only through a close examination of individual emotions but also through a general consideration of definition in the context of demonstrative science. I am thinking especially of the *Posterior Analytics*, in which Aristotle tells us that questions of essence (*ti esti*) and questions of cause (*dia ti*) are one and the same (*An. post.* 2.2 90a15). His stock example is that of the lunar eclipse. The essential definition is one that not only speaks of a deprivation of light but also states the efficient cause: obstruction by the earth (*An. post.* 2.2 90a16). Diminution of the moon's light resulting from any other cause may have the same appearance, but it is essentially different, for the lunar eclipse is by definition attributable to the interposition of the earth.[12] The application to emotions is obvious, and Aristotle will not have missed it. He recognized the importance of thought as the cause of emotional response, and in the case of anger, he offers a definition that mentions not only a final cause, revenge but also an efficient cause, the appearance of being slighted (*Rhet.* 2.2 1377a31–3).

In my preceding remarks, I have found it helpful to emphasize Aristotle's use of the preposition "on account of" (*dia*). To avoid any misunderstanding, I want to state clearly that Aristotle does not always use this preposition when referring to the efficient cause; and that is true both of the *Posterior Analytics* and of the *Rhetoric*. In the former work, we find him substituting "by" (*hypo*); for example, to the question of what an eclipse is, he replies, "A deprivation of light from the moon by the obstruction of the earth" (*An. post.* 2.2 90a15–16).[13] In the latter work, prepositions such as "resulting from" (*ek*) or "concerning" (*peri*) are found; for example, fear is defined as "a pain or disturbance resulting from the appearance of a future evil which is destructive or painful" (*Rhet.* 2.5 1382a21–2), and shame as "a pain or disturbance concerning those evils which appear to contribute to bad reputation" (*Rhet.* 2.6 1383b12–13). There is no confusion here. In the early stages of an investigation, it is often useful to avoid variation in terminology, but once clarity is achieved, consistency in the use of single words and phrases becomes unimportant and perhaps misleading. For the student may fail to appreciate the many different ways in which the same notion is expressed in everyday language.

A rhetorical definition of emotion

In *Rhet.* 2, prior to the discussion of individual emotions such as anger and fear, Aristotle offers a general definition of the emotions: "The emotions are all those feelings on account of which men so change as to differ in judgment, and which are followed by pain and pleasure" (*Rhet.* 2.1 1378a20–2). By way of clarification, Aristotle adds a short list of emotions: "for example, anger, pity, fear and all other such emotions and their opposites" (*Rhet.* 2.1 1378a22–3). The reference to opposites is clear enough. Aristotle is looking forward to the subsequent treatment of individual emotions, in which opposites are discussed together; for example, anger is paired with calmness (*Rhet.* 2.2–3), pity with indignation (*Rhet.* 2.8–9), and fear with confidence (*Rhet.* 2.5). More important is the list of particular emotions, because without this list the definition might be taken inclusively, so that it covers diseases and bodily drives. For these passions, at least in some forms, not only involve pain and pleasure but also affect one's judgment.

A different way to eliminate diseases and bodily drives from consideration is to include within the definition a reference to thought as the efficient cause. If the argument of the preceding section is correct, Aristotle was capable of giving such a definition, but he chose not to do so. Instead, he refers to change of judgment as a consequence of emotions such as anger, pity, and fear. That almost certainly reflects Aristotle's concern with rhetoric and, more precisely, his interest in the power of emotional appeal. The orator who cannot persuade listeners by arguing the issue may try to effect a change in judgment by working on their emotions. In another context, that effect might be ignored or dismissed as a consequence of emotional response and not an essential feature. But in the context of rhetoric, Aristotle makes it a defining mark, for he is interested in a particular group of emotions: those strong emotions that orators arouse when argument fails. Weak emotions that do not affect the critical capacity of the audience are of no use and therefore excluded by defining emotions in terms of altered judgment.

So much is clear. But there are problems with the definition in the context of Aristotle's *Rhetoric*. I mention two. First, it fails as a general definition of the emotions subsequently discussed. The clearest case of failure concerns hate (*misos*). This emotion is explicitly dissociated from pain. As Aristotle puts it, the angry person feels pain, but the person who hates does not (*Rhet.* 2.4 1382a12–13). The contrast is intelligible. Those who are angry are responding to personal insult and as a result feel pain. Those who hate are not so affected, for they are not responding to a personal attack; rather, their emotion is aroused by the odious qualities of persons with whom they may have no contact whatsoever. But if such a contrast is intelligible, the idea that hate occurs without pain fits poorly with the definition of emotions, for in this definition pain and pleasure are said to accompany the emotions. Without some qualifying remark that allows for exceptions,[14] it seems natural to understand pain and pleasure as essential to emotional response; but in that case hate fails to qualify as an emotion and is oddly included among the several emotions discussed in *Rhet.* 2.

Something similar can be said about kindness (*charis*). Aristotle defines this emotion without any reference to pain or pleasure. It is said to be "service to one in need, not in return for something, nor in order that something may be gained by the person rendering the service, but rather by that person (who is in need)" (*Rhet.* 2.7 1385a18–19). In what follows, Aristotle focuses on the needs of the person served (*Rhet.* 2.7 1385a20–34) and on the fact that the service must be rendered freely and without consideration of personal gain (*Rhet.* 2.7 1385a34–b10). What is missing is any reference to the pain or pleasure felt by the person rendering kindness. There is, of course, mention of the pain felt by the person in need (*Rhet.* 2.7 1358a23, 25, 33), but that only serves to emphasize Aristotle's silence concerning any painful or pleasurable feelings felt by the person who does good service. Silence here may exhibit good judgment, for it is not at all clear that meeting the needs of another – that is, acts of kindness – must be accompanied by any feelings whatsoever. A person may simply think it right and proper to be helpful and therefore stand by others who are in need.[15] But that may not be the whole story, for Aristotle begins his discussion by asking a question concerning gratitude (being grateful, *charin echein*): Toward whom do men feel gratitude, for what reasons and how are they disposed (*Rhet.* 2.7 1385a16)? The subsequent discussion of acts of kindness may be viewed as an answer to the initial question: people feel gratitude toward those who do them a kindness freely and without seeking some gain.[16] But even if that is the case, it does not remove the difficulty in question. For there is nothing said concerning the pleasures and pains that may or may not be part of being grateful. Of course, we do hear of the pains that a person in need experiences, but they precede the act of kindness and are not part of the resulting gratitude.[17] I conclude that while the definition of emotions in *Rhet.* 2.1 speaks of pain and pleasure, one or more of the emotions discussed later in the same book – certainly hate and possibly gratitude and kindness – are not tied to painful and pleasant feelings.

The second problem concerns altered judgment. Introducing the discussion of emotional appeal and prior to the general definition of emotion, Aristotle speaks of preparing a judge by putting him into an emotional condition. For things do not appear the same to persons who feel friendly and feel hate, and to persons who are angered and are calm. They appear either altogether different or different in degree (*Rhet.* 2.1 1377b24, 28–9, 31–1378a1). Aristotle's words are clear enough, and they explain the inclusion of friendliness and hate (*philia* and *misos*) within a discussion of emotional appeal. Nevertheless, it is not clear that persons who feel friendly and hate are always affected in regard to judgment. It may be that emotions such as anger and pity normally (though perhaps not always) distort a person's critical faculty so that it is no better than a warped straight stick (see *Rhet.* 1.1 1354a24–6), but friendliness and hate are much less closely tied to distorted judgment. Hate, free of pain, seems the appropriate emotion for a juror who votes on the basis of the evidence to condemn a hardened criminal. And friendliness in the sense of goodwill (*eunoia*) may be thought desirable in a juror, providing it is exhibited equally in regard to both plaintiff and defendant.[18] In addition, the orator seeks to present himself as a person of goodwill: a friend of the city (*philopolis*)[19] and someone well disposed toward the audience (*Rhet.* 2.1 1377b26–7, 1378a8). Aristotle tells us that goodwill and feelings of friendship will be discussed among the emotions (*Rhet.* 2.1 1378a18–19), but certainly he does not want to say that manifesting goodwill is tantamount to an announcement of biased judgment. That may explain in part why there is no account of goodwill in the subsequent discussion of individual emotions, but I doubt that it is the whole story or even the most important factor. My guess is that the account of individual emotions (*Rhet.* 2.2–11) was transferred to the *Rhetoric* from a different context, probably from a lost work such as *Divisions* or *On Emotions: Anger*,[20] and that the account never included a discussion of goodwill distinct from that of feelings of friendship. But whatever the truth concerning the origin of the account of individual emotions, it seems clear that Aristotle's introductory remarks on preparing a judge and putting him into an emotional condition are in line with the subsequent definition of emotions as feelings that cause a change in judgment. Together they rule out those cases of friendliness and hate that are not relevant to emotional appeal – that is, those that are of no help when the orator seeks to make the weaker argument appear the stronger.

An analysis emphasizing similarity

The definition of emotions given in *Rhet.* 2 is oriented toward emotional appeal and therefore not intended as a general definition covering all the emotions felt by human beings. In a rhetorical context, that is understandable and even commendable, but we are left wondering whether Aristotle ever offered a truly general definition of emotional response. He may have done so in one or both of the lost works mentioned in the preceding section, but if he did, the definition is lost along with those works. My suspicion, however, is that Aristotle would have rejected a general definition in favor of an inclusive analysis that emphasizes similarity, for the phenomena in question have almost no common core, and to the extent that they have one, it is determinable rather than determinate.[21]

In developing this idea, it may be helpful to begin by looking at Book 8 of the *Nicomachean Ethics*, for there we have a rather clear example of the kind of analysis that Aristotle could have offered in the case of emotion. I am thinking of the discussion of friendship.[22] Aristotle recognizes three types of friendship: that of the virtuous, that of pleasure-seekers, and that of those associated for the sake of utility. He is not in doubt that each of these types is properly called friendship, but he never offers a general definition applicable to all three. Instead, he focuses on the several ways in which the friendships resemble each other. He tells us that the three types exhibit common features: reciprocal affection, wishing (one's friend) well, and awareness (*Eth. nic.* 8.1 1155b27–1156a5). These are the necessary marks of friendship, such that the absence of any one of them is sufficient to rule out friendship. But these features are not all there is to friendship. Each of the three types has its own goal: what is good, pleasant, and useful (*Eth. nic.* 8.1 1155b18–21); and these goals serve not only to mark off the types but also to relate them through similarity based on analogy. For as the good is to virtuous friends, so the pleasant is to friends of pleasure and the useful to persons associated for the sake of utility. Finally, there are features shared by two of the types but not by all three. These features are the qualities of being pleasant and being useful. The friendship of the virtuous has both, while the friendship of pleasure-seekers is pleasant but not useful, and vice versa for the friendship of those associated for utility. Accordingly, the friendships based on pleasure and utility resemble friendship based on virtue; and through that type of friendship they are related indirectly to each other.[23] In sum, friendship based on virtue is complete, in that it has all the qualities looked for in a friendship; and for that reason, it is a kind of perfect or paradigm case. In comparison, the other types are incomplete; but still they are friendships, for they not only possess the necessary qualities but also exhibit similarity based on analogy and a relationship that is mediated through the perfect or complete friendship of the virtuous.

Returning now to the emotions, I suggest that Aristotle will have offered – or more cautiously, was capable of offering – a similar analysis. He could have pointed out that all emotions resemble each other, in that they have thought as their efficient cause. As such, thought is not just a common feature; it is a necessary one, so that any passion resulting from a different cause is not an emotion. Aristotle could also take note of the goals that not only differentiate between emotions such as anger and fright but also relate them through similarity based on analogy. For as the angry person acts with revenge as his goal, so the frightened person has safety as his goal. In addition, Aristotle could observe that some emotions lack features that others have. Feelings of pain and pleasure come immediately to mind: although characteristic of most emotions, they are missing from hate and perhaps from kindness.[24] Something similar can be said of goals. Anger and fright necessarily involve goals that lead to action. Angry individuals strive for revenge, and frightened individuals seek safety. Hence, Aristotle tells us that anger is absent when revenge appears impossible (*Rhet.* 1.11 1370b13), and that fear requires some hope of safety, for fear makes people deliberate, and no one deliberates concerning things considered hopeless (*Rhet.* 2.5 1383a5–8). In contrast, there are other emotions that do not exhibit a necessary connection with goal-directed behavior. Pity and shame are examples. People can and often do feel pity when they perceive others suffering an evil for which there is no remedy; and they experience shame when they realize that they themselves have committed wrongs that are impossible to reverse.[25] For our purposes, the important point is that here, as with different types of friendship, we have the possibility of mediating a relationship. Kindness involves goal-directed action, but it lacks a close connection with feelings of pleasure or pain; pity is marked by feelings of pain, but there is no necessary tie to goal-directed behavior. Nevertheless, both emotions resemble central cases such as anger and fright, and through these central cases, they are related to each other.

A difference between the analysis of types of friendship and the proposed analysis of emotions is the number of common characteristics. In the case of friendship, there are four characteristics possessed by each of the three types: being goal-oriented (a similarity established by analogy), reciprocal affection, wishing (one's friend) well, and awareness (all necessary if friendship is to exist). In the case of emotions, the number is less. Goal-directed behavior is characteristic of many but not all emotions, and the same is true of pain and pleasure. What is characteristic of all emotions is a single feature: thought as the efficient cause. But having said that, I emphasize that thought here is determinable, much like wishing well in the case of friendships. When pleasure-seekers and persons associated on the basis of utility wish each other well, the wish is self-interested and dependent upon the attainment of some pleasure or advantage. In the case of the virtuous, wishing well is very different; instead of self-interest, there is concern for the moral goodness of the parties involved.[26] Similarly in regard to emotions, no one thought is the efficient cause. In the case of anger, it is the thought of an unjustified slight, and in the case of fear, it is the thought of imminent danger. That suffices to mark a distinction between the two emotions, but these thoughts are not sufficient for the occurrence of anger and fright. There must also be action directed toward the appropriate goal and feelings of pain and pleasure. In the case of other emotions such as pity and kindness, one or the other of these additional features may be missing, but there is always thought in a determinate form.

Emotions and the body

Before going any further, I should make note of Aristotle's remarks in *De an.* 1.1, for there we are told that emotions such as anger and fright do not occur apart from bodily changes and that a complete scientific definition of such emotions is complex. It includes mention of some bodily change as well as a judgment and a desired goal. For example, being angry is by definition "a certain movement of a body of such and such a kind, or a part or capacity of it (caused) by this thing for the sake of that" (*De an.* 1.1 403a26–7). Here we have mentioned not only the efficient cause ("[caused] by[27] this thing"; i.e., on account of an apparent slight) and the final cause ("for the sake of that"; i.e., for revenge) but also the material cause. In the case of anger, this third kind of cause is a certain movement of a body or, more precisely, "a boiling of the blood and hot stuff around the heart" (*De an.* 1.1 403a31–b1). Beginning as we have from the *Philebus*, this emphasis on bodily factors is important, for in the Platonic dialogue Socrates assigns emotions such as anger and fright to the class of pains and pleasures that belong to the soul itself. In the context of the dialogue, the assignation is useful, for it helps to mark off these passions from others whose primary cause is bodily: a diseased state of the body or a depletion needing replenishment. But it also can give a misleading impression of emotional response, for when people become angry or frightened, the body too plays a role: it must be predisposed to the emotion, and the bodily changes that occur during the emotion have effects that are both public and private.

Concerning predisposition to emotional response, I offer two observations. First, Aristotle is careful to point out that the condition of the body may be a factor in explaining both strong and weak responses to a particular situation. He tells us that when the body is aroused, people are angered by trivia, but when the body is not aroused, they fail to exhibit exasperation. Similarly with fear, a person may be so disposed by the body as to experience fright even though nothing frightening is occurring; or a person may fail to be frightened despite the presence of dangers that are severe and clear (*De an.* 1.1 403a19–24). Second, the fact that people may be predisposed to extreme emotional response raises the question whether the predisposition can be altered in order to avoid unwanted responses. My suspicion is that Aristotle's answer would be bipartite. He would say that a temporary condition can be altered. An invasive medical procedure might remove accumulated blood or bile from a particular part of the body, or (less dangerously) a homeopathic treatment might be tried. A visit to the theater might result in an intense fright or a good laugh, so that the offending fluids are burned off and the person returned to a desirable condition.[28] But Aristotle would also say that a long-standing condition, whether innate or acquired, is not easily removed. Indeed, there may be no permanent cure. For an example, I turn to his pupil Theophrastus, who in *On Comedy* told how the people of Tiryns tried to remedy their propensity to laughter. They asked the oracle at Delphi how they might be released from their condition and were told that they would be released if they performed a sacrifice without laughing. Fearing that a child might laugh, they attempted to remove all the children from the place of sacrifice; but one child escaped notice and made an absurd remark that resulted in laughter.[29] In this way, the people of Tiryns learned that their long-standing habit was incurable (ap. Athenaeus, *Deipn.* 6.79 261D–E [=709.1.10 FHSG]). What role this story played in the Theophrastean treatise *On Comedy* is uncertain. It may have been introduced to illustrate verbal humor or perhaps the possibilities of a comic plot revolving around a fixed disposition; but equally it could have served to underline the need for homeopathic therapy. Like the Tirynthians, many of us are given to excessive laughter; and since there is no permanent cure, we would do well to attend the comic theater and to obtain short-term relief through laughter.

I have said that the bodily changes occurring during emotional response have effects that are both public and private. In speaking of "public" effects, I am thinking of superficial changes of the body such as change in color and the appearance of sweat. In regard to change in color, I cite Aristotle, who tells us that turning red is typical of shame, whereas turning pale is a mark of fright (*Eth. nic.* 4.9 1128b13–14). In regard to sweat, I turn to Theophrastus, who observes that sweat appears on the feet of those who are nervous, and it does so because of an increase in bodily heat (*On Sweat* 36.226–30 F).[30] By "private" effects, I mean painful and pleasurable sensations. When an angry person says, "I feel pain," this may refer to a special mental feeling; but equally, and in my judgment more probably, it may refer to bodily discomfort whose proximate cause is a change in the body, such as the boiling of blood around the heart. I will return to bodily sensations in the next section of this essay, but here I want to underline that there is no contradiction in saying that the painful sensations of anger are caused by bodily change and that anger is caused by the thought of being unfairly slighted. The latter comes first and causes change in the body, which in turn produces an unpleasant sensation.

Difference in degree

In the preceding section, I had occasion to mention Theophrastus in regard to laughter and the bodily changes that accompany emotional response. I now want to call attention to his treatment of anger (*orgē*) and two closely related emotions: faultfinding and rage (*mempsis* and *thymos*). I begin with anger, which Theophrastus, following Aristotle, regarded as a complex phenomenon. A fragment preserved by Stobaeus and another translated into Latin by Seneca make clear that Theophrastus viewed anger as a desire for revenge on account of injustice (Stobaeus, *Flor.* 3.19.12 Hense [=526.4 FHSG]; Seneca, *Ira* 1.12.3 [=446.1 FHSG]). A report by Marcus Aurelius tells us that Theophrastus recognized the involvement of pain in anger (*Meditations* 2.10 [=441.3–4 FHSG]); this same text and another found in Simplicius inform us that Theophrastus did not ignore the bodily changes that accompany anger (*On Aristotle's Physics* 965.1 Diels (1882–95) [=271.3 FHSG]). In sum, Theophrastus analyzed anger in terms of thought, goal-directed behavior, feelings, and bodily change.

What is new in Theophrastus is the introduction of difference in degree in order to distinguish between closely related emotions. Our source is Simplicius, who cites the Theophrastean work *On Emotions* and tells us that according to Theophrastus, faultfinding, anger, and rage differ in respect to "the more and less" (*to mallon kai hētton*) and are not identical in kind (*On Aristotle's Categories* 253.7-8 Kalbfleisch [1907] [=438.6-8 FHSG]). To this report, Simplicius adds a short list of other closely related emotions – friendliness and goodwill, savagery, bestiality and anger, appetite and lust – and then observes that in general, the more shameful emotions, when intensified, change into another kind (*On Aristotle's Categories* 253.8-13 Kalbfleisch [1907] [= 438.8-12 FHSG]). It is not entirely clear whether the additional list of related emotions is taken from Theophrastus, nor is it clear whether Theophrastus regarded difference of degree as merely compatible with or actually determinant of difference in kind. My inclination is to believe that the list is Theophrastean in origin and that Theophrastus did introduce the more and less in order to establish difference in kind. I offer three reasons in support of my belief. First, the list follows on faultfinding, anger, and rage without noticeable interruption. Second, the mention of appetite and lust (*epithymia* and *erōs*) within the list invites comparison with Theophrastus' definition of lust. That definition is preserved by Stobaeus: "Lust is an excess of an unreasoning appetite, whose coming is swift and parting slow" (*Flor.* 4.20.64 [=557.1-2 FHSG]). The definition fits neatly with Simplicius' observation concerning the more shameful emotions that, when intensified, become different in kind. It also supports the idea that difference in degree – here represented by excess, swift and slow – may be determinant of difference in kind and therefore mentioned in the essential definition. Third, there are parallels in Theophrastus' botanical works. I cite *Research on Plants*. In the introduction, Theophrastus makes special mention of the more and less (*Hist. plant.* 1.1.6); and in the subsequent discussion of related kinds of plants – for example, the date palm and the doum palm – he introduces difference in degree in order to distinguish between kinds.[31]

No text reports the details of Theophrastus' analysis of faultfinding, anger, and rage; however, if the preceding remarks are correct, it seems likely that he applied difference in degree to one or more of the features involved in anger. He may have said that anger is caused by a greater injustice than faultfinding, involves a stronger desire for revenge, greater bodily disturbance, and more pain. In contrast, anger falls short of rage in regard to the perceived injustice, desire for revenge, disturbance, and pain. That is the simplest case: difference of degree applied to all features. But it is not the only possibility. At least in regard to faultfinding, it is easy to imagine an analysis in which a feature is said to be absent, either occasionally or always. Some faultfinders may have a weak desire for revenge, but do they all have such a desire? To be sure, they all voice a complaint, but it is not clear that they always aim to hurt another person. Similarly with pain, many or most faultfinders may feel some minor discomfort, but it seems reasonable to believe that some faultfinders simply express annoyance without feeling anything that can reasonably be called pain. In this regard, a passage in Aristotle's *Eudemian Ethics* may be instructive. I am thinking of the second book, where Aristotle calls emotions "such things as rage, fright, shame, appetite and generally things that are in themselves accompanied for the most part by sensory pleasure and pain" (*Eth. eud.* 2.2 1220b12–14). If I understand Aristotle, he introduces the qualifier "sensory" (*aisthētikē*) because he is referring to pleasant and painful sensations that are caused by bodily changes; and he says "for the most part" (*hōs epi to poly*) because he thinks that these sensations are not always present. On one interpretation, he means that there are whole kinds of emotion that are marked by an absence of sensation (Leighton 1984). Hate is a case in point, and faultfinding might be another. On a different interpretation, one that I find more plausible, Aristotle is taking account of individual occurrences in which sensations are not experienced (Fortenbaugh 1985: 217–19).[32] Faultfinding, for example, is normally accompanied by pain, but occasionally the bodily disturbance is so weak that no painful sensation is experienced. Here again, it may be helpful to cite the introduction to Theophrastus' *Research on Plants*, for Theophrastus states clearly that a part that belongs to the nature of a plant can be absent in a particular specimen; and when it is absent, there is always an explanation such as disease or old age or mutilation (*Hist. plant.* 1.1.2). Similarly with emotions, Theophrastus may well have said that pain is a normal feature that in particular cases and for a particular reason may fail to be present. And if he did say that, he may have gone on to cite faultfinding as an example. But whatever the truth concerning this emotion, it does seem likely that Theophrastus would recognize that an adequate analysis of related kinds will consider absences as well as differences in degree.

Emotion, good character, and moral virtue

In the first section of this essay, I discussed Aristotle's explanation of the involvement of thought in emotional response. I now want to emphasize that for many emotions the thought in question has both a factual and an evaluative component. Take anger as an example. A person who is angry believes that someone has done something – perhaps made a hand gesture or passed by in silence – that is deemed to be unjustified behavior. Here there is not only factual apprehension – seeing a gesture or noticing silence – but also evaluation. The angry person assesses another person's action negatively and expresses this assessment in seeking revenge. Aristotle understands that; and in defining anger, he chooses to emphasize evaluation. He first mentions an apparent "slight" (*oligōria*) as the cause of anger and then adds "the slight being unjustified" (*tou oligōrein mē prosēkontos*) (*Rhet.* 2.2 1378a32–3, cf. 2.2 1379b11–12).[33] Without that assessment, without deeming the slight unjustified, there would be no anger. For example, for a person who acknowledges having done wrong and being punished justly, a painful emotion is possible, but it will not be anger (cf. *Rhet.* 2.3 1380b16–18).

Similarly in regard to fear, it is not enough to observe that bodily harm is imminent. The frightened person must also assess the harm negatively and manifest this assessment in seeking safety. As Aristotle puts it, the frightened person is necessarily in preparation (*Rhet.* 2.5 1382b3–4). The involvement of evaluation in other emotions is, I think, clear enough.[34] It may, however, be helpful to add two qualifying remarks. First, although the frightened person, like the angry one, expresses a negative assessment in goal-directed behavior, there are emotions in which evaluation need not lead to action. Indignation and pity are examples. Both emotions involve a negative evaluation – "The good fortune of that person is unmerited"; "The suffering of another is unmerited" (*Rhet.* 2.8 1385b13–14; 2.9 1386b9–14) – but neither need be expressed in action. Rectification may be quite impossible, so that any action would be no more than an expression of displeasure. Second, not all emotions involve evaluation. A clear example is finding something funny.[35] The cause is always a thought, but there need not be an assessment of the situation as merited or unmerited, just or unjust; rather, people often laugh at, for instance, the unexpected or word play such as a pun or clever repetition.[36] That will have been recognized by Aristotle, Theophrastus, and other Peripatetics who discussed the matter in works on comedy and more generally on the ridiculous.[37]

The involvement of evaluation in emotions such as anger, fright, indignation, and pity means that these emotions can express character. In the *Rhetoric*, Aristotle makes the point explicitly when he says that both pity and indignation belong to good character (*ēthos chrēston*), for people ought to feel pity for those whose suffering is unmerited, and to feel indignation when success is unmerited (*Rhet.* 2.9 1386b12–14). Aristotle goes on to say that indignation is attributed to the gods (*Rhet.* 2.9 1386b15–16), but he never refers indignation or pity to moral virtue (*ēthikē aretē*). That is because he thinks of moral virtue as a disposition to act and therefore as a disposition tied to emotions that regularly manifest themselves in action.[38] Good temper (*praotēs*) is the moral virtue related to anger, and the person of good temper is one who both assesses the situation correctly – is not mistaken in perceiving an unjustified slight – and seeks revenge in an appropriate manner. Similarly, courage (*andreia*) is the moral virtue related to fear, and the courageous person is one who assesses danger correctly and confronts it as the situation demands.[39]

These appropriate responses are made possible by moral training during youth (*Eth. nic.* 2.3 1104b11–13). For example, a young man is taught to respect other people according to their merit. He learns that respectful treatment is a fine thing and that disrespectful treatment is something bad. In this way, he acquires moral principles that are action-guiding. When disrespectful treatment occurs, he recognizes an unjustified slight, and should the slight be directed toward himself or those close to him, he exhibits his virtue by becoming angry and seeking appropriate revenge. As Aristotle says, "Virtue when outraged always chooses to act" (*Rhet.* 2.5 1382a35–b2); and as Theophrastus puts it, "Good men are angered on account of wrongs done to their own (close friends and relatives).... It cannot happen that a good man is not angered by evil" (ap. Seneca, *Ira* 1.12.3, 14.1 [=446.1, 6–7 FHSG]).

Similarly with fear, a young man is taught to despise danger and to express this evaluation in action (*Eth. nic.* 2.2 1104b1–3). He learns to remain steadfast because doing so is fine or noble (*Eth. nic.* 3.7 1115b12, 23; 3.7 1116a11, b31). Here too education has conveyed principles that govern action.[40] This education is not an eradication of fear. On the contrary, the courageous person will feel fear, but this fear will be moderate and appropriate to the occasion. Generally, the courageous person is not frightened out of his mind (*Eth. nic.* 3.7 1115b11) and as a result is able to reflect on the situation and to deliberate about means to meet the impending danger.[41] If reflection shows that the situation is not what it appeared to be, the response will be altered; and if deliberation shows that one way to meet the danger is better than another, the better way will be chosen.

These reflections and deliberations are not, in themselves, emotional responses; rather, they are acts of reasoning that follow on emotional response. In the absence of moral virtue they might not occur, for strong emotions interfere with reasoning.[42] However, it is not moral virtue that guarantees the correctness of the reasoning itself; that is the work of practical wisdom (*phronēsis*). What moral virtue does do is guarantee the appropriateness of emotional response. Of course, an initial response may turn out to be second best or worse. The facts of the situation sometimes are different from what they appear to be. Nevertheless, the morally virtuous person will always respond according to principles, choosing, for example, to stand on guard rather than flee, for courageous action is something noble and a good in itself. Aristotle makes the point in regard to sudden dangers (*Eth. nic.* 3.8 1117a17–20). When the situation allows time for deliberation, a person who lacks courage may choose to stand on guard because a consideration of the options brings the realization that the apparent danger can be safely met. But when the immediacy of the situation rules out deliberation,[43] character is revealed in emotional response: the coward flees, while the courageous person, believing it noble to do so, stands firm.

If the foregoing is clear, it should also be clear why Aristotle connects moral virtue with the goal of action, and practical wisdom with the means to accomplish the goal (*Eth. nic.* 6.13 1145a4–6). He is thinking in terms of emotion and reasoning – that is, goal-directed emotional responses such as anger and fright and the deliberations that are occasioned by these emotions and determine how best to realize the goals involved in them. Aristotle's statement becomes difficult only when we dissociate emotion from thought or so emphasize the connection of emotion with pleasure and pain that we obscure other elements: the evaluations and goals that are part of emotions such as anger and fright.[44] We need to keep in mind that emotional responses are not locked into the present: revenge and safety typically are goals that can be realized only at some future time. And we need to remember that the moral education of young people conveys principles concerning what is fine or noble: general directives that not only provide an orientation for one's life but also determine how one responds to particular situations.

In conclusion, I want to be clear that the early Peripatetics recognized the limitations of moral education. Acquiring principles and being trained to respond in accordance with these principles are, of course, important first steps toward moral perfection, but real excellence involves an independence that is not conveyed by training during youth. That training produces obedience to one's superiors: parents, rulers, and the laws of the state. What is needed for perfection is an understanding of why these authorities offer certain directives and not others, and how the directives relate to each other and to human happiness. Such understanding is, of course, not easy to come by; it requires sound training in youth, considerable experience over many years, and careful reflection on law and custom. Few will complete the process, but those who do will be transformed into autonomous moral agents. Aristotle makes the point in the *Politics* when he describes the virtue of the good person – one who has acquired practical wisdom as well as moral virtue – as "fit to rule" (*Pol.* 3.4 1277a28) and "different in kind" (*Pol.* 3.4 1277b17). So too Theophrastus tells us that practical wisdom gives the just person "his special form" (ap. Stobaeus, *Flor.* 2.7.20 [=449 A.35 FHSG]). For both Peripatetics, the addition of wisdom to moral virtue works the same effect. The individual is freed from strict obedience to the directives of authority because he or she can appreciate the limitations of such directives and recognize situations that call for exceptional behavior.[45]

Notes

1 For fright, see, for example, *Il.* 3.30–7; 22.136–7 (Paris is frightened of Menelaus, and Hector flees as Achilles approaches); for pity, *Il.* 22.59; 24.516 (Priam calls [vainly] on Hector for pity, and Achilles feels pity for the gray-haired Priam); for laughter, *Il.* 2.270; cf. 1.599 (the Achaeans laugh at Thyrsites; cf. the gods laughing at Hephaestus).
2 There are innumerable examples, and each person will have personal favorites. Here are some of mine: lyric, Anacreon 44 (the poet laments old age and expresses fear of death); tragedy, Euripides's *Medea*, passim (the eponymous heroine is so consumed by anger that ultimately she kills her own children); comedy, Aristophanes' *Clouds* 1481–509 (Strepsiades is so upset that he rejects a lawsuit in favor of burning down the Thinkery); history, Herodotus's *Histories* 7.35 (when Xerxes learned that a storm had broken up the bridge across the Hellespont, he had the Hellespont scourged with 300 lashes); rhetoricians, Gorgias's *Helen* 15–19 (love is an excuse for bad behavior); philosophers, Plato's *Republic* 439E–40 A (disgust fails to keep Leontius from running to view corpses lying beside the road).

3 See the entries for Fortenbaugh in the bibliography.
4 I will be modifying my view of the relation between Aristotle's rhetorical definition of emotion and his discussion of individual emotions ("A rhetorical definition of emotion"), adding an analysis emphasizing similarity ("An analysis emphasizing similarity") as well as illustrative material from Theophrastus ("Emotions and the body") and dealing with recent criticism concerning good character and the goal of action ("Emotion, good character, and moral virtue").
5 The *Philebus* is Plato's penultimate dialogue. Since his last work, the *Laws*, was left unfinished, we can say that the *Philebus* was Plato's last completed dialogue. Stylistic studies establish a close connection between the *Philebus* and the middle books of the *Laws*. That suggests contemporaneous composition. See Billig 1919: 233–4; Brandwood 1990: 184, 206.
6 See *Phileb.* 46A10; 47C2. In the first passage, *pathē* occurs; in the second, *pathēmata*. In both cases, the first kind of *pathos* is under discussion.
7 See *Phileb.* 47D8, where Socrates quotes Homer, *Il.* 18.108–9: "sweeter by far than dripping honey." Cf. Aristotle, *Rhet.* 2.2 1378b5–7, where Homer, *Il.* 18.109–10 is quoted.
8 On the date(s) of the *Topics*, see Brunschwig 1967: lxiii–civ; Rist 1989: 283–5.
9 I do not follow Brunschwig (1967: 109) in deleting *oligōrias* at *Top.* 4.6 127b31. See Fortenbaugh 1997: 174 n. 30.
10 Book 8 may date to 343–340 BCE, when Aristotle was in Macedonia (see Rist 1989: 285). But whatever its precise date, it probably is a later part of the *Topics*, and the straightforward way in which the definition of anger is advanced may well reflect acceptance of the definition.
11 The qualifier "unjustified" emphasizes the evaluation involved in anger. See below, the beginning of "Emotion, good character, and moral virtue."
12 See *An. post.* 2.8 93b5–6, where rotation of the moon and extinction are mentioned as possible causes that are ruled out by an essential definition that includes the cause.
13 In Aristotle, *De an.* 1.1 403a27, *hypo* occurs in the definition of anger. See below, "Emotions and the body," where the definition is quoted.
14 See below, "Difference in degree" on *Eth. eud.* 2.2 1220b13.
15 It may be significant that the account of kindness emphasizes action. The emotion is defined as a service (*hypourgia*) (*Rhet.* 2.7 1385a18), and the subsequent discussion refers to people who render service (*Rhet.* 2.7 1385a19), stand by (*paristasthai*) (*Rhet.* 2.7 1385a26), and help (*hypēretein*) (*Rhet.* 2.7 1385a26–7). For Aristotle, it seems, action is central to kindness, and feelings of pain and pleasure are largely or wholly irrelevant.
16 At *Rhet.* 2.7 1385a29–30, Aristotle tells us that the initial question has been answered.
17 Gratitude may well be Aristotle's primary concern in *Rhet.* 2.7, but if it is, we are left wondering why we are given a definition of kindness (*Rhet.* 2.7 1385a18–19) and not of gratitude. See Fortenbaugh 2002: 107–9.
18 Cf. Isocrates, *Antid.* 22, where the Athenians are criticized for not exhibiting common goodwill toward competing parties. Earlier, in *Antid.* 21, Isocrates refers to the oath that bound jurors to listen "equally." Apparently, common goodwill is thought of as a guarantee of impartiality.

19 Cf. Thucydides, *Hist.* 2.60.5 (Pericles on himself); Plato, *Apol.* 24B (Socrates ironically of Meletus).
20 See Kennedy 1991: 122; Fortenbaugh 1997: 173–80.
21 In his commentary on Aristotle's *Nicomachean Ethics*, Aspasius tells us the he was unable to find a definition of emotion among the older Peripatetics (Heylbut 1889: 44.20–1). His search may have been faulty, but more likely there was none to be found. See Fortenbaugh 1981.
22 Aristotle's word for "friendship" is *philia*, the same word used in the *Rhetoric* for "friendly feelings."
23 See Fortenbaugh 1975b: 56.
24 And possibly gratitude; see above "A Rhetorical Definition of Emotion."
25 Aristotle recognizes that pity is aroused by death, old age, and ugliness (*Rhet.* 2.8 1386a8, 11), all of which are irremediable. In defining shame, he mentions painful sensations but omits any reference to action (*Rhet.* 2.6 1383b12–14), for no action is necessarily involved in experiencing the emotion. We may call these emotions "nonpractical" in contrast to "practical" emotions such as anger and fear. For a fuller discussion, see Fortenbaugh 1975a: 79–83.
26 See Aristotle, *Eth. nic.* 8.3 1156a9–14.
27 Here the preposition "by" translates *hypo*. See above, the end of "Emotions distinguished from other passions."
28 On intense fright, see Aristotle, *Poet.* 14 1453b5: the plot of a tragedy should produce shuddering in one who hears a tragedy read. By using the verb "to shudder" (*phrittein*), Aristotle indicates that the listener feels fear intensely and in doing so undergoes bodily change (see Janko 1987: 105). For purgation through laughter, see *Tractatus Coislinianus* 10–11 (Koster 1975: 64 [=IV in Janko 1984: 24]), where the definition of comedy ends with these words: "through pleasure and laughter accomplishing the catharsis of such emotions."
29 The child confused two cognate Greek words: *sphageion* ("sacrificial bowl") and *sphagion* ("sacrificial victim"). The child wanted to ask the adults whether they were frightened that he would overturn a bowl; but he mixed up the cognate words and asked whether they were worried that he would overturn the victim, which in this case is a bull.
30 The reference is to my edition of *On Sweat* (Fortenbaugh *et al.* 2003: 46); cf. Ps.-Aristotle, *Problems* 2.26.
31 See Theophrastus, *Hist. plant.* 2.6.6–11; for more detailed discussion see Fortenbaugh 1985: 213–14.
32 In agreement with Woods 1982: 110.
33 I have translated *oligōria* with "slight" not only because it is close to the root meaning of *oligōria* but also because one can easily speak of a justified as well as an unjustified (deserved as well as undeserved) slight. That would not be true if *oligōria* were translated with, for example, "outrage," as occasionally I have done elsewhere (e.g., Fortenbaugh 1975a: 11).
34 For fuller remarks on evaluation and its application to Aristotle's analysis of emotions, see Fortenbaugh 1969: 164–7; in more recent literature see, for example, Nehamas 1994: 264.
35 I speak of "finding something funny" instead of "laughter" because the former seems to me more restrictive, suggesting a response caused by thought and

therefore ruling out cases of laughter caused by tickling and the like. But most of the time, laughter is caused by thought and therefore is part of an emotional response. See Fortenbaugh 2003: 91–106 and 2006: 88–92.

36 See above, "Emotions and the body" on the Tirynthians.
37 See the *Tractatus Coislinianus* 13–30 (Koster 1975: 63–4 [=V–VI in Janko 1984: 24–36]), where the causes of laughter are divided into language and situations (*lexis* and *pragmata*).
38 Moral virtue is repeatedly said to be a disposition concerning emotions and actions (*Eth. nic.* 2.3 1104b13–14; 2.6 1106b24–5; 3.1 1109b30).
39 I soon will introduce a qualification. Although the good-tempered person and the courageous person normally assess the situation correctly, there are occasions when the situation is not what it appears to be. In such cases, reflection may lead one to alter or to abandon an initial emotional response.
40 While principles may be learned from parents and tutors who give general directives concerning virtuous action, they also may be acquired through song and poetry and literature in general. For example, to teach a youth the importance of facing danger bravely, he might be asked to read or listen to an elegy of Tyrtaeus, in which the poet describes the death of a young soldier as something fine or noble (frg. 10.30). See Fortenbaugh 1987: 251 (=1991: 103).
41 I use two different verbs, "to reflect" and "to deliberate," in order to emphasize that a person may ponder both the appropriateness of a response to a particular situation (Is there a real danger here? Is my response too weak or too strong?) and the means to realize a desired goal (Is this or that the better way to achieve safety?). Nevertheless, I want to be clear that my usage is arbitrary: "to deliberate" can be used for both cases, as can *bouleuein* in Greek.
42 Cf. Theophrastus, ap. Stobaeus, *Flor.* 3.19.12 [=526.2–4 FHSG], where we are told that strong anger prevents a person from acting with forethought; in a rage, such a person is, as it were, drunken with contentiousness and subject to impulse.
43 In offering a résumé of my earlier work, A. Smith attributes to me the following view: "In many situations, indeed in all where action is immediately required, wisdom is superfluous" (A. Smith 1996: 62). To me, this statement seems misleading, for to say that "wisdom is superfluous" suggests that wisdom might be present; that is, the deliberations of practical wisdom might occur. A sudden situation, however, rules out any exercise of wisdom; there is only emotional response. On responding to a sudden situation without hesitation, see Fortenbaugh 2002: 101–2.
44 I am responding here to A. Smith (1996: 70–3), who contrasts being motivated by pleasure and pain with following reason. In many contexts the contrast is unobjectionable; but it distorts the framework within which Aristotle sets out his view of moral virtue.
45 For fuller discussion, see Fortenbaugh 1990: 463–5. A. Smith misrepresents my view when he describes it as one that "implies that wisdom is ethically wholly otiose" (A. Smith 1996: 64).

3

THE PROBLEM OF THE PASSIONS IN CYNICISM

David E. Aune

The Cynic focus on a lifestyle "according to nature" rather than "according to custom" and their fundamental emphasis on freedom were not based on philosophical theory, nor did the Cynics constitute a Hellenistic philosophical school comparable to the Stoics, with whom they were often associated. In the chreiai and doxography of early Cynics, hints of the extirpation of the passions are attributed to Antisthenes, but this typically Stoic doctrine is missing from both Diogenes and Teles. Dio of Prusa, projecting his own brand of Stoicized Cynicism in his "Diogenes speeches," emphasized the antithesis between πόνος ("hardship") and ἡδονή ("pleasure"), maintaining the latter should be completely avoided, though no supporting philosophical arguments are advanced. The *Cynic Letters* again emphasize the antithesis between πόνος and ἡδονή, with the latter serving as a slippery slope leading to further evils.

Introduction

The task of delineating the Cynic view of the πάθη (*pathē*), the "emotions" or the "passions," is difficult for several reasons. The literature produced by early Cynics has largely perished, and our knowledge is largely confined to sayings and anecdotes of doubtful historical value. Cynic views of the πάθη, as well as nearly every other theme typical of Hellenistic philosophical inquiry, were never given a systematic or theoretical basis in dialogue with other philosophical positions. This led Hegel to express the opinion, "There is nothing particular to say of the Cynics, for they possess but little philosophy, and they did not bring what they had into a scientific system" (Hegel 1995: 1.479). A.A. Long (1996b: 29) advocated that the temptation to follow Hegel's advice should be resisted, though his otherwise excellent synthetic treatment of Hellenistic philosophy contains no separate discussion of Cynicism (Long 1986). Furthermore, in Long and Sedley's important two-volume source book and commentary on Hellenistic philosophy, the Cynics are again omitted (along with Cyrenaeics, Megarians, and Dialecticians) as influential though "nonstandard" Hellenistic philosophers (Long and Sedley 1987: 1.xii). In her important book on Hellenistic ethics that focuses on the therapeutic function of philosophy, M. Nussbaum chooses to omit any discussion Cynicism with the following justification:

> The Cynics are certainly important in some way in the history of the idea of philosophical therapy; and the reader of Diogenes Laertius' life of Diogenes the Cynic will find them fascinating figures. On the other hand, there is, I believe, far too little known about them and their influence, *and even about whether they offered arguments at all*, for a focus on them to be anything but a scholarly quagmire in a book of this type. With some regret, then, I leave them at the periphery.
> (Nussbaum 1994b: 8 [italics added])

Here the vague phrase "important in some way" catches the eye, while the phrase "leave them at the periphery" actually means that they will not be mentioned again. The fact that Long, Sedley, and Nussbaum have not discussed Cynic views in the context of the main Hellenistic philosophical traditions suggests that the attempt to do so is difficult and problematic.

The Cynics were important for Hellenistic philosophical tradition for at least three reasons: (1) following the model of Socrates, they pointed out the irrationality of conventional values; (2) they liberated the goal of εὐδαιμονία (*eudaimonia*, the "flourishing life") from external circumstances with a vengeance; (3) they provided the model of the independent sage with the "far-out" lifestyle who was unaffected by the needs and passions that beset others (Long 1996b: 44–5). The early influence of Cynic sages such as Diogenes and Crates waned with the rise of philosophical schools such as Epicureanism and Stoicism that successfully placed some of the early concerns of Cynics on a more systematic theoretical basis.

After whining about some of the major problems confronting the modern study of ancient Cynicism, which makes my assigned topic difficult, I will propose a relatively simple strategy for accessing various Cynic positions on the passions or emotions: the use of the lexemes found in semantic fields associated with the term πάθος (*pathos*) in ancient philosophical contexts as a means for identifying appropriate texts that on other grounds have a relatively clear connection to Cynic teaching and practice. It is important at the outset, however, to stress the tentative and problematic nature of this discussion.

Some problematic features of Cynicism

The modern student of ancient Cynicism is faced with a host of problematic issues that stand in the way of a satisfactory understanding of how the widespread philosophical occupation with the theme of the πάθη and related concepts function in this ancient countercultural tradition.

What is Cynicism?

There is widespread agreement that Cynics should be identified primarily by their appearance and behavior and secondarily by certain key concepts that they publicly propounded and embodied. The appearance of the Cynic remained relatively constant throughout antiquity: a threadbare cloak (τρίβων, *tribōn*), a leather pouch (πήρα, *pēra*), a staff (βακτηρία, *baktēria*), and disheveled hair (Epictetus, *Diss.* 3.22.9–10; Julian, *Or.* 6.190D, 201A); some even begged for a living. However, none of these characteristics were monopolized by those who thought of themselves as part of the Cynic tradition. There were a number of concepts associated with the Cynic way of life, although ἐλευθερία (*eleutheria*) and all that it implies certainly lies at the heart of Cynicism. The Cynic emphasis on ἐλευθερία, however, is largely negative, as it is construed as freedom *from* various types of entanglements that are generically described with the umbrella metaphor of "slavery." Cynicism is essentially a negative reaction to the social and cultural environment, but its proponents' chief failure was to propose a program that would prove to be a positive counterpart to their criticism (Billerbeck 1991: 150). Cynic ἐλευθερία is not only freedom from concerns about food, clothing, home, wife, family, and from the demands of the state, the law, and custom, but also freedom from the πάθη, the passions or emotions. Concepts that are clustered with ἐλευθερία, forming a semantic field, include αὐτάρκεια (*autarkeia*, "self-sufficiency"),[1] παρρησία (*parrhēsia*, "freedom of speech"), ἀπάθεια (*apatheia*, "freedom from emotion"), and ἀναίδεια (*anaideia*, "shamelessness"). Whereas αὐτάρκεια and ἀπάθεια are concepts important for Stoicism, the Cynic understanding of these terms typically was devoid of any theoretical basis. Together these constitute an ἔνστασις βίου (*enstasis biou*) or ἄσκησις (*askēsis*), a "pattern of living," which could alternately be described as πόνος (*ponos*, "striving"). A.J. Malherbe puts all these pieces together and proposes this generally acceptable definition of Cynicism:

> What made a Cynic was his dress and conduct, self-sufficiency, harsh behaviour towards what appeared as excesses, and a practical ethical idealism, but not a detailed arrangement of a system resting on Socratic-Antisthenic principles.
>
> (Malherbe 1982: 49–50)

The emphasis on behavior rather than theory meant that Cynicism could be regarded as compatible with views that shared its ethical demands even if they were at cross-purposes with its fundamentally different teaching in other matters. Diogenes was the hero of Cynicism because his outrageously countercultural behavior made him the most radical exponent of the Cynic quest for εὐδαιμονία.

Was Cynicism a philosophical school?

Although Cynicism is described as a philosophy in ancient sources, it was not a Hellenistic philosophical school in any way comparable to Stoicism, Epicureanism, or Scepticism, for it lacked two basic features that characterize all other Hellenistic philosophical traditions: (1) an organizational structure; (2) a central body of teaching. The absence of these two institutional features of philosophical schools can be construed as a conscious rejection by Cynics of conventional society and culture. The succession of Cynic teachers presented by Diogenes Laertius in the sixth book of his *Lives of Prominent Philosophers* is largely fabricated on the analogy of the succession traditions of other philosophical schools. Diogenes Laertius proposed two criteria for a philosophical sect or school: (1) a philosophical αἵρεσις (*hairesis*) should follow some λόγος (*logos*, "principle"); (2) a philosophical αἵρεσις should have a positive body of doctrines (Diogenes Laertius 1.20). He treats Cynicism as one of the important Hellenistic philosophical schools even though he expresses some doubt about whether it should be categorized as one at all (Diogenes Laertius 6.103). Whether Cynicism constituted a philosophical school was a matter of debate among the ancients themselves (see Goulet-Cazé 1986: 28–31). Hippobotus, in a lost work entitled Περὶ αἱρέσεων, discusses nine philosophical schools, but he ignored Cynicism, Elianism, and Dialecticism (Diogenes Laertius 1.19; 2.88; see Runia 1998). Unlike other Hellenistic philosophical traditions, Cynicism never produced a system of philosophic doctrines, whether in esoteric oral form or in exoteric written form, that could be subject to discussion, criticism, and elaboration in a school setting (Julian, *Or.* 6.186B).

Actions speak louder than words

Since Cynicism focused on lifestyle rather than philosophical theory and argument, the structure of Cynic practice remained relatively stable throughout its entire discontinuous history. Diogenes Laertius, citing the analogous example of the Stoic Ariston of Chios, claimed that the Cynics ignored logic and physics and focused instead on ethics (Diogenes Laertius 6.103). Yet if by "ethics" one means a *system* of moral principles, even this way of characterizing the Cynic philosophical perspective is an exaggeration. Julian spells out the behavioral focus of Cynicism very clearly:

> For it [Cynicism] seems to be in some ways a universal philosophy, and the most natural, and to demand no special study whatsoever.

> But it is enough simply to choose the honourable by desiring virtue and avoiding evil; and so there is no need to turn over countless books.
>
> (Julian, *Or.* 6.187D)

Cynics thought that attitudes followed behavior, and therefore they emphasized orthopraxy rather than orthodoxy, deeds rather than words (Julian, *Or.* 6.189A), a view with superficial Aristotelian support.[2] This "operant conditioning" (to use a Skinnerian behaviorist motto) stands in striking contrast to Stoic theory. For Stoics, action was a rational enterprise, following the assent to impulse (Annas 1992: 89–102).[3] In Ps.-Crates, *Ep.* 21 (to Metrocles the Cynic), the emphasis is on action rather than education: "For the way that leads to happiness through words is long, but that which leads through daily deeds is a shortened regimen."[4] One definition of Cynicism from the imperial period that appears to emphasize action over study is attributed to Crates: τὸ δὲ κυνίζειν τὸ συντόμως φιλοσοφεῖν, "to live as a Cynic is a shortcut to philosophy" (Ps.-Crates, *Ep.* 16; cf. Ps.-Diogenes, *Ep.* 12). This slogan first appears in a fragment of Apollodorus of Seleuceia, a Stoic (*SVF* 3.261 [Apollodorus, frg. 17]; Diogenes Laertius 7.121), but it is found also in a general Cynic doxography in Diogenes Laertius 6.104 (Goulet-Cazé 1986: 22–4 nn. 22, 23), which may go back to Antisthenes (Emeljanow 1965). This slogan means that the Cynics, alone among the Hellenistic philosophical traditions, opposed the study of the liberal arts as a prerequisite for the study of philosophy (Diogenes Laertius 6.103–4). For Varro, "Cynicism" was a term applied to a variety of different philosophical positions whose only common denominator was the Cynic mode of living (Augustine, *Civ.* 19.1.2–3). Many regarded Cynicism as an ἔνστασις βίου, "style of living," rather than a philosophy (Diogenes Laertius 6.103; cf. Julian, *Or.* 6.181D, 189B, 201A). Writing in the late fourth century CE, Julian characterized Cynicism as a sort of universal philosophy (*Or.* 6.182C), and he regarded neither Antisthenes nor Diogenes as its founder, but maintained that it was practiced before the time of Heracles (*Or.* 6.187C–D).

The discontinuous history of Cynicism

The Cynic ideal continued in one form or another (i.e., as either a social reality or a literary ideal) from the fourth century BCE through the fifth century CE and is generally structured in three main historical phases, of which the first and third are obviously the most significant: (1) classical Cynicism (fourth and third centuries BCE); (2) a period of low visibility, perhaps even extinction (second and first centuries BCE); (3) a revival during the late first century CE that lasted until the early fifth century CE. While other Hellenistic philosophical traditions resist synchronic description because of the changes and developments that they underwent during the Hellenistic and Roman periods, the emphasis that Cynics placed on behavior rather than on theory produced a basic structural stability throughout the tradition's history, making a synchronic description possible.

A brief discussion about the sources for the first and third phases of Cynicism is necessary. The beliefs and practices of the earlier Greek Cynics (fourth and third centuries BCE) must be deduced from a mass of anecdotes (most of doubtful historical value) and doxographical traditions, for with the exception of some fragments, all classical Cynic literature has been lost.[5] There is little evidence for the existence of Cynicism during the second and first centuries BCE. Some scholars have maintained that Cynicism had essentially died out,[6] suggesting that it was the Stoics who were chiefly responsible for the revival of Cynicism in the first century CE. Others argue that Cynicism maintained a shadowy and obscure existence during this period.[7] The Cynic revival in the first century CE is linked to the interest of prominent Stoics in the figure of the ideal Cynic and is also associated with Cynic virtuosos such as Demetrius, Dio Chrysostom, Demonax, Peregrinus, and Oenomaus of Gadara. The views of later Greek Cynics are expressed in pseudonymous epistolary literature attributed to famous philosophers of an earlier period (such as Heraclitus, Socrates, Anacharsis, Diogenes, and Crates), and in the writings of prominent Stoic philosophers (such as Seneca). Since ancient doxographical traditions agreed that Stoicism had emerged from Cynicism (Diogenes Laertius 1.15; 6.19, 104), it was natural that Cynicism be given the role of representing the more radical form of Stoicism (Billerbeck 1991: 149). Furthermore, Cynics and Cynicism of the first century CE are refracted primarily through the perspectives of Stoic interpreters (Malherbe 1982: 48).

Cynicism experienced a revival in the Julio-Claudian era, when economic prosperity was on the increase. Since the Romans had a greater respect for practical philosophy compared with more speculative philosophy, and therefore were open to Stoicism and Cynicism, the unpopularity of Cynicism sometimes was the cause for the expulsion of some Stoic philosophers, whom the authorities tarred with the same brush (B.F. Harris 1977). Several Roman Stoics displayed a propensity for Cynic asceticism, including Attalus and Musonius Rufus (Billerbeck 1991: 151–2). In the Greek world, figures such as Dio of Prusa, Demonax, Oenomaus,[8] and Peregrinus (d. 165 BCE)[9] pursued the Cynic way of life. The strongest effect of the Cynic heritage was the fact that their ethical teaching was aimed at the practice (μελέτη, *meletē*) and the training (ἄσκησις, *askēsis*) of moral behavior rather than the intellectual ability to penetrate the fundamentals of doctrine (Billerbeck 1991: 153).

The πάθη or παθήματα

The word πάθος (*pathos*) has many connotations, but generally it means "something that happens," referring either to an event or to a person affected by an outside agent; that is, it can mean "event" or "experience" (the latter can be either a good or a bad, a happy or an unhappy experience). Although some have argued that πάθη (*pathē*) should be translated "passions" (Inwood 1985), a term widely used in the western philosophical tradition, the term "emotions" often is more appropriate. Although Hellenistic philosophical traditions made both implicit and explicit distinctions between the πάθη of the body and the πάθη of the soul (and sometimes their interrelationship), the πάθη of the soul, according to Aristotle, are accompanied by either pleasure or pain (*Eth. nic.* 2.5.2 1105b). Much of what the Hellenistic philosophers discussed under the heading of πάθη is what we could consider "emotions" or "feelings," terms that are essentially neutral in English, while the word "passion" has the connotation of excess. The Greeks tended to regard strong emotions as outside agents, and both πάθος and its Latin equivalent *passio* mean something that "happens to" a person who is regarded as a passive victim (Dodds 1951: 185; Gould 1990: 63).

In the surviving textual evidence from Cynics, whether in doxographies, in Stoic accounts of Cynic teaching and behavior, or in the pseudepigraphical Cynic letters, the term πάθος occurs only rarely, and there is not even the rudiments of a systematic discussion of the term. Therefore, I will begin by considering how other Hellenistic philosophical traditions construed πάθος and its constituent emotions as a heuristic device to search for the same clusters of lexemes in Cynic sources. The "passions" or "emotions" were a concern of Hellenistic philosophical traditions, particularly the topic of ἡδονή (*hēdonē*) or *uoluptas* (Aulus Gellius, *Noct. att.* 9.5). The Cyrenaics had the most positive stance toward the πάθη, which functioned for them as a basic epistemological category, since they maintained that one could have no knowledge of things in the world except through the medium of the πάθη (Tsouna 1998). Plato was hostile to certain physical pleasures, but he (and Aristotle even more so) insisted that there were pleasures of intellect and virtue, so that the passions were no longer an infection of external origin, but rather a necessary part of the life of the mind. Antisthenes (a proto-Cynic) and Cynics such as Diogenes and Crates, on the other hand, maintained an austere view of pleasure (Gosling and Taylor 1982: 294). Plato (*Tim.* 42A–B) refers to two features of the embodied soul: first, αἴσθησις (*aisthēsis*, "sensation") proceeding from violent παθήματα, and second, ἔρως (*erōs*, "sexual love") mingled with ἡδονή (*hēdonē*, "pleasure") and λύπη (*lypē*, "pain"), together with φόβος (*phobos*, "fear"), θυμός (*thymos*, "anger"), and so forth. If these passions are mastered, people can live justly; if not, they will live unjustly. In *Tim.* 69C–D this is somewhat clearer. There Plato refers to the mortal part of the soul that has within it fearful and unavoidable παθήματα, including ἡδονή ("pleasure," a powerful lure to evil), and λύπας ("pains," which cause good to flee), and other παθήματα as well, including θάρρος (*tharros*, "audacity" [a rare negative use of a lexeme that normally means "courage, confidence"]) and φόβος ("fear") (both called "foolish counselors"), then θυμός ("anger") and ἐλπίς (*elpis*, "hope"). In *Leg.* 1.644C–D Plato speaks of two antagonistic and foolish counselors, called ἡδονή ("pleasure") and λύπη ("pain"), and in addition, each person has two opinions about the future (called ἐλπίς, "hope"); the one anticipating λύπη is called φόβος ("fear"), while that anticipating ἡδονή, is called θάρρος ("confidence"). While there are other lists of the passions in Plato (see *Phileb.* 47E), the basic distinction between pleasant and unpleasant emotions, ἡδονή ("pleasure") and λύπη ("pain"), is picked up by Aristotle and the Stoics (Knuuttila and Sihvola 1998: 14).

Aristotle provides longer and more systematic classifications of the passions. In *Eth. nic.* 2.5.2 1105b, for example, he provides a longer list of πάθη, including ἐπιθυμία (*epithymia*, "desire"), ὀργή, (*orgē*, "anger"), φόβος (*phobos*, "fear"), θράσος (*thrasos*, "confidence"), φθόνος (*phthonos*, "envy"), χαρά (*chara*, "joy"), φιλία (*philia*, "friendship"), μῖσος (*misos*, "hatred"), πόθος (*pothos*, "longing"), ζῆλος (*zēlos*, "jealousy"), and ἔλεος (*eleos*, "pity"), each of which is accompanied by ἡδονή ("pleasure") or λύπη ("pain"). Other Aristotelian catalogues of the emotions are found in *Rhet.* 2.1 1378a; *Eth. eud.* 2.2 1220b; *De an.* 1.1 403a (Leighton 1996). For Epicureans, pleasure (i.e., the consciousness of being in a good state) was a central concern because it was considered the good, since according to Cyrenaic and then later Epicurean epistemology, appearances are true and reliable (Long and Sedley 1987: 1.78–86).

The Stoics, who have the most negative view of the passions among Hellenistic philosophical traditions, expended a great deal of effort in classifying and defining them.[10] In view of the close associations, both real and imagined, between aspects of Stoicism and aspects of Cynicism, it is possible that the Stoic views of the πάθη may be used as a heuristic structure for understanding the Cynic view of the πάθη, for a great deal is known about the epistemological theory and practice of Stoic ethics, and it may be instructive to learn the extent to which the bits and pieces of our knowledge of Cynic ethics can be compared or contrasted with the ethics of Stoicism. The main types of πάθη distinguished by Stoicism included λύπη ("pain" or "grief"), φόβος ("fear"), ἐπιθυμία ("desire"), and ἡδονή ("pleasure") (Diogenes Laertius 7.111).[11] Each of these primary passions also has many subtypes.[12] Zeno defined passion as "an irrational movement of the soul contrary to nature, or as an excessive impulse" (Diogenes Laertius 7.110 [=*SVF* 1.205]), indicating that assenting to passions is a violation of a person's rational nature (Stevens 1993: 242). The radical Stoic view of the πάθη was that they were diseases – that is, excessive and irrational impulses (*SVF* 1.206). The wise person, who is ἀπαθής (*apathēs*), is therefore a person without πάθη (Diogenes Laertius 6.117), for passions are by definition wrong (Inwood 1985: 130). From this perspective, then, the striking Stoic emphasis on the complete elimination of the πάθη, which are diseases, makes good sense. Rather than accept the model that moral action arises out of a struggle between various elements within the person, Stoicism preferred the model that moral action is based on the sickness or health of the individual. Nevertheless, for the Stoics, the πάθη were peripheral because they denied that human beings had a natural impulse toward pleasure (*SVF* 3.178 [=Diogenes Laertius 7.85–6]), and they ranked them among things considered to be ἀδιάφορα (*adiaphora*, "indifferent"), a category within which some Stoics distinguished between "preferred" things and "unpreferred" things, though other Stoics refused to regard ἡδονή or any of the other passions as "preferred" (Gosling and Taylor 1982: 415–27).

While the wise person, according to Stoicism, is free from passion in the sense of movements of the soul contrary to reason, he or she does experience εὐπαθείαι ("good emotional states"), the rational counterparts of passion, "the harmonious motions of the soul acting in accordance with reason" (Stevens 1993: 251): joy, caution, and wishing (Diogenes Laertius 7.116).

Majority opinion versus nature

In Hellenistic philosophical traditions, the term δόξα (*doxa*) is used to mean both "opinion" and "judgment." Plato distinguished between ἐπιστήμη (*epistēmē*, true knowledge) and δόξα (an inferior type of knowledge or opinion). The early Stoics were rationalists who considered πάθη to be κρίσεις (*kriseis*) – that is, "[incorrect] intellectual judgments" (Diogenes Laertius 7.111; Edelstein and Kidd 1989, no. 152; *SVF* 3.456, 461; Rist 1969: 22–36). The term κρίσις (*krisis*) can be used also in a positive sense of assent to propositions, while δόξαι (*doxai*) are by definition *incorrect* judgments (Inwood 1985: 130 n. 11), and so constitute a subset of κρίσεις (Stevens 1993: 241). The Stoics posited a complete disjunction between true knowledge and ignorance (or opinion) and denied that there was any validity to any intermediate between oppositions such as virtue and vice, wisdom and folly, sanity and insanity (Long and Sedley 1987: 1.257). Frequently, Cynic sources distinguish between living κατὰ δόξαν, "according to opinion" (often described using the metaphor of slavery), and living κατὰ φύσιν, "according to nature" (Ps.-Diogenes, *Ep.* 7; 10.2), which as the opposite of slavery is ἐλευθερία, "freedom," the focal Cynic value (cf. Diogenes Laertius 7.121). Several important features of Cynicism are included in this definition by Julian (*Or.* 6.193D):

> Now the end and aim of the Cynic philosophy, as indeed of every philosophy, is happiness, but happiness that consists in living according to nature [ἐν τῷ ζῆν κατὰ φύσιν, *en tō zēn kata physin*] and not according to the opinions of the multitude [τὰς τῶν πολλῶν δόξας, *tas tōn pollōn doxas*].

Pseudo-Diogenes suggests a definition of Cynicism that centers on the term φύσις (*physis*): ὁ γὰρ κυνισμός, ὡς οἶσθα, φύσεώς ἐστιν ἀναζήτησις, "For Cynicism is, as you know, an investigation of nature" (Ps.-Diogenes, *Ep.* 42). Here ἀναζήτησις (*anazētēsis*, "investigation"), which suggests a detailed, systematic inquiry, is used hyperbolically. While the epistemology of Stoicism reflects a suspicion about "appearances," the Cynic view tends to polarize the view of most people (which is necessary wrong), and the view of Cynics themselves who live "according to nature." Although they do not provide an abstract definition of what this means, they embody its meaning by their behavior.

Early Cynics

While the writings of the early Cynics have not survived, many anecdotes of dubious historical value have been attributed to them. Antisthenes (ca. 445–365 BCE), the proto-Cynic, regarded as the founder of Cynicism by the ancients (Diogenes Laertius 1.19), expressed a profound rejection of ἡδονή, regarded as the most deadly of the passions and the antithesis of πόνος ("struggle"), which is in accordance with nature and makes happiness possible: *Antisthenes Socraticus summum malum dicit*, "Antisthenes the Socratic called [pleasure] the greatest evil" (Aulus Gellius, *Noct. att.* 9.5.3). The antithesis between πόνος and ἡδονή in Antisthenes suggests that the latter is more than an emotion; it is pleasurable behavior. When ἡδονή occurs in Cynic sources, as it frequently does, it tends to have the concrete meaning of pleasurable acts. Also attributed to Antisthenes was the saying "I would rather go mad than experience pleasure" (Aulus Gellius, *Noct. att.* 9.5.3; Diogenes Laertius 6.3; Antisthenes 27, 29 in Paquet 1988: 23). However, in the collections of chreiai associated with Diogenes (Diogenes Laertius 6.20–81 [see Paquet 1988: 49–100]), traditionally a disciple of Antisthenes, the supposed Cynic antipathy toward the passions is not prominent. Diogenes was a countercultural gadfly with a ready wit and a sharp tongue who delivered devastating social and cultural critiques to anyone foolish enough to be within earshot. The anecdotes portray him as an advocate of the simple life "according to nature" (Diogenes Laertius 6.31, 37, 44, 71), a tireless critic of those whose words were not consistent with their actions, those who emphasized theory over actions, and those who preferred written rules to true physical training (Diogenes Laertius 6.28, 48, 64). According to one chreia (Diogenes Laertius 6.54), Diogenes, when asked what wine he found pleasant (ἡδέως, *hēdeōs*) to drink, replied, "That for which other people pay." Note that no critique of ἡδονή is even implied. In another chreia (Diogenes Laertius 6.67) he declared that lovers derive their pleasure (ἡδονή) from their misfortune; that is, they derive pleasure from pain. Again, no critique of ἡδονή is expressed. Yet another anecdote about Diogenes concludes with this statement: "He said that servants obey their masters, and bad men obey their desires [ἐπιθυμίαις, *epithymiais*]" (Diogenes Laertius 6.66), implying the negative character of ἐπιθυμίαι, which certainly would accord with the Stoic view. Though one cannot legitimately expect to mine much didactic material from the chreiai attributed to Diogenes, it is noteworthy that the theme of the passions is striking by its virtual absence.

While the doxographical material attributed to Diogenes of Sinope in Diogenes Laertius 6.70–1 may not actually be from the writings of Diogenes himself, it nevertheless surely constitutes one of the more important sources of early Cynic teaching.[13] The passage consists of a threefold argument: (1) ἄσκησις (*askēsis*, "training") has both a psychical and physical character; (2) ἄσκησις is indispensable; (3) psychical ἄσκησις is the more important of the two. As we have seen, one of the primary categories of the passions in ancient philosophical tradition was ἡδονή, "pleasure." In a context in which he emphasizes the importance of the training of the soul using the analogy of the training of the body, Diogenes is said to have claimed, paradoxically, that the despising of pleasure can, with practice, itself be pleasurable (Diogenes Laertius 6.71), so that "those whose training has been of the opposite kind derive more pleasure from despising pleasure than from the pleasures themselves"; that is, there is a "higher" form of pleasure which is "according to nature" (Goulet-Cazé 1986: 206). This is the most extensive discussion of ἡδονή in the limited doxographical tradition attributed to Diogenes, and its paradoxical character gives it an authentic ring. Furthermore, the phrase τῆς ἡδονῆς ἡ καταφρόνησις (*tēs hēdonēs hē kataphronēsis*, "the despising of pleasure" [repeated in a verbal form]), reflects a conviction shared by Antisthenes and the Stoics, but is itself the subject of criticism.

The seven fragmentary discourses of Teles (fl. 240 BCE), preserved in Stobaeus, who in turn epitomized the epitome of Theodoros, are the earliest examples of the diatribe style and are one of the oldest texts emphasizing characteristic Cynic themes that we possess. The fact that he quotes the earlier writings of Bion (seven times) and Crates makes his work important for the history of Cynicism. The fifth fragment of Teles, based on the earlier teaching of Crates, is entitled "Pleasure Is Not the Goal of Life" and is essentially a refutation of the view that human happiness (εὐδαίμων, *eudaimōn*) is based on an excess of pleasure (ἡδονή). Teles counters this view by narrating a generic version of human life from childhood to old age, a sort of "Unheilsgeschichte" emphasizing all the hardships, punishments, and privations that punctuate each phase of life. The implied conclusion is that an emphasis on pleasure is simply an unrealistic goal for normal human living. There is no hint at any point in this pragmatic argument that a theoretical basis exists for the denigration of pleasure. This rejection of pleasure as part of a complex of appropriate attitudes that enable a person to live a life free from distress is emphasized in the second discourse, Περὶ αὐταρκείας, "On Self-Sufficiency."[14]

> But if you consider yourself as one who looks down on pleasure [ἡδονή,], as one who does not discredit hard work [πόνοι], and as one

who holds good and bad reputation as equal, and as one who does not fear death, it will be possible for you to do whatever you want without distress.

This cluster of attitudes clearly reflects the Cynic view of life, particularly in the antithesis between ἡδονή and πόνος, and again it appears likely that ἡδονή should be understood concretely as "pleasurable acts."

In fragment seven, Περὶ ἀπαθείας ("On Freedom from Passion"), Teles maintains that "the happy person will also be beyond passion and mental disturbance [τοῦ πάθους καὶ ταραχῆς]," but the person who is "in distress and pain and fear (ἐν ὀδύνῃ καὶ λύπῃ καὶ φόβῳ)" is neither satisfied nor happy. It is clear that the terms πάθος ("passion") and ταραχή (*tarachē*, "mental disturbance") are evaluated negatively, are close synonyms, and are judged the antithesis of happiness. Further, the other emotions that Teles mentions (distress, pain, fear) are all aspects of πάθος or ταραχή. Essentially, his argument (if it may be called that) is that happiness is the antithesis of pain and fear, and therefore a happy person will not be bothered by either pain or fear or other forms of emotional perturbation. Teles then articulates a rather simple-minded injunction (O'Neil 1977: 65):

> Therefore, he should be a happy man, so that he is not pained over the death either of a friend or a child, nor even over his own death. Or don't those people seem to you cowardly who await their own death ignobly and not at all boldly?

Countering the δόξα ("popular opinion") that a woman who does not weep for a dead child is "hard-hearted," he gives examples of women whose primary concern is not that their sons have died in battle but rather that they died courageously. What Teles has done here is to juxtapose two δόξαι, or forms of popular opinion: one that judges a woman unfeeling who does not mourn the death of her child and one that judges a woman noble who is proud of the courageous death of her son. At the end of the day, however, Teles provides no epistemological basis for discerning which of the two δόξαι is correct; rather, he relies on commonsense arguments whose validity is based on their implicit acceptance by his audience.

Several tentative conclusions can be drawn from these explorations of some of the fragmentary evidence attributed to early Cynics. First, the conception of the necessity of the complete extirpation of the passions, which has echoes in Antisthenes and became fully developed in Stoic thought, has no analogy in the chreiai or doxography of the early Cynics. Second, when Cynics express negative opinions about the πάθη, and particularly ἡδονή, such opinions never appear to be placed in the most basic theoretical structure, such as the elemental opposition between ἡδονή and λύπη that first appeared in Plato and was accepted as constitutive by Aristotle and the

Stoics alike. Third, there appears to be an implicit opposition between ἄσκησις and πόνος on the one hand and the πάθη on the other, though this is never worked out in even a general way.

Imperial Cynicism

Epictetus on the ideal Cynic

In Arrian, *Epict. diss.* 3.22, Epictetus the Stoic discusses the ideal Cynic in a diatribe entitled Περὶ κυνισμοῦ, "On Cynicism" (see Billerbeck 1978). In this discourse, he presents a programmatic exposition of the major features of a heavily Stoicized ideal Cynicism, emphasizing the complete eradication of sensual desire, ambition, and emotion that frees the governing principle (ἡγεμονικόν, *hēgemonikon*). According to Epictetus (Arrian, *Epict. diss.* 3.22.13), the aspiring Cynic is to have no anger (ὀργή), no rage (μῆνις), no envy (φθόνος), no pity (ἔλεος). While no Cynic worthy of the name would deny this statement, this mini-elaboration of the emotions bears a suspiciously close resemblance to Stoic catalogues of emotions that reflect the distinctively Stoic goal of the complete elimination of the passions. The fact that this radical systematic rejection of the passions is Stoic is confirmed in part by the emphasis on the correct use of impressions, φαντασίαι (*phantasiai*), a term derived from Stoic epistemology (Arrian, *Epict. diss.* 3.22.20) and one never used by hard-core Cynics. Since no one can compel a person to assent to what appears false, and to refuse assent to what appears better, there is something within a person that is ἐλεύθερον φύσει, "free by nature" (Arrian, *Epict. diss.* 3.22.42), a sentiment that reflects both Cynic and Stoic views but is Stoic by virtue of its theoretical basis. According to M. Billerbeck,

> Epictetus, whose teaching of ethics largely conformed to the standards of Roman Stoicism, found an elegant way of removing from Cynicism the taint of antisocial attitude while defending at the same time the Cynic concept of absolute independence. The rôle of the Cynic, as Epictetus depicts it, is an exceptional one. Cynicism is not a way of life for everybody who is interested in moral progress. Cynicism has a raison d'être only so long as mankind has not been converted to wisdom. Cynicism is not an aim of life, but is a profession taken up for the period of transition. In order to fulfill his mission the Cynic – who is a messenger of Zeus – must put his own natural needs last. In order to be at the disposal of everyone he must dispense with his personal rights and duties in civic life. Accordingly, the Cynic will avoid marriage and having children, not because he disapproves of this on principle but because he is unlikely under the present circumstances to find a wife who would be willing to share his Cynic vocation and who would be prepared to

accept the renunciation necessary to carry out the mission of conveying the Cynic message to the world.

(Billerbeck 1991: 163)

Epictetus must have based this conception of Cynic αὐτάρκεια on Socrates, who was remembered for his abstemious way of living (Xenophon, *Mem.* 1.3.5; 1.2.14),[15] but Plato attributes the αὐτάρκεια of Socrates to his awareness of a mission that leaves him little time to attend to worldly affairs:

Therefore I [Socrates] am still even now going about and searching and investigating at the god's behest anyone, whether citizen or foreigner, who I think is wise; and when he does not seem so to me, I give aid to the god and show that he is not wise. And by reason of this occupation I have no leisure to attend to any of the affairs of the state worth mentioning, or of my own, but am in vast poverty on account of my service to the god.

(Plato, *Apol.* 23B)

Dio Chrysostom, Oration 8.12–35

In several of his later *Orations*, Dio of Prusa purports to repeat five "Diogenes speeches" (*Or.* 4; 6; 8–10). While some have argued that Diogenes is actually a mouthpiece for Antisthenes, others have maintained that the speeches are based on a fourth-century compendium of Cynic teaching (Höistad 1948: 59). In my view, it is more likely that such speeches are rhetorical devices to convey Dio's own views (Jones 1978: 47). In one of these "Diogenes speeches," entitled "On Virtue," the bulk of the oration consists of a speech attributed to Diogenes of Sinope (*Or.* 8.12–35). The narrative setting is Corinth on the occasion of the Isthmian games. Diogenes had moved to Corinth, according to Dio, precisely because just as a good physician should go where the sick are most numerous, so also the sage should go where the most ignorant people are to be found in order to convict them of their ignorance and correct them (8.5). Some foreign visitors gathered about Diogenes to hear him speak, and one of them asked him whether he came to see the games. When, to the questioner's surprise, Diogenes replies that he intends to participate, the incredulous questioner asks who his competitors are. The protreptic response of Diogenes in 8.12–35 falls into two sections. In the first section (8.12–19), Diogenes speaks of the really difficult antagonists, which are πόνοι (*ponoi*, "hardships") such as hunger, cold, thirst, exile, and contempt (8.16), with the lasting prize consisting of εὐδαιμονία (*eudaimonia*, "happiness") and ἀρετή (*aretē*, "virtue") (8.15). When treated with contempt, these antagonists are conquered, but when regarded with fear and caution, they win. In the second section (8.20–35), Diogenes focuses on the greatest battle of all, that against ἡδονή ("pleasure"), which he treats through allegorizing aspects of the story of Circe in the *Odyssey* (8.20–6), and the life of Heracles (8.27–35).

Diogenes provides no theoretical framework for his discussion of ἡδονή, nor is ἡδονή defined; Diogenes simply assumes that this major subcategory of the passions must be completely avoided. The alternatives are either to flee as far as possible from ἡδονή or to be enslaved by it; there is no middle ground. This absolute polarization between slavery to ἡδονή and freedom from ἡδονή is similar to the Stoic rejection of an intermediate stage between virtue and vice (Diogenes Laertius 6.105, 127 [=SVF 1.187; 3.49]). Like the magic drugs of Circe, ἡδονή enslaves and transforms people into, as it were, pigs or wolves. Ἡδονή works through all of the senses of sight, hearing, smell, taste, and touch, through food and drink and sexual desire (8.21); that is, ἡδονή is a behavior more than an emotion. Turning to Heracles (the primary Cynic hero), he interprets the labors as the conquest of those enslaved to various pleasures by the ascetic Heracles. When he could no longer continue his struggles due to disease, he voluntarily ended his life.

The antithesis between πόνοι and ἡδονή that occurs both explicitly and implicitly in the fragmentary documentary evidence on the early Cynics appears here as a major feature of the Cynic mode of living. While the absolute opposition to ἡδονή in all its forms is programmatically Stoic, the fact that it is not given a theoretical underpinning suggests the distinctively Cynic orientation of this moral program in a life of action rather than thought.

The Cynic Letters

Apart from the fragments of Oenomaus, the pseudepigraphical *Cynic Letters* are the only literary expressions of imperial Cynicism that have been preserved (Goulet-Cazé 1990: 2805–6). Yet it is probably true to say that neither the Cynicism of Diogenes nor the Cynicism of the Roman Empire is decisively illuminated by the "literary Cynicism" found in these letters, since they were written by various authors over a long period of time.

The letters of Pseudo-Diogenes

Fifty-one letters are included in the collection of letters attributed to Diogenes, the largest group of Cynic letters. Of the five occurrences of πάθος in the letters of Pseudo-Diogenes,[16] three are particularly relevant to the present discussion. In *Ep.* 5 (to Perdiccas), Pseudo-Diogenes uses martial language in referring to fighting δόξαι ("opinions"), which are enemies more formidable than the Thracians and Paeonians, and equates this battle with subduing τὰ τῶν ἀνθρώπων πάθη, "the human passions."[17] In this telling passage, then, opinions are virtually equivalent to the passions, presumably because the passions are formidable only when people act in accordance with the opinions of the majority. In *Ep.* 27 (to Anniceris) Diogenes, complaining that the Spartans had expelled him from their city, claims that they have surrendered their unprotected souls to the passions (τοῖς πάθεσιν, *tois pathesin*). In *Ep.* 50 (to Charmides) Pseudo-Diogenes was less than impressed by the rhetorically polished arguments of Euremus, a student of Charmides, and points out that his love of money, which is the cause of all evil, reveals that he should have extirpated all passion (τὸ σύμπαν πάθος, *to sympan pathos*) through philosophy. The adjective ἀπαθής (*apathēs*, "unmoved by passion") is used of people who think their own possessions to be adequate for patient endurance and decline to marry and have children (Ps.-Diogenes *Ep.* 47).

The term ἡδονή, "pleasure," occurs six times in Ps.-Diogenes. In *Ep.* 12, the Cynic is enjoined, as part of ἄσκησις, "training," to resist the twin adversaries of ἡδονή and πόνος, "pleasure" and "hardship" (again using martial imagery), while the masses embrace ἡδονή. In the role of "spokesman for indifference" (ὁ τῆς ἀπαθείας προφήτης, *ho tēs apatheias prophētēs*), Pseudo-Diogenes speaks of those who have sexual intercourse for pleasure rather than to reproduce and maintains that they are living a deluded life (*Ep.* 21). The enjoyment of pleasure is sure to end in pain and suffering (*Ep.* 28.5). There is, in fact, pleasure in avoiding pleasure (*Ep.* 37.6), an allusion to a view attributed to Diogenes in Diogenes Laertius 6.71.

The letters of Pseudo-Crates

The term πάθος does not occur in the letters of Pseudo-Crates, but ἡδονή is used some six times. In a paraenetic letter to his students (Ps.-Crates, *Ep.* 15), Pseudo-Crates suggests that ἡδονή and πόνοι are basically antithetical, the former being the cause of evil, and the latter the cause of good. The worst of evils, ἀδικία (*adikia*, "injustice") and ἀκρασία (*akrasia*, "self-indulgence"), are caused by ἡδονή, but neither is generally considered to be among the πάθη; it is obvious that certain passions associated with the term ἡδονή are the equivalent of a moral slippery slope leading to greater evil. While ἡδονή gives rise to injustice and self-indulgence, πόνοι produce self-control and perseverance. Odysseus, whom some called "the father of Cynicism," doubtless because of his legendary πόνοι, is criticized for seeking pleasure above everything else (*Ep.* 19). On being asked, "Who, being free, needs a master?" he replied, "Those who are evil," according to *Ep.* 34.4, "and who honor pleasure but dishonor toil" (οἱ φαῦλοι καὶ τιμῶντες μὲν ἡδονήν, ἀτιμάζοντες δὲ πόνον). The summum bonum for most Hellenistic philosophical traditions was εὐδαιμονία, a good that Pseudo-Crates claims should not be confused with ἡδονή (*Ep.* 3).

Conclusions

The Cynic attitude toward the πάθη like their attitudes toward virtually everything else is governed by the core principle of ἐλευθερία: freedom from the slavery of a life governed κατὰ δόξαν (the customs and laws of culture), so as to live an unencumbered life κατὰ φύσιν (the self-evident design of nature), which is by definition ἐλευθερία. The *Cynic Letters* from the Roman imperial period contain a vague definition of Cynicism that focuses on the term φύσις and gives Cynicism a pseudo-philosophical orientation: ὁ γὰρ κυνισμός, ὡς οἶσθα, φύσεώς ἐστιν ἀναζήτησις, "For Cynicism is, as you know, an investigation of nature" (Ps.-Diogenes, *Ep.* 42). Ἐλευθερία entailed a cluster of other Cynic values, including αὐτάρκεια ("self-sufficiency"), παρρησία ("freedom [of speech and behavior]"), ἀπάθεια ("freedom from emotion"), and ἀναίδεια ("shamelessness"). Cynicism was not, strictly speaking, a philosophical school, but rather more an ethical tradition that emphasized the ἔνστασις βίου ("style of living") over against philosophical theory and argument. The phrase τῆς ἡδονῆς ἡ καταφρόνησις ("the despising of pleasure"), which is found in both Stoic and Cynic sources and has its roots in the Antisthenean strictures against pleasure as the most deadly of the passions, certainly reflects the attitude of both traditions. Yet this motto itself appears to have been the object of a critique by Diogenes, if we can accept the basic historicity of the chreia in which he refers to those who derive pleasure from despising pleasure. The anecdotal tradition associated with Diogenes also indicates his negative attitude toward ἐπιθυμίαι, also typical of Stoicism. Teles opposed the view that the flourishing life can be attained through pleasure, and he opposes the positive concept of πόνος to its negative opposite, ἡδονή, following Antisthenes. Furthermore, passion and disturbance are virtual synonyms for Teles and are considered the opposition of happiness or the flourishing life. Characteristically, however, Teles provides no philosophical arguments or epistemological basis for his condemnation of pleasure. Neither the anecdotes about Diogenes nor the diatribes of Teles reflect the view that the passions must be completely extirpated (the general Stoic view with antecedents in Antisthenes). Epictetus's discussion of the Cynic mission is heavily Stoicized, apparently with the intention of domesticating the Cynic tradition in order to make it acceptable to Roman *gravitas*. Dio Chrysostom attributes to Diogenes an oration in which martial imagery is used to describe the antithesis between πόνος and ἡδονή, the latter again conceived as a behavior rather than an emotion (*Or.* 8.12–35). Dio allows no middle ground between slavery to ἡδονή and freedom from ἡδονή, a characteristically uncompromising Stoic position. The use of martial imagery in Pseudo-Diogenes is applied to both the struggle against δόξαι, which are enemies that prevent the conquest of the human passions, and the human πάθη themselves. In the letters of Pseudo-Diogenes and Pseudo-Crates the theme of the struggle between πόνοι and ἡδονή appears again, and the latter functions as the slippery slope leading to further evils. While these probes into some of the fragmentary literary evidence for Cynic attitudes toward the πάθη have produced relatively meager results, there is little reason to think that the analysis of a broader spectrum of witnesses would appreciably alter the findings.

THE PROBLEM OF THE PASSIONS IN CYNICISM

Notes

1 The Cynic concept of αὐτάρκεια on the material level means contentment with the bare necessities of life, and on the moral level a complete detachment from the world and worldly values – that is, a stern renunciation of the world that held that nothing that could be derived from a source external to the Cynics had any value for them or could affect them in any way (see Rich 1956: 23). The true Cynic aimed at αὐτάρκεια as it was exemplified in the conduct of Diogenes, a conduct both celebrated and exaggerated in the anecdotal tradition. To practice αὐτάρκεια in the Cynic sense meant to be antisocial; the person who needs nothing and nobody has no reason to participate in the life of the community (Rich 1956: 27). Epicureans and Sceptics likewise wanted to banish the passions from life. For the former group, αὐτάρκεια involved holding correct opinions about people and gods; for the latter group, it involved holding no opinions at all.
2 Note Aristotle, *Eth. nic.* 2.4.5–6 1105b: "It is correct therefore to say that a man becomes just by doing just actions and temperate by doing temperate actions; and no one can have the remotest chance of becoming good without doing them. But the mass of mankind, instead of doing virtuous acts, have recourse to discussing virtue, and fancy that they are pursuing philosophy and that this will make them good men."
3 See Cicero's discussion of Chrysippus's explanation of human actions in *Fat.* 41–2 (very close to Aristotle, *De an.* 3.10–11; cf. Hamlyn 1967: 151–4).
4 The same "Cynic" notion is found in Seneca, *Ep.* 108.35–7: "We should so learn them [i.e., precepts that will help us] that words may become deeds [*ut quae fuerint verba, sint opera*]. And I hold that no man has treated mankind worse than he who has studied philosophy as if it were some marketable trade, who lives in a different manner from that which he advises." In the storm of life, he maintains, "One must steer, not talk [*non est loquendum, sed gubernandum*]."
5 The surviving fragments of Cynic authors and the testimonia regarding Cynics and Cynicism are collected in Paquet 1988.
6 See Bernays 1879: 27–8; Zeller 1919–23: 3/1.287–8, 791–2; Billerbeck 1991: 148.
7 See Dudley 1967: 117–24; Billerbeck 1979: 3–4.
8 See Hammerstaedt 1990.
9 See Hornsby 1933.
10 See the collection of fragments in *SVF* 3.92–102 under the rubric *De affectibus*.
11 An identical list is found in Andronicus (*SVF* 3.391).
12 See Diogenes Laertius 7.111–14 (=*SVF* 3.407, 396, 400). (1) The nine subtypes of λύπη include ἔλεος (*eleos*, "pity"), φθόνος (*phthonos*, "envy"), ζῆλος (*zēlos*, "jealousy"), ζηλοτυπία (*zēlotypia*, "rivalry"), ἄχθος (*achthos*, "load of grief"), ἐνόχλησις (*enochlēsis*, "annoyance"), ἀνία (*ania*, "distress"), ὀδύνη (*odynē*, "anguish"), σύγχυσις (*sygchysis*, "distraction"). (2) The six subtypes of φόβος include δεῖμα (*deima*, "terror"), ὄκνος (*oknos*, "hesitation"), αἰσχύνη (*aischynē*, "shame"), ἔκπληξις (*ekplēxis*, "consternation"), θόρυβος (*thorybos*, "panic"), ἀγωνία (*agōnia*, "mental distress"). (3) The seven subtypes of ἐπιθυμία include σπάνις (*spanis*, "craving"), μῖσος (*misos*, "hatred"), φιλονεικία (*philoneikia*, "contentiousness"), ὀργή (*orgē*, "anger"), ἔρως (*erōs*, "love"), μῆνις (*mēnis*, "wrath"), θυμός (*thymos*, "resentment"). (4) The four subtypes of ἡδονή include κήλησις (*kēlēsis*,

"ravishment"), ἐπιχαιρεκακία (*epichairekakia*, "malevolent joy"), τέρψις (*terpsis*, "delight"), διάχυσις (*diachysis*, "transport").

13 See Höistad 1948: 37–47; on this passage see Goulet-Cazé 1986.
14 See Hense 1909: 2; the text of Hense, with translation, is in O'Neil 1977: 11.
15 Xenophon attributes this saying to Socrates: "To have no wants is divine; to have as few as possible comes next to divine" (Xenophon, *Mem.* 1.6.10). Later, the same saying was attributed to Diogenes (Diogenes Laertius 6.104).
16 In one instance, πάθη clearly means "[physical] suffering" (Ps.-Diogenes, *Ep.* 33.4), while the use of πάθη in *Ep.* 32.3 (to Aristippus) is unclear to me.
17 The translation of the first sentence of Ps.-Diogenes *Ep.* 5 by B. Fiore (in Malherbe 1977: 97) is problematic: (1) the important term δόξα Fiore translates as "appearances," whereas here it must mean "opinions"; (2) the last part of the sentence is introduced by a circumstantial participle, καταστρεφόμενος τὰ τῶν ἀνθρώπων πάθη μεταπέμπου με, and modifies the main verb, πολεμεῖς, and so should be translated "by subduing the passions," but Fiore turns the phrase into a second main clause by translating the phrase "and if you are trying to subdue the human passions."

4

THE PASSIONS IN NEOPYTHAGOREAN WRITINGS

Johan C. Thom

This essay surveys the way the passions are treated in four types of Hellenistic and Neopythagorean writings: the pseudepigraphic treatises, the Pythagorean letters, Pythagorean sayings collections, and biographical traditions about Pythagoras. Only the first group treats the passions in a theoretical and systematic manner. According to these treatises, all moral action is accompanied and influenced by passions, which are considered the very matter of virtue. They favor the Aristotelian ideal of *metriopatheia* and are strongly opposed to the Stoic *apatheia*. In the other three groups, the focus is on the practical, moral implications of the passions and on appropriate ways of dealing with them. We find a wide spectrum of views, ranging from a temperate approach recommending moderation to a highly ascetic and apathetic view.

Introduction

When using the term "Neopythagorean," one should keep its imprecise character in mind. Neopythagoreanism does not constitute a conceptually homogeneous philosophical tradition, nor does it have very definite chronological boundaries. The notion of a Neopythagorean movement distinct from the earlier tradition inaugurated by Pythagoras is based on two ancient sources: Aristoxenus of Tarentum and Cicero. According to Aristoxenus, a student of Aristotle and one of the earliest historians of Pythagoreanism, the Pythagorean movement had disappeared in his time, the late fourth century BCE.[1] Cicero also referred to the Pythagorean *disciplina* as extinct for several centuries but lately revived by his friend Nigidius Figulus (*Tim.* 1.1). This revival is today known as Neopythagoreanism. However, neither Aristoxenus's nor Cicero's reports should be taken at face value.[2] Aristoxenus clearly is biased toward a specific form of Pythagoreanism, and he deliberately ignores other Pythagoreans known to have lived from his own time onward (e.g., the "Pythagorists" of Middle Comedy; a certain Lycon).[3] Cicero's statement of the "revival" under Nigidius Figulus perhaps should also be taken *cum grano salis*; there is very little evidence that Nigidius was indeed a Pythagorean; Cicero's statement may have been no more than a clever compliment for his polymathy.[4]

At least some of the numerous pseudepigraphic Pythagorean texts collected by H. Thesleff (1965a) should be dated in the Hellenistic age,[5] while other Pythagorean writings usually considered late may also have their origin in this period.[6] Consequently, some form of Pythagoreanism (or perhaps more than one) probably existed in the interval between Aristoxenus and the first century BCE. Whether to call texts from this period Hellenistic or Neopythagorean is a moot point: the former description prejudges the dating of the texts, while the latter unnecessarily implies a decisive break with the earlier tradition, as well as some form of conceptual unity.[7] The term "Neopythagorean" in the title of this essay is used merely as a matter of convenience and should not be taken either to imply a late date or to denote a homogeneous movement. As we will see, the writings to be considered indeed derive from diverse literary and ideological traditions.

These writings may be divided into four rough categories: (1) the pseudepigraphic treatises; (2) the Pythagorean letters, including letters purportedly by Apollonius of Tyana; (3) Pythagorean sayings collections; (4) the biographical traditions about Pythagoras and the Pythagoreans.[8] As far as I could determine, the topic of the passions is not treated in the extant writings and fragments of the Neopythagorean philosophers Moderatus of Gades, Nicomachus of Gerasa, or Numenius of Apamea.[9] Of these four groups, only the first – that is, the Pseudopythagorica – discusses the passions in a theoretical and systematic manner within the context of philosophical ethics; the others are more interested in the practical, moral implications of the passions.

The pseudepigraphic treatises

The pseudepigraphic Pythagorean treatises, mostly written in Doric, show a remarkable homogeneity in their views of the passions.[10] References to the passions occur in a considerable number of the treatises, but the most important texts on this subject are Archytas's *On Law and Justice* (Περὶ νόμου καὶ δικαιοσύνης = *De leg.*) and *On Moral Education* (Περὶ παιδεύσεως ἠθικῆς = *De educ.*), Metopus's *On Virtue* (Περὶ ἀρετῆς = *De virt.*), and Theages's *On Virtue* (Περὶ ἀρετῆς = *De virt.*).[11]

The framework for the ethics of the Pseudopythagorica is a psychology that assumes the existence of two opposing forces in the soul that at the same time are capable of being harmonized. This concept leads to a binary division of the soul into rational and irrational elements, although the latter usually is subdivided to form the well-known Platonic tripartite division of rational, spirited, and appetitive parts.[12]

Moral virtue results from the harmony (συναρμογά, *synarmoga*) of the irrational with the rational element.[13] It does not exist independently from the passions but is intimately involved and concerned with the passions.[14] Just like Aristotle, the Pseudopythagorica recognize that all moral action is accompanied and influenced by passions such as pleasure and pain,[15] which they called the "ultimate" (ὑπέρτατα, *hypertata*) passions,[16] but they go a step further in considering passions the very "matter" (ὕλα, *hyla*) of virtue.[17] Virtue emerges precisely by applying the measure of moral duty in pleasure and pain.[18]

From the preceding, it should be clear that the Pseudopythagorean authors not only favor the Aristotelian ideal of μετριοπάθεια (*metriopatheia*), moderation of the passions, but indeed strongly oppose the Stoic ἀπάθεια (*apatheia*), which entails the elimination of passions.[19] Virtue is viewed as the mean (μεσότας, *mesotas*) between the vices of deficiency and excess, or as the "due proportion" (συμμετρία, *symmetria*) of passions.[20] (In this way, the Pythagorean–Platonic notion of justice as a balance, a proportionality between parts, becomes associated with the Peripatetic doctrine of the mean.) It is explicitly stated that "the passions should not be removed from the soul ..., but joined in harmony with the rational part" (οὐκ ἀφελὲν ὧν δεῖ τὰ πάθεα τᾶς ψυχᾶς ..., ἀλλὰ συναρμόσασθαι ποτὶ τὸ λόγον ἔχον). "Virtue does not consist ... in eliminating the passions from the soul, but in bringing them into harmony" (οὐκ ἐν τῷ ὑπεξελέσθαι τὰ πάθεα τᾶς ψυχᾶς ἁ ἀρετὰ πέπτωκεν ἀλλ' ἐν τῷ ταῦτα συναρμόζεσθαι).[21]

In the view of the Pseudopythagorica, the Stoic ethical doctrine of *apatheia* is untenable for two reasons. First, this ideal is unattainable: it is just as impossible for the moral agent to be free from emotional "pain" as it is for the body to be free from illness and suffering. One therefore should not expect human beings to accomplish something that clearly is beyond their ability.[22] Second, such an ideal also is counterproductive because *apatheia* renders the soul inert and without enthusiasm for what is beautiful; it enervates what is noble in the soul.[23] Passion is just as necessary to virtue as shadows and lines are to a painting that is meant to be realistic and vivid; colors alone are insufficient.[24] Virtue arises from the passions and grows along with them;[25] thus it is not feasible to destroy the passions.[26]

According to F. Becchi, the Pseudopythagorica's emphasis on the importance of the passions and the strong stance against *apatheia* are a deliberate attempt to provide a more humane theory of moral action: instead of the perfect and inhuman Stoic σοφός (*sophos*), a "professional of rationality" without any emotion, they propose the ἀγαθός (*agathos*), who "incarnates the ideal of moral excellence that does not exist in purifying the soul of passions, but in moderation and self-control, in a just equilibrium vis-à-vis pleasure and pain, ... thus tempering pleasure with moral rectitude" (Becchi 1992: 116; cf. 107–8).[27]

The Pythagorean letters

The Pseudopythagorean letters and the letters attributed to Apollonius of Tyana deal with the topic of the passions in a very practical manner.[28] It occurs in Pythagoras's letter to Hieron, in two letters by Theano, and in a handful of letters by Apollonius.

In Pseudo-Pythagoras's letter to Hieron (*Ep. Pyth.* 1.2.9–12), the tyrant is informed that "a good disposition is not engendered by sex or food, but by poverty which leads a man to virtue. Diverse and uncontrolled pleasures enslave the souls of weak people."

Theano's letter to Euboule (*Ep. Pyth.* 5) is addressed to a mother who spoils her children. Instead of weakening their characters with pleasure and luxury, she should educate them to live prudently.[29] Against this background, Theano gives the mother the very robust advice to expose and accustom children to frightening situations, even if it causes them to suffer, in order that the children do not become slaves of passions such as fear (*Ep. Pyth.* 5.2.11–15).[30] In another letter, to Nicostrate (*Ep. Pyth.* 6), Theano tells her friend how to deal with her husband's unfaithfulness.[31] She has to distinguish carefully between his passion for the courtesan and his rational love for her (*Ep. Pyth.* 6.2.19–20); most importantly, she should not counter his passion with her own passion – that is, pain and jealousy (*Ep. Pyth.* 6.6.47–8; 6.7.62–4). His passion will best be extinguished by her patience (*Ep. Pyth.* 6.7.66–7).

Jealousy and anger are also the passions treated in Apollonius's letters.[32] In a letter to his chief opponent, the Stoic philosopher Euphrates (*Ep. Apoll.* 1), Apollonius juxtaposes being a philosopher and "treating one's emotions" (θεράπευέ σου τὰ πάθη), especially that of jealousy. A few other letters all deal with anger in epigrammatic fashion: "A quick temper blossoms into madness" (*Ep. Apoll.* 86); "If the emotion of anger is not conciliated and treated [καθομιλούμενον μηδὲ θεραπευόμενον], then it becomes a physical disease" (*Ep. Apoll.* 87); "If a person displays excessive anger over small offenses, he does not allow one who commits an offense to distinguish his lesser wrongdoings from his more serious ones" (*Ep. Apoll.* 88).[33]

In all these letters, it is recommended that the passions be dealt with in a positive and constructive manner. Interesting is the association between anger and disease; anger also should be "treated" (θεραπεύειν, *therapeuein*). The need to distinguish between situations expressed in the last letter cited is an aspect of the Pythagorean notion of the καιρός (*kairos*), doing what is appropriate to the occasion.[34]

Pythagorean sayings collections

Various sayings collections were in existence in the Hellenistic and imperial periods that either were attributed to the Pythagoreans or had a demonstrably Pythagorean origin. These collections differ considerably in style and content, and they cannot be traced back to a single Pythagorean group. The best-known collections, which will be discussed here, are the *Golden Verses*, the *Sentences of Sextus*, the *Sentences of Clitarchus*, the *Pythagorean Sentences*, and the *akousmata*. Apart from these, a considerable number of sayings ascribed to Pythagoras are preserved as quotation fragments in numerous ancient authors. These will not be considered here.[35]

It may be objected that the Pythagorean *akousmata* (also known as *symbola*) do not belong here, since it is generally acknowledged that they represent some of the oldest teachings of Pythagoreanism. What interests us here, however, is not the early, original meanings of these precepts and taboos, but rather the moral interpretations that they received from the Hellenistic age onward, and that therefore do fall within the chronological ambit of this investigation.[36] The most frequent passion dealt with by the *akousmata* (i.e., according to their Greco-Roman interpreters) is anger. According to one *akousma*, "One should not stir a fire with a knife," which is universally interpreted, "Do not increase someone's anger by arguing with him."[37] "Turn a sharp knife [or, according to another witness, 'acidity'] away from you" means "Keep away from anger."[38] "Wipe out the marks of a pot in the ashes" indicates that one should not allow any trace of anger to remain after it is spent, but that all remembrance of evil must be erased from the mind.[39] "Do not roast what was boiled" means "Gentleness does not need anger."[40] Two other *akousmata* also have to do with emotions: "Do not eat the heart" is interpreted to mean "Do not wear yourself out by worrying."[41] "Do not be overwhelmed by unchecked laughter" apparently needs no interpretation, but according to one ancient commentary, laughter here represents the passions (παθῶν, *pathōn*) in general; the *akousma* indicates that one should control the instability of the passions by means of the philosophical reason.[42]

In the *Golden Verses*, the first "virtue" to be mastered is self-control, which includes control of anger and lust, as well as of one's appetite and desire to sleep (*GV* 9–11). One should not be angry at suffering or one's lot in life, but rather heal it as far as possible (*GV* 17–19). Moderation in all things is the ideal (*GV* 33–4, 38).[43]

In view of the many repetitions and parallelisms between the *Sentences of Sextus*, the *Sentences of Clitarchus*, and the *Pythagorean Sentences*, I will discuss them together.[44] Passions are viewed in a very negative light.[45] They enslave the soul; it is not possible to be free when controlled by passions; it is harder to serve the passions than to serve tyrants (*Sent. Sext.* 75a; 75b; *Sent. Clit.* 85; 86; *Pyth. Sent.* 21; 23; 71). Persons who allow their passions free rein become like them (*Sent. Sext.* 435). Passion is an illness and an enemy of reason (*Sent. Sext.* 205; 207); it is therefore also a danger to one's salvation (*Pyth. Sent.* 2b; 116). Whatever is done in passion will be regretted (*Sent. Sext.* 206). In Sextus' Christianized terminology, a faithful person (πιστός, *pistos*) is immune to passions; conversely, one can only be considered faithful if one has put passions aside (*Sent. Sext.* 204; 209). The goal of education is the removal of passions; *sophrosyne* is the light of a passionless (ἀπαθοῦς, *apathous*) soul (*Pyth. Sent* 2c; 88).

It is clear that the sayings collections represent a wide spectrum of views on the topic of the passions. This ranges from a moderate view emphasizing self-discipline and moderation in the *Golden Verses* at one end of the spectrum to a highly ascetic and apathetic approach in the *Sentences of Sextus* at the other end, with the fairly austere view expressed by the *akousmata* in the middle. In all these texts, the main passions targeted are anger and bodily pleasures.

Biographical traditions

The biographical traditions portray Pythagoras and other famous early Pythagoreans as moral role models. Many of these traditions are mediated by Neopythagoreans such as Apollonius of Tyana and Nicomachus of Gerasa, although it is doubtful whether they were the sole sources for later authors. The subject of the passions is briefly referred to in a source on Pythagoreanism used by Diodorus of Sicily and in Porphyry's biography of Pythagoras, but it is treated extensively and repetitively in Iamblichus's *On the Pythagorean Way of Life*, which, as the title indicates, is more of a handbook of the Pythagorean life than a biography proper.[46] Thus, I will concentrate on the latter, since it includes all the material on this topic found in the other two authors.[47] Iamblichus does not discuss the passions systematically, as he often does with other topics; thus, we have to systematize his scattered observations.

In a conversation that Pythagoras was supposed to have had with the tyrant Phalaris and the "wise man" Abaris,[48] he revealed "the truth about the nature of the soul and its abilities and emotions" (*VP* 218), thus locating the discussion on the passions within the framework of a psychology.[49] His views on the passions in general are understood to agree with the Peripatetic doctrine, as opposed to Stoic:[50]

> ἀσκῆσαι δέ φασιν αὐτὸν καὶ τὰς μετριοπαθείας καὶ τὰς μεσότητας καὶ τὸ σύν τινι προηγουμένῳ τῶν ἀγαθῶν ἕκαστον εὐδαίμονα ποιεῖν τὸν βίον, καὶ συλλήβδην προσευρεῖν τὴν αἵρεσιν τῶν ἡμετέρων ἀγαθῶν καὶ προσηκόντων ἔργων.

> He is also said to have practiced moderation of the passions and the doctrine of the mean and the concept of making a happy life for oneself by directing it in accordance with one dominant good. In

sum, he discovered the concept of a choice of goods and deeds relative to them.

(*VP* 131)

Because extreme passions have to be avoided, the Pythagorean ideal is, however, sometimes described as "freedom from emotion," ἀπάθεια (*apatheia*) (*VP* 234).[51] In one list, these emotions are described as "pains and angers, pangs of pity, absurd jealousies and fears, all sorts of desires, outbursts of indignation, yearnings, feelings of superiority, bouts of laziness, and outbreaks of violence" (λύπας καὶ ὀργὰς καὶ ἐλέους καὶ ζήλους ἀτόπους καὶ φόβους, ἐπιθυμίας τε παντοίας καὶ θυμοὺς καὶ ὀρέξεις καὶ χαυνώσεις καὶ ὑπτιότητας καὶ σφοδρότητας) (*VP* 64).

Two metaphors are used to describe the way one should deal with these passions. The bushes in which passions such as sexual desires and greediness dwell have to be cleared away, "both with fire and sword and all the devices of science," to provide space for "something good" to be planted in the rational part of the soul (*VP* 78; cf. 228). The second metaphor was perhaps not really perceived as such. If ever Pythagoreans were overcome by an emotion such as anger, despondency, confusion, or grief, they retired and attempted "to heal the passion" (ἰατρεύειν τὸ πάθος) (*VP* 196; 225).[52]

This principle is illustrated by an anecdote about Archytas of Tarentum. When he returned to his farm after a period of absence, he noticed that the servants had been exceedingly negligent, and he became angry. The servants went unpunished, however, because he would not act in anger (*VP* 197).[53]

Moderation of the passions does not mean an absence of emotion but rather an avoidance of extremes: *sophrosyne* as regards the intellect (διάνοια, *dianoia*) entails that one does not oscillate between merriment and despondency, but rather observes "an equitable and calm joy" (ἐφ' ὁμαλοῦ πράως χαίροντες) (*VP* 196). Thus, prospective Pythagoreans were tested to make sure "that they would not be excited immoderately by feeling or desire" (*VP* 94).

At the same time, however, Pythagoreans were cautious about pleasure, "for nothing so disconcerts us or causes us to err as this emotion" (*VP* 204). Physical desire in particular needs special care and training, since the majority of human desires are acquired and developed by humans themselves. Human desires have no natural end, but continue almost indefinitely (*VP* 205–6).

In sum, one should only act in accordance with "right reason" (ὀρθοῦ λόγου) and not be diverted by pleasure, trouble, any emotion, or danger (*VP* 223).

An interesting aspect is the use that Pythagoreans made of music in treating the passions.[54] Pythagoras is attributed with the belief "that the first level of care [ἐπιμέλειαν] for humans is that brought about through sense perception." Although this includes visual perception of beautiful shapes and forms, most attention is given to the use of music: Pythagoras is supposed to have composed special musical arrangements (ἐξαρτύσεις τε καὶ ἐπαφάς) and melodies to turn harmful emotions around and to reharmonize the soul's faculties; these tunes "corrected [emotions] in the direction of moral excellence" as if they were health-giving drugs (*VP* 64). Such therapy he called "medical treatment through music" (τὴν διὰ τῆς μουσικῆς ἰατρείαν): certain melodies were designed against despondency and mental suffering (ἀθυμίας καὶ δηγμούς), others against rages, angers, and mental disturbance (πρός τε τὰς ὀργὰς καὶ πρὸς τοὺς θυμοὺς καὶ πρὸς πᾶσαν παραλλαγὴν τῆς τοιαύτης ψυχῆς), still others against desires (πρὸς τὰς ἐπιθυμίας) (*VP* 110–11; 224). Only the lyre was used as musical instrument, since the pipe has an adverse effect on emotions (*VP* 111–13).[55] At certain times of the day, or even of the year, Pythagoreans sang special odes and used special incantations to induce the emotion needed: vigor and energy early in the morning, peace of mind at night, feelings of joy in the spring (*VP* 110; 114).[56]

Finally, the principle of appropriateness – that is, the notion of the καιρός (*kairos*) – also applies to emotions. There are indeed opportune occasions to experience anger or desire or indeed any other emotion, but "the use of the opportune time ... is a complex and many-faceted art," and not easily taught (*VP* 181–2; cf. 180). Unfortunately, Iamblichus does not give examples of appropriate experiences of emotions. He does give examples of inappropriate emotions, however: no kind of anger on the side of a younger toward an older person is ever appropriate (*VP* 180); anger between friends should also be avoided, because it is not conducive to the preservation of friendship (*VP* 230; 233).[57]

To summarize: The "Pythagorean" approach to the passions, according to the biographical traditions, appears to be strongly influenced by the Peripatetic view of *metriopatheia*. Even so, its strong emphasis on control often reminds one of the Stoic *apatheia*. What is of considerable interest is the psychagogical principles involved in dealing with the emotions: students are carefully chosen on the basis of their ability to handle emotions; certain emotions have to be cleansed from the soul before any moral and intellectual progress can be made; passions should receive treatment, just like physical illnesses; the use of music plays an important role in this process; and finally, students should be taught how to apply the principle of appropriateness in expressing emotions.

Conclusion

On balance, a *metriopathetic* approach to the passions predominates in the writings under consideration here, although some do take a more negative view. Like other philosophical traditions of the Greco-Roman period, Neopythagorean authors attempted to teach their students appropriate ways of dealing with their passions. However, this varies from using the passions in a positive manner to promote moral excellence, on the one hand, to a strict control that allows very little scope for the modern ideal of spontaneity and self-expression, on the other.

Notes

1 In Iamblichus, *VP* 251; Diogenes Laertius 8.46 = Aristoxenus frgs 18, 19 Wehrli (1967); cf. Diodorus of Sicily 15.76.4 ("certainly based on Aristoxenus" [Burkert 1972: 200]).
2 See Thom 1995: 84–6; Kingsley 1995: 323–5.
3 See Fritz 1963: 174–5; Burkert 1972: 198–200; Riedweg 2002: 138–9.
4 See Thesleff 1965b; Riedweg 2002: 161–2. A somewhat more positive view of the sources is taken in Centrone 1996: 164–70.
5 In an earlier work, Thesleff (1961) gives a brief survey of these texts, dating all of them between the fourth and the first centuries BCE; see esp. the summarized chronology on pp. 113–16. Thesleff's early dating has not found general acceptance; see, for example, the debate between him and W. Burkert in their respective contributions in Fritz 1972: "On the Problem of the Doric Pseudo-Pythagorica: An Alternative Theory of Date and Purpose" (Thesleff, pp. 59–87); "Zur geistesgeschichtlichen Einordnung einiger Pseudopythagorica" (Burkert, pp. 25–57). However, Burkert too accepts a Hellenistic dating for some of these texts; see Burkert 1961; 1962. A summary of various positions on the dating of these texts is given in Centrone 1990: 14 n. 3; see also Centrone 1996: 148–63; Giani 1993: 8–12; Riedweg 2002: 158–61.
6 Recently, I have argued that the Pythagorean *Golden Verses* should be dated in the early Hellenistic period, rather than in the late Hellenistic or early imperial period, which is the majority opinion; see Thom 1995: Ch. 5; 2001. An earlier date is defended also in Reale 1990: 259.
7 For recent discussions of the problem, see Reale 1990: 237–49; Kingsley 1995: 317–34; Centrone 1996: 144–8.
8 A similar classification has been followed in a previous essay; see Thom 1997.
9 For a survey of these authors, see Dillon 1977: 341–83; Reale 1990: 251–72. Reale suggests that these Neopythagorean authors be distinguished from the earlier Pseudopythagorica, by describing the latter as "Middle Pythagoreanism."
10 There is one apparent contradiction: in *De leg.* 33.17–18, attributed to Archytas, he appears to be in favor of *apatheia*, while in another text, *De educ.* 41.16–18, he strongly argues for *metriopatheia*. This discrepancy will be discussed in more detail below. For summaries of the Pseudopythagorica's views on the passions, see Moraux 1984: 661–6; Centrone 1990: 18–30; Becchi 1992. For the doctrinal homogeneity of the Doric Pseudopythagorica in general, see Centrone 1996: 153–9. All citations of the Pseudopythagorica, unless otherwise indicated, are by page and line number in the collection by Thesleff (1965a).
11 Since the *Tabula of Cebes* is not usually considered a "Pythagorean" text, it will not be treated here (*pace* Sorabji 2000: 294–5). For discussions of this text, see the essays by White and Fitzgerald in this volume.
12 See Moraux 1984: 656; Becchi 1992: 104. For the binary division see, for example, Archytas, *De leg.* 33.14–18; for the tripartite division, Aresas, *De nat. hom.* 49.3–8; Diotogenes, *De regn.* 73.9–15; Callicratidas, *De dom. felic.* 103.5–10; Theages, *De virt.* 190–3; Timaeus, *De univ. nat.* 217–18 (=43–7 Marg [1972]) (also Alexander Polyhistor in Diogenes Laertius 8.30 = Anonymus Alexandri 235.29–36.4 [Thesleff 1965a]; Anonymus Photii 240.5–26 [Thesleff 1965a]); for an explicit derivation of the one from the other, Metopus, *De virt.* 118.1–6.

13 Cf. Archytas, *De leg.* 33.17: γίνεται γὰρ ἐκ τᾶς ἑκατέρων [sc., τὸ λόγον ἔχον καὶ τὸ ἄλογον] συναρμογᾶς ἀρετά ("For virtue results from the harmony of both [sc., the rational and the irrational element]"); Metopus, *De virt.* 119.28–20.1: καθόλω μὲν ὦν ἀρετὰ συναρμογά τις ἐντὶ τῶ ἀλόγω μέρεος τᾶς ψυχᾶς ποτὶ τὸ λόγον ἔχον ("In general, therefore, virtue is a harmony of the irrational part of the soul with the rational element"); Theages, *De virt.* 193.15. Unless otherwise indicated, all translations are my own.

14 Metopus, *De virt.* 119.8–9: περὶ ταῦτα [sc., τὰ πάθεα] γὰρ καὶ ἐν τούτοις ἁ ἀρετά ("For virtue is concerned and involved with these things [sc., the passions]").

15 Cf. Theages, *De virt.* 192.30–193.7.

16 Theages, *De virt.* 192.6; cf. Metopus, *De virt.* 119.8–10.

17 Cf. Aristotle, *Eth. nic.* 2.2.1104b4–24; Metopus, *De virt.* 119.8–10; Theages, *De virt.* 192.24–193.7; discussed by Moraux, who points out that Peripatetics of the imperial period also considered passions the matter of virtue (Moraux 1984: 661).

18 Metopus, *De virt.* 120.1–2: γίνεται δὲ αὐτὰ [sc., ἀρετά] τῷ κατ τὰν ἁδονὰν καὶ τὰν λύπαν ὅρον ἐπιδέξασθαι τὸν τῶ δέοντος ("It [sc., virtue] arises by applying the measure of duty in pleasure and pain").

19 See Becchi 1992: esp. 107–16; Giani 1993: 30; cf. Moraux 1984: 662–4; Centrone 1990: 25. The only apparent exception is Archytas, *De leg.* 33.17–18: γίνεται γὰρ ἐκ τᾶς ἑκατέρων συναρμογᾶς ἀρετά, αὕτα δὲ καὶ ἀπὸ τᾶν ἁδονᾶν καὶ τᾶν λυπᾶν εἰς ἀρεμίαν καὶ ἀπάθειαν ἀπάγει τὰν ψυχάν ("For virtue results from the harmony of both [sc., the rational and the irrational element], and it leads the soul away from pleasures and pains to quietude and freedom from passions"). Because of the contradiction between this passage and Archytas, *De educ.* 41.16–18, which stresses the need to practice *metriopatheia*, Moraux (1984: 662 n. 285) suggests that the texts derive from two different authors. Becchi (1992: 114–15) argues persuasively that *apatheia* cannot result from a virtue that owes its existence to the "harmony" of the irrational with the rational. He therefore suggests that the text, defective due to haplography (εἰς ... εἰς), should receive the following insertion: ... τᾶν λυπᾶν <εἰς μετριοπάθειαν, μὴ> εἰς ἀρεμίαν.... The resulting text could then be translated as "it [sc., virtue] leads the soul away from pleasures and pains < to the moderation of passions, not > to quietude and freedom from passions."

20 Metopus, *De virt.* 120.4–5, 23–5; Theages, *De virt.* 191.28–9; 192.11. See Becchi 1992: 111.

21 Metopus, *De virt.* 121.10–12; Theages, *De virt.* 192.7–8. See Becchi 1992: 112.

22 Archytas, *De educ.* 41.9–18; cf. Diotogenes, *De regn.* 74.9–11. See Moraux 1984: 663; Becchi 1992: 112; Giani 1993: 30.

23 Metopus, *De virt.* 120.25–21.1; Archytas, *De educ.* 41.13–14. See Moraux 1984: 663; Becchi 1992: 112.

24 Metopus, *De virt.* 121.2–5. See Moraux 1984: 663–4.

25 Metopus, *De virt.* 121.7–8: γίνεται γὰρ ἐκ τῶν παθέων ἁ ἀρετά, καὶ γενναθεῖσα πάλιν συναύξεται τούτοις ("For virtue arises from the passions, and when it has come into existence, it in turn grows along with them").

26 Metopus, *De virt.* 121.10–12. See Moraux 1984: 664; Becchi 1992: 112–13.

27 Becchi (1992: 117–20) points out that this anti-Stoic polemic is found also in other early imperial authors such as Plutarch, Aspasius, Galen, and Lucian. See also Giani 1993: 26–31, 34–7.

28 For these texts, see Städele 1980; Penella 1979.
29 Städele 1980: 290–1.
30 Städele 1980: 166.
31 Städele 1980: 302–4.
32 For a brief introduction to Apollonius, see Centrone 1996: 170–2.
33 Translations of Apollonius's letters (some slightly adapted) are from Penella 1979.
34 See Thom 1995: 124–5, 161.
35 Except for the *akousmata*, the Pythagorean sayings tradition is all but ignored in most surveys of Pythagoreanism. A good case in point is the otherwise excellent recent introduction by B. Centrone (1996).
36 For a brief introduction with further references, see Thom 1994, esp. 94–6. To this should now be added Centrone 1996: 78–83, 86–92; Riedweg 2002: 55–67.
37 The oldest attestation of the *akousma* is by Anaximander the Younger of Miletus (ca. 400 BCE) in *Suda*, s.v. Ἀναξίμανδρος. The interpretation goes back to Androcydes the Pythagorean (before first century BCE) (see Thom 1994: 95 n. 11); cf., for example, Trypho in *Rhetores Graeci* 3.194.7 Spengel (1854–85); Ps.-Plutarch, *Lib. ed.* 12E; Athenaeus, *Deipn.* 10.77; Porphyry, *VP* 42; Diogenes Laertius 8.18; Iamblichus, *Protr.* 21 pp. 107.6; 112.24–13.7. References to Iamblichus's *Protrepticus* are to the edition of Pistelli (1888).
38 Diogenes Laertius 8.17; Iamblichus, *Protr.* 21 pp. 107.7; 113.8–18.
39 Plutarch, *Quaest. conv.* 727C, 728B; Clement of Alexandria, *Strom.* 5.5.27.8.
40 Iamblichus, *VP* 154.
41 Cf. Athenaeus, *Deipn.* 10.77; Ps.-Plutarch, *Lib. ed.* 12E; Diogenes Laertius 8.18; Porphyry, *VP* 42.
42 Iamblichus, *Protr.* 21 pp. 107.29; 121.9–25.
43 For a text and translation with an extensive commentary of the *Golden Verses*, see Thom 1995; for commentary on the sayings cited here, see pp. 126–30, 140–5, 156–63.
44 For Sextus, see Chadwick 1959; Edwards and Wild 1981. The text of Clitarchus is found in Chadwick 1959: 76–83; that of the *Pythagorean Sayings* in ibid., 84–94. See also the brief description in Thom 1997: 87.
45 Cf. in general the disparaging remarks about pleasure in *Sent. Sext.* 70; 71b; 72, and the sayings about marriage and sex in *Sent. Sext.* 230a–40.
46 For a text and translation of this work, see Dillon and Hershbell 1991. All translations of Iamblichus's *De vita Pythagorica* are from this work (sometimes slightly adapted).
47 On using these texts as evidence for a Neopythagorean point of view, see Thom 1997: 82–3.
48 On the fictional character of this conversation and its sources see Dillon and Hershbell 1991: 215 n. 2.
49 According to Pythagoras's statements in this conversation, human psychology is structurally analogous to the organization of the cosmos (cf. Anonymus Photii, pp. 240.5–26 [Thesleff 1965a]), but it is unclear to me what implications this view has for the passions.
50 Dillon and Hershbell 1991: 151 n. 10.
51 On the possible source of this passage, see Dillon and Hershbell 1991: 229 n. 4. See also Marg's (1972) emendation of εὐπείθεια to ἀπάθεια in his edition of Timaeus

of Locri, *De univ. nat.* 224.7 (Thesleff 1965a [=82 Marg]), in a context describing Pythagorean *sophrosyne*.
52 Cf. *Golden Verses* 18–19, with the commentary in Thom 1995: 144–5.
53 Cf. Diodorus of Sicily 10.7.4. A similar story is told about Plato, but the one about Archytas may well be the original; see Dillon and Hershbell 1991: 203 n. 10. The same principle is also attributed to Cleinias (*VP* 198).
54 See Porphyry, *VP* 30.
55 Iamblichus, *VP* 112–13 contains examples of how Pythagoras and Empedocles used music to calm the anger of youths.
56 For the Pythagorean practice of purification by music, see Boyancé 1936: 106–7; John 1962. As far as I could determine, no reference to Pythagoras's "medical treatment through music" occurs in Nicomachus's *Harmonicum enchiridion*.
57 See also Thom 1995: 122–5.

5

"BE ANGRY AND SIN NOT": PHILODEMUS VERSUS THE STOICS ON NATURAL BITES AND NATURAL EMOTIONS*

David Armstrong

Recent scholarship has sometimes tended to emphasize the reserve with which Epicurus and his school regarded emotion, and to assimilate them to the Stoics in this point. Though they were not emotionalists without reserve, however, it can be shown that the texts of Epicurus and his school, especially Philodemus's *On Frank Criticism*, *On Anger*, and *On Death*, do not support this view, but encourage a surprising range of emotional reactions as being "natural." In an appendix, it is shown that Philodemus's opponents in *On Anger*, whatever their differences with him, were Epicureans and were themselves arguing, as he tries to, for anger in the Epicurean sage as "natural."

Introduction

ὀργίζεσθε καὶ μὴ ἁμαρτάνετε· ὁ ἥλιος μὴ ἐπιδυέτω ἐπὶ [τῷ] παροργισμῷ ὑμῶν, μηδὲ δίδοτε τόπον τῷ διαβόλῳ.
Be ye angry, and sin not: let not the sun go down upon your wrath: Neither give place to the devil.
                                                                      (Eph 4:26–7 AV)

---

* I am very much obliged to John Fitzgerald for his sensitive and detailed editing of this article and his expert help with the NT references. All errors that remain are of course my own. I must also thank the Mellon Foundation for a Mellon Emeritus Fellowship that has supported my work in 2006 and 2007 while I wrote and corrected it.

In this well-known verse of the Pauline Epistle to the Ephesians the author begins by quoting the opening words of the LXX version of Ps 4:5 (4:4 Eng.), "Be ye angry and sin not." The initial word in the Hebrew text, by contrast, probably means, "Tremble" (JB, NAB, NJPS, etc.), not "Be angry,"[1] and the psalm continues in a way that is not at all, either in Hebrew or Greek, like what follows in the rest of Eph 4:26–7, so that the writer has made his LXX quotation into something quite new.[2] Furthermore, whereas the psalmist is admonishing his adversaries about a false accusation, the author of Ephesians is exhorting fellow believers about the proper attitude toward anger. Although he not just wishes but commands, in the words of the LXX psalm, his Christian readers to feel *real anger*, he warns them to make it short-lived if they are to avoid error and evil. And thus, perhaps not entirely accidentally, he reproduces the teaching of the Epicureans of the first century BCE, at least as represented in Philodemus's *On Anger*.

In other schools anger was considered, if justified, to involve *pain* worth feeling even by wise men at a slight to themselves or their family and friends, and *pleasure* worth feeling in vindication or even in revenge, as Aristotle classically defines it in *Rhet.* 2.4. Or, the Stoics argued, it was always assent, even if originating in a justified feeling of momentary outrage, either to a false proposition about the facts or to false values about what was truly important in life, or both, and always, both as pleasure and pain, to be condemned and cut out of oneself to the extent possible – that is, at least ideally, entirely. So also were all the other ordinary emotions, except a specified few exalted feelings such as "joy" in virtue (and its opposite, "aversion" from vice), in friendship with other virtuous people, and in the good government of the universe.

By contrast, Philodemus's *On Anger* offers a clever variation from the Epicurean side on Aristotle's classic definition. The *pleasure* of anger is joy in revenge, a prime example of an untrustworthy and unnecessary "kinetic" pleasure, more likely to end in damaging the angry person than the object of revenge, and likely to become an obsession and an addiction spreading over all of the angry person's life, making him or her repulsive and ridiculous and leading to self-damage. The *pain* of anger and indignation is unavoidable by any human being at some time in life, and is a "natural" emotion given to us, not of course by the gods, who in Epicurus's view live at a great distance from our affairs and our world and take no part in it, but by what Epicurus called "blessed Nature" (ἡ μακαρία φύσις, *hē makaria physis*), to help us defend ourselves against wrong and injustice. Or to put it more strictly, "natural" emotions helped our species survive and can still help each of us. We can know that our anger is "natural" by its *brevity*, for in Epicurus's view no one pursues pain, but wants to be rid of it instead. It is the pleasure of revenge that lasts, becomes obsessive, and is the bad side of the emotion, and we must guard against it. And of course "unnatural" and "empty" anger causes and involves still more pain to oneself and others, which is "unnatural" pain. But the pleasure a person takes in revenge, and the fit of temper's lasting too long, are treated as the chief signs that one is feeling "empty" anger and should check oneself. It is not impossible that this argument had drifted down to the author of Ephesians in some form and helped shape his words.

Now, both the author of Ephesians and the writer of the Epistle of James, who says, "Be...slow to wrath [βραδὺς εἰς ὀργήν, *bradys eis orgēn*], for the wrath of man worketh not the righteousness of God" (Jas 1:19–20 AV), were writing in the first century CE, and are to some extent influenced by philosophical language of the period, in which the emotions were lavishly discussed. The quotation from James might be thought more or less to agree with the position of the Stoics, who disparaged emotion and distrusted it. But Paul and the Pauline writings are, as has long been seen, here and there influenced both by the Stoics and by the language of the Epicureans, who gave some emotions, at least, a cautious welcome as being "natural."

This does not mean that the Epicureans welcomed violent emotional feelings into the ideal philosopher's soul without reservation, or that they were not suspicious of the emotions as threats to their ideal wise person's freedom from disturbance (*ataraxia*). Most of what we know about their opinion, however, does not come from the founders of the school. The predominant use of the word *pathos*, "emotion," in the texts that survive from the writings of the founder of Epicureanism and his contemporaries in the school concerns the two feelings all-important in Epicurean ethics and psychology: pleasure and pain. If these count as emotions or emotional experience, all people, including Epicurean sages, are continually in one *pathos* or the other, for merely living without pain and intelligently also constitutes pleasure.

Philodemus on the emotions

Our best evidence for how the Epicureans treated what the other schools, in accordance with more normal Greek usage, called "emotions," *pathē*, comes from later Epicurean texts, especially the Herculaneum papyri, and particularly from the treatises in which Philodemus of Gadara (ca. 110–30 BCE), the author of the large majority of these, explained Epicureanism to his Roman audience. Philodemus in turn is not usually giving his readers his own original thoughts, but rather is following the theories of his teacher Zeno of Sidon (ca. 150–70 BCE), the head of the school in Athens in his youth.[3] Zeno's theories were shaped by argument against Diogenes of Babylon (ca. 240–152 BCE) and his pupil Panaetius (185–109 BCE), the fourth and fifth heads of the Stoa after its founders, Zeno of Citium, Cleanthes of Assos, and Chrysippus of Soli. Although Stoicism was founded by Zeno of Citium, who was six years younger than Epicurus (341–270 BCE), when Epicurus's school was already well established, and given its most characteristic form still later by Chrysippus (ca. 280–207 BCE), the language and arguments of Philodemus's treatises, and thus probably of his teacher Zeno of Sidon also, reflect arguments and technical language borrowed from or shared with the Stoics in the course of generations of argument with them.

In particular, it is well recognized that in Zeno's and Philodemus's period Epicureanism (without departing from its founder's basic tenets) made efforts to discover answers to questions not extensively treated in the founders' texts, such as the place of music, rhetoric, and poetics in the philosopher's life, which were dealt with richly by the other Hellenistic schools but neglected by the founders of Epicureanism; or how a Roman nobleman or a king should deal with political responsibilities that cannot be laid aside (Philodemus's *On the Good King According to Homer*); or the right behavior of the wise person in the face of threats from tyrants and other extreme situations that threaten one's happiness, a topic that previously had been a particular province of the Stoics (Philodemus, *On Death* 33.37–35.34);[4] or the technical problems of mathematics, which Epicurus had thought made little contribution to the happiness of the wise and consequently encouraged his followers to neglect, and to which Zeno of Sidon made contributions that were still remembered in late antiquity.[5] For that matter, whatever the impatience with which the Master and his circle had regarded mathematics, geometry, philology, and literature as pursuits for the wise, the school had indulged itself pretty liberally since the death of Hermarchus, the last of the founders, in the study of all of these, as long as no clear dissonance with the basic tenets of the founders resulted.[6]

Philodemus provides some of our best evidence of how Epicureans such as he and Zeno dealt with what ordinary Greeks called "emotions." To some extent we can find in his writings better evidence about how Epicureans' prescriptions for their role in the wise person's life and their psychological therapy for the standard list of emotions worked, a topic on which Epicurus himself and his companions, the founders of the school, had written less explicitly. But it became an unavoidable topic of discussion for later Epicureans under the radical challenge of the Stoics.

In this essay I examine some texts from three of these treatises, *On Frank Criticism*, *On Anger*,[7] and *On Death*, that suggest that when dealing with such standard "emotions" discussed by the ancient ethical philosophers from Aristotle onward as *shame, anger, gratitude*, and *fear*, the Epicureans show themselves far less "facile eudaemonists" in their theory of what is fitting to a "happy" human being than they sometimes are taken to be. *Parrhēsia*, frank criticism, sometimes may be quite painful both to the student and the teacher of philosophy because it involves shaming for the teacher and being shamed for the student, but is nonetheless both necessary and beneficial. The pleasure of anger – revenge – is disturbingly unlimited and obsessional, and damages the person who feels it in the end more than the object of revenge. But the pain of anger is "natural" to all human beings, and is to be accepted even by the wise. It is *anekpheukton anthrōpōn physei* (*On Anger* col. XL.20–1), inescapable by and for human nature, and it is well that is so, for evils cannot be remedied without the spur it provides. The fear of death is in many cases equally "natural" because it keeps us alive, and for entirely good purposes, and we are not wrong to lament and weep over the frustration of these good purposes, or even (we have Epicurus's own word for it) just for the death of family members and good friends. In the end this fear and this grief ought not to prevail over our thankfulness for life and friendship and our acceptance, indeed our constant, conscious contemplation, of the facts of life and death. These emotional feelings Philodemus calls variously "harsh" (*sklēron*), "painful" (*lypēron*), and "biting" (*dēktikon*), describing them as "stings" or "bites" (*nyxeis, dēgmoi*), and comparing them at least twice to submitting to a medical operation with the knife, or to a nauseating drug, wormwood (*apsinthion*). But they all are natural (*physikon*), by which Philodemus means worthy of acceptance by a human being, and that in a fairly strong sense. And they are all produced by a correct understanding that some state of affairs is true; they are not mere first reactions as with the Stoics. Gratitude, which requires in ancient terms the acceptance of reciprocal obligations, is too "natural," at least toward philosophical friends and teachers, to need even to be called that. It is just approved, even (in a less intense form) for other benefits given by friends in ordinary life.

Zeno of Sidon's contemporary, the Epicurean Demetrius Laco, whose opinion is also preserved in the Herculaneum texts (*On Textual and Exegetical Problems in Epicurus*, cols 67–8 Puglia [1988]), defines "natural" in contexts such as (1) what we feel by uncorrupted natural impulse (*adiastrophōs*), (2) what we feel inescapably (*katēnankasmenōs*), (3) what we feel that is advantageous for ourselves (*sympherontōs*), and (4) what we feel that corresponds reliably with external reality, like the first and primitive meanings of words, according to Epicurean theories of the origin of language. It can be shown that the pangs of these "natural" emotions of Philodemus all fit one or more of these definitions, most of them all four.[8]

Therefore, although no modern theorist of the emotions as essentially healthy feelings would be remotely satisfied with these Epicurean concessions to them – because they are, always, thought of as concessions to be watched carefully before they get out of hand – they really do contradict the Stoic theory both of what emotions are and how to manage and treat them, and give us a good reason why the Stoics treat these concessions with adamant hostility throughout the rest of the long battle between the two schools lasting until the third century CE. There is a title preserved in Galen of a book by the otherwise obscure Epicurean Antonius, of uncertain date: *Peri tēs tois idiois pathesin ephedreias*, *On Ephedreia* (or, *Keeping a Watch*) *over One's Personal Emotions*. Galen quotes the title at the beginning of his own treatise *On the Diagnosis and Therapy of the Emotions in the Soul* (5.1–2) and says that by *ephedreia* Antonius meant the watching over (*paraphulakē*), analysis (*diagnōsis*), and improvement (*epanorthōsis*) of one's own emotional reactions. The Epicureans allow for real emotions, but they must be watched carefully. The emotions, however, are natural and should be there. That is all that I would claim for them, but it seems important to establish that on this point the Epicureans were by no means (or at all) merely agreeing with the Stoics in different words.

Julia Annas on the Epicureans

But this was the claim of J. Annas (1992: 196–9). According to her, the Epicureans insisted on "a transformation of emotional life nearly as drastic as Plato's in the *Republic*" (Annas 1992: 196). Philodemus, she argues on the basis of *On Anger* cols XXXIV.24–XXXV.6, does not permit real human anger.

> The behavior may appear the same, but its causes are so different that we do not really have the same emotion. Philodemus, however, does not use distinct words, for an Epicurean the revised kind of anger is a true kind, of which the ordinary kind is a distortion or corruption.
>
> (Annas 1992: 197 n. 27)

"The Epicurean remedies that take the damaging heat out of anger turn out to leave us cold in areas where this is not so clearly a good thing" (Annas 1992: 198), though unless it is a good thing in itself to be angry, Philodemus's point that one should be angry in order to prevent wrong to oneself or to one's friends seems to me to cover all the "good" bases. Moreover, to feel real pain at being slighted and wronged and use that as a motivation to redress oneself is not to be "cold" in any sense that I can accept.

> The affectively transformed Epicurean will, like the ideal Stoic, be free from the disturbances of emotion in our everyday sense, and motivated by emotions which have been transformed by a total restructuring of the beliefs that sustain them. Their behavior will not be quite the same – the Stoics have no room for approved forms of the hostile or negative emotions like anger, and the Epicureans do – but they will be *equally far* from our everyday state. It is somewhat ironical that this is the end result of a theory allegedly based on uncomplicated feelings which all share. We start from common sense, but we end very far from it.
>
> (Annas 1992: 198–9 [italics added])

Again, Annas (1993: 199), although she acknowledges that the point of Philodemus's *On Anger* is to prove that anger is unavoidable and natural, even for the wise, claims that the wise person according to Philodemus only *pretends* anger, and does not feel it. She translates *On Anger* col. XXXIV.31–8, "In general, we should know that the person who is purely unangered [καθαρῶς τις ὢν ἀοργητός, *katharōs tis ōn aorgētos*] will give the appearance of an angry person, but not for long, and if he gives it for longer is not deeply [angry], but just not such as he seems to be." But in fact *aorgētos* is the opposite of *orgilos*, "irascible" – that is, by nature. It is not said of not being angry on this or that occasion; and indeed, LSJ translates *aorgētos* as "not irascible." It is not a person "purely unangered" whom Philodemus means, but a person "wholly unirascible" (Indelli 1988: 122, "assolutamente non irascibile"), for καθαρῶς (*katharōs*) has nothing to do with purity, and just means "entirely," as it does now and then in Philodemus and later Greek (see LSJ, 851, s.v. καθαρός II.6 [Adv.]). The passage that Annas cites really means this (according to Indelli's [1988: 122] translation):

> <If we see the unirascible acting like>[9] irascible people, we should know that <both these things and> all the other things that we have given an exposition of come about without the emotion and disposition to it, and the things that *they* [i.e., the Peripatetics, whom Philodemus has just finished dealing with] claim result from these. But sometimes it happens that they can be changed in temper, by people who drive them out of their minds and by the augmentation of those characteristics by which they appear irascible, even to the point of making them really irascible. But generally speaking, one should know that a man entirely nonirascible will not give the appearance of an irascible man for a long time, or if he does so for a longer time, is not such to the core, but only not such a person as he seems. At any rate, they appear to that extent to have the opposite disposition to their real one, that even a wise person, as, for example, Epicurus, has given some the impression of being such.
> (*On Anger* cols XXXIV.16–XXXV.5)

The point is the reverse of what Annas claimed. Though not as the Peripatetics wanted a sage to be when angry – that is, taking pleasure in anger as well as feeling pain (or so Philodemus claims they did) – even the most peaceful-tempered sage sometimes will be angry. Nor will it always be momentary anger, as Philodemus recommends (Horace's *irasci celerem, tamen ut placabilis essem*, "swift to anger, but nevertheless in a way that I can be calmed down" [Horace, *Ep.* 1.20.25]).[10] The sage will be angry as long as is appropriate to achieve the desired purposes, and will not care, as Epicurus did not, if taken to be bad-tempered because of it. Indeed, the passage goes on (*On Anger* cols XXXV.5–XXXVI.21) to show Philodemus in a long, uphill battle against historical evidence – of which he admits there is much – that Epicurus himself and many Epicurean teachers frequently behaved like extremely "irascible" people, rebuking friends harshly, criticizing and losing their temper with their slaves for trifles, sometimes without justice ("before realizing completely that the offence was by chance" [*On Anger* col. XXXV.18–20]). He hopes that this "appearance" is explained by "a greater liability to natural anger, as I have already said, or to the causes I have set forth in *On Frank Criticism* or because (provoking) things like this happened more often to them" (*On Anger* col. XXXVI.13–21). But Philodemus seems to admit that his Epicurean adversaries, who argued, whether in rebuke or in admiration, that a hot temper had not been thought by the founders of the school to detract from the sage's wisdom or happiness, had evidence that was necessary to answer.[11] "People who drive them out of their minds" (μανιοποιοῦντας ἀνθρώπους, *maniopoiountas anthrōpous*) would have sounded strange enough to the Stoics: what people can do this to the Stoic sage? None, according to their claim.

It is more reasonable of Annas to make a point of Philodemus's claim that although it is true that anger and gratitude are based on our knowledge of other's intentions toward us, the sage does not feel *intense* gratitude or *intense* anger. Here, however, his adversaries are other Epicureans, who hold that the sage will feel both! Philodemus is arguing that the sage feels "natural anger," *orgē*, but not transporting rage, *thymos*. His adversaries' argument, reported at *On Anger* col. XLVI.17–35, is that since gratitude and anger are parallel emotions, and we feel neither to inanimate things that do us good or evil, the emotion is moved in us by our belief that good or evil is done to us intentionally. Therefore we will always feel anger or gratitude on those conditions. And our reaction will vary in intensity according to the good or evil done us. Philodemus replies,

> To the first of their syllogisms [*epilogismoi*] one can offer this argument. "If we are naturally impelled to feel intense gratitude to those who intentionally do us good, we are stirred naturally to intense anger at those who by choice [*prohairesis*] harm us; for as the wise man is grateful ... [four lines missing]."
>
> (*On Anger* col. XLVIII.3–16)

The adversaries' contention ended in the gap, and Philodemus's reply, or what survives of it, was "... since he considers external benefits small; so not only in the case of evil done but good he will suppose nothing external very important." "But he is very grateful," the adversaries reply, "not only to those who made him wise, but to those who got for him certain other things." "But," apparently Philodemus replies, "if a person will say that he does that looking at their *prohairesis*, obviously he will accept that in the case of anger" (*On Anger* col. XLVIII.17–32). As is often (frustratingly) true in Philodemus, one needs the four missing lines to be certain what he actually argued. It appears that he thinks that the importance of the benefit or damage is of greater weight than the person's intention who makes us either grateful or angry. One must limit this importance by considering that externals are never of great weight.

But it seems even possible for there to have been something *in the gap* about intense gratitude at least for instruction in wisdom – as opposed to the external things that the sage regards as trivial – that Philodemus, who was as willing as Lucretius to regard the Master as a Savior God, and to feel intense gratitude to Epicurus and Zeno of Sidon for giving him wisdom, admitted was appropriate.[12] Otherwise, it is hard to see why the adversaries are made to reply, "But there are other things besides having made one wise that provoke intense gratitude."

At any rate, Philodemus had Epicurean adversaries who explicitly believed in the sage's intense gratitude and intense anger. Both Epicurus and Metrodorus claimed that only the sage knows how to feel gratitude (Seneca, *Ep.* 81.11 [Usener 1887, frg. 589]). The context in Seneca shows that they did not mean that they felt gratitude a mere duty, as Annas claims of Philodemus and Epicureans in general.

> He will repay benefits and make graceful gestures but will think of these things merely as what has to be done; he will not feel grateful in the way that we do. For our feelings of gratitude, just as much as our feelings of anger, are based on empty beliefs: we think that things like retaliation and gratitude matter, and to a good Epicurean they do not.
> (Annas 1992: 198)

The evidence does not support this. The question in the passage that she cites was whether we should feel *transports* of either emotion, not whether we should feel gratitude and anger as genuine, fully experienced, conscious emotions, which Philodemus and his adversaries both believe. And even there the adversaries, Epicureans like himself, believed in feeling them intensely. And probably he himself believed in intense gratitude (which for the living included the eager doing of favors) to one's teachers – including himself, in his relationship to his students and to Epicurus and his circle. As for gratitude to his own teacher Zeno of Sidon, Philodemus says that he was Zeno's "very faithful admirer [*erastēs*] while he was living and the tireless hymner of his praises [*akopiatos hymnētēs*] now that he is gone" (P. Herc. 1005, col. 14.8–9 Angeli [1988]).

Annas's arguments on these points are trifling errors in two very major books. They also are something of an early reaction to G. Indelli's 1988 edition, with translation and commentary, which is the first really reliable presentation of the treatise as a whole since it was discovered.[13] Nonetheless, they have been influential in a period of Epicurean scholarship where there has been a recent trend to claim that if the Epicureans thought of themselves as preachers of friendship and good feelings, their materialism left them without good arguments for it, and perhaps they even were insincere. These are connected questions. Modern discussions of ancient emotions so far do little justice to Aristotle's contention (*Rhet.* 2.4) that friendship and hatred are primary emotions, whatever other characteristics he gives friendship in the *Nicomachean Ethics*, but the passage is there, and a great deal of what is said about emotions in the treatises of Philodemus that I am discussing involves what one feels about friends, family, and enemies, as in fact a great deal of what is said about emotions by anyone must.

The views of Mitsis, Rist, and Brennan

P. Mitsis (1988: 98–128) has argued that although the Epicureans ascribed an almost mystical value to friendship as the foundation of all human happiness, and Epicurus held that any sacrifice for friends, including one's life, was justified by it, they could not really justify doing this if pleasure were the end, and what arguments they can offer to the contrary do not work as arguments. The Herculaneum papyri can help, in my opinion, for some texts in *On Frank Criticism* and *On Death* are the basis of a reexamination of this problem that I am writing concurrently with the present essay. The issue is a current one, for Mitsis's position has now been endorsed emphatically by J.M. Rist (2002: 45–50), who compares Epicurus, not favorably, to Machiavelli and Hobbes. Similarly, T. Brennan (1999: 77) claims that an Epicurean attending a friend's – he says a wife's – deathbed will console himself with pleasant thoughts, such as those of his next meal, rather than allowing himself to grieve or even shed a single tear.

Again, Brennan's is just a momentary aberration in a dissertation about something else, but it contradicts not just Philodemus's views in *On Death*, but Epicurus's own words. He wept over his brother Neocles' death, at which he was present, advised many friends in his letters to act the same way, and considered "toughing it out" in such situations to be silly pretense. And Plutarch, who reports these events and views directly from a rereading of Epicurus's letters (so he claims), clearly thinks that the Epicureans are "girlie men" – to borrow the phrase brought into notoriety by California governor Arnold Schwarzenegger – for taking this view (Plutarch, *Suav. viv.* 1097E; 1101A). It goes against both the surviving texts and the tenor of all the criticisms made of the Epicureans by the Stoics and Plutarch and the rest of their adversaries to make their anti-emotionalism this severe. Those of us who work on the Herculaneum papyri tend to take a different view, as one can see, for example, from the work of V. Tsouna[14] and in a recent and very pleasing article by J. Porter (2003).

Richard Sorabji on the Epicureans and Stoics

R. Sorabji (2000; 2004) recently has discussed "pangs" and "bites" such as Philodemus mentions for the Stoics, who originated the idea to describe "first movements" or, as Philo of Alexandria called them, "pre-emotions" (*propatheiai*), the emotional pangs felt as immediate reactions in provocative situations even by the wise, who may still withhold assent to them before they become "emotions" in the full sense, and he has traced their history in patristic and medieval Christian thought, where they are the "beginnings" that one ought to "resist" as a Christian in the well-known maxim *obsta principiis*.[15] Sorabji shows that Philodemus also used the same language of "bites" and "stings" as the Stoics, along with being influenced in his descriptions by the school's language in other ways. That of course is not unexpected in an Epicurean such as Philodemus, writing two hundred years after the Master's death, and as part of a history of debate between the schools. (I review Philodemus's usage of these words later in the present essay.) Philodemus was indeed a "Panaitios des Kepos," as M. Erler (1992a) has called him, an Epicurean who modernizes the Epicurean school's discussion topics as Panaetius and Posidonius did those of the Stoa. I also agree with Erler that as far as Philodemus and Zeno went in discussing topics left alone or little treated in the writings of the early Epicureans, they compromised none of the sect's basic beliefs.

Sorabji, however, overemphasizes Philodemus's language, and its coincidences with Stoic language of the emotions, and he underrates the real underlying difference. Philodemus's opponent Nicasicrates, probably a fellow Epicurean, as Sorabji notes, in *On Anger* "differs from the Stoics in thinking that not even the wise person can ever be free from anger. Philodemus seems to differ from the Stoics on this point only in name" (Sorabji 2000: 202). So then, Sorabji, like Annas, finds that at least Philodemus's view of anger, although (significantly) not that of all Epicureans, is just the Stoics' view put in different words. But this is not consistent with what Sorabji (2000: 202–3) immediately adds: "What is sought is described as punishment (*kolasis*), not retaliation. And it is sought not as something pleasant. It is seen as very necessary, but *very unpleasant*" (italics added), "like a drink of medicinal wormwood" (*apsinthion*) "or surgery." Sorabji of course means, and Philodemus's text shows, that the unpleasantness is to the philosopher forced to be angry and seek redress, not to the person punished. But whether the emotion is *very* unpleasant or just mildly unpleasant, like a Stoic "bite," is just what the argument was all about.

This slight contradiction, I think, turns out to be quite significant when one looks at all the texts together in *On Frank Criticism*, *On Anger*, and *On Death* where Philodemus describes *accepting the pain* of natural emotions. In that context Philodemus's "stings" and "bites" can be seen clearly to be not those of Stoic *propatheiai*, but of the real *pathē* themselves, as the Epicureans understood them. For Philodemus, acceptance of the "natural" "stings" and "bites" and the "bitterness" (*pikrotēs*) and "harshness" (*sklērotēs*) of real emotions – although their most damaging aspects, such as the joy of revenge or inflicting insult, or extravagant grief over reasons that turn out to be illusory, are vigorously warned against – turns out to be part of obeying the Master's dictum that although pleasure is the end of the good life and pain its worst enemy,

> it is for this very reason that we do not choose every pleasure, but often pass over many a pleasure because more trouble than pleasure

results to us from them; and consider many painful things [*algēdonas*] more valuable than pleasure, since greater pleasure follows for us when we have finished enduring the pains for however long a time.
(Epicurus, *Letter to Menoeceus* 128)

Philodemus clearly believes that the pain of anger is a pain worth enduring in just this sense.

Ancient theories of emotions currently are enjoying a vigorous revival of attention because of their clear relevance to modern theories, medical, psychological, and philosophical, just as Epicurus's and Democritus's atomism came in for renewed study and comment in the light of contemporary physics in the seventeenth and eighteenth centuries, and the Stoics' continuum physics and sophisticated logical systems did in the mid-twentieth century as adumbrations of the newest discoveries in those fields. How vigorous the Hellenistic schools were in their enmity to the emotions is of course a central topic of debate in everything written about them in this context. Freud's doctrine that repression (sometimes it seems that he means of any kind whatever) is identical with psychological dishonesty has had a long life and seems destined to have a longer one. It has survived almost every other key psychological doctrine that Freud preached, and the Stoic wise person, who eradicates all emotions but a few as being assents to false propositions about value, is easily accused of inhumanity, repression while pretending restraint, and "facile eudaemonism," pretending to happiness without really having attained it in any satisfying and human way. In Sorabji's edited volume of essays *Aristotle and After* (1997a), assembled while *Emotion and Peace of Mind* (2000) was on the way, he has B. Williams (1994; 1997) as a determined opponent, attributing "lethal high-mindedness" (Sorabji 1997b: 203 n. 36) to the Stoics in their treatment of emotion. Sorabji contends not a bit the less that "the rigorous philosophical treatment of the emotions by the Stoics is of great therapeutic value" (Sorabji 1997b: 197).

Indeed, the major value of Sorabji's *Emotion and Peace of Mind*[16] is to have contested objections like Williams's and accomplished a convincing picture of how the Stoics conquered all kinds of new philosophical territory in the study and therapy of emotions, for themselves and for their successors to the end of the Roman Empire and after, just by their daring and bravery in attempting to eradicate the emotions instead of offering any kind of compromise with them. One learns so much from Sorabji's *Emotion and Peace of Mind*, perhaps the most comprehensive treatment of Stoic emotional theory yet written, and from his article in the collection by Strange and Zupko (2004), that it seems presumptuous to take issue with his treatment of the Epicureans' theory of emotion, which is very much a side issue in this enthralling story, taking only a few pages of his monumental book. But I am encouraged to dispute his lack of interest in the details of their more humane therapy of the emotions by the striking essay by L. Becker (2004), which, like his *New Stoicism* (Becker 1998), evaluates Stoic theories – in this case, their theory of emotion – in modern terms for someone who wants to profit from Epictetus and Marcus Aurelius while accepting the results of modern psychology and science. Becker argues in very attractive and human terms that the rejection of normal and not excessive emotions is nonessential to Stoicism, because clearly they do no such damage as Chrysippus thought. Whatever the value of this argument may be for ancient Stoicism, which was convinced in its pure form that any radical departure from the perfection of the founders' system rendered it incoherent, Becker's essay encouraged me in writing this one. I argue that the Epicureans thought, very much as Becker does, that the acceptance of normal and not excessive emotions, real emotions, was innocent, and in particular that shame, grief, and anger had a status guaranteed by (the beneficent and helpful side of) Nature itself as valuable to us. Their various restraints on emotion surround and protect an acceptance of certain forms of it, especially grief and even a certain amount of fear of death, at least in certain specific forms. Philodemus's theories of the emotions, in treatises where we have enough continuous text to judge, show both a conscious rejection of all the principal Stoic positions on emotion and an acceptance of some kinds of "natural" emotion that is unambiguous and explicit.

In Sorabji's story, which is couched in less friendly terms than these and told in what I think is too little detail, the Epicureans and in particular Philodemus are nearly as hostile to emotions as are the Stoics themselves. Epicurus approved only "selective" emotions, and Philodemus uses language like that of the Stoics, like that of "bites" and "goads," to describe them, and limits them nearly as narrowly as do the Stoics. This section of his book is called "Epicureans: From Selective Emotions to Compromise with Stoics" (Sorabji 2000: 201–3), but I cannot find that either "selective emotions" or "compromise with Stoics" correctly describes anything that the Epicureans said about the emotions. Epicurus held that the wise man "will be *more* susceptible of some emotions [*pathesi*] than other men: that[17] can be no hindrance to his wisdom" (Diogenes Laertius 10.117).[18] That "some" emotions can be summed up as only "selective" emotions Sorabji tries to prove by citing the opening sentence of the same paragraph: βλάβας ἐξ ἀνθρώπων ἢ διὰ μῖσος ἢ διὰ φθόνον ἢ διὰ καταφρόνησιν γίνεσθαι, ὧν τὸν σοφὸν λογισμῷ περιγίνεσθαι. Hicks (1925: 2.643) in the LCL edition translates, "There are three motives to injurious acts among men – hatred, envy, and contempt; and these the wise man overcomes by reason." Sorabji (2000: 201) paraphrases, "The same passage ascribes to the wise pity and distress, but dissociates them from hatred, envy and contempt."

Something is wrong here. One would not suppose a priori that the sage would have any reason not to *hate* tyrants or *despise* wealth and political power. As for *kataphronēsis*, "contempt," it is more like "caring not a fig for something" – not an emotion, but an attitude. Aristotle uses it as an equivalent of *oligorēsis*, "slighting," in his discussion of anger in *Rhet*. 2.4. It provokes an emotion, but it is not one itself. So the three nouns do not add up if taken as emotions to be selected or deselected by the sage.

There is a better solution. In fact βλάβας ἐξ ἀνθρώπων (*blabas ex anthrōpōn*), "harms from (other) human beings," is parallel to the common Epicurean phrase ἀσφάλεια ἐξ ἀνθρώπων (*asphaleia ex anthrōpōn*), "safety from other human beings," which is provided by the sage's law-abiding conduct. So the phrase must indicate that the damage done by other people's hatred, envy, and undervaluing the philosopher *as a philosopher* is something the recipient of these rises above. Bollack (1975) translates it correctly, "Les blessures causées par les hommes sont le fait ou bien de la haine ou bien de l'envie ou bien du mépris; autant de maux que l'homme sage domine par le raisonnement": "The damages caused by men are created by hatred or envy or slighting, evils which the sage rises above by reasoning." So also Usener (1887, frg. 536) understood it, as is clear from his heading to frgs 536–9, *De securitate ex hominibus paranda*, "On securing safety *from other men*" – that is, nonphilosophical ones. And indeed it is commonplace that all philosophy, not just Epicurean philosophy, can easily inspire hatred, envy, and contempt in the nonphilosophical.[19] These aren't the sage's emotions in the first place; they are other people's feelings against the sage.

There is nothing wrong with Sorabji's idea in intention or general result, for of course there are emotions that the Epicureans reject as foolish or vicious, as Aristotle rejected *phthonos*, malicious envy, for the good person, but approved of *nemesis*, righteous indignation (*Rhet*. 2.9). But in fact such emotions as Epicureans accept or refuse they would have claimed not to select or deselect but to accept or refuse on the basis of intense attention to the study of nature, *physiologia*, and the facts, *pragmata*. As another philosopher whose work is preserved in the Herculaneum papyri puts it, we are freed from such emotions "only by what we have called the true study of nature as it really is" (Polystratus, *On Irrational Contempt* 19.3–8 Indelli [1978]). As for a more accurate understanding of why and how Philodemus uses Stoic terms for the emotions without a Stoic meaning, it is better to look at his larger treatises that concern the emotions in detail.

If we are to contrast Philodemus's views with those of the Stoics, Sorabji's is by far the best current exploration available of the Stoic theory of the emotions, but only a brief summary is possible here. The Stoics, at least of the school of Chrysippus, held that although everyone experiences emotional "first feelings," any emotion, except of clearly defined and very limited kinds, constitutes the acceptance of a false proposition about what is good and evil, only virtue being good and only vice being evil. Thus desire, anger, fear, and even pity have nothing virtuous or natural about them. Feeling a "bite" (*dēgmos*) or "goad" (*nyxis*) is inevitable. Assent to it or, rather, to the proposition that something painful or desirable is present, since that is what a real emotion is, is always wrong, and even more wrong is action on it, because one always goes against truth by the first and against God-governed Nature by the second. And even what look superficially like right actions, with the wrong motivation (such as emotion always provides), are damaging. This is in accord with the Stoic theory of the soul, which has parts: the five senses; the faculty of speech; the generative faculty in all animals, which we share with them, the *spermatikon*; and the governing faculty, *logos* or the *hēgemonikon*. Only the *hēgemonikon* is responsible for accepting the "first feelings" and making them into emotions proper.

There are exceptions: what the Stoics called *eupatheiai*, which Sorabji and many others resist translating as "good emotions," preferring "dispositions" or "good feelings," though if it is right to rejoice in rediscovering the similarly formed word *propatheia* from someone as early as Philo, not just the Greek Fathers, for "pre-emotion," why not?[20] That certainly does not make their list very comprehensive. One can have joy (*chara*) over the good government of the universe and the virtues of oneself and one's husband or friends; one can will what is right (*boulēsis*) and disdain and avoid what is wrong (*ekklisis*) as a substitute for valuing pleasure and desire on the one hand, and fear and anger on the other. Moreover, these good emotions or emotional feelings, which are truly present, or mostly, only in the perfect sage, seem not to be subject to prohibition or even limit, for they can be indulged without shame. And these good emotions are capable of various forms and objects that transform them – in a "virtuous" way – into the equivalents of several others among the standard list of emotions. But that is not much of a concession. I agree that even if we take this drastically reduced list of emotions as emotions of a kind, they may well remind present-day readers of many a current diet that offers "all you can eat," but only of things such as grapefruit, celery, and carrots. That even what we would take for obvious and virtuous emotions are forbidden is shown by the saying attributed to the Stoic of Pliny the Younger's day, Euphrates of Tyre, who said when his wife died, "Philosophy, your demands are tyrannical. You say 'Love!' but when one loses the person, you say 'Don't be upset!' " (Stobaeus, *Flor.* 4.35.34 [trans. Frede 1997: 1]).

No one ever should have argued that Philodemus or Epicurus (who himself had never heard these propositions) believed this or anything like it. If they do not offer at first sight so much to discuss, it is that basically their definitions of emotions are like Aristotle's in the second book of *Rhetorica*, summaries of common language and *ta nomizomena*, what is usually implied by them in poetry and nonphilosophical common language, and never could have generated so much excitement and stimulation as the Stoics' exciting paradoxes and radical counterintuitive positions about them did. Epicurus did not undervalue joy, *chara*, in enlightenment, sometimes using it where he might have used *hēdonē* ("pleasure"), and Philodemus uses *chairein* ("to rejoice") as a fit word for the result of enlightenment also. But they consider other emotions, more like what we consider and the ancient world considered to be within the normal range of emotions, valuable also, and in Demetrius Laco's sense, "natural." And much of Epicurean moral philosophy from Epicurus onwards is about choices and avoidances, περὶ αἱρέσεων καὶ φυγῶν (*peri haireseōn kai phygōn*). But Philodemus rejects Stoic "divisions of the soul" and will have nothing to do with first emotions or the theory that emotions *tout court* must involve a further assent to propositions to become real emotions.

How hostile were the Stoics and Epicureans to sexual experience and to nonpassionate love? Not very. Sorabji is masterly in showing that the Stoics had never heard of the sexual asceticism that characterized Judaism in some forms and Christianity in most of its forms. They accepted the same rules as everyone else, or nearly, in antiquity, that matrons and virgins and male and female children *of free families* rich and poor had a right to be free from sexual harassment. Casual sex with slaves, prostitutes, and unmarried free people who are no longer children was otherwise unexceptionable. Sex with one's wife deepened the personal relationship by adding physical to friendly intimacy, and even older men and younger men whose principal interest in each other was dependent on character and intelligence could fall into a sexual relation based on the older man's admiration of whatever youth and beauty the younger man possessed and the younger man's acceptance of him. The Stoics do not think that dangerous emotions and self-indulgent passion necessarily enter into any of these situations (Schofield 1991: Ch. 2, esp. 32–46; Inwood 1997; Sorabji 2000: 277–87).

In the case of Lucretius's account of sex and passionate love in book 4 of *De rerum natura*, Sorabji, like Annas before him, seems to revert to the older view that Lucretius has little good to say about it. Annas (1992: 196) says that Lucretius offers "a transformation of emotional life nearly as drastic as Plato's in the *Republic*," and Sorabji cites him only for the propositions that it is better to satisfy oneself with prostitutes than to have passionate love relationships, and that marriage should be "a source of procreation, but not one from which contentment can particularly be expected" (Sorabji 2000: 283). I suppose that if only a bottom-line summary a hundred words long survived of this amazing passage, one could say that. Though even so, I would have thought that the half-humorous passage about giving up passion for marriage and longer-term companionship at the end offered one precisely contentment in place of passion (Lucretius, *De rerum nat.* 4.1282–7). But I prefer the more sympathetic comments of M.C. Nussbaum (1994a,b: 140–91) and the commentaries of J. Godwin (1986) and particularly R.D. Brown (1987), who gives an account of this brilliant, sexy, subtle, amusing, and, above all, forgiving passage of Lucretius's about the sex life of the upper-class Roman adolescent before its inevitable end in marriage, family, and a quieter life that puts it squarely into the Roman Republic of Cicero's *Pro Caelio*, not Plato's *Republic*. That this is what it really is, not a condemnation of "sex" and "love," I take as axiomatic. As Brown says in a perceptive passage, the finale of *De rerum natura* 4 has topics arranged in a logical sequence, beginning ... with the initial urges of adolescence, full-fledged desire and passionate love, and ending with problems associated with reproduction; the final paragraph (1278–87), with its glimpse of a long-term domestic relationship, brings the discussion to an appropriate close.

(Brown 1987: 61)

The element of biography, beginning with childhood, progressing to adolescence and passion, and ending with marriage, is too much neglected by those who call this passage a diatribe against "sex" and "love," as though Lucretius considered neither to be important in a healthy life. Lucretius seems rather to advise that the young grow to learn the futility of violent adolescent passions by means of hands-on experience (quite a lot of it), after which they can discover the quieter pleasures of marriage and family. If this idea that Lucretius's so-called lecture against love is essentially a *Bildungsroman* for the young could be true, it certainly seems that Lucretius envisages wisdom, and full recognition of the humanity of one's lovers instead of using them as mere objects of passion,[21] as coming after quite a bit of sexual experience. Evidently this will not have done permanent damage, either. The Stoics' view was more severe, as one learns from a famous passage in which Seneca quotes Lucretius's older contemporary Panaetius as giving very much more restrictive advice to the young (Seneca, *Ep*. 116.4–5; see Inwood 1997: 60–1).

One might as well say that Philodemus is anti-love because he closes a book of erotic epigrams about his youthful adventures with the straight-faced comment that inasmuch as "he is now thirty-seven" – a fairly generous allowance for adolescence in the ancient world – he intends to take up not chastity, but a simpler Muse and a soberer girlfriend (*Epigram* 4 Sider = *AP* 11.41 = 17 GP). Or he says (echoed by Horace, *Ep*. 1. 14.36, and Propertius 1.14.19–25) that he

> fell in love. Who hasn't? I reveled. Who is not an initiate of revels? ...
> Let it go, for already grey hair rushes in to take the place of black ...
> And when it was right to play we played; and since it is right no longer, we shall lay hold of *loftier* thoughts (italics added).

This is D. Sider's (1997: 78) translation, but for λωίτερης (*lōiterēs*) LSJ (1069, s.v. "λωίων") offers *"more desirable, more agreeable, better,"* rather than Sider's "loftier" (*Epigram* 5 Sider = *AP* 5.112 = 18 GP).

Epicurus and the Epicureans

This topic needs longer treatment, and the status of Epicureans such as Lucretius and Philodemus as poets and philosophers of love life, not to mention at least para-Epicureans such as Horace and Vergil, can be left for another essay. As for grief, Plutarch's testimony about Epicurus is unambiguous: he recommended that one should give way to real grief and real tears at the loss of a friend or a family member, and with perfect confidence that one would not be damaged – a recommendation that Plutarch treats with unattractive contempt. M. Wigodsky reminds me that Epicurus's own words are quoted in this passage, that "remembering [his brother] Neocles' last words he let himself melt away in the unique [*idiotropos*] pleasure that comes with tears," τῶν ἐσχάτων Νεοκλέους λόγων μεμνημένος ἐτήκετο τῇ μετὰ δακρύων ἰδιοτρόπῳ ἡδονῇ (Plutarch, *Suav. viv.* 1097E [Usener 1887, frg. 186]).[22] I think that Usener must be right to take the words quoted as essentially Epicurus's, perhaps changed to the third person from the first. Ἰδιότροπος (*idiotropos*) occurs in *On Nature* and *The Epistle to Herodotus*, and τοιουτότροπος (*toioutotropos*) in Epicurus and Philodemus, also ὁμοιότροπος (*homoiotropos*) (not in the Stoics or other philosophers that we know of), and that probably guarantees as Epicurus's own also the strong word τήκεσθαι (*tēkesthai*), "melt," more common in poetry (Homer onward) than prose. To which Plutarch adds this comment: "a thing no sane man could call true felicity or joy." I would even argue that Epicurus, for all his affectation of contempt for poetry, was silently echoing the words of Andromache when she laments that Hector had not offered her his hands from his deathbed and spoken words that she might remember (μεμνῄμην, *memnēmēn*) day and night with tears (Homer, *Il.* 24.743–5); he was also implying that he remembered the fine old Homeric expression "satisfy oneself with grief" (τέρπεσθαι γόοιο, *terpesthai gooio*) as one satisfies oneself with food or wine. Certainly Epicurus's thought comes from the world where words such as Andromache's were still common *topoi* at family funerals, not just quotations from ancient epic. For that matter, in modern Greece they still are ("these things come from real life" [*tauta biōtika*], says one of the scholiasts of Andromache's words, on *Il.* 24.745).

Plutarch's later testimony at *Suav. viv.* 1101A–B (Usener 1887, frg. 120) is that

> they disagree with those who would do away with grief and tears and lamentations at the death of friends, and say that an absence of grief that has become unemotional [*apathes*] stems from another greater evil: hardheartedness or a passion for reputation [*doxokopia*] both inordinate and insane... they say it is better to feel some emotion [*paschein ti*] and feel pain and have eyes glittering with tears [*lipainein*] and melt [*tēkesthai*].... Epicurus has said this in many places, especially when he wrote about the death of Hegesianax to Sositheus and Pyrson the father and brother of the deceased. You see I recently happened to run through his letters.
> (trans. Einarson and De Lacy 1967: 109, 111, altered)

This must also, therefore, contain words quoted from Epicurus.[23]

Sorabji (2000: 234) cites this treatise for Plutarch's criticism of Epicurus's theory that one could calm *excessive* grief or fear about death by reflecting on previous joys (*Suav. viv.* 1088F–1089C), but not for these striking passages. Yet they had their impact on Philodemus, as my discussion of *On Death* will show. And Epicurus's words about his grief for Neocles suggest not only that he endured his grief but also that he was not ashamed to indulge and cherish it. It seems worth remarking that though Epicurus's criticism of "hardhearted" ostentation of lack of grief cannot have been directed at the Stoics, there is an ode of Horace on the theme, written in an explicitly Epicurean context, that *is* directed at them. We know now (Gigante and Capasso 1989) that his and Vergil's friend Quintilius formed part of a band of friends among the addressees of Philodemus's treatises along with Vergil himself, Varius, and Plotius Tucca. The ode (*Carm.* 1.24) consoling Vergil for Quintilius's recent death begins, *quis desiderio sit pudor aut modus/tam cari capitis*? "What shame, what limit could there be to our longing for so dear a friend?" These words, in their heavily Epicurean context, are an implicit gesture of contempt to the Stoics who had been the explicit butt of so many of the *Satires* – or so it should now be seen.[24] Even the recommendation of patience at the end of the ode is a slam at them: *durum, sed levius fit patientia/quidquid corrigere est nefas*, "harsh; but that which it is *a sacrilege to set right* becomes lighter by bearing it" – an oxymoron reminding us that we live, after all, in an imperfect world ungoverned by providence, as the Epicureans believed and the Stoics did not. I do not see that the still-rebellious attitude to the order of Nature (*tanta stat praedita culpa*) at the end of the poem has anything heretical about it in an Epicurean, though certainly it would in a Stoic.

Philodemus's *On Frank Criticism*

Philodemus's treatise *On Frank Criticism* (*Peri parrhēsias* = *De libertate dicendi*) is, of course, important for many things more wide-ranging than what it can tell us about how the Epicureans view the emotions of shame and indignation, Aristotle's *aischynē* (*Rhet.* 2.6) and *nemesis* (*Rhet.* 2.9), and gratitude, his *charis*. It gives us a precious look at the inside of a philosophical school like Philodemus's and Siro's at Naples, where apparently a lecture setting forth the principles by which the teachers taught, counseled, and reproved could be read at length not just to the teachers, but to the students, who are everywhere implied as its audience. It supplies a therapeutic model of free speech and frank criticism by which the philosopher establishes equality of rank with his pupils, wealthy and powerful though they may be, which illuminates what we know from literature and history of philosophers of all schools, especially the Stoics as well as the Epicureans, in their relations with Roman students in late republican and imperial times. This model parallels that laid out for the use of *parrhēsia* in ordinary life between friends of different rank in works such as Plutarch's *How to Tell a Flatterer from a Friend*. It may even help us understand "teaching" situations in religious cults influenced by philosophical language and protocols, as has been proposed for Paul and his circle by C. Glad (1995), one of the translators and editors for the Society of Biblical Literature's Greek text and English translation of *On Frank Criticism* (Konstan et al. 1998).[25] It certainly helps immensely in understanding the use, by Roman writers such as Horace or Seneca to such of their literary addressees as possess philosophical qualifications or pretensions, of almost theatrically harsh "frank criticism" like that which Philodemus describes.

For the present essay, however, the emotional implications of frank criticism between teacher and student are most relevant in seeing how Epicureans deal with unpleasant but supposedly "natural" and helpful emotions. If we had a better text, we would find that the emotions of shame (*aischynē*), which the student must be made to feel, whether by friendly or by harsh and painful *parrhēsia* on the teacher's part, and the anger that the student suspects the teacher feels, but that the teacher must at all times beware of unless it is needed to make the right impression, are the predominant ones that Philodemus is discussing. As it is, the hints in the text are clear enough. Aristotle (*Rhet.* 2.6) defines *aischynē* as the fear of *adoxia*, of being thought stupid, cowardly, or immoral by others. Where we can check Philodemus's usage of these two Greek words in the treatise, they are well enough in accord with this definition. According to frg. 39, the student is exhorted to

> [remember that it is un]becoming not to cast [his private affairs], as it were, upon the teachers [*kathēgoumenoi*] and pay attention to them alone, just as it is not (unbecoming) in the case of the acquisition of good things, and that it is utterly shameful [*aischron*], while playing a part themselves in the care of their body and not needing doctors in everything, where it concerns the soul not to try (the teacher's counsel).
>
> Perhaps out of shame [*hyp' aischynēs*] a student will avoid the wise man, thinking of his reputation among his other friends and wary of becoming too like him [(*tē*)*n apomimēsin phylattōn*].
>
> (col. XIIIa.7–13)

> We have spoken about how we should never give up, nor grasp at everything, when we apply frank criticism, and also about the loss of reputation [*adoxia*] (which philosophy brings) among the many, and about separation from one's family.
>
> (frg. 3)

> [They think that it is merely friendly to apply frank criticism and] rebuke others, but to do oneself what provokes rebuke is disgrace and condemnation [*adoxian kai katagnōsin*]. And thinking they are practicing a friendly work, they find it fun, but being themselves rebuked, no such thing, and that they are not liable to error; for they

would not be able to see and to transfer the others' faults, in that case, to themselves.

(col. XIXb)

It may be out of the usual male chauvinism that Philodemus supposes, in a striking passage, that women are more sensitive to shame than others of his students:

> They are more likely to suppose they are being reproached, and more crushed by ill-repute [*hypo tēs adoxias*], and more suspicious of evil things against their admonishers, and find everything that bites people in general [*di' ha tines daknontai*] more threatening, and are bolder and vainer and fonder of their reputation [*philodo(xoterai)*].... [And they expect] their weaker nature to be pitied and find forgiveness, and not to be ridiculed on purpose by those stronger (in philosophy) than they. Which is why they resort quickly to tears, thinking they are being criticized because one despises them [*apo kataphronēseōs*].[26]
>
> (cols XXIIa–XXIIb.1–9)[27]

"Strong" (*ischyros*) in this treatise means "more advanced in philosophy" or rather "in the philosophical life," as well as "strong-natured" or "stubborn," since it is not only by assenting to Epicurean arguments, but by living one's life in obedience to them that one becomes an Epicurean. "Stronger" students can take harsher and more biting frank criticism, and they need it more because they have more experience of the therapeutic and (presumably) more vanity about their progress so far.

> We shall admonish others with great confidence [*pepoithēsis*],[28] both now and when we have attained eminence by having become offshoots of our teachers in this manner; and the encompassing and most important thing is that we shall give obedience to Epicurus, according to whom we have chosen to live [*kath' hon zēn eirēmetha*].
>
> (frg. 45.1–10)

> For the most part he (the teacher) will be subtle [*diaphilotechnēsei*] in such a way, but sometimes he will be quite simple in his frank criticism, thinking he must risk it, if otherwise they do not obey; and in fact those who are very strong both by nature and through the progress they have made [*prokopēn*][29] with all passion and [reviling, (*ka*)*ki*(*smōi*)].... (He will expect them) rather to give pleasure, even, with the watchfulness with which he will inquire into them; and after that will set forth the difficulties that follow and are inevitable to people that are like this again [and again], saying "you do [ill]...."
>
> (frgs 10–11)

But if he does not make it clear that it is all for the pupil's good, "his labor will accomplish nothing good, rather will discourage" (frg. 12.4–6). The "good" of this frank criticism Philodemus underscores with medical analogies, most amusingly at frgs 63–5, where the harsher forms of frank criticism are compared to purges and clysters that a doctor must not be ashamed to use over and over until at last the desired result is achieved.

The confrontational tactics used with these "strong" subjects are spoken of throughout in terms of "stings/stinging" and "goading" (*dēgmos/daknō, nyttō*), as we will see the pains of anger and fear are in *On Anger* and *On Death*. Even the "light" kind of rebuke suited to the weaker student is described thus, as a "gentle irony biting all in general" (*epieikōs daknousēs hapantas eirōneias*) (frg. 26.9–10). Wise persons will accept the "bite" of frank criticism from each other and apply it to themselves in "the gentlest way and feel gratitude for it" (*dexontai dēgmon heautous ton ēpiōtaton kai charin eidēsousi*) (col. VIIIb.11–13), for even the wise, unlike the Stoic sage, are still in need of improvement. And although this might be like the Stoic use of "bites" for *propatheiai*, it is also used of stronger forms of appeal to shame by frank criticism. Women, as we noted above, dislike being "bitten" by frank criticism and shamed. As we will see of being angry and accepting it in *On Anger*, submitting oneself to really merciless "frank criticism" is like submitting to an operation.

> When they fully see that their character is prone to error they are bitten [(*d*)*aknontai*], and as people employing skilled doctors for an operation, when those apply the scalpel to sick persons, so when for these the biting [*dēktikon*] part of frank criticism becomes visible and they believe they will commit no error, or no one will know it no matter how often they err, they ask one to admonish ... [more gently, presumably].
>
> (col. XVIIa)

Pleasingly enough, it is the teacher who feels, when he must "without pleasure" use the "harsh" (*sklēron*) (frg. 7.10) kind of frank criticism, as if he is drinking wormwood (*apsinthion*) (col. IIb.8). This indicates that he must resign himself to feeling real anger, for the language is the same as in *On Anger* col. XLIV.19–20, where the sage is said to accept anger without pleasure as he would drink *apsinthion* or endure surgery.

Philodemus's *On Anger*

Now, in terms of my argument, this way of talking is invoked simply to establish that Philodemus did indeed, as Sorabji shows, share the imagery of "bites" and "goads" in common with the Stoics' way of speaking about "preemotions." When, however, he recommends that the teacher not to be angry overmuch, and to blend in praise for effect when it seems right, he clearly considers that the teacher can and must, if necessary, risk being very blunt, and do so with students who are not only of higher social rank but also as much the product of Mediterranean shame culture as he. The treatise *On Anger*, interestingly, is at several points clearly also a lecture "to the school." It speaks of student life explicitly and anger's role in making students unpopular "with fellow students and teachers" (col. XIX.14–16), and cols XIX–XXI can be taken as illustrating how the teacher's "frank criticism" deals with excessive and wrong-headed anger in philosophical students, thus providing readers of *On Frank Criticism*, at least in its present very fragmentary form, with much-needed actual examples of exactly how the ideal Philodemean teacher rebukes pupils and what he rebukes in them. *On Anger* is in fact an extension of *On Frank Criticism*, and it takes *On Frank Criticism* "as read," mentioning it by title (col. XXXVI.22–6). Philodemus indicates that he had written another discourse of the kind on "erotic desire," *erōtikē epithymia* (col. VII.19–20). If it was as vivid a diatribe as the surviving one against the bad kind of anger (cols VII.26–XXXI.24), which Philodemus premises by arguing that Chrysippus and Bion of Borysthenes were right to deliver such diatribes[30] against the awful effects of bad emotions, and offering to give the school one of his own, it must have been very striking.

However, the section establishing the naturalness and rightness of what Philodemus defines as "reasonable anger," *eulogos orgē* (col. XX.24–5), and "natural anger," *hē physikē orgē* (cols XXXVI.20; XXXVIII.6, 36; XXXIX.26, 30, etc.) concerns us most here. In *On Frank Criticism* Philodemus does not separate out bad shame and good shame (bad shame being the shame of telling one's teachers one's doings and feelings, which is to be deplored, but not a serious vice) or use the word "natural" of the emotions that he discusses. Here he distinguishes "natural" anger from the bad kind that involves obsessive pleasure in revenge; for these are evils "which we would say the reasonable person does not encounter; but he most certainly falls in with the natural kind of anger, for which reason we argued that it is inescapable [*anekpheukton*] to human nature" (col. XL.16–22). Note that Philodemus definitely thinks it an argument that not just the wise person, but all human beings, must feel this kind of anger. And it is not "pre-anger," but full-fledged anger itself. We see here that "natural" anger satisfies at least one of the requirements of the "natural" in feelings defined by Demetrius Laco (as quoted above): it is felt "by strong necessity," *katēnankastōs*. I cannot find where Philodemus says that anger is felt "by uncorrupted impulse," *adiastrophōs*, as Demetrius Laco said, but it is certainly implied in its being common "to human nature." It is also profitable to us, since it inspires us to remove offense without damaging us, if we take no pleasure in it, and although the Epicureans refuse to agree with the Stoics that emotions are assents to propositions, false or true, certainly the good kind corresponds like the "first" and primitive uses of words to reality, *ta pragmata*, for Philodemus claims that

> we Epicureans teach that the emotion, taken in isolation and *per se*, is an evil, since it is painful or resembles what is painful, but taken in conjunction with one's character as a whole it is something that can even be called a good, as we think; for it results (when good) from an examination of what the nature of states of affairs [*hē physis tōn pragmatōn*] really is and from accepting no false perception in our comparative estimation of the damage done and in our punishments of those who damage us. So that in the same way we call the pointless kind of anger an evil, because it results from a worthless disposition of character and entails all sorts of further troubles, one must call the natural kind of anger a non-evil, but, as it is something biting [*dēktikon*] ...[31] (just as, when it results from) a good (disposition), it is not an evil thing, but even a good, so also we will call it a bad thing not to experience it ... and a good thing to experience it.
> (cols XXXVII.20–XXXVIII.34)

Thus the fourth of Demetrius Laco's definitions, that "natural" emotions should correspond to reality, proves to be justified about "natural" anger.

We also see, as here, that Philodemus uses the imagery of "bites." Both the "bad" and the "good" kind of anger, in fact, are "biting." The person in an unnatural rage is *dakōn*, or "biting" (col. XLI.8), and the emotion itself is *daknēron* whether good or evil (col. XXXVII.19). This suggests to me that Philodemus is very clearheaded, in his use of the vocabulary of "bites" and "stings," in differentiating it from the Stoics'. In fact he is describing full-blown anger, even destructive anger, in these words; the emotion itself, and not any kind of first manifestation or "pre-emotion," in which the Epicureans refuse to believe because they do not believe there are such "pre-emotions" followed by mental assent. It may be that the passage seems at first to imply something rather like the Stoics' idea that the wise person's emotions are always based on truth and not on illusion. But in fact, as we will see in examining *On Death*, this is not what Philodemus means. The "goodness" of his "natural" emotions results not from meditations on virtue and the good, but from his continual and unremitting attention to something very different: actual facts, *ta pragmata*, and what is in accordance with them, *to pragmatikon* – a meditation quite different from that of the Stoic sage.

Before we go on to *On Death*, however, I think that I can offer a suggestion as to why writers such as Annas and Sorabji have thought Philodemus's position on anger and related emotions in *On Anger* so near that of the Stoics. It is because in the diatribe section, cols VIII.16–XXXI.23, the longest surviving section, he agrees with them that the pleasure of revenge is vicious and insane, and he delivers a long, vivid attack on it, a Stoic diatribe of his own. In fact, Teubner editor K. Wilke (1914: xxx–liv) argued at great length in the Latin preface that its main source was Chrysippus's *Therapeutikos Logos*, the fourth book of his *On Emotions*, which was more widely read in antiquity than the other three books.[32] It has been argued to have been more accessible and popular in tone, perhaps even more protreptic, than the other three. This last opinion was so general in the nineteenth century that in 1886 Karl Buresch[33] conjectured that Philodemus's *On Death*, whose surviving part resembles a protreptic popular lecture and comes, as the subscription tells us, from book 4, was itself a *Therapeutikos Logos*, in imitation of Chrysippus's famous example, that succeeded three books of more technical philosophy on the same subject.

The reason why Wilke thought this is interesting. Not long before the diatribe section Philodemus argues that his fellow Epicurean Timasagoras was wrong to depreciate Bion of Borysthenes' lecture *On Anger* and Chrysippus's *Therapeutikos Logos*, because although it was wrong solely to inveigh against the angry and do nothing more, it had genuine therapeutic and even medical value to put the horrors of rage *pro ommatōn* – vividly, before their eyes:

> For such reasons he tried to prove that reproach is crazy, but indolently as he was wont; and in fact if he reprimands those who only reproach and do little or nothing else, like Bion in *On Anger* and Chrysippus in the *Therapeutikos Logos* of *On Emotions*, his conclusions might be reasonable; but as it is in taking the putting of these things before people's eyes to be ridiculous and crazy, he himself is [ridiculous and crazy]....
> (*On Anger* col. I.7–27 [Indelli 1988])

Philodemus goes on to argue (cols II.6–VIII.8) that such diatribic reproaches and putting things *pro ommatōn*, "before the eyes," of the afflicted – philosophical arguments being left out or left for later – have true medical and therapeutic value.[34] He then launches into his own long diatribe that indeed offers no strictly philosophical arguments, just a garishly vivid catalogue of the pure human horrors and insanities caused by obsession with revenge. Its vigorous conclusion is that "[nothing is reliable] except canonic argument" (i.e., Epicurean logic),

> and on the contrary everyone is your opponent, those on the one hand who are non-philosophers egging you on in every way, parents and all your relatives for the most part even rejoicing over you [i.e., in your anger] as being manly, and of the philosophers some talking rubbish in their "consolations," and some even strengthening your anger by their advocating it, for I dismiss orators and poets and all such trash.
> (col. XXXI.11–24)

Is this last a slam at Chrysippus's habit of quoting the poets as authorities on the emotions? Philodemus quotes epic, tragedy, and comedy in the diatribe section much more richly than is his wont except in his treatises explicitly about poetry, and this was one of Wilke's main arguments that Philodemus is using Chrysippus, and imitating his tendency to cite the poets, in accordance with his argument that "putting things before the eyes" of the sufferer is a valid method where philosophy as such is irrelevant. Wilke does not cite Origen, but "putting things before the eyes" instead of using technical argument from one's own philosophy resembles Chrysippus's well known saying in the *Therapeutikos Logos*, quoted by Origen, that he could convince anyone of any philosophy that emotions were dangerous. Chrysippus said that he would rather argue with a Peripatetic who believed in three levels of goods – psychic, bodily, and external – on the grounds that emotions helped one acquire none of them; or with an Epicurean who believed pleasure to be the good, that emotions were no means to that end. He considered it inappropriate when a person was actually in the grip of emotion to use the technical arguments of one's own school, right as the school might be (Origen, *Cels.* 8.51 = *SVF* 3.474). It is at least suggestive, as Wilke says, that in the section after the diatribe that Philodemus gives his own school, there is a brief set of rather rhetorical and protreptic arguments against the Peripatetics for advocating revenge as a proper pleasure for the wise person (cols XXXI.24–XXXIV.6; see Wilke: 1914: xl–xvi). Perhaps Philodemus echoes Chrysippus's arguments intended to calm both an angry Epicurean and an angry Peripatetic.

However, as Indelli (1988: 24–7) notes, J. Fillion-Lahille (1984), in her book on the sources of Seneca's *De ira*, accused Wilke of special pleading and extremism in arguing that it was the *principal* source of that part of *On Anger*, since almost none of the scanty fragments of the *Therapeutikos Logos* actually correspond – at least in a way that would prove the point beyond doubt – to Philodemus's diatribe or to his criticism of the Peripatetics.[35] Wilke thought that there was almost nothing of Bion of Borysthenes in the diatribe section, but others have disagreed, particularly W. Crönert (1906: 31–6, esp. 32–3). Yet Crönert supposes that Philodemus got the passages that may be ascribed to Bion from the *Therapeutikos Logos* (which he thinks Chrysippus quoted from Bion, who wrote several decades earlier).

At any rate, Indelli points out many of the same parallels to Chrysippus as Wilke did, and more in his commentary on the diatribe section. It may well be that we can recover some of the tone of the more vivid "before the eyes" presentations in Chrysippus, of which a sample very much like Philodemus's ranting is found in *SVF* 3.478 (see Tieleman 2003: 178–81). Both Sorabji's *Peace of Mind* and Tieleman's *Chrysippus' On Affections* do much to facilitate further research. In favor of Wilke's idea is the fact that Philodemus – and most ancient authors who did not trouble themselves to take down several scrolls at once to refer to – is most often, where he does not reveal his sources, taking them one at a time. Perhaps Philodemus's knowledge of Bion was indeed mediated through Chrysippus.

But my point is that since so much of the book is taken up with a parody (if quite a seriously intended parody) of Stoic diatribe against the madness of anger, and so little with the theory of anger that Philodemus wants to present, no wonder it could be misconstrued. In the context of the whole work, much more than half of which at the beginning is lost (Indelli 1988: 37–9), that is misleading. Philodemus's diatribe against the bad kind of anger, the *pleasure* of revenge and vindictive self-assertion, is a side issue to his positive view, which must have dominated the treatise as a whole, that the *pain* of anger is a good and natural motivation to self-defense. There will have been a full statement of Philodemus's view at the beginning, which will have put the Epicureans' positive view of "natural" anger in a much stronger light. As it is, what is preserved to us begins with the long diatribe *against* bad anger, and there follows an attack on the Aristotelian concept of anger as allowing pleasure in it; and there is only the final section from cols XXXIV.16–XLVI.15 to argue for the "natural" anger that Philodemus recommends as necessary even to the sage. Since he argues against Epicureans who argued from Epicurus's and other Epicureans' known propensity to bursts of anger and harshness, he restricts natural anger to the pain that motivates retribution and redress, thus not including vengefulness or pleasure in getting one's way. Nonetheless, Philodemus's "natural" anger is a real emotion, and sometimes deeply unpleasant, and longer lasting, as circumstances dictate, than pain just considered as pain should be. As the pleasure-pain principle of Epicureanism would dictate, being suspicious of the pleasure and accepting only the pain of anger would ensure that the emotion is controllable and limited in a sensible person – even the unphilosophical or un-Epicurean addressee of a diatribe, let alone a sage. No one wants more pain than has to be endured. As for the pleasure of anger, even unphilosophical Greeks since Homer's time (*Il.* 18.104–11) had been suspicious of it as counterproductive. Like Epicurus's notions about grief, Philodemus's theory of anger is meant to be grounded in universal human reactions, and it does not require radical self-transformation, as Annas claimed, to accept.

Philodemus's *On Death*

In *On Death* we find several more suggestive uses of the concept of "bites" and "stings," this time as the "natural" bites and stings of the prospect of dying; and although Lucretius *appears* to pass over these in his (to many readers) rather too contemptuous lecture on the theme that death is "nothing to us" (but see Fish 1998), Philodemus as therapist finds that some of the fearful things about the prospect of dying are not only worthy of a philosopher's sympathy, but are things that philosophers will themselves feel, in some cases more, not less, than others, and with perfect reason. In the end, their intense meditation not on illusions but on the facts of life, the *pragmata*, will provide the strength – the *bene praeparatum pectus*, "the well-prepared heart," as Horace calls it – to accept life as a paradoxical gift and to accept death as a reality that makes no mockery at all of the happiness they enjoyed in it. But just as Epicurus told his disciples over and over that there was no point in refusing to weep, even at length, about the loss of friends and family members, so also Philodemus's patients will be encouraged to express their grief – but only at certain aspects of dying, not others.

    I have argued in a recent article (Armstrong 2004a) that *On Death* is not addressed to the school, but is a showpiece for a general audience, arguing for the excellence of Epicureanism above other schools in its attitude toward death and dying. It uses very little in the way of Epicurean technical language, though it cites Epicurean popular aphorisms; it quotes Epicurus, but less often than in *On Frank Criticism* and *On Anger*, treatises addressed to the school; it praises philosophers in general, not only Epicureans, and also ordinary people of ordinary courage for their brave reaction to the prospect of death and even expresses openness at one point to "whatever one considers the elements of matter to be," not a phrase that one could easily use to an audience of convinced Epicurean believers (*On Death* 32.30–1). And it seems considerably more carefully composed; the sections on the relevance or irrelevance of various fears of the dying and the peroration on how the wise person's acceptance of the reality of death makes that person's life more beautiful and death fearless, however unexpectedly it may come, have a rhetorical finish and impact rare in Philodemus's frequently careless writing, which also mark the treatise as "protreptic" rather than technical in tone. Here I take an opportunity to thank J. Warren for using both my complete draft translation of the treatise and my article, offering improvements as he does so, in his *Facing Death: Epicurus and His Critics* (Warren 2004), and for his very helpful discussions of both. I plan to take these into account in my articles and other work on *On Death*. "Natural bites" did not attract Warren's attention as they did Sorabji's, so here I must return to them and conclude, and argue further elsewhere for the "protreptic" rather than technical nature of the treatise and its assumption of a general audience of philosophers of all schools and nonphilosophers.

    The references to the "natural bite" of dying are all (in the surviving portions of the treatise) in the part that lists and discusses various painful things about dying, which lasts from col. 12 to the end. Every instance Philodemus gives, however, is not the result of a "pre-emotion" but of the full realization of one's situation with regard to dying. Dying too young Philodemus treats at length. Long life and short life are equally valueless for the unwise, he argues, to our feeling rather unsympathetically – although, as he says unexpectedly at the end, "this part of one's pain is probably forgivable [*syngnōston*]" (*On Death* 20.1–3). A young person who has achieved full philosophical enlightenment, however, has little to complain of, he argues, for this person has enjoyed all the pleasure that life can offer. But certainly it is reasonable for the person who is making progress in philosophy to complain of dying young: *physik[on] men t[o n]yttes[th]a[i t]on to[iou]ton*, says Philodemus, "It is a natural thing for such a one to be stung by this" (*On Death* 17.35–6), and "a sensible man" (*noun echōn anthrōpos*) will indeed desire to live a while longer (*oregesthai prosbiōnai tina chronon*) for this purpose or even as long as possible (*hos pleiston chronon zēn*) (*On Death* 14.5–10; 13.37). Long life is not a value, to him as to Epicurus and Lucretius, as also to the Stoics, compared to the good life (see the texts cited in Sorabji 2000: 241 n. 93); but this and the other "natural" pangs of death that he mentions in the treatise imply that all people, not just philosophers, may quite reasonably desire to stay alive at least awhile for their own good purposes and be hurt that they cannot. For that matter, once one has attained enlightenment, there is no reason not to live and enjoy it as long as one can; it is natural in itself (*oikeion*), even though death itself cannot deprive one of the joy that enlightenment gives (*On Death* 19.3–11, 30–3). Even enlightenment itself requires *some* additional time to live and enjoy (*poson chronon epizēsai*) (*On Death* 19.1–2). And yet, Philodemus argues, even the happiness that the student has already enjoyed and the example that he has been to many others mean that he is to be admired as having found much greater good than evil (*On Death* 17.36–18.16).

Philodemus contrasts with this reasonable desire to live longer and be wiser the absurdity of caring whether one will no longer be able to defend one's reputation against one's enemies (*On Death* 20.3–22.9). However, surprisingly, he concedes that it gives one a "natural bite" to think of being mocked by enemies, at least during life (*On Death* 20.7–8).[36] It is equally absurd to be filled with grief because one leaves no children behind to inherit one's goods or name (*On Death* 22.9–25.2). By contrast, he says with surprising emphasis,

> to leave behind parents or children or a spouse or others of one's familiars, who are going to be in misfortunes because of our death or even lack the necessities of life, has quite admittedly the most natural of bites [*physikōtaton dēgmon*] and rouses sheddings of tears [*dakryōn proeseis*] in the intelligent person, in him uniquely or most of all [*monon ē malista*].
>
> (*On Death* 25.2–10)[37]

Here the text becomes unintelligible for twenty lines (and nothing more of significance can be done, even with the new Brigham Young MSI photographs), making Philodemus's further attempt to console those in this situation unintelligible: what is badly preserved of it at col. 25.30–7 is not enlightening. However, the sentence quoted above makes impressively clear that at least for Philodemus's kind of Epicurean, even the fully enlightened can indeed encounter situations where the appropriate reaction is summed up in the title of B. Rollin's (2000) excellent book about dealing with cancer, *First, You Cry*. Of course, neither she nor Philodemus holds that crying is the only thing you do, but rather just the first; however, it is clear that as a therapist, Philodemus was prepared to let even the sage allow "natural bites" to take their full effect in tears of frustration before offering the consolations of philosophy.

The next "natural bite" is equally surprising and sympathetic: dying in a foreign land (*epi xenēs*) (*On Death* 25.38). This brings another natural (*phy[sikon]*) pang "to philosophers" (*philologois*),[38] and especially if they are leaving parents and other relations behind in their homeland – "but only so as to goad one [*nyttein monon*], not so as to create pain, and that great, as one dies, over and above the difficulties of living in a foreign land" (*On Death* 26.1–7). This, of course, is partly an elegant joke for the benefit of his audience of Romans and transplanted Greeks. And, he goes on after this unexpected piece of sentimentality about Gadara,[39] the wise person has no concern at all about being entombed abroad, tombs being a matter of indifference to Epicureans. Yet even in this minor instance he brings out that "the wise person will feel emotions more deeply" (Diogenes Laertius 10.117). Nor should one worry about dying passively in bed and winning neither military nor civic glory to leave behind, for it diminishes the glory of Pericles and Themistocles no more than Epicurus's or Metrodorus's or that of "the greater part of the philosophers" (*hoi pleistoi tōn philosophōn*) (*On Death* 29.10–11 [another uncharacteristic reference to the excellence of philosophers not of his own school]) that they all have died in bed. Other reasons good and bad I have summarized in my essay "All Things to All Men" (Armstrong 2004a), along with the peroration. In the end Philodemus shows, whether convincingly to a philosopher or not, but certainly with much powerful rhetoric and vivid illustration of what he means, that the only secure relief from these painful yet natural emotions is the continual, religious contemplation of facts not fancies about the omnipresence, immediacy, and inevitability of mortality. This contemplation, he believes, pursued deliberately and continually, makes life more precious and enjoyable, not less (*On Death* 38.14–39.25).

When Philodemus echoes Stoic terminology, then, he is using it in a very wide-awake way. There are some secure texts in which he uses the characteristic Stoic language *prokopē, prokoptein*, of progress in philosophy (in *On Death, p[roko]ps[ai* is rather insecurely restored at 17.33, and *p[r]okopsei[n* much more securely at 17.38; note also *hapantes hoi kata tēn hairesin hēmōn prokopsantes* at 23.7–8). But Philodemus's moving portrait of his youthful progress-maker feeling a "natural bite" at not being able to complete his studies, yet having achieved greater happiness and glory than his pain already, is very far from the gloomy Stoic portrait of the *prokoptontes* in philosophy as being as liable to folly and slavery as any ordinary person, and the sage alone being secure. That must be an intentional "gently biting irony," as he says in *On Frank Criticism*, but here aimed at Stoics in the audience.

Similarly, Philodemus knows perfectly what he is doing in using the idea of "stings" and "goads," even if he found them first in the Stoics. These are not "pre-emotions"; they are the emotions themselves. Stings and goads can in fact kill, but in their "natural" form they prompt feelings that are valuable to a good life, not hostile intellectual evaluation and rejection. Shame leads us to moral improvement, and anger leads us to repel harm; intense gratitude to our teachers in philosophy is no vice; the "natural" objections to death that make us dread it lead us to wish, perfectly reasonably, for as long a life as we can have (ὡς [π]λεῖστον [χ]ρό[ν]ον ζῆν, *hōs [p]leiston [ch]ro[n]on zēn* [*On Death* 13.37]). This last feeling turns to "natural" sting and goad when the facts of life tell us that our end is near, and the Epicurean therapist must offer sympathy. Yet in themselves, all the objections that Philodemus recognizes as "natural" objections to dying – the desire of the young to live longer, "forgivable" in itself and all the more natural in young people who have begun to learn wisdom and want to learn more; the wish to further the welfare of one's family and friends, and the fear that they will be in danger on their own; even the desire to die at home rather than abroad, if one only could – correspond perfectly to Demetrius Laco's four criteria of the "natural," like "natural" anger. They are felt by uncorrupted natural impulse, not civilized illusion; they are necessarily felt by all; they correspond to the facts; and they are profitable, until the inevitability of death turns them into frustrations that only utter realism about death itself can calm (the realism recommended in the peroration of the treatise, by which Philodemus tries to show how "natural bites" can be both accepted and transcended). And the pain of all these emotions, not of "pre-emotions" awaiting assent, the wise feel as fully as, or in some instances – because they know the facts, τὰ πράγματα (*ta pragmata*) – even more than, the unwise do. They belong to the class of pains that one should actively choose, just as the pleasure of revenge belongs to the class of pleasures that one must decline. But the pain of "natural" emotions at least can be overridden by two things: the joy that one has known by enlightenment, and firm grounding in simple reality. Where Epicurus strikingly said that we should give thanks (χάρις, *charis*) to "blessed Nature" for making what is necessary to us so easy to attain (frg. 469 Usener [1887]), Philodemus even more emphatically says that the wise person το[ῖς] πράγμασιν εὐχα[ρ]ιστεῖ, "gives thanks to the facts" (*On Death* 38.25).

Conclusion

It thus seems wrong to disparage Epicurus's and Philodemus's or even Lucretius's attitude toward the emotions as merely a milder version of the Stoics'.[40] They do indeed allow that feeling at least some real emotions, and those important ones, is "natural" in the terms that they lay down; and they do not see that these "natural" emotions do any great damage. When Philodemus talks of "stings" and "bites," he indeed is talking of what both the ancients and we would call "emotions," and not something else. All the Epicureans also encourage what even in today's English we would call "a philosophical attitude" – that is, the cultivation *in the end* of some kind of distance from the situation, some kind of *ephedreia*, "watchfulness," over one's emotions, as Galen's Antonius the Epicurean called it; but for those who think that this is a bad thing, no ancient philosopher is going to be more than a certain amount of help.[41]

Additional note: Philodemus's opponents in *On Anger*

The loss of Philodemus's full statement of his own position and that of his opponents, frequently otherwise little-known contemporaries of Zeno of Sidon, and the necessity of inferring his and their positions from arguments that assume these at the end of a treatise, very often all we have, are a well-known difficulty in interpreting him. However, this can be dealt with when we have enough text, as D. Obbink does in his edition of *On Piety* (Obbink 1996), and especially (since he is struggling against even greater difficulties and obscurities) R. Janko does in his edition of book 1 of *On Poems* (Janko 2000).[42] Enough work has been done on this problem in *On Anger* to arrive at a pretty fair understanding anyway.

1   Philodemus's "diatribe" sections open the surviving part of the work that can be numbered in columns. Several fragments precede them. It seems from frgs 1 to 4 that he was discussing the pain of anger theoretically; in frgs 6–13 he inveighs against its horrors; the name of Nicasicrates, without a restorable context, occurs in frg. 7; in frgs 14–17 he seems to have returned to theoretical discussion. In col. I, where a more continuous text begins, he is criticizing an opponent who thought that it was "raving nonsense" to deliver diatribes against anger, like "Bion in his *On Anger* or Chrysippus in the *Therapeutikos Logos* of the *On Emotions*" (lines 15–19). Philodemus agrees that it was right to fault them for reviling anger and its effects without doing anything further about it, but he considers that in thinking it "ridiculous" to put the horrible results of anger vividly *pro ommatōn*, "before the eyes," the opponent was himself "ridiculous and raving" (lines 20–26). He argues, using a wealth of medical imagery, that just as a doctor sometimes needs to show the horrible results of disease that a patient will suffer unless the patient makes changes, so also passionate people need this kind of warning about their passions (cols II–VIII.8). At col. V.16–25 Philodemus says, "And certainly the disasters that were to follow upon his rage against Basilides and Thespis were not visible to *him*, though he thought he had set limits to his own harshness in argument." Basilides and Thespis were leaders of the Epicurean school in Athens about 150 BCE, otherwise little known. Apparently they took the same favorable view of the virtues of diatribe therapy, even as practiced by eclectics such as Bion of Borysthenes or Stoics

such as Chrysippus, as also by Zeno of Sidon and Philodemus after them. At col. VI.6–9 the opponent is at last revealed by the surviving text to be Timasagoras, who refuses to believe that angry people can be reasoned with by any therapeutic opposition, however "vivid."

The longer "diatribe" section properly so called now follows, mostly eclectic in philosophical tone and vividly warning against the horrors of anger, though part of it (cols XVIII.34–XXI) is specifically about the horrors of anger in creating dissidence among students and disobedience to teachers in a school such as Philodemus's own. As H. Ringeltaube said about this section, "in philosophi scholam aliquam nos remissos esse putamus," we feel in these columns as if we have been sent back to school to an ancient philosopher (Ringeltaube 1914: 39). There are other indications, such as a quotation from Metrodorus (col. XIII.22–30), that show that the speaker is Epicurean, and that, as Procopé says, it is "a distinctly Epicurean sermon" (Procopé 1993: 382). But most of the diatribe could come from Chrysippus or Bion as plausibly as from Philodemus, except for the occasional "but I pass over all that" or "and all that sort of thing," phrases that show that Philodemus is reworking material that he assumes is already well known.

2   As the "diatribe" section closes, Philodemus vividly criticizes not just poets and orators who encourage emotionalism by their writings, but philosophers, "some of them talking nonsense in their exhortations and some of them even strengthening one's anger by encouragement" (col. XXXI.18–21). It immediately turns out that among these are "some of the Peripatetics, at least, whom earlier we mentioned by name [*dia prosōpōn*]" (lines 24–26). Philodemus attacks them in cols XXXI.21–XXXIV.7 (Indelli's section 6), not entirely fairly (since he fails to mention any reservations that the Peripatetics had about violent or irrational anger, which certainly they did), and is still talking about them at col. XXXIV.21 (the beginning of Indelli's section 7), where he says,

> If we see people not irascible looking like irascible people, we should know that it is without the emotion itself and the disposition and the results they [= the Aristotelians] ascribe to it that all the other things happen which we have given an account of.
> (col. XXXIV.16–24)

He goes on to say,

> Sometimes, however, it turns into that, because of people driving one crazy and increasing the characteristics through which one appears irascible, even to the extent of making them irascible in truth. But generally we may suppose that a person genuinely not irascible will not give a prolonged impression of irascibility, or if he does will not be such profoundly, but just not the sort of person he seems. At any

rate they appear to that extent (irascible) even when their disposition is quite opposite, so that even the wise man, for instance Epicurus, has made this sort of impression on some; and the cause was sometimes qualities so many and such that ... [about nine lines missing] ... and then out of friendship there is frequent rebuking of all or most of his disciples, and quite intense, often even (amounting to) reviling because of his quickness of soul, and before he had considered completely that the misbehavior was an accident; the outbursts of anger occasionally seen in him, though some (philosophers) thought right that the wise man should be invulnerable to emotion; the austerity in his relations (for the most part) with the public; his severe style of refutation, in both writing and verbal argument, of philosophers who committed errors of reasoning; the desertion of some of his friends because of his frank speaking or his refusing (them something); sometimes even hatred against him from the embittered (among them), intemperate as they are; the falling foul of servants who have done wrong; and many other things ... so that some wise men present the appearance of irascible men more than others, those (that is) in whom there is more natural anger present; or are more outspoken for the reasons we set forth in our *On Frank Criticism*; or because such things (as provoke one) happen to them more often. Those in whom anger is not naturally present, and to whom such things as we are speaking of do not happen, will not present such an appearance.

(cols XXXIV.24–XXXVI.30)

Philodemus is in some trouble here. He is having to fight uphill because he is obliged to admit that Epicurus might at least superficially be thought to be a poor example for the "restrained," pleasure-free, and brief anger that he is advocating, and that according to the Master's own literary remains and official biography.[43] For the rest of the treatise he defends himself – and not by abuse, as he did against Timasagoras, but with considerable restraint and respect in reporting arguments – against two kinds of adversaries.

First, there is Nicasicrates, who thought that the wise person sometimes will do self-harm through anger – "harming himself, which Nicasicrates claims that even the wise man sometimes does" (col. XXXVII.4–6) – and that even "natural" anger damages one's reason and friendships:

In Nicasicrates we read that natural anger not only gives pain by its very nature, but darkens one's reasonings to the extent it can and prevents an entirely acceptable and trouble-free life with friends and brings many of the disadvantages enumerated; not having compared it with the "empty" anger and....

(cols XXXVIII.34–XXXIX.8)

Philodemus does not subject Nicasicrates to any such sarcasm and abuse as Timasagoras, either. The severest thing that he says against this point of view is that anger is admitted to be inescapable to human nature "and indeed Nicasicrates himself, I dare say, since he shares in human nature, could not escape all anger but must at all events be capable of some of it" (col. XL.21–5). (This justifies, I think, my inference that Nicasicrates, in more familiar Epicurean technical language, had held anger to be "natural but not necessary" instead of "natural and necessary" as Philodemus believes.) Philodemus also objects that the sage "could not be called by this appellation, if anger is that great an evil; also, how can we still say anything with freedom of speech against the arguments of those who refuse the sage every kind of anger?" (col. XXXIX.19–25). If Nicasicrates is right, the Epicurean wise person is *not* wise, since this person suffers anger to so great and so damaging an extent; and also Nicasicrates has "let down the side," since if anger entails such horrors, how can we confront the Stoics, who will not admit any anger in the wise at all?

Second, there are also Epicureans who believe, from textual study of the Master's literary remains and his circle's, that the sage will experience rage (*thymos*) or intense anger (*entonos orgē*). They reason from the use of the word *thymos* and its cognates in the founders' texts (cols XLI.31–XLVI.13), and they offer and are answered by *epilogismoi* (LSJ: "reflections, considerations," which the Epicureans opposed to *apodeixis*, "complete demonstrations"). Again, one can see from the passage quoted above why they thought that the texts encouraged such a view. Nor does Philodemus answer them with sarcasm, but rather with serious argument. These have to be Epicureans, since they believe in the sacred texts of the founders and in *epilogismos* in the technical Epicurean sense (on *epilogismos* see Erler 2003).

But who were Timasagoras and Nicasicrates? Earlier editors, given that Philodemus says at col. XXXI.24–27 that he has mentioned Peripatetics who encouraged anger "by name" earlier, and seeing both names in earlier columns, supposed that they must be Peripatetics who encouraged anger. This was the opinion of Wilke (1914: xxi–xxvi) and Crönert (1906: 89–91). In a slightly different form it is revived by Asmis (1990: 2396–8), who thinks that Timasagoras was a Peripatetic of the times of Basilides and Thespis, and Nicasicrates was an Academic who admitted the existence of "natural" anger as a ploy against the Epicureans.

However, the evidence is overwhelming that both were Epicureans.[44] Ringeltaube already saw this correctly in 1914; he thought that Timasagoras, like the Epicureans whom Philodemus answers at the end of *On Anger*, was for fewer limits on the sage's anger than was Philodemus, and Nicasicrates was against it in any form, but both were Epicureans anyway. It is worth noting that like Asmis, Ringeltaube (1914: 40–6) perceives that Philodemus treats them differently, and not as if they were somehow a pair.[45] So does Procopé (1993: 377–86), who both considers them Epicureans and sees clearly that they were two different items.[46] Strictly speaking, we do not know what Timasagoras thought except that he insulted Basilides and Thespis about the usefulness of diatribes as therapy. But Ringeltaube may well be right; it is possible that Timasagoras was "for anger" in the sense that he thought that Chrysippean diatribe assumed the wrongness of all emotions, and that to compliment such writing or quote it was to back off from the Epicurean view that some emotions are all right in the context of an overall good life. Nicasicrates thought that anger was "natural" but damaging – in Epicurean terms, "natural but not necessary" and not attractive either. We might define his position with another Pauline quotation: πάντα ἔξεστιν, ἀλλ' οὐ πάντα συμφέρει· πάντα ἔξεστιν, ἀλλ' οὐ πάντα οἰκοδομεῖ, "All things are permitted, but not all things are expedient; all things are permitted, but not all things edify" (1 Cor 10:23). Nicasicrates admitted from the evidence of the Master's and his circle's writings that the sage could be angered; but why not voluntarily renounce such a troublesome possibility, permitted or not?[47] No wonder one could confuse not Philodemus but at least one of his adversaries with the Stoics; anger could be natural, and the sage could feel it, but could refuse it anyway. But as Procopé says, not even Nicasicrates' position was like theirs: "in Stoic eyes there is no difference between Nicasicrates or Philodemus or the wildest Peripatetic" (Procopé 1993: 385) – not to mention the other Epicurean adversaries, cited at the end of *On Anger*, who took the earlier literature of the Epicureans at what looked like its word about the permissibility to the wise person not just of anger, but of intense anger or even rage.

In fact, what Procopé (1993: 367 and esp. 385) took for bad writing in the final sections of *On Anger* is more like the reflection of Philodemus's own difficulties in sustaining his medialist position. In his view "natural" anger consists only in pain; pleasure in one's anger and the persistence of the feeling when no pragmatic object is served by it are warning signals. But he had to argue this position, which no doubt was Zeno of Sidon's before him, against minimalists such as Nicasicrates, and maximalists such as (perhaps) Timasagoras, and certainly the fellow Epicurean opponents at the end. It is a reasonable position, as is shown by the lasting impression that his and Zeno of Sidon's arguments for it made on Atticus (see n. 10), Vergil, and Horace. But he could not take it for granted as canonical. Philodemus will have had an easier row to hoe in discussing erotic passion with his students, since, like Lucretius, at least in M.C. Nussbaum's exposition, he could easily show that less dramatic human relationships, such as marriage, or realistic, long-term love affairs *concedentes humanis rebus*, making concessions to others' humanity and faults, have more value than fleeting and imaginary passions. His poems may have suggested thirty-seven as the age to discover this, but he will have had little trouble explaining that away. In *On Death* he discriminates very sensitively between fears about dying that are based on real values and deserve sympathy, and those that are not and do not. If Lucretius sounds harsher in the diatribe at the end of book 3, it is only because he, aiming at livelier dramatic effect, chose to do the harsh and not the friendly form of "frank criticism" as Philodemus understands it. (As Fish [1998] shows, Lucretius knew that the other possibility was there.) But on anger there was quite a lively debate, and his Epicurean opponents on both the other sides are not "heretics" and cannot merely be dismissed with invective. Lucretius (*De rerum nat.* 3.294–319) had said that some human beings are as angry as lions by nature, some as fearful as deer, some as invulnerable to fear and anger as placid cows; but though these temperaments cannot be completely uprooted, "so trivial are the traces of different natures that remain, beyond reason's power to expel, that nothing hinders our living a life worthy of gods" (Lucretius, *De rerum nat.* 3.320–2, trans. Rouse [1992: 213]). Evidently, the records of the Master and his circle had rendered a range of views possible in the school about how extensive, in the case of anger, these trivial traces of different natures, these *parvula naturarum vestigia*, should be.

The difficulties of Philodemus's struggle to maintain his own and Zeno of Sidon's position, even against other Epicureans, are obvious at times – for example, in his contention (against Nicasicrates, who thought that we should voluntarily refuse to imitate the Master's angry moods) that a wise person in the grip of natural anger makes himself only *slightly* discreditable ("these feelings only bring with them a little additional discredit [ὀλίγον δέ τι μόνον ἀνευδοκησίας συνε[πι]φέρονται][48] in the eyes of those who will admit that it is a natural thing and in the wise man's case brief" [cols XXXIX.39–XL.2]). It sounds as if, had he been giving the lecture to an audience with representatives of the other schools in it, especially Stoics, and not just his own admiring students, a trying question period might naturally have followed.

Notes

1 The Hebrew word *ragaz* indicates agitation caused by either awe or anger. Although some modern translations follow the LXX in interpreting the verse in terms of anger (NEB, NIV, etc.), it is much more likely that the psalmist is telling his adversaries to tremble in awe before God, who hearkens to the faithful when they call upon him (Ps 4:4 [4:3 Eng.]).
2 The Hebrew text continues with the words, "Commune with your own heart upon your bed, and be still" (AV). The LXX, on the other hand, has, "Speak in your hearts, and be pricked on your beds."
3 D. Sedley (1989) offers a thorough analysis of Philodemus's special relationship with and allegiance to Zeno. See texts and discussion in Angeli and Colaizzo 1979.
4 Citations of Philodemus's *On Death* are from the edition of Kuiper (1925).
5 See Vlastos 1966; Angeli and Colaizzo 1979: 63–8, frgs 27, 81–5, 123–5. For a good review of Zeno as a mathematician (did he anticipate non-Euclidean geometry, or were his views merely skeptical and negative?) and the scholarship of this question, see O'Connor and Robertson 1999.
6 This is very amusingly brought out by M. Erler, to whose treatment of Epicureanism I am indebted throughout (Erler 1994: 209–14).

7 For Philodemus's *On Anger*, see Indelli 1988; for *On Frank Criticism*, see Konstan et al. 1998.
8 See Procopé 1993: 372–3. The importance of this passage in Demetrius Laco was pointed out to Procopé by D. Sedley.
9 The restorations are those of Wilke (1914).
10 I have argued that this paraphrases Philodemus's doctrine that anger, if limited to pain and excluding the pleasure of revenge, should be brief (Armstrong 2004b: 281, 296 n. 21). I show from Cicero, *Att.* 1.17.4 that Cicero's friend Atticus, as an Epicurean, was expected to hold this doctrine also. *Nam si ita statueris, et irritabilis animos esse optimorum saepe hominum, et eosdem placabilis* [= Horace's *irasci celerem, tamen ut placabilis essem*, where the commentaries cite this passage of Cicero, and which I argue is a paraphrase of Philodemus's doctrine] *et esse hanc agilitatem, ut ita dicam, mollitiamque naturae plerumque bonitatis et, id quod caput est, nobis inter nos nostra sive incommoda sive vitia sive iniurias esse tolerandas, facile haec, quemadmodum spero, mitigabuntur; quod ego ut facias te oro:* "For if you have decided to think this [the future perfect *statueris* means that this is supposed to be Atticus's fixed belief] – that even the best men's spirits are irascible, and at the same time placable, and that this nimbleness/sensitivity of disposition is generally a sign of goodness, and, that which sums it all up: for us and among ourselves, our unattractive qualities or vices or misdoings are to be put up with – these things will easily be mitigated as I hope they will, which I beg you to do." I claim that Cicero is appealing to Atticus's Epicurean principles about anger and friendship, which he must have learned from Zeno and Phaedrus, not Philodemus. I would also point out that the second part of the sentence quoted, about condoning friends' lesser vices as the Stoics supposedly refused to do, is the theme of Horace, *Sat.* 1.3, which comes from Horace's explicitly Epicurean period and is full of allusions to Epicurus and Lucretius. On the knowledge that Vergil shows of this doctrine about anger, and how it fits in the psychology of his Aeneas and Turnus, see Galinsky 1988; 1994; Erler 1992b; Fish 2004.
11 Some, including many nineteenth-century scholars who discussed *On Anger*, thought that Philodemus's opponents all admitted anger as a valid emotion, including even its vengeful side to some extent, and must therefore have been Aristotelians. From references elsewhere in the corpus Longo Auricchio and Tepedino Guerra (1981: 32–9) have demonstrated that Timasagoras and Nicasicrates were Epicureans, probably from Rhodes, and that the *tines* were also Epicureans, that is, the "certain people" who advanced the arguments (discussed by Philodemus in the last section) that the sage feels intense anger or rage as well as the more limited "natural anger" that Philodemus tries to define. See, at the end of the present essay, "Additional note: Philodemus's opponents in *On Anger*."
12 Philodemus's and Epicurus's doctrines on gratitude are collected in Tepedino Guerra's (1997) edition of *On Gratitude*. As Erler (1994: 322–3) points out, even in the brief fragments that she edits the theme of gratitude to one's teachers (*kathēgētai*) stands out; col. 8, for example, has *eucharistia, peithein, paideuesthai,* "thankfulness, persuasion, education."
13 W.V. Harris (2001: 102–4) offers a perfectly reliable summary of *On Anger* and Philodemus's and Lucretius's views that better reflects the treatise's continuing

assimilation into the scholarly picture since Indelli. So does Procopé (1993), and so do general accounts of the treatise by Asmis (1990: 2396–9) and Erler (1994: 323–5). A newer and indispensable discussion is Angeli (2000). Wilke's (1914) Teubner text offered only a Latin summary in the introduction, which helped neither with Philodemus's thorny Greek nor with the doubts inevitable in those days about the reliability of the text and the means by which it was gotten from the papyrus and the *disegni* (hand-drawn copies of the papyrus made when they were first opened). Indelli's edition has changed all that.

14 See especially Tsouna (2001), a very sympathetic and perceptive review of Epicurean "therapy."
15 "Bites" as the Stoics saw them are a major topic in Sorabji's *Emotion and Peace of Mind* (2000) and the focus of his essay "Stoic First Movements in Christianity" (2004), although that essay leaves the Epicureans aside.
16 See also the essays in response to Sorabji by C. Gill (2005) and A.W. Price (2005).
17 Or, emending by inserting a relative pronoun, "which."
18 The LCL translation of Hicks (1925) has been slightly altered and italics added. Bignone's (1920) addition of τιοι (*tisi*) after πάθεοι (*pathesi*), which Marcovich (1999) accepts and Sorabji (2000: 201) is tempted by, is not *textually* necessary, though it clarifies the meaning. Diogenes Laertius, as he so often does, is taking one sentence after another out of context, and it is more probable that the context itself made clear that not all passions were felt by the sage more deeply than others, only the natural ones.
19 Cf., for the same mistranslation, "Epicurus said that the wise person will be more gripped by certain emotions than other people. They are dissociated from hatred, envy, and contempt, but they feel pity and distress (DL 10.117–18)" (Knuuttila 2004: 83).
20 Graver (1999), Sorabji (2000: 319–56). Graver considers the translation "good emotions" and rejects it, but I am still impressed by A.C. Lloyd's claim that it is "one-sided to speak, as is common today, of the Stoics' intellectualism: as much as they made will or the passions intellectual they could here be said to have made the intellect volitional and passionate" (Lloyd 1978: 242). So perhaps purely intellectual emotions might deserve to be called such.
21 See Brown (1987) on Lucretius 4.1190 and 4.1191, and the striking treatment of the whole passage by Nussbaum (1994a: 172–87), making it turn on these lines (and saying explicitly that "the goal of Lucretian therapy is to make a good marriage possible" [Nussbaum 1994a: 185]). Nussbaum thinks, probably quite rightly, that the ideal Epicurean husband still does not find enough "intense excitement and beauty in being needy and vulnerable before a person whom one loves" and is thus too godlike in his self-sufficiency: "What neither the sick patient nor the cured pupil have found, it seems, is a way in which being simply human can be a source of erotic joy" (Nussbaum 1994a: 190–1). But in fact Nussbaum is the first scholar I know to have brought out firmly and clearly that Lucretius's addressee starts to find real happiness and the prospect of a longer-term relationship and/or a family the minute he acknowledges his mistresses' essential humanity, *humanis concedere rebus*.
22 On the relation of this passage to Epicurus's piety toward friends see Obbink 1996: 412–14, on lines 797–9. Capasso (1988: 71–82) offers an excellent and

comprehensive review of the texts that show why, though one's grief for the loss of a friend does not lead an Epicurean to conclude that the friend was unhappy in death, the school thought grief "natural" and in the end something appropriate, a stage in the journey to happy memory and thus enjoyment of the friendship even after death. Metrodorus too, this time to Seneca's disgust, found the same "pleasure" in grief as Epicurus and the average classical Greek (Seneca, *Ep.* 98.9 = Metrodorus, frg. 35 [Körte 1890]); as Capasso comments about both these passages, "un tema non insolito nella tradizione greca: il piacere delle lacrime," the pleasure of tears is a familiar theme in the Greek tradition (Capasso 1988: 76).

23 See the comments in Bignone (1973: 1.542–3).

24 I am grateful to James Inman for making this point in my Horace seminar. Nisbet and Hubbard (1970), for example, come fairly close to saying this *ad loc.*, although the evidence for Quintilius's Epicureanism was not available to them. For more Horatian references and for a timely reminder that even Lucretius censures only *excessive* grief over death and dying, not grief itself, see Fish's (1998) brief but important essay.

25 In citing the translation of *On Frank Criticism* by Konstan *et al.* (1998) for this essay, I have been careful to pick passages of whose text and translation one with experience in editing Philodemus over a number of different treatises can be fairly certain. D. Obbink and D. Konstan, I have been told, are preparing a more complete and reliable edition. It is to be hoped that the new methods of photography by multiple spectrum imaging (MSI) introduced by Brigham Young University's team at the turn of the new millennium will speed the day when we can form an idea of everything to be found in the papyrus itself. Meanwhile, although one must be grateful to the editors of *On Frank Criticism* for the best text of the Greek so far and the first English translation of any kind, it needs to be noted that even with the supplementary emendations of R. Philippson (many of them too speculative) and M. Gigante, which the editors have added to Olivieri's old Teubner text of 1914, we have nowhere near a complete text of what survives, and that although there is a better-preserved set of columns that Olivieri numbers I–XXIV after the *disegni*, with only middle parts missing for the most part, the ninety-four fragments that come before them give us at best roughly forty or fifty Greek words apiece with gaps between them that must have included as many words and more. The translations given, though they mostly follow those of Konstan *et al.* (1998), are my own. I have kept their Arabic numerals for fragments, in which they follow Olivieri, and Roman numerals for columns, as with *On Anger*, though not in citing *On Death*, where I also intend to publish my own translation, and where I think that the columns should have Arabic numerals. If this seems inconsistent, it is one way of expressing my gratitude to Indelli for his text and commentary, which I have consulted throughout, and Konstan and his fellow editors for making the text available at last with English translation and notes.

26 *Kataphronēsis* is another important term in the vocabulary of shame.

27 In analyzing this extraordinary passage, so significant for the relationship between philosophers and women, I might mention that there seems to be good evidence that not just Calpurnius Piso Caesoninus, Julius Caesar's father-in-law, was one of Philodemus's adherents in Epicureanism, as Cicero testifies at length in the *In*

Pisonem, but also his daughter Calpurnia, the wife of Caesar, and at least one of her freedwomen and the freedwoman's young son; see the note on Calpurnia in Armstrong 1993: 200–1 n. 29, and the article on *CIL* 6.14211 (= Bücheler, *Carm.* 964) by P. Boyancé (1955). I should have added that Plutarch's words about Calpurnia's dream before Caesar's murder, that Caesar was the more inclined to believe in it because "he had never seen any womanish superstition [*gunaikismon en deisidaimoniai*] in her before" in the fifteen years of their marriage (Plutarch, *Caes.* 56), show that Plutarch's tradition made her out to be an Epicurean. If Epicurean women of rank and culture such as Calpurnia heard this lecture, which is possible, Philodemus will have been joking with them; but perhaps he is just expressing the usual ancient male prejudices.

28 *Pepoithēsis* is a word found more in Hellenistic Jewish writers, according to LSJ, than in pagan ones: 4 Kgdms 18:19; Eph 3:12 and five more times in the Pauline writings; Philo; Josephus.

29 *Prokopē* is a Stoic term for "progress in philosophy" that Philodemus uses occasionally, like "bites," although he also uses *probasis* and *probainein*.

30 It has been argued (Moles 1996) that the diatribe was not a recognized literary genre, but Philodemus appears to use the word *diatribē* thus at *On Anger* col. XXXV.28, and the section satirizing bad anger and revenge certainly seems to fit the traditional definition of the word.

31 The next words as restored would mean "happens about the most trifling things" (π[ερ]ὶ ἐλάχιστ[α γίνε]ται [Indelli 1988: "si verifica per cose minime"]) "and in the way in which we adduce" (κ]αὶ κα[θ' ὃν τρόπον ἐ]πιφ[έρομεν) (col. XXXVIII.9-10 [as Indelli has it, following Wilke]), but I am very suspicious. The sense to be expected should be "as it is something painful, it should be confined (or indulged) to the least possible extent," but I have not found the right supplement.

32 On this work see Tieleman 2003, in which the fourth chapter is devoted to the reconstruction of the *Therapeutikos Logos*. Tieleman (2003: 179) notes that in *On Anger* Philodemus mentions vivid descriptions of the repulsiveness and madness of anger as taking up "a lot of space" in Chrysippus' *Therapeutikos*, although he stops short of considering that *On Anger* might itself give us an idea of what these were.

33 The conjecture appears in Buresch's (1886) discussion of Greek and Roman consolation, which includes an essay "Epimetrum de Philodemi περὶ θανάτου libro" (142–64, at 143). "Epimetrum" indicates that Buresch had just time to take into account Mekler's (1886) edition of *On Death*, which came out just as his book was being printed. Buresch also argued that some of the material for *De morte* actually came from Chrysippus, who (he had earlier argued) had included much "consolation of grief" material in his own *Therapeutikos* (Buresch 1886: 37).

34 See Tsouna 2003. She cites my forthcoming translation of *On Anger*, on which we have worked together, for a first version of the opinions that I give here about Philodemus's mock-Stoic "diatribe" (Tsouna 2003: 243 nn. 3, 6).

35 See Fillion-Lahille 1984: 229–36. She believes that resemblances between Seneca and Philodemus's diatribe section come from Seneca's having read Philodemus, not the use by the two of them of Chrysippus as a common source, and is doubtful that *On Anger* gives us any new fragments of Chrysippus, at least for certain. Indelli (1988: 24–6) does not seem to take her arguments as decisive.

36 ἐνοχλεῖ δὲ φυσικῶ[ς] ἐπε[γ]γελῶν ἐχθρός, "an enemy laughing at you troubles you naturally," which is also an important footnote to Philodemus's theory of natural anger in *On Anger*.
37 Cf. "The wise person will feel emotions more deeply" (Diogenes Laertius 10.117), discussed earlier.
38 But cf. LSJ, s.v. "*philologos*" II.1, "fond of philosophical argument," citing Epicurus, *SV* 74, and Philodemus, *Lib.* col. VIIIa.7–9, where *sophos, philosophos,* and *philologos* form a threefold description of the philosopher.
39 On Gadara, Philodemus's native city, see Fitzgerald 2004.
40 I say *even* Lucretius's because I think that with the peroration of *On Death* to guide us, the central contention in Segal 1990, that Lucretius's feelings about death were darker as a poet than his philosophy could really embrace, is not true. They exemplify, just like the last columns of *On Death*, the continuous attention and meditation, *epibolē*, on reality and Nature as it is, the making of death so continuous an undercurrent of one's thoughts – as Philodemus explains, that it is never absent even when one is thinking about something else on the surface – that the school really did recommend. But that too as a principle in Lucretius is for another essay. It is worth noting, however, that the apparent gap between Lucretius's austere tone in the diatribe on death at the end of book 3, and Philodemus's more friendly therapy in *On Death*, is in fact merely the difference in *On Frank Criticism* between the "harsh" or "biting" kind of frankness and the more affectionate and consoling one used for pupils who are more sensitive and require a friendlier tone. Lucretius and Philodemus are the "bad cop" and the "good cop," one might say, though they make the same point in the end, and though sarcasm is not lacking in Philodemus, nor sympathy in Lucretius. "If Philodemus's audience in *On Death* included philosophers from various schools, the caustic rhetoric of Lucretius, with its harsh elements such as *stulte* (III,939) and *improbe* (III,1026), would have been altogether inappropriate. But for Lucretius, whose intended reader was the ambitious Roman nobleman, such a harsh and vivid portrayal of moral illness would fit the occasion more than precise definitions as to allowable emotions. Each adapts himself to his audience, as does Horace himself, who anticipates an audience of different philosophical persuasions and levels of education" (Fish 1998: 102).
41 I am grateful to Voula Tsouna, Benjamin Henry, Jeffrey Fish, and Michael Wigodsky for help and criticism without which I could not have written this essay; of course, all errors of fact, argument, and emphasis are my own.
42 Janko's "Philodemus' Sources and Opponents" (Janko 2000: 120–89) disentangles Philodemus's euphonist opponents and their similar but different theories from a tangled text with a success that one would not a priori have thought possible. By comparison, the opponents in *On Anger* are easy work.
43 Or if we suppose that the lacuna covered a change of subject from Epicurus himself to biographical facts known about other philosophers accepted as sages in the school, the problem is not much different. Jensen thought that the whole passage referred to Epicurus; Philippson suggested that after the nine-line lacuna the subject had changed to Zeno and Phaedrus and to *their* displays of anger (see Indelli 1988 on col. XXXV.17). But that would make Philodemus's difficulties in arguing down his opponents greater, not less.

44 The evidence given in Longo Auricchio and Tepedino Guerra 1981: 32–9 seems overwhelming. Timasagoras is named by both Cicero (*Acad.* 2.80) and Aetius (4.13.6 [36]) as a dissident Epicurean, and it means nothing that the manuscripts of both authors shorten his name to "Timagoras." Nicasicrates, known only from the Herculaneum papyri, praised Democritus, not an authoritative reference point to anyone but atomists. There are many other testimonies in Philodemus to each of them singularly (never together) that go to prove the same point.

45 Ringeltaube argues that Timasagoras and the Epicureans answered at the end of the book "quamquam eiusdem disciplinae erat atque Philodemus, tamen amplioribus quam ille cancellis sapientium libertatem irascendi circumscribi vellent," "though of the same school as Philodemus they wanted to confine the sages' right to be angry within more generous limits" (Ringeltaube 1914: 43). About Nicasicrates ("Stoicorum quam similis") he says, "Philodemus indignatione exardescit, quod Nicasicrates summa cum severitate sapientem etiam naturali ira carere vult," "Philodemus burns with indignation, that Nicasicrates with the greatest severity wants the sage to lack even natural anger" (Ringeltaube 1914: 44); but I do not see that Philodemus is at all as angry with Nicasicrates as with Timasagoras, who attacked the school's heads by name.

46 Procopé (1993: 379, 382) thinks that Timasagoras was contemporary with Basilides and Thespis, but that Nicasicrates was contemporary with Philodemus himself.

47 This seems more in line with the side of Nicasicrates that Philodemus twice mentions in surviving texts (*De dis* 3 frg. 65 and *De ira* frg. 7.15 Indelli) that Procopé (1993: 382 n. 80) cites as having always had to "add something of his own" than Procopé's (1993: 382) other speculation that Nicasicrates might have been a "hard-liner" in Epicureanism. The first to call attention to Philodemus's observation about Nicasicrates was H. Diels (see Indelli 1988: 138; Procopé 1993: 382 n. 80).

48 On *aneudokēsia*, a *hapax legomenon*, see Indelli 1988 on this passage (with his note on ἀνευδόκητά, *aneudokēta* [col. XXV]). Nicasicrates had claimed that natural anger "brought with it in addition (συνε[πι]φέρειν) many disadvantages" (col. XXXIX.5–7).

6

ΠΑΘΗ AND ΑΠΑΘΕΙΑ IN EARLY ROMAN EMPIRE STOICS

Edgar M. Krentz

Stoicism in the early Roman Empire concentrated its interest on ethics, whereas early Stoicism gave priority to logic and physics. These Roman Stoics considered the *pathē* (emotions) when discussing ethics. Arius Didymus and Epictetus, two first-century Roman Stoics, illustrate this. Arius Didymus gives us the fullest, coherent account of ethics we have from the period. He first describes the principles on which ethics is based, then discusses the four basic emotions. One has to reconstruct Epictetus's interpretation of the *pathē* from remarks scattered throughout his *Dissertations*. Both make clear that the four basic emotions (appetite, fear, pain, and pleasure) contradict the rational character of the human being. Thus, one must weigh emotions against the essential character of humans.

Introduction

"In classical philosophy as well as later patristic thought, the human passions presented a moral but inevitably also an ontological, or else physical, dilemma" (Blowers 1996: 57). So P.M. Blowers writes in the introduction to his recent article on Maximus the Confessor. He is certainly correct with respect to Stoic philosophy and its early Roman Empire representatives, Arius Didymus and Epictetus.

According to Plutarch (*Ant.* 80; *Praecept. ger. rei publ.* 814D; *Apophth. Lac.* 207A–B), Arius Didymus, a philosopher, accompanied Caesar Augustus when he entered Alexandria in 30 BCE.[1] He was still active in 9 BCE, when he composed a consolation for Livia on the death of Drusus. A century and a half ago, he was identified by A. Meineke (1859) as the author of the section in John Stobaeus titled "The Beliefs of Zeno and Other Stoics about the Ethical Part of Philosophy" (Stobaeus, *Ecl.* 2.7.5–12 [Wachsmuth and Hense

[1884–1912]: 2.57–116]), an identification more recently supported by A.A. Long (1996a: 108–10).[2] Long calls this epitome "the longest and most detailed surviving account of Stoic ethics," deriving from a source of "unimpeachable orthodoxy."[3]

Epictetus lived about a century later. A slave in his early life, for some time the property of Epaphroditus, himself a freedman and official in Nero's court, he was a student under Musonius Rufus, educated into a Stoicism that had a long history.[4] He lived from about 50 to 120 CE, being banished by Domitian in 89 or 92 CE. Arius Didymus and Epictetus taught in Greek, not Latin. Thus, they are basic for understanding the philosophic thought of Stoicism in the early period of the Roman Empire.[5]

Early Roman Empire Stoicism had a stress different from that of earlier Stoicism. Between the founders of Stoicism and Caesar Augustus had come the Roman conquest of the East. Polybios characterizes the period of conquest with the phrase ταραχὴ καὶ κίνησις (*tarachē kai kinēsis*), "terror and movement" (Walbank 1972: 30). Rome destroyed both Carthage and Corinth in 146 BCE, while 133 BCE ushered in a century of unrest in Roman public life that finally ended only with Octavian's entry into the principate.[6] Consistent throughout that history was the conviction that the emotions (πάθη, *pathē*) were inimical to the true philosophical life, which aimed at life governed by reason (λόγος, *logos*). Julia Annas describes early Stoicism thus:

> The methodology of Stoicism is wholistic: there is no foundational part which supports the others. Different Stoics disagreed radically both over the correct structure of their position and the correct order of teaching it. Thus the theory can be fully understood only as a whole, one of the respects in which it is markedly "ideal" and makes high demands on the student.
>
> (Annas 1996: 1446)

She describes Roman Stoicism as tending to "edifying and moralizing discussion" that "gave little indication of the philosophical structure of their positions" (ibid.).

That is certainly true of Arius Didymus and Epictetus, who in a sense assumed the conclusions of earlier Stoics on logic (τὸ λογικὸν μέρος, *to logikon meros*) and physics (τὸ φυσικὸν μέρος, *to physikon meros*) as they centered their philosophy on ethics (τὸ ἠθικὸν μέρος, *to ēthikon meros*). Zeno, as reported by Diogenes Laertius (7.110), already defined πάθη, definitions that Epictetus inherited. Thus, πάθος (*pathos*) is "an irrational and contrary-to-nature motion of the soul."[7] The second definition, also in Diogenes Laertius 7.110, is "desire run rampant" (ἡ ὁρμὴ πλεονάζουσα, *hē hormē pleonazousa*). Chrysippus defined τὸ πάθος as decision-making.[8] Both Arius Didymus and Epictetus assume such understandings without expressly citing them.

Τὰ πάθη ("emotions" is a standard translation but may be too constrictive)[9] are the reactions in the soul to external impressions (φαντασίαι, *phantasiai*) brought to the soul. These reactions may be emotions or, more generically, sense impressions, feelings caused by external stimuli. They lead to actions, whether physical or mental, that are motions of the soul. The goal of ethics is to bring such movements of the soul under control, and that is done by relating them to reason (λόγος, *logos*) and nature (φύσις, *physis*).[10] The earlier Stoics had identified four general classes of emotions: "appetite (ἐπιθυμία, *epithymia*) and pleasure (ἡδονή, *hēdonē*) are assent to an impending or present good, fear (φόβος, *phobos*) and distress (λύπη, *lypē*) are assent to an impending or present evil."[11] Each of them involves both a belief (δόξα, *doxa*) and an impulse (ὁρμή, *hormē*).

Arius Didymus on the πάθη[12]

Arius Didymus discusses ethics in a very orderly fashion. A.A. Long says that "his detailed material in the Stoic section is probably more accurate and certainly fuller than anything else we possess" (Long 1996a: 130). Arius lays down principles on which he bases his discussion of Stoic ethics. By the time he turns to discussing the πάθη, he has a foundation on which to build. He first discusses the categories "goods" (τὰ ἀγαθά, *ta agatha*) and "evils" (τὰ κακά, *ta kaka*),[13] in which he also discusses "things indifferent" (τὰ ἀδιάφορα, *ta adiaphora*) and "preferred things" (τὰ προηγούμενα, *ta proēgoumena*) (Arius Didymus 5a = Stobaeus, *Ecl.* 2.59).[14] Arius develops what follows from his definitions in that initial discussion (Long 1996a: 111). First he discusses goods and evils (Arius Didymus 5b1–6f = Stobaeus, *Ecl.* 2.57–79). Then he discusses τὰ ἀδιάφορα, "things indifferent" (Arius Didymus 7–7 g = Stobaeus, *Ecl.* 2.79–85). This extended discussion includes material on virtue and the goal of life, blessedness (εὐδαιμονία, *eudaimonia*). There follow discussions of τὸ καθῆκον (*to kathēkon*), the "appropriate," and ἡ ὁρμή (*hē hormē*), "impulse" (Arius Didymus 8–9b = Stobaeus, *Ecl.* 2.85–8). This long discussion prepares for his treatment of the *pathē*.

Arius Didymus describes the πάθη as follows:[15]

> They say a passion is an impulse [ὁρμή] which is excessive, disobedient to the choosing reason [τῷ αἱροῦντι λόγῳ] or an <irrational> motion of the soul contrary to nature [φύσις] (all passions belong to the controlling part [τὸ ἡγμονικόν] of the soul). Hence also every agitation [πτοία] is a passion, <and> again <every> passion is an agitation. As passion is like this, it must be assumed that some passions are primary and fundamental [πρῶτα καὶ ἀρχηγά], while others have reference to these. First in genus are these four: appetite, fear, pain, and pleasure [ἐπιθυμία, φόβος, λύπη, ἡδονή]. Appetite and fear lead the way, the former toward the apparently good, the other

toward the apparently evil. Pleasure and pain come after them: pleasure whenever we obtain that for which we had an appetite or escape from that which we feared; pain whenever we fail to get that for which we had an appetite or encounter that which we feared. With regard to all the passions of the soul, when they say they are opinions [δόξαι], "opinion" is employed for "feeble assumption" [ἀσθενὴς ὑπόληψις] and "fresh" for "that which is stimulative of an irrational contraction <or> elation."

The terms "irrational" and "contrary to nature" are not used in the usual sense, but "irrational" as equivalent of "disobedient to reason" [ἀπειθὲς τῷ λόγῳ]. For every passion is overpowering, just as when those in the grips of passion often see that it would be useful not to do this, but carried away by its violence, as if by some disobedient horse, are led to doing this.... "Contrary to nature" [παρὰ φύσιν] in the description of passion is taken as something which occurs contrary to correct and natural reasoning [παρὰ τὸν ὀρθὸν καὶ κατὰ φύσιν λόγον]. All those in the grips of passion turn their backs on reason, not in the same way as those who have been thoroughly deceived in any matter, but in a special way. For those who have been fooled, for example, that there are invisible first elements, when taught that they do not exist, abandon this judgment. But those in the grips of passion, even if they know or have been taught that they need not feel pain or be afraid or be involved at all in the passions of the soul, nevertheless do not abandon them, but are led by their passions to being governed by their tyranny.
(Arius Didymus 10–10a = Stobaeus *Ecl.* 2.88.8–90.6
[=*SVF* 3.378, 389 in part])[16]

Arius then further defines the four primary passions and lists the emotions subsumed under each (10b). Under appetite, he lists anger, violent cases of erotic love, cravings, yearnings, and cases of fondness for pleasure or wealth or esteem. Under pleasure, he lists joy at others' misfortune, self-gratification, charlatanry (γοητεῖαι, *goēteiai*). Fear includes hesitancy, anguish, astonishment, shame, commotions, superstitions, dread, and terror. Pain encompasses distress, jealousy, pity, grief, worry, sorrow, annoyance, mental distress, and vexation.

This is an illuminating passage. Arius clearly shows how important the discussion of the passions was in Stoic thought.[17] He argues that reason can control the passions, which are a misuse or perversion of reason, contrary to that which should control human beings, their nature as rational beings. Since we can control our judgments, we are responsible for our passions and so are to blame for them. In this, he picks up the "cognitive" interpretation of the passions presented earlier by Chrysippus.[18] Indeed, the cognitive interpretation triumphs in early Roman Empire Stoicism, as a consideration of Epictetus will support.

Epictetus on the πάθη

As Arrian (Lucius Flavius Arrianus) himself tells us, he recorded Epictetus's discourses and more informal conversations "word for word" (*Introductory Letter* 2). It is likely that he also arranged them in the four books we have. Although it is difficult to discern a coherent structure that runs through the four books, the first book seems to provide the background for the other three.[19]

There is an interrelated set of terms significant for our discussion: self-control (ἐγκράτεια, *enkrateia*), freedom from the passions (ἀπάθεια, *apatheia*), and so on. Yet one cannot begin by considering directly Epictetus's views on the emotions. Instead, one must do as he did – first lay the groundwork for understanding his ethical teaching in general and then examine his view of the passions in particular. Here we can only begin to unravel his teaching.

Epictetus asserts the primacy of reason (ἡ λογικὴ δύναμις, *hē logikē dynamis*)[20] at the outset in 1.1.[21] It is the only faculty that stands in judgment over itself (αὐτῆς θεωρητικῆς, *autēs theōrētikēs*) (*Diss.* 1.1.4)[22] and over all other faculties as well. Because the rational faculty makes use of external impressions or appearances (ἡ χρηστικὴ δύναμις ταῖς φαντασίαις, *hē chrēstikē dynamis tais phantasiais*), it can make distinctions, judge, and approve the use of all other faculties – for example, music and grammar (1.1.5–6).[23] "The correct use of appearances [by the rational faculty] comprehends the whole of ethics for Epictetus" (De Lacy 1943: 114), because "the gods put only this, the best thing that controls all others, in our power, the use of appearances" (τὸ κράτιστον ἁπάντων καὶ κυριεῦον οἱ θεοὶ μόνον ἐφ' ἡμῖν ἐποίησαν) (1.1.7).

A.A. Long calls attention to the Stoic definition of πρόσωπον (*prosōpon*, Latin *figura*). "By the time of Roman Stoicism, the term *prosōpon*, 'role', had become a way of designating a person's character and the 'performance' expected of one." (Long 2006b: 15; cf. 2006c: 335: "*Persona* is not primarily what a human being is, but rather a role or status a human being has or maintains or undertakes or bears or assumes...."). Epictetus, *Diss.* 1.2 bears the title "How one can preserve one's πρόσωπον in every respect." Its opening words are "For the rational being only the irrational is unbearable, but the rational is bearable." *Diss.* 2.10 shows how one may have many *prosōpa*, and how rationality has implications for each. Rationality is fundamental to understanding the human being.

This rational faculty can draw inferences (ἡ παρακολουθητικὴ δύναμις, *hē parakolouthētikē dynamis*) [1.6.15]) so that one can act according to method in an orderly fashion (1.6.15). Indeed, one's decisions (προαίρεσις, *prohairesis*) are all that is in one's power (τὰ ἐφ' ἡμῖν, *ta eph' hēmin*); therefore, ethical action lies in moral decision (2.5.4–5) (Striker 1996b: 279).

Humans, endowed with reason, avoid the irrational (τὸ ἄλογον, *to alogon*) but endure the rational (1.2.1). Nature (φύσις, *physis*) becomes the criterion of the rational, since humans are to live according to nature (κατὰ φύσιν ζῆν, *kata physin zēn*), in logical consistency with nature (ὁμολογουμένως τῇ φύσει, *homologoumenōs tē physei*), and in harmony with nature (συμφώνως τῇ φύσει, *symphōnos tē physei*) (3.1.25; 1.2.6). Therefore, an understanding of nature (ἡ φύσις) and its significance for the human being are essential.[24]

What distinguishes a human being from all other living beings is the rational faculty; that determines the nature of humans. Only the irrational is unbearable for a rational being (τῷ λογικῷ ζῴῳ μόνον ἀφόρητόν ἐστι τὸ ἄλογον, *to logikō zōō monon aphorēton esti to alogon* [1.2.1]). Thus, the goal of philosophy and of life is to learn what does not conform to the rational, since different people distinguish the rational and irrational differently (ἄλλῳ δ' ἄλλο προσπίπτει τὸ εὔλογον καὶ ἄλογον, καθάπερ καὶ ἀγαθὸν καὶ κακὸν ἄλλο ἄλλῳ καὶ συμφέρον καὶ ἀσύμφορον [1.2.5]). Therefore, we need education (παιδεία, *paideia*) "to learn to correlate our concept of rational and irrational to particular cases in a manner consonant with nature"[25]; for that, each one uses not only valuations of externals but also valuations of what things are congruent with our own self-understanding (τῶν κατὰ τὸ πρόσωπον ἑαυτοῦ, *tōn kata to prosōpon heatou* [1.2.7]).

Reason determines whether we rush toward external appearances or away from them, whether we desire them or avoid them.[26] Epictetus places ethical actions in the realm of the internal rationality, which unites humans with the gods. In 1.1, he stresses the rational character of ethics, and in 1.2 the need to live "in accordance with [one's] nature" (συμφώνως τῇ φύσει, *symphōnos tē physei* [1.2.6]). That means that one must know one's nature and act accordingly (1.2.7).

How does one do this? A key text is 1.4, "On Progress" (Περὶ προκοπῆς, *Peri prokopēs*). Epictetus begins by citing a "philosopher's truism" in the first sentence, which sets the tone. He introduces three *topoi* that are crucial for ethical decisions: (1) desire and avoidance, which deals with passions; (2) impulse and repulsion, which deals with duty; and (3) avoidance of error and precipitous judgment, which is fitting for those who are making progress, concerned with being unimpeded (ἀσφάλεια, *asphaleia*) in the first two.[27]

> He who is making progress, having learned from the philosophers that desire is for good things and avoidance is toward bad things, and having also learned that impassivity and a good flow of life are not otherwise attained than through unerring desire and unfailing avoidance – such a person has removed desire from himself altogether, or else deferred it to another time, and exercises avoidance only toward things within the sphere of choice.
> (1.4.1 [trans. Dobbin 1998: 9])[28]

Note that a good flow of life and impassivity – that is, freedom from *pathē* – are coordinated, as are εὐδαιμονία, ἀπάθεια καὶ εὔροια in 1.4.3: "Virtue [ἡ ἀρετή, *hē aretē*] promises to produce happiness, freedom from passions, and serenity; certainly the progress in relation to each of these is progress" [1.4.3]).[29] Serenity is the function or product (ἔργον, *ergon* [1.4.5] of virtue. Reading books, even all of those written by Chrysippus,[30] does not produce progress. Rather, one asks whether one properly uses choice and avoidance, whether one trembles or has grief or does not (1.4.5–12).[31] Thus, the emotions work against progress in virtue because they enslave one and prevent true freedom. Epictetus later says that reading Chrysippus's treatise Περὶ τοῦ ψευδομένου (*On Falsehood*) will only produce sadness and trembling (πενθῶν ἅπαν ἀναγνώσῃ καὶ τρέμων πρὸς ἄλλους ἐρεῖς [2.17.34]).[32] What counts is "how you move toward a goal or away from it, how you are enamored and how you avoid, how you approach things, put them together, and how you prepare yourself, whether in a manner harmonious to nature or discordant" (1.4.14).[33] Progress lies in recognizing what is in one's power (τὰ ἐφ' ἡμῖν, *ta eph' hēmin*) and working to bring one's desires into concord with nature.[34] Then choice is "lofty, free, unhindered, unimpeded, trustworthy, pious."[35] To desire or flee things not in one's power is to be at the mercy of externals.[36]

Then what is the utility of reading? Epictetus does not think that Greek tragedies are useful, since they stress the emotions of people that arise from externals (1.4.26). What, then, is the goal of reading? It is

> to practice to remove from his life mourning and expressions of sorrow [πένθη καὶ οἰμωγαί] and that "Woe is me" and that "O wretch that I am" and ill fortune and failure [δυστυχία καὶ ἀτυχία] and to learn what death is, what exile is, what a prison is, what hemlock is, in order to be able to say in prison, "My dear Crito, if it is dear to the gods, let it happen in this way,"[37] and not that "Wretch that I am, an old man, for such things have I preserved my gray locks" (1.4.23–4).[38]

But Chrysippus can aid: "What does Chrysippus offer us? That you may know that these things are not false, from which serenity and *apatheia* meet us, take my books and recognize how the things that make me free from *pathē* are logical and congruent to nature."[39] Thus, reading philosophy can instruct the mind, and so it is useful for controlling the passions.

Ἀπάθεια, that is, a life unencumbered by human passions or emotions, was one aspect of such a life. For Epictetus, these emotions are ultimately four in number: fear, desire, grief, pleasure (φόβος, *phobos*; ἐπιθυμία, *epithymia*; λύπη, *lypē*; ἡδονή, *hēdonē*).[40] Emotions (πάθη) arise when that which makes human beings what they are, their logical and rational nature (the governing [faculty], τὸ ἡγεμονικόν, *to hēgemonikon*), no longer governs their life. Epictetus did not call it τὸ ἡγεμονικόν for no reason. Emotions are internal motions of the mind that react to external stimuli (φαινόμενα, *phainomena*).

The philosopher differs from the nonphilosopher (ἰδιότης, *idiotēs*) in this respect. Nonphilosophers grieve because of their child, their brother, or their father. The philosopher says οὐαί μοι δι' ἐμέ ("Woe to me because of myself," 3.19.1); that is, the cause for grief is internal, not external. It is the result of a faulty upbringing (3.19.5).[41] Nothing can prevent προαίρεσις (*prohairesis*); it can only hamper or injure itself (3.19.2). Therefore, if one aims at proper choice, so that "whenever we fail, we blame ourselves and recall that there is no other cause of unrest or upset than our opinion, then I swear by the gods that we are making progress" (3.19.3).[42]

Epictetus applies this fundamental insight to a whole series of possibilities. One must control desires and so avoid emotions. It is externals that disturb and cause emotions. An ἀπορία (*aporia*, perplexity)[43] comes to people from externals (περὶ τὰ ἐκτός, *peri ta ektos*) (4.10.1). Therefore, one must learn not to desire things that are not one's own and to avoid all things not in one's control (4.10.6). One must control impressions that come from the outside by recognizing that they do not affect one. No news, good or bad, can upset you (3.18): not news of a death, of calumny, of disinheritance, of the guilt of impiety. Your function is to speak your apology firmly, with proper respect, without anger (εὐσταθῶς, αἰδημόνως, ἀοργήτως, *eustathōs, aidēmonōs, aorgētōs* [3.18.6]). If you are free from fear, you are ἄλυπος (*alypos*). Providence (πρόνοια, *pronoia*) has outfitted us by nature to use our unique equipment (κατασκευή, *kataskeuē*) to see God and be his interpreter (1.6.19). Illness should cause no fear, for "everything that is according to nature comes to be in a correct manner" (πᾶν τὸ κατὰ φύσιν γινόμενον ὀρθῶς γίνεται [1.11.5]). Even those emotions that arise from sympathy with another are not good – unless it is the συμπασχεῖν (*sympaschein*) that one feels with what is in heaven (1.14.2)! What, then, is virtue (ἀρετή, *aretē*)? Zeno (or Chrysippus) defined it as follows: "a disposition and faculty of the governing principle of the soul brought into being by reason, or rather: reason itself, consistent, firm and unwavering."[44]

In 3.22.13, "On the Cynic," Epictetus sums it up as follows:

> It is necessary for you to remove desire absolutely, to turn your avoidance to the things that are within the province of your choice [ὄρεξιν ἆραί σε δεῖ παντελῶς, ἔκκλισιν ἐπὶ μόνα μεταθεῖναι τὰ προαιρετικά]; you should have no anger, no wrath, no envy, no mercy [σοὶ μὴ ὀργὴν εἶναι, μὴ μῆνιν, μὴ φθόνον, μὴ ἔλεον]; no little girl should appear fair to you, no little public reputation, no young boy, no little darling [μὴ κοράσιόν σοι φαίνεσθαι καλόν, μὴ δοξάριον, μὴ παιδάριον, μὴ πλακουντάριον]. In short, say no to all emotions, positive or negative, in all areas of life.

In 2.21, he deals with emotions that people value falsely because they are involuntary: timidity (τὸ δειλόν, *to deilon*), pity (τὸ ἔλεος, *to eleos*), jealousy (τὸ ζηλότυπος, *to zēlotypos*). Epictetus denies that they are not under the control of the will. God "has turned you over to yourself [as a rational being] and says [to you], I have no one else more trustworthy than you; keep yourself such as you are by nature: reverent, faithful, elevated, unaffected by events, without passion, undisturbed" (2.8.23).[45]

In 4.8.20, he presents himself as a model: "Note how I eat, how I drink, how I sleep, how I endure, how I abstain, how I co-operate, how I use desire, how aversion, how I maintain the natural or contrived relationships without confusion and without obstruction. Judge me from that, if you can."[46] Epictetus runs together the mundane things of life with the technical vocabulary of ethics. The passions relate to all, without exception. Although he uses himself as a model, he also uses others as models of control of the passions. The list is too long to enumerate here; it includes philosophers, athletes, mythical figures, and so on. But one negative example is instructive: How do we harmonize our preconceptions to specific cases? What happens if you want something and do not get it (2.17.18). It caused Medea to kill her children. She (and the hearer) should have given up everything but what God wanted (2.17.19–22).[47] Epictetus then provides a long list of externals that one should give up (2.17.24). The study of syllogisms will not make one ἀπαθής (*apathēs*), free from *pathē*. Rather, let a young man seek to live without impediments and without grief, which is the first field of study, and he will be without passions and not be disturbed (2.17.31).

Julia Annas (1992: 103–20) discusses the emotions in Stoicism under six headings: "Emotions as Irrational Movements in the Soul"; "Emotions as Beliefs"; "Emotions as Involving a 'Fresh' Belief"; "The Taxonomy of the Emotions"; "Good Feelings"; and "The Unity of the Soul." She draws primarily on Arius and Galen in discussing these topics, not once referring to Epictetus. But her categories fit him too.

Epictetus urges ἀταραξία (*ataraxia*) and ἀπάθεια (*apatheia*).[48] By these, however, he does not mean noninvolvement or disinterestedness; rather they describe imperturbability, the triumph of mind over disturbance arising from without, the mastery of circumstances, against which anger, fear, love, hatred, despair, friendship, desire, and the like work. One should not be apathetic like a statue; no one must keep the natural and acquired states, as a pious person, a son, a brother, a father, a citizen (3.2.4). In 1.27, he considers the fear of death an example of how to provide aids against impressions (φαντασίαι, *phantasiai*). One must not allow something that distresses to become a habit (ἔθος, *ethos*) (1.27.3). One needs to recognize the inevitability of death; therefore, as W.A. Oldfather (1925–8: 1.172 n. 1) notes, death is not an evil (1.27.9). Epictetus continues, "Although not able to escape fear of it, still, shall I die while lamenting and trembling? For this is the birth of πάθος (emotion, suffering), to desire something and not have it come to pass."[49]

One needs to struggle against external impressions. Every habit and faculty is strengthened and confirmed by reciprocal actions – true of physical action, it is also of mental. Get angry and you have strengthened that habit. If you once desire money, bring reason into the perception of evil; then the desire is stopped and the governing principle is restored to its original authority (2.18.8). Therefore, there are three fields of study in which the καλὸς καὶ ἀγαθός (*kalos kai agathos*) must be trained: (1) concerning desires and avoidances (ὀρέξεις καὶ ἐκκλίσεις, *orexeis kai ekkliseis*); (2) choice and refusal (ὁρμὴ καὶ ἀφορμή, *hormē kai aphormē*) and in general duty (τὸ καθῆκον, *to kathēkon*); (3) concerning avoidance of error and rashness in judgment, in general about cases of assent (ἀνεξαπατησία, *anexapatēsia*; συγκαταθέσεις, *synkatatheseis*). These must, in the first place, deal with the emotions (3.2.3–5)! *Pathos* arises when desire or aversion fails, as is made clear by examples of passions that make it impossible to listen to reason.

The theory of emotions has a long history.[50] Much later, Maximus the Confessor believed that ἀπάθεια was the goal of the spiritual life and held that true Christians are those who "pass beyond the disturbances brought about by the passions."[51]

There is much more that one should discuss in both Arius Didymus and Epictetus. A partial list of additional topics would include the use of θεραπεία (*therapeia*) and ἁρμονία (*harmonia*) as images for the control of the emotions; the possible correlation of the four *pathē* with the four virtues; the use of positive language about some emotions;[52] Epictetus's own use of emotions as teacher; and so forth.

Juvenal wrote lines that reflect this Stoic attitude and serve as a fitting conclusion to this discussion:

> Pray for a brave heart, which does not fear death,
> which places a long life last among the gifts
> of nature, which has the power to endure any trials,
> rejects anger, discards desire....
> If we have common sense, Chance, you are not divine:
> it is we who make you a goddess, yes, and place you in heaven.[53]

Notes

1 Pomeroy (1999: 2–3) provides a useful summary of what can be known about Arius Didymus.

2 Long (1996a: 107–33) calls attention to parallel accounts of Stoic ethics in Diogenes Laertius 7.84–131; Cicero, *Fin.* 3.16–76.

3 A.A. Long (2002: 34) says that the most comprehensive treatment of Epictetus's life, dated but useful, is that of Th. Colardeau (1903).

4 On Stoicism in antiquity, see esp. Barth (1946), Pohlenz (1964), Edelstein (1966), Rist (1969), Frede (1986), and Erskine (1990).

5 Seneca, who writes in Latin, is the only other first century source we have. For his view of the emotions, see Inwood 1993. For an overview of Roman Stoicism, see Arnold 1911.

6 For a characterization of the Augustan era, see Galinsky 1996.

7 ἔστι δὲ αὐτὸ τὸ πάθος κατὰ Ζήνωνα ἡ ἄλογος καὶ παρὰ φύσιν ψυχῆς κίνησις (Diogenes Laertius 7.110 [=*SVF* 1.205]; cited according to H.S. Long 1964). Translations of Diogenes Laertius are my own, although instructed by R.D. Hicks's edition (1925) in the LCL. Arius Didymus gives similar definitions (Stobaeus, *Ecl.* 2.88); cf. Cicero, *Tusc.* 4.11: *aversa a recta ratione contra naturam animi commotio*. References are from Bonhöffer 1890: 262.

8 δοκεῖ δ' αὐτοῖς τὰ πάθη κρίσεις εἶναι, καθά φησι Χρύσιππος ἐν τῷ Περὶ παθῶν. ἥ τε γὰρ φιλαργυρία ὑπόληψίς ἐστι τοῦ τὸ ἀργύριον καλὸν εἶναι, καὶ ἡ μέθη δὲ καὶ ἡ ἀκολασία ὁμοίως καὶ τἄλλα: "The *pathē* seem to be decisions, as Chrysippos says in his 'On *Pathē*.' Love of money is the supposition that silver is good, and drunkenness, and in similar fashion debauchery, and the others" (Diogenes Laertius 7.111).

9 J. Annas comments, "*Pathos* does not mean 'emotion'; it is a more general term, which can cover a wide range of what one 'suffers' or what is done to one (*pathein*). However, what the Stoics (and Epicureans and a wide range of ancient philosophers) are discussing is clearly, from the key examples and key theses, emotions such as anger, fear, and joy. The discussion also covers some cases of what we would call feelings that do not amount to emotions, such as desires and feelings of pleasure or repulsion. However, 'emotions' seems a better general term in English than 'feelings,' and it is certainly more suitable for the Stoics, although the Epicurean account makes feelings more central" (Annas 1992: 103 n. 1).

10 For an extended discussion of the passions in early Stoicism, see Inwood 1985: 127–81.

11 Striker 1996: 271 (in her essay "Following Nature: A Study in Stoic Ethics"). See also Brennan 1998: 30–1.

12 A.A. Long (1996a: 130–3) gives a helpful "Table of ethical theses in Stobaeus II, pp. 57–85." H. Diels (1929: 69–88) discusses the authorship of the doxographical fragments of Arius found in Eusebius, *Praeparatio Evangelica* and scattered throughout Stobaeus.

13 I follow the structure worked out by A.A. Long 1996a: 111–22.

14 In what follows, I restrict myself to citing Pomeroy's 1999 edition and giving the equivalent text in the edition of Stobaeus by Wachsmuth and Hense 1884–1912.

15 I insert the key Greek terminology into the text in brackets.

16 The translation is that of Pomeroy 1999: 57, 59. This text is also cited in a slightly different translation in Long and Sedley 1987: 1.410–11, no. 65A.

17 For a good discussion, see Long and Sedley 1987: 1.419–21.

18 M. Nussbaum argues that there are two Stoic interpretations of the passions. Posidonius presents the "non-cognitive view," which was held earlier by Diogenes of Babylon. He views the passions as "movements of a separate irrational part of the soul" that are not affected by rational thought (Nussbaum 1993: 100, 109–21). The "cognitive view" of Chrysippus (and probably also of Zeno [Nussbaum 1993: 100]) holds that passions are rational judgments that assent to appearance and hence are subject to intellectual education. Nussbaum says that both Seneca and Epictetus follow Chrysippus, to whom we can add Arius Didymus.

19 R.F. Dobbin observes that Book 1 is "philosophically the richest of the four, which is one reason why a detailed commentary on it can serve almost as a complete guide to Epictetus's thought" (Dobbin 1998: xix).

20 This dependence on logic for ethics is characteristic of Stoic philosophy in general. See A.A. Long's essay "The Logical Basis of Stoic Ethics" (in Long 1996b: 134–55). Long more recently wrote that "... the ancient Stoics, like some contemporary philosophers, rejected the idea that emotions are the manifestation of an irrational or non-rational component to our minds. Rather they proposed that, far from being animal-like drives, emotions actually are judgements, issuing from the mind in its motivational function, and manifesting complex beliefs and propositional attitudes; they are activities of a uniformly rational mind because only a rational mind could be subject to human emotions" (Long 2006d: 379).

21 I am indebted here to De Lacy 1943: 112–25.

22 I cite Epictetus from Schenkl 1965. References to the *Dissertationes* (*Diss.*) of Epictetus are by standard book, chapter, and section numbers.

23 1.1.12 introduces key terms: "impulse for" (ὁρμητική, *hormētikē*) and the "impulse away from" (ἀφορμητική, *aphormētikē*), the impulse that desires (ὀρεκτική, *orektikē*) and the impulse that avoids (ἐκκλιτική, *ekklitikē*).

24 J. Annas comments, "In all areas of philosophy there is appeal to the notions of nature and of reason, which have two roles, in the world as a whole and in us humans" (Annas 1996: 1446).

25 μαθεῖν τοῦ εὐλόγου καὶ ἀλόγου πρόληψιν ταῖς ἐπὶ μέρους οὐσίαις ἐφαρμόζειν συνφώνως τῇ φύσει (1.2.6).

26 ἐδώκαμέν σοι μέρος τι ἡμέτερον, τὴν δύναμιν ταύτην τὴν ὁρμητικήν τε καὶ ἀφορμητικὴν καὶ ὀρεκτικήν τε καὶ ἐκκλιτικὴν καὶ ἁπλῶς τὴν χρηστικὴν ταῖς φαντασίαις: "We have given to you some portion of ourselves, the faculty both to move toward and to move away, both to desire and to avoid, and in short the faculty to use sense impressions" (1.1.12; cf. 1.20.15–16).

27 These three *topoi* are presented here and, more fully, in 3.2.2. See Dobbin 1998: 92–3.

28 ὁ προκόπτων μεμαθηκὼς παρὰ τῶν φιλοσόφων ὅτι ἡ μὲν ὄρεξις ἀγαθῶν ἐστιν, ἡ δὲ ἔκκλισις πρὸς κακά, μεμαθηκὼς δὲ καὶ ὅτι οὐκ ἄλλως τὸ εὔρουν καὶ ἀπαθὲς περιγίνεται τῷ ἀνθρώπῳ ἢ ἐν ὀρέξει μὲν μὴ ἀποτυγχάνοντι, ἐν ἐκκλίσει <δὲ> μὴ περιπίπτοντι, τὴν μὲν ὄρεξιν ἦρκεν ἐξ αὑτοῦ εἰσάπαν καὶ ὑπερτέθειται, τῇ ἐκκλίσει δὲ πρὸς μόνα χρῆται τὰ προαιρετικά.

29 εἰ δὲ ἡ ἀρετὴ ταύτην ἔχει τὴν ἐπαγγελίαν εὐδαιμονίαν ποιῆσαι καὶ ἀπάθειαν καὶ εὔροιαν, πάντως καὶ ἡ προκοπὴ <ἡ> πρὸς αὐτὴν πρὸς ἕκαστον τούτων.

30 Diogenes Laertius 7.189–202 gives a long, if incomplete, list of Chrysippus' works.

31 Epictetus uses the athlete's jumping weights (οἱ ἁλτῆρες, *hoi haltēres*) as a marvelous example of the function of philosophical writing; they are aids, not an end (1.4.13).

32 For Epictetus on Chrysippus and the emotions, see 2.17.29–34.

33 πῶς ὁρμᾷς καὶ ἀφορμᾷς, πῶς ὀρέγῃ καὶ ἐκκλίνεις, πῶς ἐπιβάλλῃ καὶ προτίθεσαι καὶ παρασκευάζῃ, πότερα συμφώνως τῇ φύσει ἢ ἀσυμφώνως.

34 εἴ τις ὑμῶν ἀποστὰς τῶν ἐκτὸς ἐπὶ τὴν προαίρεσιν ἐπέστραπται τὴν αὑτοῦ, ταύτην ἐξεργάζεσθαι καὶ ἐκπονεῖν, ὥστε σύμφωνον ἀποτελέσθαι τῇ φύσει, ὑψηλὴν ἐλευθέραν ἀκώλυτον ἀνεμπόδιστον πιστὴν αἰδήμονα· ... οὗτός ἐστιν ὁ προκόπτων ταῖς ἀληθείαις: "If one of you moving away from externals turns to his own choice, works this out and labors at it so as to bring it into conformity with his nature, exalted, free,

unimpeded, without obstructions, trustworthy [or true], pious, ... he is the one making progress in true things" (1.4.18, with some omissions).
35 ὑψηλὴν ἐλευθέραν ἀκώλυτον ἀνεμπόδιστον πιστὴν αἰδήμονα (1.4.18).
36 μεμάθηκέν τε, ὅτι ὁ τὰ μὴ ἐφ' αὑτῷ ποθῶν ἢ φεύγων οὔτε πιστὸς εἶναι δύναται οὔτ' ἐλεύθερος, ἀλλ' ἀνάγκη μεταπίπτειν καὶ μετα<ρ>ριπίζεσθαι ἅμα ἐκείνοις καὶ αὐτόν, ἀνάγκη δὲ καὶ ὑποτετάχέναι ἄλλοις ἑαυτόν, τοῖς ἐκεῖνα περιποιεῖν ἢ κωλύειν δυναμένοις: "he has learned that one is not able to be faithful or free while desiring or fleeing things not in his power, but must necessarily change and be disturbed along with them, and must also subject himself to others, who can obtain those things [for him] or prevent them" (1.4.19).
37 Citing Plato, *Crito* 43D.
38 A stock phrase in tragedy.
39 Τί οὖν ἡμῖν παρέχει Χρύσιππος; ἵνα γνῷς, φησίν, ὅτι οὐ ψευδῆ ταῦτά ἐστιν, ἐξ ὧν ἡ εὔροιά ἐστι καὶ ἀπάθεια ἀπαντᾷ, λάβε μου τὰ βιβλία καὶ γνώσῃ ὡς ἀκολουθά τε καὶ σύμφωνά ἐστι τῇ φύσει τὰ ἀπαθῆ με ποιοῦντα (1.4.28).
40 Bonhöffer 1894: 46 (ET, 1996: 77).
41 Bonhöffer 1890: 274.
42 ὅταν δυσοδῶμεν, αὑτοὺς αἰτιᾶσθαι καὶ μεμνῆσθαι, ὅτι οὐδὲν ἄλλο ταραχῆς ἢ ἀκαταστασίας αἴτιόν ἐστιν ἢ δόγμα, ὀμνύω ὑμῖν πάντας θεούς, ὅτι προεκόψαμεν (3.19.3).
43 Oldfather (1925–8: 2.397) translates this as "difficulty."
44 Zeno, *SVF* 1.202 (Plutarch, *Virt. mor.* 441C): κοινῶς δὲ ἅπαντες οὗτοι τὴν ἀρετὴν τοῦ ἡγεμονικοῦ τῆς ψυχῆς διάθεσίν τινα καὶ δύναμιν γεγενημένην ὑπὸ λόγου, μᾶλλον δὲ λόγον οὖσαν αὐτὴν ὁμολογούμενον καὶ βέβαιον καὶ ἀμετάπτωτον ὑποτίθενται· καὶ νομίζουσιν οὐκ εἶναι τὸ παθητικὸν καὶ ἄλογον διαφορᾷ τινι καὶ φύσει ψυχῆς τοῦ λογικοῦ διακεκριμένον, ἀλλὰ τὸ αὐτὸ τῆς ψυχῆς μέρος, ὃ δὴ καλοῦσι διάνοιαν καὶ ἡγεμονικόν, διόλου τρεπόμενον καὶ μεταβάλλον ἔν τε τοῖς πάθεσι καὶ ταῖς κατὰ ἕξιν ἢ διάθεσιν μεταβολαῖς, κακίαν τε γίνεσθαι καὶ ἀρετήν, καὶ μηδὲν ἔχειν ἄλογον ἐν ἑαυτῷ· λέγεσθαι δὲ ἄλογον, ὅταν τῷ πλεονάζοντι τῆς ὁρμῆς ἰσχυρῷ γενομένῳ καὶ κρατήσαντι πρός τι τῶν ἀτόπων παρὰ τὸν αἱροῦντα λόγον ἐκφέρηται· καὶ γὰρ τὸ πάθος εἶναι λόγον πονηρὸν καὶ ἀκόλαστον, ἐκ φαύλης καὶ διημαρτημένης κρίσεως σφοδρότητα καὶ ῥώμην προσλαβόντα: "All these men agree in taking virtue to be a certain character and power of the soul's commanding-faculty, engendered by reason, or rather, a character which is itself consistent, firm, and unchangeable reason. They suppose that the passionate and irrational part is not distinguished from the rational by any distinction within the soul's nature, but the same part of the soul (which they call thought and commanding-faculty) becomes virtue and vice as it wholly turns around and changes in passions and alterations of tenor or character, and contains nothing irrational within itself. It is called irrational whenever an excessive impulse which has become strong and dominant carries it off towards something wrong and contrary to the dictates of reason. For passion is vicious and uncontrolled reason which acquires vehemence and strength from bad and erroneous judgement" [trans. Long–Sedley 1987: 1.378, 61B].
45 παραδέδωκέ σοι σεαυτὸν καὶ λέγει· οὐκ εἶχον ἄλλον πιστότερόν σου· τοῦτόν μοι φύλασσε τοιοῦτον οἷος πέφυκεν, αἰδήμων, πιστός, ὑψηλός, ἀκατάπληκτος, ἀπαθής, ἀτάραχος.
46 βλέπε πῶς ἐσθίω, πῶς πίνω, πῶς καθεύδω, πῶς ἀνέχομαι, πῶς ἀπέχομαι, πῶς συνεργῷ, πῶς ὀρέξει χρῶμαι, πῶς ἐκκλίσει, πῶς τηρῶ τὰς σχέσεις τὰς φυσικὰς ἢ ἐπιθέτους ἀσυγχύτως καὶ ἀπαραποδίστως· ἐκεῖθέν με κρῖνε, εἰ δύνασαι.

47 καὶ ἁπλῶς μηδὲν ἄλλο θέλε ἢ ἃ ὁ θεὸς θέλει. καὶ τίς σε κωλύσει, τίς ἀναγκάσει; οὐ μᾶλλον ἢ τὸν Δία (2.17.22).
48 For ἀταραξία (*ataraxia*), see 1.4.27; 2.1; 2.5.2; 2.18.29; 4.6.9; and Xenakis 1969: 81–2.
49 οὐ δύναμαι τὸν θάνατον ἀποφυγεῖν· τὸ φοβεῖσθαι αὐτὸν μὴ ἀποφύγω. ἀλλ' ἀποθάνω πενθῶν καὶ τρέμων; αὕτη γὰρ γένεσις πάθους θέλειν τε καὶ μὴ γίνεσθαι (1.27.10).
50 For a history of theories concerning feelings and emotions, see Gardiner *et al.* 1937.
51 Maximus the Confessor, *Quaestiones ad Thalassium*, Ins. 71–2 (cited in Wilken 1995: 146).
52 Brennan (1998: 34–5) mentions joy, volition, and caution, called εὐπάθειαι.
53 orandum est ut sit mens sana in corpore sano;
fortem posce animum mortis terrore carentem,
qui spatium vitae extremum inter munera ponat
naturae, qui ferre queat quoscumque labores,
nesciat irasci, cupiat nihil
... si sit prudentia: nos te,
nos facimus, Fortuna, deam caeloque locamus.
(Juvenal, *Sat.* 10.356–66 [trans. MacInnes 1955: 279])

7

PLUTARCH ON MORAL PROGRESS

Richard A. Wright

This essay illustrates Plutarch's understanding of moral progress from his essay *Progress in Virtue*. In contrast to certain Stoic understandings of progress, Plutarch argued that visible indicators are absolutely essential for making progress toward virtue. Without such signs, progress is impossible. Plutarch was very much a part of the larger Hellenistic moral philosophical context in his treatment of the topic. He understood the passions to be at the core of the problem that students of philosophy had to address. He argued that the passions must be domesticated (not eradicated) but that when that task was accomplished, they assisted in progress toward virtue. Having argued for the observability of indicators of progress, Plutarch outlined a number of signposts that, if observed, assist the philosophical traveler on the journey toward virtue.

Introduction

Plutarch takes up the topic of moral progress in his essay *Quomodo quis suos in virtute sentiat profectus* (hereafter referred to as *Progress in Virtue*, and cited as *Virt. prof.*).[1] This treatise provides a convenient entry into Plutarch's ideas about the possibility of progressing toward virtue and his identification of signposts along the way.

Progress in Virtue fits in the context of Plutarch's larger collection of writings against the Stoics.[2] Even though Plutarch does not explicitly identify the Stoics as his opponents in this essay, he begins his discussion with a critique of two ideas concerning moral progress that he elsewhere links explicitly with the Stoics.[3] First, Stoics had argued that there are no gradations of errors: only virtue is good, and only vice is bad; everything else is morally indifferent.[4] Stoics who held such views offered several illustrations to make their point: just as a stick is either straight or crooked, so also a person is either virtuous or not (Diogenes Laertius 7.127); a person drowning is unable to breathe whether he or she is near the surface of the water or at the bottom of the pool; a puppy about to open its eyes is no less blind than a newborn.[5] From such a perspective, only one's current moral state is of any import: either one is swimming, living a virtuous life, or one is drowning in a vicious life. The fact that the person might be rising toward the water's surface rather than sinking toward the bottom is not taken into consideration, at least from Plutarch's perspective.[6]

Second, Stoics also claimed that having attained wisdom, one would not necessarily notice the change.[7] This assertion struck Plutarch not only as enigmatic (αἴνιγμα, *ainigma*) but as outright absurd (*Virt. prof.* 76A). Because of the sharp contrast that Stoics drew between virtue and vice, one would expect the change from the vicious state to the virtuous to be dramatic. Plutarch argued,

> Why, it seems to me that anyone who, like Caeneus, were made man from woman in answer to prayer, would sooner fail to recognize the transformation, than that anyone made temperate, wise, and brave, from being cowardly, foolish, and licentious, and transferred from a bestial to a godlike life, should for a single second not perceive what had happened to him.
>
> (*Virt. prof.* 75E–F)[8]

To Plutarch, these Stoic concepts of progress emptied the idea of any meaning. Against these Stoic tenets, Plutarch argued that for there to be any hope of making progress toward virtue, one must be aware that changes are taking place. In his opening statement in *Progress in Virtue* Plutarch asks,

> What possible form of argument ... will keep alive in a man the consciousness that he is growing better in regard to virtue, if it is a fact that the successive stages of his progress produce no abatement of his unwisdom, but, on the contrary, vice constantly besets all progress ...?
>
> (*Virt. prof.* 75A–B)

Plutarch wants to make two points here. First, studying philosophy is analogous to learning many skills or trades. In order to become more proficient, one has to be able to observe signs of improvement. Signs indicate the direction that one must travel to make progress. Plutarch points to musicians and grammarians as occupations that use such signs to tell practitioners where and how to make improvements (*Virt. prof.* 75B–D). Without observable signs of progress, the student will be unable to know how or where improvement is needed.

The second point is related to the first. If signs offer clues to progress, then without these clues, a person is more likely to grow discouraged and give up the pursuit of virtue.

> Those who at the outset [of philosophical pursuit] engage in long excursions into its realms and later meet with a long series of obstacles and distractions without becoming aware of any change toward the better, finally get wearied out, and give up.
> (*Virt. prof.* 77A–B)

For progress to be made toward virtue, then, the student needs cues to identify the path toward the goal and to stave off discouragement caused by lack of feedback.[9]

Although Plutarch begins the essay in an anti-Stoic context, this fact should not lead us into reading the work as primarily written against the Stoics; rather, these ideas provide Plutarch with a necessary springboard from which to launch into his subject. Because the early Stoa had defined progress in a way that, to Plutarch, made it impossible even to take up the subject in any meaningful way, Plutarch must have felt compelled to dispel those ideas.[10] Before Plutarch could address the topic of moral progress proper, he had to establish that such progress is both possible and observable. Once the possibility of observing progress had been established, Plutarch could drop his attack against specific opponents and turn to an extended discussion of the topic.

Moral progress and philosophical therapy

Although Plutarch is careful in *Progress in Virtue* to assert the necessity that progress toward virtue be both possible and visible, he does not attempt to define precisely from what state a person begins to progress. For Stoics, progress was an intermediate stage between vice (κακία, *kakia*) and virtue (ἀρετή, *aretē*).[11] In *Table-Talk* (636B), Plutarch describes progress as a phase between good nature (εὐφυΐα, *euphuia*) – not vice – and virtue. However, this passage is difficult to interpret. The statement is made in an offhand way to support an argument that has nothing to do with issues of moral progress.[12] For the purposes of this essay, it is less important to define precisely where Plutarch placed progress on the continuum from vice to virtue than it is to recognize his insistence that progress must take place and that it be observable.[13]

Plutarch shared a number of ideas with other moral philosophers of the Hellenistic and Roman periods. The overall framework for a discussion of moral progress was commonplace. M. Nussbaum, in her book on therapy in Hellenistic ethics, observes, "According to the Hellenistic philosophers, society is not in order as it is; and, as the source of most of their pupils' beliefs and even their emotional repertory, it has infected them with its sicknesses" (Nussbaum 1994b: 26).[14] Nussbaum's description provides two clues to understanding Plutarch's discussion of moral progress. First, external cues from the world are not trustworthy – their source is corrupt. The student of philosophy must struggle against misperceptions supplied by the environment. Second, many of the terms and analogies that make up the discussion will come from the medical field. The student of philosophy begins the pursuit morally ill and must be cured through the practice of philosophy.

It is in such a context that we should understand Plutarch's emphasis on the need to test ideas and actions. The work of the student of philosophy is to examine the circumstances of, and events in, his or her life in order carefully to construct a moral life. Plutarch explains that "those who are making progress ... do not indiscriminately accept for it [their lives] a single action, but, using reason to guide them, they bring each one into place and fit it where it belongs" (*Virt. prof.* 86A). The emphasis here is that each action must be examined and then categorized on the basis of the examination. The student must refuse to accept, without reflection, external impressions. The student must take seriously each misstep as something that must be changed.[15] Adherence to such a practice will gradually detach the student from the bad habits with which he or she has been infected.

The second cue has to do with the internal struggle that the student of philosophy wages against passions. The description of this struggle often was cast in terms of analogies with medical practices.[16] Moral philosophers of the Hellenistic and Roman periods understood their task to be directly comparable to the work of the medical doctor. As Nussbaum argues,

> Philosophy heals human diseases, diseases produced by false beliefs. Its arguments are to the soul as the doctor's remedies are to the body. They can heal, and they are to be evaluated in terms of their power to heal. As the medical art makes progress on behalf of the suffering body, so philosophy for the soul in distress.
>
> (Nussbaum 1994b: 14)

Plutarch uses the analogy to medical practice regularly. In speaking about the necessity of progress being observable, Plutarch argues that just as the person who is sick requires visible signs of getting better in order to know whether the treatment received is working, so also the student of philosophy must be able to discern that progress is taking place (*Virt. prof.* 75B–C). Again in reference to progress:

> For just as the turning aside of a disease into the less vital parts of the body is an encouraging symptom, so it is reasonable to assume that when the vice of those who are making progress is transformed into more moderate emotions, it is being gradually blotted out.
>
> (*Virt. prof.* 84A)

Like most other moral philosophers of this period, Plutarch associates the passions with sickness or disease.[17] However, the passions play a complex role in Plutarch's description of the journey toward moral health. A full treatment of this topic is beyond the scope of this essay, but we must briefly look at the topic in order to understand Plutarch's description of progress.

To begin with, Plutarch argues in his *On Moral Virtue* that moral or ethical virtue (ἠθικὴ ἀρετή, *ēthikē aretē*) differs from theoretical virtue (θεωρητικὴ ἀρετή, *theōrētikē aretē*) primarily in that the former has the emotions as its matter (ὕλη, *hylē*) (*Virt. mor.* 440D).[18] Passions are thus intrinsic to ethical virtue and cannot be excised without damaging the moral life. Operating from a Platonic–Aristotelian standpoint,[19] he divides the soul into three states: (1) capacity or potentiality (δύναμις, *dynamis*), (2) passion (πάθος, *pothos*), and (3) acquired or settled disposition (ἕξις, *hexis*).[20] He describes capacity (or predisposition) as passion's starting point (ἀρχή, *archē*) and matter (ὕλη, *hylē*), such as a person's proneness to anger (ὀργιλότης, *orgilotēs*); passion proper as a stirring of the soul's capacity by, for example, anger (ὀργή, *orgē*)[21] or shame; and the acquired disposition as the settled state of passion. This state can be either vicious or virtuous, depending on how the passion has been educated (*Virt. mor.* 443D).[22]

For example, on those occasions when a person's philosophical studies get interrupted, the soul becomes stirred. Those who are making progress experience something similar to hunger or thirst when they must temporarily put aside their philosophical pursuits (*Virt. prof.* 77C). Those less disciplined become irrational (ἄλογος, *alogos*) and are driven impulsively (πόθος, *pothos*) back toward philosophy when separated from it (*Virt. prof.* 77C). The same stirring can thus generate very different responses.

In such an understanding, passions are crucial to moral progress.[23] Reason (λόγος, *logos*) is the "form" (εἶδος, *eidos*) that must be imposed on the "matter" (ὕλη, *hylē*) of the emotions if progress is to occur (*Virt. mor.* 440D). Provided that reason molds and controls the passions, they can serve as powerful catalysts stimulating virtuous behavior. Furthermore, when held in moderation, the passions can assist reason by intensifying virtues (*Virt. mor.* 451D–452A). "Reason makes use of the passions when they have been subdued and are tame and does not hamstring or altogether excise that part of the soul which should be its servant" (*Virt. mor.* 451D).[24] Plutarch even talks favorably about the passion that a "progressing" person has for the dispositions of those whom he or she is trying to emulate (πάθος, ὧν ζηλοῦμεν τὰ ἔργα τὴν διάθεσιν φιλεῖν καὶ ἀγαπᾶν) (*Virt. prof.* 84E).[25]

The intent of the moral philosopher, according to Plutarch, is not the eradication of the passions (ἀπάθεια, *apatheia*), which he views as neither possible nor desirable; the goal is rather their domestication, which consists in limiting their scope through the setting of a firm boundary (ὅρος, *horos*) and in establishing order (τάξις, *taxis*) in regard to them. The ethical virtues produced by reason do not eliminate the passions but are the "due proportions of the passions" (συμμετρίας παθῶν, *symmetrias pathōn*) and a proper "mean" (μεσότητας, *mesotētas*) between them (*Virt. mor.* 443C–D).[26] It is, above all, practical reason (φρόνησις, *phronēsis*) that has "to do away with defects and excesses of the passions, and to find the proper mean, μεσότης, between the ἔλλειψις [deficiency] and ὑπερβολή [excess] which, according to Aristotelian teaching, is the characteristic of ethical virtue" (Hershbell 1978: 138).

The key is to have the proper training so that a passion acquires a virtuous rather than a vicious state. One uses reason and discipline (ἄσκησις, *askēsis*) to accomplish this task. Accordingly, to emphasize the importance of reason, Plutarch can even cite Zeno's prescription that the passionate part of the soul should be dissolved by reason (τῆς ψυχῆς ... παθητικὸν διακεχυμένον ὑπὸ τοῦ λόγου) (*Virt. prof.* 82 F = *SVF* 1.234). He underscores the indispensability of discipline by saying that it must take hold of the passionate part of the soul (τῆς ψυχῆς τοῦ παθητικοῦ τὴν ἄσκησιν ἐπιλαβομένην) (*Virt. prof.* 83C).[27] As a result of constant training, the rational use of the passions becomes habitual, and it is through habituation that moral character is formed. Without the emotions, moral character is impossible, for it is a quality of the irrational (ποιότης τοῦ ἀλόγου) part of the soul. To make his point, Plutarch uses a word play, saying that moral character (ἦθος, *ēthos*) is properly named because of the key role played by habit (ἔθος, *ethos*) (*Virt. mor.* 443C).

It is not only the case, though, that passions *may* assist in progressing toward virtue. In fact (as was mentioned above), Plutarch warns that the absence or loss of passions for philosophy may lead to a person giving up the philosophical pursuit altogether (ἐξερρύη τὸ πάθος αὐτῶν ἐκεῖνο, καὶ ῥᾳδίως φέρουσιν) (*Virt. prof.* 77B). The reason for this unfortunate occurrence is clear. When one begins the study of philosophy, the soul is weak and less able to keep external laws and opinions from infecting it (*Virt. prof.* 83D). The lack of training allows the passions to control the student's responses and actions. Plutarch likens the student to

> persons who have left behind the land which they know and are not yet in sight of the land to which they are sailing. For having given up the common and familiar things before gaining knowledge and possession of the better, they are carried hither and thither in the interval, and oftentimes in the wrong direction.
> (*Virt. prof.* 77E)

Novices are unable to control the passionate part of the soul. So when obstacles arise, they may give up all together or may embody irrational desires for "good" things, as when an undisciplined student is driven "impulsively" (πόθος, *pothos*) back toward philosophy after having been separated from it (*Virt. prof.* 77C). The fact that the desire to study philosophy is a good thing does not change the fact that "impulse" reactions are not beneficial. The one making progress, on the other hand, "hungers" to attain the goal. When difficult times occur, doubts of one's ability to accomplish the task may enter (*Virt. prof.* 78A). Yet when good sense (φρόνημα, *phronēma*) quickly and easily conquers such thoughts, a person can be sure that progress is being made.

The passions, therefore, play an important role in making progress toward virtue. Progress toward virtue involves disciplining the passions so that they can help move the student toward the goal.

Diagnosing progress

In depicting the pursuit of the virtuous life in terms of a journey, Plutarch identifies only two states on the path: a person is either progressing or regressing. There is no holding state. A person who stops making progress, unless he or she changes course again quickly, begins to lose whatever progress had previously been made. Vice immediately pulls the person back down (*Virt. prof.* 76D). Plutarch uses the image of a constant war raging against the various pleasures that act as soldiers sent by Vice (*Virt. prof.* 76E). Territory lost during the war must be regained before one can move ahead again.

Throughout the essay, Plutarch identifies a number of areas in which one can look for progress. Because the student of philosophy hones a variety of skills valued by the larger society (but valued for the wrong reasons), one can tell that he or she is making progress by the choices one makes in these areas.

The practice of rhetoric is one area valued by society that requires discipline on the part of the student of philosophy. Therefore, one's approach to rhetoric is a good location for evaluating one's progress. The tendency is to pursue those forms of discourse that will secure a reputation among one's peers, focusing on flash rather than on substance (*Virt. prof.* 78E–F).[28] The student must move beyond ostentatious styles of discourse (e.g., πανηγυρικός, *panēgyrikos*) to styles that deal with character and passion (*Virt. prof.* 79B). The goal for one's discourse should be reasonableness and mildness in discussions: "To avoid a sort of arrogance over success in argument and exasperation over defeat, are the marks of a man making adequate progress" (*Virt. prof.* 80B–C).

Likewise, the student making progress no longer seeks attention from others when having done well or when having refrained from performing some vice (*Virt. prof.* 81A). Immature, self-centered attitudes decrease as one makes progress toward virtue.

Progress is also indicated when one begins to derive benefit from sources in which others only find pleasure. For example, it is a sign of progress when one discovers something profitable in poetry, which others read purely for pleasure (*Virt. prof.* 79D).[29]

Making progress toward the virtuous life is not, however, simply a matter of acquiring sufficient knowledge. It is not enough to know the preferred forms of discourse or where to find knowledge beneficial for virtue. Once one comes to understand what will help lead to virtue, the person who is truly making progress begins to put this knowledge into practice. The ability to put knowledge into practice distinguishes the person making progress from the one who is merely using philosophy to acquire skills that will allow a good appearance before peers (*Virt. prof.* 80A).[30] One needs to "pay careful attention, not only to one's words, but also to one's actions, to see whether the element of usefulness in them prevails over ostentation, and whether their whole aim is the truth rather than display" (*Virt. prof.* 80E). One's actions must arise out of the proper mind set. "Good" or "appropriate" deeds done for the sake of being seen are an indication that one has further to go on the road toward virtue.[31]

Plutarch emphasizes that "the translating of our judgments into deeds, and not allowing our words to remain mere words, but to make them into actions, is above all else, a specific mark of progress" (*Virt. prof.* 84B). After all, in each area where judgments must be made, the societal values are different from those of the virtuous person. To break free from the errors presented by society and translate judgments into correct actions, one has to find and use proper models.[32] Plutarch describes the key tools for achieving the goal in terms of admiration (θαυμάζειν, *thaumazein*) and emulation (ζηλοῦν, *zēloun*).

Because society is infected, people who take up the philosophical quest for virtue will receive criticism from both friends and enemies for this decision. There will be pressure from such people to admire and emulate the wrong things. The tendency is to want to value what the majority value. Unfortunately, society deceives. Plutarch acknowledges that "to cease emulating what the great majority admire is impossible, except for those who have acquired the faculty of admiring virtue" (*Virt. prof.* 78C).

Plutarch recommends that the student make self-comparisons with a good and perfect person.[33] Any shortcomings discovered as a result of the comparison should produce a hope and stimulate a passion to effect change (*Virt. prof.* 84D). As one progresses, one develops a feeling of affection for the disposition of the person being emulated.

> A peculiar symptom of true progress is found in this feeling of love [φιλεῖν, *philein*] and affection [ἀγαπᾶν, *agapan*] for the disposition shown by those whose deeds we try to emulate, and in the fact that our efforts to make ourselves like them are always attended by a goodwill which accords to them a fair meed of honour.
> (*Virt. prof.* 84E)

The comparison identifies the goal toward which one wants to move, and then along the way one is able to tell whether one is closer to obtaining the goal or moving farther away.

The student needs to get to the point of being able to call to mind those who are to be emulated for support when difficulties arise.

> It is also true that the thought and recollection of good men almost instantly comes to mind and gives support to those who are making

> progress towards virtue, and in every onset of the emotions and in all difficulties keeps them upright and saves them from falling.
> (*Virt. prof.* 85B)[34]

As we noted earlier, the passion that stimulates the soul to admire can, left to its own, lead away from virtue. Thus one must be careful not excessively to admire great people. Upon meeting someone of importance, Plutarch warns, the student should not become flustered (*Virt. prof.* 85C). One must be able to distinguish between the disposition to be admired and the person displaying the disposition.

In many ways, this discussion of the emulation and imitation of great persons should be seen as the key to Plutarch's understanding of how one makes progress toward virtue. Several factors contribute to such an understanding. Plutarch spends more time on this discussion than on any other individual topic (*Virt. prof.* 84B–85D). In addition, it is noteworthy that the essay is dedicated to Sosius Senecio, to whom Plutarch also dedicated his *Parallel Lives*.[35] *Progress in Virtue* probably should be read as a companion volume to the *Parallel Lives*, with the former emphasizing what ought to be gained from reading the latter. Plutarch expected Senecio to compare his own life to those included in the *Parallel Lives* and, based on his reading, to find the areas of his life that needed to be improved.[36]

Again, taking up our analogy with medical practices, just as those who have medical ailments seek out a physician to cure them, so also the student of philosophy ought to seek out those who can help cure moral ills (often referred to as a director of souls or psychagogue). Plutarch indicates that it is crucial for success in progressing toward virtue that one be willing, first of all, to recognize and admit shortcomings and further to share that knowledge with someone who can help get rid of those faults (*Virt. prof.* 82C). Plutarch argues,

> And for a man who is in error to submit himself to those who take him to task, to tell what is the matter with him, to disclose his depravity, and not to rejoice in hiding his fault or to take satisfaction in its not being known, but to confess it, and to feel the need of somebody to take him in hand and admonish him, is no slight indication of progress.
> (*Virt. prof.* 82A)

The task of the psychagogue becomes training the student to understand what will help strengthen the soul and provide it with training that leads to virtue (*Virt. prof.* 79F).

One of the tools that the psychagogue as moral physician uses is frank speech or criticism (παρρησία, *parrhēsia*).[37] This tool provides the recipient with trustworthy information with which to correct errors derived from the misperceptions presented by society. How a person receives frank criticism is another indication of the progress being made toward virtue. Plutarch argues that "the incurable are those who take a hostile and savage attitude and show a hot temper toward those who take them to task and admonish them, while those who patiently submit to admonition and welcome it are in less serious plight" (*Virt. prof.* 82A).[38]

In *On the Delays of the Divine Vengeance* (*De sera numinis vindicta*), Plutarch describes god as an additional guide for the journey toward virtue. God provides each individual with a portion of virtue at birth (*Sera* 551D). Because god gives the portion of virtue, he also knows the constitution of each person's soul. As a good physician, god knows the right time to administer medication for the soul in the form of punishment. Not everyone requires the same medication, nor do those who receive the same medicine necessarily require the same dosage (*Sera* 551D–E). Furthermore, Plutarch argues that human beings are in no position to second-guess god's prescriptions (*Sera* 549F–550B).

Another location where one can discern whether progress toward virtue is being made is in a person's dream life. Dreams provide a strong indication of one's progress toward virtue. A person who acts in dreams in ways that he or she would not act while awake still has a distance to go toward virtue. Plutarch recalls Zeno's conclusion that a person was making progress toward virtue

> if he observed that during his period of sleep he felt no pleasure in anything disgraceful, and did not tolerate or commit any dreadful or untoward action, but as though in the clear depth of an absolute calm there came over him the radiant thought that the fanciful and emotional element in his soul had been dispelled by reason.
> (*Virt. prof.* 82F–83A)

Plutarch also quotes Plato to the effect that the irrational part of the soul would reveal its level of maturity in a person's dreams:

> "It attempts incest," and feels a sudden hunger for a great variety of food, acting in lawless fashion, and giving loose rein to the desires which in the daytime the law keeps confined by means of shame and fear.
> (*Virt. prof.* 83A)[39]

These ideas about the capabilities of dreams to indicate the health of the soul are part of a larger recognition in antiquity of the usefulness of dreams for diagnostic purposes. Not all dreams were viewed as meaningful, but those that did have meaning could be divided into subcategories for the purpose of interpretation.[40] Many medical doctors believed that dreams were an important indicator of the body's health.[41] Dreams are frequently discussed in the Hippocratic corpus of writings.[42] In this body of literature dreams are considered a source of information about the health of the body. The fourth chapter of Hippocrates' *Regimen in Acute Diseases* (*Vict.*) is dedicated to a discussion of dreams. According to this treatise, during the day, the soul operates in the service of the body. It divides itself up to provide the necessary functions for the body to operate: seeing, hearing, touching, and so on. While the body sleeps, however, those faculties operate to diagnose the state of the body.[43] The physician, then, is to interpret the dream in order to understand how to treat the patient.

> Those dreams that repeat at night the daily activities or thoughts of a person as happening the same way as they were done or thought during the daytime over a just and right affair are good for a person; for they signify health, since the soul stands by its daily resolutions, and has been mastered by neither surfeit nor depletion nor anything that has fallen from without. But when the dreams are the opposite of the daily actions and some struggle or triumph concerning them occurs, then this signifies that there is a disturbance in the body.
> (Vict. 4.88)[44]

Just as dreams that act out actions contrary to what a person would normally do during the day indicate either the presence of disease or the impending onset of disease, so also dreams evoking immoral actions indicate a soul still in need of treatment and, perhaps, the kind of treatment required.[45]

Conclusion

This essay has illustrated Plutarch's understanding of moral progress. In contrast to certain Stoic understandings, Plutarch argues that for progress toward virtue to be made, it is absolutely essential that there be observable indicators. Without such signs, progress is impossible. Plutarch is very much a part of the larger Hellenistic moral philosophical context in his treatment of the topic. He understands the passions to be at the core of the problem that students of philosophy had to address, but unlike many of his colleagues, Plutarch believes the passions to be an important component for making progress toward virtue. By bringing discipline to passions, the student creates aids for progress toward virtue. Along the way, it is imperative to pay careful attention to the available cues. These signs can be seen in many aspects of a person's life, from the kinds of discourse that one employs to the information derived from one's dreams. For Plutarch, the key to completing a successful journey seems to have been the finding of exemplars in the lives of human beings (or even gods). By gradually bringing one's daily habits into alignment with the model(s), one could in fact progress toward virtue.

Notes

1 For a brief discussion of this treatise and an attempt to relate it to early Christian literature, see Grese 1978. See also the edition and French translation of the treatise by Philippon in Klaerr et al. 1989: 143–87.

2 *On Stoic Self-Contradictions; The Stoics Talk More Paradoxically Than the Poets; On Common Conceptions.* In *Progress in Virtue*, Plutarch uses extensively what had become a Stoic technical term for talking about moral progress: προκοπή (*prokopē*) (and variants). For the most part, Plutarch restricts his use of the term to this particular essay. He uses it once in *The Education of Children* (2A) (although many doubt that Plutarch wrote this essay); once in *On Praising Oneself Inoffensively* (543E); three times in *Table-Talk* (631A [once]; 636B [twice]); once in *The Cleverness of Animals* (962A); and nine times in *On Common Conceptions*. Although the Stoics were not the only ones to use the term, its extensive usage in this essay combined with the anti-Stoic beginning suggests that Plutarch was trying to wrest the term from a peculiarly Stoic understanding.
3 The fact that Plutarch seems to assume that his readers will know to whom these ideas belong, combined with the fact that he does identify these ideas as Stoic in his essay *On Common Conceptions*, leads D. Babut (1969b: 47–52) to argue that *Progress in Virtue* was written after *On Common Conceptions*.
4 Cf. *Comm. not.* 1062E–1063B. Zeno, Persaeus, and Chrysippus reportedly argued that all errors are equal, which implies that the one whose errors are little and the one whose errors are great are equally not perfect (*SVF* 3.527 = Diogenes Laertius 7.120). Note also Cicero: "Moral goodness (*honestum*), in the true and proper sense of the term, is the exclusive possession of the wise and can never be separated from virtue; but those who have not perfect wisdom (*sapientia perfecta*) cannot possibly have perfect moral goodness, but only a semblance of it" (*Off.* 3.3.13 [translations of *De officiis* are from Miller 1913]).
5 *Comm. not.* 1063A; Cicero, *Fin.* 3.14.48.
6 For the purposes of this essay, I do not wish to enter into the long-standing debate about how accurately or fairly Plutarch has depicted the Stoic positions that he wishes to refute (on this issue see Babut 1969b, with the review of Hershbell 1972). My concern is to present Plutarch's own view of moral progress, which he develops in part by using the Stoics as a foil for his arguments.
7 Cf. *Comm. not.* 1062B–1063C; *Stoic. rep.* 1042E–1043A; *Stoic. abs.* 1058B. See also Philo, *Agr.* 160–1 (=*SVF* 3.541, in part) and Arius Didymus, *Epitome of Stoic Ethics* 11n Pomeroy (1999) (=Stobaeus, *Ecl.* 2.7.11n, p. 113 Wachsmuth [in Wachsmuth and Hense 1884–1912] = *SVF* 3.540). For discussions of the Stoic sage who is unaware of his attainment of wisdom, see Pomeroy 1999: 126 n. 211 and esp. Alesse 1997.
8 Translations of *Quomodo quis suos in virtute sentiat profectus* are from Babbitt 1927, occasionally slightly modified.
9 Malherbe (1987: 39–40, 83–4) rightly emphasizes that one of Plutarch's chief concerns in this treatise was the disappointment experienced by beginners who were making slow progress in philosophy and the concomitant need to give them proper encouragement.
10 Toward this end, it does not really make any difference whether Stoics contemporary with Plutarch held these positions. Because the arguments had been made, Plutarch would need to dismiss them before he could properly begin his own discussion of progress.
11 See Luschnat 1958 and Roskam 2004.

12 Plutarch is caught up here in the age-old argument concerning which came first: the chicken or the egg.
13 See Roskam 2004 for a critique of the classic article by Luschnat (1958) and a more nuanced approach to understanding the *Table-Talk* passage.
14 For a detailed treatment of Plutarch in terms of a therapeutic method see Ingenkamp 1971: 74–145.
15 Self-examination was widely practiced by Greco-Roman philosophers, including Epicureans, Middle Platonists, Neopythagoreans, and Stoics, for it was "the *sine qua non* for any progress in virtue" (Thom 1995: 163). See esp. GV 40–4, which was the best known and most quoted section of the Pythagorean *Golden Verses* in antiquity: "Do not welcome sleep upon your soft eyes before you have reviewed each of the days's deeds three times: 'Where have I transgressed? What have I accomplished? What duty have I neglected?' Beginning from the first one go through them in detail, and then, if you have brought about worthless things, reprimand yourself, but if you have achieved good things, be glad" (trans. Thom 1995: 97). Similarly, Epictetus argues from a Stoic perspective the necessity of examining what one finds or experiences in the world: "Make it, therefore, your study at the very outset to say to every harsh external impression [φαντασίᾳ τραχείᾳ], 'You are an external impression and not at all what you appear to be.' After that examine it and test it by these rules which you have" (*Ench.* 1.5 [trans. of Epictetus are from Oldfather 1925–8]).
16 For a discussion of medical imagery in the moral philosophers and the Pastoral Epistles see Malherbe 1989a. Malherbe discusses the use of medical imagery in Plutarch's *How to Tell a Flatterer from a Friend* (in particular, Plutarch's use of παρρησία [*parrhēsia*] on pp. 134–5, including a brief reference to *Progress in Virtue*).
17 Cf. *Virt. prof.* 76 A. For a more detailed discussion of the passions in Plutarch, see Ingenkamp 1971: 74–98.
18 On this work, see esp. Babut 1969a and Hershbell 1978.
19 For the Aristotelian aspects of Plutarch's *On Moral Virtue* (*De virtute morali*), see Etheridge 1961. For the contention that Plutarch remains, despite the Aristotelian components of the treatise, authentically Platonic, see Babut 1969a: 66–75.
20 See esp. Aristotle, *Eth. nic.* 2.5.1–2, and Arius Didymus, *Epitome of Peripatetic Ethics* ap. Stobaeus, *Ecl.* 2.7.20, p. 139 Wachmuth (in Wachsmuth and Hense 1884–1912).
21 For a discussion of the inconsistency in Plutarch's position with respect to anger, see Harris 2001: 118–20.
22 Cf. Aristotle, *Eth. nic.* 2.5.2: "we have a bad disposition in regard to anger if we are disposed to get angry too violently or not violently enough, a good disposition if we habitually feel a moderate amount of anger" (trans. Rackham 1934: 87).
23 For a discussion of Plutarch's treatment of the educational benefit of poetry in this regard, see Schiesaro 1997: 102–4.
24 Translations of *De virtute morali* are from Helmbold 1939. In *Progress in Virtue*, Plutarch can define progress as the "abatement of excess and keenness of passions" (*Virt. prof.* 84A), or as the moderation of passions (*Virt. prof.* 83E). The means by which vice gets eliminated is through a moderation of the passions (*Virt. prof.* 84A) or a lightening of the passions (*Virt. prof.* 79A).
25 The concept of emulation in Plutarch is discussed further below.

26 Again, Plutarch is following the Academic-Peripatetic attempt to moderate the passions over against the early Stoic position that the passions must be extirpated. For a basic discussion of Plutarch and passions, see Dillon 1977: 193–5. For Plutarch and μετριοπάθεια (*metriopatheia*), the moderation of the passions, see Hadzsits 1906: 29–32, and for the debate between Chrysippus and Plutarch, see Dillon 1983: 511–16. For more detail, see Ingenkamp 1971: 90–8.
27 For a discussion of discipline in Plutarch, see Ingenkamp 1971: 99–124.
28 Compare Augustine, who confessed that when he began to frequent Ambrose's sermons, he was listening not to the content, but to Ambrose's style, to see if Ambrose lived up to his stylistic reputation (*Conf.* 5.13–14).
29 Cf. *Adol. poet. aud.* 15F–16A: "Wherefore poetry should not be avoided by those who are intending to pursue philosophy, but they should use poetry as an introductory exercise in philosophy, by training themselves habitually to seek the profitable in what gives pleasure, and to find satisfaction therein" (trans. Babbitt 1927: 81).
30 Cf. Cicero, *Off.* 1.18.60: "So the rules for the discharge of duty are formulated, it is true, as I am doing now, but a matter of such importance requires experience also and practice." Also Epictetus, *Diss.* 1.4.16: "Never look for your work in one place and your progress in another."
31 The Stoics shared a similar concern. In the final analysis, right motive and true knowledge marked the difference between the sage and everyone else. According to Sextus Empiricus, "[The Stoics say] the virtuous man's function is not to look after his parents and honour them in other respects but to do this on the basis of prudence. For just as the care of health is common to the doctor and the layman, but caring for health in the medical way is peculiar to the expert, so too the honouring of parents is common to the virtuous and the not virtuous man, but to do this on the basis of prudence is peculiar to the wise man" (*Math.* 11.200–1 [trans. Long and Sedley 1987: 1.362, 59G]).
32 On the importance of personal example in Hellenistic moral philosophy, see Fiore 1986. Cf. Seneca, *Ep.* 6.5: "I shall therefore send to you the actual books.... Of course, however, the living voice and the intimacy of a common life will help you more than the written word. You must go to the scene of action, first, because men put more faith in their eyes than in their ears, and second, because the way is long if one follows precepts, but short and helpful if one follows patterns" (translations of Seneca are from Gummere 1917). Epicurus also encouraged the use of examples and models among his students. He wrote books about each of his brothers and five concerning Metrodorus (Diogenes Laertius 10.27–8). As D. Clay (1983: 266) has emphasized, these persons became models for the Epicurean of how to die.
33 Plutarch also indicates that god can provide a model for human beings. Specifically, the slowness with which god punishes should be imitated by humans when they punish wickedness (*Sera* 550D–F). D.A. Russell (1973: 87–8) offers a brief discussion of the role of the divine in Plutarch. According to Plutarch, he wrote *On the Delays of the Divine Vengeance* (*De sera numinis vindicta*) to answer Epicurus's denial of divine providence based on the observation that the gods are slow to punish the wicked.
34 Cf. Seneca, *Ep.* 11.9–10: "Happy also is he who can so revere a man as to calm and regulate himself by calling him to mind! ... Choose therefore a Cato; or, if Cato

seems too severe a model, choose some Laelius, a gentler spirit. Choose a master whose life, conversation, and soul-expressing face have satisfied you; picture him always to yourself as your protector or your pattern. For we must indeed have someone according to whom we may regulate our characters."

35 Q. Sosius Senecio, a friend of Emperor Trajan and Pliny the Younger, was *consules ordinarii* in 99 and 107 CE. He was a familiar friend of Plutarch's family, not merely an indifferent patron (cf. *Quaest. conv.* 612E; 666D; 734E). Senecio helped Plutarch obtain public honors. See the discussion in Jones 1971: 55; see also Jones 1970.

36 For a treatment of the difficulties involved in deriving ethical practices from the *Lives*, see T. Duff 1999: 66–71.

37 The use of frank criticism was a prominent feature of Epicurean psychagogy. Philodemus gives the example of Heraclides, who, "deeming the censures for the things that would be revealed to be less {important} than their benefit, he disclosed to Epicurus his errors" (*Lib.* frg. 49 [trans. Konstan *et al.* 1988: 61]). For a more extensive treatment of Philodemus and Epicurean use of frank criticism see Glad 1995; 1996. For Plutarch's use of *parrhēsia* as a sign of friendship, see his *How To Tell a Flatterer from a Friend* and the discussion of this treatise by Engberg-Pedersen 1996.

38 Philodemus, in *On Frank Criticism* (*De libertate dicendi* [*Peri parrhesias*]), raises numerous questions about how to deal with those who resist receiving frank criticism violently (*Lib.* frg. 5); whether one ought to use frank criticism with those unable to endure it (*Lib.* frg. 67); why women (*Lib.* col. XXIb) and persons of repute (*Lib.* col. XIIb) do not receive frank criticism very well.

39 The reference to Plato, from *Resp.* 571D, is repeated in *Virt. vit.* 101 A. Epicurus also argued that if one trained oneself with Epicurean precepts, "then never, either in waking or in dream, wilt thou be disturbed" (*Ep. Men.* 135 = Diogenes Laertius 10.135 [trans. Hicks 1925: 2.659]). Plutarch also suggested that god used dreams as a source for divine punishment: "For visions in dreams, apparitions by day, oracles, the fall of thunderbolts, and all else that gets ascribed to the agency of god bring agonies of terror to those in this state" (*Sera* 555A [trans. De Lacy and Einarson 1959: 221]).

40 See Oberhelman 1993.

41 The exception was physicians who were identified as methodists (Oberhelman 1993: 137–8).

42 That Plutarch had studied the Hippocratic literature is made clear both in *Progress in Virtue* and other treatises: "But the man who is making true progress takes as his example Hippocrates, who published and recorded his failure to apprehend the facts about the cranial sutures" (*Virt. prof.* 82D; cf. *Tu. san.* 122B–137E).

43 See Oberhelman 1993: 130–1.

44 Quoted in Oberhelman 1993: 133.

45 The interpretation of the dream, however, was subject to a consideration of context. A symbol that signified something good under one set of circumstances might signify something bad under another set (Oberhelman 1993: 133).

Part II

PHILOSOPHY AND LITERATURE

8

PASSION AND PROGRESS IN OVID'S *METAMORPHOSES*

S. Georgia Nugent

This essay explores relations between the passions and progress in Ovid's epic poem, the *Metamorphoses*, by focusing on six tales of disastrous passion. In each instance, physical impasse – an inability to progress – provides a means of representing moral impasse of the type Aristotle characterized as *akrasia*. Each of the female protagonists in these tales attempts to master her passion (and thus to progress) through the manipulation of language, but (with one exception – arguably the only tale in the *Metamorphoses* with a positive outcome) none is successful. The physical impasse experienced by these heroines is often followed, after a moment of crisis, by dramatic movement; but that movement is impetuous or even mad – it does not represent moral progress. In fact, in each of the tales – again, with the exception of the anomalous "happy ending" in the case of Iphis – disordered passion not only impedes moral progress, it introduces the element of murder in the family, thus threatening perhaps the most basic form of progress, the chronological succession of generations.

Introduction

This essay explores relations between the passions and progress in Ovid's epic poem, the *Metamorphoses*. Passions abound in the *Metamorphoses*; indeed, a once popular paperback translation proclaimed on its cover that the poem is "an epic of love." Few readers today would endorse that description, since much of what passes for love in this work would more accurately be called rape, or at least lust.[1] Still, Ovid's epic makes of the passions its subject matter more explicitly and consistently than does any of its classical counterparts. Indeed, it is most often passion – not necessarily love, but often anger, fear, greed, or shame – that appears to cause the transformations that give the poem its title. And metamorphosis itself may represent a kind of progress insofar as it is change, movement from one state to another. But metamorphosis may also halt or even negate progress, resulting in fixation in an eternal present or even "regress" on an evolutionary chain – for example, from human to nonhuman, or animate to inanimate. In this sense, metamorphosis often appears in Ovid's narrative as a kind of *deus ex machina*. It terminates, but offers no real progress beyond, the impasse to which Ovidian characters often are led by disordered passion.

In relating passion to progress, our central concern is, of course, in *moral* progress, the development of the human soul and the ways in which the passions may influence, impede, or enhance that development. In Ovid's work, however, which avowedly attempts nothing less than a history of the world from the cosmogony to the poet's own day, the senses of progress that we encounter will be more directly chronological and kinetic: progress understood as the passage of time and the ability to move forward. Yet this is not to say that the moral dimension is missing; rather, I would argue that Ovid approaches moral progress obliquely, his characters' movement in space and time rich with signification for our understanding of their moral strides – or their standstill. In the concluding books of the *Metamorphoses*, the poet is drawn again and again to explore the situation in which a protagonist (always female), torn between her illicit desires and her own sense of rationality and shame (or perhaps only cultural protocol), stands at an impasse. As metamorphosis in Ovid often presents a physical analogue to a moral condition,[2] so the moral impasse between desire and decorum is literally embodied by Ovid's heroines as an inability to progress physically, to take the next step.

As one critic has dryly remarked, "What most interested Ovid and provided him with a limitless field for exploration ... was human behaviour under stress" (Kenney 1982: 436). Several of the best-known and most frequently studied passages of the poem are stories in which an intense but illicit love is held in equipoise by a countervailing emotion, and the individual experiencing these emotions debates her course of action in an internal monologue. In a number of cases, the passion of love is restrained or offset by *pudor*: shame or a sense of propriety.[3] This particular scenario of agitated internal debate occurs with a series of women, including Medea, Scylla, Althea, Byblis, Iphis, and Myrrha. These six Ovidian episodes are interrelated in many ways.[4] In each case, the heroine's moral dilemma results in her being "stuck" for a time as conflicting passions render her unable to progress. Yet these six heroines display a kind of paradoxical relation between passion and progress. On the one hand, they are fixed fast by the moral choice that confronts them, while on the other hand, their passion ultimately drives them to actions that propel them across the boundaries of sanctioned human behavior. Paralysis of the will had merely suspended them on the threshold of transgression. In each case but one (that of Iphis, who, as we will see, presents a singularly positive denouement), these characters, when they break out of moral and physical impasse, plunge forward both impetuously and tragically.

Trapped by choice

What is the philosophical context for Ovid's consideration of these issues? For an author whose reputation is colored still by Quintilian's characterization of him as *nimium amator ingenii sui*, "too much in love with his own cleverness" (*Inst.* 10.1.88), this may seem a strange question to ask. Did this witty and irreverent poet, who clearly relished and fostered his own image as a cosmopolitan bon vivant, a "bad boy" in the regime of a moralizing Augustus, have an interest in the systematic philosophies of his time? Ovid's description of the origins of the universe clearly bears traces of Lucretius's *De rerum natura*, but it also includes Platonic and Stoic elements. Although few would consider Ovid to be consistently Epicurean, Stoic, or Pythagorean (despite the extended "speech" of Pythagoras with which the epic culminates), the poet seems to have been not indifferent to the philosophical currents of his time, but rather, as we might expect, eclectic in his relationship to philosophical schools.

The specific narrative *topos* that concerns us here – instances in which passion wars with rationality, causing the individual to be trapped between these two opposite impulses, often literally rendered immobile, incapable of progress – may be illumined by yet another philosopher. Ovid's repeated anatomy of this problem seems to present a narrative and indeed an explicitly kinetic correlative to the philosophical state that Aristotle diagnosed as *akrasia* (*Eth. nic.* 7.1–10), a kind of paralysis of the will in which a moral agent correctly perceives the "better" course but fails to act upon it.

While the Hellenistic philosophers are extremely concerned with the correct ordering of the will, with what M. Nussbaum (1994b) has appropriately called "the therapy of desire," it is Aristotle who perhaps provides the most complete diagnosis of the condition that afflicts the heroines of Ovid. In the seventh book of the *Nichomachean Ethics*, Aristotle addresses his analytical powers to the puzzle of the akratic individual, someone who correctly perceives that the action that he (or, exclusively in the case of Ovid, she) is about to undertake is wrong and yet chooses that action nevertheless. Plato's Socrates had argued that this was impossible, that every moral agent acts in accordance with his (or her) best understanding of "the good." But Plato's contemporary Euripides clearly disputed this view in a number of his theatrical works, including *Medea*. And Plato's student Aristotle, drawing on empirical observations as was his wont, grapples with the reality that we perceive in our own time as well: individuals do in fact (even with alarming regularity) perceive the better course and choose the worse (*Eth. nic.* 7.2.1–10). What train of thought, what rationalizations lead moral agents to behave in this way?

The philosopher sets himself the question: Does the akratic individual, who apparently knows what he or she should do but acts in contradiction to that knowledge, actually *have* knowledge, and if so, in what sense? Aristotle pursues an intriguing analysis of this problem that seems particularly illuminating in the case of Ovid's heroines. First, he frames the problem as one of faulty logic by assuming that a moral agent's choice essentially takes the form of a practical syllogism (*Eth. nic.* 7.3.6). For example,

> Daughters should not betray their fathers. (major premise)
> I am a daughter. (minor premise)
> Therefore, I should not betray my father. (conclusion)

The akratic individual, Aristotle argues, correctly recognizes the major premise, the general rule, but fails in the formulation of the appropriate minor premise, the application of the universal to the particular. We surely see Ovid's deliberators behaving in just this fashion, performing elaborate mental gymnastics to enable themselves to slip the noose of the syllogism. Often, this takes the form of attempting to rename, recategorize, or otherwise redeploy language so as to detour from the inexorable path of the logic.

In the instance above, for example, the skewed logic might take this form:

> Daughters should not betray their fathers.
> I am a lover (more than a daughter).
> Therefore, I may betray my father.

In other instances, it seems that two quite distinct syllogisms are inappropriately commingled. For example,

> Incest is forbidden for humans.
> I am a human.
> Therefore, incest is forbidden for me.

> The gods' behavior is appropriate.
> The gods commit incest.
> Therefore, incest is appropriate.

In the ruminations of a Byblis or Myrrha, these two are melded into a misshapen syllogism, something like this:

> Incest is forbidden for humans.
> But the gods commit incest.
> Therefore, I can commit incest.

How does this faulty logic come about? Aristotle argues that even if, in some way, the akratic individual "knows" what is right – that is, knows how to construct the practical syllogism correctly – under the influence of passion such knowledge is not really present to the individual. The knowledge is not operative, any more than it might be to one who is asleep or drunken or mad (*Eth. nic.* 7.3.7). Furthermore, Aristotle draws the analogy that under those circumstances a person apparently speaking the language of knowledge is simply mouthing the words, like an actor speaking a part (*Eth. nic.* 7.3.8). This phenomenon, too, one can observe in Ovid's akratic heroines, who in several instances clearly recall dramatic heroines[5] and at other times seem to conceive themselves almost as actors in a play. I do not claim direct Aristotelian influence on the *Metamorphoses*, but the philosopher's analysis of the akratic individual can shed light on Ovid's representation of characters who are driven by their passions to act in a way that they "know" is wrong.

Medea

The poster child for akratic conflict clearly is Medea, in a narrative tradition that dates back to Euripides's *Medea*:

> I know indeed what evil I intend to do,
> But stronger than all my afterthoughts is my fury,
> Fury that brings upon mortals the greatest evils
>   (*Medea* 1078–80 [trans. R. Warner,
>   in Lattimore 1955])

In this famous formulation, "I see the better, but I do the worse," Euripides had thrown down the gauntlet to a Platonic philosophical understanding that individuals act in accordance with their knowledge of the good. Ovid's Medea voices essentially the same sentiment as she launches into a troubled soliloquy that explores both her emotional state and possible actions and outcomes:

> si possem, sanior essem;
> sed trahit invitam nova vis, aliudque cupido,
> mens aliud suadet: video meliora proboque,
> deteriora sequor!
>   (*Metam.* 7.18–21)

> I'd act more sanely, if only I could,
> but this new power overwhelms my will;
> reason advises this, and passion, that;
> I see the better way, and I approve it,
> while I pursue the worse.[6]

At the conclusion of her deliberations she reiterates even more forcefully that she understands the enormity of her choice and acts, not ignorant of the right but overcome by passion:

> quid faciam, video, nec me ignorantia veri
> decipiet, sed amor!
> *(Metam.* 7.92–3)

> I clearly see what I'm about to do:
> not ignorance beguiles me now, but love.

The very explicit terms in which Ovid's Medea voices her decision (self-perceived as immoral) make it clear that the poet is self-consciously participating in the philosophical controversy, with origins at least four centuries before him, about whether an individual, conscious of the right, can choose the wrong. Ovid explores the individual's moral conflict in such a case through the development of both rhetorical and physical analogues for the conflict. Medea and her counterparts in the *Metamorphoses* engage in elaborate rhetorical formulations of their dilemmas, often employing paradox and irony as means of reconfiguring the reality that they face. G. Tissol has offered an excellent analysis of the way in which, through these rhetorical ploys, "we observe language stretched and exploited, made to promote the worse argument over the better." "Semantic slippage," Tissol notes, "allows desire to ... prepar[e] fertile ground for both the generation and the reception of specious arguments" (Tissol 1997: 51).

In addition to negotiating their inner conflicts through rhetorical ploys, however, Ovid's heroines also project their moral dilemmas into a spatial dimension. As she wrestles with the conflicting emotions caused by her infatuation with Jason, who has come to her father's kingdom as an enemy (*frustra ... repugnas* [*Metam.* 7.11]), Medea represents her inner indecision to some extent in terms of external physical forces or paths of action. Although she exhorts herself to thrust aside (*excute* [7.17]) her passion, she is unable to do so. She is dragged along (*trahit* [7.19]) by some alien force; she also speaks of a god standing in opposition to her (*nescio quis deus obstat* [7.12]). We realize that as she debates inwardly, enjoining herself to dispense with delay (*omnem pelle moram* [7.47–8]), she is paralyzed by these conflicting forces, incapable of action.

It appears briefly that Medea may succeed in following her better judgment and banishing her passion (*et victa dabat iam terga cupido* [*Metam.* 7.73]; *et iam fortis erat, pulsusque resederat ardor* [7.76]). However, as soon as she lays eyes on Jason again, her infatuation overcomes her. Alluding again to the clarity with which she perceives her own course to be wrong (*quid faciam, video: nec me ignorantia veri decipiet* [7.92–3]), she nevertheless proceeds. If the epitome of *akrasia* is the paralysis of the will, with the moral agent poised on the razor's edge, unable to make the right choice, unable to refrain from the wrong, this interminable moment is narratively represented in Medea's case by her fixed gaze on Jason. She is unable to turn her eyes from him, frozen in time (*lumina fixa tenet* [7.87]; *nec se declinat ab illo* [7.88]).

The rhetorical couplings in which Medea presents her possible alternatives represent them almost as physical destinations to be approached or fled:

> non magna relinquam,
> magna sequar:
> (*Metam.* 7.55–6)
>
> ... quin adspice, quantum
> adgrediare nefas, et dum licet, effuge crimen!
> (7.70–1)
>
> I do not leave
> greatness, but elope with him to seek it!
> ... Just look ahead:
> how great a sin it is you're thinking of!
> Turn from this crime and flee while you are able.

Of course, in Medea's case there is a particular rationale for framing her moral choice in terms of a physical itinerary, for she will either remain in her father's household or, an exile from her land, set sail with Jason. In the event, having fled from her native land with Jason, Medea embarks on a seemingly endless circling of the globe. Her extraordinary journeys, undertaken via magical chariot, are more extensive than any other travels described by Ovid. They are occasioned either by Medea's search for baneful herbs for her potions or by the need to escape the scenes of the crimes that she has effected through those potions. To map Medea's moral choices onto geographical coordinates, then, is particularly appropriate. Yet this tendency to formulate moral dilemma in terms of physical impasse, which is established paradigmatically in Medea's case, then extends beyond her to a series of subsequent narratives that do not necessarily entail actual physical relocation. Each of these presents a woman who engages in an anguished interior monologue in which she debates whether to undertake an action that she initially believes to be amoral, but to which she is driven by passion.

Scylla

The brief tale of Scylla opens book 8, much as Medea's narrative opened book 7, and her situation bears the closest similarity to that of Medea. As Jason came seeking the Golden Fleece, a source of power for Medea's father, likewise King Minos is a handsome and daring hero who has come to besiege the kingdom of Nisus, Scylla's father. And Scylla, like Medea, finds herself intensely drawn by the sight of the enemy leader. As the power of Medea's father, Aeetes, depended on his possession of the Golden Fleece, similarly Nisus's kingship depends upon a magical lock of purple hair. Scylla resolves to cut this lock of her father's hair and present it to Minos, thereby betraying her father and handing over her city to the attacker.

Scylla's passion stirs her to contemplate a headlong rush to Minos's side (*impetus* [*Metam.* 8.39]). In her mind, she imagines leaping down into his camp from the tower whence she has watched him for six months or flying to him on wings:

> O ego ter felix, si pennis lapsa per auras
> Gnosiaci possem castris insistere regis.
> (*Metam.* 8.51–2)

> Thrice happy would I be if I had wings
> to fly into the camp of the Cretan king.

But in fact she simply sits (*sedebat*) and gazes at him (8.38–42).

In Scylla's case the impasse to which her passion has brought her means not only that she is unable to rouse herself to action, but also that she is unable even to determine whether she is happy or sad: " '*laeter*,' *ait* '*doleamne geri lacrimabile bellum, in dubio est*' " "What should I feel about this dreadful war? Should I rejoice or grieve? I cannot say" (*Metam.* 8.44–5). In the brief internal debate that follows, however, Scylla develops several rationalizations for action, imagining why it will actually be a good thing to betray her city, including the justice of Minos's cause and the idea that by curtailing the war, she will be preventing bloodshed. As Tissol has noted, these specious arguments make a space for desire to inhabit, and Scylla determines to move boldly forward. Noting that what stands in the way of love (*obstaret* [8.75]) should simply be destroyed, she resolves to forge ahead, though fire and sword should bar her path (*ire per ignes et gladios ausim* [8.76–7]).

In fact, however, as Scylla notes, fire and sword do not block her path; it is only her father who stands in her way. This is the sole obstruction to desire that, she opines, any similarly determined girl would delight in destroying (*perdere gauderet* [*Metam.* 8.75]). She expresses the wish that she had no father (*di facerent, sine patre forem!* [8.72]), and it is clear that the cutting of her father's talismanic lock of hair is actually a symbolic murder of the father. Once she has decided to snip this lock, essentially the deed is done: her father and her city are betrayed. Minos, however, rejects her gift and herself, while nevertheless taking the proffered city.

Whereas the lovelorn Scylla merely passively contemplated Minos, the spurned Scylla actively casts herself after him, madly plunging into the sea and clinging to his departing ship. At this juncture antagonism between father and daughter is revisited as Scylla's father, who now has been transformed into a bird, swoops down and attacks her, tearing at her with his hooked beak.[7] In the metamorphic denouement of the tale, however, she too is transformed into a bird, thereby both escaping the attacks of her father and realizing her earlier wish to take flight.

Althea

Later on in the same book another tortured heroine debates her course of action at considerably greater length. This is Althea, mother of Meleager. Althea is driven not by erotic love, but by two conflicting loves and loyalties, one owed to her male child and another to her male siblings. This account follows upon the story of the Calydonian boar, in which Meleager is triumphant over the boar, but in a fray that subsequently breaks out he also kills his two uncles, Althea's brothers. When she learns of her brothers' deaths, and of her son's responsibility for their demise, she resolves to take vengeance on her son (Ovid characterizes her impulse as *poenae amor*, a passion for vengeance [*Metam.* 8.450]). Again, a magical element is involved in this tale. It happens that at his birth, the Fates decreed that the length of Meleager's life would be equal to the life of a particular wooden log. Althea snatched this log from the fire and has kept it safe in her possession. To avenge her brothers, she determines to burn it.

In Althea's case, the paralysis of will resulting from her conflicting passions is elaborated in great detail.[8] She builds a fire, but she cannot bring herself to place the log upon it, stopping and starting, not just three times, but four:

> tum conata quater flammis inponere ramum
> coepta quater tenuit:
> (*Metam.* 8.462–3)

And then she tried – four times – to thrust the branch
into the fire, and drew back each time.

Several times, Althea's dilemma is formulated as one of conflicting roles and names:

> pugnat materque sororque,
> et diversa trahunt unum duo nomina pectus.
> (*Metam.* 8.463–4)

Mother and sister strove with one another
and those two names were tugging at one heart.

> incipit esse tamen melior germana parente.
> (*Metam.* 8.475)

The sister, nonetheless, began to win.

nunc animum pietas maternaque nomina frangunt.
(Metam. 8.508)

And now the mother in me melts my heart.

In Althea's case, we may easily perceive a kind of flawed syllogism underlying her dilemma:

A mother should not kill her son.
I am not a mother (but a grieving sister).
Therefore, I must kill my son.

This conclusion might have resulted from the melding of two distinct syllogisms, both of which Althea perceives as applicable to her:

A mother should not kill her son.
I am a mother.
Therefore, I should not kill my son.

A sister must avenge her brothers.
I am a sister.
Therefore, I must avenge my brothers.

Aristotle notes that in such cases where two arguments are (or appear to be) in contradiction, passion (*pathos*) may lead one to act as if under the influence of madness (*mania*).[9]

Althea's inability to act is explicitly compared to the plight of a ship caught in conflicting currents. In a brilliant rhetorical formulation, Ovid says that she repeatedly takes up and puts down her wrath (*ira* [*Metam.* 8.474]), yet surely one feels that *ira* is a synecdoche for the log that is synonymous with her son's life:

utque carina,
quam ventus ventoque rapit contrarius aestus,
vim geminam sentit paretque incerta duobus,
Thestias haud aliter dubiis affectibus errat
inque vices ponit positamque resuscitat iram.
(Metam. 8.470–4)

as when a ship,
driven in one direction by the wind
and in the other by an opposing tide,
feels those two equal forces struggling,
and yields herself uncertainly to both;

that was Althea, wandering between
wavering passions; now her burning rage
is stifled, now it's started up again.

One aspect of Althea's dilemma concerns not only her own conflicting kinship roles as mother and sister, but also the importance of the father/son relationship. She finds it unbearable that her husband, Oeneus, may still enjoy a son, while her own father, Thestius, has been deprived of both of his sons:

an felix Oeneus nato victore fruetur,
Thestius orbus erit? melius lugebitis ambo!
(Metam. 8.486–7)

Shall fortunate
Oeneus rejoice in his son's victory?
Shall Thestius mourn? Better you both grieve.

Ultimately, she will determine that Meleager must die, thereby destroying his father's hopes:

pereat sceleratus et ille
spemque patris regnumque trahat patriaeque ruinam!
(Metam. 8.497–8)

Let him die,
the criminal, and with him take the hopes
his father had for him and for his kingdom.

At last, she determines to go through with the act, and she invokes her brothers' *manes* (spirits). Yet, once again, she hesitates and refrains, unable to bring her hand to the deed:

quo rapior? fratres ignoscite matri!
Deficiunt ad coepta manus!
(Metam. 8.491–2)

What am I rushing into here?
Brothers, forgive a mother's wavering,
my hands rebel from what they have begun!

Her equivocation rises to a crescendo – *et cupio et nequeo*, "but I cannot accomplish what I wish for" (*Metam.* 8.506) – and it seems that she may never be able to escape the vortex of indecision and the inability to complete the movement that will both avenge her brothers and murder her son. Finally, in a posture of *contraposto* that provides a perfect physical analogue to the tergiversations of her soul, averting her eyes but extending her hand, she completes the act:

> Dixit dextraque aversa trementi
> funereum torrem medios coniecit in ignes.
> (*Metam.* 8.511–12)

> She turned away and with a trembling hand
> flung the funeral torch into the fire.

Having taken the step of throwing the log on the fire and thereby ending the life of her son, Althea proceeds at once to end her own life as well, driving a sword through her heart (*exegit poenas acto per viscera ferro* [8.532]).

Whereas Medea had debated two courses of action that literally entailed different destinations, and Scylla formulated sophistries that appeared to transform betrayal into benefit, in Althea's story Ovid has taken both the physical and the rhetorical analogues of passionate dilemma to a new plane. Althea's decision to take or not take a physical action (tossing the log on the fire) will have a remote consequence (causing her son to die) rather like what we are accustomed to in the virtual world. Ovid has abstracted the heroine's dilemma from a directly physical analogue (Medea will stay or sail away) to a mediated action (Althea's disposition of the log will have consequences for her son) that assumes a significance far beyond itself. Similarly, Althea's tale moves the conflict that she feels between her obligations as a mother and those as a sibling to a level of abstraction where it is not only loyalties or emotions, but also abstract designations, *nomina*, that vie with one another. The heroine's rumination on how disordered passion either causes or is reflected by a disorder in language itself will be reiterated and taken further by subsequent figures, particularly Byblis and Myrrha.

Byblis

The tragic tale of Byblis is introduced specifically as an exemplum to be avoided: *Byblis in exemplo est, ut ament concessa puellae*, "Byblis serves to illustrate a moral: that girls should not desire what's forbidden" (*Metam.* 9.454). Thus the narrator introduces an awareness of this narrative *as a narrative*, a tale intended for an audience and, more specifically, to effect a particular moral outcome in that audience. This self-consciousness about the transaction between the writer and the reader is particularly apt for the Byblis episode, for it mirrors the action of the narrative, in which Byblis herself becomes an extremely self-conscious writer.

This lover's deliberations with herself are the most extensive in the work. Furthermore, in a way that itself reflects her divided mind, her deliberations take place in two separate monologues. Having wavered over what course of action to take, and then taken it, Byblis then revisits that original decision and determines that she will proceed in a different way. Whereas the first episode is marked by a great deal of hesitation and questioning, stopping and starting, the second appears straightforward: Byblis makes a decision and acts on it. To some extent, this becomes yet another stage in the initial quandary, another opportunity to change one's mind and backtrack. More significantly, however, once Byblis has decided to act, she is propelled madly forward, her crossing of the bounds of propriety ultimately leading her to traverse physical boundaries as well.

When Byblis recognizes, initially through the experience of very vivid erotic dreams, that she loves her brother in more than a sisterly way, she, like the other heroines we have seen, formulates novel rationalizations for her impulses, laments what stands in her way (*quod obest* [*Metam.* 9.494]), and utters the telltale exclamation, *Quo feror?*, "Where is this leading me?" (9.509), a signal in Ovid's text that the speaker, like an individual swept away in a flash flood, has lost the sense of agency and feels borne along disastrously by forces that she (or he) cannot control.[10]

For Byblis, even more so than for Althea, a great deal revolves around the power of names:

> iam dominum appellat, iam nomina sanguinis odit:
> Byblida iam mavult, quam se vocet ille sororem.
> (*Metam.* 9.466–7)

> She calls him "Master" now, and now detests
> the thought that they are siblings, and prefers
> that he should call her "Byblis" and not "Sister."

> O ego, si liceat mutato nomine iungi,
> (*Metam.* 9.487)

> If I could be allowed to change my name
> and marry you . . . .

Althea wrestled with the mutually exclusive actions apparently mandated by her multiple designations as sister and as mother. Byblis, however, not content to be so constrained by her designation as sister, perceives that she must change the names themselves, must take control of the power of naming.

After a particularly specious argument, Byblis decides that she will indeed confess to her brother her incestuous love (*Metam.* 9.514). Love compels her (*coget amor* [9.515]), but shame restrains her (*pudor . . . tenebit* [9.515]) from speaking out. Trapped between speaking and not speaking, she chooses an alternative path: she will write a letter.

> "ipsa petam. poterisne loqui? poterisne fateri?
> coget amor, potero; vel, si pudor ora tenebit,
> littera celatos arcana fatebitur ignes!"
> Hoc placet, haec dubiam vicit sententia mentem.
> (*Metam.* 9.514–17)

165

> "I will go after him! Can you admit this?
> Will you be able to confess it?
> Compelled by love, I will be able to!
> If Shame should press her finger to my lips,
> a silent letter will confess my hidden feelings."
> This purpose pleases her and overcomes
> her mind's uncertainties.

The writing of Byblis's letter is a quite extraordinary event, and one that Ovid chooses to describe at length in vivid physical detail. The extended agony that we have just seen in Althea's case, as she steels herself for the dreadful act of infanticide, yet cannot bring herself to it, yet cannot abandon her plan – all this is condensed, in Ovid's portrayal of Byblis, into a kind of paroxysm of indecision:

> incipit et dubitat; scribit damnatque tabellas;
> et notat et delet; mutat culpatque probatque
> inque vicem sumptas ponit positasque resumit.
>   (*Metam.* 9.523–5)

> She starts and stops. Sets down – and then condemns.
> Adds and deletes. Doubts; finds fault with; approves.
> She throws the tablet down, then picks it up!

The standoff between *audacia* and *pudor* (9.527) seems to render the poor girl almost palsied, but she does indeed proceed with her letter-writing:

> in latus erigitur cubitoque innixa sinistro ....
> et meditata manu componit verba trementi.
>   (*Metam.* 9.518, 521)

> Still in her bed,
> she lifts herself up and leans on her left elbow: ...
> Her shaking hands set down the practiced words.

Expressing the effect of her passion to some extent with metaphors of motion, she notes that she fought at length (*pugnavique diu* [*Metam.* 9.543]) against Cupid's weapons but was unable to flee (*effugere* [9.544]). Finally, she has been driven by overwhelming passion (*cogor* [9.546]; *cogeret ultimus ardor* [9.562]). The dire outcome destined for Byblis's letter is itself presaged by a kinetic sign: as the sister entrusts her missive to a servant for its delivery to her brother, it falls to the ground.

> cum daret, elapsae manibus cecidere tabellae;
> omine turbata est, misit tamen.
>   (*Metam.* 9.571–2)

She dropped the tablets she was giving him,
but sent them anyway – despite that omen.

When this ill-fated letter reaches its recipient, very much like Minos in the case of Scylla, Byblis's brother Caunus is horrified and repulsed by her overture. Informed of his reaction by the servant who delivered her letter, Byblis initially is frozen with terror:

> palles audita, Bybli, repulsa,
> et pavet obsessum glaciali frigore corpus.
> *(Metam.* 9.581–2)

When she heard the news
of his rejection, Byblis lost all color
and shivered uncontrollably from chills.

Recovering quickly, however, she launches into a second monologue to plot a new strategy. From this point on, her earlier indecisiveness of action, as she starts and stops, inscribes and erases, takes up and puts down her writing tablet, is essentially reversed. No longer trapped in indecision, she now propels herself forward, tragically, into immediate and indeed ceaseless action:

> vincetur! repetendus erit, nec taedia coepti
> ulla mei capiam, dum spiritus iste manebit.
> *(Metam.* 9.616–17)

He will be overcome! I will pursue him
once more, and not give up while I have breath!

> iamque palam est demens, inconcessamque fatetur
> spem veneris, siquidem patriam invisosque penates
> deserit, et profugi sequitur vestigia fratris.
> *(Metam.* 9.638–40)

Her madness unconcealed now, she confesses
the hope of her forbidden love, and flees
her homeland and its now-detested hearth,
and sets out after her self-exiled brother.

She relentlessly importunes her brother, who finally flees from his homeland in despair. Yet Byblis continues to pursue, her passion leading to a mad and frenzied flight across the earth, until she finally drops in exhaustion and is transformed into a fountain, still endlessly flowing.

Iphis

Following directly on the tale of Byblis's impossible love in Ovid's text is the story of yet another impossible love, that of Iphis. Byblis's erotic object choice was inappropriate because it was her brother; Ovid represents Iphis's choice as equally hopeless, because she is a woman in love with another woman. Iphis finds herself in this predicament because she has been disguised as a male all her life. Her mother (on the advice of the goddess Isis) raised her this way because had her true gender been known, she would have been put to death at birth as an unwanted female child. Iphis's father, Ligdus, had mandated exposure if his wife should give birth to a female child. The father is successfully deceived, however, and he, believing his child to be a son, betroths him to a young woman, Ianthe – a particularly poignant situation because Iphis has in fact become enamored of this young woman.

Iphis reflects upon her dilemma in ways very similar to the other akratic heroines. She perceives herself to be trapped in an impossible situation and draws a series of analogies, as do Byblis and Myrrha. However, whereas Byblis and Myrrha seek to sanction their illicit passions by reference to the behavior of the gods or animals, Iphis finds no such anodyne. Even among the animals, she laments, a passion like hers is unknown.

The inability to proceed is very concretely represented in the narrative by the repeated attempts of Iphis's mother to stall and delay the wedding that the father has arranged. Despite the ostensibly hopeless situation, however, this is one of the rare narratives in the poem, indeed perhaps the only one, in which metamorphosis appears to provide an unequivocally positive outcome. Through the miraculous intervention of the goddess Isis, Iphis is metamorphosed into the male whom her father Ligdus and betrothed Ianthe believed her to be, and she is united with her beloved. This extraordinarily positive outcome is quite literally represented in the form of progress: the initial sign of Iphis's transformation is the fact that as she approaches the wedding ceremony, which can no longer be put off, she begins to march forward with the longer stride of the male gait (*sequitur comes Iphis euntem, quam solita est, maiore gradu* [*Metam.* 9.786–7]).

Myrrha

Even more so than in the case of Byblis, Ovid's narrator prefaces the story of Myrrha with warnings about its dreadful nature. So horrible is the story, the poet avers, that he even urges his own work be left unread or receive no credence:

> dira canam: procul hinc natae, procul este parentes,
> aut, mea si vestras mulcebunt carmina mentes,

> desit in hac mihi parte fides, nec credite factum;
> vel, si credetis, facti quoque credite poenam!
> (*Metam.* 10.300–3)

> I sing of dire events: depart from me, daughters,
> depart from me, fathers; or, if you find my poems charming,
> believe that I lie, believe these events never happened;
> or, if you believe that they did, then believe they were punished.

As several of the Ovidian heroines have wished away the existence of their progenitors, in this case the narrator's voice proclaims that it would have been better if Cinyras's daughter had never been born:

> si sine prole fuisset,
> inter felices Cinyras potuisset haberi.
> (*Metam.* 10.298–9)

> if he had only been childless,
> Cinyras would be regarded as one of the blessed.

At a later point in the narrative Myrrha will also express the wish that she were not the daughter of Cinyras (*non essem Cinyrae, Cinyrae concumbere possem* [*Metam.* 10.338]). In another paradoxical formulation the narrator asserts that while it is a crime to hate one's parent, love like this is an even greater crime:

> scelus est odisse parentem;
> hic amor est odio maius scelus!
> (*Metam.* 10.314–15)

> Hating a parent is wicked, but even more wicked
> than hatred is this kind of love.

Unlike Byblis, Myrrha is not deceived about her own incestuous passion; she knows it for what it is. Indeed, her first-quoted words in the text are symptomatic: *Quo mente feror?* "What have I begun?" (*Metam.* 10.320). The troubled interior monologue that follows is, in her case, a series of rhetorical riffs on the paradoxical aspects of her situation, variants of what both Byblis and Iphis have articulated. Myrrha dwells at particular length on the confusion of names that incest threatens, as mother and daughter become rivals, and the incestuous mother is sister of her son, and so on.[11]

It is not directly in this interior monologue that Myrrha fully displays the syndrome of conflicted passion that we have been examining, but rather in the narrator's description (in the third person) of the sleepless night that follows for her. As is true for the other lovers, shame and desire war within

Myrrha (*pudetque et cupit* [*Metam.* 10.371-2]), and she does not know how to proceed (*quid agat, non invenit* [10.372]). Similar to the metaphorical description of Althea as a ship caught in conflicting eddies, Myrrha is compared to a great tree, struck by an axe, balanced precariously before crashing down in one direction or another:

> utque securi
> saucia trabs ingens, ubi plaga novissima restat,
> quo cadat, in dubio est omnique a parte timetur,
> sic animus vario labefactus vulnere nutat
> huc levis atque illuc momentaque sumit utroque,
> nec modus et requies, nisi mors, reperitur amoris.
> (*Metam.* 10.372-7)

> She wavers,
> just like a tree that the axe blade has girdled completely,
> when only the last blow remains to be struck, and the woodsman
> cannot predict the direction it's going to fall in,
> she, after so many blows to her spirit, now totters,
> now leaning in one, and now in the other, direction,
> nor is she able to find any rest from her passion
> save but in death.

Although Myrrha settles on a plan to end her life by hanging, she is found and rescued by her nurse, who wheedles out of the demented girl the source of her agony. Again Myrrha is caught, unable to confess or to remain silent (*conataque saepe fateri saepe tenet vocem* [*Metam.* 10.420-1). The nurse, as such stories always go, proves to be a resourceful procurer and in fact arranges a means for Myrrha to realize her desire and come to her father's bed under cover of darkness. Reminiscent of the omen of Byblis's fallen tablets, Myrrha thrice stumbles on the threshold of her crime, both literally and metaphorically: *ter pedis offensi signo est revocata*, "thrice Myrrha stumbles and stops each time at the omen" (10.452). Yet she crosses the threshold and goes forward to the crime.

Father and daughter cohabit not once, but many nights. Ultimately, Cinyras wants to know the identity of his mysterious young lover (*Cinyras avidus cognoscere amantem post tot concubitus* [*Metam.* 10.473]). He calls for light and, with a speed enhanced by grammatical zeugma, "recognizes at once his daughter and his crime" (*inlato lumine vidit et scelus et natam* [10.473-4]). His reaction is equally immediate: he draws his sword to kill her (*pendenti nitidum vagina deripit ensem* [10.475]). Myrrha flees, and she succeeds in escaping the murderous intention of her father (*intercepta neci est* [10.477]).

Myrrha's escape bears comparison to Scylla's in that both daughters are spared attack at their fathers' hands, and her mad flight, ended only by exhaustion, recalls that of Byblis. Another striking similarity between the tales of Scylla and Myrrha is that the curse that Minos hurled at Scylla, that she might be banished from the world, denied both land and sea (*di te submoveant, o nostri infamia saecli, orbe suo, tellusque tibi pontusque negetur!* [*Metam.* 8.97–8]), finds an echo in Myrrha's final words. This time, however, the possibility of being removed beyond the known world becomes not a curse, but a prayer, Myrrha's own petition for herself:

> ne violem vivosque superstes
> mortuaque extinctos, ambobus pellite regnis
> mutataeque mihi vitamque necemque negate!
> (*Metam.* 10.485–7)

> Lest I should outrage the living by my survival,
> or the dead by my dying, I do not turn away
> from the terrible sentence that my misbehavior deserves;
> drive me from both of these kingdoms, transform me
> wholly, so that both life and death are denied me.

Passion, progress, and progeny

We have noted that each of these six women encounters an impasse when her passion comes into conflict with her rational assent to social mores. This impasse is real; there is in fact no way for the heroines to reconcile their desires with the cultural protocols that they believe, at some level, to be rational. Hence their akratic predicament. But there are further similarities among these six scenarios.

Each heroine resorts to the power of language as a means of freeing her from the perceived constraints of her circumstances; in some cases, it is language as incantation (Medea), in others as prayer (Iphis), but most frequent is the attempt to regain agency through the power of redescription. The akratic character's desire to escape the constraints of kinship, ethnicity, or gender through the reassignment of names and designations is not unrelated to her construction of faulty syllogisms, in the Aristotelian analysis ("This holds true for X, but I am not X..."). The possibility of renaming is also obviously related to metamorphosis itself, which may make of one a different entity entirely. In a sense, the heroines attempt to transform themselves, to effect their own metamorphosis, through the power of language. In one case, that of the prayer for Iphis, this metamorphosis will be successful. In the majority of instances, however, these figures' exercise of language in a transformative effort results in the unmaking both of themselves and of the family.

A number of broad structural relations connect the dilemmas, choices, and outcomes in the tales of these six women. Two of the characters, Medea and Scylla, betray their fathers and their cities for the sake of a handsome stranger. Another two, Byblis and Myrrha, attempt incest – Byblis (unsuccessfully) with her brother, and Myrrha (successfully) with her father. These two, paired narratives represent extreme end points along an axis of exogamy and endogamy. By pursuing incestuous relationships, Byblis and Myrrha exemplify an unacceptably strong form of endogamy, wishing to marry not just within the cultural group but within the conjugal family.[12] Medea and Scylla appear to have made less disastrous choices, in their desire for exogamous partners, but they too have gone to extremes. In both their cases, the action that serves as a declaration of love is simultaneously the betrayal of the father and his kingdom.

At first glance, the stories of Althea and Iphis do not show the surface similarities that render Medea and Scylla, Byblis and Myrrha, almost doublets of one another. Yet both Althea's and Iphis's tales involve a mother's miraculous saving of a newborn child – an action that is revisited and questioned when the child becomes an adult. Telethusa's decision to raise her daughter Iphis as a male is miraculously affirmed by Iphis's metamorphosis into a male.[13] In stark contrast, Althea's earlier salvation of her son is reversed, as she determines that she must destroy him in order to avenge her brothers (and, ultimately, her father).

Among the many structural relations that connect these six tales, one of the most surprising is that all (save that of Byblis)[14] involve the notion of intrafamilial murder, either parent killing child or child killing parent. If Medea presents the paradigm of the akratic heroine, she also embodies the epitome of murderous intrafamilial conflict. Medea not only murders her own children but also engineers the murder of Jason's uncle Pelias at the hands of his own daughters, and she is very narrowly prevented from arranging the death of Theseus at his father's hands. In the narrative of Scylla, although daughter attempts to murder father and father returns the favor, both killings are deflected via metamorphosis. Althea, albeit indirectly, kills her son. Iphis's father decreed her death (although he is circumvented). And Myrrha's father, horrified by his complicity in crime with his daughter, attempts to kill her.

In his study of tragic drama, psychoanalyst and critic Bennett Simon has highlighted the centrality of intergenerational violence in that genre in ways that are relevant to these tragic narratives in Ovid. Simon's analysis alerts the reader to "a sense of terrible warfare within the family" in which "the family is at risk of destroying itself, either by literally destroying its own progeny or by making propagation impossible" (Simon 1988: 2). Although the situations of Ovid's heroines appear to involve erotic passion rather than hatred, they result almost uniformly in a lethal relationship between the generations. And of course metamorphosis itself often represents a radical alternative to propagation, snatching the metamorphosed individual out of the generative cycle and creating a new species, not through reproduction, but by fixating him or her as the instantiation of that species. Simon notes as well that the narrative impasse that pits the generations of the family against one another is also often reflected on the formal level of language as "an anxiety and concern about generating and propagating stories...an uneasiness about storytelling" (Simon 1988: 4). This anxiety around the use of language and storytelling, too, is prevalent in these six Ovidian tales, dramatically enacted in Byblis's fraught letter-writing and culminating in the poet's preface to the story of Myrrha, when he takes the extraordinary step of urging his audience not to read it. "Twisted and interrupted narration, including silences," Simon argues, "signifies and is consonant with twisted and interrupted generational relationships" (Simon 1988: 8).

In the Ovidian universe, progress is hard-won, and passion, although it may have a creative dimension, more often threatens to destroy. The fundamental cosmogonic progression from chaos to cosmos, for example, is not decisively accomplished but must be reinstituted several times, as the passions – first of Jove's anger, second of Phaethon's pride – cause reversion to a chaotic state. The most basic metric of progress in the *Metamorphoses* is that of chronology, signaled by Ovid's grounding the poem in cosmogony at its opening and in the contemporary reign of Augustus at its close. Although there is by no means a strict chronological progress between these two points, in part because no such fixed timeline for mythology exists, by and large Ovid's tales follow a generational progression (Galinsky 1975: 85). In the six narratives that we have been examining, however, Ovid suggests that the passions with which these heroines contend have the potential not just to impede forward movement, but, more tragically, to dismantle the most basic dimension of human progress: the succession of the generations.

Notes

1 L.C. Curran (1978) counts "some fifty or so occurrences of forcible rape, attempted rape, or sexual extortion hardly distinguishable from rape." Cf. Segal 1969, esp. "Metamorphosis and the Moral Order," pp. 86–94.
2 The paradigmatic case is the first transformation in the epic, that of Lycaon, whose predatory nature as a human being is manifested in his transformation into a wolf (*fit lupus et veteris servat vestigia formae* [*Metam.* 1.237]).
3 An early example occurs when Jupiter is confronted by Juno, who suspects the truth about Io, even though Jove has already transformed his paramour into a cow. When Juno asks her husband to hand over this bovine creature, *pudor* persuades one way, *amor* another (*pudor est, qui suadeat illinc, hinc dissuadet amor* [*Metam.* 1.618–19]). On the human plane, *pudor* is the force that, for example, restrains the young Medea's impulse to embrace Jason (*obstitit incepto pudor* [7.146]); in Byblis, *pudor* vies with *audacia* (9.527); in Myrrha with desire (*pudetque et cupit* [10.371–2]).
4 Medea and Scylla, for example, seem to be narrative doublets, as each betrays her father for a handsome stranger. The incestuous desires of Byblis and Myrrha have obvious similarities. Myrrha and Iphis utilize almost diametrically opposed

arguments, as one rationalizes and the other repudiates her desires by reference to the behavior of the animals. Meanwhile, Byblis offers exactly the same rationalizing arguments as those of Myrrha, but looks to the gods rather than the animals as exemplars.

5 Cf. Medea's echo of the speech of Euripides' Medea, as noted above, and Myrrha's echo of Phaidra's dramatic action in her attempted suicide and subsequent confession to the nurse.

6 With a few exceptions, all translations of Ovid's *Metamorphoses* are those of C. Martin (2004), occasionally modified. For the Latin text, I have used mainly the edition of W.S. Anderson (1972–97), though I have not followed him in capitalizing the initial letter of each line and have sometimes changed his punctuation.

7 Scylla had already anticipated capital punishment at the hands of her father (*Metam.* 8.126–7).

8 Tissol (1997: 14–15) sensitively examines Ovid's use of paradox in this tale.

9 In a number of instances Ovid alludes to his heroines being driven mad by their passion. Of Medea: *ratione furorem vincere non poterat* (*Metam.* 7.10–11); of Scylla: *vix sua, vix sanae virgo Niseia compos mentis erat* (8.35–6); of Byblis: *dubiaque ita mente* (9.473); *incertae tanta est discordia mentis* (9.630); *tum vero maestam tota Miletida mente defecisse ferunt, tum vero a pectore vestem deripuit planxitque suos furibunda lacertos, iamque palam est demens* (9.635–9).

10 Cf. *Metam.* 10.320 (Myrrha) and *Ars* 3.667 (the *praeceptor amoris* expresses dismay that he is letting women in on men's secrets).

11 The locus classicus for such confusion in kinship relations is, of course, the tale of Oedipus, as rendered in Sophocles' tragedies on the theme.

12 Although neither Byblis nor Myrrha marries her kinsman, both express this as their desire (Byblis: *Metam.* 9.487–94; Myrrha: 10.356–64).

13 The intervention of the goddess Isis, on whose promises Telethusa had relied, is certainly at stake here. Behind this uniquely positive denouement in the *Metamorphoses*, however, lies a unique relationship to the father in the tale. Ovid's text makes an extraordinary effort to portray the father, Ligdus, in a positive light. Despite the fact that he would have exposed and killed his daughter at birth, he weeps along with his wife even as he gives her this order (*Metam.* 9.670–82), and he is explicitly characterized as blameless (*inculpata* [*Metam.* 9.673]).

14 Somewhat like Scylla, who wishes that she had no father, Byblis identifies a previous generation as the source of her problem: if she and Caunus did not share the same grandparents, she avers, her amorous suit would be acceptable (*Metam.* 9.491). That grandfather is the river Maeander, which, as Ovid reminds us in introducing the tale, continually turns back upon itself (*totiens redeuntis eodem* [9.451]). This is, of course, just what his granddaughter Byblis has done by directing her passion back upon her own twin brother rather than outward, resulting in the impasse of incestuous passion rather than the progress of generations.

9

THE PASSIONS IN GALEN AND THE NOVELS OF CHARITON AND XENOPHON*

Loveday C.A. Alexander

Galen's *On the Passions of the Soul* provides a useful contemporary matrix in popular moral philosophy for examining the treatment of the passions in two early Greek novels. As in the novels, Galen's dramatic depiction of the effects of passion functions as a kind of "aversion therapy." Both focus on the objective dramatization of the effects of passion, leading to a blurring of the boundaries between *pathos* ("emotion") and *ethos* ("character"); yet both also feature a small number of characters who are depicted subjectively, as moral subjects capable of moral choice. For the novelists, however, the conflict between passion and reason is a conflict that the philosopher cannot hope to win: no amount of rational debate can resist the onslaught of love.

Introduction

Galen's short treatise *On the Passions of the Soul* presents an eclectic compendium of popular (mainly Stoic) philosophical teaching on the passions.[1] This text provides a useful contemporary framework for examining the treatment of the passions in the earliest Greek novels, those of Chariton of Aphrodisias and Xenophon of Ephesus. I am not primarily interested here in raising questions of dependence or influence (in either direction), but simply in using this framework to suggest some ways in which the early novels may usefully be read against the moral philosophy current in their time.[2]

At first sight, indeed, they appear to have little in common: the novelists celebrate the triumphs of *erōs*, while in Galen, *erōs* appears to be a wholly

---

* I am grateful to John Fitzgerald and the members of the SBL Hellenistic Moral Philosophy and Early Christian Section for comments on this essay.

regrettable lapse in moral control. But on closer inspection, the two are not so far apart as we might expect. I suggest that the novelists show at least four points of commonality or continuity with Galen's philosophical approach to the passions and one major point of contrast. Galen's narrative depiction of the passions, especially of passion as emotion, provides a useful key to the characterization of the novels. In both, this dramatic depiction of the effects of passion functions in some way as a kind of "aversion therapy," a way of displaying the full awfulness of uncontrolled passion and the depths to which sufferers will sink under its sway. In the novels, as in Galen, this is largely an objective realization of the effects of the passions, leading to a certain blurring of the boundaries between *pathos* and *ethos*, or what we would call "emotion" and "character." But the whole philosophical tradition of moral therapy implies that at least the narrator and the narrator's interlocutor are depicted as moral subjects, capable of moral choice. The novels also contain a number of characters who are portrayed in this more subjective fashion – that is, as personalities torn between conflicting passions and not just as passion personified.

But what of the central theme of the novels, the irresistible power of sexual attraction? Even here there is continuity as well as contrast: arguably, love in the novels is viewed objectively as a *pathos*, a tragic event that brings suffering (even when it is innocent, and even when it is returned), in precisely the same way as grief, for Galen, is a "pain" that the philosopher naturally seeks to avoid. But the novelists' most striking tribute to the moral philosophers is at the point where they are most self-consciously opposed, in their vivid portrayal of the power of love over reason. This is presented as a triumph for the deities of Love: the unfortunate human who tries to "philosophize" in the face of their onslaught is not so much a hero as a fool.

Galen's depiction of the passions

The Passions of the Soul illustrates well how readily narrative could be used in the service of moral discourse. "Everybody knows," according to Galen, "that the passions are anger and wrath [*thymos* and *orgē*] and fear and grief and envy and excessive desire"; and he adds his personal view that "loving or hating anything too much" should also be regarded as a *pathos* (*Passions* 1.3, p. 32 = *SM* 1, p. 5.18–22 [my translation]). Only the best (wisest) of humans can escape these morbid conditions, which are illustrated by a series of graphic narrative vignettes showing the actual effects of the passions in the lives of Galen himself and his family and friends. Extremes of passion are easily recognized:

> Whenever a man becomes violently angry over little things and bites and kicks his servants, you may be sure that this man is in a state of passion. The same is true in the case of those who spend their time in drinking to excess, with prostitutes, and in carousing.
> (*Passions* 1.2, pp. 29–30 = *SM* 1, p. 3.17–20)

Moderate states of passion are less easy to diagnose: being "moderately upset over a great financial loss or a disgrace" and eating cakes "rather greedily" are the examples given (*Passions* 1.2, p. 30 = SM 1, p. 3.20–4).[3] But it is the extremes, as we might expect, that attract Galen's most vivid descriptive powers, and especially the passion of anger:

> When I was still a youth ... I watched a man eagerly trying to open a door. When things did not work out as he would have them, I saw him bite the key, kick the door, blaspheme, glare wildly like a madman, and all but foam at the mouth like a wild boar.
> (*Passions* 1.4, p. 38 = SM 1, p. 12.5–11)

Even more than the furniture, clearly it is the unfortunate household slaves who bear the brunt of this kind of anger. Galen rather prides himself on his self-restraint in resolving

> never to strike any slave of my household with my hand. My father practiced this same restraint. Many were the friends he reproved when they had bruised a tendon while striking their slaves in the teeth; he told them that they deserved to have a stroke and die in the fit of passion which had come upon them.
> (*Passions* 1.4, pp. 38–9 = SM 1, p. 13.1–6)[4]

Even the emperor Hadrian had been seen (in a chilling anecdote that should warn us against the easy assumption that household slavery was a relatively humane institution) to gouge out a slave's eye with a stylus that he happened to have in his hand.[5]

The moral function of these dramatic scenes is made clear in Galen's closing summary of his recommended method for "curing" the soul of the "disease" of passion. Watching these scenes is part of the cure: "We must observe what is shameful and to be shunned in the instances of those who are caught in the violent grip of these diseases, for in such men the disgrace is clearly seen" (*Passions* 1.7, p. 53 = SM 1, p. 27.15–17). In other words, extreme instances of passion-controlled behavior act as a kind of aversion therapy – an effect to which Galen can give personal testimony in the effect of his mother's uncontrolled anger on his own youthful self:

> My mother, however, was so very prone to anger that sometimes she bit her handmaids; she constantly shrieked at my father and fought with him – more than Xanthippe did with Socrates. When I compared my father's noble deeds with the disgraceful passions of my mother, I decided to embrace and love his deeds and to flee and hate her passions. Just as in these respects I saw the utter difference between my parents, so also did I see it in the fact that my father

<seemed> never to be grieved over any loss, whereas my mother was vexed over the smallest things. Surely, you know, too, that children imitate the things in which they take pleasure but that they shun the things on which they look with disgust.
(*Passions* 1.8, p. 57 = *SM* 1, p. 31.12–22)

A similar emphasis on the importance of narrative depiction within moral training is found a century earlier in Philodemus's treatise *On Anger*, which seems to imply a view that where simply piling up "blame" is ineffective in moral teaching, the graphic depiction of the full results of a particular passion "before the eyes" will achieve a much more telling effect.[6] Here again, the engagement of the moral will is largely achieved by a powerful appeal to the sense of shame: passion-controlled behavior simply makes you look "silly and ridiculous" (ληρώδης καὶ καταγέλαστος, *lērōdēs kai katagelastos*).

The ultimate aim of philosophical therapy is to induce self-discipline, seen as a system of "training" (*askēsis*) comparable to a prolonged course of training in rhetoric or medicine (*Passions* 1.4, p. 41 = *SM* 1, p. 16.1–4). This ultimately will enable the addressee to live a life in which the passions are firmly under the control of the rational mind:

> If you do this, some day you will be able to tame and calm that power of passion within you which is as irrational as some wild beast. Untamed horses are useless, but horsemen can in a short time make them submissive and manageable. Can you not take and tame this thing which is not some beast from outside yourself but an irrational power within your soul, a dwelling it shares at every moment with your power of reason? Even if you cannot tame it quickly, can you not do so over a longer period of time? It would be a terrible thing if you could not.
> (*Passions* 1.5, pp. 45–6 = *SM* 1, p. 20.12–19)

In other words, the passions are, in principle, correctable faults or, as Galen would prefer, diseases of the soul that can be cured. But there are limits to what this kind of moral training can achieve. Unchecked, passion can take such a hold that a cure is no longer possible:

> Strive to hold the impetuosity of this power in check before it grows and acquires an unconquerable strength. For then, even if you will to do so, you will not be able to hold it in check; then you will say what I heard a certain lover say – that you wish to stop but that you cannot – then you will call on us for help but in vain, just as that man begged for someone to help him and to cut out his passion. For there are also diseases of the body so intense that they are beyond cure.
>
> Perhaps you have never thought about this. It would be better, then, for you to think now and consider whether I am telling the

truth when I say that the concupiscible power often waxes so strong that it hurls us into a love beyond all cure, a love not only for beautiful bodies and sexual pleasures but also for voluptuous eating, gluttony in food and drink, and for lewd, unnatural conduct.
(*Passions* 1.6, p. 48 = *SM* 1, p. 22.8–22)

Nevertheless – and this is illuminating for the relationship between passion and character – the soul's susceptibility to the passions is a matter of nature as well as nurture. This is clear, Galen says, if you look at children:

Not only, then, are the natures of the young predisposed to grief but they are also readily inclined to anger and sumptuous eating, passions which I have spoken about at length up to now. Besides the types of young men I have already mentioned, you can see some who are shameless, others who are respectful; some have good memories, others are unmindful and forget; some work hard at their studies while others are careless and lazy.... Therefore, all who observe children call some modest and others shameless.... They further say that they are either cowards or contemptuous of blows; and they put other such names on them according to their natures. In this way, then, we see that some children are naturally truthful or liars and have many other differences of character about which there is now, in all likelihood, no need to speak, because some of these children are very easily educated while others benefit not at all.
(*Passions* 1.7, pp. 55–6 = *SM* 1, pp. 29.15–30.15)

This view, of course, provides a useful excuse for the moral educator: "If their nature will accept the advantage of our care, they could become good men. If they should fail to accept this attention, the blame would not be ours" (*Passions* 1.7, p. 56 = *SM* 1, p. 30.17–20). It also reveals a deep-rooted ambivalence about the nature of the moral character that is highly relevant to the study of characterization in the novels. If one is born with a natural predisposition to greed, say, or anger, does that make the exercise of the passion less culpable? Galen probably would have thought the question nonsensical. From the point of view of the moral educator, such a nature simply makes one more difficult to train. From everybody else's point of view, it makes such a person a more shameful and pitiable sight – that is, all the more an example to be avoided by the right-thinking individual anxious to achieve the philosophical way of life. The distinction between "natural" character as something one is born with and "moral" character as something for which one can be held morally responsible (or about which one should feel guilt) does not seem to enter into the discussion.

This view of the moral character as something that is both innate and affected by training and discipline persists right down to the Victorian moralists who devoted so much attention to the nurture of the young. For the ancient novelist, it means that there is no need to distinguish between expressions of character that are "innate" or intrinsic to a personality and those that reflect moral choices for which the individual can be held responsible. Character is depicted objectively from a unitary, external perspective that allows for the presentation of certain patterns of behavior as shameful or honorable – that is, as examples of good behavior to be followed or as types of bad behavior to be avoided – without troubling the spectator with the question of the moral responsibility of the individuals for their own behavior. One of Galen's longest narratives depicts a friend from Gortyna who (despite his other estimable qualities) is characterized as "so prone to anger that he used to assail his servants with his hands, even sometimes his feet, but far more frequently with a whip or any piece of wood that happened to be handy" (*Passions* 1.4, pp. 39–40 = *SM* 1, p. 14.1–7). An unseemly display of anger (with potentially fatal consequences) is followed by an equally unseemly – and equally violent – display of remorse (*Passions* 1.4, pp. 40–1 = *SM* 1, pp. 14.25–15.17). Interestingly, Galen treats both anger and remorse with the same amused contempt: his friend's emotional apologies are seen not as a properly penitent response to moral failing, but simply as a further example of excessive *pathos*.[7]

The therapeutic enterprise, however, to retain credibility, must also maintain the possibility of moral improvement in response to training: some people at least must be treated as moral subjects, not simply as object lessons in the effects of the passions. In Galen's treatises, the only moral subjects in this sense are the narrator (who makes moral choices in response to his observation of the passions in those around him) and, by implication, the addressee (who is exhorted to make such choices). This inevitably encourages a kind of moral voyeurism in which only the "I" and the "you" of the discourse have real choices; the many other characters introduced as examples of the passions simply provide a kind of ethical peep show, eternally cranking through their despicable – or pitiable – behavior patterns at the behest of the philosopher and his pupil.

The depiction of passion in the novels

Against this background, we can now move to examine the depiction of passion in the novels, noting four major points of comparison and one of contrast.

First, Galen's narrative depiction of the passions, and especially of passion as emotion, provides a useful key to reading the characterization of the novels. The novelists specialize in the portrayal of emotion: bags of emotion, emotion of all kinds, larger than life and splashed all over the screen in great tear-jerking dollops. Their ethos is caught exactly in tabloid coverage of a 1996 episode in the popular British television soap opera *Coronation Street*:

> I LOVE HER MORE THAN LIFE ITSELF[8]
> The heartbreaking *Coronation Street* exit of Raquel will be spread across three episodes next week – including a one-hour special on Wednesday.
> And today the *Mirror* can give an exclusive moment-by-moment preview of the Raquel-Curly parting that will bring tears to living-rooms across the land.
> Actress Sarah Lancashire's performance as Raquel was so moving that cast and crew sobbed themselves as the final moments were shot.
> Curly, played by Kevin Kennedy, says in the depths of his despair that if he had a gun, he would shoot them both rather than see her go.
> "I love her more than life itself," says Curly as his rejection unfolds in one of the most poignant stories in the Street's 36 years of happiness and heartbreak.
> *The glamour-girl barmaid makes her last exit next Friday, but Weatherfield's tear-filled week begins like this . . .*

The point is well observed in Gaselee's introduction to the protonovelistic collection of mythological tales which appears under the name of Parthenius:

> The mythological tales which Parthenius has given us in his collection have little interest in the way of folk-lore or religion; the mythology is above all made the groundwork for the development of emotion. Cornelius Gallus [to whom the collection is dedicated], or any writer with an artistic sense who determined to found his work on the summaries given him in these skeleton *Love Romances* [Pref. §1 τὴν ἄθροισιν τῶν ἐρωτικῶν παθημάτων, *tēn athroisin tōn erōtikōn pathēmatōn*] would find that the characteristics lending themselves best to elaboration would not be their religious or historical elements, but rather those of emotion; jealousy, hatred, ambition, and above all unhappy and passionate love. Take away the strictly mythological element (substitute, that is, the names of unknown persons for the semi-historical characters of whom the stories are related), and almost all might serve as the plots for novels, or rather parts of novels, of the kind under consideration.
> (Gaselee 1916: 409–10)

It is the portrayal of emotion – principally, but not entirely, "unhappy and passionate love" – that makes these adaptations of episodes from mythology or history "novelistic." Like the legendary film directors of the silent era, the novelists like their heroes and heroines to be able to register their emotions on screen, so that the effect of a particular passion (anger, fear, lust) is graphically illustrated "before your very eyes." There is a markedly dramatic element in this portrayal of *pathos*, sometimes explicitly so, as in Chariton's description of the sudden appearance of Chaereas in the courtroom in Babylon:

> What reporter could do justice to the scene in that courtroom? What dramatist ever staged such an extraordinary situation? An observer would have thought himself in a theatre filled with every conceivable emotion [μυρίων παθῶν, *myriōn pathōn*]. All were there at once – tears, joy, astonishment, pity, disbelief, prayer. They blessed Chaereas and rejoiced with Mithridates; they grieved with Dionysius; about Callirhoe they were baffled. She herself was totally confused and stood there speechless, gazing with eyes wide open only at Chaereas: I think that on that occasion even the king would have wished to be Chaereas.
>
> (Chariton 5.8.2–3)

The novelists are fond of this kind of emotional conglomerate, either in the big crowd scene where every emotion in turn runs across the face of the actors, or with individuals who experience all the emotions together. When pirates break into her tomb, Callirhoe is "seized with every emotion at once: fear, joy, misery, amazement, hope, disbelief" (Chariton 1.9.3). In Xenophon's novel, there are similar lists of mixed emotions (πάθη συμμιγῆ, *pathē symmigē*), as, for example, when Perilaus, on discovering Anthia apparently dead, is seized with grief, fear, and astonishment.[9]

The dramatic portrayal of passion through speech (dialogue and soliloquy) is, of course, nothing new in Greek literature; this was something developed centuries before in Greek theater and deeply embedded in rhetorical training through the *progymnasmata* (Hock 2005). But the novelists can add to it a relatively simple and direct narrative style (at least in the early novels) that allows them to realize the full effects of passion on their characters through explicit description of action and emotion as well as through direct speech. Very often, as in the philosophers, it is the trivial physical actions (biting, kicking, rolling on the ground) that give the portrayal its graphic force. Chariton is particularly good at this kind of narrative depiction of the effects of passion: Dionysius, "overcome with grief" for his first wife, "refused for the most part even to go out, though the city sorely missed him; he remained in his room as if his wife were still with him" (Chariton 2.1.1). Later, we are told that he (having transferred his affections to Callirhoe) lies "prostrate with grief, and his body too was emaciated. On hearing that Callirhoe was there, he could not speak, and a mist spread over his eyes at the unexpected news" (Chariton 2.7.4; cf. 3.1.3). Callirhoe, waking up in the tomb,

> called Chaereas, thinking he was asleep at her side. But when neither husband nor servants answered, and all was dark and lonely, she began to shiver and tremble, unable by reasoning to guess at the truth. As she slowly came to her senses, she touched the funeral wreaths and ribbons, and caused the gold and silver to clink. There was a prevalent odor of spices. She next remembered the kick and the

ensuing fall and eventually realized that as a result of her unconsciousness she had been buried. Then she screamed at the top of her voice...
(Chariton 1.8.2–4)

Chariton gives a particularly vivid dramatic portrayal of Chaereas's fateful outburst of jealousy (ζηλοτυπία, *zēlotypia*),[10] which in turn hinges on his capacity to believe fabricated slanders against his wife: both the anger and the mistaken belief are, according to Galen, "commonly called errors":[11]

> Chaereas... rushed in as though possessed. Finding the chamber still shut, he banged on the door vigorously. When the maid opened it and he burst in upon Callirhoe, his anger was changed to sorrow and he tore his clothes and shed tears. When she asked him what had happened, he was speechless, being able neither to disbelieve what he had seen, nor yet to believe what he was unwilling to accept. As he stood confused and trembling, his wife, quite unsuspicious of what had happened, begged him to tell her the reason for his anger. With bloodshot eyes and thick voice, he said, "It is the fact that you have forgotten me that hurts so much."
> (Chariton 1.3.3–5)

Although the lovers are reconciled on this first occasion, it is no surprise that Chaereas's youthful propensity for jealousy and his inability to control his anger eventually precipitate the tragedy that motivates the novel's plot:

> He could find no voice with which to reproach her; but overcome with anger, he kicked at her as she ran forward. His foot struck the girl squarely in the diaphragm and stopped her breath.... Thus Callirhoe lay without speech or breath, presenting to all the appearance of death.... [But] Chaereas, still inwardly seething, locked himself up all night.
> (Chariton 1.4.12–5.1)

Second, as in the philosophers, the novelists' dramatic depiction of the effects of passion functions as a kind of "aversion therapy," displaying the full awfulness of uncontrolled passion and the depths to which sufferers will sink under its sway. This feature is especially clear in the portrayal of "barbarian" and lower-class characters. These tend to be depicted in monochrome tones as "lustful" or "devious," the implication being that the novels's heroines and heroes, being both noble and Greek, are free of such defects. Chariton delights in presenting the eunuch Artaxates as prey to "all kinds of emotion [μυρίων παθῶν μεστός, *myriōn pathōn mestos*] – anger at Callirhoe, sorrow for himself, and fear of the king" (Chariton 6.6.1). Artaxates has already been characterized as a combination of the "cunning slave" and "pimp" characters of New Comedy, with a continual stress[12] on his status as "slave" (worse, as "eunuch") and "barbarian," working shamelessly on the passions of first the Great King (Chariton 6.3–4) and then Callirhoe (Chariton 6.5). His success is varied. The barbarian King, as we will see, is completely enslaved to Love and easily swayed by Artaxates' arguments, and Artaxates, on his part, is encouraged to see his own success as a smart career move. The narrator makes it absolutely clear that this character's motives are anything but disinterested:

> Artaxates was in high spirits too; he thought that he had undertaken valuable service and would be holding the reins at court from now on, since both would be grateful to him, especially Callirhoe. He judged that it would be an easy matter to handle; he was thinking like a eunuch, a slave, a barbarian. He did not know the spirit of a wellborn Greek – especially Callirhoe, chaste Callirhoe, who loved her husband.
> (Chariton 6.4.10 [trans. Reardon 1989a: 94])

But Callirhoe's reactions to the eunuch's proposition are beyond his comprehension; not only is she completely impervious to his indecent proposal, but she is also able to control her immediate anger and prevaricate to get herself out of a dangerous position, while contriving a monumental put-down for the eunuch at the same time:

> Callirhoe's first impulse was to dig her nails into the eyes of this would-be pimp and tear them out if she could; but being a well-brought-up and sensible woman [πεπαιδευμένη καὶ φρενήρης, *pepaideumenē kai phrenērēs*], she quickly remembered where she was, who she was, and who it was who was talking to her. She controlled her anger and from that point on spoke evasively [κατειρωνεύσατο, *kateirōneusato*] to the barbarian. "Oh," she said, "I hope I am not so deranged as to let myself believe I am fit for the Great King. I am like the servants of Persian women. I beg you, please do not talk about me to your master anymore. You can be sure that even if he is not angry now, he will deal with you severely later on, when he realizes you have thrown the ruler of the whole world to Dionysius's slave-girl. I am surprised that with all your intelligence you fail to realize how humane the King is: he is not in love with an unfortunate woman, he is taking pity on her. We had better stop this talking; someone may misrepresent us to the Queen." With that she hurried off, leaving the eunuch standing there all agape; he had been brought up in a highly despotic society and could not conceive that there was anything impossible – even for himself, let alone the King.
> (Chariton 6.5.8–10 [trans. Reardon 1989a: 95–6, with modifications drawn from Goold 1995: 305])

The contrast between Greek and barbarian is underlined yet again through the familiar trope of the "despotism" of the Persian court; it is interesting to speculate what the resonances of this might be for Greek readers living under the Roman Empire, or, if the early dating is right, for Roman readers in Neronian Rome (Goold 1995: 5).

Third, as in Galen, this dramatic realization of the effects of the passions leads to a certain blurring of the boundaries between pathos and ethos, or what we would call "emotion" and "character." The novels contain many "flat" characters, often little more than stock figures used to dramatize certain emotions. The emphasis is on displaying certain patterns of behavior associated with a particular emotional situation, not on considering the possible causes or cure for such behavior. In fact, in some cases at least, the implication is that certain races or classes (barbarians, eunuchs, slaves) have an innate predisposition to certain patterns of behavior; but there is no question of diminished responsibility. None of these characters ever seeks to claim (like the street kids in Bernstein's *West Side Story*), "Hey! I'm depraved on account I'm deprived!" Like the negative examples in Galen, these characters are considered purely objectively, as samples of passion-controlled behavior and its shameful and degrading consequences, irrespective of the question of moral responsibility. As readers, we are meant not to consider apportioning relative degrees of guilt, but rather to take note of them as negative examples and at all costs to avoid falling into the same state.

The novels's heroes themselves often provide textbook examples of the kind of unbridled passion (anger, fear, jealousy) that Galen deplores. Sometimes this is clearly culpable behavior, as with Chaereas's initial fit of jealous rage that propels Chariton's plot, and for which Chaereas is justly punished by Aphrodite (Chariton 8.1.3); at other times the varied emotions of grief and fear (or, as we will see, love itself) are simply represented, as they are in Galen, as forms of "pain" that any sensible person will seek to avoid (*Passions* 1.7, p. 54 = *SM* 1, p. 28.9–12.). But it is above all in the stock villains of the novel plots that we can see this "objective" depiction of passion. Xenophon's heroine and hero are constantly seeking to maintain their chastity against the most devious wiles and assaults of assorted pirates, barbarians, and other outsiders:

> A few days later Apsyrtus went off on another venture to Syria, and his daughter Manto fell in love with Habrocomes. She was beautiful and already of marriageable age, but not nearly as beautiful as Anthia. Through her day-to-day contact with Habrocomes this Manto became uncontrollably [ἀκατασχέτως, *akataschetōs*] infatuated, and she did not know what to do. For she did not dare to speak to Habrocomes; she knew that he had a wife, and never expected to win him round; nor did she dare to tell any of her own household for

fear of her father. Because of all this, her feelings were all the more inflamed and she was in a bad state.

(Xenophon 2.3.1–3)

She decides to confide in Anthia's (Greek) maid Rhode, and the encounter allows Xenophon to underline Manto's dubious and uncontrollable status as a barbarian: "You must realize that you are my slave and that if you hurt me, you will experience the anger of a barbarian woman!" Rhode is all too well aware of it, as she confides to her partner and fellow-slave Leucon:

> The daughter of our master... is madly in love with Habrocomes and is threatening to do us terrible harm if she does not succeed. So consider what we must do. It is dangerous to thwart this barbarian woman but impossible to come between Habrocomes and Anthia.
>
> (Xenophon 2.3.4–8)

And their fears prove to be well founded: when Manto receives a letter of rejection from Habrocomes, we read,

> [She] could not control her anger. All her feelings were confused: she felt envy, jealousy, grief, and fear, and was planning how to take her revenge on the man who was turning her down.
>
> (Xenophon 2.5.5)

And, of course, she does. In a later episode, Habrocomes gets another dose of the same treatment in Egypt, from a Potiphar's wife character called Kyno (Xenophon 3.12), who is not only in the grip of uncontrollable passion, but ugly as well:

> [Araxus] had a wife who was hideous to look at and much worse to listen to; she was amazingly insatiable, and her name was Kyno. This Kyno fell in love with Habrocomes the moment he was brought to the house and could not contain herself any longer; she was terribly passionate and determined to indulge her lust.
>
> (Xenophon 3.12.3)

Anthia, meanwhile, is having to fend off the attacks of an Indian merchant prince called Psammis:

> This man saw Anthia at the merchants' quarters, was ravished at the sight of her, paid the merchants a large sum, and took her as a maidservant. The moment he bought her the barbarian tried to force her and have his will with her. She was unwilling and at first refused, but at length gave as an excuse to Psammis (barbarians are

superstitious by nature) that her father had dedicated her at birth to Isis till she was of age to marry, which she said was still a year away. "And so," she said, "if you offend the goddess's ward, she will be angry with you and take a terrible revenge." Psammis believed her, paid homage to the goddess, and kept away from Anthia.

(Xenophon 3.11.3–5)

Despite the fact that Anthia arouses exactly the same reactions in the respectably married prefect of Egypt (Xenophon 5.4) and uses a very similar delaying tactic with the brothel keeper in Tarentum (Xenophon 5.7), Xenophon's narration leaves a strong impression that both Psammis' passion and his religious scruples (*deisidaimonia*) are typically "barbarian."

Fourth, it would be a mistake, however, to take this monochrome characterization at face value. Both Xenophon and Chariton also feature a number of characters who are depicted subjectively, as moral subjects capable of moral choice – in other words, as personalities torn between conflicting passions and not just as passion personified. For Xenophon it is principally the heroine and hero who get this more nuanced treatment, but Chariton has a whole range of multifaceted characters whose humane portrayal belies Chariton's rather conventional rhetoric of Greek versus barbarian.

Dionysius provides one of Chariton's most successful examples of a personality struggling with conflicting passions. He is introduced as grieving for his dead first wife, "wearing mourning and sad-faced" (Chariton 1.12.6). He is also, prophetically, described as "rich and susceptible to women" (Chariton 1.12.7). His first sight of Callirhoe, however, sends him home "already aflame with love" (Chariton 2.3.8), and he hides himself in a vain attempt to conceal love's "wound" (Chariton 2.4.1):

> Not wanting his servants to look down on him, or his friends to think him immature, he kept a tight rein on himself throughout the whole evening, thinking he would not be noticed, but making himself more noticeable by his very silence.
>
> (Chariton 2.4.1)

(Note the implication that giving way to love is seen as potentially shameful and "immature" behavior.) In a vain attempt to evade the inevitable, "he prolonged the drinking as long as possible since he knew that he would be unable to sleep, and in his wakefulness he needed the company of friends" – but to no avail.

> Still he could get no sleep. In his mind he was at the shrine of Aphrodite, and he recalled every detail: her face, her hair, how she had turned round and looked at him, her voice, her figure, her words; her very tears were setting him on fire.
>
> (Chariton 2.4.2–3)

What is described here in graphic detail is the first *agōn* (Chariton 2.4.4) in a sustained campaign in which Dionysius is successively brought under the control of a personified and belligerent Love. Yet Dionysius remains throughout a moral subject, able to reflect on his passion and to attempt resistance:

> Then you could observe a struggle between reason and passion, for although engulfed by desire, as a noble man he tried to resist, and, rising above the waves, as it were, he said to himself, "Are you not ashamed, Dionysius, the leader of Ionia in worth and reputation, a man whom governors, kings, and city-states admire – are you not ashamed to be suffering the heartache of a boy? You fell in love at first sight, and that too while still in mourning and before you have propitiated the spirits of your poor wife. Is this why you came to the country, to celebrate a new marriage still clothed in black – and that too with a slave girl who may even belong to another man? Why, you do not even have legal title to her!"
>
> (Chariton 2.4.4–5)

The second phase of the campaign, aided and abetted by the schemes of Plangon, reaches a climax when Callirhoe stumbles into Dionysius's arms and he kisses her: "That kiss sank deep into Dionysius's heart like poison, and he could no longer see or hear. He was completely taken by storm [ἐκπεπολιορκουμένος, *ekpepoliorkoumenos*] and could find no remedy for his love" (Chariton 2.8.1). Yet even when Dionysius is fully committed to the marriage, he can attempt to control his passion with reasoned reflection:

> His passion [ἐρωτικὸν πάθος, *erōtikon pathos*] mounted and brooked no delay to the marriage: control is irksome when desire can be indulged. Though well brought up, Dionysius was caught in the tempest and his heart was engulfed [ἐβαπτίζετο, *ebaptizeto*]. Yet he forced himself to rise above the billows of his passion [ὅμως δὲ ἀνακύπτειν ἐβιάζετο καθάπερ ἐκ τρικυμίας τοῦ πάθους, *homōs de anakyptein ebiazeto kathaper ek trikymias tou pathous*]. And so he gave himself over to the following reflections [λογισμοῖς, *logismois*] ...
>
> (Chariton 3.2.6)

The "siege" of Dionysius is balanced in Chariton's novel by a parallel assault on the chastity of Callirhoe. Such assaults, as we have noted, are standard episodes in novel plots, and usually they are repelled by the hero or heroine without much sign of internal struggle. Callirhoe is different in that she does actually (and, in effect, bigamously) marry her suitor, but only as the result of a prolonged but completely different *agōn*:

> [At first] Callirhoe proved completely invincible and remained faithful to Chaereas alone. Yet she was overcome by the stratagems of fortune, against whom alone human reason [λογισμὸς ἀνθρώπου, *logismos anthrōpou*] is powerless. She is a deity who likes to win [φιλόνεικος, *philoneikos*] and is capable of anything. So now she contrived a situation that was unexpected, not to say incredible. It is worth hearing how Fortune laid her plans to attack the girl's chastity.
> (Chariton 2.8.2–4)

Fortune's unexpected trump card is Callirhoe's pregnancy, which forces her into the unwelcome position of having to choose between fidelity to her husband and the interests of her child. The piquancy of the situation (enhanced by the reader's knowledge that Callirhoe's first husband is not actually dead) is exacerbated by Plangon's brutal insistence that there is no time to lose if Callirhoe intends to seek an abortion as her only realistic alternative to marriage:

> The more Plangon urged her to destroy the unborn child, the greater became her pity for it. "Give me time to consider," she said. "My choice lies between two vital matters, my honor or the life of my child." Plangon again praised her for not choosing hastily, saying, "A decision either way can be justified, in the one case by a wife's fidelity, in the other by a mother's love. But this is no time for protracted delay. By tomorrow at the latest you must choose one way or the other, before your condition becomes known."
> (Chariton 2.10.7–8)

The whole situation, with Callirhoe's emotional monologue setting out her options on both sides, reads like a dramatic reconstruction of a bizarre but conceivable dilemma in moral philosophy: faced with such a choice, what should the philosopher do?

But what, finally, of the central theme of the novels, the irresistible power of love? Here there is at first sight little room for common ground with Galen. Sexual attraction, for the philosopher, is simply one example of the kind of inordinate desire that the wise man will do his best to curb:

> When a man's anger makes his behavior unseemly, it is a disgraceful thing to see. It is just as disgraceful when his unseemly behavior is due to erotic desire and gluttony and to drunkenness and luxuriousness in eating, which are actions and passions belonging to the concupiscible power of the soul.
> (*Passions* 1.6, pp. 46–7 = SM 1, p. 21.4–7)

Galen himself prefers not to dwell on erotic desire, but to focus on the control of gluttony as an example of the need to control all the "concupiscible powers"

(*Passions* 1.6, pp. 49–51 = *SM* 1, pp. 23.30–25.15). In the novels, by contrast, the passion of love is not merely tolerated, but is celebrated as a divine power that not even the best and noblest can resist. Thus, paradoxically, the lustful desires of their various captors, however regrettably they reflect on the moral character of the individuals concerned, are at the same time right and proper responses to the divine beauty of the novels's heroines and heroes. This is particularly clear in Chariton, where Callirhoe's every appearance is accompanied by tributes to Aphrodite: "Her beauty was not so much human as divine, not that of a Nereid or a mountain nymph, either, but that of Aphrodite herself" (Chariton 1.1.2).[13]

The power of Aphrodite and her capricious offspring is explicitly acknowledged as a motive force in the plots of both novels. Chariton's hero offends Aphrodite not through resistance to Eros, but by allowing his love to be overpowered by jealousy. At the end of the story we discover that Aphrodite's anger has been behind the couple's protracted torments:

> By now [Aphrodite] was becoming reconciled to Chaereas, though earlier she had been intensely angered at his intemperate jealousy; for, having received from her the fairest of gifts, surpassing even that given to Alexander surnamed Paris, he had repaid her favor with insult [ὕβρισεν εἰς τήν χάριν, *hybrisen eis tēn charin*]. Since Chaereas had now made full amends to Love by his wanderings from west to east amid countless tribulations [διὰ μυρίων παθῶν, *dia myriōn pathōn*], Aphrodite took pity on him, and, as she had originally brought together this handsome pair, so now, having harassed them over land and sea, she resolved to unite them again.
> (Chariton 8.1.3)

Xenophon's plot is notoriously lacking in direction, but the closest it gets to ethical motivation is supplied at the outset by Habrocomes' refusal to recognize the power of Eros:

> He had a high opinion of himself, taking pride in his attainments, and a great deal more in his appearance. Everything that was regarded as beautiful he despised as inferior, and nothing he saw or heard seemed up to his standard. And when he heard a boy or a girl praised for their good looks, he laughed at the people making such claims for not knowing that only he himself was handsome. He did not even recognize Eros as a god; he rejected him totally and considered him of no importance, saying that no one would ever fall in love or submit to the god except of his own accord. And whenever he saw a temple or statue of Eros, he used to laugh and claimed that he was more handsome and powerful than any Eros....
>
> Eros was furious at this, for he is a contentious god and implacable against those who despise him. He looked for some stratagem to

employ against the boy, for even the god thought he would be difficult to capture. So he armed himself to the teeth, equipped himself with his full armory of love potions, and set out against Habrocomes.
(Xenophon 1.1–2)

Here love itself appears to be a punishment inflicted on the hero for his *hybris*, and this suggests one possible point of community between Galen and the novelists. There does seem to lie somewhere behind the novels – and more importantly, perhaps, behind their somewhat implausible plots – a common perception that the *pathos* of sexual love is precisely that: it is a *pathos*, something that happens to people (πάσχω, *paschō*), that is outside their control, and that can have tragic and disastrous consequences. This seems to be the way the word is used in Parthenius; and indeed, most of the *erotika pathēmata* that he relates are tragic rather than romantic episodes where love, however innocent, is disastrous for the persons concerned. Xenophon includes a couple of mini-episodes of tragic love in this manner in the stories of Hippothous's doomed love for Hyperanthes (Xenophon 3.2) and of the fisherman Aegialeus and his dead wife (Xenophon 5.1). On this view, love is a *pathos*, a tragic event that brings suffering (even when it is innocent, and even when it is returned) in precisely the same way as, for Galen, grief is a form of psychic *pathos* analogous to the physical pain that affects the body (*Passions* 1.7, p. 54 = SM 1, p. 28.9–12). This mode of thought, I suggest, helps us to understand the apparent lack of motivation in Xenophon's plot, especially in the launching of the fateful voyage (which seems so obviously the wrong response to an oracle predicting disaster at sea [Xenophon 1.6.2]). If the story of Anthia and Habrocomes were known – or invented – as an example of "tragic love" in the manner of Parthenius's tales, then the initial collocation of love and disaster might be less surprising. In this context, the classic voyage motif sits well enough as an example of the sufferings (*pathos* can also mean "tribulation," as in Chariton 8.1.3) that are love's natural concomitants.

But arguably, the novelists' most striking (if backhanded) tribute to the moral philosophers is at the point where they are most self-consciously opposed, in their vivid portrayal of the power of love over reason. Even here, the underlying sense of *pathos* as suffering is never very far away. Consistently, for hero and heroine as much as for the villains, falling in love is presented as a painful condition that nobody in his or her right mind would enter voluntarily. Passion is a "wound," a "disease," a poison in the heart. Chaereas, when he first sees Callirhoe, is depicted as "a hero mortally wounded in battle, ... too proud to fall but too weak to stand" (Chariton 1.1.7); the whole city was united in concern as "a well-bred and spirited youth began to waste away" (Chariton 1.1.8), and when the young people found out the cause of his sickness (τῆς νόσου, *tēs nosou*), "all felt pity for a handsome youth who seemed likely to die from the passion of an honest heart [διὰ πάθος ψυχῆς εὐφυοῦς, *dia pathos psychēs euphyous*]" (Chariton 1.1.10).[14]

Passion is also depicted as a "fire" that engulfs its victims. Compare Chariton's description of the effects of love on his heroine and hero: "The ensuing night brought torment to both, for love's fire was raging. But what the girl suffered [ἔπασχεν, *epaschen*] was worse" (Chariton 1.1.7–8); or on the hapless Dionysius: "Leonas, I am utterly ruined and you are the cause of my misery. You have brought fire into my house, or rather, into my heart" (Chariton 2.4.7).[15] Xenophon combines the images of sickness and fire in his depiction of the plight of Habrocomes and Anthia:

> As time went on, the boy was unable to go on; already his whole body had wasted away and his mind had given in, so that Lycomedes and Themisto were very despondent, not knowing what had happened to Habrocomes, but afraid at what they saw. Megamedes and Euippe were just as afraid for Anthia, as they watched her beauty wasting away without apparent cause. At last they brought in diviners and priests to Anthia to find a remedy to her plight. They came and performed sacrifices, made libations of all sorts, pronounced foreign phrases, alleging that they were placating some demons or other, and pretended that her malady came from the underworld. Lycomedes' household too kept offering prayers and sacrifices for Habrocomes. There was no relief for either of them from their malady, but their love burned still more fiercely. Both, then, lay ill; their condition was critical, and they were expected to die at any moment, unable to confess what was wrong. At last their fathers sent to the oracle of Apollo to find out the cause of their illness and the antidote.
> (Xenophon 1.5.5–9)

So far, the moral philosophers probably would agree: Galen himself talks of love as a "diseased" condition for which the patient often leaves it too late to seek help (*Passions* 1.6, p. 48 = *SM* 1, p. 22.8–24). The difference, of course, is in the remedy. Galen asserts that there is a well-tested "way" (ὁδός, *hodos*) to achieve self-control, "the usual one for recognizing and curing all diseases of the soul" (*Passions* 1.7, p. 53 = *SM* 1, p. 27.5–7):

> The chastisement [κόλασις, *kolasis*] of the concupiscible power consists in not furnishing it with the enjoyment of the things it desires. If it does attain to this enjoyment, it becomes great and strong; if it is disciplined and corrected, it becomes small and weak. The result is that the concupiscible power does not follow reason [τῷ λογισμῷ, *tō logismō*] because it is obedient but because it is weak.
> (*Passions* 1.6, p. 47 = *SM* 1, p. 21.13–18)

In the world of the novels, on the contrary, it is dangerous to try to suppress love's fire, and the remedy sought is the exact opposite. As the cynical

Artaxates tells the Great King, "The remedy you seek has been already found by Greeks as well as Persians. There is no other remedy for love except the loved one. This after all is the meaning of the famous oracle, 'He who wounded shall heal'" (Chariton 6.3.7). In Xenophon's story it is the oracle of Apollo that points the way to the necessary remedy: "Why do you long to learn of the end of a malady, and its beginning? One disease has both in its grasp, and from that the remedy must be accomplished" (Xenophon 1.6.2). Achilles Tatius's Charmides uses a similar argument:

> I am about to battle against the Rangers, but another battle is being waged in my soul. The enemy within is besieging me with his bow, harassing me with arrows: I have lost the fight; I am bristling with his shafts. Call the doctor, sir, and quickly; my wounds demand immediate attention. True, I fight mortal enemies with fire, but Eros hurls his own burning brands at me. O Menelaos, quench this fire first. Premartial sex is a good omen for success. Let Aphrodite set me up for Ares.
> (Achilles Tatius 4.7 [trans. Winkler 1989: 225])[16]

But the novelists also know of an alternative therapy, one that, significantly, they call "being a philosopher." Chariton displays this particularly clearly in his description of the moral *agōn* inflicted by Love on the virtuous Dionysius, a struggle between *pathos* and reason (*logismos* [Chariton 2.4.4, cited above]). Dionysius, unlike most of the other would-be suitors of the novels's heroines, has had a good education and knows that being in love is not a state to which the well-brought up Greek male will readily admit: "Dionysius, love-smitten, tried to conceal the wound, as became somebody well-brought up who made especial claim to manliness" (Chariton 2.4.1). Love, in other words, will naturally conflict with ἀρετή (*aretē*): neither "manly prowess" nor "moral excellence" (both meanings are appropriate here) will allow itself to be overpowered by passion. Xenophon's Habrocomes has a similar concept of the essential opposition between manly virtue and passion:

> Habrocomes pulled at his hair and tore his clothes; he lamented over his misfortunes and exclaimed: "What catastrophe has befallen me, Habrocomes, till now a man [ἀνδρικός, *andrikos*], despising Eros and slandering the god? I have been captured and conquered and am forced to be the slave of a girl. Now, it seems, there is someone more beautiful than I am, and I acknowledge love as a god. But now I am nothing but a worthless coward [ἄνανδρος, *anandros*]. Can I not hold out this time? Shall I not show my mettle and stand firm? Will I not remain more handsome than Eros? Now I must conquer this worthless god. The girl is beautiful; but what of it? To your *eyes*,

Habrocomes, Anthia is beautiful; but not to *you*, if your will holds firm. You must make up your mind to that: Eros must never be my master."

(Xenophon 1.4.1–3)

Galen would probably have agreed; but for the novelists, this is a conflict that the philosopher cannot hope to win. No amount of rational debate can successfully resist love's onslaught:

> But Love snapped his fingers at these sensible thoughts, considering his self-restraint [σωφροσύνη, *sōphrosynē*] an insult, and for that reason inflamed all the more a heart which attempted to philosophize with love [ἐπυρπόλει σφοδρότερον ψυχὴν ἐν ἔρωτι φιλοσοφοῦσαν, *epyrpolei sphodroteron psychēn en erōti philosophousan*].
>
> (Chariton 2.4.5)

Chariton's Persian King goes through a similar (and equally fruitless) moral battle. Love is a ruthless foe who "invades" his heart and takes him captive (Chariton 6.3.2); yet when Artaxates suggests that the easiest remedy is to indulge his passion and take Callirhoe by force, the King shows himself rather more of a philosopher than the eunuch had expected: "I am mindful of the laws.... Do not accuse me of lacking self-control [*akrasia*]. I am not overcome to that extent" (Chariton 6.3.8). So, balked by his own sense of honor from giving free rein to his passion, the King pleads with Artaxates to help him find another remedy:

> That is a noble thought, Your Majesty.... Do not apply to your love the same remedy that other men use, but rather the more potent and kingly one of fighting with yourself [ἀνταγωνιζόμενος σεαυτῷ, *antagōnizomenos seautō*]. For you alone, master, can overcome even a god. So distract your thoughts [ψυχὴν, *psychēn*] with every pleasure.... It is better to spend your time hunting than in the palace and close to the fire.
>
> (Chariton 6.3.8–9)

Galen could hardly have put it better himself, but the ill-concealed *hybris* in the eunuch's words leaves the reader in little doubt that this philosophical "remedy" will prove futile. Love, as the novelists repeatedly tell us, is a deity who "likes winning and enjoys unexpected triumphs" (Chariton 1.1.4; cf. 2.8.1). The result of this battle is a foregone conclusion:

> The king saw no horse, though many riders raced with him; no beast, though many were pursued: he heard no hound, though many were baying; no man, though all were shouting. He saw only Callirhoe,

though she was not there; he heard only her, though she was not speaking. In fact Love had accompanied him to the hunt, and being a god who likes to win and seeing that the king was opposing him with well-laid plans, as he thought, Love turned his own strategy against him, and used the very cure to set his heart on fire. Love entered his mind and said, "How wonderful it would be to see Callirhoe here, with her dress tucked up to her knees and her arms bared, with flushed face and heaving bosom...." As the king so pictured and imagined her, his passion flared up.

(Chariton 6.4.5–7)

Only the fortunate pair whose mutual passion forms the pivot of the novel's action is able to quench the flame of unrequited desire in the legitimate pleasures of the marriage bed:

With this they relaxed in each other's arms and enjoyed the first fruits of Aphrodite; and there was ardent rivalry all night long, each trying to prove they loved the other more. When it was day, they got up much happier, and much more cheerful after fulfilling the desires they had had for each other for so long.

(Xenophon 1.9.9–10.1)

For them – and for them almost alone in the narrative world of the novels – the fulfillment of passion is wholly unreprehensible: far from upbraiding these couples for the intensity of their mutual passion, the novels reward them.[17] Eros is properly honored by those who surrender to his shafts, but only if they are married.[18]

Conclusions

The two novels studied here testify to a popular view that "acting the philosopher" means being able to exert control over the passions, especially sexual passion. Interestingly, Galen uses a similar phrase in another context to describe the admirable sexual restraint exercised by Christians of all social classes (Walzer 1947: 15). The passions in this perspective are viewed as pathological conditions, and the "philosophical" ability to control them also happens to coincide with patterns of behavior that are characteristic of the Greek (as opposed to the barbarian), and of the free (and preferably noble) as opposed to the slave. The novelists, like Galen, thus testify to a complex network of ethical patterns deeply embedded in Greek thought in which shame and honor (pride of birth, pride of race) are inextricably interwoven with the "manly" virtue of self-control (although it is significant that their female characters are also capable of displaying this kind of virtue – or at least, their heroines are).

But it is also characteristic of the novelists that they refuse to take the "philosophical" ideal of self-control too seriously. The stories of Chariton and Xenophon tap into a rich seam of dramatically represented emotion in Greek literature in which Eros is not only a *pathos*, but a god: there is a touch of *hybris* about the notion of resistance to his power. The novels thus present at times an embryonic "anti-philosophy" or "religion of Love" comparable to the "anti-religion" of courtly love in the Middle Ages (Lewis 1936). In the later novelists (especially Achilles Tatius), this takes on a darker, more violently erotic tone that is developed much more intensely in the *peri erōtos* literature. But in the early novels, the dominant tone is not so much hostile to philosophy as playful and gently mocking. Philosophy, above all, is something that should not be taken too seriously: like Epictetus's worldly old man (though in a different context), the novelists say, "Listen to me, my son; one ought of course to philosophize, but one ought also to keep one's head; this is all nonsense" (Epictetus, *Diss.* 1.22.18 [trans. Oldfather 1925–8: 1.149]).

Notes

1 Unless otherwise stated, all translations of Galen's *On the Passions of the Soul* (*De affectuum dignotione*), cited hereinafter as *Passions*, are those of Harkins (1963), sometimes slightly modified. The Greek text is cited according to vol. 1 of the *Scripta Minora* edition of Galen's minor works, edited by Marquardt, von Mueller, and Helmreich (1884), cited hereinafter as *SM* 1 (with page and line). For Galen and the passions see Hankinson 1993.

2 Unless otherwise stated, all translations of Chariton's *Callirhoe* are those of Goold (1995), although occasionally modified slightly. For Xenophon, I have used the Greek text of Dalmeyda (1962) and, unless otherwise stated, the translation of G. Anderson (1989) in the collection of ancient novels edited by Reardon (1989b). This collection provides convenient and informed access to the Greek novels in English, but I have not attempted here to provide an up-to-date bibliography of this burgeoning field. Note especially Bowie 1985; Brant, Hedrick, and Shea 2005; Hägg 1971; 1983; 2004; Helms 1966; Morgan and Stoneman 1994; Schmeling 1996; and Tatum 1994.

3 This section of the Greek text is bracketed by the editors.

4 Note that it is not the punishment that is reprehensible here, but the exercise of passion. Galen and his father clearly belonged to the "never hit a slave in anger" school of thought; you should wait until your anger had cooled down, and then punish "with reflection" (*Passions* 1.5, p. 42 = *SM* 1, p. 16.20–2).

5 *Passions* 1.4, p. 39 = *SM* 1, p. 13.14–15. Note also *Passions* 1.5, p. 43 (= *SM* 1, p. 17.5–10): even though Galen admits that "inflicting an incurable injury on a human being is the act either of someone slightly insane or of an irrational, wild animal," he still holds that "those who strike their servants with their own hands are not such great sinners as those who bite and kick stones, doors, and keys," presumably because the latter exhibit the more uncontrolled and shameful behavior.

6 Philodemus, *Ira*, col. 1.20–7 (Indelli 1988). Cf. col. 3.13–18, and also col. 4.4–19, where there is a comparison with doctors who describe the dangers and sufferings

7 So Helms (1966: 36), probably rightly, cites the penitence of Chaereas as an example of moral "weakness."
8 *Daily Mirror*, 8 November 1996, p. 2.
9 Xenophon 3.7.1; cf. 5.13.3. Cf. also Achilles Tatius 5.19.1: "On reading this, my feelings exploded in all directions – I turned red; I went pale; I wondered at it; I doubted every word. I was rapt with joy and racked with distress" (trans. Winkler 1989: 243).
10 On jealousy see now Konstan 2003; 2006: 219–43.
11 Galen distinguishes "error" (arising from mistaken reasoning) from "passion" (arising from "an irrational power within us which refuses to obey reason"), but he acknowledges that both are commonly called "errors" (ἁμαρτήματα, *hamartēmata*): (*Passions* 1.1, p. 28 = *SM* 1, p. 2.5–10).
12 See Helms 1966: 101–6. Artaxates displays "a typically servile attitude manifested in an eagerness to please, a shrewdness in adapting to changing fortune.... The interest is centered mainly in the dialogues between Artaxates and Callirhoe which reveal so vividly the vast gulf separating the moral character of an oriental slave from that of a noble and free-born Greek woman" (Helms 1966: 102).
13 Cf. Chariton 1.14.1; 2.2.2–8; 2.3.5–9; 2.5.3; 3.2.17.
14 For love as wound see Chariton 2.4.1; 5.5.5; 6.3.3; for love as poison see Chariton 2.8.1. Cf. the similar extended description of the physical effects of passion on Habrocomes and Anthia in Xenophon 1.4–9.
15 Cf. Chariton 1.1.8; 2.3.8; 2.4.3, 5; 6.7.1; Xenophon 1.3.4. On the metaphor of "burning" see Alexander 1998.
16 Cf. Achilles Tatius 5.26.2: "However angry you make me, I still burn with love for you.... Make a truce with me at least for now; pity me.... A single consummation will be enough. It is a small remedy I ask for so great an illness. Quench a little of my fire" (trans. Winkler 1989: 247–8).
17 Xenophon provides two more examples of happy and fulfilled passion in the slave couple Leucon and Rhode (Xenophon 5.13), and in Hippothous, who is allowed in the end to find happiness with Cleisthenes (Xenophon 5.9, 13). But Leucon and Rhode are servants, whose own mutual devotion hardly figures in the narrative itself; and Hippothous has already been imprinted on our minds as the subject of an unhappy love affair that ended in tragedy (Xenophon 3.2). Only Habrocomes and Anthia share the distinction of narrated passion that achieves a happy ending.
18 On the mutuality of passion between Chaereas and Callirhoe, see Chariton 2.8.4; cf. Konstan 1994. On the ambivalence of the philosophers toward passion within marriage see Deming 2004: 47–104; Alexander 1998.

Part III

PHILOSOPHY AND RELIGION

10

PHILO OF ALEXANDRIA ON THE RATIONAL AND IRRATIONAL EMOTIONS*

David Winston

Philo's theory of the passions is essentially that of the Stoics with occasional modifications. Although Posidonius's Platonizing version of the Stoic theory was of considerable help to Philo, he nevertheless used this paradigm rather selectively. Philo's knowledge of Stoic philosophy is quite extensive, and he even makes use of some of the most esoteric of the technical terms of that school. Philo's portrait of Moses is that of a supersage who transcends even the impossible ideal projected by the many Stoic paradoxes that attracted the ridicule of their numerous critics. Moreover, in the final analysis, the most effective therapy for removing the passions is to counter them with the most powerful emotion of all, our love of God.

Introduction

According to Galen, Posidonius asserts in the first book of his work *On the Passions* that the examination of things good and evil, ends and virtues, depends on the right inquiry into the passions (*PHP* 5.6, line 15 [De Lacy 326] = Posidonius, frg. 30 Edelstein and Kidd).[1] The same may be said to be true of Philo, who, like Posidonius and Chrysippus, apparently devoted a separate treatise to this topic, which unfortunately is no longer extant, although it may represent a project that was never consummated (*Leg.* 3.139).[2] In any case, Philo's vast oeuvre is liberally interwoven with numerous and vivid analyses of the canonical four generic passions (appetite, fear, distress, and pleasure [*SVF*

---

* I thank Prof. Tony Long for his helpful comments on this essay.

3.378]) that were designated by the Stoics as the sources of all vice.[3] In Middle Platonic fashion, Philo adopted the Platonic tripartition of the soul that located each soul-part in a particular area of the body (cf. Plato, *Tim.* 69–70), although this was construed as a fundamentally bipartite dichotomy of the rational and the irrational, with the affective part (παθητικόν, *pathētikon*) subdivided into spirited (θυμητικόν, *thymētikon*) and appetitive (ἐπιθυμητικόν, *epithymētikon*) (*Leg.* 2.99; 3.115–18; *Agr.* 30; *Her.* 167, 185, 232; *Congr.* 26; *Spec.* 4.92–4; *QG* 2.33).[4] When his biblical exegesis demands it, however, Philo freely utilizes the eightfold Stoic division of the soul, again within the bipartite framework that contrasts the undivided rational commanding faculty (ἡγεμονικόν, *hēgmonikon*) and the irrational five senses along with the faculties of speech and reproduction (*Opif.* 117; *Agr.* 30; *Mut.* 111; *Abr.* 29).[5] The fusion of Platonic and Stoic terminology and conceptuality in Middle Platonism enabled Philo to superimpose the monistic Stoic analysis of the passions, which he found so appealing, on his dualistic Platonic understanding of the human psyche.[6] This particular conflation of Platonic and Stoic doctrine, already found in Cicero's *Tusculanae disputationes* (4.10–11), turns up, as B. Inwood has noted, in many later authorities (many of which do not claim to be offering an account of old Stoic views), including Arius Didymus (Stobaeus, *Ecl.* 2.38–9), "who is often an excellent source of information on the old Stoa" (Inwood 1985: 141).[7] Finally, it should be observed that although Philo might have found it especially convenient to follow the Platonizing theory of the passions of the Middle Stoic Posidonius, his own affinity to much in the Old Stoic view constrained him to use that paradigm rather selectively.

Before turning to a detailed analysis of various aspects of Philo's theory of the emotions, we will look at a broad general outline of his position. Philo's sage is virtually a mirror image of the Stoic sage and echoes many of the paradoxes attached to the figure in that philosophical tradition.[8] Moreover, Philo's sage is as rare as the Stoic counterpart, and for the same reasons.[9] Like the Stoics, Philo notes that all learning must be built on a foundation receptive of instruction; otherwise, all else is futile: "Those ungifted by nature seem to differ not at all from an oak or mute stone, for nothing can adhere or fit into them" (*Mut.* 211).[10] Similarly, Zeno says, "Some fools are so foolish as to be utterly incapable of attaining wisdom" (Cicero, *Fin.* 4.56), and Epictetus writes, "When a man who has been trapped in an argument hardens to stone, how shall one any longer deal with him by argument?" (*Diss.* 1.5.2). Seneca points out that when the natural disposition is aided by precepts, it grows stronger, "provided only that the chronic trouble has not corrupted the natural man. For in such a case, not even the training that comes from philosophy, striving with all its might, will make restoration" (*Ep.* 94.31).

Agreeing with Cleanthes that one must be glad to attain virtue at life's approaching end (Sextus Empiricus, *Math.* 9.90; Philo, *Her.* 307), Philo asserts that we must be content with the overthrow of vices, "for the complete possession of virtue is impossible for man as we know him" (*Mut.* 50; cf. 225;

Mos. 2.147; Seneca, *Ep.* 75.13–15; *Ira* 2.10.6). He goes on to say that "it is a mark of great ignorance to believe that the human soul can contain the unwavering, absolutely steadfast excellences of God," and that "happy is he to whom it is granted to incline towards the better and more godlike part through most of his life, for to do so throughout the whole of his life is impossible" (*Mut.* 181–5). Elsewhere he insists that all perfection, joy, and gladness belong to God alone (*Her.* 121; *Cher.* 86), although in one passage, after asserting that absolute sinlessness belongs to God alone, he cautiously adds "or possibly to a divine man," which may be an allusion to Moses (*Virt.* 177; *Fug.* 157; *Deus* 75; *Somn.* 2.146; *Spec.* 1.252).

The chief characteristic of the Stoic sage, however, clearly is *apatheia*, the complete elimination of the irrational emotions. Although this *apatheia* was not conceived by the Stoics in a purely negative manner, but also positively as a state in which the *pathē* have been replaced by *eupatheiai*, their critics sought to brand the Stoic sage as not only passionless, but also as a completely unfeeling and bloodless automaton of reason. Philo, on the contrary, who was a keen student of Greek philosophy and possessed a detailed and accurate knowledge of Stoic theory, was a great admirer of their conception of the sage and passionless virtue.[11] Indeed, the ideal of *eupatheia* so intrigued him that he ascribed it not only to the wise, but also in a way to God himself – although the early Stoics may have anticipated him in this.[12] The three canonical *eupatheiai* are *boulēsis* (willing or wishing), *eulabeia* (watchfulness or caution), and *chara* (joy), and it is clear that Philo was in no way embarrassed to apply at least two of these (*boulēsis* and *chara*) to God.[13] Thus Philo is led to the depiction of Isaac as an exemplar of the apathic ideal, and to a depiction of Moses that would appear to transcend even this virtually unattainable moral standard. The impression that one gets from Philo's description of Moses' ethical level is of one who no longer even has automatically to withhold assent from irrational impulses in the manner of the Stoic sage, inasmuch as he enjoys the unique privilege of having entirely eliminated his irrational soul-components, a privilege commensurate with his unique status as a heavenly soul that was sent down on loan to mere earthlings to whom it is appointed as god, the bodily region and its ruling mind having been placed in subjection to it (*Sacr.* 9; cf. *Det.* 161–2; *Leg.* 1.40; *Migr.* 84; *Mut.* 19).

Yet in spite of Philo's fascination with the ideal of *apatheia*, he is at times content with the milder Peripatetic view. In *Deus* 162–5, he espouses the Aristotelian mean, identifying the middle path with the royal road leading to God (cf. *Spec.* 4.102; *Post.* 101). Moreover, although at *Det.* 6–9 he explicitly attacks the Peripatetic view of the triple good, which includes external goods (Aristotle, *Eth. nic.* 1.1098b; *Rhet.* 1.1360b), at *Her.* 285–6 he apparently follows the compromise adopted by Antiochus of Ascalon, who distinguished the *vita beata*, which depends only on virtue, from the *vita beatissima*, which requires also the possibility of using external goods (Cicero, *Acad.* 1.22; 2.22; 2.134). Furthermore, at *Abr.* 257 we are told that at the death of Sarah, Abraham chose not *apatheia*, but *metriopatheia*, moderating his grief instead of extirpating it.[14] Thus it is not all that surprising to find Philo identifying *apatheia* as the highest ethical ideal, while at the same time indicating the usefulness of the passions.[15]

Finally, in line with his mystical tendency to refer all human action to God, Philo finds the most effective antidote to the ravages of the passions in the vision of the Beautiful, the best and most sublime gift bestowed by the all-beneficent Deity. We turn now to a closer inspection of the issues surveyed above.

The four passions

Philo is fond of elaborate descriptions of the onset and impact of the passions in which he employs a blend of Platonic and Stoic terminology. At *Prob.* 159, for example, he writes,

> For if the soul is driven by desire [πρὸς ἐπιθυμίας ἐλαύνεται], or enticed by pleasure [ὑφ' ἡδονῆς δελεάζεται (cf. *Agr.* 103)], or turns away from its course [ἐκκλίνει] by fear, or is contracted [στέλλεται (some MSS: συστέλλεται)] by distress, or is gripped [τραχηλίζεται (cf. *Mos.* 1.297)] by anger, it enslaves itself and makes him whose soul it is a slave to a host of masters.[16]

A more vivid description, similarly replete with Stoic terminology, is given at *Her.* 269:

> "And the slavery is for four hundred years" [Gen. 15:13]; thus he shows the powers exercised by the four passions. When pleasure rules, the temper is high flown [μετεωρίζεται] and inflated, uplifted [ἐξαιρόμενον] with empty levity. When desire is master, a yearning for what is not arises and suspends the soul on unfulfilled hope as on a noose. For the soul is ever athirst yet never able to drink, suffering the torments of a Tantalus. Under the sovereignty of distress it is pinched and contracts [συστέλλεται], like trees that shed their leaves and wither.... While desire has a power of attraction [ὁλκὸν ἔχουσα δύναμιν] and forces us to the pursuit of the desired object even though it flee from our grasp, fear on the other hand creates a sense of estrangement [ἀλλοτριότητα] and sunders and removes us from the sight we dread.[17]

Especially striking is Philo's use of some of the more technical terms of the Stoic psychology of action, the precise meaning of which is, for lack of adequate evidence, somewhat obscure. At *Mut.* 160, after giving some examples of how Nature provides signs that indicate future happenings beforehand, Philo goes on to say that this kind of occurrence is called ὄρουσις (*orousis*) by those who practice word-coining – that is, the Stoics. The soul, he continues, experiences much the same thing:

When good is hoped for, it rejoices in anticipation, and thus in a way feels joy before joy, gladness before gladness.... Similarly, the presence of evil produces distress, and its expectation fear. And so fear is distress before distress, just as hope is joy before joy.
(*Mut.* 161–3)[18]

According to Arius Didymus's doxography of Stoic ethics preserved by Stobaeus (*Ecl.* 2.7.9, p. 87 Wachsmuth[19] [=*SVF* 3.169]), ὅρουσις is "a movement of the mind to something in the future" (φορὰν διανοίας ἐπὶ τι μέλλον).[20] Inwood classifies πρόθεσις (*prothesis*), ἐπιβολή, (*epibolē*), ἐγχείρησις (*encheirēsis*), and παρασκευή, (*paraskeuē*) as subtypes of ὅρουσις, and ἐπιβολή is defined in Stobaeus as "an impulse before an impulse" (ὁρμὴν πρὸ ὁρμῆς) (*SVF* 3.173).[21] Philo also uses the term ἐγχείρησις, defined in Stobaeus as "an impulse of something already in hand" – that is, an impulse to a future action that could begin with some sort of action on something present (*Somn.* 2.200). Finally, πρόθεσις, defined in Stobaeus as "an indication of accomplishment," which Inwood (1985: 232) suggests probably means a self-conscious impulse to a future action involving deliberation and self-conscious planning, apparently is used by Philo in this sense at *Mos.* 2.280.

Influenced by Platonic imagery, Philo is fond of comparing the passions to wild beasts, "because savage and untamed as they are, they tear the soul to pieces" (*Leg.* 2.11), and he describes the belly as "the manger of the irrational animal, desire, which drenched by wine-bibbing and gluttony, is perpetually flooded with relays of food and drink" (*Spec.* 1.148; 4.94).[22] He also utilizes Plato's famous myth of the soul's chariot in *Phaedr.* 246–7, where the *logikon* appears as the charioteer, and the *thymikon* and *epithymētikon* as the nobler and baser horses, respectively (*Leg.* 1.72–3; 3.118, 136; *Agr.* 73 [Long and Sedley 1987: 1.411, 65A]), and he refers to the driver's lack of skill causing the team to be swept down precipices and gullies (*Agr.* 76; *Leg.* 1.73; *Somn.* 2.161, 276; *Spec.* 4.79; cf. *T. Reu.* 2.9; Galen, *PHP* 44.2.43 [De Lacy 246]).[23]

Philo's fanciful interpretation of the meaning of the punishment of Cain, the first fratricide (Gen 4:13–15), involves the notion of his living forever in a state of dying. This was effected by God's cutting out of Cain by the roots the two passions that are concerned with the good, pleasure and desire,

so that never by any chance should he have any pleasant sensations or desire anything pleasant, and by engrafting in him only the pair on the bad side, distress and fear, producing grief unmixed with cheerfulness and fear unrelieved. For Scripture says that God laid a curse upon the fratricide that he should ever "groan and tremble."
[Gen 4:12 LXX] (*Praem.* 68–73)

Desire and pleasure

Philo's tirades against pleasure in particular echo similar rhetorical effusions of various Greek philosophers ranging from extreme statements such as that attributed to Antisthenes, "I'd rather be mad than feel pleasure" (μανείην μᾶλλον ἢ ἡσθείην) (Diogenes Laertius 6.3), to the relatively mild remark of Aristotle that "we must be especially on our guard against pleasure, for when it comes to pleasure we cannot act as unbiased judges" (*Eth. nic.* 2.9 1109b).[24] He begins on the somewhat positive note that desire, ruled by the serpent pleasure, unites reason with sense-perception, but he goes on to say that whereas sense-perception is an "intermediate" (μέσον, *meson*), and in itself neither bad nor good, irrational pleasure is bad in itself. Hence, unlike Eve/Sense-perception, the serpent pleasure is not given the opportunity to defend itself (*Leg.* 3.65–8).[25] Pleasure cheats the maimed sense of that power of apprehension which it could have had through reason by compelling the soul to employ unseeing guides (*Leg.* 3.107–10). The serpent pleasure is also the most cunning of all things (Gen 3:1), for all things are in thrall to it, and the things that yield pleasure are obtained through cunning of every kind (*Leg.* 2.107). Moreover, whereas other creatures seek pleasure only through taste and the organs of reproduction, human beings do so through the other senses as well, pursuing with their ears and eyes all such sights and sounds as can afford delight (*Opif.* 162; cf. *Leg.* 2.74–5). The popular philosopher Dio Chrysostom similarly writes, "Pleasure hatches no single plot but all kinds of plots, and aims to undo men through sight, sound, smell, taste, and touch" (*Or.* 8.21).[26] Finally, as the starting point and foundation (ἀρχὴ καὶ θεμέλιος, *archē kai themelios*) of all the passions, Philo considers pleasure the worst of them: "Desire comes about through love of pleasure [ἔρωτος ἡδονῆς (cf. *SVF* 3.394)]; distress [λύπη] arises with its withdrawal; fear is engendered owing to the anxiety of being without it" (*Leg.* 3.113; cf. 3.139).

In an effort to explain why of all the passions desire is singled out in the Decalogue for special condemnation, Philo says that it is the hardest one to manage.[27] Whereas each of the other passions,

> impinging from the outside and attacking from without [θύραθεν ἐπεισιὸν καὶ προσπῖπτον ἔξωθεν], appears to be involuntary, desire alone originates with ourselves and is voluntary.... When a person conceives an idea of something good that is not present and is eager to get it, and propels his soul to the greatest distance and strains it to the greatest possible extent in his avidity to touch the desired object, he is, as it were, stretched upon a wheel, all anxiety to grasp the object but unable to reach so far.
>
> (*Decal.* 142, 146; cf. *Somn.* 2.13)[28]

Although H.A. Wolfson (1948: 2.225–37) claims that this distinction between desire and the other passions is in direct opposition to the view of the Stoics, "for whom all the passions are judgments (κρίσεις) and therefore voluntary," his argumentation ultimately is dependent on his idiosyncratic and highly unlikely view that Philo held a theory of absolute free will. What Philo is actually saying is that the passions of fear, distress, and pleasure only "seem" to be involuntary because they derive from external causes, whereas desire is often generated by the soul from within, as when its objects are not present but future goods.[29] Philo's motivation clearly is exegetical, and his claim that the other passions appear to be involuntary is similar to a presumed objection to Aristotle's own definition of voluntary action, of which he readily disposes (*Eth. nic.* 3.1 1111a24–b4), and surely is not to be taken as a serious philosophical position that Philo intended to maintain in opposition to both the Stoics and the Peripatetics.[30]

Apatheia/eupatheia

Inasmuch as according to Philo, God is completely ἀπαθής (*apathēs*) (*Deus* 52, 59; *Sacr.* 95–6; *Plant.* 35; *Abr.* 202), his ὁμοίωσις θεῷ (*homoiōsis theō*) formula clearly implies that the highest ethical human goal is constituted by a state of *apatheia*.[31] Thus, in his depiction of Isaac and Moses, Philo introduces them as prototypes of a higher ethical level than that of the ordinary individual. Although both Isaac and Moses exemplify soul-types that achieve perfect virtue without toil, Moses presumably represents for Philo a higher type than does Isaac, inasmuch as ultimately he is translated to a higher station than that of the latter, being placed beside God himself, above genus and species alike (*Sacr.* 8). Isaac thus symbolizes the sage whose psyche, being *apathēs*, generates only *eupatheiai* or rational emotions, and so is analogous to the Stoic sage who acts out of a fixity of disposition, no longer having to struggle in order to make rational decisions. The one difference between Isaac and his Stoic counterpart is that the former, like Moses, achieves this level without toil, being αὐτομαθής (*automathēs*), self-taught or God-taught (cf. Homer, *Od.* 22.347), whereas the Stoic *sophos* has had to struggle to attain it. This apparent difference, however, is probably not very significant, as Seneca is able to say that some are so blessed with good natural endowments (εὐφυΐα, *euphuia*), that they seemed to have attained wisdom virtually without effort (*Ep.* 95.36). Philo's intent probably is the same. Isaac and Moses both require some training, but their natural εὐφυΐα is such that their acquisition of wisdom is virtually automatic. As Philo notes with regard to Moses, "His happy natural gifts anticipated his teachers' instruction, so that it seemed to be a case of recollection rather than of learning, and he himself devised conundrums for them" (*Mos.* 1.21–2). Moses, on the contrary, would appear to symbolize the Godlike man "given as a loan to earthlings" (*Sacr.* 8) – that is, belonging to that category of rational souls that ordinarily never leave the supernal sphere for embodiment below. He is one who has achieved a state of absolute *apatheia*, living, as it were, in the disembodied realm of pure *nous*. Thus he is contrasted with Aaron, the one who is still making moral progress and practices only μετριοπάθεια or moderation of the passions (*Leg.* 3.129).[32]

Before embarking upon an analysis of Philo's description of the Mosaic form of *apatheia* in *Leg.* 3.129–59 and *Migr.* 67, we will find it useful to examine the preceding section of *Leg.* 3.114–28, which presents a number of exegetical problems. Citing Gen 3:14 LXX, "on your breast and belly shall you go" (the Hebrew text does not include the word "breast"), Philo, in accordance with Plato's theory of a tripartite soul, with each part localized in a specific area of the body, refers this verse to the fact that "passion has its lair in these parts of the body." He also notes Posidonius's view that the so-called parts of the soul ought to be described as δυνάμεις (*dynameis*) or faculties rather than μέρη (*merē*) or parts (Edelstein and Kidd 1988: 2.542, 677), though in line with his own exegetical needs he follows the Platonic trilocation. Then he points out that pleasure certainly is not to be found in the head, where reason, which is at war (μάχεται, *machetai*) with pleasure, resides, but rather in the breast and the belly, the seat of the irrational portions of the soul, "where our judgment [ἡ κρίσις ἡ ἡμετέρα] and the passions are to be found."[33] Heinemann correctly noted that this statement is looking ahead to the placing of the "oracle of judgment" (λόγιον τῶν κρίσεων, *logion tōn kriseōn*), together with the "showing and the truth" (δήλωσιν καὶ ἀλήθειαν, *dēlōsin kai alētheian*), upon Aaron's breast, which represents the healing of passion by reason, accompanied by truthfulness and distinctness (Exod 21:30), and it stands in sharp contradiction to Chrysippus' teaching that the passions are judgments (κρίσεις, *kriseis*) of the *hēgemonikon* and can be entirely removed by reason's self-healing (Diogenes Laertius 7.111).[34] It would seem that Philo here is following Posidonius, who contested Chrysippus' position, abandoning his monistic analysis and highlighting the crucial role of the soul's irrational powers in deflecting us from the path of reason.[35] Although Galen's evidence for Posidonius's position is insufficiently clear, Kidd has suggested the following understanding of it. The human psyche has three different *oikeiōseis* or affinities, not one, as Chrysippus thought. There are those who thus

> mistakenly suppose that what is suitable to the irrational powers of the soul is suitable without qualification [ἁπλῶς οἰκεῖα]; they do not know that to experience pleasure and to rule over one's neighbors are objects sought by the animal-like part of the soul [τοῦ ζῳώδους τῆς ψυχῆς], but wisdom and all that is good and noble are objects sought by that (part) which is rational and divine.
> (Galen, *PHP* 5.6, line 18 [De Lacy 330–1])

Only wisdom, good, and beauty are absolutely good (ἁπλῶς οἰκεῖα, *haplōs oikeia*). If one's *logistikon* is weak, the false beliefs (ψευδεῖς δόξαι, *pseudeis doxai*) that pleasure and victory are absolute goods trigger an excessive impulse, which through its "emotional pull" (παθητικὴ ὁλκή, *pathetikē holkē*) compels assent. Thus we are left (if I have understood Kidd correctly) with a corrupt disposition (ἕξις [*hexis*] or διάθεσις [*diathesis*]) that inclines us to pleasure and victory and distorts the *logistikon*'s decision (κρίσις, *krisis*) to a particular act. "So the main αἰτία [of the πάθη]," writes Kidd,

> remains the emotional pull, although it is preceded by the 'false belief' from our lower affinities and a weak *logistikon*. But the κρίσις is not the δόξαι but comes at the end of the process as a result of the παθητικὴ ὁλκή.
> (Edelstein and Kidd 1988: 2.622)[36]

We are now in a position to understand Philo's remark that it is in the irrational part (ἄλογον, *alogon*) of the soul that our judgment and the passions are to be found. When a weak *logistikon* allows the false beliefs generated by the irrational movements of the παθητικόν to trigger an excessive impulse (ὁρμὴ πλεονάζουσα, *hormē pleonazousa*) that compels assent, we have a situation in which, as Philo puts it, the mind abandons the contemplation of the intelligibles, which are proper to it, and becomes the prisoner (δορυάλωτον, *doryalōton*) of the παθητικόν (*Leg.* 3.116). Under these circumstances, it may be said that the real locus of the *logistikon*'s decision is now in the παθητικόν, inasmuch as the mind itself is now captive in that realm.[37]

After pointing out that Moses, unlike Aaron, who can only control his passions, cuts out the breast, or the warlike spirited element in his soul, with all its passions (*Leg.* 3.128–40), Philo adds a further, analogous distinction between these two figures. Not only does Moses exscind the spirited element entirely, but in a corresponding manner he also scours away and shakes off pleasures, whereas Aaron, once again unable to act in so radical a fashion, admits simple and necessary pleasures, declining only what is superfluous and excessive in the way of delicacies (ἐπεντρώσεις [*epentrōseis*], an Epicurean term; frg. 413 Usener 1887).[38] Thus we read, "And he washed with water the belly and the feet of the whole burnt-offering" (Lev 9:14); that is, he washes out the entire belly and the pleasures that it and the parts adjoining it yield, rejecting even necessary food and drink, being fed instead by the contemplation of things divine. So we read in Exod 24:28 that "for forty days he ate no bread and drank no water" when he was on the holy mountain listening to divine communications (*Leg.* 3.140–1; cf. *Somn.* 1.36). Moreover, Moses does all this without God's bidding, while Aaron acts under orders (cf. Epictetus, *Ench.* 48; Plutarch, *Virt. mor.* 446E). Furthermore, in refusing pleasure, Moses practically renounces the other passions too, for the filling of the belly is the very foundation of the latter (*Leg.* 3.113). Finally, Philo notes the significance of Scripture's subtle distinction between Moses' "removal" of the breast and his "washing" of the belly. The perfected one, although able utterly to eliminate every element of high spirit, is powerless to exscind the belly: "Even the man of fewest needs who scorns the very necessaries of life and trains himself in abstinence from them is forced by nature to take necessary food and drink" (*Leg.* 3.147). In short, Philo seems to be saying that whereas Aaron eliminates only unnecessary pleasures – that is, inessential types of food such as delicacies – Moses contents himself with the absolute minimum of food necessary for bare sustenance, and even that not for the pleasure that it affords.[39]

É. Bréhier (1909: 246 n. 1) had already noted the apparent contradiction between *Leg.* 3.141–2, where we are told that Moses rejected even necessary food and drink, and *Leg.* 3.147, where it is said that he was forced by nature to take necessary nourishment. R. Radice (in Reggiani and Radice 1987) dismisses this difficulty by insisting that Philo is not a systematic philosopher, and that apparent contradictions of this kind are a result of his predominant exegetical intention. Although it certainly is true that Philo's exegetical concerns often generate minor contradictions, it is unlikely that he has so directly contradicted himself within the short space of two pages. The contradiction, however, may readily be disposed of if one notes that at *Leg.* 3.141 Philo says only that Moses had such contempt for the pleasures of the belly that he would eliminate even necessary food and drink for "limited" periods of time when he was totally absorbed in divine contemplation (cf. *Leg.* 3.161). Clearly, Philo had no intention of claiming that Moses was entirely exempt from the physical constraints of his bodily frame.

We may now turn to the important passage in *Migr.* 67, where, from a somewhat different perspective, Philo once again cites the curse in Gen 3:14 upon the serpent, who now represents every irrational and passion-loving person. A sharp antithesis is drawn between the fool, who jettisons intellect while retaining irrational elements, and the individual of opposite character, who has cut out (*ektetmētai*) irrational parts, *thymos* and *epithymia*, and has chosen the divine Logos as patron:

> Even so, Moses, best beloved of God, when offering the whole burnt sacrifices of the soul, will "wash out the belly" [Lev 8:21], that is, will cleanse away the whole class of *epithymia* [ὅλον τὸ ἐπιθυμίας εἶδος], while "the breast from the ram of consecration he will take away" [Lev 8:29]. This means, we may be sure, the warlike spirit in its completeness, and the object of taking it away is that the better portion of the soul, the rational that is left, may employ its truly free and noble-minded impulses towards all things beautiful, with nothing tugging at it any longer and diverting it [μηδενὸς ἀντισπῶντος ἔτι καὶ μεθέλκοντος].[40]

Philo's pointed contrast here between the two opposite poles of the ethical continuum – the utter fool and the supremely perfect sage – apparently leads him to a more refined portrait of Mosaic perfection, one that transcends that presented in *Leg.* 3.129–59. There he offered two parallel sketches of Moses' supreme ethical achievement. In the first sketch, Moses is portrayed as one who has completely eliminated the spirited or competitive component of his psyche (*thymos*), a feat that is indicated in Scripture by his "removal [ἀφεῖλεν, *apheilen*] of the breast from the ram of consecration" (Lev 8:29). This is paralleled in the second sketch by Moses' analogous removal of all pleasure, which is indicated in Scripture by his "washing the belly of the whole burnt-offering" (Lev 9:14). The appetitive element as such, however, he is unable to remove, as is subtly indicated by Scripture's choice of the word "wash" instead of "cut out" (*Leg.* 3.147). Nonetheless, since for Philo pleasure is the foundation of all the passions, Moses' ethical preeminence once again consists in the complete extirpation of his passionate nature. In *Migr.* 67, on the contrary, Moses is depicted as cutting out (ἐκτέτμηται, *ektetmētai*) not only his *thymos*, but also his *epithymia*, again indicated in Scripture by his "washing out the belly" (Lev 8:21) and "removing the breast of the ram of consecration" (Lev 8:29). Here Moses dispenses not only with the spirited element (*thymētikon*), but also with his appetitive element (*epithymētikon*), so that his reason (*logistikon*) operates in a sort of passional vacuum. Thus he appears to consist solely of body and rational soul, his bodily sensations producing none of the lower impulses in his single-tiered psyche, to which his reason must either give or withhold assent. The account in *Leg.* 3.129–59 operates within the framework of Plato's tripartite soul, but no explicit attempt is made there to portray Moses as eliminating both of his irrational soul-components, as is the case in *Migr.* 67.[41]

It would seem, then, that Philo has provided us with the extraordinary phenomenon of a supersage, whose perfected reason requires no epithymetic impulse to motivate it to compute the body's needs and satisfy them in the best possible way. Its own proper affinity for knowledge and truth includes an impulse to know the body with which it is associated and to guide all its activities. Thus Moses' mind lives in lower, impulse-free conjunction with his body, and with the sole exception of joy (*chara*), it is unaccompanied by the ordinary sage's rational emotions. The Mosaic mind is accordingly the closest possible approximation to the Divine Mind, as neither of them is characterized by the usual rational emotions. As I have indicated elsewhere, it is highly likely that the only rational emotion that Philo allows God is joy, provided that it is applied to God analogically, inasmuch as the divine joy differs from that of the sage in that it involves no elation or change whatever.[42] Here, at last, the Mosaic mind falls short of the Divine, since unlike the latter's eternal and elationless joy, that of Moses is constituted by the expansion of his psychic *pneuma* upon his arrival at maturity and wisdom.

Usefulness of the passions

In addition to the help of the senses, Philo also recognizes the aid provided by the passions:

> For pleasure and desire contribute to the permanence of our kind: pain and fear are like bites or stings warning the soul to treat nothing carelessly: anger is a weapon of defense that has conferred great boons on many, and so with the other passions (*Leg.* 2.8 [trans. Whitaker, LCL]).

Indeed, the essential nature of the passions in the cosmic scheme of things is shown by the fact that they constitute "ideas" within the Divine Mind (*Leg.* 2.12).[43] The view that the passions are an important and indispensable component of human nature and therefore cannot be eliminated is a Peripatetic position (Cicero, *Tusc.* 4.43; *Acad.* 2.135, where it is also attributed to the old Academy; Seneca, *Ira* 3.3.1; Alcinous, *Did.* 32.4).[44] It is apparently also the view of Posidonius, who aimed not at the eradication of the irrational elements, but at their submission to reason (frgs 31, 161, 187 Edelstein and Kidd). According to Posidonius, the irrational "team" of the soul should not be too strong, for the emotional movements must be blunted (ἀμβλυνθῆναι, *amblynthēnai*) by habitual good practices (Galen, *PHP* 5.5.29 [De Lacy 322]), but not too weak either (see frg. 31 Edelstein and Kidd, with Kidd's commentary [1988: 160]). Thus Philo is following the Peripatetics and Posidonius in this passage (unless Cooper is right that Galen has misrepresented Posidonius's view). Elsewhere, however, as we have already seen, he subscribes to the Chrysippean view of the eradication of the passions (*Leg.* 2.100–2; 3.131, 140; *Prov.* 1.56, 66), although he softens his harsh characterization of the προκόπτων (*prokoptōn*) as vicious by emphasizing the Stoic recognition that "although he who makes progress is still numbered with the fools, yet he is separated from them by a long interval" (*Somn.* 2.234–6; cf. *Fug.* 202, 213). At the same time, he omits entirely the vicious classification of the first half of this statement.[45]

Removing the passions

In Philo's mystical theology, it is God who is the true author of all human perfection, virtue, and happiness. Since the passions are the chief obstacle to spiritual bliss, Philo frequently refers all success in this domain to the divine power and compassion (*Cher.* 50; *Somn.* 1.173; 2.25, 266–7; *Post.* 30–1; *Leg.* 2.86; 3.219). It behooves the soul not to ascribe to itself its toil for virtue, but to refer it to God (*Leg.* 3.136). The human condition, being mortal, is by nature vulnerable to the oppression of the passions, although it is the Deity's will to lighten that burden (*Her.* 272–3).

Philo frequently likens the activity of the passions to that of a consuming flame.[46] The irrational and unmeasured impulse is called Amalek, "people licking up," for its force, like that of fire, licks up and destroys all that stands in its path (*Congr.* 55; *Post.* 71; cf. *Fug.* 158; *Leg.* 3.160, 248; *Spec.* 4.83, 113; cf. Galen, *PHP* 4.7.28 [De Lacy 286]: παθητικὴν φλεγμονήν [*pathētikēn phlegmonēn*]). But Philo evokes a counterimage that is equivalent to fighting fire with fire. In a charming allegory, he speaks of God leading his people out of Egypt – that is, out of their bodily passions. As they journeyed along the track barren of pleasure, they encamped at Marah, which had only water that was wholly bitter (Exod 15:23); for the delights, appetites, and sexual lusts bewitched them, consistently casting their spells over them, so that they came to abhor labor as utterly bitter and repugnant, and they planned to retrace their steps and return to Egypt, the refuge of licentiousness. And they might have done so, had not the Savior taken pity on them and cast into their soul a sweetening tree like a syrup, producing love of labor. For being the Creator, he knew that it was impossible for them to rise superior to anything whatever unless a vehement love of such effort be implanted in them (cf. Cicero, *Tusc.* 4.44); for the lover of virtue, set on fire by the brilliant appearance of the beautiful, burns up the pleasures of the body and then chops and grinds them up (*Post.* 155–9, abbreviating Colson's LCL translation). Thus it is the mind set ablaze by the dazzling vision of the Beautiful, a vision graciously bestowed by God, that ultimately counters the dark glow of the flaming passions and extinguishes them.[47] Like Plato and Spinoza, Philo knows that in the conflict of emotions, weaker emotions are removed by stronger ones, and the most powerful emotion of all is the intellectual love of God.[48]

Notes

1 Citations of Galen's *De placitis Hippocratis et Platonis* (*On the Opinions of Hippocrates and Plato*) are given according to the CMG edition of De Lacy (1978–84), and the fragments of Posidonius according to the edition by Edelstein and Kidd (1972–99).

2 According to R. Radice (contra Bréhier, Whitaker, and Mondésert), *logos* (in the phrase ὥς τις κατ' ἐξαίρετον λόγος μέμνηται) can be rendered "argumentation" instead of "treatise," since Philo may be referring not to a specific treatise but more generally to one of the many passages in which the same theme is discussed (see Reggiani and Radice 1987: 493). Cf. Yizhak (Isaak) Heinemann's translation: "wie die besondere Lehre von ihnen ergibt" (in Cohn, Heinemann, and Adler 1909–38: 3.130). M. Pohlenz (1965: 1.353) observes that no part of Greek philosophy appears so frequently in Philo as the Stoic doctrine of the passions.

3 Cf. Timaeus Locrus, *On the Nature of the Cosmos and the Soul* (Marg 1972: 72). Although Plato frequently refers to these four passions (Ariston's so-called tetrachord), nowhere does he describe them as the sources of vice, as the Stoics do (*SVF*

1.211, 370; 3.378; Plato, *Lach.* 191D; *Symp.* 207E; *Theaet.* 156B; *Resp.* 4.429C; 430B–C). See Baltes 1972: 204.

4 For the παθητικόν (*pathētikon*), not an old Stoic term for a faculty of the soul, cf. Posidonius ap. Galen, *PHP* 5.5, line 25 (De Lacy 320); Alcinous, *Did.* 17; 24. (Posidonius, however, rejected the Platonic trilocation of the three soul faculties.) As Dillon has noted, "It had been Platonist doctrine since the time of the Old Academy, attested to earliest, perhaps, in the Peripatetic *Magna Moralia* 1.1.1182a24 (although the imagery of charioteer and horses in the *Phaedrus* would appear already to depict such a doctrine, and Xenocrates, at least, would seem to have held it), that the fundamental division of the soul was bipartite. In Chapter 24, Alcinous begins by presenting the soul as tripartite, but the basic bipartition reasserts itself before the chapter is over" (Dillon 1993: 139); see also Vander Waerdt 1985. D.T. Runia has pointed out that "bipartition is faithful to the spirit of the *Timaeus*, where Plato speaks of the immortal and mortal part of the soul. This division facilitated a comparison with the macrocosm, the rational part being parallel to Heaven, the irrational part to the sublunar region (Cicero *Acad.* 2.135; *Tusc.* 4.43; Seneca *De Ira* 3.3.1)" (Runia 1986: 305).

5 The Stoics themselves made no such contrast, since for them the soul was unitary. See Long and Sedley 1987: 1.315, 53H. Furthermore, in *QG* 2.59 (cf. *Opif.* 67) Philo makes a tripartite division of the soul that is more Aristotelian than Platonic, distinguishing as its three parts the nutritive (θρεπτικόν, *threptikon*), the sensitive (αἰσθητικόν, *aisthētikon*), and the rational (λογικόν, *logikon*). See Wolfson 1948: 2.225–37; Dillon 1977: 174; Runia 1986: 304.

C. Lévy (1993) thinks that Philo's use of the Platonic metaphor of the marionettes at *Opif.* 117 profoundly subverts the Stoic psychology, since the parts of the soul are likened to objects that are of themselves inert. This dichotomy between a living and autonomous *hēgemonikon* and inert instruments is foreign to Stoic hylozoism and represents a Platonizing of Stoic psychology. The fact is, however, that Philo is fond of the marionette analogy (used again at *Fug.* 46; *QG* 3.48) because it illustrates so vividly that the real author of all things is God, who energizes the *hēgemonikon* and is thus ultimately the one who pulls the strings of the senses. The key element in the analogy is that the marionettes are moved by an invisible power; their inertness is irrelevant. There need not be a one-to-one correspondence between all the components of an analogy. Cf. Ps.-Aristotle, *Mund.* 398B, where the point of the analogy is somewhat different. For an eighteenth-century example of the use of this analogy, note the words of Khwajir Mir Dard: "And the string of predestination is hidden from the view of all, and the player [is hidden] in the screen, and the puppets are visible" (Schimmel 1975: 278). Lévy (1993: 276–7) admits, however, that Philo's metaphors at *Leg.* 1.28 and especially at *Agr.* 30 are fully in the spirit of Stoic psychology.

6 Atticus, for example, adopted the doctrine that virtue is sufficient (αὐτάρκη, *autarkē*) for happiness, a characteristically Stoicizing move (frg. 2.4.2 [Des Places 1977]). Alcinous's definition of πάθος (*pathos*) as an "irrational emotion of the soul, in response either to something bad or to something good" is Stoic (*SVF* 1.205; 3.378), but more probably, as Dillon suggests, "Alcinous derives it, immediately or otherwise, from the Peripatetic Andronicus (as reported by Aspasius in *EN* 44.21–2)" (Dillon 1993: 193). Although Antiochus, like Philo, accepted the Stoic ideal of *apatheia*, unlike Philo, he nowhere uses Plato's tripartite scheme of the soul. See Dillon 1993: 178, 193; 1977: 102.

7 Cf. J. Annas's comment: "Cicero in *Tusculan Disputations* 4 makes a gallant attempt to compromise by combining Stoic accounts of the emotions with a Platonic division of the soul into rational and irrational parts. The result is merely edifying muddle: Cicero persists in treating the Stoic ideal of banishing *pathē* as a more rigoristic version of other theories' demand to moderate the *pathē*, failing to see that within the different theories *pathē* have quite different implications" (Annas 1992: 118).
8 For a detailed discussion of the paradoxes see Winston 1995.
9 For the rarity of the good see Philo, *Leg.* 1.102; *Ebr.* 26; *Migr.* 51, 59, 63, 123; *Mut.* 34–56, 213; *Spec.* 2.47; *Virt.* 10; *Abr.* 19; *Prob.* 63, 72; *Agr.* 180; Cicero, *Off.* 3.16–17; Seneca, *Constant.* 7; *Ira* 2.10.6; *Ep.* 42.1.
10 Translations of Philo and other ancient authors are either my own or those of the LCL, sometimes modified.
11 For further discussion of this widely misunderstood Stoic concept see Winston 1984: 400–5.
12 See Winston 1992. On Philo and the Stoic *eupatheiai*, see also Dillon and Terian 1976–7.
13 *Lypē*, "distress," had no rational counterpart.
14 Since Abraham was a sage, if Philo were strictly following Stoic theory, he should have described Abraham's grief and tears as a sort of "sting and slight convulsions of the soul" (*morsus et contractiunculae quaedam animi* [Cicero, *Tusc.* 3.82]). Indeed, in *QG* 4.73 (Greek frg. in Marcus 1953a: 220]), it is said that Abraham experienced not a *pathos*, but only a *propatheia* ("pre-passion"), but according to Petit, this fragment should be restored to Eusebius of Emesa: "Eusebius was certainly inspired by *QG* 4.73, but he has completely modified the redaction of this source" (Petit 1978: 168 [cf. Royse 1991: 25 n. 51]). Pohlenz (1961, 2.151) had already realized that the word *propatheia* here belonged to Procopius, not to Philo. On the contrary, Graver (1999) has now made a strong case for the use of the term *propatheia* by the Old Stoa on the basis of the Armenian version of *QG* 4.73. Philo there solves the difficulty of Abraham's grieving for Sarah by noting that Scripture does not represent him as actually mourning, but only "coming to mourn." "For things," says Philo, "that unexpectedly and against his will strike the pusillanimous man weaken, crush and overthrow him, whereas everywhere they merely bow down the man of constancy when they direct their blows against him, and not in such a way as to bring their work to completion, since they are strongly repelled by the guiding reason, and retreat." Graver explains, "Both the ordinary and the virtuous person may be 'struck' unexpectedly and against their will by 'things' – i.e. by events ... perceived as unfortunate. Grief does not occur, however, unless these things 'bring their work to completion' in a further mental event described, with metaphorical violence, as if it were the knockout in a psychological boxing-match or the collapse of a building subject to bombardment. In the virtuous person, this latter event does not take place. ... Such a person may indeed be affected in some way, but that is merely the experience of being 'bowed down' under the assault. ... This is not even a limited or moderate form of grief" (Graver 1999: 306–7). Graver further notes that this is recognizably the same sequence of steps as found in frg. 9 of Epictetus, and that "there is a curious similarity, as well, in the purposes for which Gellius and Philo invoke the προπάθειαι" (Graver 1999: 308). Graver correctly

points out that the term *propatheia* was known to Philo, since it appears in *QG* 1.79 (Greek frg. [Petit 1978: 73]).

Nonetheless, it should be noted that Philo's use of the term *propatheia* in that fragment refers to what he elsewhere calls an *orousis* (*Mut.* 160). Thus there is no explicit evidence for Philo's application of the term *propatheia* in the context of responses that are literally "pre-passions" – that is, if assented to would constitute full-fledged "passions" (*pathē*). It may be, however, that the term *propatheia* did occur in the original Greek text of *QG* 4.73 and somehow was obliterated in the Armenian version.

Finally, it should also be noted that Seneca himself, who generally follows a strict Stoic line in this matter, does on occasion yield to the Peripatetic *metriopatheia* (*Polyb.* 18.5.6; cf. *Helv.* 16.1; *Marc.* 7.1; *Ep.* 99.15–21. See Bonhöffer 1890: 307–11). Moreover, we know that *metriopatheia* was especially commended in treatises of consolation. Plutarch (*Cons. Apoll.* 102D) advocates *metriopatheia* in bereavement in similar terms and quotes the Academician Crantor's *Peri Penthous* to the same effect. The same passage from Crantor is quoted in Cicero, *Tusc.* 3.12, as noted by Colson in Colson and Whitaker 1929–62: 6.598–99.

15 In commenting on this passage É. Bréhier (1909) had already pointed out the incongruities inherent in *Leg.* 2.8. He noted the unusual, positive evaluation of the passions, in addition to the dualistic Platonic psychology that frames a discussion couched in Stoic terms. For a survey of various attempts to resolve the incongruities see Reggiani and Radice 1987: 387–92.

16 Cf. Plato, *Resp.* 9.573E: ὥσπερ ὑπὸ κέντρων ἐλαυνομένους τῶν τε ἄλλων ἐπιθυμιῶν (cf. *Phaedr.* 240D); *Tim.* 69D: ἡδονὴν μέγιστον κακοῦ δέλεαρ; *SVF* 3.391: λύπη μὲν οὖν ἐστιν ἄλογος συστολή ... φόβος δὲ ἄλογος ἔκκλισις. In *Mos.* 2.139 Philo writes, "Let him [the priest] who shall be purified with water, bethink him that the mirrors [donated by the women and melted down by Moses for the making of the laver for lustration] were the material of this vessel, to the end that he himself may behold his own mind as in a mirror; and if some deformity [αἶσχος] appear of unreasoning passion, either of pleasure, uplifting and raising him to heights contrary to nature [παρὰ φύσιν ἐπαιρούσης καὶ μετεωριζούσης (cf. *Decal.* 143)], or of its converse pain, making him contract and pulling him down [στελλούσης ἔμπαλιν λύπης καὶ καθαιρούσης], or of fear, diverting and distorting the straight course to which his face was set, or of desire, pulling and dragging him [ἑλκούσης καὶ ἀποτεινούσης] perforce to what he has not got, then he may salve and heal the sore and hope to gain the beauty that is genuine and unalloyed." This passage is cited in *SVF* 3.392. Cf. Philo, *Agr.* 103; *SVF* 3.391; 2.54; Plato, *Resp.* 439D, 589A; *Prot.* 352C; Aristotle, *Eth. nic.* 1145b24. For πλεονάζουσα ὁρμή (*pleonazousa hormē* [Philo, *Spec.* 4.79]) cf. *SVF* 3.377–8, 479.

17 For ὁλκός (*holkos*) cf. Philo, *Spec.* 4.113; Posidonius, frg. 169 Edelstein and Kidd (= Galen, *PHP* 5.5, line 25 [De Lacy 320]): παθητικὴ ὁλκή (*pathētikē holkē*), a term that, according to Kidd, probably was coined by Posidonius to convey the action of his "emotional movements" (frg. 153 Edelstein and Kidd). "The idea of ὁλκή, was perhaps derived from Plato *Laws* 644E: 'These inward affections, like sinews or chords drag us along (σπῶσι) and being opposed to each other, pull one against the other (ἀλλήλαις ἀνθέλκουσιν) to opposite actions'" (Edelstein and Kidd 1988: 2.622). Cf. Plato, *Resp.* 439B, and Philo, *Abr.* 59, where Philo says that God counters the ὁλκὴ παθητική (*holkē pathētikē*) and with his ὁλκῇ δυνατωτέρᾳ (*holkē dynatōtera*) draws (ἐπισπάσηται, *epispasētai*) the soul to himself. For ἀλλοτριότης

(*allotriotēs*) cf. Diogenes Laertius 7.85; *SVF* 1.197. For πτοία (*ptoia*, "fluttering"), ἀγωνία (*agōnia*, "anguish"), and δειματόω (*deimatoō*, "frighten") (*Decal.* 145) cf. *SVF* 1.206; 3.409, 476, 900. For ὀρέγω (*oregō*, "reach after") (*Decal.* 146) cf. Galen *PHP* 5.7.29 (De Lacy 342).

18 Cf. *Leg.* 3.86–7; *Praem.* 161; *QG* 1.79, where *elpis* is called a *propatheia tis chara pro charas*. It should be noted, however, that the Stoic position, as represented by Hecaton, is that one should cease to hope, for if one ceases to hope, one will also cease to fear, since the two go together (Seneca, *Ep.* 5.7–9).

19 References to Stobaeus are to the edition of Wachsmuth and Hense 1884–1912.

20 "By means of the various kinds of ὅρουσις," writes Inwood, "the Stoics would be in a position both to account for planning and long-range intentions and also to hold people responsible for the moral quality of the plans they make even if, by some chance, they should not carry them out" (Inwood 1985: 231). The Greek text of Arius Didymus's epitome of Stoic ethics and an English translation are now conveniently accessible in the edition of Pomeroy (1999).

21 Cf. Philo, *Leg.* 3.86–7; *Praem.* 161; *QG* 1.79; *Sobr.* 18; *Migr.* 32; *Somn.* 2.200; *Mos.* 1.26; *Spec.* 3.180; 4.5; *Praem.* 50; and possibly *Post.* 79, 83, where ἐπιβολή appears in an Epicurean context but seems to be used in its Stoic sense. See Whitaker's note in Colson and Whitaker 1929–62: 2.499 n. 79. "One could say," writes Inwood, "that an ἐπιβολή is an impulse to an action A preceding an impulse to another action B. The two actions, A and B, must be closely connected, so that the ἐπιβολή causes A but is logically connected to B, which is further in the future and will have its own impulse.... We hold a man responsible for getting himself into a situation where an action of his which he intended to do (A) leads to another (B), even if he did not consciously acknowledge where his initial action would lead" (Inwood 1985: 233).

22 Cf. *Leg.* 3.113; *Gig.* 35; *Abr.* 32; *QG* 2.57; Plato, *Tim.* 70F; *Resp.* 9.571C, 588C–590A; Alcinous, *Did.* 32 (Dillon 1993: 43), where the emotions are divided into wild and tame.

23 Cf. Posidonius, frgs 31, 166 Edelstein and Kidd. Inwood (1985) notes Philo's use of both the one-horse and two-horse versions of the Platonic comparison of the irrational part of the soul struggling against its driver, reason (*Leg.* 2.99; 3.118, 136). At *Leg.* 2.100 Philo, exegeting Gen 49:18, writes, "It is well that the soul does not fall forwards [εἰς τοὔμπροσθεν οὐ πίπτει]: let him not get in advance of the passions, but be behind them, and he shall learn self-control.... For if the mind, after starting out to do wrong, drops behind and falls backwards [πέσῃ εἰς τὸ ὀπίσω], it will not do the wrong deed." The same imagery is used by Galen when expanding on Chrysippus's likening of an excessive impulse to the condition of one who is running: "The person who draws the weight of his body backward [εἰς τοὐπίσω] as he runs has full control over stopping, but the person who draws it forward [εἰς τὸ ἔμπροσθεν] is prevented by it from stopping" (*PHP* 4.2, line 34 [De Lacy 244]).

24 "This passage," writes Annas, "is surprising because it embodies the idea that pleasure is itself inherently dangerous or dubious; the good man should avoid it, like a seductive but fatal Helen. This tone of popular moralizing sits oddly with the repeated insistence throughout this book that the good man is the man who takes pleasure in virtuous activities" (Annas 1980: 291).

25 Y. Amir (1984) has pointed out that one of Hercules's twelve labors is his battle with the Hydra, and that a Stoic source identifies the latter as the embodiment of

sensual pleasure against which the wise man must struggle (Heraclitus, *All.* 33.8; 33.1). This Stoic allegory of Wisdom's endless war with carnal pleasure is repeated by Philo: "When one enemy is subdued, there grows up another, in every respect stronger, as with the many-headed Hydra" (*Somn.* 2.14).

26 For Cynic elements in Philo see Bréhier 1950: 264.

27 The Hebrew תחמד לא is rendered in the LXX as οὐκ ἐπιθυμήσεις.

28 For θύραθεν ἐπεισιὼν καὶ προσπῖπτον ἔξωθεν cf. Plato *Tim.* 33 A, 44A; *Resp.* 8.561C; Aristotle, *Gen. an.* 2.736b28; Galen, *PHP* 4.6.35 (De Lacy 278): persons angered move "in conformity with some force external to themselves" (κατ' ἄλλην τινα βίαν ἔξωθεν αὐτῶν).

29 As Cicero reports, "The Stoics hold that there are divisions of disorder originating in two kinds of expected good and two of expected evil ... lust and delight [*libidinem et laetitiam* (i.e., ἐπιθυμία and ἡδονή)], in the sense of delight in present good and lust of future good, originate in what is good; fear and distress, they consider, originate in what is evil, fear in future and distress in present evil" (*Tusc.* 4.11 [trans. LCL, King 1927]). Philo is careful to describe fear as occurring when an evil is "not yet lodged inside us nor pressing hard upon us but is on the point of arriving and sending in its van trepidation and distress, messengers of evil presage, to sound the alarm" (*Decal.* 145). Cf. Epictetus, frg. 180 (in Oldfather 1925–8: 2.450).

30 Cf. *Spec.* 4.79–105 for a long tirade on desire, where it is called ἀρχέκακον (*archekakon*), source of all evils, and *Ebr.* 6, where Philo calls it the most painful (ἀργαλεωτάτη, *argaleōtatē*) of the soul's passions (although at *Det.* 119 he says that fear and distress are the more painful (ὀδυνηρότερα, *odynērotera*) of the four passions). For a critique of Wolfson's ascription of a theory of absolute free will to Philo, see Winston and Dillon 1983: 181–95.

31 The Old Academy, as well as Middle Platonism, adopted the goal of μετριοπάθεια (Cicero, *Acad. pr.* 2.131; Plutarch, *Virt. mor.* 443 C, 444B, 451C; Alcinous, *Did.* 30.5–6; Taurus, ap. Aulus Gellius, *Noct. att.* 1.26.11). Apuleius seems to be the only exponent of Middle Platonism who has openly adopted ἀπάθεια instead of μετριοπάθεια. See Lilla 1971: 60–117; Dillon 1977: 151–2; 1983; 1993: 188.

32 Cf. Josephus, *A.J.* 4.328–9.

33 Cf. Alcinous, *Did.* 24.2: "Since the affective and the rational parts are different in nature, it is proper that they occupy different locations, for they are found in conflict with one another. But any single thing cannot be in conflict with itself, nor can things that are in opposition to each other occupy the same place at the same time." See Plato, *Resp.* 4.436 A, 440A; Plutarch, *Virt. mor.* 446E.

34 See Heinemann in Cohn, Heinemann, and Adler 1909–38: 3.123 n. 2.

35 Panaetius may also have adopted a form of psychological dualism. See Rist 1969: 182–4; Inwood 1985: 292 n. 19.

36 Kidd's interpretation is driven by the need to account for Galen's statement that according to Posidonius, the passions were neither judgments (κρίσεις, *kriseis*), nor followed on (ἐπιγιγνόμενα, *epigignomena*) judgments, but were caused by the spirited and desiring power or faculty (frg. 34.10 Edelstein and Kidd; cf. frg. 152 Edelstein and Kidd; De Lacy 292).

37 As for Philo's emphatic expression ἡ κρίσις ἡ ἡμετέρα (*hē krisis hē hēmetera*), it may perhaps be explained by the fact that according to Posidonius, "the cause of the passions, that is, of the lack of harmony [ἀνομολογία] and of the life of misery [κακοδαίμων βίος], lies in not following in everything the daemon within, which is

kin [συγγενής] to the one that rules the whole world, but rather to live in subjection to the worse and brutish [ζῳώδης]" (Galen, *PHP* 5.5.6 [De Lacy 326], trans. Kidd, in Edelstein and Kidd 1988]). (For this kinship cf. Plato, *Tim.* 47B–C; 90A–D). Thus the emphatic "our" may refer to our following our own inferior brutish part rather than the daemon within us, which we share with the world-governing daemon. According to Radice (in Reggiani and Radice 1987: 486–7), the expression "our judgment" is to be understood in the sense of "that which we Hebrews understand by judgment, i.e., 'the oracle of judgment' and its significance" (see *Leg.* 3.118). It should be noted that in *Leg.* 2.6 Philo appears to be noncommittal with regard to Chrysippus's view that the passions are themselves judgments of the commanding faculty. On the contrary, as Pohlenz (1965: 1.354) has noted, from *Spec.* 2.89 it would appear that Philo accepts the Stoic view that the passions are formed in the *hēgemonikon*. See also Kidd 1971.

The larger question of how to interpret Galen's presentation of Posidonius's view of the passions is beyond the scope of this essay. Annas cites the interesting suggestion of J. Cooper that "Galen is unfairly representing Posidonius as much more of a Platonist than he was, and that his real view was consistent with orthodox Stoicism." Galen thus misidentifies the παθητικαὶ κινήσεις (*pathētikai kinēseis*) with the emotions themselves, whereas in truth they are to be identified only as a predisposing condition. See Annas 1992: 118–20; also Gill 1997, esp. 225–8. See now Cooper 1999: 449–84; Sorabji 2000: 93–132. If Cooper's interpretation should prove to be correct, then Philo would appear in the present passage to have veered from the orthodox Stoic position in the interests of his scriptural exegesis.

38 Noted by Heinemann in Cohn, Heinemann, and Adler 1909–38: 3.130 n. 2. For Epicurus on necessary and unnecessary pleasures see *Rat. sent.* 149: "Among desires some are natural (and necessary, some natural) but not necessary, and others neither natural nor necessary, but due to idle imagination [κενὴν δόξαν]." The scholium explains this as follows: "Epicurus regards as natural and necessary desires those that put an end to pain, as for instance drink in the case of thirst; natural and not necessary are those that merely vary the pleasure but do not remove pain, as for instance expensive foods: neither natural nor necessary are for instance crowns and the setting up of statues." See Bailey 1926: 100–2, 367.

39 It is interesting to note a somewhat similar attempt at compromise reached by the Hasidic master R. Nahman of Bratslav. "In his early childhood, we are told, he sought to overcome the pleasure he took in eating. Realizing that he could not do without eating altogether, he began to eliminate chewing, swallowing his food in large pieces so that he should not enjoy the taste" (Green 1979: 28). The Stoic sage, on the contrary, would not be disturbed by the unavoidable agreeable physical feelings that accompany various experiences. See Sandbach 1975: 62; Winston 1984: 408. Cf. Stobaeus, *Ecl.* 3.18, p. 526, lines 6–7 Hense (= Musonius Rufus, frg. 18B ["On Food"], p. 101, line 17 Hense 1905): (One should eat) οὐχ ἵνα ἥδηται, ἀλλ'ἵνα τρέφηται, "not for pleasure but for nourishment" (cited by Wendland 1895: 13); Seneca, *Ep.* 8.5. See also Brennan 1998: 36.

40 The collocation of ἀντισπῶντος (*antispōntos*) and μεθέλκοντος (*methelkontos*) is fairly frequent in Philo, especially in the context of the attractive force of the irrational soul components. See *Post.* 25; *Ebr.* 53; *Her.* 46; *Somn.* 1.152; *Abr.* 73; *Mos.* 2.165.

41 To me, Whitaker's LCL translation, "*but* the breast for the ram of consecration he will take away," seems wrong because the context makes it clear that here there is no contrast being made between the "washing" and the "taking away" as in *Leg.* 3.147. Although from a purely linguistic point of view, one could explain the ἐκτέτμηται as referring only to the *thymos* and not to the *epithymia*, the context shows, I think, that Philo is intent on portraying Moses, in contrast to the fool, as entirely eliminating the irrational part of his soul. Indeed, he makes no allusion here to the subtle distinction that he had introduced in *Leg.* 3.147, which is irrelevant to his purposes in *Migr.* 67. In any case, in light of his refined portrait of Moses, he is now suggesting that the latter has not even the desire to take nourishment, and that it is only his *logistikon* that calculates his bodily needs and determines how they are to be met.

42 It should be noted, however, that even when Philo attributes the *eupatheia* of *chara* to God, he undoubtedly is referring not to God as he is in himself (what is called in *QG* 2.62, Greek frg., ὁ πρὸ τοῦ λόγου θεός [*ho pro tou logou theos*]), but to God qua Logos – that is, God in his Logos aspect.

43 Bormann (1955: 28) notes that this notion is incongruous with Philo's view that God is never the cause of evil (*Opif.* 75; *Mut.* 30; cf. Plato, *Tim.* 42D; *Resp.* 10.617C), and he cites the suggestion of Heinemann, who follows Bréhier, that Philo here is influenced by Aristotelian doctrine, although his use of it here is occasioned by the wording of the biblical text; Bormann further notes that the wild beasts or passions are called "helpers" only *katachrēstikōs*, i.e., by a straining of language, "since in reality they are found to be our actual foes" (*Leg.* 2.10). See also Heinemann in Cohn, Heinemann, and Adler 1909–38: 3.55 n. 2.

44 See also Graver 2002: 163–5.

45 Seneca (*Ep.* 75.8–14) distinguishes three classes of *proficientes*, although Chrysippus (*SVF* 3.510) and Epictetus (*Diss.* 4.2) recognized only the first two; cf. Cicero, *Fin.* 4.56: "[Zeno] maintains that Plato, even if he is not wise, is not in the same case as the tyrant Dionysius: Dionysius has no hope of wisdom, and his best fate would be to die, but Plato has hope of it, and had better live." See Rist 1969: 90–1; Winston in Winston and Dillon 1983: 209–10, 370 n. 444.

46 At times, however, Philo speaks of the flood of the passions threatening the soul (*QG* 2.12; *Conf.* 24–25, 30; *Somn.* 2.13; *Virt.* 14).

47 Cf. *Abr.* 170, where Abraham's love for God enables him to overcome the love-charms of family ties. It should be noted that Philo's descriptions of Abraham (see also *Abr.* 243–4) indicate his need to overcome the passions. Even if we assume that what he battles is only *propatheiai*, clearly he differs from the Stoic sage, whose perfected mind automatically refuses assent to *propatheiai* without having to do battle with them. Abraham, then, is not *apathēs* in the Stoic sense of that term. This accords with Philo's statement in *Det.* 46 that Isaac is the only example of *apatheia* in his family line (ἐν γενέσει, *en genesei*) and removes any inconsistency with Philo's characterization of Moses as *apathēs*. For this translation of γενέσει cf. Plato, *Leg.* 691D. I agree with D.C. Aune that "the context in *Det.* 46 clearly suggests a comparison between Isaac and his family members (Abraham and Jacob)" (see Aune 1994: 125–58, esp. 130, 150 n. 28).

48 See Plato, *Tim.* 86B–90E; Spinoza, *Ethics* 5.1–20. For ἀγάπησις (*agapēsis*) as a subform of βούλησις (*boulēsis*) see *SVF* 3.432; Bonhöffer 1890: 287–8.

11

PASSIONS IN THE PAULINE EPISTLES: THE CURRENT STATE OF RESEARCH

David Charles Aune

Scholarship in the past three decades has recognized significant points of contact between the New Testament writings and popular philosophical understandings of the passions. This essay focuses on Pauline scholarship, demonstrating that although Paul accepts and utilizes particular methods for describing and treating certain passions, he avoids philosophical models for mastery of the passions. The first section surveys traditional twentieth-century approaches that dismissed Paul's passion language as inconsistent and nonphilosophical in content. Then follows a detailed discussion of three themes: (1) Paul's descriptions of his suffering and emotional hardships; (2) Paul's treatment of grief, anxiety, and anger in his communities; (3) Paul's strong rejection of "sinful" passions and desires. The essay concludes with suggestions as to why Paul avoids therapeutic models of self-mastery in his moral instructions for early Christian communities.

Introduction

In his masterful survey of research dealing with Hellenistic moral philosophy and NT literature, A.J. Malherbe (1992) challenges contemporary scholars to move beyond superficial comparisons and the uncritical use of parallels.[1] In particular, Malherbe laments the scholarly tendency to emphasize distinctions without offering constructive formulations.[2] Although Malherbe's article contains no specific information about the topic of passions in Paul's letters, his observations remain an important starting point for my inquiry.

The present essay outlines the current state of research on passions such as grief, anxiety, anger, and various desires as they are depicted in the undisputed Pauline letters.[3] Given the theme of the present volume, I am especially interested in the relationship between control of the passions and progress in moral virtue. I begin with a brief survey of traditional approaches to Paul's passion language, demonstrating that NT scholars generally have viewed Paul as rejecting the perspectives of Hellenistic philosophy. Following this, I provide an overview of late twentieth-century scholarship that moves beyond these traditional approaches. Paul's references to various emotions and desires can best be understood in conversation with Greco-Roman cultural perspectives and literary treatments of the passions. Finally, I conclude with brief comments about Paul and the theme of philosophical self-mastery.

Traditional approaches to Paul's passion language

For most of the twentieth century, discussions about Paul's passion language often focused upon the substantial differences between Paul and the prevailing philosophical conceptions of his time. Scholars recognized that Paul commonly uses both the noun πάθημα (*pathēma*) and the cognate verb πάσχω (*paschō*) to describe various sufferings rather than "passions" that need to be subdued.[4] However, in two instances (Rom 7:5; Gal 5:24) Paul uses the plural form of πάθημα to describe sinful behaviors associated with "the flesh." Even more curious for those familiar with Greco-Roman philosophy, Paul connects the specific term πάθος (*pathos*) with illicit sexual behavior and other behaviors associated with pagan society (Rom 1:26; 1 Thess 4:5; cf. Col 3:5). Based upon these observations, scholars traditionally portrayed Paul as using passion language in a distinctly nonphilosophical manner.[5]

Thus A. Bonhöffer (1911: 124), in his influential study of Epictetus and the NT, acknowledged Paul's familiarity with Greco-Roman philosophy but argued that Paul directly rejected Stoic notions of the passions. Specifically, Bonhöffer recognized that Paul's use of the term πάθος describes negative activity associated with pagan practices rather than unbridled or excessive emotions. For Bonhöffer, Paul's direct association of πάθημα with sin (Rom 7:5), as well as his characterization of ungodly Gentiles as being afflicted with the "passion of desire" (1 Thess 4:5), demonstrated a decisive departure from current philosophical arguments on the subject.[6]

In his study of virtue and vice lists, A. Vögtle (1936) provided further arguments to distinguish Paul's passion language from categories developed in ancient philosophy. According to Vögtle (1936: 208), Paul's placement of πάθος and ἐπιθυμία (*epithymia*) in a vice list along with various other negative behaviors (Col 3:5) would have seemed illogical for anyone trained in Greco-Roman philosophy. Instead, Vögtle (1936: 209) maintained that Paul's consistent identification of πάθος with sexual desire is best understood in light of early Jewish paraenetic material, not Hellenistic moral philosophy.[7] Perhaps most importantly, Vögtle (1936: 211–12) noted that a wide ideological gap exists between Stoic notions of freedom from the soul's irrational movements and Paul's notion of "putting to death" one's earthly passions.[8]

Some of the most strenuous arguments for Paul's direct rejection of Stoic conceptions of the passions came from M. Pohlenz (1949: 70, 76–7), who characterized Paul's statements about the anger of God in Rom 1:18 as "thoroughly unhellenistic" and claimed that Paul intentionally rejected the Stoic conception of divine "Nature" permeating the world. Regarding passion language, Pohlenz (1949: 81–2) built upon Vögtle's observations about Paul's distinctly nonphilosophical use of πάθος and ἐπιθυμία by citing Paul's failure to use common philosophical terminology such as ἀπάθεια (*apatheia*), ἀταραξία (*ataraxia*), and εὐδαιμονία (*eudaimonia*).[9] In the end, Pohlenz (1949: 80–1) viewed Paul as advocating a mystical, faith-based approach to moral issues that differs substantially from the Stoic emphasis upon philosophical self-mastery.[10]

In partial response to the view that Paul rejected popular philosophical notions about the human condition, most NT scholars in the mid-twentieth century shifted their focus to the distinctiveness of Paul's theological anthropology.[11] Thus R. Bultmann (1951: 104–5, 239–46), who otherwise recognized substantive parallels between Paul and the Stoics, discussed Paul's conception of the passions in the context of an anti-Christian existence characterized by "flesh" and "sin."[12] In this regard, Bultmann (1951: 241–4) considered ἐπιθυμία ("desire") to be the most troublesome passion for Paul, but he argued that other emotional dispositions, such as μέριμνα (*merimna*, "care" or "anxiety"), φόβος (*phobos*, "fear"), and even καύχησις (*kauchēsis*, "boasting"), could also be morally problematic if they demonstrated self-reliance or lack of trust in God.[13]

R. Jewett (1971) modified this theological approach by arguing that Paul's passion language, along with his other anthropological terms, developed in response to his opponents in various conflict settings. For example, Jewett proposed that the mainly Gentile Thessalonian community would not have fully grasped Paul's arguments about the problems of idolatry and impurity associated with πάθος and ἐπιθυμία. Furthermore, according to Jewett (1971: 101–11), Paul clarifies his position in Galatians, exposing the false promises of his libertine opponents by associating destructive passions with the "flesh" in Gal 5:19–21. In addition, Jewett (1971: 145–6) argued that Paul associates the particular "sinful passions" of Rom 7:5 neither with the "sensual character of the flesh" nor with general pagan practices, but rather with the "sinful desire to gain righteousness" through works of the law.[14]

Another traditional approach has been to interpret Paul's passion language almost exclusively in light of nonphilosophical Jewish sources. Most prominently, W.D. Davies (1955: 17–31; 1957) maintained that Paul's association of sexual desire with sin and "the flesh" directly drew upon Jewish conceptions of the [יצר הרע] (*ytsr hr'*, "evil inclination").[15] Davies (1955: 21–3) noted that in early Jewish literature, the evil inclination is particularly associated with sexual passion and idolatry. Therefore, for Davies, Paul's connection between idolatry, sinful desires, and other evils in Gentile society could best be explained as an articulation of the "doctrine of the two impulses."[16] This view has been promoted more recently by J. Marcus (1986), who argues that the "*yēser* doctrine" underlies most, if not all, of Paul's references to passions and sexual desire.[17]

In the past four decades a growing number of scholars have refined and modified previous approaches to Paul's passion language. Moving beyond narrow fields of inquiry and particular theological agendas, scholars have argued that Pauline references to emotion and desire are best understood in relation to conventional treatments in Greco-Roman pagan and Jewish sources. Four particular areas have received the most attention: (1) Paul's rhetorical use of emotional appeal; (2) Paul's descriptions of his own sufferings and emotional endurance; (3) Paul's treatment of grief, anxiety, and anger in his communities; (4) Paul's negative assessment of sexual passions and desires.[18]

Paul's rhetorical use of emotional appeal (*pathos*)

Many contemporary scholars have used categories from ancient rhetoric to help interpret Paul's emotionally charged language, especially as related to his methods of argumentation and persuasion.[19] Admittedly, as T. Olbricht (2001: 7–8) has recently observed, there exists very little agreement about the precise definition and application of the rhetorical category of πάθος (emotional appeal). Nevertheless, a great deal of progress has been made. In what follows, I have selected some recent scholarly discussions that explore the purpose and function of "rhetorical πάθος" in three Pauline letters.[20]

In his rhetorical analysis of 1 Thessalonians, B. Johanson (1987: 81–108) claims that Paul relies heavily upon πάθος appeals throughout the first part of the letter to commend the members of the Thessalonian community for their imitation of Paul's faithfulness to God and to affirm the strong emotional bond that he has with them.[21] Johanson (1987: 98) also identifies Paul's strong polemical statement in 1 Thess 2:15–16 as a form of *vituperatio* intended more to foster group solidarity than to turn his audience against their persecutors. According to Johanson (1987: 58), these πάθος appeals combine with other persuasive strategies to strengthen a community that was especially shaken by the unexpected deaths of fellow Christians.[22] T. Olbricht (1990), while accepting some of the details in Johanson's analysis and acknowledging that Paul's language is filled with emotion, argues that Paul uses very little πάθος in the Aristotelian sense of the term. Instead, claims Olbricht (1990: 227, 230), Paul relies far more heavily upon ἦθος and λόγος for the main purpose of "reconfirming" this community in its primary faith affirmations. More recently, E. Krentz (2000) has argued that Paul blends ἦθος and πάθος in 1 Thessalonians for the purpose of urging the community to make correct choices about serving God. Krentz (2000: 311) cites 1 Thess 4:9–12 as an example of πάθος because Paul uses his appeal to the community's love for God as the basis for exhortations to live virtuously in society.

The identification of πάθος appeals throughout 2 Corinthians has been used for various interpretations. Some scholars have pointed to the heightened use of πάθος in 2 Cor 10–13 as evidence for the integrity of the entire letter.[23] Other scholars have focused on specific sections. Thus M. DiCicco (1995: 429–32) claims that Paul's seemingly odd mixture of indignant and reproachful language with his statements about love for the community and fear of divine judgment in 2 Cor 10–13 are in fact an effective technique for persuading the Corinthians to accept his apostolic authority.[24] J. Sumney (2001) discusses rhetorical πάθος in 2 Cor 1–7; 10–13, focusing upon Paul's attempts to elicit favorable emotional responses toward himself while at the same time heightening negative feelings of shame and enmity toward his opponents. According to Sumney (2001: 160), this emotional argumentative strategy demonstrates that Paul views certain emotions as "intelligent and discriminating parts of the personality."[25] Focusing upon the conciliatory portions of 2 Corinthians, L. Welborn (2001) draws upon rhetorical theory to demonstrate that Paul elicits the emotions of pity, anger, and zeal in his readers. According to Welborn (2001: 57–60), Paul's overriding purpose is the transformation of these emotions into hope, love, and confidence as they are experienced through a communal participation in the sufferings of Christ.

A growing number of scholars have also identified and explored Paul's rhetorical use of πάθος in Galatians. L. Thurén (1999) highlights Paul's angry statements and other emotionally charged language throughout Galatians but rejects those interpretations that view Paul himself as being overwhelmed by emotions. Instead, argues Thurén (1999: 317), Paul uses πάθος and other rhetorical strategies to dramatize the theological differences between himself and his opponents.[26] R.D. Anderson (1998: 142–89) likewise identifies many examples of rhetorical πάθος in Galatians, characterizing the letter as primarily a strong rebuke of the Galatian Christians who have been influenced by Paul's opponents.[27] T. Martin (2001) focuses on Gal 4:12–20, using Aristotelian categories to argue that Paul seeks to arouse in his readers the emotions of friendliness toward himself, shame for inappropriate actions, and anger toward those who are agitating the community. Finally, S. Kraftchick (2001) claims that Paul needed to rely on both character appeals (ἦθος) and emotional persuasion (πάθος) throughout Galatians because his opponents' claims could not be countered with logical argumentation alone. According to Kraftchick (2001: 42–7), Paul's use of πάθος should not be expected to follow established rhetorical guidelines, but rather can be best understood as a form of "original argumentation" intended to change the thoughts and actions of the Galatian community.[28]

Paul's descriptions of suffering and emotional endurance

In his study of the *"agon* motif" in Paul's writings, V. Pfitzner (1967) argues that Paul portrays his endurance of various sufferings as a requirement of his particular apostolic calling, not a general moral struggle to be undertaken by all Christians.[29] Likewise, when Paul commends his churches for sharing in his struggles and sufferings for the sake of the gospel, there is no notion of a "moral *agon*" against the passions (Pfitzner 1967: 109–29).[30] According to Pfitzner (1967: 93–4), Paul emphasizes the proclamation of Christ rather than any personal moral achievement in his endurance of emotional and physical hardships.[31]

J.T. Fitzgerald (1988) further clarifies Paul's perspective on the endurance of suffering and emotional distress in his study of *peristasis* catalogs ("hardship lists") in the Corinthian correspondence. Fitzgerald identifies three basic positions regarding the control of the passions in Greco-Roman moral philosophy: moderation of the passions (μετριοπάθεια, *metriopatheia*), freedom from the passions (ἀπάθεια, *apatheia*), and lack of pain (ἀναλγησία, *analgēsia*).[32] Influential proponents of Stoic philosophy argued that a philosophical sage could maintain ἀπάθεια despite the physical manifestations of groaning and tears. According to Fitzgerald (1988: 199–201, 204–7), Paul adopts and adapts philosophical traditions that use hardship lists to depict the sage as enduring intense suffering without being inwardly shaken. More precisely, Paul defends the authenticity of his apostolic calling and describes the character of his ministry (διακονία, *diakonia*) through vivid descriptions of his hardships, pain, grief, and other emotional distresses. Rather than taking credit for his ability to endure, however, Paul consistently credits God for enabling him to maintain composure in the midst of these remarkable hardships (Fitzgerald 1988: 166–72, 207).

Building upon the work of Fitzgerald and others, S. Garrett (1990) has argued that Paul's struggle against worldly afflictions blends Hellenistic themes with important elements from early Jewish apocalypticism. According to Garrett, Paul does draw upon the common motif of the philosophical sage conquering his passions. However, when the causes of suffering are identified with evil forces in this world, Paul's struggles against affliction are depicted as spiritual warfare rather than the endurance of hardships.[33]

F.G. Downing (1998: 141–73) maintains that Paul's descriptions of his struggles find their closest affinities in Cynic, rather than Stoic, sources.[34] Thus throughout 2 Corinthians when Paul emphasizes his foolish behavior and admits to being weighed down by various kinds of emotional distress, his audience would have recognized similarities with ancient depictions of Odysseus (Downing 1998: 157–8).[35] Downing further argues that unlike the Stoic sages, Paul never refers to himself as having an undisturbed mental composure (ἀταραξία, *ataraxia*). Therefore, claims Downing (1998: 166–7), Paul promotes the typical Cynic ideals of pragmatic action and physical stamina rather than a concern about the quality of one's inner disposition.

Paul's treatment of grief, anxiety, and anger in the community

Contemporary scholars have convincingly shown that Paul, when dealing with grief, anxiety, and anger in the community, often uses various methods of consolation, correction, and rebuke described by moral philosophers as "therapeutic treatment" for "diseases of the soul."[36] In this regard, Malherbe has focused upon Paul's use of consolatory language in the Thessalonian correspondence.[37] Malherbe (1989b: 64–5) demonstrates that Paul's treatment of "grief" (λύπη, *lypē*) in 1 Thess 4:13–18 has striking similarities with the consolation offered in Greco-Roman philosophical sources.[38] Paul's theological instructions about the resurrection and return of Christ provide the basis for appropriate grief in the Christian community (Malherbe 1989b: 65–6).[39] Malherbe further argues that Paul's heightened use of emotional language in 1 Thess 2–3 functions both to strengthen his relationship with the Thessalonian community and to demonstrate his concern for their experiences of distress.[40]

D. Balch (1983) has surveyed Roman Stoic views on the topic of marriage as they pertain to Paul's instructions in 1 Cor 7:32–35 about being "free from anxiety" (ἀμέριμνος, *amerimnos*) and "undistracted" (ἀπερισπάστως, *aperispastōs*) in one's devotion to the Lord. Balch concludes that Paul, like many of the Stoics, recognizes the negative aspects of emotional distress and offers adaptable instructions about marriage on the basis of whether it will cause inappropriate "anxiety" and "distractions."[41] In a presentation of Paul as a "worldly ascetic," V. Wimbush (1987) further clarifies Paul's perspective about various desires and emotional distresses as articulated throughout 1 Cor 7. Wimbush (1987: 49–66) claims that Paul exhorts the Corinthians to live "as if" (ὡς μή, *hōs mē*) worldly attachments are unimportant so that they will be undivided in their "devoted care" (μέριμνα, *merimna*) to the Lord.[42] Drawing upon insights from social science, Wimbush (1987: 66–71) concludes that Paul, like the Stoics, offers rational arguments about inner detachment that reflect the ancient urban experience.[43]

Regarding the passion of anger, scholars have shown that whereas Paul considers certain kinds of anger to be appropriate in the community, most kinds of anger are not.[44] Paul's exhortations against vengeance in Rom 12:19–21 have been interpreted as a concession to retributive anger. For example, K. Stendahl (1962) has argued that Paul does not expect a lessening of anger against one's enemies as the community awaits God's impending judgement. Against this view, W. Klassen (1962: 348–9; 1984: 120), J. Piper (1979: 114–19), F.J. Ortkemper (1980: 122–3), and others have claimed that Paul exhorts the Christian community to conquer their desire for retribution through active deeds of love.[45] G. Zerbe (1992: 191–4) articulates a growing consensus on this issue: whereas Paul considers certain forms of anger to be appropriate within the community, he recognizes the danger of retributive anger and admonishes his audience in Rom 12 not to retaliate against outsiders.[46]

C. Glad (1995: 186–93, 315–25) has provided a particularly helpful framework for understanding Paul's treatment of troublesome forms of grief, pain, and anger in his communities. According to Glad, Paul uses therapeutic arguments as an integral part of his "psychagogic activity" – that is, the work of providing spiritual guidance through nurture and the correction of faults. As evidenced especially by his comments pertaining to the "wrongdoer" in 2 Cor 2:3–11; 7:8–13, Paul not only was vulnerable to the pain (λύπη) caused by others, but also willing to inflict a certain amount of emotional pain for the purpose of correction and communal health. According to Glad (1995: 316–17), Paul's concerns about the harshness of his comments and the potential damage of "excessive grief" have close parallels in Greco-Roman moral literature.[47] Glad (1995: 318–19) provides a coherent reconstruction of Paul's relationship with the Corinthians, emphasizing that Paul sought healing in the community through mutual reconciliation while at the same time defending his own harsh words because they resulted in repentance.[48]

Paul's negative assessment of sexual passions and desires

As we have seen, Paul repeatedly connects specific terms for "passion" (πάθος, πάθημα) and "desire" (ἐπιθυμία, ὄρεξις [*orexis*]) with immoral behaviors.[49] Paul's negative characterization of these passions fits within a larger complex of issues, including idolatry, impurity, and various sexual practices. Recent studies have focused on the precise relationship between fleshly desire, immoral behavior, and Paul's conception of sin and sexuality.

J. Boswell (1980: 107–13) initiated a great deal of controversy by arguing that Paul, in Rom 1:26–7, condemns not homoerotic desire, but rather homosexual acts committed by heterosexual persons.[50] For Boswell (1980: 113), the language of dishonor and shame (ἀτιμία, *atimia*; ἀσχημοσύνη, *aschēmosynē*) associated with the passions in Rom 1:26–7 indicates that Paul is mainly concerned about social disgrace, not sexual desire as such.[51] Although Boswell's specific arguments have not fared well among NT scholars, his work has prompted a careful reexamination of the particular social and cultural context in which Paul's passion language should be understood.[52]

L.W. Countryman (1988: 104–23) moves in a different direction by interpreting Paul's negative references to the passions in Rom 1:26–7 and 1 Thess 4:3–5 as pertaining mainly to the ritual impurity of idol-worshiping Gentiles. According to Countryman (1988: 111–12), the Gentile desires of Rom 1:24–5 are essentially different from those of the Jews because Gentiles had been "surrendered" to this condition by God.[53] Most importantly, Countryman (1988: 110, 117) argues that since Paul refrains from using the language of sin in this description of Gentile passions, he views these passions as impure but not morally evil.[54]

Building upon the work of Countryman, B. Fiore (1990) has argued that the related conceptions of "intemperate passion" (πάθος ἐπιθυμίας, *pathos epithymias*) and "competitive greed" (πλεονεξία, *pleonexia*) connect the diverse topics in 1 Cor 5–6. Fiore (1990: 141–3) notes striking similarities between Plutarch's polemic against the Epicureans and Paul's strong admonitions to the Corinthians, suggesting that Paul saw the need to warn against Epicurean influence. Furthermore, Paul's use of rational argumentation throughout this section of 1 Corinthians also suggests that he accepts the philosophical distinction between reason and irrational passion.[55] However, Fiore (1990: 139) distinguishes sharply between "Plutarch's philosophical idealism and Paul's pneumatic faith."

Considerable work has been done to clarify the concept of ἐπιθυμία ("desire") in Paul's writings and explain its direct connection with immoral behavior and sin.[56] Of particular importance is the argument in Rom 7:7–8, where Paul cites the LXX translation of the tenth commandment (οὐκ ἐπιθυμήσεις, "do not desire") as an example of the law's demand. Scholars have recognized that Paul here draws upon a common Hellenistic Jewish conception identifying ἐπιθυμία ("desire" in the sense of "covetousness") as the source of sin and other evils.[57] Scholars have also interpreted Paul's reference to "desiring evil things" in 1 Cor 10:6 as a warning against idolatry, sexual immorality, and other sinful actions detailed in this text.[58] Based on this research, scholars often have related Paul's negative evaluation of ἐπιθυμία to rebellion against God and the wide range of destructive, antisocial behaviors resulting from human disobedience.[59]

Scholars have also utilized methodologies from the social sciences in an attempt to clarify Paul's understanding of sinful desires. For example, in a psychological interpretation of Pauline theology, G. Theissen (1987: 177–265) analyzes Paul's depiction of inner conflict in Rom 7 and describes Paul as promoting a type of "cognitive restructuring" through his use of Christ symbolism. K. Berger (1991: 158–68) takes a different approach, emphasizing that Paul was not concerned with the analysis of emotions as such. Nevertheless, according to Berger (1991: 159–60), Paul's arguments against sinful desire are grounded in a rational belief structure that is best described as an "ecstatic rationalism." R.G. Hamerton-Kelly (1992: 90–101, 161–82) applies the theories of René Girard to Paul's account of sinful desire in Rom 1–7, claiming that mimetic union with Christ's sacrificial death provides a means for reforming the "deformed desires" caused by Adam's sinful rebellion against God.

In a creative engagement with Paul's letters, D. Boyarin (1994: 162–79) argues that "fleshly desire" refers specifically to sexual lust. To support his position, Boyarin claims that throughout Rom 7 Paul was primarily concerned about sexual sin aroused by the command to "be fruitful and multiply."[60] In this reading, Paul declares Christians as having been freed from the "law" to produce physical progeny so that they can live fully in the Spirit, bearing "spiritual fruit" (Boyarin 1994: 165–70).[61] Therefore, Boyarin (1994: 176–9) depicts Paul as a "proto-encratite" who privileges the celibate life of spiritual union with Christ and admonishes the Christian community to remain free from worldly entanglements.[62] Importantly for our purposes, Boyarin distinguishes between Paul's conception of the "desires of the flesh" (sexual desire) and the "works of the flesh" (the destructive social outcome of these desires). In the end, Boyarin's Paul does not view fleshly desire as inherently evil, but he repeatedly warns against its tendency to pull Christians into sin, away from their spiritual calling (Boyarin 1994: 174–7).

D. Martin (1997) argues, in the clearest and strongest possible terms, that Paul consistently rejects all sexual desire as inherently dangerous and polluting for the body of Christ.[63] According to Martin (1997: 203), Paul does not differentiate between "homosexual" and "heterosexual" desires; both are condemned.[64] Indeed, in 1 Cor 7 Paul's goal was to eliminate or quench sexual desire so that it does not damage the Christian community (Martin 1997: 202).[65] Rather than resorting to subjective "common sense" solutions for Paul's statements, Martin turns to selected Greco-Roman medical and philosophical writers who likewise seek to control or extirpate sexual desire. When placed alongside these other ancient writers, Paul is seen as sharing a particular cultural understanding of sexual desire. Desire is like a dangerous disease that affects both body and soul; it can be healed or completely removed through proper "therapies." However, Martin (1997: 204–7) emphasizes that Paul's viewpoint contrasts sharply with the Stoic ideal of self-sufficiency, an ideal closely connected with aristocratic values in the Greco-Roman world.[66]

In a "rereading" of Romans, S. Stowers (1994) provides a framework for understanding Paul's depiction of Gentile passions in Rom 1:18–32 as a particular cultural problem.[67] According to Stowers, Paul accounts for the sexual practices and antisocial behaviors of Gentile society by emphasizing God's role in judging the Gentiles for their idolatry. In his description, Paul combines two themes already present in the anti-Gentile polemic of his day: impurity and lack of self-mastery.[68] Importantly for Stowers (1994: 97–100), Paul's account has striking similarities with other Hellenistic "decline of humanity" narratives that likewise emphasize the proliferation of evil in Greco-Roman society.[69] Stowers reads Paul as offering a culturally specific characterization of Gentile unbelievers rather than a general description of the depraved condition of humankind.[70]

B. Brooten (1996) has further emphasized the culturally specific aspects of Paul's negative comments about sexual passion in Rom 1:18–32, especially as related to same-sex love between women.[71] Brooten draws upon a vast body of ancient literature to argue that Paul shares a general cultural assumption about "natural" sexual behavior in which men are dominant and active but women are inferior and passive.[72] Regarding the specific comments of Rom 1:24–7, Brooten (1996: 237–8, 254–5) claims that Paul's negative characterizations of "desire" and "passion" were likewise shaped by cultural influences.[73] Brooten (1996: 255–6) concludes that Paul holds persons responsible for their behavior, despite a theological framework that emphasizes God's action in surrendering persons to their passions.[74]

Current discussions of homosexuality in light of Scripture continue to focus upon the precise meaning of the "dishonorable passions" and "inflamed desires" referred to in Rom 1:26–7. D. Fredrickson (2000) marshals a great deal of evidence from philosophical sources to argue that the specific terms used by Paul in this passage constitute an attack on erotic love, not homosexuality as such. According to Fredrickson, it is the failure to control sexual passion that brings dishonor and shame. In this reading, uncontrolled passion is inherently dishonorable; thus Paul condemns same-sex intercourse as an example of unrestrained passion, not as an "unnatural" violation of a heterosexual norm (Fredrickson 2000: 207–15, 222). But even those scholars who accept a more traditional reading of Rom 1:24–7 often claim that Paul viewed all sexual desires, not merely homoerotic desires, as inherently problematic.[75] This leads us, then, to the concluding question of philosophical self-mastery in Paul's writings.

Conclusion: Paul and philosophical self-mastery

To summarize this discussion thus far, we have seen that scholars throughout most of the twentieth century dismissed Paul's passion language as intentionally nonphilosophical in its content. Despite this, more recent scholarship has shown significant points of contact between Paul's writings and popular philosophical understandings about the passions. This is particularly evident in Paul's rhetorical use of emotional language, his endurance of emotional hardships, his treatment of emotional distress in the community, and his negative assessment of certain desires. However, one important question remains: Why does Paul not provide a well-designed plan for mastering the passions similar to those developed in the philosophical schools of his day? Stated differently: Why does Paul accept and apply "therapeutic methods" to treat certain passions but reject "therapeutic models" of self-mastery for overcoming desires of the flesh?

Scholars have long recognized that Paul's conception of "self-mastery" (ἐγκράτεια, *enkrateia*) differs substantially from various conceptions developed in Hellenistic philosophy. Thus M. Hill (1977) distinguishes Paul's notion of "having power over" sexual desires from the philosophical notion of "having power in oneself." The agent of self-mastery for Paul is the Spirit (Gal 5:23), not human reason. Regarding Paul's description in 1 Cor 7:9 of persons who are not controlling their sexual desires, Hill (1977: 78) argues that the exercise of self-mastery is not itself part of Paul's "remedial action" and therefore not an essential requirement for maintaining a moral life.

In his study of the Corinthian body, D. Martin (1995a: 212–17) contrasts Paul's complete rejection of sexual desire with the views of ancient medical writers who did promote various forms of physical and philosophical self-mastery.[76] Since Paul conceives of desire as inherently hostile and foreign to Christ's body, he does not promote any method for controlling the sexual passions; they must be completely avoided. Those members of the Corinthian community whom he designates as "the strong" are, in Martin's (1995a: 217) interpretation, misguided to think that they could indulge desire even within marriage.

Stowers (1990; 1994: 42–82, 273–84) has provided the most thorough explanation for Paul's rejection of philosophical self-mastery. According to Stowers (1990: 274–84), the so-called wise members of the Corinthian community were promoting a therapeutic model of Christianity, privileging human reason in an "epistemically irresponsible" manner. Therefore, throughout the Corinthian correspondence Paul rejects therapeutic models as hierarchical, elitist, and destructive of the Christian community (Stowers 1990: 284–6).[77] Similarly, in Paul's letter to the Romans, Stowers (1994: 42–6, 66–7) claims that Paul's opponents had combined an elitist ethic of self-mastery with Jewish teachings to provide a method for controlling passions among Gentile converts. Here, Paul again rejects therapeutic models of self-mastery because they were associated with his opponents. Rather than providing specific instructions about how to control one's desires, Paul exhorts his audience to identify with Jesus Christ and allow Christ's Spirit to reverse their experience of moral decline (Stowers 1994: 255–7, 273–84).

Unquestionably, Paul's conceptions of the passions cannot be properly understood apart from the philosophically informed cultural codes that permeated Greco-Roman society. Nor can the passions be understood apart from Paul's basic convictions about the life, death, and resurrection of Jesus — what W. Meeks (1993: 196) has described as the "Christ-story." Paul does indeed, to quote Meeks, "suggest, cajole, argue, threaten, shame, and encourage [his] communities into behaving, in their specific situations, in ways somehow homologous to that fundamental story" (Meeks 1993: 196). Paradoxically, then, Paul uses emotional language both to persuade his audience about the value of living according to the gospel of Christ and to proscribe those passions that are, in his view, destructive to a shared life in Christ.

Notes

1 For a critical appraisal of the use of parallels in the study of early Christianity see J.Z. Smith 1990: esp. 54–84, 116–43, and also White and Fitzgerald 2003: 13–39.
2 Thus, in regard to certain studies comparing the writings of Paul and the Stoics, Malherbe contends that "dissimilarity as the decisive criterion in comparison does not enrich our understanding of Paul" (Malherbe 1992: 300).
3 Since most serious research on passions in the NT has centered upon Paul's writings, I have limited this essay accordingly. For a general discussion of desire, fear, and other emotions throughout the NT see Berger 1991: 158–224 [ET 2003: 128–77]. Selected studies dealing with specific passions in particular NT texts deserve special mention. For the passions of anger, desire, and anxiety in Matt 5–6 see Betz 1995: 198–239, 460–86. For an overview of emotion language in Mark's Gospel but without reference to philosophical sources see Pauw 1997. For the passion of fear in Mark's Gospel see Allen 1947; Lincoln 1989. For Luke's description of Jesus as overcoming grief in the Gethsemane narrative see Neyrey 1980. For an overview of emotion language in Acts see Pauw 1995. For the polemical use of passion language in the Pastoral Epistles see Johnson 1978; Malherbe 1989a. For philosophical self-mastery in the Epistle of James see Johnson 1990. For the development of philosophical conceptions about the passions in other early Christian literature see Sorabji 2000: 343–417.
4 For πάθημα as "suffering" to be endured by both Paul and his readers see Rom 8:18; 2 Cor 1:5–7; Phil 3:10; cf. Col 1:24; 2 Tim 3:11. For πάσχω as "the experience of suffering" see 1 Cor 12:26; 2 Cor 1:6; Phil 1:29; 1 Thess 2:14; cf. 2 Thess 1:5; 2 Tim 1:12. In at least one instance (Gal 3:4) Paul uses the verb πάσχω in the neutral sense of "experiencing things" (in this case, experiencing them in the Spirit). A complete listing of emotion language is available in D.C. Aune 1995.
5 To underscore the difference between the traditional approaches that dominated the first two-thirds of the twentieth century and the more recent studies and approaches that appeared with increasing frequency during the last third of the century, I use primarily the past tense in this section but the present tense in the following sections of this essay.
6 On this point Bonhöffer is particularly forceful: "Especially in this regard Paul would have thought all the less of the philosophical teaching about the affections, since he refers to being afflicted with the emotion of ἐπιθυμία as a distinguishing mark of the 'Gentiles, who do not know God'" (Bonhöffer 1911: 125, my translation).
7 Citing Ps.-Phocylides 193; T. Jos. 7:8. Vögtle also noted that many of the vices that figure prominently in Paul's letters (e.g., πορνεία [porneia] and ἀκαθαρσία [akatharsia]) are not known in the vice lists of popular philosophy.
8 For a concise overview of ancient vice lists and their relationship to the "passions" see Fitzgerald 1992.
9 As an example of Paul's lack of interest in (or awareness of) technical Stoic ethical categories, Pohlenz claimed that "the equation of the concept of πάθος with its

species ἐπιθυμία [Col 3:5] was a logical impossibility for the Stoics" (Pohlenz 1949: 82, my translation).
10 Similar conclusions were reached by Sevenster (1961: 76–84, 140–6).
11 Remarkably, analyses of the passions were absent from most major studies of Pauline anthropology and anthropological concepts written during this period, including Gutbrod 1934; Kümmel 1948; Stacey 1956; Sand 1967; Brandenburger 1968; Käsemann 1971: 1–31. Stacey provides an explanation for this omission: "[Paul's] aim was not to present coherent psychology and the fact that his terms were confused would not have worried him. [Paul's] great vision of how man stands before the God he found in Christ, he did convey, and that was enough" (Stacey 1956: 238).
12 See also Bultmann 1967. On Bultmann's recognition that Paul adapts other Stoic concepts see Colish 1992: 370–3.
13 The influence of Bultmann on this topic is inestimable.
14 Although most scholars have not accepted Jewett's reconstruction of the particular conflict settings in Paul's letters, his work represents an important step forward in the attempt to identify the moral teachings of Paul's opponents.
15 In the development of his arguments, Davies relied heavily upon the work of F.C. Porter (1902).
16 More precisely, D. Flusser (1958: 255) argued for a direct connection between the יצר בשר (*ytsr bsr*, "inclination of the flesh") in the Qumran literature and Paul's notion of ἐπιθυμία σαρκός (*epithymia sarkos*, "desire of the flesh") in Gal 5:16. So also W. Michaelis (1968: 928–9), who cited the work of Bonhöffer, Vögtle, and Pohlenz to argue that Paul's description of "passion" departs from Stoicism and instead has much in common with nonphilosophical Jewish sources from the Second Temple period.
17 According to Marcus, however, Paul subverts important Jewish traditions by rejecting his opponents' claim that observance of Torah will weaken or destroy the "evil inclination" and its desires. For a fuller discussion of the Jewish background see Marcus 1982.
18 My discussion of current research in the following sections is selective, not comprehensive. Those whose contributions are discussed were selected because of the importance of their work or because they are representative of a contemporary approach to Paul's use of passion language.
19 Philosophers and rhetoricians (esp. Aristotle, Cicero, and Quintilian) advocated various kinds of "invention": persuasive proofs that relied upon λόγος (*logos*, examples and rational argumentation), ἦθος (*ēthos*, moral character and conduct), and πάθος (*pathos*, emotional appeal). These writers likewise provided detailed analyses of various emotions and their usefulness for effecting particular results in one's audience. For explanations of these categories and their use see Kennedy 1963; 1972; Wisse 1989.
20 I intentionally use the term "rhetorical πάθος" to describe emotional appeals in the context of persuasion and argumentation. Other studies dealing with this topic in Paul's letters, not discussed at length here, include Snyman 1993; Poster 2001; Keck 2001.
21 Citing 1 Thess 1:6; 2:17–20; 3:5, 9–13 as some of the strongest evidence for this.
22 Johanson argues that the problem addressed in 1 Thess 4:13–5:11 is the "primary

exigence to which the various persuasive strategies of the letter as a whole are directed."
23 Witherington 1995: 429–32. A similar argument is developed more fully in Thompson 2001.
24 At times, DiCicco does not make careful distinctions between Paul's personal feelings and Paul's use of emotional language to effect certain results in his readers.
25 Sumney refers to M. Nussbaum's (1996) assessment of Aristotle.
26 This argument is developed also in Thurén 2000: 58–94.
27 Although Anderson's discussion of ancient epistolary theory is helpful, the analysis fails to integrate the important section of paraenesis in Gal 5:13–6:10.
28 For the concept of "original argumentation," Kraftchick draws upon P.C. Smith 1998.
29 See esp. Pfitzner 1967: 97–8 (on the athletic imagery in 1 Cor 9:24–27): "[Paul's] immediate concern is to defend his apostolic actions and the principle of self-negation demanded by his special office.... The Agon of Paul is not that of every Christian, but the eventual necessity for restriction of personal liberty is a rule which applies...."
30 With particular reference to Rom 15:30; Phil 1:27–30; Col 1:29–2:1; 1 Thess 2:14. Later, Pfitzner (1967: 162–4) maintains that Paul uses military rather than athletic imagery to depict the moral struggle against passions associated with sin.
31 For the concept of self-mastery as related to Paul see my conclusion below.
32 Fitzgerald (1988: 65–70) draws mainly upon the writings of Seneca to provide a sensible discussion of ἀπάθεια in later Stoicism.
33 Thus Garrett claims that "once Paul has identified his opponents with the perishing and with the god of this age ..., Paul is not just the *sophos* whose endurance commends him, but the warrior against the rulers of this present evil age" (Garrett 1990: 117). See also Garrett 1995.
34 Downing draws heavily upon Ebner 1991.
35 Referring esp. to 2 Cor 6:10; 11:28; 12:10–12.
36 For a survey of the literature and examples of various methods see Malherbe 1992: 301–4. A thorough discussion of this theme in Hellenistic philosophy is provided in Nussbaum 1994b, but see also the essays in Sihvola and Engberg-Pedersen 1998, and the wider range of literature discussed in Braund and Gill 1997. For Paul's use of "therapeutic treatments" see esp. Glad 1995 (discussed further below).
37 See Malherbe 1987: 57–8, 61–7, 79–81; 1983.
38 In addition to the wealth of sources cited by Malherbe, see the detailed study of Plutarch and the consolatory tradition by Martin and Phillips (1978), in which parallels to 1 Thess 4 are noted (p. 413).
39 On Paul's use of eschatological arguments to provide comfort for grief in this passage see Wimmer 1955.
40 Thus Malherbe (1989b: 52–3) explains that Paul's descriptions of desire (ἐπιθυμία, *epithymia*), longing (ἐπιποθέω, *epipotheō*), and other emotions in 1 Thess 2:17; 3:6, 10 have a philophronetic function: Paul emphasizes his friendship and care despite his physical distance from the community. For this epistolary strategy see Malherbe 1988: 12–14, 33.
41 So, esp., Balch 1983: 434–5: "Like these three Roman Stoics [Antipater, Epictetus,

and Hierocles] ... Paul advises the Corinthians that marriage is helpful for some, but not advantageous for others."

42 Against Balch, Wimbush argues that Paul views the concept of μεριμνᾶν as neutral or even positive when applied to serving God.

43 In this regard, Wimbush finds a close parallel between the Stoic concept of ἀπάθεια and the Pauline notion of living "as if" (ὡς μή) one has no worldly attachments.

44 Various kinds of anger can be distinguished: Paul dismisses "acts of rage" (θυμοί, *thymoi*) in the vice lists of 2 Cor 12:20 and Gal 5:20 and argues against "seeking vengeance" (ἐκδικέω, *ekdikeē*) in Rom 12:20, whereas he commends a certain kind of "indignation" (ἀγανάκτησις, *aganaktēsis*) and "vengeance" (ἐκδίκησις, *ekdikōsis*) in 2 Cor 7:11. Anger is probably also indicated by numerous statements throughout 2 Cor 11, especially the description of "burning" (πυροῦμαι, *pyroumai*) in 2 Cor 11:29. Importantly, in the undisputed letters Paul limits the concept of ὀργή (*orgē*, "wrath, retribution") to God (as in Rom 1:18; 2:5; 9:22; 1 Thess 2:16) or those acting directly on God's behalf (as in Rom 13:4). For an assessment of early Christian perspectives on anger see W. Harris 2001: 391–9.

45 For a recent survey of approaches and a thorough analysis of this passage see Zerbe 1992.

46 Harris (2001: 393–6) emphasizes the ambiguities that develop from Pauline and other early Christian teachings about anger.

47 Glad cites pertinent examples from Philodemus, *Lib.* frg. 61.1, and numerous discourses by Plutarch, including *Adul. amic.* 55C; 66B; 70D–E; 73D–E; *Alc.* 23.5; *Virt. mor.* 452C; *Tranq. an.* 476F; *Exil.* 599A–C.

48 Glad connects not only 2 Cor 2:6–7 with 7:9–11, but also 1 Cor 4:14–21, 2 Cor 13:1–10, and other sections of the Corinthian correspondence.

49 Paul makes specific reference to πάθος ("passion") as illicit sexual desire in Rom 1:26; 1 Thess 4:5; cf. Col 3:5. Other, related passages include the negative depiction of πάθημα ("passion") in Rom 7:5; Gal 5:24, ἐπιθυμία ("desire") in Rom 1:24; 6:12–13; 13:13–14; 1 Cor 10:6–10, and ὄρεξις ("desire, craving") in Rom 1:27.

50 Boswell interprets the phrase παρὰ φύσιν (*para physin*) as "in excess of one's nature" rather than "unnatural" to argue that the same-sex activities of Gentiles are excessive and degrading but not evil.

51 A similar emphasis is developed by H. Moxnes (1988: 213).

52 For arguments against Boswell see esp. R.B. Hays 1986; J.B. DeYoung 1988.

53 In this regard, Countryman accepts the central thesis of Boswell but views Paul as describing "Gentile culture as a whole." At the same time, Countryman presents Paul as agreeing with contemporary cultural notions about the need for mature persons either to subdue their sexual desires or to express them within the context of marriage.

54 This argument is developed also by J. Siker (1994).

55 As evidence of rational argumentation Fiore (1990: 138–9) cites Paul's concern with judgment, knowledge, truth, wisdom, and deception throughout 1 Cor 5–6.

56 Admittedly, Paul can use the term ἐπιθυμία to describe the admirable desires for companionship with others (1 Thess 2:17) or union with Christ (Phil 1:23). However, when used without a specific object (as in Rom 7:7–8) or with particular reference to "evil things" (as in 1 Cor 10:6), the concept clearly suggests transgression of God's law.

57 So, esp., S. Lyonnet (1962: 157–62), who cites evidence from 4 Macc 2:6; Philo, *Decal.* 142–53; *Spec.* 4.84. See the discussion in D.C. Aune 1994: 126–7, 134–5.
58 Perrot 1983; Willis 1985: 144–6; Collier 1994. Alternatively, W. Meeks (1982) argues that Paul uses the verb παίζω (*paizō*, "to play") to summarize the specific sins listed in this passage.
59 See esp. Murphy-O'Connor 1982: 109–11.
60 According to Boyarin (1994: 163–4), the "speaker" of Rom 7 is Adam, and the "law of sin in the members" (Rom 7:23) refers to the commandment in Genesis regarding procreation.
61 This reading is consistent with Boyarin's (1994: 27–32, 57–85) argument that Paul absorbed many ideas from Middle Platonism, resulting in a modified dualism that distinguishes "spirit" from "matter."
62 Boyarin therefore views Paul's rejection of "fleshly desire" as anticipating later forms of Christian asceticism.
63 See also Martin 1995a: 198–228; 1995b.
64 Citing Rom 1:24–7; 1 Thess 4:3–8; 1 Cor 10:6–10.
65 Martin interprets Paul's concession in 1 Cor 7:1–5 as a method for guarding "weak Christians from the pollution of *porneia*" and claims that Paul "nowhere mentions a positive kind of desire as opposed to the 'burning' that he hopes marriage will quench." So also Martin 1995a: 215–16.
66 Responding in particular to arguments about the Stoics made in Nussbaum 1994b.
67 See esp. Stowers 1994: 88–100.
68 Stowers cites parallels with the Wisdom of Solomon to demonstrate that Paul's writings reflect "an ethnic caricature developed by certain Jews that draws upon two major cultural codes, the ethic of self-mastery and a Jewish code of purity and pollution" (Stowers 1994: 94). However, Stowers argues that Paul, unlike his opponents, does not utilize therapeutic models for the mastery of one's passions. These arguments are discussed further in my conclusion.
69 Stowers rejects any interpretation that reads into this passage the Adamic fall narrative and views Paul as providing a general diagnosis for the human condition.
70 So, esp., Stowers 1994: 92: "Paul describes not a timeless ontological truth but how certain humans created by God became the idolatrous and passion-dominated nations." For connections with 1 Thess 4:3–5 see Stowers 1994: 97; Yarbrough 1985: 65–87.
71 Brooten offers a succinct statement of her argument: "Paul's condemnation of homoeroticism, particularly female homoeroticism, reflects and helps to maintain a gender asymmetry based on female subordination" (Brooten 1996: 302).
72 See esp. Brooten 1996: 298–302.
73 Brooten remarks that philosophically informed readers would have recognized Paul's references to excessive passions and desires but not his theological diagnosis of the problem.
74 *Pace* Boswell and Countryman.
75 Thus, for example, W.R. Schoedel: "In Philo [as well as in Paul], it is the abhorrence of pleasure for the sake of pleasure or the abhorrence of impurity that provides the real impetus to the rejection of same-sex eros" (Schoedel 2000: 49).
76 So also Martin 1997: 202–4.
77 Stowers focuses upon Paul's arguments in 2 Cor 10; 1 Cor 8.

12

THE LOGIC OF ACTION IN PAUL: HOW DOES HE DIFFER FROM THE MORAL PHILOSOPHERS ON SPIRITUAL AND MORAL PROGRESSION AND REGRESSION?

Troels Engberg-Pedersen

The essay compares the logic that underlies Paul's exhortation and talk of progression and regression with the logic of the active, "self-determining self" that is part of the philosophy of action, emotion, deliberation, and more in the ancient Greco-Roman philosophical tradition. Are the two logics the same, or do they differ? Claims for difference have been made from two sides. A. Malherbe articulates a traditional theological insistence that the pervasive notion in Paul's thought of God's agency distinguishes him fairly sharply from the philosophers. D. Martin articulates a modern theological idea to the effect that Paul did not at all operate with a notion of the self like that of the philosophers. The essay argues for an intermediate position that claims that the two logics in Paul and the philosophers are in fact the same, while also allowing (with Malherbe) that the notions of God's agency and demonic agency provide an additional, very important dimension in Paul's thought, and (with Martin) that the Pauline notion of the self is a fairly "flat" one (as was the similar notion in the philosophers) in comparison with certain modern notions of the self (e.g., existentialist ones). Toward the end, a solution is proposed to the hackneyed question of the relationship between indicative and imperative talk in Paul's writings, again with the aim of articulating the basic logic that underlies his exhortation and talk of progression and regression.

Introduction

This essay discusses two questions that help to define the overall framework within which we should understand Paul's talk of spiritual and moral progression and regression. First, did Paul basically operate within the same paradigm of understanding progression and regression as did the Greco-Roman moral philosophers (including those who were his contemporaries), a paradigm that presupposes that in the field of action and emotion, which is also that of progression and regression, something is, as they said, "up to us"? In that case, what role should we ascribe to the agency of demons – and of God? Second, is there any room for progression and regression within Paul's understanding of conversion to the Christ faith? Is conversion not rather an all-or-nothing affair? All through, my concern will be to lay bare the underlying logic of action and emotion that frames Paul's talk of progression and regression. A number of issues that might be discussed in relation to progression and regression will not be touched upon at all. Instead, I will attempt to stay rigorously on target.

A few quotations will focus the first basic question for us.

J. Fitzgerald writes of Epictetus,

> His prayer is not a request for external blessings but either a call for God to be his helper... or an expression of gratitude. He thanks God for placing his *prohairesis* under his own control so that he is able to derive what is truly good from himself.
> (Fitzgerald 1990, 92)

A passage from Epictetus makes the point particularly clearly:

> God has not merely given us the faculties that enable us to bear all that happens without being degraded or crushed thereby, but... He has given them to us free from all restraint, compulsion, hindrance: He has put the whole matter under our control without reserving for Himself any power to prevent or hinder.
> (*Diss.* 1.6.40 [trans. Oldfather 1925–8: 1.49, with one change])

God has put the whole matter under our control, *eph' hēmin*, and he has left no power, *ischys*, for himself to interfere. Epictetus here introduces the notion of something being "under our control" or "up to us," as I translate *eph' hēmin*. The notion played a crucial role in Greek moral philosophy from at least Aristotle onward as a way of capturing the basic perspective within which the moral philosophers spoke of virtue and vice, of praise and blame, of a self who deliberates, decides, acts, and is formed in his or her character in accordance with those other things, and finally of the self as responsible (for his or her deliberations and so forth). At the risk of being misunderstood, we may speak of a "self-determining self," who by the use of the faculty of reason (viewed as a formal capacity) comes to see and understand things and to feel and act in accordance with this. I will not attempt to define this perspective any further here. Any page in the ethical treatises of Aristotle, the Stoics, Epicurus, the Academics, or the Sceptics presupposes it. Here I quote just one particularly striking example from Aristotle's *Nicomachean Ethics*:

> The question is also raised whether it [happiness, *eudaimonia*] is something acquired by learning [*mathēton*], by habituation [*ethiston*] or else by some other form of training [*askēton*] – or whether it comes to be present by some divine apportionment [*theia moira*] or else by luck [*tychē*]. Now if there be some other gift [*dōrēma*] too from the gods to human beings, it is reasonable that happiness too is godgiven, and the more so since it is the best of human affairs. However, that issue may be more germane to another investigation, still [here comes Aristotle's own view], even if it is not godsent, but comes to be present through virtue [*aretē*] and some kind of learning [*mathēsis*] or training [*askēsis*], it does seem to be one of the most godlike things. For the prize and end of virtue seems to be the best thing and something godlike and blessed. But it would also seem to be very widely shared. For it is possible for it to be present through some form of learning [*mathēsis*] and care [*epimeleia*] for all who are not maimed with a view to virtue.
> (*Eth. nic.* 1.9.1–4, 1099b9–20)

Here, Aristotle emphatically insists that happiness is something that may be brought about by human beings themselves, by learning, habituation, training, or some combination of these, and in all events by human care. Elsewhere (*Eth. nic.* 3.5) he goes out of his way to argue that moral virtue and vice too are "up to us" (see *Eth. nic.* 3.5.2, 1113b6–7), and that we are at least "ourselves in some way co-responsible for our mental states" (*Eth. nic.* 3.5.20, 1114b22–23), and of course also for the acts that spring from them (see *Eth. nic.* 3.5.22, 1114b31–32 and 3.1 as a whole). Indeed, as he claims, "man is a moving principle [*archē*] and a begetter [*gennētēs*] of his actions as of his children" (*Eth. nic.* 3.5.5, 1113b18–19). I will refer to the basic perspective expressed in this way by speaking of the logic that underlies exhortation, of a "self-determining human self," and occasionally even of the "rational self" of the moral philosophers. So, can or should we ascribe to Paul the same logic underlying exhortation that we find in the moral philosophers? In particular, does Paul handle the issue of moral and spiritual progression and regression from within the perspective of a self-determining self?

Most people will deny this. I quote from A. Malherbe, whose knowledge of and interest in the moral philosophers no one will question:

> The similarities between Paul and the philosophers should not be pressed.... Of major significance is that, whereas the philosophers stressed the importance of reason and reliance on self in moral growth, Paul refers the moral life to God and the power of the Holy Spirit. The philosophers, furthermore, through character education aimed at virtue and happiness, for the attainment of which one could be justly proud. Paul, on the other hand, while he does speak of a transformation, as the philosophers do, has in mind a metamorphosis of the intellect that rejects conformity to the world and aims at discerning the will of God.
> (Malherbe 1987: 32–3)

I suspect that Malherbe's points will resonate widely among Pauline scholars: reason *versus* God; reliance on self *versus* being led by the power of the Holy Spirit; character education of which one may be justly proud *versus* a metamorphosis of the intellect that aims at discerning the will of God. All these contrasts have a strongly theological flavor. Basically, they reflect a concern about the contrast between God and the human self. If Malherbe's contrasts are rightly drawn, we must answer our question in the negative. In spite of similarities (and indeed, as Malherbe would insist, substantial similarities), the basic logic that underlies exhortation in Paul's writings and those of the moral philosophers is not the same. But are these dichotomies rightly drawn?

There is another perspective that yields the same result even though it comes from what initially appears to be a very different direction. Where Malherbe's perspective is traditional and theological, the other is postmodern and purportedly nontheological, in fact steeped in cultural anthropology. Whereas from Malherbe's perspective what makes the crucial difference is God, from the other perspective it is the demons in Paul's demon-filled world, his *Geisterwelt*.

The view I have in mind has a fine pedigree, in M. Dibelius (1909) and in A. Schweitzer (1930) (conversely, Malherbe's perspective may draw sustenance from, for instance, R. Bultmann).[1] It has more recently been placed on the map again with gusto by D. Martin (1995a). In Martin's reading, not only does a large number of motifs that belong under the theme of exhortation in Paul's writings get very short shrift, but it also almost appears as if there is no self left in Paul's thought to function in a logic underlying exhortation. Such a self is, Martin claims, a modern construction. The ancient self, by contrast, had no firm boundaries and in Paul's view was basically exposed to its surroundings, including the *Geister*.[2] Within such a perspective it makes very little sense to speak of certain things as being "up to us." Conversely, if that idea is basic to the logic of exhortation as presupposed by the moral philosophers, then the difference between them and Paul will be vast.

From two sides, then, doubts have been raised whether Paul handles moral and spiritual progression and regression from within the perspective of a self-determining self as the ancient philosophers understood this. My first question is whether we should agree or disagree.

The second question was whether there is at all room for progression and regression within Paul's understanding of conversion. Further articulation of this question will be postponed until the end because the articulation itself presupposes the answer that will be given to the first question.

A few more introductory remarks are in order. When I speak of "the moral philosophers," I have in mind primarily the Stoics, both those representing the basic Stoic system of ethics and philosophy of action and also Paul's (near) contemporaries Seneca and Epictetus. I do not, however, intend to exclude any school of Hellenistic moral philosophy. Even an eclectic such as Plutarch, who wrote *How a Man May Become Aware of His Progress in Virtue*, is relevant. But neither do I intend to go into detail on any specific theory about what is "up to us." The schools differed on the details, but they also agreed on the basic conception of the "rational self," which they had in fact taken over from the pre-Hellenistic philosophers headed by Aristotle. And it is this conception that is relevant for a comparison with Paul.

I should also make explicit that I have felt free to draw indiscriminately on all seven of the supposedly genuine Pauline letters. There are some relevant differences of emphasis among them,[3] but there is no indication of a real change in Paul's presuppositions with regard to human responsibility for action. Thus all of them may serve for the present discussion.

Finally, I will take it, without argument, that there is no discernible difference in Paul's thought between progression and regression that is either "spiritual" or "moral." The categories themselves are, of course, non-Pauline. They might for all that be applied. In fact, however, all deliberation and action on the part of Christ-believers was seen by Paul as so many ways of expressing the Christ faith and hence as being "spiritual." There is no distinctly "moral" area in Paul's thought, no "moral" area that does not also relate to faith.[4]

The overall picture of progression and regression in Paul's thought

Before turning to the two basic questions, let us try to sketch the two basic parameters for Paul's talk of progression and regression: a cosmological and an anthropological one. The cosmological is centered on the idea of God's agency. In the Christ event, God has done something new that pertains to the world as a whole. He has set it on a path that moves in one direction, toward salvation, which is a future event when God will act again in connection with the resurrection of human beings, the final judgment, and a declaration of justice.[5] God has also done something to Paul. He too has been set on a path, that of making God's act and plan known to the Gentiles

(Gal 1:12–16; Rom 1:5). Finally, God has, through Paul, done something to Paul's addressees, who have been set on the same path leading to salvation (2 Cor 5:19–20). However, it is important to keep in mind that one aspect of God's agency concerns the world as a whole, not just Paul and his addressees.

We can represent the cosmological picture in the following figure (Figure 1):

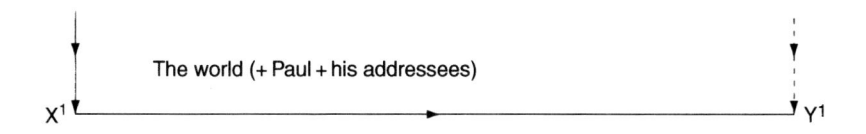

[Figure 1: a horizontal line from X^1 to Y^1 labeled "The world (+ Paul + his addressees)"]

Figure 1

In addition to this cosmological pattern there is an anthropological one. The two schemes interact not just at beginning and end, but all through. Thus one formulation of our first basic question might be to ask exactly how the cosmological pattern shapes and influences what occurs at the anthropological level.

The anthropological pattern might seem to be quite straightforward. Paul and his addressees have been called, and they have come to faith. They have been baptized, and they have received the spirit. In so doing, they have turned their backs completely on everything that does not fall within the compass of God's call (and faith and the spirit) – that is, "the world." In fact, however, there is a certain complication that pertains directly to the issue of progression and regression. In spite of indications to the contrary, it appears that Paul and his addressees have been set on what is precisely only a path *toward* salvation, with some distance to be covered before they will reach the projected goal. Furthermore, although they have all turned their backs on the world, they are not necessarily all placed in exactly the same place on the line going from the world to the final goal. They may be placed at different points on the one path toward the final goal,[6] or they may in principle even be placed on different paths, provided that they all lead to the same final goal.[7] We can represent this picture in the following figure (Figure 2):

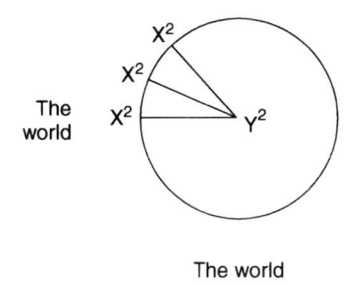

[Figure 2: a circle labeled "The world" with interior points X^2, X^2, X^2 and Y^2 with arrows toward Y^2]

Figure 2

Against this picture we have the one hinted at a moment ago, according to which Paul would expect the entrance into the circle of the holy ones to be in fact an all-or-nothing affair. In this picture, there would be no room for talk about being set on a path *toward* the center; rather, the circle would be, as it were, constituted by its geometrical center alone. If you were in, you would be wholly in.[8] How this conception relates to the one given in Figure 2, where there is a real circle with different positions in relation to the center, is a topic to which we will return when we look at our second basic question.

To complete the picture, we should bring our two figures together in the following way (Figure 3):

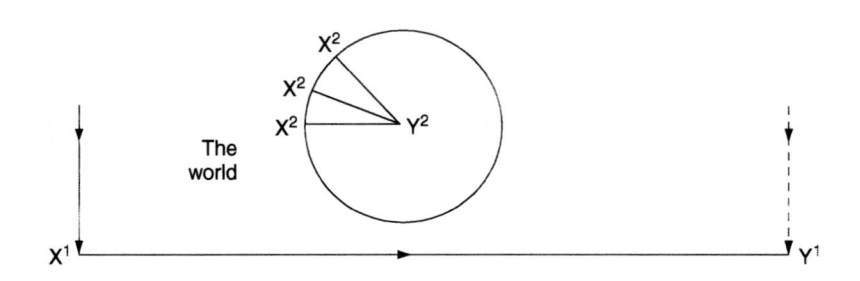

Figure 3

Note here that the two parts of the combined figure do not fit completely together, since the center of the circle (Y^2) and the general resurrection on the Day of the Lord (Y^1) stand for the very same thing even though they are spatially separated in the figure. What this points to is the fact that Paul's writings contain two very different descriptions of the final event: either (Y^1) as a physical, cosmic change and act of God through Christ or (Y^2) as the acquisition of a final *insight* on the part of believers, a future all-comprising grasp corresponding to believers having been grasped by Christ or God in the present (see, e.g., 1 Cor 13:12). There are two wholly different types of description, then. The first basic question that we will address asks in more detail how the two types may be related.

Meanwhile, a passage such as Phil 3 shows that Paul himself intended to keep the two descriptions tightly together. On the one hand, Paul's conversion had the final goal of making him "know" (*gnōnai*) Christ, the power of his resurrection, and a fellowship with his sufferings through being conformed with his death (Phil 3:10). Paul has not already "seized," or indeed "grasped" (*lambanein*), this state, but he strives (*diōkein* [Phil 3:12, 14]) to catch hold of it (*katalambanein*), corresponding to the fact that he has been caught hold of (*katelēmphthēn*) by Christ and called by God through

Christ (Phil 3:12–14).[9] On the other hand, there is also the aim of "arriving at" (*katantan*) the general resurrection from the dead (Phil 3:11), which presumably is also the "prize" of God's upward call in Christ (Phil 3:14) – namely, the resurrection, when the Lord Jesus Christ will return from the heavenly *politeuma* as savior (Phil 3:20) and accomplish the final metamorphosis of the lowly human body that makes it conform to his own body of glory (Phil 3:21). The two goals were probably seen as distinct by Paul. After all, the former was a cognitive grasp on the part of a believer such as Paul himself, whereas the latter was a physical, cosmic event brought about by God. Still, the way they are intertwined in the text shows that he probably also thought that the cognitive grasp would only be fully reached at, or even as part of, the cosmic change. This fact is highly relevant to our theme. The final *event*, engineered by God and effected by Christ, and the final human *insight, striven for* (see Phil 3:12) in the meantime by human beings, were not seen by Paul as being in opposition to one another. On the contrary, they would lie side by side.

With the two first figures combined in the third one, we have a full picture of the basic parameters within which Paul spoke of moral and spiritual progression and regression, but only in the form of a map. I now turn to the first basic question, which addresses in more detail how we may see the relationship between Y^1 and Y^2, between an event brought about from the outside and an insight acquired from within. I can only attempt here to present a grouping of the relevant Pauline texts together with some indication of how they should be read. I first address the relationship between human agency and the intervention of demons,[10] and then in two sections the one between God's agency and human agency, which is in effect the relationship between the two patterns in Figure 3. Throughout, the question will be whether what Paul says in the various groups of texts places him outside the logic of a self-determining self as this underlies moral philosophical exhortations to progression and warnings against regression.

Texts and answers 1: Demons and the self-determining self that underlies exhortation

On the side of similarities there can be no doubt that in its actual practice Paul's exhortation closely follows the pattern employed by the moral philosophers. We might therefore expect that it also has the same logical underpinning. There is, for instance, the motif of (moral and spiritual) growth.[11] There is the appeal to remembrance of who they are (their identity).[12] There is the appeal to advantage.[13] And there is more. All of this seems to presuppose a logic of moral deliberation and reform of the self that relies on the notion of self-determination in the sense of people undergoing changes in knowledge, as opposed to being exposed to the inroad of external, personal, superhuman powers.

On what is apparently the side of dissimilarities, however, there is the relatively frequent reference to the role played by a number of personal, superhuman agents below God. This situation gives rise to the following thesis:

> (1a) In the case of some Pauline invocations of the inroad of superhuman external powers, there is a complete *parallelism* of what Paul says in "power language" and what he says in a "moral language."

A few examples from 1 Cor 5–7 will substantiate this: 1 Cor 7:5 ("in order that Satan not tempt you"), followed immediately by the phrase "because of your lack of self-control"; 1 Cor 5:6–7 (the old leaven, *zymē*, viewed as an agent that may, in spite of its small size, infect the whole dough), followed by 1 Cor 5:8, the old leaven of "vice and wickedness";[14] 1 Cor 6:11 (the Corinthians have been washed clean, made holy and justified in baptism), in support of a claim that as a result of the baptismal ritual cleansing from all worldly infection they are (or should be!) just (1 Cor 6:9) in a straightforward, moral sense (1 Cor 6:7–8).

A second thesis runs like this:

> (1b) There is a relation of *insufficiency* between the superhuman external powers and what is up to the human beings involved.[15] In other words, there *is* something that is up to them.

An example: 1 Cor 10:1–12, on the insufficiency of the old Israelites' "baptism" and "Eucharist" in the desert. The passage unequivocally implies that the ritual cleansing of baptism and the eucharistic getting into touch with so much powerful "stuff" provided by God were and are, in and of themselves, not a sufficient guarantee against destruction. Something more is needed: people must not set their desires on bad things (1 Cor 10:6); each person must take care not to fall (1 Cor 10:12). By contrast, if they themselves do not do this, *then* they are liable to be punished by the inroad of external powers, in the way the Israelites were punished by snakes (1 Cor 10:9) and by Satan (1 Cor 10:10), who, incidentally, was operating in accordance with God's wishes (1 Cor 10:5).

A third thesis runs like this:

> (1c) Knowledge – that is, a thorough and complete grasp in the understanding – is *sufficient* to guard against external powers. There is a relation of sufficiency between what is (in principle) up to human beings and the superhuman external powers.

An example: 1 Cor 8:1–13, on *gnōsis* (knowledge) and a strong *syneidēsis* (conscience) as sufficient to counteract any detrimental effects of eating idol food. Paul's argument suggests the following picture. The strong Christ-believers have *gnōsis* to the effect that idols or false gods do not in fact exist, at least in the sense of being gods comparable to the Jewish and Christian God. This knowledge, so Paul implies, is sufficient to guard them against any inroad from those lesser powers, which in some sense do exist (cf. 1 Cor 10:19–20). The weak ones, by contrast, lack the relevant *gnōsis*. Due to their habit of reckoning with the false gods, they eat the food as sacrificial food, and because of the weakness of their "self-consciousness" (*syneidēsis*) – that is, of their own inner awareness of what they are doing when they eat it – that consciousness is "polluted." In other words, *because of their incomplete cognitive state they fall back into the sphere where the false gods do play a role*. And so they are actually destroyed. Or as Rom 14:23 has it, since they are in doubt when they eat the food, they are judged because they do not eat out of faith.[16]

As a direct consequence of 1c we can make room for all Paul's extended talk of self-examination and self-testing (*dokimasia* and *dokimazein heauton*, *peirazein heauton*, *blepein* lest one fall, and the like).[17] It all presupposes that there is an area, in relation to the operation of external powers, where it is genuinely up to human beings themselves to think and act in such a way that the inroad of those powers is precluded. What we had was this: parallelism, insufficiency of the powers, sufficiency of the human understanding. What I have not been able to find, by contrast, is any sign of the idea that external powers might be responsible for some good or bad action on the part of human beings in such a way that the causal influence of the powers on those actions would completely bypass the minds of those to whom this experience would occur and be in no way reflected in the way they would understand things. Such an idea could not be captured within the logic that underlies exhortation in the thought of the moral philosophers. I submit that it cannot be found in Paul's writings either. On the contrary, no matter how much Paul may have been thinking in terms of the inroad of external powers, he also always writes as if he would hold his addressees responsible for all their actions, and indeed always as if those actions reflected the state of their own understanding. Whenever Paul refers to the powers, he also refers to the understanding of his addressees. His account always has a *double aspect*.

Here an adherent of the demon reading of Paul might come back and argue that whenever Paul appears in his exhortation to appeal to a self-determining self to whom it is up to do this or the other thing, he in reality presupposes that some power other than the one to be resisted is operative too – for instance, the *pneuma* or even God himself. There is no *independent* self, it will be said, apart from these powers, no self who ultimately is personally responsible for and the creator of the ways in which he or she sees the world. For this reason the Pauline picture of the self-determining self that underlies exhortation will remain radically different from the one found in the moral philosophers.[18]

The conclusion does not follow. In Stoicism, for instance, something being "up to us" is tied to the understanding. What is "up to us" is our seeing something in this or that way. But there is no suggestion that, as it were *behind* our seeing, there is an independent self that is personally in some strong sense ultimately responsible for the seeing and in this sense free in relation to it. Rather, our "freedom" lies *in* the seeing, which includes the ability to acquire a better seeing when the world presents itself to us in such a way that we feel the need to change our understanding of it.[19] The moral philosophical (Stoic) notion of the "self" underlying the idea of what is "up to us" is what we may call a flat one. It is not one that would go against the suggestion that "it all comes from external powers." Still, it is not so flat as to be nonexistent. There is an idea of a self engaged in deliberation and character formation, in reflecting on whether to see the world in this or that way and gradually acquiring a character that conforms with this. The very same idea underlies Paul's exhortation.

In this connection it is worth looking a bit more closely at Rom 8:5–13. This is one of the passages in which the flesh (*sarx*) and the spirit (*pneuma*) are most clearly presented as cosmological, superhuman agents, each with its own "mind-set" (*phronēma*) (Rom 8:6–7). Individuals are also located within each of the two spheres, both in the abstract (Rom 8:5, 8) and as an indicative fact about Paul's Roman addressees (Rom 8:9a). So is there any room here for an individual self to whom it is up whether to be in the flesh (Rom 8:8) or in the spirit (Rom 8:9)? Indeed, there is. Paul's indicative statements (Rom 8:9–11) constitute the background to other statements with an imperatival force (Rom 8:12–13), and the latter do presuppose the flat notion of the self that I introduced. It is in fact up to the Romans themselves to decide whether they are in the flesh or in the spirit. How so? By their acts. For instance, when Paul says, "Anyone who does not have Christ's spirit does not belong to him" (Rom 8:9), the force of the statement is an imperatival one telling the Romans that one cannot belong to Christ without having his spirit and so *acting* upon it (cf. Rom 8:13: killing the acts of the body *by means of* the spirit). In other words, one's own acts decide whether one has the spirit and so belongs to Christ. Or again, if one does not act in accordance with the spirit (and so shows that one does have it), one does not belong within the circle of those belonging to Christ. All in all, Rom 8:5–13 is a particularly clear example of how Paul's final appeal is to his addressees themselves, and indeed to their understanding of what is at stake.[20]

Texts and answers 2: God's agency and human agency

The demons are not all there is. If there is no opposition between talk of a self-determining self that underlies the language of exhortation and talk of external superhuman agents, how is it with Paul's emphasis on God's agency? Does this emphasis go against ascribing to him a notion of the self-determining self like the one we find in the moral philosophers?

THE LOGIC OF ACTION IN PAUL

In addressing this question, we will come across a number of motifs that have traditionally received a strong theological reading that focuses on the idea of a fundamental opposition between God's agency and human self-reliance (as opposed to mere agency). I have organized the texts on a line of gradually ascending theological power. Although all the texts belong on a single line, I have divided the discussion into two sections. The present section begins from texts that give no sign whatsoever that God's agency should in any way be contrasted with human agency (2a); then follows a group of texts that emphasize God's sole agency (2b). As I bring in further motifs and texts, we will finally arrive, in the next section, at the possibility of a conflict between God's agency and human "self-reliance." Throughout, my aim is to determine whether in his handling of these various motifs Paul should be seen as presupposing a notion of the "acting self" that differs from what we find in the moral philosophers.

A first thesis runs as follows:

> (2a) In some passages Paul mixes references to God's agency and human agency so intimately that the two types of agency must be thought of as running in close parallel.

A few examples:

Phil 2:12–13: The Philippians must work (*katergazesthai*), each one of them, on their own salvation with fear and trembling, for it is God who is at work (*energein*) in them, making them wish and work actively (*energein*) in response to his good will (with regard to them).[21] This speaks for itself.

1 Cor 1:4–10: Paul first (1 Cor 1:4–9) very strongly emphasizes God's agency in relation to the Corinthians, employing a whole string of "divine passives" (1 Cor 1:4, 5, 6, 9), which are in one instance (1 Cor 1:8) turned into a direct "divine active" to the effect that Christ will secure that they are irreproachable on the final day. Next (1 Cor 1:10), in the *prothesis* to the whole letter, he brings in a piece of exhortation (*parakalō de hymas ... hina ...*) to the effect that they should behave properly. His use of the expression *ēte de katērtismenoi* here is revealing. We should translate it with a marked emphasis as follows: "but be rather *yourselves reformed.*"[22] In other words, Paul is speaking of progression following on some form of regression, but apparently he did not feel that type of language to be in any conflict with the earlier idea that God and Christ will strengthen them until the end. There is no opposition here, but neither is there "cooperation"; rather, the two types of agency lie side by side and are so intimately connected that one may wonder whether they do not, in the final analysis, come to the very same thing.

1 Cor 10:13 (on the testing of the Corinthians): Here we find all three components that we have been operating with, and all three are conceived of as full agents. There is the demon or Satan, who is at work testing the Corinthians; there are the Corinthians, who are themselves capable of putting

up with the testing; and behind the scene there is God, who ultimately is responsible both for the testing itself (and so for the activity of the demon or Satan) and for its resolution (and so for the response of the humans involved). Clearly, there is no opposition whatsoever in Paul's mind between the two last types of agency, but rather a total parallelism.

A second thesis runs as follows:

(2b) In other passages where Paul emphasizes God's sole agency he is nevertheless keen on stressing that God is working through the understanding of human beings.

Some examples:

Passages speaking of human obedience (*hypakoē/hypakouein*) to God. Paul uses the term almost technically for the initial conversion.[23] This is brought about by God's agency, which has been working directly on Paul himself and his addressees in the cosmological pattern that we noted earlier. In this pattern, the idea of slave obedience as to a master is central.[24] A good example of the pattern is found in Rom 10:14–16. Here Paul speaks of the hoped-for conversion (*hypakouein* [Rom 10:16]) of those to whom his mission is addressed and brings it back by stages to his own having been sent forth on that mission (Rom 10:14–15). They should "call on" (*epikalesasthai*) the name of the Lord, through having come to "have faith" (*pisteuein*), through having "heard" (*akouein*), through having had the gospel "preached" to them (*kērychthēnai*) – all of which presupposes that Paul on his side has been sent forth as an apostle (*apostalēnai*), and of course by God. So God is the ultimate, real agent. In addition to offering this picture, Paul apparently took it that God's *Herrenwort* was also operative in the words of his apostles *after* the initial conversion.[25] In either case, we may ask whether Paul thought that in some way God was acting directly on the Christ-believers by means of his *Herrenwort*, as if bypassing their understanding. The answer is no. In the Romans passage referred to, Paul precisely goes on to distinguish mere hearing (*akouein*) the message (Rom 10:18) from also understanding or grasping (*gnōnai*) it (Rom 10:19). In other words, God works *through* the understanding.

Passages using cognitive terms in a divine passive. One example must stand for many: Gal 4:9 (the Galatians had come to know [*gnōnai*] God, or rather [*mallon de*], had been known [*gnōsthēnai*] by him).[26] What Paul means by the claim that one is "known by" God is presumably that it is God who has made one know him and have the knowledge of him that one has.[27] And so one does have some knowledge (of God), brought about by God. Why does Paul employ this rather convoluted thought? Probably because he wishes to validate the kind of knowledge and grasp that he is talking about as the proper knowledge and grasp (God is himself responsible for it!), one that in the given context is contrasted with some other kind of knowledge. Thus in

Gal 4:9 the Galatians had already come to know God. Indeed, they had been known by him or given knowledge (of God) by God. What this means is that they already had the proper and correct knowledge of God (presumably that he had set the Christ event going); why, then, do they now wish to behave in a different manner vis-à-vis God?[28] Thus when Paul uses cognitive verbs in a divine passive, he need not be talking of a specific type of knowledge that in some formal sense bypasses the minds of human knowers so as not really to be a matter of *their* knowing; rather, he is probably speaking of knowledge as human beings normally have this: a state of understanding arrived at in the usual ways. In terms of its content, however, it is also God's knowledge, the *correct* grasp and knowledge (of God and Christ), one that is wholly in line with God's ways of ordering the world.

Passages referring to the specific idea of God's revelation (*apokalypsis/apokalyptein*). Again a single example must stand for many: Gal 1:12, 16. Do we not find here the idea of a kind of knowledge for which God alone is responsible? Certainly. Paul's overall point is clear. He came to see something that had to do with God's son (Christ) and with what Paul himself should do (Gal 1:16). However, he was not made to see this by any other human being, either through some tradition or by having it directly taught to him by somebody (Gal 1:12). Nor did he come to see it through his own means, since he was precisely violently opposed to the whole idea (Gal 1:13–14). Neither anyone else nor Paul himself did anything to make him see what he came to see. No human being was in that sense responsible for it. Instead, God was responsible, in whatever he did to Paul. We know what God did do. He first staged the Christ event, and next he showed it (in whatever way) to Paul. So God was responsible. This emphasis makes Paul's talk of revelation closely similar to (indeed, probably just a strong form of) his use of cognitive terms in a divine passive. We may therefore be tempted to read it in the same way. Paul's rhetorical purpose with this type of locution will then have been to insist against all opponents that what he had come to see was wholly correct: it stemmed directly from God. That fits the context in Gal 1. But if we then go on to ask whether Paul himself might also in a different sense be held responsible for his new insight, the answer should undoubtedly be yes. Paul himself was in possession of the new insight once he had acquired it (or indeed received it). Not only that: Paul himself was adamantly convinced of its truth (cf. Gal 2:5, 14), so much so that he did not even feel the need to discuss it with anybody else (Gal 1:16c). In terms of a Stoic understanding of the logic that underlies exhortation, Paul would therefore himself be eminently responsible for his new insight. As we saw, the flat conception of the self that underlies exhortation in no way goes against the suggestion that "it all comes from external powers," in this case, directly from God. This is the point: no actual *doing* is required for a human agent to be personally responsible for seeing the world in this or that way; it is enough that the seeing is his or hers.

Passages stressing the actual inability of human beings to reach the required knowledge without God's active interference. Large parts of Romans are relevant here. For instance, Rom 9:10–23 (on God's sovereign election of whom he chooses, his mercy toward and hardening of whom he wills), and indeed Rom 1–8 as a whole (on the universal "moral" impotence of Greeks and Jews that was overcome by God's intervention).[29] But of course it is Paul's point in these passages that human beings did reach some *knowledge* as a result of God's intervention (see Rom 6:1–14). Also, he is particularly keen on stressing that those who have not reached this knowledge are themselves responsible for their faulty understanding.[30] Thus Paul is not out to emphasize God's sovereign agency in *opposition* to a supposed notion of the role of the self in coming to know, as if only the idea of God bypassing human minds so that it is no longer they who come to know will generate the proper relationship with God. It *is* true that human beings were not, in Paul's view, themselves able to reach that relationship, but not because there is an element in human agency that needed to be eradicated (the "rational self"). On the contrary, God made something happen that made it possible *for human beings themselves* to *acquire* the proper mind-set, that in which they, on their side, would stand in the proper relationship to God and to one another.

We may reasonably conclude that there is no opposition or conflict so far between talk of God's agency and that of human beings. The reason why this has not generally been seen is that theologians have regularly been operating with an overblown notion of the self of human agency and a concomitant overblown notion of responsibility as presupposing that the agent has personally *done* something to *generate* whatever seeing he or she is counted responsible for. This is a philosophical mistake. We have noted that the ancient moral philosophical self was a flat one. There is no reason to ascribe a thicker one to Paul.

Texts and answers 3: God's agency and human "self-reliance"

We have been moving from human acting to human understanding and gradually to an ever greater involvement on God's part. We must now take up a few ideas in Paul's thought that have traditionally played a central theological role, not least in Dialectical Theology, which remains a powerful source of false emphases in the understanding of his thought. I have in mind certain ideas relating to grace (*charis*), to works (*erga*), and to boasting or pride (*kauchēsis*). In the traditional reading, these ideas have been taken to focus on the notion of human self-reliance in opposition to God. As we will see, a notion of self-reliance is not entirely beside the point, though it does come out rather differently from how it has usually been taken. The main issue, however, is to determine whether there is any indication in Paul's handling of these ideas that, viewed from his (as we will say) specifically religious perspective, the notion of the acting human self will turn out to be in some way religiously suspect. To put it more bluntly: Did Paul think that there was an element in the notion of the self-determining self as the moral philosophers used it that was inherently sinful because it would necessarily lead to a religiously detrimental "self-reliance"? In that case, we would have to say that the way in which Paul understood moral exhortation and progression and regression was different from the way these things were construed by the moral philosophers. (But it would also be quite unclear how Paul would in fact understand it.)

My argument is that Paul's ideas about grace, works, and boasting do not have these consequences. The moral philosophical notion of the self-determining self is a formal one, and there is nothing in Paul's thought to indicate that he took this formal notion to have any substantive, religiously detrimental implications. It is true that when we consider what he says about grace, works, and boasting in substantive terms, as connected with so many human attitudes, Paul does come out as having a target. However, the target is not a specifically "religious" one in the sense of an attitude of self-reliance in relation to God. Rather, as we will see, it is one that we should term "moral," an attitude of a mistaken relationship with other human beings.

That is important, for a moral self-reliance – that is, self-reliance over against other human beings – is a target for the moral philosophers too (at least some of them), while a religious self-reliance over against God is not. But then, as I claim, it is not a target for Paul either. So even if Paul had thought that the formal phenomenon of a human self-determining self would in some way inherently lead to sin, the kind of sin that he would have had in mind was one that was also a target for the moral philosophers, not a specifically religious one that fell outside their perspective. Thus even in this highly charged area of grace, works, and boasting, Paul sides with the moral philosophers.

A first thesis, which is about grace and works, runs as follows:

> (3a) What Paul says about God's grace and about works does not pertain to human doing or acting as such, but is specifically directed toward the issue of Jews and Gentiles.

For instance, the idea is not something like this: God has shown by his act of grace that he alone is in charge, and human beings must respond to this by relying exclusively on God in some form of ultimate obedience that implies that they will have given up any form of acting or doing "on their own." Rather, Paul's point is intended to open up access for Gentiles to the Christ event on equal terms with Jews by allowing them to bypass completely the requirements of the Jewish law. Paul is saying this: God's grace as shown in the Christ event means that righteousness and salvation are available not through the Jewish law, but rather in a direct response to that act of grace:

through faith – and hence also to Gentiles who remain Gentiles.[31] When Paul refers to God's grace, he means something very specific: "and so not through the Jewish law." This also provides the proper understanding of Paul's rejection of works. Works generally are to be understood as works of the Jewish law, and Paul's target is once more the exclusive insistence on those as the only valid route of access to righteousness and salvation. It is not human doing or acting of an ordinary kind, as if that would intrinsically turn a person away from God. Paul's emphasis on God's grace and his rejection of works were not intended to introduce a special form of human acting ("God-infused acting") to counter a religiously suspect notion of a human self-determining self. It could not be this, since God's grace, as a distinct thing, was not a continuous phenomenon, but rather a single, one-time act – the Christ event itself.[32] Correspondingly, Paul's works were not works as such – doing, acting, working – but something far more specific: the works of the Jewish law understood as an entity that through its very specificity set up boundaries between Jews and Gentiles.[33]

This reading of grace connects closely with the earlier point that human beings are themselves unable to reach the proper relationship with God and with one another. God therefore stepped in, functioning as "a kind of divine psychagogue" (Stowers 1990: 261).[34] He did it once, in the Christ event, in a manner that once and for all changed the route of access for human beings to righteousness and salvation. But as before, it remained up to human beings whether or not they would respond to the new act of God in the way he intended. What the reference to God's grace does not bring in is any idea of grace as being continually operative in human beings (of faith) in such a way that the whole, logical form of their acting and doing is changed. God's grace, for Paul, is not a phenomenon that is "continually operative" in that sense. And it is not introduced by Paul in opposition to some categorically or logically other form of attitude, one characterized by a spirit of "working." In neither case was Paul's target a form of reliance on oneself (in acting) that might render the formal notion of the self-determining human self religiously suspect.

A second thesis, which is about boasting (and partly again about works), runs as follows:

> (3b) When Paul criticizes boasting, what he has in mind is not boasting over against God, but rather boasting over against other human beings, though possibly, as it were, standing *before* God.[35] Such boasting may be found not only among Jews, who would point to the special quality of their own works (of the Jewish law), but also among Gentiles.

Rom 2:17–24 provides a very clear example of how Paul construed Jewish boasting. It is a boasting *of* God (Rom 2:17), which consists in pointing out *to* non-Jews the wonderful treasure that Jews have in their law. There is no trace of boasting *to* God by referring to their works of the law, or even of *relying* on the law over against *God*. There is only boasting to non-Jews. *They* do not have what *Jews* have (in relation to God). In fact, Paul does not even limit to Jews the charge of boasting. Christ-believing Gentiles too (to judge from 1 Cor 1:29, 31; 3:21) may be prone to boasting, this time of their *sophia* and again understood as a special asset that they themselves have in *relation* to God. But here too their boasting is targeted not *at* God, but at their fellow believers.

Once more we see that Paul's target is not the sheer formal notion of a self-determining human self. Nor is it a substantive attitude of opposition to God that he might have seen from his peculiar religious perspective to be inherently rooted in the formal notion.[36] His target, rather, is a substantive attitude toward other human beings, a sense of superiority over against other human beings that is a *form* of self-reliance, *moral* self-reliance. However, this is not derived by Paul from the formal notion of a self-determining human self. It is rooted in something else: a lack of *substantive* directedness toward God.

The last point brings us to a center of Paul's thought in a manner that is also directly relevant to our present concerns. It is a constant Pauline theme, which even constitutes the basic idea that runs through Rom 1–8, that directedness toward God and Christ (in other words, faith) is what will save human beings from sin. In Gal 2:19 Paul states this idea by saying that he has died, as an individual self (an *egō*), in order that he might live for God. The passage is particularly noteworthy in our context because it almost explicitly operates with a distinction between the formal notion of a self-determining human self (call it I^1) and a substantive notion of the self (I^2) that may generate an obnoxious form of self-reliance. The latter, substantive, self may be engaged in sin and must then die. It will be engaged in sin when it is not directed wholeheartedly toward God in the manner in which Paul says that he himself is. If the substantive self focuses on everything (body, status, and the like) that most immediately belongs to itself and helps to identify it as that particular self, then it will remain in the sphere of sin. By contrast, the substantive self dies when a person gives attention wholeheartedly to God (in "living for God"), thereby putting on an altogether different version of the substantive self: Christ. But *who* does this? Obviously, the other self, I^1.[37] The point is this: Paul's crucial idea of a complete turn toward God and Christ in faith presupposes the continuing existence of a formal, self-determining self: the one who *makes* the turn. That self is a notion that Paul never thought of giving up, and he would have been baffled if anybody had suggested to him that that notion should be considered religiously suspect.

Summarizing, we may conclude that there is nothing in what Paul says of grace, works, and boasting that should in the least be understood as making problematic, from within Paul's own perspective, the formal notion of a self-determining human self, the self who may come to see things (through God's gracious intervention) and who is personally responsible for seeing or not seeing God's truths about the world as made known in the Christ event. Not only is there a close parallelism between Paul and the moral philosophers in the logic that underlies exhortation and the area of human agency in general, but this parallelism also carries over into areas that lie at the heart of Paul's theologizing: his idea of God's grace, his rejection of works and boasting, and his idea of participation in Christ (Gal 2:19–20). Nowhere have we come across a manner of viewing the human self in relation to the world and to God, or conversely the impingement of God and the world on the self, that places it outside the basic picture of the self that we find in the moral philosophers. We should conclude that what Paul says of moral and spiritual progression and regression not simply looks as if it belongs within the parameters set up for the same kind of language in the moral philosophers: it does belong there.

Texts and answers 4: Conversion and progression/regression

Now to my second basic question. We have seen that there is the same kind of logical room for exhortation and human agency in Paul's thought as we find in that of the moral philosophers. But do we need such room? Indeed, how may we at all make sense of the phenomena of progression and regression within Paul's understanding of conversion to the Christ faith? In some passages, at least, it looks as if conversion is an all-or-nothing affair. In that case, once a person has been converted to Christ, there will be no need for progression because the convert has, as it were, already arrived at the final destination. The extension of the circle that we noted has been reduced to its very center. Nor will there be any possibility of regression, since that would imply that the person had not really been converted after all.

On the other side there are several passages that seem to leave plenty of room for both progression and regression and even to require it. Indeed, the root fact about Paul's letters, which is that they are all so many different specimens of exhortation, points very strongly in that direction, to say the least. Why exhort if there is no need for progression and no possibility of regression?

When we look at passages for and against, we very quickly realize that the two viewpoints are presented in close proximity to one another. In short, we have something of a problem.

A first thesis about conversion runs as follows:

(4a) Conversion allows for progression and regression.

A few passages that clearly imply this idea. Phil 1:6: begin (*enarxasthai*) and bring to completion (*epitelesein*); see also Gal 3:3; 2 Cor 8:6, 10–11;[38] Phil 1:12, 25: progress (*prokopē*), in the second case clearly a matter of progression on the part of Paul's addressees; later in the letter Paul presents himself extensively as a model for just such progression (Phil 3:12–14); Gal 6:1: a clear case of regression (*paraptōma*) on the part of a member of the congregation whom the other Galatians must reform (*katartizein*); 1 Cor 5:1–5: the man who has slept with his stepmother; 1 Cor 6:1–11: Corinthians who act unjustly toward their fellow believers.

This last passage raises the problem particularly clearly. Those who act unjustly (*adikein*) (1 Cor 6:8) are also those who have been made just in baptism (1 Cor 6:11) and who already know that unjust people will not inherit God's kingdom (1 Cor 6:9).

A second thesis about conversion runs as follows:

(4b) Conversion is an all-or-nothing affair.

A few passages that suggest this idea. Gal 3:25–8; 4:6–7: being baptized, the Galatians *have* become one in Christ and *have* received the spirit; still, of course, they are in grave danger of regressing completely (cf. Gal 1:6: *metatithesthai*); Gal 6:14: Paul himself *has* been crucified to the world, and the world to him; still, as he states elsewhere (Phil 3:12), he is not yet perfect; Gal 5:24: the Galatians too *have* crucified the flesh (insofar as they do "belong to Christ") and *are* filled by the fruits of the spirit (Gal 5:22) so as no longer to do the acts of the flesh (Gal 5:17–24); still, there apparently is a need for further exhortation (Gal 5:25–6).

By now it will have become clear that the issue raised by these passages is neither more nor less than the famous one of the indicative versus the imperative, only here I am construing it in the straightforward pre-Bultmannian sense (against which Bultmann reacted) of taking both linguistic modes to be about the very same thing: having been *made* free of the flesh and having *to* free oneself from that same flesh. Also, the underlying problem is clearly focused on baptism. Through faith, baptism, and reception of the spirit, Paul's addressees have come to belong to Christ. Then why is there a need for further exhortation? How is progression at all possible? And indeed, how is it possible to regress?[39]

A solution may be found by considering certain points in 1 Cor 1–3 that highlight the crucial role in Paul's thought of the notion of "cognitive development," a notion that is part and parcel of his agreement with the moral philosophers on the role of the self-determining self. As a premise, we need the point just hinted at, that faith, baptism, and reception of the spirit go indissolubly together in Paul's mind.[40] If we then combine and contrast 1 Cor 2:1–5 and 1 Cor 3:1–3 with 1 Cor 2:6–16, we obtain the following picture. (1) When Paul came to Corinth for the first time, the Corinthians acquired faith (1 Cor 2:5), were baptized, and received the spirit, all on the basis of Paul's "demonstration of [God's] spirit and power" (1 Cor 2:4). It is almost certain, therefore, that Paul thought of them, and they thought of themselves, as people who had received the spirit, as *pneumatikoi*.[41] (2) However, says Paul (1 Cor 3:1), he was not able to speak to them then "as" spiritual beings. Instead, he had to speak to them "as" fleshly beings (*sarkinoi*, which they actually no longer were). And the same is true now, since they remain fleshly (*sarkikoi*) (1 Cor 3:3).[42] What matters here is Paul's use of "as" (*hōs*). The Corinthians *were* and *are* spiritual beings (if one likes: in terms of substance), but Paul could not and cannot speak to them as such, since they were and are only "children" in Christ (1 Cor 3:1). They had not, and still have not, grown sufficiently into Christ to be and function as what we may call "adults in Christ." (3) What is wrong with them? They are lacking in understanding, in grasping the full extent of God's revelation, the full cognitive content of Paul's initial *kērygma* – in fact the very content that Paul is setting out in these chapters of the letter.

On such a reading, the whole passage combines two ideas. There is first the idea of an initial conversion that is, in a sense, the crucial one, an event that brings a person within the circle of Christ-believers through faith, baptism, and reception of the spirit. But there is also an idea of progression toward a full understanding and grasp of the cognitive content of God's revelation (1 Cor 2:10) in the crucified Christ (1 Cor 2:2), the "mystery" that it is (1 Cor 2:1, 7). It is the span set up by this framework that generates the need for progression and also makes regression possible. As the passage makes abundantly clear, the span is itself a cognitive one. It is all a matter of growth in the understanding.

This model in effect disposes of the supposed problem of the indicative and the imperative. The indicative is about entering the circle of Christ-believers. It contains a statement about what has occurred to Paul's addressees: faith, baptism, reception of the spirit and a pledge of final salvation. It is also a statement to the effect that through faith, baptism, and reception of the spirit Christ-believers have, in principle, *become* just and for that very reason (as I would say) secure candidates for salvation (cf. Gal 5:5). In spite of the revolutionary character of entering the circle of Christ-believers, however, there remains an area or span short of completion, the span from the periphery of the circle to its center, from X^2 to Y^2 in Figure 3. It is the existence of this "cognitive span" that gives rise to the need for imperatives and for applying all the forms of appeal and techniques for generating cognition that go into Paul's exhortation. It is here, as it were between the indicative and the end point to which the imperatives look, that Paul's letters operate.

Does this picture in fact dispose of all the traditional problems connected with the indicative and the imperative? In particular, if at point X^2 converts have not yet reached Y^2, then how can Paul's "indicative," which in this proposal is about X^2, state that they have reached it? Or in other words, what lies behind the small phrase "in principle" that I smuggled in a few sentences back? Here is the answer that I believe will finally dispose of the supposed problem of the indicative and the imperative. The problem was this: if the indicative statements hold, then what is the purpose of the imperatives? Notice, then, that Paul makes his indicative statements precisely when he intends to speak in the imperative, as *part* of that. This suggests that the supposed "problem" has formulated the issue upside down. The logic is not this: you *have* reached the final destination (Y^2), so move *toward* it. That is, of course, incoherent and baffling. Instead, the logic is this (addressed to people who have in fact arrived at point X^2): what X^2 (where you *have* arrived) actually means (though you may not yet quite have grasped it) is this ... (the indicative), so *do* that (so as *finally* to bring yourselves *from* X^2 to Y^2) – that is, try to bring it about; *that* (Y^2) is where you (*already*) want to go, and now you also know it. Or applied to 1 Cor 1–3: what faith (X^2) actually means is this ... (the Christian *sophia*: Y^2), so do *that*. Construed in that way, the logic of the interplay of indicative and imperative is both coherent and totally meaningful.

One more question: in Paul's picture of the relationship between X^2 and Y^2, is progression a condition of salvation? Hardly. A text a little further on in 1 Corinthians (1 Cor 3:11–15) suggests that final salvation will be the lot of all who have entered the circle of those who build on the one shared foundation that is "Jesus is the Christ" (1 Cor 3:11) – in other words, the foundation of the initial faith. They may differ in other respects, and the activity or work (*ergon*) of some may even be burned up on the Day of the Lord and the people themselves made to pay, but they will all be saved, albeit through fire (1 Cor 3:15).[43] In spite of this, however, there is plenty of room for them to deepen their grasp of what has, in principle, already occurred to them and in that way to move further in the direction of the center of a circle to which they already do belong.[44]

Conclusion

I have been concerned throughout this essay with the logic that underlies Paul's talk of moral and spiritual progression and regression. In many respects the overall picture that frames that talk differs vastly from what we find in the thought of the moral philosophers. In Paul's thought the whole world is on the move toward a single event that will occur at a specific time in the (near) future. Also, a corresponding event has already occurred that constitutes a single fact about the world that also operates as the one and only criterion of value, thereby dividing the world up completely between good and evil. Nothing of this can be found in the moral philosophers, at least not once it is understood as speaking in completely realistic terms of actual facts about the world.

It is also important to note that the idea of a movement toward salvation provides a very different overall shape to what we might call moral and spiritual "deliberation" in Paul's thought. It is true that Paul's exhortation is to some extent, and indeed quite importantly, intended to appeal to what has already occurred to his addressees. They *have* received the spirit. They *have* been washed clean of sin. They *have* become just. In short, they already (in principle) are where Paul intends to bring them. And so there is no need of any extrinsic motivation for making them go there. That is something they already want. In spite of this, however, the idea of a movement toward salvation also appeals to an almost utilitarian sense of their own advantage. They must think and act in a manner that will make them remain within the circle of Christ-believers (thereby avoiding the risk of regression) and even hopefully move further in the direction of its center (thus experiencing progression) in order finally to reach salvation. Nothing of this is found in the moral philosophers.

What I have mainly concentrated on, however, is the question of whether we should or should not see, alongside these important dissimilarities, an extensive overlap between Paul and the moral philosophers with regard to the picture of the self that is involved in human deliberation, decision, action, and character formation – in short, the whole logic that underlies Paul's exhortation. Epictetus, living after Paul, said that God has put the whole matter under our control without reserving for himself any power to prevent or hinder. And Aristotle, living at the beginning of the ancient ethical tradition proper, had said that happiness (a this-worldly goal of no interest whatever to Paul) comes to be present through virtue and some kind of learning or training. My first basic question has been whether the understanding of the self-determining self that is encapsulated in these two sentences was also Paul's. The answer has been that it was. Had Paul been working explicitly with the categories in which the Greek moral philosophers had brought out the logic that underlies exhortation, he would have agreed completely with both Epictetus and Aristotle. We can see this from what he does say in his handling of the ideas that he *also* has about demonic and divine agency. Throughout, Paul presupposes the kind of self-determining self who makes up his or her own mind, and who is, as it were, an individual "understanding in action." Underlying Paul's letters is a complete logic of exhortation, a large and central area of presuppositions concerning the human self and human deliberation, decision, action, and character formation that is completely and unproblematically shared by Paul and the moral philosophers. It is within this area that Paul speaks in his exhortation. And it is this area that allows us to speak quite straightforwardly about progression and regression in Paul's thought.

This conclusion also allowed an answer to my second basic question, of whether there is at all room for progression and regression in Paul. With a self-determining self understood as an individual "understanding in action," there is plenty of room for both progression and regression in the form of cognitive development and relapse. Already in Paul we meet the cognitive span that lies between "faith and understanding." But note well: These two lie on a *single* line, from a rudimentary grasp to a full one. They do not constitute two different categories, as a later tradition has seen them.

The relationship between my findings and later tradition is in fact intriguing. D. Martin claimed that the self-determining self is a modern invention not to be found in Paul's thought. That, I have argued, is incorrect. It is indeed found in Paul's thought, but without being in opposition to his *Geisterwelt* (as Martin thinks it would have been.) Here I side with tradition, which has always recognized, if only implicitly, that Paul's exhortation does presuppose the notion of a self of the moral philosophical kind.

Tradition, however, has misconstrued its own position. Thus A. Malherbe's very precise rendering of the traditional view of a number of (radical) contrasts (reason versus God; reliance on self versus guidance by the Holy Spirit; one's own character education leading to pride versus discernment of God's will) is evidence of what I have argued is a conflation of two crucially distinct levels: a formal one and a substantive one. Formally, Paul agrees completely with the moral philosophers when he presupposes a self-determining self with a nuclear role in the very logic that underlies exhortation. It follows that this fundamental level provides no basis for Malherbe's traditional, radical contrasts. (That is the brunt of my argument.) The next question then becomes whether substantively there are, after all, some differences between the moral philosophers and Paul. The best candidate for this lies, I suggest, in the area of pride. Did the moral philosophers have a different attitude toward pride (over against other human beings) from Paul's, namely, a more positive one? To some extent they probably did. However, since that is not a question of a difference in categories (but rather of the substantive content of this or that moral and religious view), there will probably also be differences among the moral philosophers themselves – say, among Seneca, Epictetus, and Marcus Aurelius.

I have not delved into this question, interesting though it is. What mattered to me was the logic that underlies Paul's exhortation and talk of progression and regression. By arguing that Paul presupposes the moral philosophical notion of the self-determining self, I have sided with tradition against Martin. By distinguishing sharply between the formal and the substantive levels of speaking of the self, I have left behind tradition as represented here by Malherbe. What it all comes down to is the claim that there is no basic contrast of categories in this whole area between Paul and the moral philosophers. The belief that there is reflects later theology. It does not stand up to a scrutiny of the historical facts.

Notes

1 See in particular "Fleisch und Sünde," §23 in Bultmann's *Theologie des Neuen Testaments* (1968).
2 See Chapter 1 in Martin 1995a. Martin writes, for example, "The self was a precarious, temporary state of affairs, constituted by forces surrounding and pervading the body, like the radio waves that bounce around and through the bodies of modern

urbanites. In such a maelstrom of cosmological forces, the individualism of modern conceptions disappears, and the body is perceived as a location in a continuum of cosmic movement. *The body – or the 'self' – is an unstable point of transition, not a discrete, permanent, solid entity*" (Martin 1995a: 25 [italics added]).

3 Thus demons play a far larger role in 1 Corinthians (e.g., 1 Cor 10) than in, for instance, Philippians. Also, Romans (e.g., Rom 9) raises the question of human freedom versus a God-generated determinism far more directly than does any other Pauline letter.

4 Certainly, it is both possible and necessary to distinguish, in the analysis of Paul's thought, between the intentional relationship of a Christ-believer with Christ and God, on the one hand, and with other human beings, on the other. The former relationship might then be termed "spiritual" and the latter "moral." But that distinction must be drawn for purely analytical purposes. In actual fact, there is no idea in Paul of a "spiritual" relationship that is not also a "moral" one and vice versa. For more on this see Engberg-Pedersen 2000: 136–8. The first version of the present essay was written before I authored that book. It presupposes a number of ideas that I went on to elaborate in the book. Where these ideas are not properly discussed or argued for here, I will refer to further discussion in the book. The topic itself of the present essay is not discussed directly in the book. At an even later stage, I developed some of the ideas presented in this essay in a discussion of divine and human agency in Epictetus and Paul (2006).

5 This comes out most clearly in Rom 5:8.

6 The principal evidence for this is Phil 3:12–16.

7 Thus it could be argued that Jewish Christ-believers and Gentile Christ-believers will find themselves on different paths that move in the direction of the same final goal.

8 This point is based on passages such as Gal 5:13–26 and Rom 6, where Paul is straightforwardly arguing that those who have "died with Christ" have thereby also died to sin. It is well known that there are traditional theological readings of these passages that deny that Paul is thinking of an actual, empirical death to sin in the sense of a state in which there is no longer any sinning. Such views are based not on what Paul says (which itself is unmistakable), but on general theological considerations combined with the observation that he makes this point in passages that are paraenetic. And paraenesis, people think, presupposes that the addressees are precisely not dead to sin.

9 The interplay between catching and being caught hold of in Phil 3:12 suggests that the grammatical object of *elabon* ("seized") in that verse is in fact Christ, and hence that *elabon* should be understood in a cognitive sense. That fits immediately with Phil 3:10, where Paul speaks of "getting to know" (*gnōnai*) Christ. In that case, Phil 3:11, which speaks of reaching the resurrection, will be left in a somewhat subsidiary position. For more on the intertwined relationship that I am elaborating between cognitive and cosmic understandings of the final goal see Engberg-Pedersen 2000: 121–5.

10 This issue pertains to the relationship between demonic agents and human agency within the circle of Christ-believers (on the line X^2–Y^2).

11 For example, Phil 1:9–10. Incidentally, note that Paul here *prays* that their love will grow and so on, but evidently he also appeals to them to *do* something about

it. For formulations of what we probably would call specifically spiritual growth see 1 Thess 3:10 ("what you are lacking in faith," *ta hysterēmata tēs pisteōs hymōn*) and 2 Cor 10:6 ("when your submission has been made complete," *hotan plērōthē hymōn hē hypakoē*).

12 Passim (*ouk oidate hoti ...*) and, for example, 1 Cor 6:9–11, 19–20.
13 For example, 1 Cor 6:9–10.
14 Here Paul obviously is worried about pollution. D. Martin (1995a) is surely right that Paul construes pollution very much as a "material" phenomenon. That only makes his immediate translation of the talk of leaven into moral language all the more striking.
15 This might also explain Paul's use of *dia* in 1 Cor 7:5: "lest you be tempted by Satan *because of* your lack of self-control."
16 Contrast D. Martin's (1995a: 179–89) downplaying of *syneidēsis* and his reading of *gnōsis* as a sort of prophylactic charm that has little or nothing to do with the phenomenon of understanding. To me, these pages are among the least persuasive in a first-rate book. The view of the relationship between knowledge and the demons that I am advocating is supported by Paul's discussion of the Eucharist a little later in 1 Corinthians, in particular by his famous idea stated in 1 Cor 11:29 that by paying the proper kind of attention (*diakrinein*) to the Eucharist "body" (no matter what that was meant to be), the Corinthians will avoid suffering from illness and death, experiences that have been brought about by God (possibly through lesser intermediaries who are directly making an inroad on the Corinthians) as a way of educating them (*paideuesthai* [1 Cor 11:32]). Here we again see a total mixture of power language with cognitive language.
17 See, for example, 2 Cor 13:5.
18 For this line of argument see, for example, Martyn 2002; Engberg-Pedersen 2002 (my response to Martyn).
19 See Chapter 9 on Stoic freedom in Engberg-Pedersen 1990. Incidentally, what I have just said of the Stoics is even more true of Aristotle also when he speaks of "man as the begetter of his actions as of his children."
20 See the analysis of Rom 8:1–13 in Engberg-Pedersen 2000: 247–53.
21 The text appears to be saying two things: (1) the Philippians themselves, each one of them (note *heautōn*), should work on their salvation (Phil 2:12), so as to become irreproachable and pure on the final day (Phil 2:15–16); (2) they should do this all the more energetically and responsibly, with fear and trembling (Phil 2:12), since their wish to work actively – their own wish to do so – in response to God's good will in relation to them (presumably as witnessed by the Christ event) is all of his doing (Phil 2:13). How did God bring this about? Probably through the Christ event itself, which has had the intended effect on the Philippians.
22 The verb *katartizein* means "to bring something back to its earlier state" (Bauer 1988: 850: "in den alten Stand setzen"; cf. *kata*, "back" and/or "right," and *artios*, "upright"). It may also be used with God as a subject along with the terms *poiein* and *ktizein* in the sense of "prepare, produce, create" (Bauer 1988: 850: "bereiten, herstellen, schaffen"); see, for example, Rom 9:22. We may bring the two senses together by translating it as "form" (the second use) and "reform" (the first use). Is *katērtismenoi* then to be understood as a genuine divine passive (with God as the logical subject) or as medial? A passage such as Gal 6:1 shows that *katartizein* may

very well figure in the active with a human subject: here the Galatians are enjoined by Paul to reform an erring member of the community in the proper manner. And a passage such as 2 Cor 13:11 shows conclusively that the corresponding medial sense was also available to Paul: *chairete, katartizesthe, parakaleisthe, to auto phroneite*. Against this background, the translation that I propose for the strongly paraenetic verse 1 Cor 1:10 seems almost unavoidable.

23 See Rom 1:5; cf. 16:26; also 15:18; 16:19; also cf. Phil 2:12.
24 Cf. Rom 6:12 and 6:16–17.
25 Thus in Phil 2:12 Paul says that the Philippians were "always" (*pantote*) obedient. That can hardly be meant to refer only to their initial conversion.
26 Other examples: 1 Cor 13:12: Paul himself believes that on the day of the Lord he will come fully to know (*epignōsesthai*) just as he has now been fully known by God (*epignōsthēai*). Phil 3:12: Indeed, Paul pursues (*diōkein*) the goal in order to catch hold of it (*katalambanein*), corresponding to the fact that he has been caught hold of (*katalēphthēnai*) by Christ. And 1 Cor 8:2–3, which is connected both with 1 Cor 13:12 and with the very complex treatment of faith and understanding in chapters 1–3: If someone believes that he or she knows something (*gnōnai*, active voice), then that person has not yet come to know in the way in which one should know it. If, by contrast, someone loves God, then that person has been known (*egnōstai*) by God.
27 Argument: Paul does not really distinguish between what in modern parlance is knowledge by acquaintance (knowing somebody or something by direct acquaintance or "touch") and propositional knowledge (knowledge *that* something or other is the case). Or perhaps we should say that the former type of knowledge is likely to be the one uppermost in his mind. This explains why he thinks of people as "known" and "caught hold of" by God and Christ. But since he may also speak of "knowing something" (1 Cor 8:2), which we should naturally understand as being a matter of propositional knowledge, Paul probably also implied that in response to being known by God, a person not only knows God, but also has some propositional knowledge about God.
28 Similarly in 1 Cor 8:2–3: The Corinthians believe that they have the proper knowledge, but they are wrong. The proper knowledge (which includes *love* of God) is the one *given* by God. And so on.
29 One basic idea in these chapters is that God's act in the Christ event was necessary to make human beings come around to the proper relationship with each other and with God. This they could not do by themselves. The Gentiles showed this in their behavior. Even though they did realize God's existence, they did not recognize him as the sovereign God, with dire consequences (Rom 1). It is the same with the Jews, who of course recognized God, but not in such a way as to let their recognition permeate their behavior in every detail (Rom 2). They too remained sinners (Rom 3). For that reason God sent Christ to save the ungodly (Rom 4–5). With the Christ event, then, salvation became finally possible for human beings (Rom 8) as it had not previously been. For more on this see Ch. 8 in Engberg-Pedersen 2000.
30 Thus both Gentiles and Jews before Christ were *anapologētoi* (Rom 1:20; 2:1), without excuse. They knew God sufficiently to be responsible for not knowing him through and through. Furthermore, even if admitting that the noncomprehending

state may have been preordained by God even from before one's birth, a person remains responsible and has nothing on which to base a claim against God (Rom 9:14–23). Indeed, it appears to be an aim of Paul throughout much of Romans to insist on the precise amount of human freedom of action that is required for it to be possible to hold someone responsible for his or her behavior. Thus in Rom 9:14–23, without providing a reasoned answer to the question how a human being may be held responsible if it is all a matter of God's will, Paul simply brushes aside the suggestion that one might not be so: "But who indeed are you, a human being, to argue with God?" (Rom 9:20). In any case, seen from a Stoic perspective, such a person would in fact be responsible, for the failure of understanding that underlies one's behavior belongs to the individual.

31 See, for example, Gal 2:21; Rom 3:24 as concluding Rom 3:21–3.
32 For this role of God's grace see Rom 4:4–5, together with Rom 5:8 and the overall perspective of Rom 5:12–21 (a new creation). I say "as a distinct thing" because Paul may, of course, very well describe everything done by God to human beings as so many *charismata* and use the term *charizesthai* of God's continuous intervention. However, that idea does not go beyond the one discussed above in "Texts and answers 2" of God's acting in human beings.
33 The preceding remarks on grace and works evidently presuppose the so-called new perspective on Paul.
34 In general I am in strong agreement with Stowers's line of thought in that essay (particularly its first half, on the use of reason) – for instance: "Far from advocating that rational deliberation be subordinated to blind faith, authoritative revelation, or Paul's authoritative leadership, 1 Corinthians 1–7 stresses the legitimacy of reason and moral autonomy in the context of a particular community with its particular goals" (Stowers 1990: 266). Stowers is also exactly right to speak of "reason and moral autonomy," but generally I have refrained from doing so here in order not to raise unintended specters.
35 See, for example, 1 Cor 1:29. Note, however, that boasting before God is not in itself an object of criticism in Paul (see, e.g., Phil 2:16).
36 The closest Paul comes to a notion of self-reliance in opposition to God appears to be in his denunciation of the Gentiles before Christ in Rom 1:18–32. They knew enough of God for it to have been possible for them to acknowledge his sovereignty. Instead, they took themselves to be wise and so did not give glory to God. Everything in the passage seems to speak of the Gentiles as relying precisely on themselves. And yet, even here Paul does not appear to criticize the Gentiles for relying on themselves in clear and pointed *opposition* to God; rather, their main fault was and is one of negligence, of not holding on to their original insight into God's sovereign power, but rather looking away from him and in a different direction. They took themselves to be wise (Rom 1:22), but they did not necessarily pride themselves on their wisdom *over against* God; rather, they turned their gaze elsewhere (Rom 1:23). The "heroic war of humankind with God" is not a Pauline idea.
37 This, incidentally, is what Paul has in mind when he speaks in positive terms of a "boasting of the Lord" (e.g., 1 Cor 1:31). Such boasting is a kind of nonboasting, since in boasting to others of something that one has (over against them), one is precisely pointing to something (the Lord, Christ) that one does not individually

possess. For there no longer is a self-directed substantive self in which to anchor such boasting. When the object of boasting is the Lord, *kauchasthai* should be translated "rejoice." On this see Engberg-Pedersen 2000: 154–5.
38 Note the impossibility of separating "spiritual" from "moral" progression here. Is Phil 1:6 "moral" and Gal 3:3 "spiritual"? No.
39 For a more comprehensive account of the solution to these queries, partly applied to a range of passages not discussed here, see Engberg-Pedersen 2000: 138–9, 166–9, 231–3.
40 Rom 6–8 speaks strongly for this, as do Gal 3:14; 4:6 together with Gal 3:25–29.
41 This is supported (rather than the contrary) by Paul's de-emphasis on baptism in 1 Cor 1:13–17. The reason why he does not emphasize baptism and spirit reception in 1 Cor 1:26–2:5 is precisely that he wished to contrast the frame of mind of the baptized Corinthians, both then and now (cf. 1 Cor 3:1–3), with that of people who had received the spirit in the proper way, those who have the proper form of Christian wisdom (1 Cor 2:6–16). As it turned out, the Corinthians still had some way to go.
42 One might be tempted here to contrast *sarkinoi*, as denoting a substance, with *sarkikoi*, as denoting a moral character, but the suggestion probably is too weakly supported to build anything on it.
43 This picture is supported by another section of 1 Corinthians (1 Cor 12–14) where Paul intends to speak of differences among his Christ-believing addressees and begins by stating that "nobody is able to say 'Jesus is Lord' unless [doing so] in the Holy Spirit" (1 Cor 12:3). Here, faith and the spirit are mentioned together as providing the one, all-important borderline between being outside the circle and inside it. The same picture of an initial faith and a further development of it also explains why Paul can use a phrase such as *ta hysterēmata tēs pisteōs* (1 Thess 3:10).
44 I have been quite sparing in my direct references to the moral philosophers, but here a reference to the Stoic notion of *oikeiōsis* is in place. In Stoicism we find the same span between an initial grasp of the ultimate truth, which in a way contains everything, and the gradual spelling out of that grasp in particularized insights that constitute the stuff of actual living and acting (on this see Engberg-Pedersen 1990: 126–40). As is well known, the Stoics also coined a special term for the movement toward the final, complete insight. It is called *prokopē* (progress), as in Paul. However, the difference is also illuminating. Strictly, in Stoicism no human being is more than *prokoptōn* (progressing) and so not wise. The same is partly true of Pauline Christianity. It is improbable that any Pauline Christian is completely perfect. Still, in Paul the *central* borderline lies far below perfection, at the entrance to the circle of Christ-believers.

13

MORAL PROGRESS AND DIVINE POWER IN SENECA AND PAUL

James Ware

In contrast to other contemporary philosophical movements, the later Stoics emphasized the role of the divine in moral progress. The Stoic philosopher Seneca exemplifies this emphasis, perhaps most markedly in *Epistle* 41, which attributes moral advancement to the power of God at work amid human weakness. This understanding of progress provides the closest analog in antiquity to the early Christian and Pauline conception of the role of the Holy Spirit in sanctification. Indeed, whether one may speak of an essential difference between the understanding of moral progress in Paul and in later Stoics such as Seneca has been questioned. However, Seneca, unlike Paul, did not conceive of God as a power outside humanity, but identified the divine with the rational soul, which he understood as a fragment of the divine dwelling in the mortal human body. Whereas Paul thinks of an inner transformation through a supernatural union with the Spirit of God, distinct from yet mystically united with the self, the divine power of which Seneca thinks is not given by a transcendent personal God, but is intrinsic to human nature and in need only of cultivation through philosophy. This fundamental theological difference between Paul and Seneca entails profound differences in their anthropology and ethics. It is this difference that most decidedly separates Seneca's understanding of moral progress from that of Paul and the earliest Christians.

Introduction

The study devoted in recent decades to the relationship of Paul's thought to Hellenistic moral philosophy has documented the natural and creative way in which Paul engaged and adapted Greek ethical thought in his own teaching.[1] This study has led to a general consensus that there are not only important similarities but also fundamental differences between Paul's moral teaching and that of the philosophers. This consensus has been challenged on two fronts. On the one hand, T. Engberg-Pedersen has recently argued that the fundamental structure of Stoic ethics, in which the individual undergoes a change in self-understanding leading to a new social identity, was taken up by Paul and made the center of his own thought (Engberg-Pedersen 2000). Thus Engberg-Pedersen, while recognizing Paul's distinctive theological emphases, provocatively argues that Paul and Stoicism are "*centrally* identical .... as regards what I argue is comprehensively central to Paul: the focus on practice and the 'anthropology' and 'ethics' that articulate that focus" (Engberg-Pedersen 2002: 105). He therefore questions "the widespread view that in the end there remains a basic, intrinsic difference between the perspectives of Paul the (Hellenistic) Jew and the ethical traditions of the Greeks" (Engberg-Pedersen 2000: 11). On the other hand, even Paul's specifically theological accents are widely paralleled in the religious features prominent in Stoicism of the imperial period. It is the religious elements of later Stoicism in particular that have led a number of scholars to question whether any basic categorical distinction exists between Paul and the Stoics in their understanding of moral progress. For example, T. Schmeller observes:

> One can often hear that in Stoicism ethics is a function of the intellect, whereas in the NT it is a function of the existential determination of the Christian by Christ. That is true to a certain extent. But this difference is hardly to be perceived where on the one hand the Stoic ethics really becomes popular and includes a strong religious element and where on the other hand NT ethics begins to be oriented by the conventional common sense. Therefore, the problem of the *proprium* of the NT ethics is particularly pressing in view of the means of the moral instruction just mentioned.
> (Schmeller 1992: 213)

The increased stress in the later Stoa upon ethics and the possibility of ethical progress was indeed accompanied by a markedly increased religiosity. In relating moral progress to God, the Stoic view was markedly different from contemporary philosophical movements for whom moral development generally was regarded as a human achievement in which the divine played no appreciable role. Cynics generally did not view the divine, if its existence was acknowledged at all, as having any role in human affairs.[2] Epicurean theology, while affirming the traditional belief in the existence of the gods, similarly rejected the idea of any influence of the divine on the human plane.[3] The Middle Platonist understanding of the relationship of the divine to the ethical life provides a partial parallel to the Stoic view. However, even the religiously colored thought of the Middle Platonists had no room for direct, unmediated influence of the divine on human moral activity.[4] The later Stoics were distinctive among the philosophical schools in relating the moral life directly to the activity of God.

This aspect of later Stoic teaching is most prominent in the Roman philosopher Seneca. Seneca, perhaps to a greater degree than any philosopher before him, emphasized the role of the divine in human moral development.[5] Seneca stresses the part played by the divine in the attainment of moral virtue perhaps most strongly in *Epistle* 41:

> You are doing a noble and salutary thing if, as you indicate in your letter, you are continuing your progress toward good understanding. It is foolish to pray for this, since you are able to obtain it from your own self. We should not lift our hands to heaven, nor request the temple-keeper to grant admittance to the image's ear, as if we would thereby gain a greater hearing. God is near you, he is with you, he is within you. This is what I mean, Lucilius: a holy Spirit dwells within us, a watcher and guardian of our evil and good deeds. Just as this Spirit has been treated by us, so it treats us. Truly no man is good without God; can anyone rise above fortune unless he is aided by God? ... If you see a person unterrified by dangers, untouched by desires, happy in adversities, peaceful in the midst of storms, viewing other human beings from a position of superiority, the gods from a position of equality, will not a feeling of reverence for him come over you? Will you not say: "This thing is too great and too noble to believe that it is like this meager body in which it dwells. A divine power has descended upon him."
>
> (*Ep.* 41.1–4)

Seneca in this passage relates moral progress not only to the human will and the aid of philosophy, but also to the divine.[6] Much like Paul (2 Cor 4:6–10; Rom 8:6–9; 1 Cor 6:9–11; Gal 5:18–24; Phil 1:9–11; 2:13; 1 Thess 2:13), Seneca here ascribes moral progress to the divine power of an indwelling holy Spirit at work in the midst of human weakness. Seneca would seem to attribute progress in the moral life not to human ability, but to the power of God. Seneca's *Epistle* 41 constitutes the closest parallel in antiquity to the emphasis in early Christian paraenesis on the activity of the Spirit in sanctification.[7]

In a brief but magisterial article A.J. Malherbe (1998) has demonstrated the similarities and also the fundamental differences between the Christian conception of conversion and its nearest analog in antiquity: conversion to philosophy. Were there also differences in the understanding of ethical progress following conversion? Can one speak of a *proprium* of NT ethics? This question has many aspects, and a full discussion is beyond the scope of this essay. However, Seneca's understanding of the role of the divine in moral development, in providing the closest parallel among the philosophers to the Pauline notion of sanctification, may help to illumine some aspects of this question. Thus the views of Seneca in this epistle merit closer attention.

The notion of progress

In the very beginning of *Epistle* 41 Seneca praises Lucilius for his advancement toward good understanding (*ire ad bonam mentem*).[8] This sets the stage for the discussion in the remainder of the epistle of the role played by the divine in moral progress.[9] A few preliminary remarks will be helpful at this point regarding the conception of moral development that underlies Seneca's words here.

Like his Stoic predecessors, Seneca attributed virtue in the strict sense solely to the perfected wise person or sage, and he classed the rest of humanity as fools (*Ep.* 75.8).[10] However, whereas the earliest Stoics generally held to an absolute division between these two categories that admitted of no distinctions among the foolish, Seneca followed Chrysippus and other members of the early and middle Stoa in routinely distinguishing between the absolutely foolish and those making progress toward virtue (*Ep.* 6.1; 13.15; 25.5–7; 26.5–7; 34). The absolute virtue of the sage remained the ideal and was, in theory, attainable (*Ep.* 20.6; 34.3). Yet in Seneca's view such a truly virtuous person was extremely rare, coming into existence, like the phoenix, perhaps once in five hundred years.[11] Thus progress in virtue constituted for Seneca the practical aim of philosophy (*Ep.* 5.1; 7.8; 35), and one who had made sufficient progress could offer oneself, with appropriate reservations, as a model for those less advanced (*Ep.* 6.1–6; 8.2; 116.5).

Seneca also distinguished various levels of those making progress in virtue.[12] The most elaborate division is found in *Epistle* 75, where Seneca divides the *proficientes* into three classes. The first and highest class are those who, while not yet wise, have attained a stage approaching perfect wisdom.[13] These have rid themselves of all passions (*adfectus*) and vices (*vitia*), but their self-confidence in the face of fortune is as yet untried (*illis adhuc inexperta fiducia est*).[14] The second class is made up of those who have laid aside only the greatest evils and passions (*maxima animi mala et adfectus*) and, moreover, may at any time fall back into these vices (*Ep.* 75.13). The third and lowest class consists of those who, while they have escaped many great vices, have not yet conquered others (*Ep.* 75.14). Seneca describes this class elsewhere as those who have made only a beginning of wisdom (*inchoatus* [*Ep.* 71.28]; cf. *Ep.* 16.1: *sapientia . . . inchoata*).[15]

Although still numbered among the fools, a great divide separated the one making progress from the rest of humanity.[16] Although only the complete wisdom of the sage produces the truly blessed life, even the beginnings of wisdom make life at least bearable (*Ep.* 16.1). Philosophy effects a full cure of the maladies of the soul in the wise person alone, but the one making progress enjoys some amelioration of the disease (*Ep.* 6.1; 8.2; 27.1; 28.6–7; 68.8–9; 72.6). Thus here, as elsewhere, Seneca commends Lucilius for making progress in virtue.[17]

The holy spirit within

After praising him for his advancement toward good understanding, Seneca goes on to admonish Lucilius that he should not lift his hands to heaven or run to the temples for divine assistance in making moral progress (*Ep.* 41.1). God is much closer than that. Seneca assures Lucilius that "God is near you, he is with you, he is within you" (*prope est a te deus, tecum est, intus est* [*Ep.* 41.1]), and that "a holy Spirit dwells within us" (*sacer intra nos spiritus sedet* [*Ep.* 41.2]). The holy Spirit of which Seneca speaks is said to dwell within human beings and is identified with God. The passage is strikingly similar to passages in Paul's letters and elsewhere in the NT that speak of the indwelling of the Holy Spirit.[18] It is generally recognized that Seneca did not understand these words in the same way as Paul did, but the precise parameters of Seneca's understanding of the divine require clarification.

For Seneca, as for his Stoic predecessors, God is identical with the material universe.[19] "The universe in which we exist," he writes to Lucilius, "is one, and it is God."[20] "What is God?" he asks elsewhere, and answers, "All that which you see, and all that which you cannot see."[21] This pantheistic notion of the divine might seem wholly to preclude a personalist conception of the deity. And it is certain that the divine was, in large measure, conceived by Seneca in impersonal terms. This has long been recognized as a key difference between the Stoics and Paul. However, Seneca's frequent use of personal language for the divine, in evidence in *Epistle* 41 and elsewhere, raises the question of his precise understanding of the deity. On one view, Seneca's religiously colored language for the divine, like that of his fellow Stoics since the time of Cleanthes, was no more than an accommodation to the anthropomorphic conceptions prevalent in the popular religion.[22] On another reading, the warmth of Seneca's language and the elasticity of the Stoic conception of the divine permit the conclusion that Seneca thought of God in something approaching quasi-personal terms.[23] In either case, the contrast with the intensely personal God of Paul's letters is marked and significant.

The identity of God and the physical universe was qualified by the Stoics in important ways. Zeno himself identified God in the strict sense with the primary element of the universe, the creative ethereal fire (*SVF* 1.154; 1.120).[24] Chrysippus similarly located God in the purest part of the ether (*SVF* 2.644), but also he introduced the doctrine of the cosmic πνεῦμα, through which this divine element was thought to permeate the entire universe (*SVF* 2.473).[25] Stoic doctrine following Chrysippus taught that just as the spirit or soul pervades the human body, so also God, through the cosmic πνεῦμα (*pneuma*) identified with the divine λόγος (*logos*, Reason) or νοῦς

271

(*nous*, Mind), pervades the universe.[26] Seneca, too, identifies the divinity in its fullest sense, not with the cosmos itself, but with this creative Reason pervading and animating the cosmos.[27] The relation of God to the material cosmos is analogous to the relation of the soul to the human body.[28] In *Nat.* 2.45 Jupiter is described as the *animus ac spiritus mundi*, "the soul and spirit of the universe." God is "the divine spirit equally diffused through all things great and small."[29]

Although diffused in varying degrees through all the cosmos, the divine λόγος or *ratio* is present in its essence, outside of the gods, only in human beings. Thus God, the gods, and human beings share an identical nature, which is the peculiar property of humankind, separating them from plants and animals, which are not endowed with reason.[30] Thus the human soul in Seneca's thought is an ineffably great and glorious thing.[31] The rational soul is a part of God inhabiting a mortal breast.[32] It is the divine seed sown in a human body.[33] "Reason," Seneca tells Lucilius, "is nothing other than a part of the divine spirit immersed in a human body [*in corpus humanum pars divini spiritus mersa*]" (*Ep.* 66.12).[34] "What else," he asks, "would you call the great soul than God lodging in a human body [*deum in corpore humano hospitantem*]?" (*Ep.* 31.11). Thus the indwelling holy Spirit (*sacer intra nos spiritus*) in the passage under consideration is, for Seneca, not a power external to humanity, but the rational soul, which is intrinsic to human nature and which Seneca understands as a fragment of the divine.[35]

Although Seneca's language is closely similar to Paul's, the contrast with Paul's thought is evident. In Paul's very Jewish thought, the divinity is not identified with the cosmos, but is distinct from all other reality, the living God, the transcendent creator of all things (Rom 1:20–3; 4:17; 11:33–6; 1 Cor 8:4–6; 1 Thess 1:9–10). Moreover, Paul's understanding of God is eschatological, dynamic and participatory. In the fullness of time God sent his own Son to redeem humanity from the enslaving power of sin and death, in order that those united to God's Son by faith might be given his own Spirit (Rom 8:1–4; Gal 4:4–6; Phil 2:6–11).[36] Through union with God's Son in baptism, believers are endowed with the Spirit of the living, transcendent creator God (cf. Rom 5:5; 8:9–17; 1 Cor 3:16; 6:19–20; Gal 4:6; 1 Thess 2:13; 4:8). In Seneca's panentheistic theology, by contrast, the human soul is itself divine.[37] The God who is near, with, and within Lucilius is Lucilius's own mind and soul. This fundamental theological difference between Seneca and Paul is, as we will see, at the heart of striking differences in the structure of their ethical thought.

Ethics and identity

This cosmotheological understanding concerning the divine identity of the rational soul played an important role in later Stoic moral exhortation.[38] This religious element in Stoic thought generally functioned paraenetically among the later Stoics to provide warrant and motivation for the life of virtue through self-knowledge of one's exalted nature as a part of the divine.[39] This function of the concept is also present in Seneca's *Epistle* 41 and is frequent elsewhere in his work.[40] In locating the warrant for ethical behavior in a new conception of one's identity focusing on the indwelling divine Spirit, this motif is similar to the logic of moral exhortation in Paul – for example, "If we live through the Spirit, let us also live in conformity with the Spirit" (Gal 5:25).[41] In light of this similarity, Engberg-Pedersen argues that in their ethical structure Paul and the Stoics are "centrally identical" (Engberg-Pedersen 2002: 105). While fully acknowledging the great theological discontinuity between the Stoics and Paul, he argues that the anthropological movement of a "transference of identity" is essentially the same in both (Engberg-Pedersen 2000: 33–44).

But the differences are in reality profound, not only on the level of theology, but also on the level of anthropology and ethics. In the Stoic understanding, this transference takes place as reason, aided by philosophy, reveals the rational soul's own intrinsic divinity.[42] In Stoic thought this process is thus entirely a matter of change in self-understanding whereby the self grasps its true identity.[43] In Paul's thought, by contrast, the new identity comes about through faith (πίστις), which by its very nature involves a relationship of trust and dependence upon one outside the self (Rom 3:21–6; 4:19–25; 10:6–13; Gal 2:16–21; 3:1–2). Through faith in Jesus, and identification with the Son of God in his death and resurrection, believers are united with God's own Son and participate in his Spirit (Rom 6:1–11; 1 Cor 1:18–2:16; Gal 4:4–6; Phil 3:9–10). In Paul's thought the logic of moral exhortation thus depends upon a substantive new identity through supernatural union with a transcendent God, who is distinct from yet mystically united with the self.[44] For Paul, paradoxically, the self "arrives at his own identity through the mystical union with the spirit of Christ: 'I live; yet no longer I, but Christ lives in me' (Gal 2:20)" (Destro and Pesce 1998: 191).

Empowerment and virtue

Seneca's theology of the soul functions in *Epistle* 41 not only as warrant for the life of virtue but also as pointer to the divinity within as the means of empowerment for the virtuous life. After reminding Lucilius of the divine Spirit that dwells within him, Seneca immediately adds, "As this Spirit is treated by us, so it treats us. No man is good without God. Can anyone rise above fortune unless he is aided by God?" (*Ep.* 41.2). Seneca's insistence that "no one is a good man without God" (*bonus vero vir sine deo nemo est*), whom Seneca identifies here with the indwelling holy Spirit, directs Lucilius to God as the source of empowerment for the moral life. This motif, found elsewhere in Seneca (cf. *Ep.* 31.8–11; 73.12–16; 92.29–31), is expressed most markedly in this letter. This theme indeed dominates the epistle (cf. *vis isto divina*, 41.4; *caelestis potentia*, 41.5; *adminiculo numinis*, 41.5).

Seneca's emphasis in this letter on divine empowerment, which has no real analog in other Stoic writers, is similar in significant ways to the thought of Paul. The transforming power of the Spirit is at the heart of Paul's ethics and theology (e.g. Rom 8:1–17; 12:1–2; 1 Cor 6:9–11; 2 Cor 3:17–18; Gal 2:19–21; Phil 2:12–13; 1 Thess 4:7–9).[45] Yet here again the differences are striking. Whereas Paul thinks of a supernatural transformation through the Spirit of God's Son given in baptism, indwelling and empowering believers through faith (Rom 8:9-17; Gal 2:20; 4:6), the empowering holy Spirit of which Seneca thinks is the rational soul. Without this rational nature, which is divine in its origin, goodness would not be possible (cf. *Ep.* 124.23). "Why can there be no good in plants and animals?" Seneca asks, and he answers, "Because they have no reason."[46] Human beings, by contrast, possess the same rational nature as the gods, differing from them only in that whereas in the gods reason has been perfected, in human beings it is capable of perfection.[47] Thus nature has bestowed at birth the foundation and seed of virtue in each person.[48]

However, as Seneca adds in our letter, "As this Spirit is treated by us, so it treats us" (*Hic prout a nobis tractatus est, ita nos ipse tractat* [*Ep.* 41.2]). For although God and humans share the same nature, in the case of God, nature (*natura*) brings the good to perfection, while in the case of human beings, labor and study (*cura*) are necessary.[49] The soul, divine though it is, requires cultivation. A passage in *Epistle* 73 sheds light on this conception:

> God comes to human beings, indeed, he comes nearer, he comes into human beings [*in homines venit*]; no mind is good without God [*nulla sine deo mens bona est*]. Divine seeds have been sown in our human bodies [*semina in corporibus humanis divina dispersa sunt*]. If a good husbandman receives them, they spring up in the likeness of their origin and grow to be equal to those from which they are derived. If a bad husbandman receives them, he kills them, just like a barren or marshy soil, and brings forth weeds rather than fruits.
>
> (*Ep.* 73.16)[50]

In this process philosophy has a fundamental role:

> The soul does not attain virtue unless it has been instructed, educated and trained by constant practice. We are indeed born for this attainment, but not yet at birth in possession of it. Even in the best men, before you educate them, there exists only the material of virtue, not virtue itself.
>
> (*Ep.* 90.46)[51]

It is consequently through philosophy that the divinity of the human soul is fully realized. "Do you ask what makes a wise man?" says Seneca. "The same thing that makes God."[52] In the wise person there is something divine, heavenly, glorious.[53] In the unpurified soul, however, there is no room for God.[54] Thus it is philosophy that, in bringing the rational soul to perfection, makes human beings into gods.[55] "For this," Seneca writes to Lucilius, "is what philosophy promises me, that it shall make me the equal of God."[56]

The idea of the virtuous person's equality with God is prominent in Seneca. "Nature has given you such endowments that, if you do not desert them, you rise equal to God."[57] "Do you ask what will be the difference between yourself and them [sc., the gods]? They will exist longer."[58] The contrast with Paul's moral vision of humanity redeemed to love, worship and glorify God (Rom 12:1–2; 15:7–13; 1 Cor 6:19–20; 8:4–6; Phil 2:6–11; 1 Thess 1:9–10) could not be stronger. In Paul's thought, the transforming empowerment of the moral life through participation with Christ in his death and resurrection excludes all human boasting (Rom 3:27–31; 1 Cor 1:26–31; Gal 6:14–16; Phil 3:2–16). In Seneca's ethics, the moral power of the philosophic life, far from revealing the need for God or leading to worship of God, rather demonstrates one's own equality with God – so with the good person in *Epistle* 41, who looks upon the gods from a position of equality (*ex aequo deos* [*Ep.* 41.4]).

Human weakness and divine power

The virtue of every good person (*unoquoque virorum bonorum* [*Ep.* 41.2]), according to the passage under consideration, points to a power beyond the corruptible body that one inhabits. Wonders of the natural world – a grove of ancient trees, an arched cave at the foot of a mountain, hidden springs and immeasurable depths – fill us with an unmistakable sense of the divine presence (*Ep.* 41.3–4). Is not then, Seneca asks Lucilius, the moral virtue of the good person – fearlessness in dangers, freedom from desire, happiness in adversity, serenity amid the storm, superiority to other human beings and equality with the gods – likewise proof of the presence of a divine power within the mortal body?

> If you see a person unterrified by dangers, untouched by desires, happy in adversities, peaceful in the midst of storms, viewing other human beings from a position of superiority, the gods from a position of equality, will not a feeling of reverence for him come over you? Will you not say: "This thing is too great and too noble to believe that it is like this meager body in which it dwells. A divine power has descended upon him."
>
> (*Ep.* 41.4)

Seneca's use in this passage of a catalog of hardships to set forth the virtue of the good person is striking. Paul, in 2 Cor 4:6–10, employs a similar catalog of hardships in order to glorify the power of God at work in the midst of his own human weakness (cf. 2 Cor 4:7: "so that it may be made clear that this extraordinary power belongs to God and does not come from us [ἵνα ἡ ὑπερβολὴ τῆς δυνάμεως ᾖ τοῦ θεοῦ καὶ μὴ ἐξ ἡμῶν]). The connections with Seneca's *Epistle* 41 are evident. But is it the case that differences are, as Schmeller suggests, hardly to be perceived? In fact, the conception is far different. In this passage Seneca does not contrast *human* weakness with an external *divine* power at work in him, but rather contrasts the frail and mortal human *body* of the good man with the divine *soul* which indwells the body. Seneca elsewhere, as we have seen, frequently contrasts the divinity within humanity with the corruptible body in which it dwells. This rational soul is God lodging in a human body (*deus in corpore humano hospitans* [*Ep.* 31.11]); it is a portion of the divine spirit immersed in a human body (*in corpus humanum pars divini spiritus mersa* [*Ep.* 66.12]); it is a divine seed sown in a human body (*semina in corporibus humanis divina dispersa* [*Ep.* 73.16]). So here, too, the perishable human body (*corpusculo*) is contrasted with the divine power (*vis divina*) of the soul that indwells it. In 2 Cor 4:6–10, very differently from Seneca, Paul contrasts his own *human* weakness with the power of the living *God* at work in him through Christ.[59] In Paul, the contrast is not between the physical body and the divine soul, but between the whole person under the power of sin and the redeeming, empowering activity of God through participation in Christ and his Spirit (cf. Rom 8:3–4; 1 Cor 6:9–11; Gal 4:4–6).

This contrast points to another key difference in the anthropology of Seneca and Paul. For Seneca, the transference of identity which takes place through philosophy involves a disassociation from the physical body, which is understood as extrinsic to the wise person's true identity.[60] The body in Seneca's view is the prison of the soul, by which it is encumbered and from which it longs to be freed.[61] In Paul's holistic understanding, the substantive new identity through participatory union with Christ embraces the person as a whole being, body and soul. The body, created by God, is now mystically united with Christ and the dwelling place of God's Spirit, and will be raised to life in the coming renewal of creation at the advent of Christ.[62] This conception of the body, radically different from Stoicism, is a key element in the structure of Paul's ethical thought, as is evident from the foundational role this conception plays in Paul's instructions to the Corinthians regarding sexual morality: "But the body is not for sexual immorality but for the Lord, and the Lord is for the body. And God both raised the Lord, and will raise us by his power" (1 Cor 6:13–14).[63]

Seneca in *Epistle* 41 speaks of the divine power of the soul as having descended from heaven (*vis isto divina descendit* [*Ep.* 41.4]; cf. *caelestis potentia agitat* [*Ep.* 41.5]). However, the Pauline conception of the eschatological outpouring of God's Spirit in fulfillment of the promises of the God of Israel (Gal 3:13–14; 4:6; cf. 1 Pet 1:12) is foreign to Seneca's thought. Seneca rather refers to the origins of the rational soul in the ethereal regions, whence it has descended at birth into the human body.[64] The divine power resident in the soul is, for Seneca, a gift, not of grace, but of nature.[65] The virtuous person

> is the equal of the gods [*deos aequat*]; he strives toward heaven, mindful of his origins. No one is wrong in attempting to ascend to the place from which he has descended [*unde descenderat*]. Why would you not believe that something of the divine [*divini aliquid*] exists in him who is a part of God [*qui dei pars est*]?[66]

This concept of the divinity of the soul, which is emphasized in Seneca to a degree unparalleled in other Stoic writers, played a key role in his thought. H. Cancik (1998: 341–4) has called attention to the frequency of "reflexive formulas" in Seneca's writings, which reveal a focusing on the self and point to an "increasing interiorization of morals." The logical and literary connections between these reflexive patterns and Seneca's theology of the soul suggest that this inward movement in Seneca's thought was closely related to his understanding of the soul as a fragment of God.[67] In *Epistle* 41 Seneca through these formulas directs Lucilius inward, to the God within, as the source of moral empowerment.[68] Strikingly, Paul's favored formulas are not reflexive, but participatory, expressing the participatory *union* of believers with Christ.[69] Alongside these are genitive formulas expressing the *belonging* of believers to Christ.[70] Paul also frequently employs prepositional phrases expressing faith, love, and hope directed *toward* Christ and God.[71] In contrast to Seneca's reflexive patterns, Paul's participatory formulas direct the reader to a transforming union with God's Son, who is distinct from yet mystically united with the self, as the source of moral empowerment. The very different structure of Paul and Seneca's ethical thought is reflected in the structure of the syntax in which that thought finds expression.

This concept of the soul's divinity was also perhaps the most important element in Seneca's negative attitude toward traditional forms of worship.[72] The connection is explicit in *Epistle* 41, where Seneca instructs Lucilius that he must seek moral progress from himself, where divinity dwells, and not through prayer or worship in the temples.[73] This relates closely to another theme prominent in *Epistle* 41: as the gods' equal, the wise person is also worthy of worship (41.4, *veneratio eius*).[74] The central place of praise, thanksgiving and worship of God in Paul's moral exhortation stands in marked contrast.[75] Paul also prays for the moral progress of his converts, and asks that his converts pray for him (Rom 15:30–3; Phil 1:9–11; 1 Thess 3:11–13; Phil 4:7). In Seneca's view, prayer for moral progress is unnecessary, in consequence of the soul's own divinity. Through philosophy, Seneca promises Lucilius, "you begin to be the associate of the gods, not their suppliant."[76] As he writes to Lucilius at the beginning of our letter, "It is foolish [*stultum*] to pray for this, since you are able to obtain it from yourself [*cum possis a te impetrare*]."[77] The reason that Seneca gives is the deity of the soul: "God is near you, he is with you, he is within you" (*Ep.* 41.1). Prayer is foolhardy in Seneca's view, precisely because the power necessary for moral progress is not something given by an external divine being, but rather is already resident in the rational soul itself, and in need only of development through philosophy.

Conclusion

Seneca, like other Roman Stoics, and perhaps to a greater degree than any other, emphasized the role of the divine in moral progress. Seneca's understanding of progress provides the closest analog among the moral philosophers to the Pauline conception of the activity of the Spirit in sanctification. However, Seneca did not understand the divine as a power external to humanity, but rather he identified the divine with the rational soul, which he conceived as a portion of the divine essence dwelling within the corruptible human body. Herein lies, alongside numerous and important similarities, a fundamental difference between Paul and Seneca in their conception of moral progress. For Seneca, moral progress is an achievement of the rational soul, made possible because of its divine nature; for Paul, moral progress is the work of a transcendent personal God with whose Spirit believers have been endowed at baptism. What Seneca attributes to the rational self, divine in origin, Paul attributes to a transforming union with the Spirit of God's Son, dwelling in believers through faith. This radical theological difference between Paul and Seneca is at the heart of striking differences in their ethical thought, including their understanding of human identity, of the human body, and of the source of moral empowerment. The Pauline conception of the activity of God in the moral life reveals, in the last analysis, a basic and intrinsic difference between the understanding of moral progress in Seneca, and in the moral philosophers generally, and that of Paul and the earliest Christians.

Notes

1 For an overview see Malherbe 1992.
2 Zeller 1889–1903: 3/1.328–30; Gomperz 1908: 2.163–5; Goulet-Cazé 1993; Malherbe 1982: 57–8; 1978: 45–51. The religious features in Peregrinus's Cynicism reflect a later period, and possible Christian influence (Hornsby 1933: 77–84). For the debate regarding Christian influence on Peregrinus see Hornsby 1933: 81–2; Jones 1993.
3 Epicurus, *SV* 65; Lucretius, *De rerum nat.* 3.1–93; 4.823–57; 5.110–234; 6.1–95; Lucian, *Bis acc.* 2; 20; see Nilsson 1961: 2.251–2; Zeller 1889–1903: 3/1.443–4, 448–9.
4 In Middle Platonic theology the *daimones*, regarded as lesser divinities or intermediate beings of mixed mortal and divine nature, often were thought to play an

important part in human moral activity (Plutarch, *De gen. Soc.* 588C–594A; Maximus of Tyre, *Diss.* 14.7–8; 38); however, the highest God and the gods of heaven were generally understood to have no direct contact with the human realm (Ps.-Plutarch, *De fato* 572F–574D; see Dill 1905: 518–40; Dillon 1996: 317–26). The later Neoplatonist theology similarly excluded any direct influence of the divine on human moral actions.

5   See Cancik and Cancik-Lindemaier 1991.
6   See Cancik and Cancik-Lindemaier 1991: 217–18.
7   As T.R. Glover (1909: 61) remarked, Seneca's *Epistle* 41 is "curiously suggestive of another school of thought," that of Paul and the early Christians; cf. Gibson 2000: 311.
8   In Seneca's thought "good understanding" (*bona mens*) is a comprehensive term embracing the whole life of virtue (cf. *Ep.* 23.1–2; 37.1; 44.2; 73.16; 117.12).
9   On the corpus of Seneca's epistles as "a narrative performance of moral progress" see Cancik-Lindemaier 1998: 99, 101–9.
10 For the early Stoic theory see *SVF* 1.66; 1.216; 3.552; cf. Kerferd 1978: 125–8.
11 *Ep.* 42.1: *Nam ille alter fortasse tamquam phoenix semel anno quingentesimo nascitur.*
12 For Seneca's debt on this score to earlier Stoic theory, especially Chrysippus, see Rubin 1901: 54–6.
13 *Ep.* 75.9: *primi sunt, qui sapientiam nondum habent, sed iam in vicinia eius constiterunt*; cf. *Ep.* 109.15: *proficientem vicinumque perfecto*.
14 *Ep.* 75.9; cf. *Ep.* 71.34. Seneca also mentions a slightly different definition of this class (*Ep.* 75.10–12), which describes them as those who have laid aside all chronic vices (*inveterata vitia*) or diseases (*morbi*) of the soul, such as greed and ambition, but who still feel the soul's passions (*adfectus*). This is at variance with the first view that Seneca presents, according to which the nearly wise person is freed even from the passions (*Ep.* 75.9). A treatment of Seneca's theory of the passions cannot be undertaken here; see Sorabji 2000: 55–92; 1998; see also the essays collected in Braund and Gill 1997, in particular those of A. Schiesaro (1997), M. Wilson (1997), C. Gill (1997: esp. 215–28), and E. Fantham (1997: esp. 188–9, 195–9).
15 Could progress in virtue, once accomplished, be lost? In answering this question, Seneca made a distinction, not only between the sage and the *proficiens*, but also between the various classes of those making progress. Regression is an impossibility for the sage (*sapiens recidere non potest, ne incidere quidem amplius* [*Ep.* 72.6]; cf. *Helv.* 13.3; *Ep.* 20.4; 50.8; 71.35; 76.19; 117.15). Regression is also impossible for the first and highest class of *proficientes*, for although they, unlike the wise, have not yet put their virtue fully to the test, they can no more fall back into the vices from which they have freed themselves (*Ep.* 75.9; cf. 72.10). The second and third classes of those making progress, by contrast, over whom at least some of the vices and passions retain their power, run the constant risk of regression from the stage of moral progress to which they have attained (*Ep.* 71.35; 72.6, 9, 11; 75.13; cf. 20.4). Indeed, whenever one slackens in devotion to the philosophic life, regression must follow (*Ep.* 72.6; 71.35). For the untried, with little training, regression can become total and involve a complete fall from the philosophic life; they fall into, as it were, the Epicurean void, empty and without end

(*Ep.* 72.9: *imperitis ac rudibus nullus praecipitationis finis est; in Epicureum illud chaos decidunt, inane, sine termino*).
16 *Ep.* 75.8: *nam qui proficit, in numero quidem stultorum est, magno tamen intervallo ab illis diducitur.*
17 *Ep.* 41.1; cf. 5.1; 16.2; 20.6; 32.1–2; 34.1–2; 108.3. A full examination of the notion of moral progress in Seneca would involve, among other topics, Senecan themes such as the proper division of philosophy, the application of the techniques of paraenesis, and the relationship of knowing and willing in moral development. Such themes will not be elaborated here. For discussion of these and related issues see Voelke 1969; Rist 1969: 226–31; Verbeke 1991: 14–16; Kidd 1978: 251–57 (on Seneca, *Ep.* 94–5); Mitsis 1993; Börger 1980: 59–146.
18 See esp. 1 Cor 3:16 (οὐκ οἴδατε ὅτι ναὸς θεοῦ ἐστε καὶ τὸ πνεῦμα τοῦ θεοῦ οἰκεῖ ἐν ὑμῖν;); 6:19 (ἢ οὐκ οἴδατε ὅτι τὸ σῶμα ὑμῶν ναὸς τοῦ ἐν ὑμῖν ἁγίου πνεύματός ἐστιν οὗ ἔχετε ἀπὸ θεοῦ ...;); see also Rom 5:5; 8:9, 11; 1 Cor 2:12; 2 Cor 1:22; 5:5; Gal 3:2, 5; 4:6; Phil 1:19; 1 Thess 4:8; 2 Tim 1:14; Luke 11:13; Acts 2:38; 4:31; 5:32; 6:3, 5; 8:15–19; 10:47; 11:24; 15:8; 19:2–6; John 7:39; 1 John 3:24; 4:13.
19 For Zeno's pantheistic conception of the deity see *SVF* 1.163; 1.158; 1.111; cf. Jacquette 1995. On the novelty of this conception in Greek thought and its crucial role in Stoic ethical theory see Long 1996e.
20 *Ep.* 92.30: *Totum hoc quo continemur, et unum est et deus.*
21 *Nat.* 1, prol. 13: *Quid est deus? quod vides totum et quod non vides totum.* Cf. *Nat.* 2.45.
22 J.N. Sevenster (1961: 34–43), for example, argues that "Seneca is in the last resort not serious when he speaks of a personal God," and that "for Seneca the godhead was on the whole impersonal"; similarly Rubin 1901: 8–9; Glover 1909: 70–3. This also appears to have been the general perception of the Stoic religious language in antiquity. This is suggested, for example, by a passage in the Epicurean work *On Piety* (traditionally attributed to Philodemus), which attacks the Stoics as hypocritical atheists, who retain the traditional language for the gods, while in actuality doing away with the notion of the divine altogether (Gomperz 1865: cols. IV.12–VI.16, pp. 77–80). See also Henrichs 1974. For further ancient comment on the fundamentally impersonal conception of the divine in Stoic thought, cf. Athenagoras, *Suppl.* 22, and Origen, *Cels.* 5.7.
23 Burton 1909: 358–65; Riesco 1966; cf. Dill 1905: 304–7. For Stoicism as a complex and somewhat elastic fusion of pantheism and theism, see Long 2002: 142–79; Thom 2005: 20–7.
24 See Lapidge 1978: 178; Todd 1978: 139–43.
25 See Lapidge 1978: 169–71. From the surviving sources it is not entirely clear whether Chrysippus conceived of the πνεῦμα as comprised of fire (πῦρ, *pyr*) and air (ἀήρ, *aēr*) (cf. *SVF* 2.1100; see Lapidge 1978: 174) or of fire and ether (αἴθηρ, *aithēr*), which would seem more consonant with the equation of the πνεῦμα and God in Chrysippus and later Stoic sources; for this latter view see Todd 1978: 149–55.
26 Lapidge: 1978: 170–1; cf. Long 1996d: 228–34. This concept qualifies Stoic materialism by positing two principles of matter, a passive principle, identified with undifferentiated substance, and an active principle, identified with the divine reason that inheres in and gives form to matter (cf. *SVF* 2.310; Diogenes Laertius 7.134; Calcidius, *Comm. Tim.* 293).

27 *Ep.* 90.29: *aeternamque rationem toti inditam*; *Ep.* 65.12: *Ratio scilicet faciens, id est deus*; *Ben.* 4.7.1: *Quid enim aliud est natura quam deus et divina ratio toti mundo partibusque inserta?* Cf. Marcus Aurelius, *Med.* 8.54.
28 *Ep.* 65.24: *Quem in hoc mundo locum deus obtinet, hunc in homine animus.*
29 *Helv.* 8.3: *divinus spiritus per omnia maxima ac minima aequali intentione diffusus.*
30 *Ep.* 124.14: *Quattuor hae naturae sunt, arboris, animalis, hominis, dei; haec duo, quae rationalia sunt, eandem naturam habent*; *Ep.* 92.27: *Ratio vero dis hominibusque communis est*; cf. *Ep.* 92.1; 121.14; 124.8; 124.23; see Akinpelu 1968; Motto 1954–5: 181.
31 *Ep.* 102.21: *magna et generosa res est humanus animus*; cf. *Ep.* 104.23.
32 *Ep.* 120.14: *mens dei, ex quo pars et in hoc pectus mortale defluxit*; *Ep.* 92.30: *Quid est autem cur non existimes in eo divini aliquid existere, qui dei pars est?* Cf. frg. 123: *[deus] in suo cuique consecrandus est pectore.*
33 *Ep.* 73.16: *Semina in corporibus humanis divina dispersa sunt.* Thus each person is a mixture of the human and the divine: *mixtum hoc divini humanique* (*Ep.* 102.22).
34 Cf. *Helv.* 6.7: *[Mens] non est ex terreno et gravi concreta corpore, ex illo caelesti spiritu descendit.*
35 See Parker 1906: 155–6.
36 See Tannehill 2007; Sanders 1977: 453–72; Malherbe 2000: 224–41.
37 *Ep.* 92.34: *ille divinus animus.*
38 See, for example, Cicero, *Tusc.* 5.38–9, 70; *Leg.* 1.22–5; Epictetus, *Diss.* 1.14.6, 11–17; 2.8.9–17, 27–9; Diogenes Laertius 7.143; Marcus Aurelius, *Med.* 2.1; 5.27; 12:26; see Gass 2000; Long 1996e: 186–201; deSilva 1995: 555. Engberg-Pedersen's account of Stoic ethics minimizes the role of theology in Stoic moral reasoning (see Engberg-Pedersen 2000: 45–79; 1990); for trenchant criticism of Engberg-Pedersen's position see Long 1996b: 154–5.
39 See Gass 2000: 20–1, 24–37. For this function see, for example, Epictetus, *Diss.* 1.3.1–6; 1.9; 1.14.11–17; 2.8; Marcus Aurelius, *Med.* 12.26.
40 See *Ep.* 41.6–9; cf. *Ep.* 66.12–13; 102.21–30; 104.22–3; 124.21–4.
41 Cf. 1 Cor 5:7; 6:15; 6:19–20; Rom 6:1–11; 8:1–17.
42 See "Empowerment and virtue" below.
43 Cf. Gass 2000: 33–7.
44 See Sanders 1977: 453–72, 497–508, 518–23.
45 For Paul's stress on the empowerment of the Spirit see Hays 1996: 43–5; Schrage 1988: 177–9; Furnish 1968: 238–9. As Hays notes: "This notion of effective transformation through union with Christ is fundamental to Paul's theological ethics" (Hays 1996: 38).
46 *Ep.* 124.8: *Quare autem bonum in arbore animalique muto non est? Quia nec ratio.*
47 *Ep.* 92.27: *Ratio vero dis hominibusque communis est; haec in illis consummata est, in nobis consummabilis.*
48 *Ep.* 108.8: *omnibus enim natura fundamenta dedit semenque virtutum. Omnes ad omnia ista nati sumus.* Cf. *Ep.* 13.15: *natus es ad ista quae dicimus.*
49 *Ep.* 124.14: *Ex his ergo unius bonum natura perficit, dei scilicet, alterius cura, hominis.*

50 Cf. Cicero, *Tusc.* 5.38–9.
51 On the necessity of philosophy for moral progress see *Ep.* 31.8; 37.3–4; 53.8; 82.7; *Helv.* 17.5; cf. *SVF* 3.223, 225; Kerferd 1978: 128.
52 *Ep.* 87.19: *Quaeris quae res sapientem facit? Quae deum.*
53 *Ep.* 87.19: *Des oportet illi divinum aliquid, caeleste, magnificum.*
54 *Ep.* 87.21: *Hic nisi purus ac sanctus est, deum non capit.*
55 *Ep.* 73.11: *quod deos facit.*
56 *Ep.* 48.11: *Hoc enim est, quod mihi philosophia promittit, ut parem deo faciat.*
57 *Ep.* 31.9: *[Natura] dedit tibi illa, quae si non deserueris, par deo surges.*
58 *Ep.* 53.11: *Quaeris, quid inter te et illos interfuturum sit? Diutius erunt.* On equality to the gods see *Ep.* 73.12–14; 92.29; 124.21; 124.23.
59 See the perceptive treatment in Fitzgerald 1988: 166–76. For Paul it is crucial that his afflictions are entirely beyond his own power to endure (2 Cor 1:8; cf. 12:7–8), for it is precisely in the midst of his human powerlessness that God's power is revealed (2 Cor 12:9–10). See Furnish 1984: 281–2; deSilva 1995: 561–2.
60 *Ep.* 41.4–5; 65.16–22; 92.33–5; 102.21–30; 120.14–16; see Inwood 2005: 502–3.
61 *Ep.* 65.16–7; 65.21; 71.16; 92.33–4; 102.22–3.
62 Rom 8:9–11; 8:18–25; 1 Cor 6:14–20; 15:12–58; 2 Cor 4:14; Phil 3:10–11, 20–1; 1 Thess 4:13–18; 5:23–4.
63 See Sampley 2002: 862–3; Sanders 1977: 454–5.
64 *Ep.* 65.16; 65.20; 73.16; 120.15; 124.14; *Helv.* 6.7; *Marc.* 24.5.
65 *Ep.* 31.9 (see n. 57 above); *Ep.* 13.15: *Natus es ad ista, quae dicimus*; *Ep.* 92.30: *Capax est noster animus, perfertur illo, si vitia non deprimant.* Contrast 2 Cor 12:9; 1:12.
66 *Ep.* 92.29–30: *hic deos aequat, illo tendit originis suae memor. Nemo improbe eo conatur ascendere, unde descenderat. Quid est autem cur non existemus in eo divini aliquid existere, qui dei pars est?*
67 See, for example, *Ep.* 124.21–4, where Seneca's understanding of the divinity of the soul and these reflexive formulas are closely conjoined: cf. *Ep.* 124.21–2: *alienum/tuum* ("another's/your own"); *Ep.* 124.23: *extra se/in te* ("outside yourself/in yourself"); *Ep.* 124.24: *ex tibi* ("out of yourself"); see also *Ep.* 31.11; 92.32; 98.2.
68 See *Ep.* 41.1: *a te* ("from yourself"); *Ep.* 41.6–7: *alienum/suum* ("another's/one's own"); *Ep.* 41.7: *in ipso* ("in himself"); cf. *Ep.* 31.8–11; 73.16.
69 For example, ἐν Χριστῷ ("in Christ") Rom 6:11; 8:1–2; 8:39; 1 Cor 1:30; 2 Cor 5:17; 5:21; Gal 3:26; Phil 3:8; many others; εἰς Χριστόν ("into Christ") Rom 6:3; Gal 3:27; Phlm 6; σὺν Χριστῷ ("with Christ") Rom 6:4; 2 Cor 4:14; Phil 1:23; 1 Thess 4:17; 5:10. See, conveniently, Sanders 1977: 458–61.
70 E.g. Rom 8:9; 14:7–8; 1 Cor 6:19–20; 15:23; Gal 5:24. See Sanders 1977: 461–3.
71 E.g. Rom 4:24; Gal 2:16; 3:26; Phil 1:29; 1 Thess 1:8.
72 On Seneca's criticism of traditional religious practices, the reasons for which were varied, see Manning 1996.
73 *Ep.* 41.1: *Non sunt ad caelum elevandae manus nec exorandus aedituus, ut nos ad aurem simulacri, quasi magis exaudiri possimus, admittat.* See Manning 1996: 319. Note the absence of temples in Zeno's ideal commonwealth (*SVF* 1.267), and cf. Seneca, *Ep.* 90.28; Epictetus, *Diss.* 2.8.13–14.
74 For the worship accorded the divine soul in Seneca's thought, see *Ep.* 115.3–5; see also Cancik and Cancik-Lindemaier 1991: 213–16.

75 Rom 1:18–25; 4:17–25; 12:1–2; 15:7–13; Phil 3:2–3; 4:6–7; 1 Thess 3:9–10; 5:16–18.
76 *Ep.* 31.8: *Quod si occupas, incipis deorum socius esse, non supplex.* For Seneca's negative evaluation of prayer see also *Marc.* 21.6; for a more positive view see *Ben.* 4.4.1–2; 2.1.4; *Nat.* 2.35–38. Seneca seems to have approved of prayer by the virtuous person only when accompanied by the proper understanding. Instructive is *Ep.* 10.4, where Seneca invites Lucilius to call upon God boldly, adding that he will not be requesting anything that is not his own (*audacter deum roga: nihil illum de alieno rogaturus es*); that is, the gifts that he craves in fact already belong to him, as a being identical in nature with the being to whom he prays. On Seneca's view of prayer see Motto 1954–5: 182; Sevenster 1961: 43–5; Rubin 1901: 12–14.
77 *Ep.* 41.1: *quam stultum est optare, cum possis a te impetrare.*

14

MORAL PATHOLOGY: PASSIONS, PROGRESS, AND PROTREPTIC IN CLEMENT OF ALEXANDRIA

L. Michael White

Clement of Alexandria's *Who Is the Rich Man That Will Be Saved?* is an allegorical *tour de force* on the Jesus-logion of Mark 10:25. Instead of denouncing wealth, however, Clement argues that the real problem is the passions of the soul, especially greed. Clement's stance is a lesson in the morals of his day for an elite audience, and it is replete with philosophical commonplaces. Thus, suffused through its treatment of wealth is a set of assumptions about virtue, vice, and the passions. They reflect intertwined elements of the physical and moral world in terms of medicine and the physiology of the soul. Clement is the moral guide through this maze of misperceptions and is doctor for the soul. This study, then, is offered as a commentary on *Quis dives salvetur* in the light of the moralist tradition and its medical assumptions regarding passions and progress.

A rhetorician's ploy

One night in about 200 CE a Greek philosopher stood up to deliver a speech. Here is how it began:

Οἱ μὲν τοὺς ἐγκωμιαστικοὺς λόγους τοῖς πλουσίοις δωροφοροῦντες ...

Those who make gifts of encomiastic orations to the rich would rightly seem to me to be judged not only as flatterers and slaves ... but also as *impious and treacherous* [οὐ μόνον κόλακες καὶ ἀνελεύθεροι ... ἀλλὰ καὶ ἀσεβεῖς καὶ ἐπίβουλοι]. They are *impious* [ἀσεβεῖς], then, because ... they confer [God's] due honor [γέρας] [of praise] to men who are wallowing in a riotous and filthy life.... Yet they are *treacherous* [ἐπίβουλοι] as well, because – whereas mere abundance on its own is sufficient to make the *soul flaccid* [χαυνῶσαι τὰς ψυχὰς], to corrupt and frustrate it – these [encomiasts] induce a further shock [προσεκπλήσσουσι] to the organs of judgment of the rich by *arousing* [ἐπαίροντες] them with the pleasures of excessive praises and above all by causing them to be contemptuous of everything else by which they are admired, save wealth alone. In truth, they are, as the saying goes, *"piping fire to a fire"* [πῦρ ἐπὶ πῦρ μετοχετεύοντες], when they pour vanity on vanity and place an additional burden on wealth – weighed down already by its very nature [φύσει] – of the even heavier weight of conceit.... Instead, they ought to perform *amputation* [ἀφαιρεῖν] and surgical excision [περικόπτειν] as with a dangerous and deadly disease.

(Clement of Alexandria, *Quis div.* 1.1–3)[1]

So, our orator begins by offering medical attention for a *flaccid soul* that has been further *shocked* by an excess of praise and *weighed down* with conceit. It is hardly a polite way to open a speech at the end of a sumptuous banquet – rather biting, we might say.

We know little of the precise circumstances of the speech, but the intent is readily discerned from tone, style, and rhetorical posture. It is noteworthy that our orator begins by selecting the *topos* on flattery and frank speech (κολακεία καὶ παρρησία, *kolakeia kai parrhēsia*) to set the tone.[2] The philosopher – the one who cares for you as much as a true friend – is the one who will speak frankly and harshly, if need be, in order to make you better. For example, Plutarch (*Adul. amic.* 61A) uses the same adage of *"carrying fire to a fire"* (πῦρ ἐπὶ πῦρ εἰσφέρουσα, *pyr epi pyr eispherousa*) in reference to the corrosive effects of flattery in intensifying passions once they have been stimulated.[3] This rhetorical posture may also provide new insights into the setting and social dynamics of the speech, for it sounds like the kind of speech that should be delivered by a philosopher after dinner – that is, at a *symposium* – in the company of students, other philosophers, and wealthy patrons.[4] Thus, when our rhetor commences by decrying flattering encomia, it must have sounded a discordant note for the audience, since an encomium is precisely what should have been expected of the philosopher in honor of the host and patron. So it is all the more provocative, as the tone here employs the philosopher's frankness to deliver moralizing lessons to the rich people in the audience.

In this case, the orator has intentionally, in my view, reversed the typical rhetorical polarities of the symposium genre and its social conventions. By the end of the second century CE, however, such an inversion was not so unusual, even among Second Sophistic orators, for whom panegyrical displays were a commonplace. They too were influenced by the *topos* on flattery and frank speech, and the encomium had become a suspect genre. Thus, in 155 Aelius

Aristides opened his *Roman Oration* by praying for adequate words to praise Rome appropriately.[5] He may well have known Pliny's *Panegyric*, which began by decrying the mere "flattery" (*adulatio*) demanded by Domitian, and praying instead for "liberty, sincerity, and truth."[6] In other words, the praises that he was about to heap on Trajan were not *merely* encomiastic hyperbole; they were "straight talk." Pliny's contemporary Dio Chrysostom had built his reputation as rhetor and "Cynic" on regular doses of public rebuke. In the case of his famous *Trojan Oration* (*Or.* 11), he began by blasting his audience for having been deceived by that "liar" Homer. Dio's *First Tarsian Oration* (*Or.* 33) disavows flattery and empty encomia in delivering advice to cities. Frank criticism is called for, he says, like a doctor curing those who are really sick. It does little good to declaim *about* anatomy, no matter how eloquently; rather, the doctor must take action by prescribing what needs to be done: halting inappropriate diet or performing requisite surgery.[7] Dio's metaphor of the philosopher as doctor of the soul, his cutting words as drugs or surgery,[8] is reminiscent of Seneca:

> Our words should aim not to please, but to help.... The sick man does not call in a physician who is merely eloquent ... [instead, he says,] "Why do you tickle my ears? Why do you entertain me? There is other business at hand; I am to be cauterized, cut upon, put on a strict diet. That is why you were summoned!"
>
> (*Ep.* 75.6–7)

But as we will see, the notion of curing the soul is more than mere metaphor.

So, our deipnosophist follows suit; his proemium continues:

> It seems to me more philanthropic [φιλανθρωπότερον] by far to treat [τοῦ θεραπεύειν] [...][9] <them, by purging>[10] the rich <of their affinities>[11] toward vice [ἐπὶ κακῷ] <and> to shrink <their pride and conceit>[12] <in order to bring about>[13] a saving cure [σωτηρίαν] for them in every possible way ... on the one hand, by beseeching God on their behalf and, on the other, ... by healing their souls with reason [λόγῳ ... ἰωμένους τὰς ψυχὰς αὐτῶν].
>
> (*Quis div.* 1.4)

As doctor of the soul, he dares not to excite their passions further with ἐγκωμιαστικοὶ λόγοι (*enkōmiastikoi logoi*); instead, his words delivered with παρρησία (*parrhēsia*) are both scalpel and saw. In any case, the tone is significant, for pride (in wealth and status) is the disease of the soul that needs to be cured. What follows, then, is a speech on the character of wealth, its proper uses, and the dreaded effects of misuse.

Our orator was, of course, the Christian teacher and philosopher Clement of Alexandria. This speech is customarily referred to as his "sermon" entitled

Who Is the Rich Man That Will Be Saved? (Quis dives salvetur), an allegorical *tour de force* on the Jesus logion "It is easier for a camel to go through the eye of a needle than for a rich man to enter the kingdom of God" (Mark 10:25).[14] As suggested already, however, I doubt seriously that this speech was a "church sermon."[15] I suspect that it was part of the after-dinner fare at a Christian symposium for banqueting Alexandrian elites associated with the philosophical and catechetical school of Clement (i.e., Clement's own students and patrons, or perhaps some "prospectives"). Far from denouncing wealth, Clement actually claims that there is no virtue in poverty alone; rather, it is a matter of the proper attitude.[16] The same view of the Gospel passage is reflected in Clement's *Stromata* (2.5),[17] where he approvingly cites Plato on proper attitudes toward wealth and poverty. Following Plato's comparable sentiment regarding "the impossibility of the rich being good,"[18] Clement goes on to say that divestment of wealth is not the answer.[19] Thus, for those who might have followed the saying of Jesus literally by giving up their possessions, Clement now says, " As for the passions of their soul, I think they were even further intensified" (τὰ δὲ πάθη τῶν ψυχῶν οἶμαι ὅτι καὶ προσεπέτειναν) (*Quis div.* 12.2).[20] Thus poverty does not automatically make one better suited to a godly life, since giving up one's wealth can actually stimulate the passions to an equally dangerous degree, either because one becomes conceited in ascetic achievement or because one becomes even more absorbed by heightened desire for basic necessities.[21]

Clement's educational program

Clement's stance is a lesson in the morals of his day for an elite audience, and it is replete with philosophical commonplaces. Thus, suffused through its treatment of wealth is a set of assumptions about the nature of social etiquette, virtue and vice, and the passions. They reflect intertwined elements of the physical and moral world, and, as we will see, of medicine and the physiology of the soul. The philosopher/teacher is the guide through this maze of misperceptions and a doctor for the soul. So near the end of his address, Clement turns from narration and exposition to deliver this exhortation directly to his audience:

> Hence it is necessary that you who are pompous and powerful and rich should appoint for yourselves some man of God as a trainer and pilot [ἀλείπτην καὶ κυβερνήτην]. Let it be one whom you respect, one whom you fear, one whom you condition yourself [μελέτησον] to heed when he is frank and severe in his speech, all the while tending to your cure [θεραπεύοντος].
>
> (*Quis div.* 41.1)[22]

Here, of course, Clement is advocating that they listen to his own instruction. He will become the doctor of their souls. Indeed, one soon realizes that his exhortation here is intended to make them turn to his other philosophical instructions – known from his well-known treatises *The Exhortation to the Greeks (Protrepticus)* and *The Instructor (Paedagogus)*[23] – for the proper direction of Christians living in the cultured society of Alexandria.[24] A look at the precise nature of those instructions (as seen in sections on eating, drinking, and other practical matters in books 2 and 3 of the *Paedagogus*), however, makes it clear that we are still in the same cultural matrix as the moralist tradition of the previous two centuries.[25] This study, then, is offered as a commentary on *Quis dives salvetur* in the light of the moralist tradition.

Although Clement traditionally is described as the second head of the official "catechetical school" of Alexandria, this idea probably reflects the anachronizing orthodoxy of Eusebius.[26] In fact, there is no known historical connection between Pantaenus and Clement, or between Clement and Origen; nor was there an official catechetical institution of the church at this time.[27] We would do better, then, to think of Clement as a private teacher of rhetoric and philosophy, like the Stoics Musonius Rufus at Rome and Epictetus at Nicopolis. Justin Martyr had earlier established a private school of Christian philosophy at Rome.[28] Much like Musonius, Clement must lead the student from the delusions of an intellectually corrupt and depraved world into a new understanding of reality, a "conversion" to a new philosophy.[29] Like the pilgrims in the *Tabula of Cebes*, they must counteract the effects of Deceit ('Ἀπάτη, *Apatē*), who sends souls into life poisoned with delusion and error, and come to True Education (Παιδεία, *Paideia*), who leads to Happiness (Εὐδαιμονία, *Eudaimonia*).[30] The teacher is both mystagogue and athletic trainer.[31]

The idea of habituation (ἕξις, *hexis*) in vice and virtue was thought of as a physiological as well as moral condition that requires training (μελέτημα, *meletēma*, or ἄσκησις, *askēsis*), as we saw in Clement's exhortation quoted above (*Quis div.* 41). We may compare this with Epictetus's "educational system" (as Hijmans calls it), in which μελέτημα and ἄσκησις play a pivotal role.[32] For example, following Chrysippus,[33] Epictetus describes ἕξις this way:

> In general, therefore, if you want to do something, make a habit [ἑκτικόν] of it. If you wish *not* to do something, don't make it a habit, but rather accustom yourself [ἔθισον] to practice other things in its place. So it holds also in matters of the soul [ψυχικῶν]: whenever you become angry [ὀργισθῇς] know that not only has this particular vice come upon you, but also that you have augmented the habit, and you have, as it were, tossed kindling on the fire.... In this way also, of course, as the philosophers say, the diseases [of the soul] *erupt*.[34] For whenever you once develop a desire for money [ἐπιθυμήσῃς ἀργυρίου], if *logos* is applied to bring about a sense perception of the vice, then the desire will be arrested and our governing principle will be

> restored to its original state. But if you do not apply anything as a curative, then the governing principle is not restored.... And if this happens repeatedly, then the residual part [of the disease] becomes calloused [τυλοῦται], and the disease strengthens the avarice. For a man who develops a fever and then it is arrested, is yet not the same as before developing the fever, unless he has been cured once and for all. Something like this happens also with passions of the soul [ἐπὶ τῶν τῆς ψυχῆς παθῶν].
>
> (Diss. 2.18.5, 8–10)

These interconnections between religious ideas, moral exhortation, and medical assumptions are more than metaphorical or analogical.

To take but one brief example, we may look at the case of the first-century philosopher/healer Apollonius of Tyana.[35] We see the interconnections at the level of moral conditioning of the soul when we look at Philostratus's description of Apollonius as a young man. At age sixteen, he says, Apollonius abruptly announced to his beloved paedagogue, the philosopher Euxenus, that he would prefer to live according to the precepts of Pythagoras. Euxenus asked him how he would go about taking up the Pythagorean life: where would he begin? Philostratus thus reports Apollonius's sagacious reply and provides us with an insightful commentary:

> Apollonius answered, "At the point where physicians begin, for they by purging the bowels of their patients prevent some from being ill at all, and heal others." And having said this, he declined to live on (a diet of) meat, on the ground that it was impure and that it made the mind turgid [τὸν νοῦν παχυνούσας];[36] so he ate only dried fruits and vegetables, since he said that all fruits of the earth are pure. Of wine he said that it was a pure drink..., but he declared that it endangered the close order of the mind, and it muddied [διαθολοῦντα][37] the aether in the soul.
>
> (Philostratus, Vit. Apoll. 1.8.)

To put it in modern terms, Apollonius of Tyana went on a diet, not only for the sake of his body, but also for his soul. He had discovered that eating meat and drinking wine produced some sort of mental constipation, but a cure had been prescribed. We should remember that even the term "diet" stems from the same semantic and cultural matrix; δίαιτα (*diaita*) originally meant "the mode of life." In the derived nominal form, διαίτημα (*diaitēma*), it could also mean both "habit of living" and "the food by which one lives," and thus "diet" in the modern sense.[38] Thus, it had long been associated with the proper diet for the athlete in training the body.[39]

Here it is clear that the true philosophic guide for mortals is thought of as one who embodies within oneself the key principles of virtue and health. But so it is also in Clement's depiction of Christ as the Paedagogue. For he, too, knows the importance of diet in maintaining control of the passions. Clement says,

> "It is good neither to eat flesh meat nor drink wine," as both he [i.e., Paul in Rom 14:21] and the Pythagoreans agree; for this practice (diet) is more like beasts. And the rising spirits [ἀναθυμίασις] that come from them, being *muddier* [θολωδεστέρα],[40] darken the soul [ἐπισκοτεῖ τῇ ψυχῇ]. If one partakes of these things he does not sin; only let him take a portion with temperance [μόνον ἐγκρατῶς μετεχέτω], seeming to be neither slavishly dependent [ἀπηρτημένος][41] on them nor looking on them with a gluttonous eye.
> (*Paed.* 2.1[11.1])

We will return to discuss this terminology of "muddying" the soul, since Clement's language is similar, *but not identical*, to that found in the Pythagorean tradition. As we will see, his source is instead Stoic, and he read Paul – rightly, I believe – as representing a similar view.[42]

Within this moralist tradition, the philosopher as doctor of the soul, I will argue, is more than just a metaphor of spiritual health. It is more visceral than that. Clement, like the other moral guides, gives instructions on how to live better, but this means controlling both soul and body. It is not a matter of wealth versus poverty alone, but one of attitude and self-control through disciplining body and soul against the effects of the passions. Thus, to return to Clement's address to the wealthy symposiasts, he continues:

> So let a person do away [ἀφανιζέτω], *not* with his possessions, but rather with the passions of his soul [τὰ πάθη τῆς ψυχῆς], which do not allow [συγχωροῦντα] the better use [χρῆσιν] of what he possesses; so that by becoming noble and good, he may be able to use these possessions in a right manner. So, then, "to give up all one's possessions" [cf. Luke 14:33] and "to sell all one's property" [cf. Matt 19:21] must be taken in this manner, as referring clearly to the passions of the soul.
> (*Quis div.* 14.5–6)

The problem is that the passions war against the moral impulses that govern proper "use" (χρῆσις, *chrēsis*) by clouding the soul's perceptions. So, says Clement, one must

> expel [ἐξορίσαι] from the soul its opinions [δόγματα] concerning riches – its affinity [συμπάθειαν] for them, its excessive desire [ὑπεράγαν ἐπιθυμίαν], its agitation and dementia [πτοίαν καὶ νόσον] over them, its anxious cares [μερίμνας] – those thorns of daily life [βίου] which choke out the seed of the (true) life [τῆς ζωῆς].
> (*Quis div.* 11.2)[43]

But how should we do this, Clement? He replies:

> Well, it is just as in the case of athletes ... and so should the rich of this world consider himself. For the athlete who has no hope of being able to win and to obtain crowns does not even enroll himself for the contest; while another who may entertain such a hope in his heart, but who does not submit to hardships and exercises and proper food, will emerge (from the contest) uncrowned and will miss the mark of his hopes. In the same way then, let the one with riches ... not have such a hope, if he remains untrained [ἀνάσκητος] and untested [ἀναγώνιστος], who would without dust and sweat receive the crowns of incorruptibility. Instead, let him subject himself to reason as trainer [γυμναστῇ μὲν τῷ λόγῳ] and to Christ as master of the athletic contest [ἀγωνοθέτῃ δὲ τῷ Χριστῷ].
> (*Quis. div.* 3.3–6)[44]

So, now Clement, as philosophic instructor, takes on another role. Not only is he physician of the soul, who prescribes harsh medicines or surgery to cure the ill, but also he is its athletic trainer, the one who gives it appropriate exercises (ἄσκησις, *askēsis*) to provide strength and endurance for the arduous contest (ἀγών, *agōn*) of life. The enemy, however, is not wealth per se – certainly not in Clement's social circles – but avarice, conceit, and the other passions of the soul that threaten to enslave the wealthy by distorting their perceptions. Clement clearly invests these ideas with a Christian coloring, but he assumes that his cultured audience will recognize and assent to the basic outlines of his educational system because it conforms to the highest ideals of medicine and philosophy of the time. It shows the interconnections that they assumed between body and soul, between medicine and morality. For Clement and his contemporaries, the training and progress of the soul depended on the cure of the passions.

In the remaining portions of this essay my aim is to locate Clement's moral exhortation more carefully within the physiological and anthropological assumptions of his day. I will take up three related aspects: (1) the pathology of the soul and its cure, (2) moral progress as psychagogy ("direction of the soul"), and (3) the pharmacology of *logos*.

The pathology of the soul

So far, we have seen comments from Clement referring to a soul that is composed of *aether* (or some clear, airy substance), but which, depending on what one eats or drinks, can become either *flaccid, thick and distended, muddied and darkened, or cancerous and calloused*. While much of this sounds like commonsense observations on human behavior expressed in metaphorical terms, the physiological and medical assumptions are important. For much of the Greco-Roman philosophical tradition in the first and second centuries, the human soul remained a "vague kind of 'stuff.'"[45] Although Plato had characterized the soul as incorporeal (ἀσώματος, *asōmatos*), others – the Stoics and Epicureans in particular – took a materialist view. The soul itself was thought of as corporeal, or as A.A. Long says, "substance in its own right which permeates the flesh and bones body."[46]

A generation after Clement, the Platonic conception of the soul reemerged through the rise of Neoplatonism, as seen in Plotinus, Iamblichus, and Origen.[47] Throughout the first three centuries, however, Stoic physiology remained normative in both medicine and ethical theory, and it is now recognized among Jewish and early Christian moralists, including Philo, Paul, and Clement. For example, in *Strom.* 5.8(90.4–91.4), Clement discusses the important Platonic passage from *Phaed.* 112–13. He agrees that the soul is immortal, but he takes the notion of punishments in Tartarus/Gehenna as a sign that it is still sensible – that is, corporeal.[48] Thus, Clement, like Galen and other contemporaries, shows an eclectic blend of Stoic and Platonic elements, but ordered into a system of practical ethical instruction based on ideas of training and habituation, medicine and health. Moral exhortation was thus also "therapy of the soul."[49]

Medical language was a widely used *topos* among the moralist philosophers.[50] This *topos* contains three interrelated components: (1) passions and vices are diseases of the soul; (2) the philosopher is the doctor of the soul; (3) reason or philosophical instruction is the medicine or cure.[51] Yet given the assumptions about the nature of the soul, these were more than mere metaphors. So we may note in Philo where the soul is depicted as a battleground between the externals (which lead to vice) and moral excellence or virtue; the former attack the latter as disease, since the soul "is not perfectly purified, but its passions and diseases grow up and choke out its healthy principles of reason" (*Abr.* 220–3).[52] The passions stimulate and irritate the soul through "their itchings and ticklings that arise from pleasure and desire" (*Det.* 110). Recall Clement's earlier comment regarding moderation in eating meat or drinking wine: to be "neither slavishly dependent [ἀπηρτημένος] on them nor looking on them with a gluttonous eye" (*Paed.* 2.1[11.1]). The usage of ἀπηρτημένος (*apērtēmenos*) here is similar to that in Lucian, *Tim.* 36, where it clearly means "to be dependent upon something."[53] In context, Lucian refers to learning "dependence on oneself" through poverty, hence a virtual synonym for the Cynic's αὐτάρκεια (*autarkeia*).[54] Lucian thus counterposes it to the sense of enslavement to luxuries that corrupt and harm the individual. I suggest that this is Clement's sense as well. To Lucian's description of the lures of such luxuries and his notion of being abandoned to them, compare *Tabula of Cebes* 9. In this passage, the "titillation" (γαργαλισμός, *gargalismos*) of pleasure is understood as a physical effect that enslaves the individual by stimulating the passions and deluding rational perception, or what would be thought of in modern terms as the enslavement of an addiction.[55]

So compare, then, the opening lines of Clement's less well-known moral treatise, *An Exhortation to Endurance* (Προτρέπτικος εἰς ὑπομονήν).[56] It extols the cultivation of "quietness" (ἡσυχία, *hēsychia*), which keeps the soul steady, as the antidote to the passions, specifically where agitation is the trap that leads to passion and vice.

> Cultivate quietness in word [ἡσυχίαν μὲν λόγοις ἐπιτήδευε], quietness in deed, likewise also in speech and in gait; avoid impetuous rashness [σφοδρότητα προπετῆ]. For thus will the mind remain steady [νοῦς βέβαιος], and will not be agitated [ταραχώδης] by your impetuousness and so become weak and diminished in judgment and see darkly. Nor will it yield to gluttony, yield to boiling rage, or yield to the other passions [παθῶν], lying exposed before them ready to be raped [ἕτοιμον αὐτοῖς ἅρπαγμα προκείμενος]. For the mind – seated on high upon a quiet throne looking toward God – must control the passions.
> (*Exhortation to Endurance* 1)[57]

Quietness is an antidote to the unstable impulses (ὁρμαί, *hormai*) that stimulate the passions.[58]

Similarly, Plutarch talks about the need for tranquility of mind (εὐθυμία, *euthymia*) as the steady state that resists ἐπιθυμία (*epithymia*) and the other passions,[59] while Dio says that passions and vice cause "corruption" of the soul.[60] The goal is ἀπάθεια (*apatheia*), being unmoved or agitated by passions such as anger or greed: "salvation belongs to passionless and pure souls (ἀπαθῶν καὶ καθαρῶν ψυχῶν)" (*Quis div.* 20.6).[61] Clement also describes it this way:

> The most severe persecution is that from within, which proceeds from one's own soul, since it is ruined [λυμαινομένης] by godless desires, manifold pleasures, vulgar hopes, and corrupting dreams [φθαρτικῶν ὀνειροπολημάτων]; ever coveting more and enraged [λυσσῶσα] by *fierce erotic desires* [ἀγρίων ἐρώτων] and being inflamed [φλεγομένη] ... it is stung [ἐξαιμάσσηται] by its attendant passions into frenzied excitement [πρὸς σπουδὰς μανιώδεις].
> (*Quis div.* 25.4)

With the phrase "fierce erotic desires" (ἀγρίων ἐρώτων, *agriōn erōtōn*), Clement, once again, alludes to Plato regarding the deleterious effects of sexual desire.[62] Stimulating the passions, by whatever means, produces and is produced by "agitation" in soul and body.

Writing at the same time as Clement was Galen (ca. 129–200), whose works show us the physiological assumptions of moral philosophy from the medical side. In his treatise *On the Passions of the Soul* (*De affectuum dignotione*),[63] Galen says,

> Since sins occur from false opinions [ἁμαρτήματα διὰ τὴν ψευδῆ(ν) δόξαν] and passion from an unreasoned impulse [ἄλογον ὁρμήν], it seems to me that one should first free oneself from the passions, for these also make us judge wrongly. Now the passions of the soul which all acknowledge are temper, anger, fear, grief, envy and extreme desire.
> (*De affect. dig.* 3.1)[64]

Galen's works show that medical knowledge and assumptions had changed some since the Classical period. In part, these changed assumptions (and the debates that go with them) also reflect the changing social climate and cultural orientations of the shift to Roman power.[65] According to Galen, the passions were physiological distortions in the corporeal soul caused by imbalances in the four elements, the four humors, and the four qualities. The key seems to be found in Galen's idea of the passions as a product of motion or change in the soul:

> Of motions [κινήσεως] there are two sorts, alteration and change of place; when the alteration becomes an abiding condition, it is named *disease* [νόσημα], being clearly a condition contrary to nature. And sometimes, while misapplying the term, we call this condition a *pathos*.
> (*De loc. affect.* 1.3)[66]

These imbalances might be stimulated or "set in motion" either by external sense impressions or by consuming the wrong types of food and drink.[67] Similarly, Clement says,

> Impulse [ὁρμή], then, is a rush of the mind toward or away from something. Passion [πάθος] is an <u>impulse that exceeds</u> or surpasses the measure of <u>reason</u> [πλεονάζουσα ὁρμὴ ἢ ὑπερτείνουσα τὰ κατὰ τὸν λόγον μέτρα], or an impulse that is unbridled and disobedient to reason. The passions, then, are a <u>movement of the soul contrary to nature</u> [παρὰ φύσιν οὖν κίνησις ψυχῆς] in disobedience to reason.
> (*Strom.* 2.13[59.6])[68]

Ultimately, these ideas on the relationship between body and soul go back to Zeno and Chrysippus.[69]

In general, then, we may say that the later Hellenistic to the early Roman imperial period was dominated by a particular set of views of the nature of the soul (ψυχή, *psychē*) and its relation to the body (σῶμα, *sōma*). As R.J. Hankinson has shown, Galen, despite his Platonic leanings, is still heavily influenced by Stoic writers and their view of the material soul.[70] Here, Stoic metaphysics, physics, and ethics will begin to intersect. The soul, then, was the "organ" of sense and perception, but one must be on guard against those things that might distort the healthy judgments, including false perceptions (φαντασίαι, *phantasiai*) or undue stimuli that cloud the soul's rational powers.

Here we may note a peculiar feature of Stoic theory and its particular appropriation by Clement and other practical moralists. For Chrysippus held that the passions arise from false opinions, beliefs, or judgments.[71] This view led to criticism and debate over whether the rational principle of the soul could be tainted or corrupted, and thus *cause* sin. Most later Stoics modified this position in order to maintain the inviolability of the rational principle.[72] In particular, Posidonius had relegated all the passions and their effects to the irrational parts of the soul alone, thus creating a discontinuous, disjointed, or "conflicted" sense of the human self.[73] By contrast, some of the practical moralists, notably Musonius, Epictetus, and especially Galen, seem to have reverted to a more "physicalist" approach to the problem by asserting that how one cares for the body can affect the rational powers, *and thereby* the condition of one's soul. Thus, training of the soul required attention to the training of the body.[74] Galen says,

> The character of the soul [τὸ τῆς ψυχῆς ἦθος.] is corrupted by poor habits in food, drink, exercise, sights, sounds, and all the arts. Therefore the one pursuing medicine should be practiced in all these things, and should not think that it is proper only for the philosopher to shape the character of the soul.
> (*De sanit. tuen.* 1.8)[75]

Elsewhere Galen puts it terms of moral progress:

> So now at least, let those who are displeased [with the premise] that food can cause [ἐργάζεσθαι] people to be more sensible or more licentious, more in command or less in command of themselves, bold or cowardly, mild and gentle or contentious and competitive. Let them come to me and learn what they should eat and drink. For they will be greatly benefited towards ethical philosophy [εἴς τε γὰρ τὴν ἠθικὴν φιλοσοφίαν ὀνήσονται] and in addition they will improve towards virtue [ἐπιδώσουσιν εἰς ἀρετὴν] in the capacities of the rational part [κατὰ τὰς τοῦ λογιστικοῦ δυνάμεις].
> (*Quod. an. mor.* 9)[76]

In turning to Clement, we find that he at first praises those Stoics who argue that "the soul is *not* affected by the body, either to vice or disease, virtue or health" (*Strom.* 4.5[19.1]). But in the continuation of this same discussion he argues that the inclinations of the body, and especially the passions, can delude, distract, or impair the operations of the rational soul.

> When pain [of body or mind (ἀλγηδόνος)] is present, the soul appears to shrink back from it and consider riddance of its presence a gift. At

that moment, it also becomes sluggish [ῥᾳθυμεῖ] with regard to its lessons, whence the other virtues are utterly neglected [ἀπημέληνται]. And yet we do not say that virtue itself suffers (for virtue is not affected by disease). But the person who is composed jointly of both, virtue and disease, is distressed [θλίβεται] by the urgent necessity. And if he happens not to be extremely high-minded [καταμεγαλοφρονῶν], not heretofore establishing the habit of self-control [τὴν ἕξιν τῆς ἐγκρατείας], he becomes distraught, and he discovers that not enduring is equivalent to fleeing. The same reasoning holds true concerning poverty. For it compels the soul to desist [αὕτη τῶν ἀναγκαίων ... ἀπασχολεῖν βιάζεται τὴν ψυχήν] from what is necessary.

(*Strom.* 4.5[20.1–21.1])

The last comment is consistent with Clement's argument in *Quis div*. 12.2 that giving up one's possessions might lead to intensifying the passions of the soul.[77] So, Clement seems to be following a distinctive line within the Stoic tradition, in keeping with the contemporary medical thinking of Galen and the practical ascetic tradition of Musonius. This feature of his thought will become even more apparent when we look at his views on eating.[78]

Moral progress as psychagogy

Clement, like other moralists, calls for the soul to be kept quiet, not to be stirred by external impressions that stimulate the passions. Often the *hēgemonikon*, or the *logical* faculty of mind, is depicted as a charioteer or teamster straining at the bridle to rein in wild horses.[79] The metaphor is found already in Plato (*Phaedr.* 246A–D), who also likens it to difference between children and adults, whose rational faculties have developed more control. Thus, the passions and desires of the soul are likened to unruly children over against the rational principle as parent. What provides the restraint is education and training of the soul.[80] This is the notion of *psychagogy* ("direction of the soul"), a term used especially among the Roman Epicureans.[81]

This notion can be seen in the treatise known as the *Tabula of Cebes*. It is a pseudonymous work attributed to Cebes the Theban, a member of the Socratic circle, but it was actually produced in the first century CE, probably within the eclectic or practical Stoic school.[82] Often considered a metaphoric depiction of the "pathway of Life," it has sometimes been referred to as the *Pilgrim's Progress* of the Classical world. The text also reflects some of the underlying physiological and psychagogical assumptions of the moralist tradition. So, we may notice that the allegory of the tablet opens with people (presumably, anthropomorphic "souls") stationed at a gate as they are about to "enter Life" (ὁ βίος, *ho bios*). Their pathway into life is directed by the *Daimon*, as guide to the soul.[83] In their journey through life they encounter the vagaries of fickle "Fortune" (*Tychē*), who gives and takes from any and all as they pass by her. Wealth, fortune, children, health, and even life itself are random, not to be trusted or counted upon.

But why is it that most people fail to recognize this fact? Why do most people put such great hope and stock in these things? Because they have been deluded by Deceit ('Ἀπάτη, *Apatē*) as they enter life.[84] Thus they enter the world as a soul mixed with delusions and "false opinions" about what is properly in one's control and what is not, and hence, what is good and what is evil. Moreover, they are constantly seduced by alluring courtesans – the vices of Sexual Incontinence, Profligacy, Covetousness, and Flattery[85] – who lie in wait, titillate, and flatter them, and lead them astray into the realm of Luxury (ἡδυπάθεια, *hēdypatheia*),[86] so that they can no longer extricate themselves. The *Tabula of Cebes* depicts an implicit physiology of the perceptions clouded through ignorance and vice. The antidote is brought by Education (Παιδεία, *Paideia*), once again personified as a woman, who leads the pilgrim soul to true understanding and thence to Happiness herself. Happiness lives secluded in a garden of repose aloft on a rough and rocky summit.[87] The path to Happiness is harsh and calls for endurance and perseverance. But the one who endures and overcomes is crowned with happiness.

> "When someone arrives here what does she [Happiness] do?"
> "Happiness crowns him with her power... as do all the other Virtues, in the same way that one crowns those who have been victorious in the mightiest contests [ἀγῶνας]."
> "Well, what kinds of contests has he won?"
> "The mightiest... overcoming even the mightiest beasts, which previously used to devour, abuse, and enslave him.... He has mastered [κεκράτηκεν] himself, so that these beasts are his slaves just as he was once theirs."
>
> (*Ceb. Tab.* 22.1–2)

Who are these beasts that have been overcome? The answer is: "Ignorance, Deceit... Grief, Lamentation, Avarice, Sexual Incontinence, and all the other vices" (*Ceb. Tab.* 23.1–2). The vices are the passions of the soul. Although the athletic term *askēsis* ("training") does not appear in this text, the semantic complex related to the *agōn* ("contest") motif is clearly present, as seen in the passage quoted above.[88] It points to the same notion of discipline and training in order to be prepared for the contest. Wrestling with the vices (including false opinions, the passions, and sexual desires), along with perseverance and endurance of hardship, are part of the training of the moral athlete in the trials of life. Clement uses a similar image: "For the mind, seated on high on a quiet throne looking toward God, must control the passions" (*Exhortation to Endurance* 1).[89]

The *Tabula of Cebes* is more than just an allegory of life. It encodes a certain understanding of the nature of the soul and its governance. It also advocates a particular mode of life (a *diet* or *viaticum*) best exemplified by the philosophic tradition. Those who reach Happiness are expected to go back down the hill to the rest of humanity and help show them the way. But first they must undergo a repentance or reorientation (μετάνοια, *metanoia*) to a proper understanding (διάνοια, *dianoia*) through education.[90] The one who attains this state has an antidote (ἀντιφάρμακον, *antipharmakon*) to the poison of deceit.[91] By their own lives and struggles they are to exemplify the proper attitudes that will make it possible for others to live well. They are, then, the doctors of the soul for others.[92] In the final analysis, the *Tabula of Cebes* is a piece of philosophic propaganda, an advertisement for a system of psychagogy, or "soul direction."[93] These notions reflect the attitudes toward wealth, sexuality, and life found commonly among the philosophical moralists, in particular among the later Cynics and what may be called the "cynicizing" or practical Stoics. At stake, they would say, is finding the "truth" – meaning proper opinions, doctrines, and reason – that keeps the soul properly conditioned to ward off the virulent effects of passion. Traditional Stoicism, on the other hand, suffered some criticism in this area, since it seemed to suggest that one is either *sophos* or ignorant, or that the change from vice to virtue is somehow immediate. Such a critique of classical Stoic doctrine is precisely the point of Plutarch's treatise *How May One Perceive His Moral Progress toward Virtue?* (Πῶς ἄν τις αἴσθοιτο ἑαυτοῦ προκόπτοντος ἐπ' ἀρετῇ). Thus, among the practical or "cynicizing" Stoics (where I would also locate the *Tabula of Cebes*), the idea of training to achieve moral progress (προκοπή, *prokopē*) was emphasized.

This is most clearly seen in the work of the Roman Stoic Musonius Rufus (ca. 30–101 CE) and his student the Greek Epictetus (ca. 55–135 CE).[94] In general, Musonius gives more specific attention to physical training and topics concerning bodily regimen than does Epictetus. Musonius is also of considerable importance for the present discussion because Clement quotes him at length, albeit without attribution, in the practical ethical sections of the *Paedagogus*. Just as in medicine, music, or sailing it is more important to practice well than simply to understand the theory behind the art, so also in the pursuit of virtue it is better to *be* self-controlled and abstinent than to teach the same. Therefore, when one learns about a particular virtue, one should follow the lesson with "training" (ἄσκησις, *askēsis*).[95]

Musonius distinguishes two types of *askēsis*: one that is proper to the soul alone, and one that is common to soul and body together, acting in concert. The latter type involves becoming "accustomed" – the key term here is μελετάω / μελέτημα (*meletaō* / *meletēma*), a synonym for ἄσκησις[96] – to bodily discomforts, including "cold, heat, thirst, hunger, plain food, hard beds, avoidance of pleasures, and endurance of suffering" (frg. 6).[97] Musonius says,

> How then, and in what manner, should they receive such training? Since it so happens that the human being is not soul alone or body

alone, but a kind of synthesis of the two, the person in training must take care of both, the better part, the soul more zealously, as is fitting, but also of the other.... Training that is peculiar to the soul [ἰδία δὲ τῆς ψυχῆς ἄσκησις] is first and foremost seeing that proofs pertaining to apparent goods as not being real goods are always ready at hand.... In the next place it consists of practice [μελετᾶν] ... in shunning by every means those which are truly evil and in pursuing by every means those which are truly good.

(frg. 6)[98]

By such habituation to hardship[99] through endurance the body becomes sturdy and ready for work, but the soul also is trained for certain virtues, "for courage [ἀνδρείαν] through endurance and for self-control [σωφροσύνην] through avoidance of pleasures." Although one may be more concerned with the soul, as the "better" part, one should care for and train the body, which is, after all, often the instrument of virtue.[100] Thus even the cardinal virtues may be developed and strengthened, like an athlete, by *bodily* training and style of life (i.e., δίαιτα [*diaita*], "diet").[101]

It is also quite significant that Musonius thought that the lessons of philosophy should be available for women as well as men.[102] This was somewhat unusual at the time, but Musonius argued that women should be trained in philosophy, and that such training will make them more virtuous wives and daughters, better housekeepers, and more loving mothers. Still, he suggests that their ability to progress in these "womanly virtues" is dependent upon their abilities to control their passions through training and habituation, in the same way that men needed to. For men and women, according to Musonius, the goal is to establish a daily regimen that inculcates the ideal of virtue. Hence marriage, labor, or even exile is no impediment to a more virtuous life.[103] Thus, he also gives extensive discussions of proper types of food and manners in eating and drinking,[104] household furnishings,[105] as well as instructions on sexual matters.[106] These are characterized by the key Stoic terms αὐτάρκεια (*autarkeia*) and ἀπάθεια (*apatheia*), meaning "self-sufficiency" and "apathy," or rather "absence of passions." In regard to clothing, housing, and furnishings, one should choose only that which meets the basic needs of the body and avoid that which leads to excess, physical weakness, and vulnerability. The catchword for such excesses is "luxury" (τρυφή, *tryphē*).[107] Luxury is a particular danger, as it injures both the body (through weakness) and the soul (through loss of self-control and courage). As in the *Tabula of Cebes*, luxury "enslaves" or "makes one dependent" through constant titillation. Even though the mind might be shocked into awareness, full recovery requires training.

When he discusses food and eating, Musonius connects bodily regimen even more directly to the soul's health, as one might expect. Not only does he argue that cheap, natural, and easily prepared foods are best for the simple lifestyle of the philosopher, but also he notes that certain foods are better for the soul and more suitable for humans, who are like the gods and should therefore eat like the gods. Of course, the gods are satisfied with "vapors rising up from the earth and water" – not quite sufficient for most humans – so the human diet should be thin, light, and dry in imitation of divine nourishment. Meat fits none of these criteria and should be avoided, not only because it is more suited to wild beasts than to civilized humans to eat flesh, but also because meat is a "heavy" food and therefore dulls the intellect and the reasoning process, and in general "darkens" the soul. Musonius

> held that it was a heavy food and an obstacle to thinking and reasoning, since the rising spirits that come from it, being muddier, darken the soul [τὴν γὰρ ἀναθυμίασιν τὴν ἀπ' αὐτῆς θολωδεστέραν οὖσαν ἐπισκοτεῖν τῇ ψυχῇ].
>
> (frg. 18A)[108]

In fact, Musonius (rather than the Pythagoreans) is Clement's source for this idea, which he quotes verbatim in *Paed.* 2.1(11.1).[109]

The glutton, then, is the exemplar of all that is wrong with luxurious eating, but the results are obvious too: with increased girth comes increased desire and appetite. As one's desire increases, so other passions are stimulated. It is – to use an idiom apropos to the moralists – a vicious cycle. Clement says,

> For as we must use food in order not to be hungry, so also we must use drink in order not to be thirsty, guarding closely against a slip, for "the introduction of wine is dangerous" [Prov 20:1]. And thus shall our soul be pure, dry, and luminous [καθαρὰ καὶ ξηρὰ καὶ φωτοειδής]; for "the clear dry soul is wisest and best [αὐγὴ δὲ ψυχὴ ξηρὰ σοφωτάτη καὶ ἀρίστη]."
>
> (*Paed.* 2.2[29.2–3])[110]

Here we may also compare Plutarch's views on eating meat:

> When we examine the sun through moist air and clouds of rising vapors [ἀναθυμιάσεων πλήθους ἀπέπτων] we see it not pure and bright, but rather deep and misty with displaced rays of light. In the same way, then, when the body is darkened and surfeited and burdened with unsuitable[111] food [σώματος θολεροῦ καὶ διακόρου καὶ βαρυνομένου τροφαῖς ἀσυμφύλοις], because the freshness and light of the soul [τὸ γάνωμα τῆς ψυχῆς καὶ τὸ φέγγος] of necessity acquire dullness and confusion [ἀμβλύτητα καὶ σύγχυσιν] and are deluded and confounded [πλανᾶσθαι καὶ φύρεσθαι], if [the soul] lacks the brightness and tone [αὐγὴν καὶ τόνον] to work out the small and hard to perceive qualities of things.
>
> (*De esu* 1.6 [*Mor.* 995F–996A])

Clement echoes similar notions regarding the affects of the passions on the clarity and perception of the soul:

> For just as the vapors [ἀναθυμιάσεις] that rise from the earth and from marshes gather into mists and dense cloudy masses, so also the exhalations of fleshly lusts [αἱ τῶν σαρκικῶν ἐπιθυμιῶν ἀναδόσεις] inflict a bad disposition [καχεξίαν] upon the soul [ψυχῇ] since they shower phantom images of pleasure [εἴδωλα τῆς ἡδονῆς] before the soul. Thus, they spread darkness on the intelligent light [ἐπισκοτοῦσι γοῦν τῷ φωτὶ τῷ νοερῷ], when the soul drinks in the exhalations of lust and the thickening clouds of the passions by persistence of pleasures.
> (*Strom.* 2.20[115.3–116.1])[112]

Thus, diet and habit are related to the soul and its perceptions. The person who would be perfect needs a moral guide to serve as trainer and coach, as well as doctor and surgeon.

There was thus a widespread tendency among the moralists to relate habituation in all areas of life (including diet and care of the body) to ethical formation. As we begin to draw these threads together, then, it may be worth noting that the treatment of eating, drinking, decoration, and sexuality by Clement in his *Paedagogus* draws extensively on the work of Musonius along with that of Plutarch, Athenaeus, and, I now suspect, Galen.[113] As we have seen, much of it is direct quotation from Musonius.[114] In my own studies of this matter I have identified a total of forty-three direct quotations of Musonius in *Paed.* 2–3. In fact, this entire section of the *Paedagogus* is peppered with paraphrases as well as verbatim quotations from Musonius, none of them attributed,[115] even as Clement freely interweaves them with scriptural passages to create a new interpretive filter. Now even the *words* of Socrates have become the words of Jesus the Paedagogue, as we see in the case of a famous aphorism: "It is better to eat to live than to live to eat."[116] Jesus, through Clement, teaches that the ideal body is a sign of controlling the passions and the proper balance of body and soul.

The pharmacology of *logos*

The final feature of the physiological assumptions that accompanied moral philosophy is the role of *logos* – that is, reason or speech. But for Clement, of course, the *Logos* was also Christ, representing the continuum between the divine and human realms transmitted through the spirit to the soul.[117] Ultimately, it is the *Logos* that cures the passions of the soul, and thus brings about perfection, incorruption, and salvation.[118] The philosopher's *logos*, as part of the art of persuasion (or protreptic), should be a part of this continuum too.[119] Just as with diseases of the body, so also with those of the soul treatment, purgatives, medicines, and surgery are needed. The doctor of the soul must diagnose and prescribe, not only in general terms, but also for the specific symptoms of each case.

Here, we may note Plutarch's treatise on disease: *Whether the Diseases of the Soul Are Worse Than Those of the Body*. The traditional Latin rendering of the title – with *affectiones* as the translation for the Greek πάθη – sums up nicely the inextricable connections of body and soul, of medicine and morality in the ancient world:

> Many of your diseases and passions, O human, your body naturally produces of itself, and it receives also many that befall it from without; but if you lay yourself open on the inside, you will find a storehouse and treasury, as Democritus says, of all manner of evils and "polypathetic" (conditions) which do not flow from the outside, but have, as it were, subterranean and earth-born springs, which Vice, being widely diffused and propagated by those passions, causes to gush forth. And if the diseases in the flesh are detected by the pulse and biliousness, so also temperatures and sudden pains confirm their presence. But the evils in the soul escape the notice of most people, because they are worse evils, since they also deprive the sufferer of any awareness of themselves. For although reason, if sound, perceives the diseases which affect the body, yet, being itself infected with those of the soul, it can form no (sound) judgment of its own afflictions, for it is affected in the very part in which it renders judgment. And of the soul's diseases, one must count as the first and greatest, ignorance, which causes Vice beyond hope of cure to abide in most people – accompanying them throughout life and joining them in death. For the beginning of the riddance of disease is perception [αἴσθησις] which leads the sufferer to make use of what will relieve it.
>
> (*An. corp.* 2 [*Mor.* 500D–F])

In this light, we must now begin to reintegrate the rhetorical or paraenetic dimensions of the moralist tradition into its pathology and pharmacology.

As Plutarch says, because of its diseases, the soul cannot always make the decision to turn for help or seek a cure. As we saw in the *Tabula of Cebes*, some of the moralists posited that the human soul was plagued by "deceit" (ἀπάτη, *apatē*) from inception, which in turn causes it to follow false opinions and vice.[120] So, it appears on this view that the human condition is trapped in a vicious circle: ignorance produces false opinion; false opinion stirs up the passions; the passions lead into one after another vice, which in turn cause more disease, vice, and ignorance.[121] Humanity needs a doctor and guide to help turn it toward health and virtue.[122]

The philosopher's speech should be one of the tools of therapy. So, let us return once more to Clement's concluding exhortation near the end of his speech:

> Hence it is necessary that you who are pompous and powerful and rich should appoint for yourselves some man of God as a trainer and pilot [ἀλείπτην καὶ κυβερνήτην]. Let it be one whom you respect, one whom you fear, one whom you accustom yourself [μελέτησον] to heed, even when he is frank and severe in his speech [κἂν ἑνὸς παρρησιαζομένου καὶ στύφοντος], all the while tending to your cure [θεραπεύοντος]. Nay, it is not good for the eyes to remain for long times unchastened [ἀκολάστοις]; better, to weep and sting [δακρῦσαι καὶ δηχθῆναι] for the sake of better health [ὑγείας]. So, also, there is no more fatal disease [ὀλεθριώτερον][123] for a soul [ψυχῇ] than uninterrupted pleasure [διηνεκοῦς ἡδονῆς]. From its wasting effect [τήξεως], [pleasure] causes blindness (of the soul), so long as the soul remains unstirred [ἀκίνητος] by reason delivered with frankness of speech.
> (*Quis div.* 41.1)

So, notice that a soul infected by passions and mired in vice may need to be shaken out its stupor before it can be put on the road to recovery. In effect, this is what Clement means by true Christian *gnosis*.[124] Like medicine, which applied "opposites" to treat specific symptoms, so too, says Clement, frank words must be applied to treat the sick soul by "stirring" or "moving" it, by applying fear and grief to counter the enslaving passions and the dulling effects of pleasure. The right words, delivered with just the right tone depending on the nature of the problem, are like the doctor's medicines. Here we may compare Galen again:

> But if there is anyone who still is enslaved in any measure to the passions yet who is able to gain knowledge of them from the foregoing words, then, just as I have said earlier, <u>let him appoint for himself</u> [ἐπιστήσας ἑαυτῷ] someone as <u>mystagogue and paedagogue</u> [ἐπόπτην τινὰ καὶ παιδαγωγόν], who will, as the occasion arises, remind [ἀναμιμνῄσκων], scold [ἐπιπλήττων], exhort [προτρέπων], and urge [παρορμῶν] him to be better, even as he offers himself in everything as a model [παράδειγμα] of what he both says and exhorts, and shall he thus prepare him with reason to be both free and good in soul. For it would be shameful to make much of freedom in matters of human laws, and yet not to show zeal for the freedom that is actually by nature, instead to be enslaved to those shameful, wanton, and tyrannical mistresses – avarice, pettiness, love of reputation, love of rule, and love of honor. Yet I do not hesitate to say that the mother of all these is excessive desire [πλεονεξία]. Who indeed having these [passions] in his soul is able to become truly good?
> (*De affect. dig.* 10.2–4)[125]

It is worth noting, then, that Galen similarly relates an encounter that he had with a "rich young man" who was seeking guidance about becoming more perfect.[126] Galen's answer comes in terms of the need for "self-sufficiency" (αὐτάρκεια, *autarkeia*) in order to counter the effects of the passion of "insatiability" (ἀπληστία, *aplēstia*) in acquiring more wealth and civic standing.[127] Galen, like Clement, argues for a proper understanding of the "utility of wealth [lit., 'possessions']" (ἡ χρεία τῶν κτημάτων, *hē chreia tōn ktēmatōn*) and "moderation" (συμμετρία, *symmetria*) in its use.[128]

Ancient rhetoric was supposed to achieve emotional effects in the souls of its hearers. So we may compare Philostratus's description of the effects of the appeal made by Aelius Aristides to the emperor Marcus Aurelius, who was said to groan out loud and weep over Aristides' words.[129] These were calculated and intentional reactions in the art of ancient rhetoric.[130] In Quintilian and other rhetorical theorists the thoughts and impressions (φαντασίαι, *phantasiai*) stimulated by the speaker were part of the artistry of the speech, aimed to arouse passions (πάθη, *pathē*) and excite the soul to motion (κίνησις, *kinēsis*).[131] Plato had already linked psychagogy and rhetoric:

> Since the faculty of speech possesses a soul-directing quality [ψυχαγωγία], the one who is about to become a rhetorician must know what form the soul takes.... He must therefore acquire a proper knowledge of these classes and then be able to follow them accurately in practice.
>
> (*Phaedr.* 271D–E)

From Philostratus we may also infer that this is finally what distinguished the mere orators (or sophists) from true philosophers, for the latter were concerned with the properly edifying effects of their speech, and not just their emotive results.[132] Clement likewise warned against those mere "sophists" who "tickle and titillate the ears."[133]

Now we may see why, since stimulating the emotions might produce negative effects if not carefully handled. On the other hand, the philosophic doctor might use the same techniques to diagnose the moral health of the audience and respond appropriately for their cure. The type of speech selected is important. Here we may think of Epictetus's responses to the many potential students and auditors who passed through his school. Perhaps more to the point, consider Lucian's description of the effects of Nigrinus's "preaching" about the passions and virtue:

> When he had said this... he ended his speech. Until then I had listened to him in awe, fearing that he would stop. When he stopped, I felt like the Phaeacians of old, for I stared at him for a long time spellbound. Afterwards, in a great fit of confusion and giddiness, I dripped with sweat, I stumbled and stuck in my endeavor to speak, my voice failed, my tongue faltered, and finally I began to cry in embarrassment; for the effect he produced in me was not superficial

or casual. My wound was deep and visceral, and his words, shot with great accuracy, *dissected* [διέκοψε] my soul. For if I too may now adopt the language of the philosopher, my conception of the matter is that the soul of the man of good disposition resembles a most tender target.... A good bowman, like Nigrinus, first of all scans the target closely for fear that it may be either very soft or too hard for his arrow – for there are, of course, impenetrable targets. When he is clear on this point, he dips his arrow ... in a sweet, gently-working drug [φάρμακον], and then shoots with skill. The arrow, driven by just the right amount of force, penetrates to point of passing through, and then sticks fast and gives off a quantity of the drug, which naturally spreads and completely pervades the soul.

(*Nigr.* 35–6)

The philosophic doctor must, then, choose tools and medicines well.[134] Thus, like the physician reading the pulse, coloration, or general physical condition of a patient, the moralist must choose which particular type of reproach or exhortation – harsher, kinder, cajoling, scathing – to apply in order to stimulate the soul properly so as to shake it out of its stupor of passion and vice and lead it to recovery.[135] Plutarch says,

In which circumstances, then, is it necessary for a friend to be severe [σφοδρὸν] and when to employ the tone of frank speech [πότε τῷ τόνῳ χρῆσθαι τῆς παρρησίας]? [It is] when circumstances summon him [the friend] to check an impulsive rush [ἐπιλαβέσθαι φερομένης] into pleasure, wrath, or arrogance, or to curtail greed, or to recover from an *inattentive rashness* [ἀπροσεξίαν ἀνασχεῖν ἀνόητον].

(*Adul. amic.* 29 [*Mor.* 69E–F, my translation])[136]

At the beginning of his *Paedagogus*, Clement likewise distinguishes different types of exhortation and instruction that the student will need: *protreptikos* to deal with habit; *hypothetikos* to deal with proper behavior; but *paramythetikos* to deal with the passions.[137] Later he describes the role of the different types of rebuke (ψόγος, *psogos*), all of which are designed to rouse fear in the person so as to bring change and thus salvation.[138] Each one must be applied with its own degree of severity or harshness, in keeping with the particular "disease" befalling the individual.[139] It is up to the philosophic doctor to diagnose the problem correctly, choose the proper tools, and prescribe the proper treatment.

So, once again Clement sounds much like the other moralists as he blends rhetorical skill with practical instruction on daily habits to direct the souls of his hearers:

Do not relax the tension [τόνον] of the soul with feasting or indulgence in drink, but consider what is needful and sufficient for the body. And do not hasten early to meals before the time for the dinner arrives; rather let your dinner be bread, and let the earth's grasses and ripe fruits of the trees be set before you; and go to your meal with composure, showing no sign of raging gluttony. Be not a meat-eater nor a lover of wine, when no sickness leads you to it as cure. But in place of the pleasures in these things choose the joys that are in the divine words and hymns.[140]

Ultimately, says Clement, it is the pure soul unmoved by passion and bolstered with the true reason of Christ the Paedagogue that will find the impassible God.[141] Elsewhere Clement talks about the moral power of the *ipse dixit*, as if the words of the "master" had some special curative force to be passed along.[142] Nor were Christians alone in discussing the balance of divine and human causation in moral progress. Thus Seneca wrote to Lucilius,

> You do something excellent, something healthful for yourself if, as you write, you are continuing to progress [*ire*] toward a good understanding, since it is stupid to pray for this when you can obtain it yourself. It is not necessary to raise your hands to heaven or to beg the temple doorkeeper to approach the ear of a statue, as if that way we could be better heard. The god is near you, with you, inside you. This is what I am saying to you, Lucilius: a holy spirit is seated within us, a watcher and guardian of our good and bad actions. As this spirit is treated by us, so it treats us.... If you see a man unterrified by dangers, untouched by desires, happy in adversity, peaceful in the midst of storms... will not a feeling of reverence come over you? Will you not say: "This thing is too great and too noble to believe that it is like this paltry body in which it dwells. It is a divine power that has descended upon him!"
>
> (*Ep.* 41.1–4)

This may help us to understand the place of the seemingly incongruous legend about St. John and a brigand that appears at the end of the *Quis dives salvetur* (§ 42). For it is finally the mere sight of John, his former teacher and mystagogue, that brings the brigand to shameful awareness (αἰδεσθείς, *aidestheis*) of the dissolute life of passion and luxury (τρυφή, *tryphē*) into which he had fallen and causes him to groan and weep.[143] In this sense, social ills are viewed as diseases of the body politic, and brigandage is only a more advanced case of greed.[144] Clement makes the point clear: if this kind of person can be brought around by the right kind of words, so can you.

This is Clement's moral pathology. His exhaustive instructions on proper eating, dress, deportment, and cosmetics must be placed in a specific tradition regarding the proper attitude toward such luxuries. In a world that knew nothing of organ systems, submicroscopic anatomy, and microbiological causation, disease, desire, and passion were medical as well as moral conditions. In the final analysis, then, perhaps Clement had diagnosed the condition of his wealthy audience correctly after all. At the very least, for the wealthy and educated, they must have thought so.

Notes

1 Stählin (1909: 159–60, my translation). As will become clear in this study, I have retranslated the work with an eye toward the medical language and assumptions that underlie its moral exhortation. Previous English translations, especially those by G.W. Butterworth (1919: 265–367) and W. Wilson (1888: 591–605), tend to obscure or misunderstand this language. Butterworth was largely following the older work of P.M. Barnard (1897; 1901) in this regard. The work of Barnard and his predecessors was superseded by Stählin (1909), which also was consulted by Butterworth. The latter, however, opted for numerous emendations of lacunae, whereas Stählin tended to be more cautious. See especially nn. 9–13.

2 Perhaps the best-known example of the *topos* is Plutarch's *How to Tell a Flatterer from a Friend* (*Quomodo adulator ab amico internoscatur* [*Mor.* 48E–74E]). Like Plutarch, Clement starts from the assumption that frankness of speech (παρρησία, *parrhēsia*) in contrast to servile flattery, is the most appropriate way for true friends to deliver reproach and thus contribute to moral rectitude. This *topos* clearly comes from a long tradition associated with the ideals of friendship, but it is also closely attuned to key features among the moralist philosophers, as seen in Plutarch. See now also the treatise of the first century BCE Epicurean philosopher Philodemus, whose work *On Frank Speech* (*Peri parrhēsias*) was discovered among the Herculaneum papyri. The Teubner edition of A. Olivieri (1914) has been translated by the Hellenistic Moral Philosophy and Early Christianity Section of the Society of Biblical Literature (D. Konstan *et al.* 1998). As noted by the translators, however, a new critical edition is sorely needed (see White 2004). On the role of frank criticism see Fitzgerald 1996, especially the essays by D. Konstan ("Friendship, Frankness, and Flattery," pp. 7–19), C.E. Glad ("Frank Speech, Flattery, and Friendship in Philodemus," pp. 21–59), and T. Engberg-Pedersen ("Plutarch to Prince Philopappus on How to Tell a Flatterer from a Friend," pp. 61–79).

3 Compare the similar wording of Epictetus regarding the passions in *Diss.* 2.18.5 (quoted in the section "Clement's educational program" below).

4 It is noteworthy, therefore, that the satirist Lucian (writing about the same time as Clement) pokes fun at the dependency and often disreputable circumstances that many Greek philosophers had gotten into when they traded their freedom for *Salaried Posts in Great Houses*.

5 See Aelius Aristides, *Or.* 26.1–5 Keil (1898) (= *Or.* 14 Dindorf [1829]). On the panegyrical tradition at work behind *The Roman Oration* see Oliver (1953: 879).

6 Pliny, *Pan.* 1.6: *Quo magis aptum piumque est te, Iuppiter optime ... ut mihi digna consule digna senatu digna principe contingat oratio, utque omnibus quae dicentur a me, libertas fides veritas constet, tantumque a specie adulationes absit gratiarum actio mea quantum abest a necessitate* ("How much more is it proper and dutiful for me to pray to you, O Jupiter Optimus, that my speech befit the dignity of the consul, the Senate, the Princeps, and that liberty, faithfulness, and truth stand by everything

spoken by me, and that my speech of thanks be as far removed from the pretext of flattery as it is absent from constraint" [my translation]). For the context of Pliny's trope see Schowalter (1993: 31–49).

7 See Dio Chryostom, *Or.* 33.2–8. This seems to have been a regular trope for Dio. Cf. his *Or.* 38, and see the discussion in White (2003: 307–49, esp. 312–16).

8 For a similar list of treatments cf. Epictetus, *Diss.* 3.22.73.

9 On p. 1 of the Escorial manuscript (S) of the text there are several notable lacunae. In this sentence I have revised some of the conjectural emendations used by Butterworth (1919) in his LCL translation. In my view, a number of these emendations miss the underlying medical tone of Clement's language, which is key to understanding the physiological and moral assumptions of his teaching. The first one in this sentence occurs immediately after τοῦ θεραπεύειν and just before τοὺς πλουτοῦντας ("the rich" [literally, "those being wealthy"]). My proposed resolutions of the lacunae (indicated by phrases in angle brackets: < >) are tentative, but they are, in my view, more in keeping with the medical vocabulary and tone of the text. They will be discussed in detail in the following notes. References to earlier editions are based on the critical apparatus of Stählin (1909).

10 Butterworth (1919: 272–3), following Fell, supplied <ἀνελευθέρως>, thus turning the articular infinitive into a genitive of comparison: "than servile attention to the rich." This basic sense was assumed by other early editors: Lindner supplied κολακείᾳ; Schwartz, μετ' ἀσεβείας. If this sense were correct, it might be advisable to opt for the phrasing of Dio Chrysostom in *Or.* 38.1: πρὸς τὸ θεραπεύειν τοὺς ὄχλους ἐπιτηδείως ("to treat the masses with familiarity [or, 'cunningly']"), which has the connotation of one who panders to the masses. It would fit the lacuna here if we also supply αὐτοὺς (in place of Dio's τοὺς ὄχλους), thus: τοῦ θεραπεύειν <αὐτοὺς ἐπιτηδείως>. I have chosen a different reading, however, by taking τοῦ θεραπεύειν in the medical sense and as a more customary genitive articular infinitive. For θεραπεύω in the medical sense cf. *Quis div.* 41.1 (quoted in the section "Clement's educational program"). I would then supply <καθαρισμένῳ> ("by purging"). Thus the clause would now read: ἐμοὶ δὲ φαίνεται μακρῷ φιλανθρωπότερον εἶναι τοῦ θεραπεύειν <αὐτοὺς καθαρισμένῳ> τοὺς πλουτοῦντας . . . (for the remainder of the sentence see n. 13).

11 Butterworth (1919: 272–3) followed Barnard in supplying καὶ ἐπαινεῖν for the lacuna after πλουτοῦντας, hence: "and praise that does them harm." Similarly, Fell had emended with καὶ προσεπαινεῖν, while Schwartz chose καὶ ἐπαίρειν ("and excite or arouse"). Here, I propose <ἀπὸ τὰς συμπάθειας> instead to continue the medical thought. For συμπάθεια as "affinity for" or "attachment to" something cf. *Quis div.* 11.2: ἀλλὰ τὰ δόγματα τὰ περὶ χρημάτων ἐξορίσαι τῆς ψυχῆς, τὴν πρὸς αὐτὰ συμπάθειαν ("but to exorcize from the soul one's opinions concerning possessions, one's *affinity* for them"). Also quoted at n. 43.

12 Butterworth (1919: 273) followed Schwartz (not Stählin, as stated in Butterworth 1919: 272 n. 4) in supplying τὴν ζωὴν καί, thus: "if we share the burden of life and...." See Schwartz (1903). The preceding word συναίρεσθαι is a cognate of ἀφαιρεῖν just above in *Quis div.* 1.3, where it clearly means "to amputate." The compound form συναίρεσθαι can mean "to abolish, shrink, contract" and has grammatical as well as political and medical applications. Compare also the use of another cognate with medical connotations, ἐξαιρεῖν, just below in *Quis div.* 3.1, where it clearly means "to

banish or remove [their desperation]." Given this parallelism with 1.3, I propose <τὸν τῦφον καὶ ὄγκον [αὐτῶν]> in keeping with the medical imagery.

13 In the Escorial manuscript this lacuna follows τὴν σωτηρίαν αὐτοῖς. Butterworth followed Fell in emending with κατεργάζεσθαι, and almost all previous editors opted for some form of this word. I propose a simple alteration to <πρὸς τὸν ἐργάζεσθαι>. Thus, the second part of the sentence now reads: <ἀπὸ τὰς συμπάθειας> ἐπὶ κακῷ τὸ συναίρεσθαί <τε τὸν τῦφον καὶ ὄγκον [αὐτῶν]> τὴν σωτηρίαν αὐτοῖς <πρὸς τὸν ἐργάζεσθαι>.

14 Clement's citation (*Quis div.* 2.2: ῥᾷον κάμηλος διὰ τρήματος ῥαφίδος διεκδύσεται ἢ πλούσιος εἰς τὴν βασιλείαν τῶν οὐρανῶν), however, is not verbatim to any one of the Synoptic versions and has some affinities for the anarthrous wording of Luke 18:25 (cf. Matt 19:24) and textual variants in Eastern manuscripts (including Syriac, Alexandrian, and Bohairic). Clement gives the full account of the story of "The Rich Young Man" (in *Quis div.* 4.4–9), with the following statement (*Quis div.* 5.1): ταῦτα μὲν ἐν τῷ κατὰ Μάρκον εὐαγγελίῳ γέγραπται· καὶ ἐν τοῖς ἄλλοις δὲ πᾶσιν ἀνωμολογημένοις ὀλίγον μὲν ἴσως ἑκασταχοῦ τῶν ῥημάτων ἐναλλάσσει, πάντα δὲ τὴν αὐτὴν τῆς γνώμης συμφωνίαν ἐπιδείκνυται ("This has been written in the Gospel according to Mark; and the same harmony of opinion is demonstrated in all the other accepted [Gospels], even though perhaps a few of the words are changed here and there"). In fact, the quoted text seems mainly to follow Mark's version (Mark 10:17–31), but with some notable variants in wording that tend to resemble distinctive features of Luke rather than Matthew. In this version the wording of the camel aphorism is εὐκόλως διὰ τῆς τρυμαλιᾶς τῆς βελόνης κάμηλος εἰσελεύσεται ἢ πλούσιος εἰς τὴν βασιλείαν τοῦ θεοῦ, a mixture of Mark 10:25 and Luke 18:25, while the interpolated saying of Matt 19:28 clearly is omitted.

15 So note Johannes Quasten's observation: "a homily on Mark 10, 17–31, which however seems not to be a sermon delivered in a public service" (Quasten 1962–75: 2.15). By contrast, Butterworth still treats it as a regular sermon, albeit "too long to have been delivered orally on any single occasion" (Butterworth 1919: 265). Apparently, he was following the view popularized by Barnard (1901: vii, and passim), even though A.C. Coxe (introductory note in Wilson 1888: 169) refers to it only as a "practical treatise."

16 See Quasten 1962–75: 2.15.

17 = *Strom.* 2.5(22.1–5). For Clement's works I will cite the text from the GCS edition of Stählin (1909). It must be noted, however, that Stählin's edition adopts a different numbering system than that of earlier editions (as followed in most of the older English translations, including the *ANF*) by adding subsections to each major chapter. In *Quis dives salvetur* this practice causes few problems because the subsection numbers start over with each of the chapters as traditionally numbered. Such is not the case in the other major works of Clement, where the subsection numbering was continuous within each book and thus does not correspond to the traditional chapter breaks. For example, *Strom.* 7.5 in Stählin (1909: 29–37) covers subsections 35.1–49.8. In order to make it easier for readers who might not have access to Stählin's GCS edition, therefore, I have chosen to give both sets of numbers, as follows: *Strom.* 2.5 corresponds to the traditional numbering by book and chapter; the number(s) in parentheses that follow represent the subsection (and verse) numbering in Stählin (1909).

18 Clement, *Strom.* 2.5(22.2), quoting Plato, *Leg.* 5.742E: πλουσίους δ' αὖ σφόδρα καὶ ἀγαθοὺς ἀδύνατον, οὕς γε δὴ πλουσίους οἱ πολλοὶ καταλέγουσι· λέγουσι δὲ τοὺς κεκτημενους ἐν ὀλίγοις τῶν ἀνθρώπων πλεῖστον νομίσματος ἄξια κτήματα ("But it is impossible for the rich [to be] both excessively wealthy and good, at least for those whom the masses call rich. For they call rich those in few cases among humans who possess property reckoned to be worth much"). Clement's version differs only by adding εἶναι after σφόδρα. This and all translations are those of the author unless otherwise noted.

19 Clement, *Strom.* 2.5(22.4), quoting Plato, *Leg.* 5.736E: ἀμῇ γέ πῃ τῆς μετριότητος ἐχομένους καὶ <u>πενίαν</u> ἡγουμένους εἶναι μὴ τὸ τὴν οὐσίαν ἐλάττω ποιεῖν ἀλλὰ τὸ τὴν ἀπληστίαν πλείω ("possessed in some way of considerable moderation and thinking that <u>poverty</u> exists not in making one's possessions decrease, but in increasing one's greed"). Clement's quotation begins at <u>πενίαν</u> ("<u>poverty</u>"), as underlined. Again, Clement's wording contains only a minor change (ἡγητέον οὐ for ἡγουμένους εἶναι μή) to make the quotation fit his syntax. Also, on Clement's use of Plato, see F.L. Clark (1902), who argues that Clement shows first-hand knowledge of Plato's works (instead of using florilegia or compendia), and that this constitutes useful evidence for an Alexandrian edition of Plato's works current in Clement's day.

20 See also Curti (1968: 20–5).

21 Cf. Clement, *Quis div.* 12.3–5. Contrast the Cynic denunciation of wealth, wherein one learns the lessons of virtue and control of the passions from poverty and endurance; see, for example, Lucian, *Tim.* 36. Clement refers disapprovingly to this Cynic view as "empty fame and vainglory" (φήμης κενῆς καὶ κενοδοξίας) in *Quis div.* 11.4, where he explicitly mentions Anaxagoras, Democritus, and Crates.

22 We will return to this passage in the section "The pharmacology of *logos*".

23 Clement does not refer directly to these surviving works; however, in *Quis div.* 26.8 he refers the audience to his treatise *Exposition concerning First Principles and Theology* (Περὶ ἀρχῶν καὶ θεολογίας ἐξήγησις) for an explication of the "higher meaning" (σεμαινέτω ὑψηλότερον) in the passage about "the camel and the narrow way," apparently an allegorical interpretation based on Matt 7:14. No work of Clement survives under this title, nor is this title listed among his "lost works" by Quasten (1962–75: 2.16–19), but a work entitled *On First Principles* (Περὶ ἀρχῶν) is mentioned in *Strom.* 3.3(13.1) and 3.3(21.2). A work under this title is also mentioned, apparently, in a comment of John Malalas (CSHB 2.34); cf. de Faye (1923–8: 1.28). On the other hand, it is possible that these references were intended not to a work under that title but to another of Clement's known writings, perhaps even the *Stromata*, for example. Compare von Arnim's suggestion in Stählin (1909: lxiv). The introductions to books 4 and 6 of the *Stromata* bear some resemblance to the kind of interpretive discussion implied in *Quis div.* 26.8. Note especially *Strom.* 4.1(2.1–2), which announces its intent to give a study of "first principles" (περὶ ἀρχῶν) and "an excursus of theology" (τὴν ἐπιδρομὴν τῆς θεολογίας) in preparation for interpretation of the Scriptures. The only other known work attributed to Clement that seems likewise to be devoted to his allegorical exposition of Scripture would be the *Hypotyposes*, also not extant except for some short extracts. For a general description see Eusebius, *Hist. eccl.* 6.14.1; for a complete collection of the fragments and testimonia see Stählin (1909: xxviii–xxix, 195–202).

24 A. Méhat (1966: 42–54) argued that *Quis dives salvetur* was written only after Clement had left Alexandria – that is, in 203 or after. He based this view on the

fact that it contains so little Philonic material. See also Runia (1993: 144–5). The view taken here, however, is that *Quis dives salvetur* belongs squarely in Clement's Alexandrian period as an exhortation to the cultured elite to pursue his Christian educational program. On the other hand, we will see in the section "The pathology of the soul" that there are, in fact, some notable similarities between Clement's notions of the passions as reflected in *Quis dives salvetur* and those of Philo. So, one may simply attribute the differential use of Philonic material (especially direct quotations or allusions) to differences of audience and purpose.

25 Note especially Clement, *Paed.* 2.1–7(13.1–60.4), which contains numerous references to proper conduct at a symposium (esp. 2.4[40.1–44.4]) and reflects standard rules of etiquette that might be supposed at a meal. See Bradley (1998); Leyerle (1995). Bradley's essay discusses many of Clement's instructions on dining etiquette in the light of normal terminology and descriptions as found especially in Plutarch and Athenaeus and discovers a compendium of rather typical practices among the higher strata of society. The purpose in Clement is twofold: "We must consider the feelings of our table companions, and avoid disgusting or nauseating them by our crude conduct, testifying (thereby) to our own lack of self-control" (*Paed.* 2.7[60.1]). Bradley rightly notes that social politeness is typical of the culture, but the main concern in Clement is self-control, which in turn links manners to morals.

26 See Eusebius, *Hist. eccl.* 6.11.6; cf. Quasten (1962–75: 2.5).

27 G. Bardy (1937; 1942) was the first to challenge Eusebius's account. Although his view, that there was no "official" catechetical school until the time of Origen, has also been challenged, a cautious view of the situation seems justified. For discussion see Runia (1993: 132–5), but see also the more negative assessments by J. Ferguson (1991: 7–10) and D. Dawson (1992: 219–22).

28 R. Grant (1986: 180) argues for a more formal sense of "school" even in Clement's day and sees the precedent not in Philo's own work, but rather in the *Therapeutai*. Runia (1993: 134) follows Grant's view. Lurking behind much of this discussion, and in my view somewhat distorting the picture, is the somewhat controversial work of S.R.C. Lilla (1971), which was criticized by E. Osborne (1981), but more reasonably so by Runia, who questions the views of both Lilla and Osborne (Runia 1993: 153, 57) regarding Clement's use of Philo. See now also Choufrine (2002: 5–16). The problem is this: Lilla and Osborne (and now Choufrine) are concerned chiefly to describe Clement as formulating an eclectic, but still thoroughly Christian, philosophical "system." The view taken here is quite different: Clement was advocating a Christian solution to a well-established notion of the human passions and moral progress, understood as protreptic for his Christian theology. Also, on this notion of protreptic see Swancutt (2004); cf. Francis (1995: 176–7).

29 See the discussion by R. Valantasis (1999), who describes Musonius's program in these terms (esp. pp. 215, 227). See Clement *Protr.* 2(22.2–3; 25.4) (with emphasis on the notion of "delusion"); *Paed.* 1.1(3.3); 1.9(83.1–4) (on health and moral progress); cf. Behr (2000: 144–5). See also Nock (1933: 169–79).

30 See Fitzgerald and White (1983: Chs 5, 19–22).

31 Both metaphors are used in Clement, *Quis div.* 3.2 and 3.3, respectively. Compare Clement's athletic metaphor in *Quis div.* 3.3–4 with that of Epictetus in

Diss. 3.22.51–2 and 2.18.26–9 (both quoted in the section "Clement's educational program"; see text and n. 44).

32 See Hijmans (1959, esp. 70–2) for the key terms.

33 See *SVF* 3.510 (Stobaeus, *Flor.* 103.22); cf. Clement, *Strom.* 7.10(59.2–5); 6.14(111.3); Philo, *Leg.* 3.22, 210; *Cher.* 14; *Deus* 35.

34 The Greek is ὑποφεύεσθαι (*hypopheuesthai*). This unusual word, a cognate of φύσις (*physis*), appears mostly in early (fourth century BCE) writings on medicine (Hippocrates), agriculture (Theophrastus, *De causis plantarum; Historia plantarum*), and animal husbandry (Aristotle, *Historia animalium*). It means "to grow up underneath," either as an attachment (like a tumor) or as a substitute (like teeth or hooves). The term seems to come into use again during the second century CE, proximate to the time of Epictetus, and occurs in Galen's medical writings and Diogenes of Oenoanda's *Epicurus* 29 (see LSJ, s.v.). In the context here it seems to be a reference to something growing under the skin (hence my translation); so note the reference a few lines later to the forming of calluses (τυλοῦται, *tyloutai*) as a next stage. Clement clearly knows some of these medical texts at least indirectly through handbooks or contemporary writers; he cites Theophrastus (*Caus. plant.* 5.15.1) in *Strom.* 3.3(24.3), apparently drawing the reference from the Hellenistic natural historian Apollonius, *Mirabilia* 46 (second century BCE).

35 It is worth noting that Philostratus, the sophist from Lemnos who produced both the *Lives of the Sophists* and the aretalogical *Life of Apollonius*, was writing at almost the same time as Clement. Philostratus flourished before 217 CE as court philosopher of Julia Domna and teacher to the future emperor Alexander Severus. On the healing tradition in Apollonius see especially Kee 1983: 252–64, with further bibliographical discussion of the "divine man" tradition at pp. 297–9.

36 The verb παχύνω (*pachynō*) means "to make thick, fat, sluggish, dull, slow, gross." Here it must be seen as a wordplay on the idea of constipation used above. Eating meat produces constipation of the mind, presumably with a similar kind of excrement.

37 The word διαθολόω (*diatholoō*), usually translated "to darken," derives from θολός (*tholos*), meaning "mud, dirt, the ink of a squid." Thus the verb has the connotation of stirring up the muddy bottom of a pool or the way a squid squirts a jet of ink as camouflage. In both cases the swirling effect of the mud or ink in the water creates a dark cloud and is here likened to the effect on the soul.

38 Plato (*Resp.* 406A) reports that the physician Herodicus of Selymbria was the first to prescribe certain foods for training and health. See also Hippocrates, *De ratione victus salubris* (Περὶ διαίτης ὑγιεινῆς).

39 Thus note Philostratus's less famous treatise *De gymnastica*.

40 Note that this is the same term used above in the Philostratus in reference to the Pythagoreans's rationale for abstinence from meat. It suggests that Clement was familiar with a Pythagorean dictum similar to the one used by Philostratus. It also means, then, that Clement read Paul as coming from the same medical and philosophical climate – very likely a justifiable conclusion.

41 See n. 53.

42 See the discussion of the influence of Musonius Rufus on Clement in the section "Moral progress as psychagogy," especially Musonius's views on food and eating (see esp. n. 110).

43 The last phrase seems to be an allusion to the parable of the sower in Mark 4:19 (so Butterworth 1919), but another possible parallel comes from Philo, *Abr.* 220–3 (see also n. 52). The use of the term βίος (*bios*) here is also quite reminiscent of *Tabula of Cebes* 4.2; 5.2, while the affinity for false opinions and inappropriate desires is linked directly to the effects of "Deceit" on the soul in *Ceb. Tab.* 5.2–6.3; 11. In the last passage note also the role of μετάνοια (*metanoia*) – "repentance" or, perhaps better, "conversion" – in bringing about this change of understanding.

44 Cf. Epictetus, *Diss.* 2.18.26–9: "And if you form the habit of taking such exercises, you will see what mighty shoulders you develop, what sinews, what vigor.... The person who exercised himself against such external impressions is the true athlete in training. Be steady, wretch, do not get carried away [by *phantasias*]. Great is the contest; the task, divine on behalf of kingship, freedom, serenity of mind, calmness of the soul [ἀταραξία]." Cf. Epictetus, *Ench.* 29.2.

45 For a comprehensive discussion of the physiology of sexual desire and the development of Christian asceticism, especially dietary abstention, in relation to it see Shaw 1998: 27–63. See also the discussion of the evolution of Greek views of anthropology in Feher, Naddaff, and Tazi 1989, especially the essay on the Greek archaic period by J.-P. Vernant, "Dim Body, Dazzling Body" (1.18–47).

46 See Long 1986; 1980.

47 A slightly different view of the nature of the soul is found in later Platonic tradition, even though it is clearly influenced by elements of the Aristotelian and Stoic notions of the material soul. See Shaw 1998: 31. The Platonic view assumes a basic three-part division of the soul, each seated in a different part or organ of the body. The chief or controlling part is the rational soul (τὸ λογιστικόν, *to logistikon*), situated in the brain; it is incorporeal and the center of reason. The other two parts are considered "irrational soul" and are (more or less) corporeal. The "irascible or excitable soul" (τὸ θυμικόν, *to thymikon*; τὸ θυμοειδές, *to thymoeides*) is located in the heart and governs anger, passion, and courage. The "appetitive soul" (τὸ ἐπιθυμητικόν, *to epithymētikon*) is seated in the liver or belly and controls desires (including sexual desire), procreation, and nutrition. See Plato, *Tim.* 69B–72D; *Resp.* 4.435–442; *Phaedr.* 253C–254E.

48 Later, Eusebius (*Praep. ev.* 11.38) discusses Plato's view of the soul and quotes this passage from Clement. He then makes the corporeal nature of the soul more explicit by replacing the term "vessels" (ὀχήματα, *ochōmata*) in *Phaed.* 113D with "bodies" (σώματα, *sōmata*). For further discussion of the *Phaedo* passage in the development of the Christian tradition on the afterlife see de Jonge and White 2003 (esp. pp. 625–6, 628, for the comments of Clement and Eusebius).

49 See Nussbaum 1994b: 13–40, 316–58 (specifically on the Stoics); Sorabji 2000: 17–28; Annas 1992: 19–36. On eclecticism see Rist 1982. On the Stoic influence on Clement see Spanneut 1957: 170–5; Brown 1988: 122–39.

50 For references among the moralists see Malherbe 1989a: 127 n. 13.

51 See, for example, *Ceb. Tab.* 19.1–2 (education gives medicine against vice as disease); 26.1 (the philosopher, having experienced the cure, becomes doctor to others). For further references see Fitzgerald and White 1983: 151 n. 66, 156 n. 80.

52 The verb (παρευημερούντων) in Philo, *Abr.* 223 refers to a weed or tree that grows up and covers over other plants. So compare the imagery of the thorns in Clement, *Quis div.* 11 (quoted in the section "Clement's educational program" above; see

also n. 43 above). Presumably from Mark 4:7, 19, this may indicate Clement's intentional linking of biblical language with that commonly known in the moralist tradition. So compare his pairing of Paul and the Pythagoreans in *Paed.* 2.1(11.1), p. 290 above. In turn, this fact may suggest another background to the language found in the Markan parable and the changes made to it in the Synoptic parallels (noting especially Luke 8:14).
53 In Plutarch, *Mor.* 105E, the term ἀπηρτημένος (+ dative) means "closely allied with," but the usage here (+ genitive) is more like that in Lucian, *Tim.* 36.
54 So compare the transient lure of pleasure in Ps.-Diogenes, *Ep.* 28.5 Malherbe (1977).
55 On the medical imagery see Malherbe 1989a: 127–8.
56 This is the main title given in the Escorial manuscript (S) of Clement's works; it correctly denotes its genre as protreptic or paraenetic literature. The Escorial manuscript also preserves what appears to be a secondary title deriving from transmission as a work of Clement, but which wrongly describes it as a catechetical treatise for those recently baptized: Πρὸς τοὺς νεωστὶ βεβαπτισμένους Κλήμεντος παραγγέλματα (*Instructions of Clement to the Newly Baptized*).
57 Stählin 1909: 221.16–23; Butterworth 1919: 370. For the quiet summit as the place of the soul's repose cf. *Ceb. Tab.* 21.
58 Cf. Plutarch, *An. corp.* 501D.
59 See Plutarch, *Tranq. an.* 471D (the role of "impulses" [ὁρμαί] in interfering with tranquility); 473B (on discontentment stirring up the passions). Plutarch also seems to know the same basic tradition as found in the *Tabula of Cebes* regarding discontentment arising from fickle fortune (*Tranq. an.* 467B–C). See also Plutarch, *An. corp.* 500 C.
60 Dio Chrysostom, *Or.* 77/78.45: "Far worse than a corrupt and diseased body is a soul which is corrupt, not, by Zeus, because of salves or potions or some consuming poison, but rather because of ignorance and depravity and insolence, and, indeed, jealousy, and grief, and a myriad desires. This disease and *pathos* is more grievous than that of Heracles, and requires a far stronger, white-hot, cautery." For Clement also, "corruption" (φθάρσις, *phtharsis*) was a key term in describing the human condition. God is, after all, "immutable" (ἀπαθός, *apathos*) and thus "incorruptible" (ἀφθαρτός, *aphthartos*). In contrast, humans are by nature "corruptible," due to the affects of the passions on the soul; note especially Clement, *Strom.* 7.6(30.1): Καθάπερ οὖν οὐ περιγράφεται τόπῳ θεὸς οὐδὲ ἀπεικονίζεταί ποτε ζῴου σχήματι, οὕτως οὐδὲ ὁμοιοπαθὴς οὐδὲ ἐνδεὴς καθάπερ τὰ γενητά, ὡς θυσιῶν, δίκην τροφῆς, καὶ λιμὸν ἐπιθυμεῖν. ὧν ἅπτεται πάθος, φθαρτὰ πάντα ἐστί ("Therefore, just as God is not circumscribed by place, nor is he ever represented in the form of a living creature; so neither does he suffer the same passions nor have wants, like the created beings, so as to desire food out of hunger from sacrifice. But of those whom passion touches all are corruptible, i.e., mortal"). On the broader implications of this idea to Clement's apophatic theology see McLelland 1976: 64–78; on its relation to Clement's ideal of the Christian "Gnostic" through baptismal enlightenment and asceticism see Choufrine 2002: 41–53.
61 Cf. Clement, *Strom.* 3.7(59.4–60.1) and 4.23(147.1–148.2), which link true ἀγάπη (*agapē*) with ἐγκράτεια (*enkrateia*) and ἀπάθεια (*apatheia*). See Rüther 1949: 56.
62 Plato, *Phaed.* 81A; cf. *Phaedr.* 232A–233D; *Resp.* 329 C.

63 The full title of the work in Greek is Περὶ διαγνώσεως καὶ θεραπείας τῶν ἐν [τῇ] ἑκάστου ψύχῃ ἰδίων παθῶν ("Concerning the Diagnosis and Treatment of the Particular Passions in Each Person's Soul"). The companion piece, *De peccatorum dignotione*, is entitled Περὶ διαγνώσεως καὶ θεραπείας τῶν ἐν τῇ ἑκάστου ψύχῃ ἁμαρτημάτων ("Concerning the Diagnosis and Treatment of the Sins in Each Person's Soul"). Quotations here from Galen come from Kühn 1821-33. For this particular text, however, citations will also come from the edition of de Boer (1937), which gives subdivisions to each chapter that Kühn's edition did not. These two works by Galen also appear in Marquardt, Mueller, and Helmreich 1884. The connection between passions, false opinion, and sin (or mistakes in judgment) will become important later. See also n. 64.

64 Kühn 1821-33: 5.7; de Boer 1937: 6; Marquardt, Mueller, and Helmreich 1884: 5. On the use of the term "sin" (either ἁμάρτημα [*hamartēma*] or ἁμαρτία [*hamartia*]) in connection with the passions cf. Clement, *Protr.* 11(115.2): ὑμεῖς δὲ οὐ βούλεσθε τὸν οὐράνιον αὐτὸν περιάψασθαι, τὸν σωτῆρα λόγον, καὶ τῇ ἐπῳδῇ τοῦ θεοῦ πιστεύσαντες ἀπαλλαγῆναι μὲν παθῶν, ἃ δὴ ψυχῆς νόσοι, ἀποσπασθῆναι δὲ ἁμαρτίας; ("But do you not wish to have the heavenly, saving word fastened to you [as an amulet] and, trusting in a charm [incantation] of God, to be set free from the passions, which are diseases of the soul, and to be delivered from sin?").

65 See Rousselle 1988: 31-3; Temkin 1973: 10-48.

66 Kühn 1821-33: 8.32; cf. *SVF* 3.429. On passions in Stoic physiology see Rabel 1981: 392; for Galen see Hankinson 1993: 184-220.

67 See Galen, *De sanit. tuen.* 1.1, 5 (Kühn 1821-33: 6.2, 15); 4.11 (Kühn 1821-33: 6.301-2); *De nat. facul.* 3.7 (Kühn 1821-33: 2.167-8); *De loc. affect.* 3.9-10 (Kühn 1821-33: 8.173-93).

68 Lilla (1971: 85) demonstrates Clement's dependence here on the basic Stoic definition of the passions drawn from Zeno and Chrysippus (ap. Diogenes Laertius 7.110 [= *SVF* 1.205]: ἔστι δὲ αὐτὸ τὸ πάθος κατὰ Ζήνωνα ἡ ἄλογος καὶ παρὰ φύσιν ψυχῆς κίνησις, ἢ ὁρμὴ πλεονάζουσα ("According to Zeno, passion is an unreasoned movement of the soul contrary to nature, or an exaggerated impulse"). The underlined portions of *Strom* 2.13(59.6) reflect the same wording as that of Zeno. The same technical terms are also reflected in Galen's definition: *PHP* 4.5 (Kühn 1821-33: 5.397 [=*SVF* 3.479]); cf. 4.2 (Kühn 1821-33: 5.368 [= *SVF* 3.462]).

69 Cicero attributes the idea to Chrysippus: "Just as when the blood is in a bad state, or there is an excess of phlegm or bile, disorder and sickness of the body are born. So also, the disturbing effect of corrupt beliefs warring against one another despoils the soul of health and introduces disorders. Moreover, from disorders are produced, first, disease, which are called νοσήματα, and besides these are affections which are the opposite of such disease and which are accompanied by unhealthy aversion and loathing for certain things. Secondly, are produced sicknesses, which are called ἀρρωστήματα by the Stoics, and these too have corresponding aversions which are their opposites. On this point too much attention is devoted by the Stoics, especially by Chrysippus, to making comparisons between diseases of the body and those of the soul" (*Tusc.* 4.10.23). For a discussion of Galen's appropriation of Chrysippean psychology see Sedley 1993.

70 See Hankinson 1991; compare the discussion in Hijmans 1959: 12-13. The Stoics distinguished eight "parts" or "faculties" of the soul: (1) the five senses plus (2) the

voice, (3) the procreative faculty (τὸ σπερμάτικον, *to spermatikon*), and (4) the authoritative or "governing principle" (τὸ ἡγεμόνικον, *to hēgemonikon*). All animals have the same eight parts (and are enlivened by *pneuma*), but in an adult human, the "governing principle" develops rationality, which is the factor distinguishing humans from irrational animals. It is the *hēgemonikon* that corresponds most closely to mind (νοῦς, *nous*) or consciousness; when Stoics, such as Epictetus, use the term "soul" in a restrictive sense, they mean the *hēgemonikon*, since it is what activates the rest. Epictetus also thought that it was visited or overseen by *daimones*, or guardian spirits. It was centered in the area of the heart, even though it was directly concerned with mental process as well. Yet the physiology of the soul meant that all the parts must be balanced and coordinated properly. False perceptions derived from the senses might deceive the mind, while a clouded mind might upset the bodily operations. The eight "parts," therefore, were not really physically distinct, but rather were different faculties or operations of the same soul. The soul was a part of the organic whole that makes up the human corpus. See Long 1980: 7–12; Shaw 1998: 30–1.

71 See Nussbaum 1994b: 366–9. The key terms are δόξα (*doxa*) and ψευδοδόξα (*pseudodoxa*), "opinion, belief" and "false opinion/belief"; κρίσις (*krisis*), "judgment"; ὑπόληψις (*hypolēpsis*): "supposition, understanding"; see Diogenes Laertius 7.111. In Latin the terms are *opinio* and *iudicium* (corresponding to the first two in Greek); note the usage in Cicero, *Tusc.* 3.25.61 (on Chrysippus's definition of λύπη [*lypē*]).
72 See Sorabji 2000: 29–47, 244–52; Nussbaum 1994b: 367.
73 Sorabji 2000: 93–132.
74 Ibid., 258–60; *contra* Lilla (1971: 68), who aligns Galen *and* Clement directly with the position of Posidonius.
75 Kühn 1821–33: 6.40 (translation Shaw 1998: 48).
76 Kühn 1821–33: 4.808; Marquardt, Mueller, and Helmreich 1891: 67.2–16; also quoted in Sorabji 2000: 260.
77 Noted in the section "A rhetorician's ploy" above; see also Curti 1968: 20–5.
78 I am grateful to Richard Sorabji for pointing me to this feature of Clement's relationship to Galen and Musonius, when I presented a version of this essay to the Colloquium on Ancient Philosophy that he organized at the University of Texas at Austin. Jim Hankinson and Alex Mourelatos also provided useful comments on that occasion.
79 Plato, *Leg.* 808D–E: "Of all wild creatures the child is the most intractable; for insofar as it, above all others, possesses a fount of reason [i.e., the human soul] that is as yet uncurbed, it is a treacherous, sly and most insolent creature. Wherefore the child must be strapped up, as it were, with many bridles [χαλινοῖς] – first, when he leaves the care of nurse and mother, with tutors, to guide his childish ignorance, and after that with teachers of all sorts of subjects and lessons [μαθήμασιν], treating him as becomes a freeborn child" (trans. Bury 1926: 2.69, slightly modified).
80 See *Ceb. Tab.* 33.3.
81 On psychagogy see Glad 1992: 20–52.
82 Fitzgerald and White 1983: 20–7.
83 Cf. *Ceb. Tab.* 30–2; as part of the concluding exhortation of the work, these directions come back, but now to be understood in a new way: in the light of *Paideia*.

84 Cf. Dio Chrysostom, *Or.* 4.114–15; see Fitzgerald and White 1983: 139 nn. 16, 20.
85 *Ceb. Tab.* 9.1: Ἀκρασία (*Akrasia*), Ἀσωτία (*Asōtia*), Ἀπληστία (*Aplēstia*), Κολακεία (*Kolakeia*).
86 See *Ceb. Tab.* 9.2–3.
87 See *Ceb. Tab.* 19–21.
88 Cf. *Ceb. Tab.* 33.3, where is mentioned the passage from Plato, *Leg.* 808D–E (quoted in n. 79 above).
89 Stählin 1909: 221.22–3; Butterworth 1919: 371.
90 See *Ceb. Tab.* 10.4–11.1. In relation to this passage see the discussion of "conversion" to philosophy in Nock 1933: 180–3.
91 See *Ceb. Tab.* 26.3.
92 See *Ceb. Tab.* 26; cf. Dio Chrysostom, *Or.* 9.2, on Diogenes as physician to humankind. On the two elements of the medical *topos* see Fitzgerald and White 1983: 151–2 nn. 66–7.
93 See Fitzgerald and White 1983: 142 n. 33. Note especially Clement, *Paed.* 3.2, 5. But note also the reversal that one finds in Lucian and Alciphron, where the courtesans likewise are viewed as "educators" over against the selfish desires of the philosophers.
94 See the discussion in Shaw 1998: 33–8.
95 See Musonius, frgs 5–6 (Lutz 1947: 48–52).
96 See Hijmans 1959: 70. The other terms that make up this *topos* and thus form a semantic complex are ἐκποιεῖν (*ekpoiein*), γυμνάζειν (*gymnazein*), ἀσκεῖν (*askein*), μελετᾶν (*meletan*). Of these, ἐκποιεῖν is almost always used in Epictetus of "working hard on" one's *prohairesis* (*Diss.* 1.4.18), virtue (3.1.7), or *apatheia* (4.10.13).
97 Lutz 1947: 54.
98 Ibid., 52–5.
99 On the notion of "hardship" as part of this semantic complex, especially in conjunction with the *agōn* motif, see Fitzgerald 1988: 47–100. See also Höistad 1948. For other references see also Fitzgerald and White 1983: 154 n. 74.
100 See Musonius, frg. 6 (Lutz 1947: 52–4).
101 See Musonius, frg. 7 (Lutz 1947: 56–7).
102 See Musonius, frgs 3–4 (Lutz 1947: 39–49).
103 See Musonius, frg. 14: "Is Marriage an Impediment?" (Lutz 1947: 90–6); frg. 11: "What Means of Livelihood Is Appropriate for a Philosopher?" (Lutz 1947: 81–5).
104 See Musonius, frgs 18A–B (Lutz 1947: 113–21)
105 See Musonius, frgs 19–20 (Lutz 1947: 121–7).
106 See Musonius, frgs 12; 13A–B (Lutz 1947: 85–9, 89–91).
107 Or ἡδυπάθεια (*hēdypatheia*) as in *Ceb. Tab.* 9.3; 28.1; 32.3. Clement uses τρυφή, in *Quis div.* 42 in regard to the dissolute life into which the brigand had fallen. In other words, he had been corrupted by the passions. The "brigand" is discussed further in the section "The pharmacology of *logos*".
108 Lutz 1947: 112.
109 As we noted earlier, Clement's language in *Paed.* 2.1(11.1) is similar, but not identical, to that found in the Pythagorean tradition.
110 The final saying is originally from Heraclitus, frg. 74 (so Stählin 1906: 174), but Clement had taken this version directly from Musonius, frg. 18 A (Lutz 1947:

112). In fact, in Musonius's discussion this statement falls only a few lines after the quotation used by Clement in *Paed.* 2.1(11.1). Notably, Musonius also calls for the soul to be "pure and dry." Musonius, in turn, cites Heraclitus as source. So also Galen gives a version of the same saying (similarly attributing it to Heraclitus) in *Quod an. mor.* 5 (Kühn 1821-33: 4.786; Marquardt, Mueller, and Helmreich 1891: 2.47). For Galen on food see Grant 2000; see also Galen, *De sanit. tuen.* 1.8; *Quod. an. mor.* 9 (both quoted in the section "The pathology of the soul" above).

111 For ἀσυμφύλοις (*asymphylois*) cf. Plutarch, *Quaest. conv.* 7.6 (Mor. 707B), where the term is applied to dinner parties when inviting people who are incompatible in their habits – for example, a drunkard and a tea-totaler.

112 Cf. Clement, *Strom.* 2.20(105.1–106.2).

113 For Musonius see Wendland 1886; 1895: 191–200; Parker 1901; van Geytenbeek 1963. S. Lilla (1971: 99 n. 3) argues for Clement using Plutarch and Musonius along with Philo for these instructions as philosophic commonplaces; however, my own work has amply documented that Clement borrowed substantial amounts of material directly from Musonius's two discourses on food (frgs 18A; 18B), especially in *Paed.* 2.1–2 (on food). For Plutarch see Hubert 1938. For a possible allusion drawn from Galen see *De affect. dig.* 10.2–4 (quoted in the section "The pharmacology of *logos*"; see also n. 125).

114 See Gussen 1955: 56–60, s.v. index 134–6; White 1981: 331–6.

115 Whereas Clement is quite consistent in giving proper attribution to more ancient sources (such as the classical Greek philosophers cited throughout the *Stromata*), he never cites material quoted from those who were his near contemporaries, including Musonius, Plutarch, and Galen. This practice is due some further study in light of parallels among other philosophers and rhetoricians of the Second Sophistic. I rather doubt that Clement is alone.

116 See Clement, *Paed.* 2.1(1.4); Musonius Rufus, frg. 18 A.

117 Clement, *Protr.* 12(120.3; 121.1): "[Christ is speaking] 'I wish to share with you this gracious gift, supplying incorruption as its full benefaction. I favor you with *logos*; I favor you with myself, perfect, the knowledge [γνῶσιν] of God.' ... [Clement responds] 'So, let us hurry, let us run; let us take up his yoke; let us take upon ourselves incorruption; let us love Christ, the noble charioteer [καλὸν ἡνίοχον] of humans.'" For the motif of the *logos* as "charioteer" (ἡνίοχος, *hēniochos*) of the soul, a motif drawn from Plato (see n. 79 above), cf. *Paed.* 3.11(53.2); *Strom.* 5.8(52.5; 53.1). Clement also adopts the motif of the *Logos*, ruling principle of the soul, as a "helmsman"; so *Strom.* 2.11(51.6): "The rational part [λογισμός], the ruling principle [ἡγεμονικόν], when it remains unimpeded and keeps the soul in check, is called its helmsman [κυβερνήτης]." See also *Strom.* 5.8(52.5); *Quis div.* 41.1 (quoted in the present section).

118 Clement, *Quis div.* 29.2–3: "Of these wounds [i.e., fears, lusts, wraths, griefs, deceits, and pleasures], Jesus alone is the doctor [ἰατρός], since he surgically excises the passions completely and to the root [ἐκκόπτων ἄρδην τὰ πάθη πρόρριζα]"; cf. *Quis div.* 40.5–6. Cf. *Paed.* 1.1(1.2, 4): "For Persuasion cures the passions [τὰ δὲ πάθη ὁ παραμυθητικὸς ἰᾶται], being one and the same the *Logos* itself that nurtures humans.... But being both curative and preceptive [θεραπευτικός τε ὢν καὶ ὑποθετικός]..., he makes what is prescribed the subject of exhortation

[προττετραμμένον], promising the cure of the passions within us. So let us call this *Logos* [in all these roles] properly by one name, *Paedagogos*." Cf. *Paed.* 1.1(3.3); 1.2(6.1–4).

119 That human agents are part of the equation is clear from *Quis div.* 35.1–2, where Clement discusses the fact that other Christians (whom he calls "energetic soldiers and steadfast guardians") serve in various capacities, including "giving reproof with frank speech [νουθετῆσαι μετὰ παρρησίας] or kindly advice [συμβουλεῦσαι μετ' εὐνοίας]" as the need arises, and "to love you truly [φιλεῖν ἀληθῶς], not with guile, fear, hypocrisy, flattery [ἀκολακεύτως], or pretense." This description of their noble efforts on the part of others sounds very much like a foreshadowing of the concluding exhortation in *Quis div.* 41.1, where Clement himself takes on this same role, especially for the rich. So note *Quis div.* 34.3: "Obtain by means of your own wealth such people as bodyguards [lit., 'spear-bearers'], both for your body and for your soul."

120 For this motif in Clement see *Strom.* 2.2(6.4) and following, and especially *Strom.* 2.6(29.4–31.3).

121 See Clement, *Paed.* 1.6(29.4). Of course, Clement and others could easily appeal to the argument proffered by Paul in Rom 1:18–32, which in turn was derived from older Jewish sources, that "idolatry" (i.e., ignorance about the one, true God) was the cause of immorality and all the passions (e.g., Wis 13:1–9; 14:8–14), which in turn fostered more confusion and idolatry (Wis 14:15–31). Of course, such warnings against "false opinions" can also be very serviceable in sectarian polemics among competing schools of philosophy. For Galen and Clement see von Staden 1982: 96–7; cf. *Ceb. Tab.* 12–13; 33–5 (on "False Education"); also Clement's general critique of Greek philosophy.

122 Clement, *Paed.* 1.9(83.2–3): "Just as those who are sound have no need of a doctor, since they enjoy good health, but those who are sick need his skill, so also since we are diseased in life concerning disgraceful lusts, concerning reproachful impurities, and concerning the other flare-ups of the passions, we need the savior. And he administers not only mild drugs [τὰ ἤπια ἐπιπάσσει φάρμακα], but also stringent ones [στυπτικά]. The bitter roots of fear arrest the spreading cancer of sin.... Wherefore, then, we who are sick need the savior, we who are led astray [πεπλανημένοι] need one to guide us, the blind need the one who brings enlightenment, the thirsty need the fountain of life."

123 Cf. Plutarch, *Is. Os.* 73 (*Mor.* 380C), where the term is specifically linked with plague or disease. See also the note in Betz 1975: 78. Here Clement is far more in keeping with the typical usage found in Plutarch than with the metaphorical and eschatological usage found in other early Christian writers.

124 Clement, *Strom.* 4.6(39.2): "Gnosis is the purification of the ruling principle [ἡ γνῶσις τοῦ ἡγεμονικοῦ τῆς ψυχῆς κάθαρσίς ἐστι] of the soul." See also Choufrine 2002: 43–50 on the role of "enlightenment" in Clement's thought.

125 Kühn 1821–33: 5.52–3; de Boer 1937: 35; Marquardt, Mueller, and Helmreich 1884: 41. The underlined phrases are nearly identical in wording to that in Clement, *Quis div.* 41.1, and the overall thought is very similar. (Clement also uses the term μυσταγωγεῖν [*mystagōgein*], meaning "to serve as mystagogue" or "to lead into the mysteries," in this same sense in *Quis div.* 3.1.) Given Clement's

penchant for quoting contemporaries without attribution, one might now begin to suspect that he knew and used Galen's work as well.
126 See Galen, *De affect. dig.* 7.7–9.21 (Kühn 1821–33: 5.37–52; de Boer 1937: 25–35).
127 In *De affect. dig.* 9.11 (Kühn 1821–33: 5.49; de Boer 1937: 33) Galen also equates "insatiability" (ἀπληστία, *aplēstia*) with "excessive desire" (πλεονεξία, *pleonexia*), which, he says in *De affect. dig.* 10.2–4 (quoted just above in the present section), is the "mother of all the passions."
128 See Galen, *De affect. dig.* 9.13–15 (Kühn 1821–33: 5.49–50; de Boer 1937: 33–4). For "utility of wealth" and "moderation" see *De affect. dig.* 9.15 (Kühn 1821–33: 5.50; de Boer 1937: 33).
129 See Philostratus, *Vit. soph.* 561.
130 See Webb 1997: 112–15; Nussbaum 1993.
131 Webb 1997: 117–18. See Longinus, *Subl.* 15; Quintilian, *Inst.* 6.2.29–32.
132 On the distinctions see Philostratus, *Vit. soph.* 479–84, and the discussion in Bowersock 1969: 10–12.
133 See Clement, *Strom.* 1.3(22.5); see also the discussion of "titillation" in the section above on "The pathology of the soul."
134 Galen's *De affectuum dignotione* was intended to help others "discover knowledge of their own sins" (*De affect. dig.* 2.5 [Kühn 1821–33: 5.5; de Boer 1937: 5]).
135 Compare Lucian's description of the demeanor and style of Demonax (*Demon.* 6–9). For discussion see Malherbe 1986; 1987: 81–8.
136 Cf. Epictetus, *Diss.* 4.12, which deals with attention and "inattentiveness." For other terms that reflect this heedless "rush" into vice see *Ceb. Tab.* 8.1: ἀπροβούλευτοι (*aprobouleutoi*, "without forethought"); 14.3: ἀφροσύνη (*aphrosynē*, "foolishness"). Compare also the wording of the censuring (ἐπιτιμητικός, *epitimētikos*) letter in Ps.-Demetrius, *Typ. epist.* 6: "For not against your will did you commit grievous and hurtful acts to many people. It is fitting, therefore, that you meet with more severe rebuke, since in the present case it so happens that others have also been wronged" (καὶ γὰρ οὐκ ἄκων μεγάλα καὶ πολλοῖς βλαβερὰ διαπέπραξαι. προσήκει μὲν οὖν σε μείζονος ἐπιτυχεῖν ἐπιπλήξεως, εἰ δὴ κατὰ τὸ παρὸν συντετύχηκε καὶ ἐπὶ ἑτέρων τῶν ἀδικηθέντων) (my translation). Cf. Seneca, *Ep.* 75.6–7 (quoted in the section "A rhetorician's ploy" above) and 40 ("on the proper style for a philosopher's mode of speech").
137 See Clement, *Paed.* 1.1(3.3).
138 Clement, *Paed.* 1.9(76.1–81.3): "rebuke" (ψόγος*, *psogos*), "admonition" (νουθέτησις*, *nouthetēsis*), "censure" (ἐπιτίμησις*, *epitimēsis*), "blame" (μέμψις*, *mempsis*), "invective" (ἐπίπληξις*, *epiplēxis*), "reproof" (ἔλεγχος*, *elenchos*), "opening the mind" (φρένωσις, *phrenōsis*), "punishment" (ἐπισκοπή, *episkopē*), "denunciation" (λοιδορία*, *loidoria*), "accusation" (ἔγκλησις*, *enklēsis*), "complaining at fate" (μεμψιμοιρία, *mempsimoiria*), "objuration" (διάσυρσις, *diasyrsis*), and "indignation" (κατανεμέσησις, *katanemesēsis*). Note that these different modes of rebuke and censure follow the technical definitions found in, for example, the epistolary handbooks, especially Ps.-Demetrius, *Typ. epist.* 3–9, and Ps.-Libanius, *Epist. char.* 4. (The Greek terms above marked with * appear in one or both of these works, either as a letter-type itself or in the description of what the letter is intended to accomplish.)

139 For example, "censure" (ἐπιτίμησις, *epitimēsis*) aims at changing from "shameful" (αἰσχροῖς, *aischrois*) to good behavior in household matters (*Paed.* 1.9[77.1]), while "punishment" or "visitation" (ἐπισκοπή, *episkopē*) is an even harsher form of "invective" (ἐπίπληξις σφοδρά, *epiplēxis sphodra*) (*Paed.* 1.9[79.2]), and "denunciation" (λοιδορία, *loidoria*) is a "vehement or torturous" form of rebuke (ψόγος ἐπιτεταμένος, *psogos epitetamenos*) (*Paed.* 1.9[80.1]).

140 Clement, *Exhortation to Endurance* (Stählin 1909: 222.23-32; Butterworth 1919: 375).

141 See Clement, *Strom.* 4.6(39.1–40.1); cf. 4.6(27.1–3), where he allegorizes the beatitudes (specifically those regarding poverty, hunger, and persecution) to refer to "wrenching the soul away from its fleshly desires," which he also calls "the Lord's training" (ἡ κυριακὴ ἄσκησις, *hē kyriakē askēsis*).

142 See Clement, *Strom.* 2.5(24.3).

143 See Clement, *Quis div.* 42.13, 15.

144 The idea that one's soul can be corrupted by proximity to others whose passions are out of control is made explicit in Plutarch, *An. corp.* 501D–E, referring to mob reactions out of anger. In this case, the premise seems to be that his turning to brigandage was the effect of his greed having gotten out of control, since his evil companions had started him out by dabbling in luxurious banquets and then petty theft (Clement, *Quis div.* 42.5). Finally, he rushed farther and farther out of control as each new "sin" caused him to fall deeper and deeper into the pit of the passions; note especially *Quis div.* 42.6–7: "He [the robber] little by little became habituated [προσειθίζετο], and because of his bulky nature, he rushed all the more towards the pit, like an unmanageable and powerful horse bolts from the right path chafing at the bit."

SELECTED BIBLIOGRAPHY

Akinpelu, J.A. (1968) " 'Logos' Doctrine in the Writings of Seneca," *CBul*, 44: 33–7.
Alesse, F. (1997) "Il tema stoico del ΔΙΑΛΕΛΗΘΩΣ ΣΟΦΟΣ e il ΔΙΑΛΑΝΘΑΝΩΝ ΛΟΓΟΣ dell'eristica megarica," *Elenchos*, 18: 57–75.
Alexander, L. (1998) " 'Better to Marry than to Burn': St. Paul and the Greek Novel," in R.F. Hock, J.B. Chance, and J. Perkins (eds) *Ancient Fiction and Early Christian Narrative*, Atlanta: Scholars Press, 235–56.
Alexiou, E. (1999) "Zur Darstellung der ὀργή, in Plutarchs Βίοι," *Philologus*, 143: 101–13.
Allen, W.C. (1947) "Fear in St. Mark," *JTS*, 48: 201–3.
Amir, Y. (1984) "The Transference of Greek Allegories to Biblical Motifs in Philo," in F.E. Greenspahn, E. Hilgert, and B.L. Mack (eds) *Nourished with Peace: Studies in Hellenistic Judaism in Memory of Samuel Sandmel*, Chico: Scholars Press, 15–25.
Anderson, G. (trans.) (1989) "Xenophon of Ephesus, *An Ephesian Tale*," in Reardon 1989b: 125–69.
Anderson, R.D. (1998) *Ancient Rhetorical Theory and Paul*, rev. edn, Leuven: Peeters.
Anderson, W.S. (1964) *Anger in Juvenal and Seneca*, Berkeley: University of California Press.
——. (ed. and trans.) (1972–97) *Ovid's Metamorphoses*, Norman: University of Oklahoma Press.
Angeli, A. (ed.) (1988) *Agli amici di scuola (PHerc. 1005)*, Naples: Bibliopolis.
——. (2000) "Necessità e autodeterminazione nel *De ira* di Filodemo (PHerc 182 fr. 12 Indelli)," *PapLup*, 9: 15–63.
Angeli, A. and Colaizzo, M. (1979) "I frammenti di Zenone Sidonio," *CErc*, 9: 47–134.
Annas, J. (1980) "Aristotle on Pleasure and Goodness," in A.O. Rorty (ed.) *Essays on Aristotle's Ethics*, Berkeley: University of California Press, 285–99.
——. (1989) "Epicurean Emotions," *GRBS*, 30: 145–64.
——. (1992) *Hellenistic Philosophy of Mind*, Berkeley: University of California Press.
——. (1993) *The Morality of Happiness*, Oxford: Oxford University Press.
——. (1996) "Stoicism," *OCD*, 1446.
Armstrong, D. (1993) "The Addressees of the *Ars poetica*: Herculaneum, the Pisones, and Epicurean Protreptic," *MD*, 31: 185–230.
——. (2004a) "All Things to All Men: Philodemus' Model of Therapy and the Audience of *De Morte*," in Fitzgerald, Obbink and Holland 2004: 15–54.

——. (2004b) "Horace's Epistles I and Philodemus," in Armstrong *et al.* 2004: 267–98.
Armstrong, D., Fish, J., Johnston, P.A., and Skinner, M.B. (eds) (2004) *Vergil, Philodemus, and the Augustans*, Austin: University of Texas Press.
Arnim, H.F.A. von (ed.) (1903–24) *Stoicorum veterum fragmenta*, 4 vols, Leipzig: Teubner.
Arnold, E.V. (1911) *Roman Stoicism*, Cambridge: Cambridge University Press.
Asmis, E. (1984) *Epicurus' Scientific Method*, Ithaca: Cornell University Press.
——. (1990) "Philodemus' Epicureanism," *ANRW*, 2.36.4: 2369–406.
Aune, D.C. (1994) "Mastery of the Passions: Philo, 4 Maccabees and Earliest Christianity," in W. Helleman (ed.) *Hellenization Revisited: Shaping a Christian Response within the Greco-Roman World*, Lanham: University Press of America, 125–58.
——. (1995) "Passions and Desires in the Pauline Epistles: An Exploration of Paul's Moral Psychology," unpublished Ph.D. dissertation, Brown University.
Babbitt, F.C. (trans.) (1927) *Plutarch's Moralia*, vol. 1, London: Heinemann.
Babbitt, F.C. *et al.* (trans.) (1927–2004) *Plutarch's Moralia*, 16 vols in 17, Cambridge: Harvard University Press.
Babut, D. (1969a) (trans.) *Plutarque, De la vertu éthique*, Paris: Belles lettres.
——. (1969b) *Plutarque et le stoïcisme*, Paris: Presses universitaires de France.
Bailey, C. (ed. and trans.) (1926) *Epicurus: The Extant Remains*, Oxford: Clarendon.
Baillie, J. (1950) *The Belief in Progress*, London: Oxford University Press.
Balch, D. (1983) "1 Cor 7:32–35 and Stoic Debates about Marriage, Anxiety and Distraction," *JBL*, 102: 429–39.
——. (ed.) (2000) *Homosexuality, Science, and the "Plain Sense" of Scripture*, Grand Rapids: Eerdmans.
Balch, D., Ferguson, E., and Meeks, W.A. (eds) (1990) *Greeks, Romans, and Christians: Essays in Honor of Abraham J. Malherbe*, Minneapolis: Fortress.
Ballester, L.G. (1988) "Soul and Body: Disease of the Soul and Disease of the Body in Galen's Medical Thought," in Manuli and Vegetti 1988: 117–52.
Baltes, M. (1972) *Timaios Lokros: Über die Natur des Kosmos und der Seele*, Leiden: Brill.
Banchich, T. (1997) *Cebes' Pinax*, Bryn Mawr: Thomas Library, Bryn Mawr College.
Bardy, G. (1937) "Aux origines de l'école d'Alexandrie," *RevScRel*, 27: 65–90.
——. (1942) "Pour l'histoire de l'école d'Alexandrie," *Vivre et Penser*, 2: 80–109.
Barlow, C.W. (trans.) (1969) *Iberian Fathers*, vol. 1, Washington, DC: Catholic University of America Press.
Barnard, P.M. (ed.) (1897) *Clement of Alexandria: Quis dives salvetur*, Cambridge: Cambridge University Press.
——. (ed. and trans.) (1901) *A Homily of Clement of Alexandria, Entitled: Who Is the Rich Man That Is Being Saved?* London: SPCK.
Barth, P. (1946) *Die Stoa*, 6th edn by Albert Goedeckemeyer, Stuttgart: Fr. Fromann.
Barton, C.A. (1993) *The Sorrows of the Ancient Romans: The Gladiator and the Monster*, Princeton: Princeton University Press.
——. (2001) *Roman Honor: The Fire in the Bones*, Berkeley: University of California Press.

Bauer, W. (1988) *Griechisches-deutsches Wörterbuch*, 6th edn, K. Aland and B. Aland (ed.), Berlin: de Gruyter.
Baumgarten, A.I., Assmann, J., and Stroumsa, G.G. (eds) (1998) *Self, Soul and Body in Religious Experience*, Leiden: Brill.
Becchi, F. (1990) "La nozione di *orge* di *aorgesia* in Aristotele e Plutarco," *Prometheus*, 16: 65–87.
——. (1992) "L'ideale della *metriopatheia* nei testi pseudopitagorici: A proposito di una contraddizione nella Ps.-Archita," *Prometheus*, 18: 102–20.
Becker, L. (1998) *A New Stoicism*, Princeton: Princeton University Press.
——. (2004) "Stoic Emotion," in Strange and Zupko 2004: 250–75.
Behr, J. (2000) *Asceticism and Anthropology in Irenaeus and Clement*, New York: Oxford University Press.
Bekker, I. *et al.* (eds) (1831–70) *Aristotelis opera*, 5 vols, Berlin: G. Reimer.
Ben-Ze'ev, A. (2003) "Aristotle on Emotions towards the Fortune of Others," in Konstan and Rutter 2003: 99–121.
Berger, K. (1991) *Historische Psychologie des Neuen Testaments*, Stuttgart: Katholisches Bibelwerk.
——. (2003) *Identity and Experience in the New Testament*, trans. of Berger 1991 by C. Muenchow, Minneapolis: Fortress.
Bernays, J. (1879) *Lucian und die Kyniker: Mit einer Übersetzung der Schrift Lucians "Über das Lebensende des Peregrinus,"* Berlin: Hertz.
Bett, R. (1998) "The Sceptics and the Emotions," in Sihvola and Engberg-Pedersen 1998: 197–218.
Betz, H.D. (ed.) (1975) *Plutarch's Theological Writings and Early Christian Literature*, Leiden: Brill.
——. (ed.) (1978) *Plutarch's Ethical Writings and Early Christian Literature*, Leiden: Brill.
——. (1995) *The Sermon on the Mount: A Commentary on the Sermon on the Mount, Including the Sermon on the Plain (Matthew 5:3–7:27 and Luke 6:20–49)*, Minneapolis: Fortress.
Beye, C.R. (1963) "Lucretius and Progress," *CJ*, 58: 160–9.
Bignone, E. (ed.) (1920) *Epicuro: Opera, frammenti, testimonianze sulla sua vita*, Bari: Laterza & Figli.
——. (1973) *L'Aristotele perduto e la formazione filosofica di Epicuro*, 2 vols, 2nd edn, Florence: La Nuova Italia.
Billerbeck, M. (1978) *Epiktet: Von Kynismus*, Leiden: Brill.
——. (1979) *Der Kyniker Demetrius: Ein Beitrag zur Geschichte der frühkaiserzeitlichen Popularphilosophie*, Leiden: Brill.
——. (1991) "Greek Cynicism in Imperial Rome," in M. Billerbeck (ed.) *Die Kyniker in der modernen Forschung: Aufsätze mit Einführung und Bibliographie*, Amsterdam: Grüner, 147–66.
Billig, L. (1919) "Clausulae and Platonic Chronology," *JP*, 35: 225–56.
Blank, D.L. (1993) "The Arousal of Emotion in Plato's Dialogues," *CQ*, 43: 428–39.
——. (1997) "Diogenes of Seleucia," in Zeyl 1997: 192–4.
Blowers, P.M. (1992) "Maximus the Confessor, Gregory of Nyssa, and the Concept of 'Perpetual Progress,'" *VC*, 46: 151–71.
——. (1996) "Gentiles of the Soul: Maximus the Confessor on the Substructure and Transformation of the Human Passions," *JECS*, 4: 57–85.

Blundell, S. (1986) *The Origins of Civilization in Greek and Roman Thought*, London: Croom Helm.
Bollack, J. (ed. and trans.) (1975) *La pensée du plaisir: Épicure: Textes moraux, commentaries*, Paris: Éditions de Minuit.
Bonhöffer, A. (1890) *Epictet und die Stoa*, Stuttgart: F. Enke.
——. (1894) *Die Ethik des Stoikers Epiktet*, Stuttgart: F. Enke; trans. into English by W.O. Stephens and published (1996) as *The Ethics of the Stoic Epictetus*, New York: P. Lang.
——. (1911) *Epiktet und das Neue Testament*, Giessen: Töpelmann.
Bonner, G. (1986) "*Concupiscentia*," in Mayer 1986: 1113–22.
Bons, J.A.E. and Lane, R.T. (2003) "*Institutio oratoria* VI.2: On Emotion," in Tellegen-Couperus 2003: 129–44.
Börger, H. (1980) *Grundzüge der Bildungstheorie L.A. Senecas*, Frankfurt: P. Lang.
Borle, J.P. (1962) "Progrès ou déclin de l'humanité? La conception de Lucrèce," *MH*, 19: 162–76.
Bormann, K. (1955) "Die Ideen- und Logoslehre Philons von Alexandrien," unpublished Ph.D. dissertation, University of Cologne.
Boswell, J. (1980) *Christianity, Social Tolerance and Homosexuality*, Chicago: University of Chicago Press.
Bouché-Leclercq, A. (1899) *L'Astrologie grecque*, Paris: Leroux; reprinted (1963) Brussels: Culture et Civilisation.
Boughton, J.S. (1932) "The Idea of Progress in Philo Judaeus," unpublished Ph.D. dissertation, Columbia University.
Bowen, A. and Garnsey, P. (trans.) (2003) *Lactantius: Divine Institutes*, Liverpool: Liverpool University Press.
Bowersock, G.W. (1969) *Greek Sophists in the Roman Empire*, Oxford: Clarendon.
Bowie, E.L. (1985) "The Greek Novel," in P.E. Easterling and B.M.W. Knox (eds) *The Cambridge History of Classical Literature*, vol. 1, *Greek Literature*, Cambridge: Cambridge University Press, 683–99.
Boyancé, P. (1936) *Études sur le Songe de Scipion: Essais d'histoire et de psychologie religieuses*, Bordeaux: Feret.
——. (1955) "Sur une épitaphe épicurienne," *REL*, 33: 113–20.
Boyarin, D. (1994) *A Radical Jew: Paul and the Politics of Identity*, Berkeley: University of California Press.
Bracher, K.D. (1987) *Verfall und Fortschritt im Denken der frühen römischen Kaiserzeit*, Vienna: Böhlau.
Bradley, K. (1998) "The Roman Family at Dinner," in I. Nielsen and H.S. Nielsen (eds) *Meals in a Social Context: Aspects of the Communal Meal in the Hellenistic and Roman World*, Aarhus: Aarhus University Press, 36–55.
Brandenburger, E. (1968) *Fleisch und Geist: Paulus und die dualistische Weisheit*, Neukirchen-Vluyn: Neukirchener Verlag.
Brandwood, L. (1990) *The Chronology of Plato's Dialogues*, Cambridge: Cambridge University Press.
Brant, J.A., Hedrick, C.W., and Shea, C. (eds) (2005) *Ancient Fiction: The Matrix of Early Christian and Jewish Narrative*, Atlanta: Society of Biblical Literature.
Braund, S.H. (1988) *Beyond Anger: A Study of Juvenal's Third Book of Satires*, Cambridge: Cambridge University Press.

Braund, S.M. and Gill, C. (eds) (1997) *The Passions in Roman Thought and Literature*, Cambridge: Cambridge University Press.

Braund, S. and Most, G.W. (eds) (2003) *Ancient Anger: Perspectives from Homer to Galen*, Cambridge: Cambridge University Press.

Bréhier, É. (1909) *Commentaire allégorique des saintes lois, après l'oeuvre des six jours*, Paris: Picard.

——. (1950) *Les idées philosophiques et religieuses de Philon d'Alexandrie*, 3rd edn, Paris: Vrin.

——. (1951) *Chrysippe et l'ancien stoïcisme*, rev. edn, Paris: Presses universitaires de France.

Brennan, T. (1998) "The Old Stoic Theory of Emotions," in Sihvola and Engberg-Pedersen 1998: 21–70.

——. (1999) *Ethics and Epistemology in Sextus Empiricus*, New York: Garland.

——. (2003) "Stoic Moral Psychology," in Inwood 2003: 257–94.

Brinton, A. (1988) "Pathos and the 'Appeal to Emotions': An Aristotelian Analysis," *History of Philosophy Quarterly*, 5: 207–19.

Brooten, B. (1996) *Love between Women: Early Christian Responses to Female Homoeroticism*, Chicago: University of Chicago Press.

Brown, P. (1988) *The Body and Society: Men, Women, and Sexual Renunciation in Early Christianity*, New York: Columbia University Press.

Brown, R.D. (1987) *Lucretius on Love and Sex: A Commentary on De rerum natura IV, 1030–1287, with Prolegomena, Text, and Translation*, Leiden: Brill.

Brunschwig, J. (1967) *Aristote: Topiques*, Paris: Budé.

Brunschwig, J. and Nussbaum, M. (eds) (1993) *Passions and Perceptions: Studies in Hellenistic Philosophy of Mind*, Cambridge: Cambridge University Press.

Bultmann, R. (1951) *Theology of the New Testament*, vol. 1, trans. K. Grobel, New York: Scribner's.

——. (1967) "The Problem of Ethics in the Writings of Paul," in *The Old and New Man in the Letters of Paul*, trans. K. Crim, Philadelphia: John Knox, 7–32.

——. (1968) *Theologie des Neuen Testaments*, 6th edn, Tübingen: Mohr.

Buresch, K. (1886) *Consolationum a Graecis Romanisque scriptarum historia critica*, Leipzig: Hirzel.

Burkert, W. (1961) "Hellenistische Pseudopythagorica," *Philologus*, 105: 16–43, 226–46.

——. (1962) review of *An Introduction to the Pythagorean Writings of the Hellenistic Period*, by Holger Thesleff, *Gnomon*, 34: 763–8.

——. (1972) *Lore and Science in Ancient Pythagoreanism*, trans. E.L. Minar, Cambridge: Harvard University Press.

Burton, H.F. (1909) "Seneca's Idea of God," *AJT*, 13: 350–69.

Bury, J.B. (1924) *The Idea of Progress: An Inquiry into Its Origin and Growth*, London: Macmillan; reprinted (1952) with an introduction by C.A. Beard, New York: Dover.

Bury, R.G. (trans.) (1926) *Plato: The Laws*, 2 vols, London: Heinemann.

Butterworth, G.W. (ed. and trans.) (1919) *Clement of Alexandria*, Cambridge: Harvard University Press.

Cairns, D.L. (1993) *AIDŌS: The Psychology and Ethics of Honour and Shame in Ancient Greek Literature*, Oxford: Clarendon.

Campbell, G.L. (2003) *Lucretius on Creation and Evolution: A Commentary on De rerum natura, Book Five, Lines 772–1104*, Oxford: Oxford University Press.

Campbell, J.S. (1982) "The Ambiguity of Progress: *Georgics* I, 118–159," *Latomus*, 41: 566–76.
Cancik, H. (1998) "Persona and Self in Stoic Philosophy," in Baumgarten, Assmann, and Stroumsa 1998: 335–46.
Cancik, H. and Cancik-Lindemaier, H. (1991) "Senecas Konstruktion des Weisen: Zur Sakralisierung der Rolle des Weisen im 1. Jh. n. Chr.," in A. Assmann (ed.) *Weisheit*, Munich: Fink, 205–22.
Cancik-Lindemaier, H. (1998) "Seneca's Collection of Epistles: A Medium of Philosophical Communication," in A.Y. Collins (ed.) *Ancient and Modern Perspectives on the Bible and Culture*, Atlanta: Scholars Press, 88–109.
Capasso, M. (ed. and trans.) (1988) *Carneisco: Il secondo libro del Filista (PHerc. 1027)*, Naples: Bibliopolis.
Celentano, M.S. (2003) "Book VI of Quintilian's *Institutio oratoria*: The Transmission of Knowledge, Historical and Cultural Topicalities, and Autobiographical Experience," in Tellegen-Couperus 2003: 119–28.
Centrone, B. (1990) *Pseudopythagorica ethica: I trattati morali di Archita, Metopo, Teage, Eurifamo*, Naples: Bibliopolis.
——. (1996) *Introduzione a i Pitagorici*, Rome: Laterza.
Chadwick, H. (1959) *The Sentences of Sextus: A Contribution to the History of Early Christian Ethics*, Cambridge: Cambridge University Press.
Chaplin, M. (1994) "Commentary on Garver," *PBACAP*, 10: 201–10.
Choufrine, A. (2002) *Gnosis, Theophany, Theosis: Studies in Clement of Alexandria's Appropriation of His Background*, New York: P. Lang.
Clark, F.L. (1902) "Citations of Plato in Clement of Alexandria," *TAPA*, 33: xii–xx.
Clay, D. (1983) "Individual and Community in the First Generation of the Epicurean School," in ΣΥΖΗΤΗΣΙΣ: *Studi sull'epicureismo greco e romano offerti a Marcello Gigante*, 2 vols, Naples: G. Macchiarolli, 255–79.
——. (1990) "The Philosophical Inscription of Diogenes of Oenoanda: New Discoveries 1969–1983," *ANRW*, 2.36.4: 2446–2559.
Code, A.D. (1997) "Aristotle," in Zeyl 1997: 67–95.
Cohn, L., Heinemann, Y. (=I.) and Adler, M. (ed. and trans.) (1909–38) *Die Werke Philos von Alexandria in deutscher Übersetzung*, 6 vols in 4, Breslau: M. & H. Marcus.
Colardeau, Th. (1903) *Étude sur Épictète*, Paris: Librarie Thorin & Fils, Albert Fontemoing.
Colish, M.L. (1992) "Stoicism and the New Testament: An Essay in Historiography," *ANRW*, 2.26.1: 334–79.
Collier, G. (1994) " 'That We Might Not Crave Evil': The Structure and Argument of 1 Corinthians 10:1–13," *JSNT*, 55: 67–71.
Colombo, A.M. (1954) "Un nuovo frammento di Crisippo," *La Parola de Passato*, 9: 376–81.
Colson, F.H. and Whitaker, G.H. (trans.) (1929–62) *Philo*, 10 vols, London: Heinemann.
Cooper, J.M. (1998) "Posidonius on Emotions," in Sihvola and Engberg-Pedersen 1998: 71–111.
——. (1999) *Reason and Emotion: Essays on Ancient Moral Psychology and Ethical Theory*, Princeton: Princeton University Press.

Countryman, L.W. (1988) *Dirt, Greed, and Sex: Sexual Ethics in the New Testament and Their Implications for Today*, Philadelphia: Fortress.

Crönert, W. (1906) *Kolotes und Menedemos: Texte und Untersuchungen zur Philosophen- und Literaturgeschichte von Wilhelm Crönert*, Leipzig: Avenarius; reprinted (1965) Amsterdam: Hakkert.

Curran, L.C. (1978) "Rape and Rape Victims in the *Metamorphoses*," *Arethusa*, 11: 213–41.

Curti, C. (1968) *Osservazioni sul "Quis dives salvetur" di Clemente Alessandrino*, Torino: Bottega d'Erasmo.

Dalmeyda, G. (ed. and trans.) (1962) *Xénophon d'Éphèse: Les Éphésiaques; ou, Le roman d'Habrocomés et d'Anthia*, 2nd edn, Paris: Belles lettres.

Dancy, R.M. (1997) "Xenocrates," in Zeyl 1997: 568–70.

Daniélou, J. (1944) *Platonisme et théologie mystique*, Paris: Aubier.

Darwin, C. (1998) *The Expression of the Emotions in Man and Animals*, 3rd edn, with an introduction, afterword, and commentaries by P. Ekman and an essay on the history of the illustrations by P. Prodger, Oxford: Oxford University Press.

Davies, W.D. (1955) *Paul and Rabbinic Judaism: Some Rabbinic Elements in Pauline Theology*, 2nd edn, London: SPCK.

——. (1957) "Paul and the Dead Sea Scrolls: Flesh and Spirit," in K. Stendahl (ed.) *The Scrolls and the New Testament*, New York: Harper, 157–82.

Dawson, D. (1992) *Allegorical Readers and Cultural Revision in Alexandria*, Berkeley: University of California Press.

de Boer, W. (ed.) (1937) *Galeni: De propriorum animi cuiuslibet affectuum dignotione et curatione; De animi cuiuslibet peccatorum dignotione et curatione; De atra bile*, Leipzig: Teubner.

Decleva Caizzi, F. and Funghi, M.S. (1988) "Un testo sul concetto stoico di progresso morale (PMilVogliano Inv. 1241)," in A. Brancacci *et al. Aristoxenica, Menandrea, fragmenta philosophica*, Florence: Olschki, 85–124.

de Faye, E. (1923–8) *Origène, sa vie, son ouvre, sa pensée*, 3 vols, Paris: E. Leroux.

de Jonge, M. and White, L.M. (2003) "The Washing of Adam in the Acherusian Lake (Greek *Life of Adam and Eve* 37.3) in the Context of Early Christian Notions of the Afterlife," in Fitzgerald, Olbricht, and White 2003: 609–31.

De Lacy, P.H. (1943) "The Logical Structure of the Ethics of Epictetus," *CP*, 38: 112–25.

——. (ed. and trans.) (1978–84) *Galen: On the Doctrines of Hippocrates and Plato*, 3 vols, Berlin: Akademie-Verlag.

De Lacy, P.H. and Einarson, B. (trans.) (1959) *Plutarch's Moralia*, vol. 7, London: Heinemann.

Deming, W. (2004) *Paul on Marriage and Celibacy: The Hellenistic Background of 1 Corinthians 7*, 2nd edn, Grand Rapids: Eerdmans.

den Boer, W. (1976) "Prometheus and Progress," in J.M. Bremer, S.L. Radt, and C.J. Ruijgh (eds) *Miscellanea Tragica in Honorem J.C. Kamerbeek*, Amsterdam: Hakkert, 17–27.

——. (1977) *Progress in the Greece of Thucydides*, New York: North-Holland.

Des Places, E. (ed. and trans.) (1977) *Atticus: Fragments*, Paris: Belles lettres.

deSilva, D. (1995) "Paul and the Stoa: A Comparison," *JETS*, 38: 549–64.

SELECTED BIBLIOGRAPHY

Destro, A. and Pesce, M. (1998) "Self, Identity and Body in Paul and John," in Baumgarten, Assmann, and Stroumsa 1998: 184–97.

DeYoung, J.B. (1988) "The Meaning of 'Nature' in Romans 1 and its Implications for Biblical Proscriptions of Homosexual Behavior," *JETS*, 31: 429–41.

Dibelius, M. (1909) *Die Geisterwelt im Glauben des Paulus*, Göttingen: Vandenhoeck & Ruprecht.

DiCicco, M. (1995) *Paul's Use of Ethos, Pathos and Logos in 2 Corinthians 10–13*, Lewiston: Mellen Biblical Press.

Diels, H. (ed.) (1882–95) *Simplicii in Aristotelis Physicorum libros quattuor posteriores commentaria*, Berlin: G. Reimer.

——. (ed.) (1929) *Doxographi Graeci*, Editio Iterata, Berlin and Leipzig: de Gruyter.

Diels, H. and Kranz, W. (eds) (1951–2) *Die Fragmente der Vorsokratiker*, 3 vols, 6th rev. edn, Berlin: Weidman.

Dihle, A. (1957) "Der Platoniker Ptolemaios," *Hermes*, 85: 314–25.

——. (1988) "Fortschritt und Goldene Urzeit," in J. Assmann and T. Hölscher (eds) *Kultur und Gedächtnis*, Frankfurt a.M.: Suhrkamp, 150–69.

Dill, S. (1905) *Roman Society from Nero to Marcus Aurelius*, London: Macmillan.

Dillon, J. (1977) *The Middle Platonists: 80 B.C. to A.D. 220*, Ithaca: Cornell University Press.

——. (1983) "*Metriopatheia* and *Apatheia*: Some Reflections on a Controversy in Later Greek Ethics," in J.P. Anton and A. Preus (eds) *Essays in Ancient Greek Philosophy: Volume 2*, Albany: State University of New York Press, 508–17.

——. (trans.) (1993) *Alcinous: The Handbook of Platonism*, Oxford: Clarendon.

——. (1996) *The Middle Platonists: A Study of Middle Platonism 80 B.C. to A.D. 220*, 2nd edn, London: Duckworth.

Dillon, J. and Hershbell, J. (eds and trans) (1991) *Iamblichus: On the Pythagorean Way of Life*, Atlanta: Scholars Press.

Dillon, J. and Terian, A. (1976–7) "Philo and the Stoic Doctrine of *eupatheiai*," *Studia Philonica*, 4: 17–24.

Dindorf, W. (ed.) (1829) *Aristides*, 3 vols, Leipzig: Reimer.

Dion, J. (1993) *Les passions dans l'oeuvre de Virgile: Poétique et philosophie*, Nancy: Presses universitaires de Nancy.

Dobbin, R.F. (ed. and trans.) (1998) *Epictetus: Discourses: Book I*, Oxford: Clarendon.

Dodds, E.R. (1951) *The Greeks and the Irrational*, Berkeley: University of California Press.

——. (1973) *The Ancient Concept of Progress and Other Essays on Greek Literature and Belief*, Oxford: Clarendon.

Doi, T. (2005) *Understanding amae: The Japanese Concept of Need-Love: Collected Papers of Takeo Doi*, with a foreword by H. Sukehiro, Folkstone, Kent, UK: Global Oriental.

Dorandi, T. (ed.) (1982) "Filodemo, Gli Stoici (PHerc. 155 e 339)," *CErc*, 12: 91–133.

——. (1990) "Filodemo: gli orientamenti della ricerca attuale," *ANRW*, 2.36.4: 2328–68.

Downing, F.G. (1998) *Cynics, Paul, and the Pauline Churches*, London: Routledge.

Dudley, D.R. (1967) *A History of Cynicism from Diogenes to the 6th Century A.D.*, Hildesheim: Olms.

Duff, T.E. (1999) *Plutarch's Lives: Exploring Virtue and Vice*, Oxford: Clarendon.
Düring, I. (1956) "Ariston or Hermippus?" *Classica et Mediaevalia*, 17: 11–21.
——. (1957) *Aristotle in the Ancient Biographical Tradition*, Göteborg: Elanders Boktryckeri Aktiebolag.
Ebner, M. (1991) *Leidenlisten und Apostelbrief: Untersuchungen zu Form, Motivik und Funktion der Peristasenkataloge bei Paulus*, Würzburg: Echter.
Edelstein, L. (1936) "The Philosophical System of Posidonius," *AJP*, 57: 286–325.
——. (1966) *The Meaning of Stoicism*, Cambridge: Harvard University Press.
——. (1967) *The Idea of Progress in Classical Antiquity*, Baltimore: Johns Hopkins Press.
Edelstein, L. and Kidd, I.G. (eds) (1972–99) *Posidonius*, 3 vols in 4, Cambridge: Cambridge University Press.
——. (ed.) (1972) *Posidonius*, vol. 1: *The Fragments*, Cambridge: Cambridge University Press.
——. (1988) *Posidonius*, vol. 2: *The Commentary*, Part 1: *Testimonia and Fragments 1–149*, and part 2: *Fragments 150–293*, Cambridge: Cambridge University Press.
——. (1989) *Posidonius*, vol. 1: *The Fragments*, 2nd edn, Cambridge: Cambridge University Press.
——. (1999) *Posidonius*, vol. 3: *The Translation of the Fragments*, Cambridge: Cambridge University Press.
Edwards, R.A. and Wild, R.A. (eds and trans) (1981) *The Sentences of Sextus*, Chico: Scholars Press.
Einarson, B. and De Lacy, P.H. (trans.) (1967) *Plutarch's Moralia*, vol. 14, Cambridge: Harvard University Press.
Ekman, P. (ed.) (1973) *Darwin and Facial Expression: A Century of Research in Review*, New York: Academic Press.
Ekman, P., Campos, J.J., Davidson, R.J., and de Waal, F.B.M. (eds) (2003) *Emotions Inside Out: 130 Years after Darwin's The Expression of the Emotions in Man and Animals*, New York: New York Academy of Sciences.
Elsner, J. (1995) *Art and the Roman Viewer*, Cambridge: Cambridge University Press.
Emeljanow, V.E. (1965) "A Note on the Cynic Short-Cut to Happiness," *Mnemosyne*, 18: 182–84.
Emilsson, E.K. (1998) "Plotinus on Emotions," in Sihvola and Engberg-Pedersen 1998: 339–63.
Engberg-Pedersen, T. (1990) *The Stoic Theory of Oikeiosis: Moral Development and Social Interaction in Early Stoic Philosophy*, Aarhus: Aarhus University Press.
——. (1996) "Plutarch to Prince Philopappus on How to Tell a Flatterer from a Friend," in Fitzgerald 1996: 61–79.
——. (1998) "Marcus Aurelius on Emotions," in Sihvola and Engberg-Pedersen 1998: 305–37.
——. (2000) *Paul and the Stoics*, Edinburgh: T&T Clark.
——. (2002) "Response to Martyn," *JSNT*, 24: 103–14.
——. (2006) "Self-sufficiency and Power: Divine and Human Agency in Epictetus and Paul," in J.M.G. Barclay and S.J. Gathercole (eds), *Divine and Human Agency in Paul and His Cultural Environment*, London: T&T Clark, 117–39.
Erler, M. (1992a) "Orthodoxie und Anpassung: Philodem, ein Panaitios des Kepos?" *MH*, 49: 171–200.

——. (1992b) "Der Zorn des Helden: Philodems 'De Ira' und Vergils Konzept des Zorns in der 'Aeneis,' " *GB*, 18: 103–26.

——. (1994) "Epikur – Die Schule Epikurs – Lukrez," in Flashar 1994: 29–490.

——. (2003) "*Exempla amoris*: Der epikureische Epilogismos als philosophischer Hintergrund der Diatribe gegen die Liebe in Lukrez *De rerum natura*," in A. Monet (ed.) *Le jardin romain: Épicurisme et poésie à Rome; Mélangees offerts à Mayotte Bollack*, Lille: Presses de l'Université Charles de Gaulle, 147–62.

Erskine, A. (1990) *The Hellenistic Stoa*, Ithaca: Cornell University Press.

——. (1997) "Cicero and the Expression of Grief," in Braund and Gill 1997: 36–47.

Etheridge, S.G. (1961) "Plutarch's De virtute morali: A Study in Extra-Peripatetic Aristotelianism," unpublished Ph.D. dissertation, Harvard University.

Evans, D. and Cruse, P. (eds) (2004) *Emotion, Evolution, and Rationality*, Oxford: Oxford University Press.

Fantham, E. (1997) " 'Envy and Fear the Begetter of Hate': Statius' *Thebaid* and the Genesis of Hatred," in Braund and Gill 1997: 185–212.

Favez, C. (1937) *La consolation latine chrétienne*, Paris: Vrin.

Fedler, K. (2002) "Calvin's Burning Heart: Calvin and the Stoics on the Emotions," *Journal of the Society of Christian Ethics*, 22: 133–62.

Feher, M., Naddaff, R., and Tazi, N. (eds) (1989) *Fragments for a History of the Human Body*, 3 vols, New York: Zone Books.

Ferguson, E. (1973) "God's Infinity and Man's Mutability: Perpetual Progress according to Gregory of Nyssa," *Greek Orthodox Theological Review*, 18: 59–78.

——. (1976) "Progress in Perfection: Gregory of Nyssa's *Vita Moysis*," *StPatr*, 14: 307–14.

Ferguson, J. (1991) *Clement of Alexandria: Stromateis 1–3*, Washington, DC: Catholic University of America.

Field, G.C. and Hornblower, S. (1996) "Xenocrates (1)," *OCD*, 1628.

Fillion-Lahille, J. (1984) *Le De ira de Sénèque et la philosophie stoïcienne des passions*, Paris: Klincksieck.

Fiore, B. (1986) *The Function of Personal Example in the Socratic and Pastoral Epistles*, Rome: Biblical Institute Press.

——. (1990) "Passion in Paul and Plutarch: 1 Corinthians 5–6 and the Polemic against Epicureans," in Balch, Ferguson, and Meeks 1990: 135–43.

Fish, J. (1998) "Is Death Nothing to Horace? A Brief Comparison with Philodemus and Lucretius," *CErc*, 28: 97–102.

——. (2004) "Anger, Philodemus' Good King, and the Helen Episode of Aeneid 2.567–589: A New Proof of Authenticity from Herculaneum," in Armstrong *et al.* 2004: 111–38.

Fitzgerald, J.T. (1988) *Cracks in an Earthen Vessel: An Examination of the Catalogues of Hardships in the Corinthian Correspondence*, Atlanta: Scholars Press.

——. (1992) "Virtue/Vice Lists," *ABD*, 6: 857–9.

——. (1994) "The Ancient Lives of Aristotle and the Modern Debate about the Genre of the Gospels," *ResQ*, 36: 209–21.

——. (ed.) (1996) *Friendship, Flattery, and Frankness of Speech: Studies on Friendship in the New Testament World*, Leiden: Brill.

——. (ed.) (1997) *Greco-Roman Perspectives on Friendship*, Atlanta: Scholars Press.

——. (2004) "Gadara: Philodemus' Native City," in Fitzgerald, Obbink, and Holland 2004: 343–97.
——. (2007) "Early Christian Missionary Practice and Pagan Reaction: 1 Peter and Domestic Violence against Slaves and Wives," in M.W. Hamilton, T.H. Olbricht, and J. Peterson (eds) *Renewing Tradition: Studies in Texts and Contexts in Honor of James W. Thompson*, Eugene: Wipf and Stock.
Fitzgerald, J.T. and White, L.M. (trans.) (1983) *The Tabula of Cebes*, Chico, CA: Scholars Press.
Fitzgerald, J.T., Olbricht, T.H., and White, L.M. (eds) (2003) *Early Christianity and Classical Culture: Comparative Studies in Honor of Abraham J. Malherbe*, Leiden: Brill; reprinted (2005) Atlanta: Society of Biblical Literature.
Fitzgerald, J.T., Obbink, D., and Holland, G.S. (eds) (2004) *Philodemus and the New Testament World*, Leiden: Brill.
Flashar, H. (1983a) "Aristoteles," in Flashar 1983b: 175–457.
——. (ed.) (1983b) *Die Philosophie der Antike*, vol. 3, *Ältere Akademie – Aristoteles – Peripatos*, Basel: Schwabe.
——. (ed.) (1994) *Die Philosophie der Antike*, vol. 4, 2 parts, *Die hellenistische Philosophie*, Basel: Schwabe.
Flusser, D. (1958) "The Dead Sea Sect and Pre-Pauline Christianity," in C. Rabin and Y. Yadin (eds) *Aspects of the Dead Sea Scrolls*, Jerusalem: Magnes, 215–66.
Fortenbaugh, W.W. (1969) "Aristotle: Emotion and Moral Virtue," *Arethusa*, 2: 163–85.
——. (1970a) "Aristotle's *Rhetoric* on Emotions," *AGP*, 52: 40–70; reprinted in K. Erickson (ed.) (1976) *Aristotle: The Classical Heritage of Rhetoric*, Metuchen: Scarecrow Press, 205–34; and in J. Barnes, M. Schofield, and R. Sorabji (eds) (1976) *Articles on Aristotle*, vol. 4, London: Duckworth, 133–53.
——. (1970b) "On the Antecedents of Aristotle's Bipartite Psychology," *GRBS*, 11: 233–50; reprinted in J.P. Anton and A. Preus (eds) (1983) *Essays in Ancient Greek Philosophy*, vol. 2, Albany: State University of New York Press, 303–20.
——. (1975a) *Aristotle on Emotion*, London: Duckworth.
——. (1975b) "Aristotle's Analysis of Friendship: Function and Analogy, Resemblance, and Focal Meaning," *Phronesis*, 20: 51–62.
——. (1981) "A Note on Aspasius, In EN 49.20–21," *Proceedings of the World Congress on Aristotle*, vol. 1, Athens: Department of Culture, 175–8; reprinted in Fortenbaugh 2006: 39–42.
——. (1985) "Theophrastus on Emotion," in W. Fortenbaugh, P. Huby, and A. Long (eds) *Theophrastus of Eresus: On His Life and Work*, New Brunswick: Transaction Books, 209–29.
——. (1987) "Un modo di affrontare la distinzione fra virtù etica e saggezza in Aristotele," *MP*, 5: 243–58; reprinted in English as "Aristotle's Distinction Between Moral Virtue and Practical Wisdom," in J.P. Anton and A. Preus (eds) (1991) *Essays in Ancient Greek Philosophy*, vol. 4, *Aristotle's Ethics*, Albany: State University of New York Press, 97–106.
——. (1990) "Theophrastus, fr. 534 FHS&G: On Assisting a Friend Contrary to the Law," *SynPhil*, 10: 457–68.
——. (1997) "On the Composition of Aristotle's *Rhetoric*: Arguing the Issue, Emotional Appeal, Persuasion through Character, and Characters Tied to Age

and Fortune," in C. Mueller-Goldingen and K. Sier (eds) *LHNAIKA: Festschrift für Carl Werner Müller zum 65. Geburtstag am 28. Januar 1996*, Stuttgart: Teubner, 165–88.

——. (2002) Reprint of Fortenbaugh 1975a, with a new epilogue, 93–126.

——. (2003) *Theophrastean Studies*, Stuttgart: Steiner.

——. (2006) *Aristotle's Practical Side: On His Psychology, Ethics, Politics and Religion*, Leiden: Brill.

Fortenbaugh, W.W., Sharples, R.W., and Sollenberger, M.G. (eds) (2003) *Theophrastus of Eresus: On Sweat, On Dizziness, and On Fatigue*, Leiden: Brill.

Fowler, D.P. (1997) "Epicurean Anger," in Braund and Gill 1997: 16–35.

Francis, J.A. (1995) *Subversive Virtue: Asceticism and Authority in the Second-Century Pagan World*, University Park: Pennsylvania State University Press.

Frede, M. (1986) "The Stoic Doctrine of the Affections of the Soul," in Schofield and Striker 1986: 93–110.

——. (1997) "Euphrates of Tyre," in Sorabji 1997a: 1–11.

Fredrickson, D.E. (2000) "Natural and Unnatural Use in Romans 1:24–27: Paul and the Philosophic Critique of Eros," in Balch 2000: 197–222.

Fritz, K. von (1963) "Pythagoras 1A: Pythagoras von Samos," *PW*, 24/1: 171–209.

——. (ed.) (1972) *Pseudepigrapha I: Pseudopythagorica, lettres de Platon, littérature pseudépigraphique juive*, Geneva: Fondation Hardt.

Furley, D. (1989) *Cosmic Problems: Essays on Greek and Roman Philosophy of Nature*, Cambridge: Cambridge University Press.

Furnish, V.P. (1968) *Theology and Ethics in Paul*, Nashville: Abingdon.

——. (1984) *II Corinthians*, New York: Doubleday.

Fusillo, M. (1989) "The Conflict of Emotions: A *Topos* in the Greek Erotic Novel," in Swain 1999: 60–82.

Galinsky, K. (1975) *Ovid's Metamorphoses: An Introduction to the Basic Aspects*, Berkeley: University of California Press.

——. (1988) "The Anger of Aeneas," *AJP*, 109: 321–48; reprinted in P. Hardie (ed.) (1999) *Virgil: Critical Assessments of Classical Authors*, vol. 4, London: Routledge, 434–57.

——. (1994) "How to Be Philosophical about the End of the Aeneid," *ICS*, 19: 191–201.

——. (1996) *Augustan Culture: An Interpretive Introduction*, Princeton: Princeton University Press.

Gardiner, H.N., Metcalf, R.C., and Beebe-Center, J.G. (1937) *Feeling and Emotion: A History of Theories*, New York: American Book Company.

Garrett, S. (1990) "The God of This World and the Affliction of Paul: 2 Cor 4:1–12," in Balch, Ferguson, and Meeks 1990: 99–117.

——. (1995) "Paul's Thorn and Cultural Models of Affliction," in L.M. White and O.L. Yarbrough (eds) *The Social World of the First Christians: Essays in Honor of Wayne A. Meeks*, Minneapolis: Fortress, 82–99.

Garver, E. (1994) "Growing Older and Wiser with Aristotle: Rhetoric II.12–14 and Moral Development," *PBACAP*, 10: 171–200.

Gaselee, S. (1916) "Appendix on the Greek Novel," in Thornley, Edmonds, and Gaselee 1916: 403–16.

Gass, M. (2000) "Eudaimonism and Theology in Stoic Accounts of Virtue," *JHI*, 61: 19–37.

Gastaldi, S. (1987) "*Pathē and Polis*: Aristotle's Theory of Passion in the Rhetorics and the Ethics," *Topoi*, 6: 105–10.
Gatz, B. (1967) *Weltalter, goldene Zeit, und sinnverwandte Vorstellungen*, Hildesheim: Olms.
Gawlick, G. and Görler, W. (1994) "Cicero," in Flashar 1994: 991–1168.
Giani, S. (1993) *Pseudo Archita: L'educazione morale* (Περὶ παιδεύσεως ἠθικῆς), Rome: Gruppo Editoriale Internazionale.
Gibson, R.J. (2000) "Paul and the Evangelization of the Stoics," in P. Bolt and M. Thompson (eds) *The Gospel to the Nations: Perspectives on Paul's Mission*, Downers Grove: InterVarsity, 309–26.
Gigante, M. (1991) "Dossografia stoica," in F. Declevia Caizzi *et al. Varia papyrologica*, Florence: Olschki, 123–6.
Gigante, M. and Capasso, M. (1989) "Il ritorno di Virgilio a Ercolano," *SIFC*, 3rd ser., 7: 3–6.
Gigon, O. (1958) "Interpretationen zu den antiken Aristoteles-Viten," *MH*, 15: 147–93.
——. (ed.) (1962) *Vita Aristotelis Marciana*, Berlin: de Gruyter.
——. (1988) "The Peripatos in Cicero's *De Finibus*," in W.W. Fortenbaugh and R.W. Sharples (eds) *Theophrastean Studies: On Natural Science, Physics and Metaphysics, Ethics, Religion, and Rhetoric*, New Brunswick: Transaction Books, 259–71.
Gill, C. (1984) "The *Ēthos/Pathos* Distinction in Rhetorical and Literary Criticism," *CQ*, 34: 149–66.
——. (1997) "Passion as Madness in Roman Poetry," in Braund and Gill 1997: 213–41.
——. (1998) "Did Galen Understand Platonic and Stoic Thinking on Emotions?" in Sihvola and Engberg-Pedersen 1998: 113–48.
——. (2003) "Reactive and Objective Attitudes: Anger in Virgil's *Aeneid* and Hellenistic Philosophy," in Braund and Most 2003: 208–28.
——. (2005) "Competing Readings of Stoic Emotions," in Salles 2005: 445–70.
——. (2006) *The Structured Self in Hellenistic and Roman Thought*, Oxford: Oxford University Press.
Glad, C. (1992) "Adaptability in Epicurean and Early Christian Psychagogy: Paul and Philodemus," unpublished Ph.D. dissertation, Brown University.
——. (1995) *Paul and Philodemus: Adaptability in Epicurean and Early Christian Psychagogy*, Leiden: Brill.
——. (1996) "Frank Speech, Flattery, and Friendship in Philodemus," in Fitzgerald 1996: 21–59.
Glibert-Thirry, A. (ed.) (1977a) *Pseudo-Andronicus de Rhodes, Peri Pathōn*, Leiden: Brill.
——. (1977b) "La théorie stoïcienne de la passion chez Chrysippe et son evolution chez Posidonius," *RPhL*, 75: 393–435.
Glover, T.R. (1909) *The Conflict of Religions in the Early Roman Empire*, London: Methuen.
Godwin, J. (ed. and trans.) (1986) *Lucretius: De rerum natura IV*, Warminster: Aris & Phillips.
Görler, W. (1984) "Pflicht und 'Lust' in der Ethik der Alten Stoa," in J. Harmatta (ed.) *Proceedings of the VIIth Congress of the International Federation of the Societies of Classical Studies*, 2 vols, Budapest: Akadémiai Kiadó, 2.397–414.

Gomoll, H. (1933) *Der stoische Philosoph Hekaton: Seine Begriffswelt und Nachwirkung unter Beigabe seiner Fragmente*, Bonn: F. Cohn.

Gomperz, T. (1865) *Philodem über Frömmigkeit*, Leipzig: Teubner.

——. (1908) *Greek Thinkers: A History of Ancient Philosophy*, 4 vols, New York: Scribner's.

Goold, G.P. (ed. and trans.) (1995) *Chariton: Callirhoe*, Cambridge: Harvard University Press.

Gordon, P. (1996) *Epicurus in Lycia: The Second-Century World of Diogenes of Oenoanda*, Ann Arbor: University of Michigan Press.

Gosling, J.C.B. and Taylor, C.C.W. (1982) *The Greeks on Pleasure*, Oxford: Clarendon.

Gottschalk, H.B. (1987) "Aristotelian Philosophy in the Roman World from the Time of Cicero to the End of the Second Century AD," *ANRW*, 2.36.2: 1079–174.

——. (1997) "Dionysius," in Zeyl 1997: 196–7.

Gould, J.B. (1970) *The Philosophy of Chrysippus*, Albany: State University of New York Press.

Gould, T. (1990) *The Ancient Quarrel between Poetry and Philosophy*, Princeton: Princeton University Press.

Goulet-Cazé, M.-O. (1986) *L'ascèse cynique: Un commentaire de Diogène Laërce VI 70–71*, Paris: Librairie Philosophique J. Vrin.

——. (1990) "Le cynisme à l'époque impériale," *ANRW*, 2.36.4: 2720–833.

——. (1993) "Les premiers cyniques et la religion," in Goulet-Cazé and Goulet 1993: 117–58.

Goulet-Cazé, M.-O., and Goulet, R. (eds) (1993) *Le Cynisme ancien et ses prolongements: Actes du colloque international du CNRS, Paris, 22–25 juillet 1991*, Paris: Presses Universitaires de France.

Grant, Mark (2000) *Galen on Food and Diet*, London: Routledge.

Grant, Michael (1980) *Greek and Latin Authors: 800 B.C.–A.D. 1000*, New York: Wilson.

Grant, R. (1986) "Theological Education at Alexandria," in B.A. Pearson and J.E. Goehring (eds) *The Roots of Egyptian Christianity*, Philadelphia: Fortress, 178–89.

Graver, M. (1999) "Philo of Alexandria and the Origins of Stoic Προπάθειαι," *Phronesis*, 44: 300–25.

——. (trans.) (2002) *Cicero on the Emotions: Tusculan Disputations 3 and 4*, Chicago: University of Chicago Press.

Green, A. (1979) *Tormented Master: A Life of Rabbi Nahman of Bratslav*, Tuscaloosa: University of Alabama Press.

Gregg, R.C. (1975) *Consolation Philosophy: Greek and Christian Paideia in Basil and the Two Gregories*, Cambridge: Philadelphia Patristic Foundation.

Grese, W.C. (1978) "De profectibus in virtute (Moralia 75A–86A)," in Betz 1978: 11–31.

Griffin, M.T. and Atkins, E.M. (eds) (1991) *Cicero: On Duties*, Cambridge: Cambridge University Press.

Gross, D.M. (2006) *The Secret History of Emotion: From Aristotle's "Rhetoric" to Modern Brain Science*, Chicago: University of Chicago Press.

Gummere, R.M. (trans.) (1917) *Seneca: Ad Lucilium epistulae morales*, vol. 1: *Epistles I–LXV*, London: Heinemann.

——. (trans.) (1917–25) *Seneca: Ad Lucilium epistulae morales*, 3 vols, London: Heinemann.
Gussen, P.J. (1955) *Het Leven in Alexandrië: Volgens de cultuur-historische Gegevens in de Paedagogus (Boek II en III) van Clemens Alexandrinus*, Assen: Van Gorcum.
Gutbrod, W. (1934) *Die paulinische Anthropologie*, Stuttgart: Kohlhammer.
Guthrie, W.K.C. (1957) *In the Beginning: Some Greek Views on the Origins of Life and the Early State of Man*, Ithaca: Cornell University Press.
Haber, L.L. (1972) "Prokope: Stoic Views on Moral Progress in the Context of Psychological Development from Conception to Maturity," unpublished Ph.D. dissertation, University of California, Berkeley.
Hadot, P. (1995) *Philosophy as a Way of Life: Spiritual Exercises from Socrates to Foucault*, Malden: Blackwell.
Hadzsits, G.D. (1906) *Prolegomena to a Study of the Ethical Ideal of Plutarch and of the Greeks of the First Century A.D.*, Cincinnati: University of Cincinnati Press.
Hägg, T. (1971) *Narrative Technique in Ancient Greek Romances*, Stockholm: Almqvist & Wiksell.
——. (1983) *The Novel in Antiquity*, Oxford: Blackwell.
——. (2004) *Parthenope: Selected Studies in Ancient Greek Fiction (1969–2004)*, ed. by L.B. Mortensen and T. Eide, Copenhagen: Museum Tusculanum Press.
Hamerton-Kelly, R.G. (1992) *Sacred Violence: Paul's Hermeneutic of the Cross*, Minneapolis: Fortress.
Hamlyn, D.W. (ed. and trans.) (1967) *Aristotle's De Anima, Books II and III (with Certain Passages from Book I)*, Oxford: Clarendon.
Hammerstaedt, J. (1990) "Der Kyniker Oenomaus von Gadara," *ANRW*, 2.36.4: 2834–65.
Hani, J. (ed. and trans.) (2003) "Consolation à Apollonios," in vol. 2 of *Plutarque, Oeuvres morales*, 2nd edn, Paris: Belles lettres, 1–89.
Hankinson, R.J. (1991) "Galen's Anatomy of the Soul," *Phronesis*, 36: 197–224.
——. (1993) "Actions and Passions: Affection, Emotion, and Moral Self-management in Galen's Philosophical Psychology," in Brunschwig and Nussbaum 1993: 184–220.
Harder, A. (2003) "The Invention of Past, Present and Future in Callimachus' *Aetia*," *Hermes*, 131: 290–306.
Harkins, P.W. (trans.) (1963) *Galen on the Passions and Errors of the Soul*, Columbus: Ohio State University Press.
Harms, W. (1970) *Homo viator in bivio: Studien zur Bildlichkeit des Weges*, Munich: Fink.
Harris, B.F. (1977) "Stoic and Cynic under Vespasian," *Prudentia*, 11: 105–14.
Harris, W.V. (2001) *Restraining Rage: The Ideology of Anger Control in Classical Antiquity*, Cambridge: Harvard University Press.
Hays, R.B. (1986) "Relations Natural and Unnatural: A Response to John Boswell's Exegesis of Romans 1," *JRE*, 14: 184–215.
——. (1996) *The Moral Vision of the New Testament*, San Francisco: HarperSanFrancisco.
Hegel, G.W.F. (1995) *Lectures on the History of Philosophy*, trans. E.S. Haldane, 3 vols, Lincoln: University of Nebraska.

Heine, R.E. (1975) *Perfection in the Virtuous Life: A Study in the Relationship between Edification and Polemical Theology in Gregory of Nyssa's De Vita Moysis*, Cambridge: Philadelphia Patristic Foundation.
Heitz, J.H.E. (1865) *Die verlorenen Schriften des Aristoteles*, Leipzig: Teubner.
Helmbold, W.C. (trans.) (1939) *Plutarch's Moralia*, vol. 6, London: Heinemann.
Helms, J. (1966) *Character Portrayal in the Romance of Chariton*, The Hague: Mouton.
Henrichs, A. (1974) "Die Kritik der stoischen Theologie im *PHerc*. 1428," *CErc*, 4: 5–32.
Hense, O. (ed.) (1905) *C. Musonii Rufi reliquiae*, Leipzig: Teubner.
——. (ed.) (1909) *Teletis Reliquiae*, 2nd edn, Tübingen: Mohr.
Hershbell, J.P. (1972) review of *Plutarque et le stoïcisme*, by D. Babut, *AJP*, 93: 485–9.
——. (1978) "De virtute morali (Moralia 440D–452D)," in Betz 1978: 135–69.
Heylbut, G. (ed.) (1889) *Aspasii in Ethica Nicomachea quae supersunt commentaria*, Berlin: G. Reimer.
Hicks, R.D. (trans.) (1925) *Diogenes Laertius: Lives of Eminent Philosophers*, 2 vols, London: Heinemann.
Hijmans, B.L. (1959) *ΑΣΚΗΣΙΣ: Notes on Epictetus' Educational System*, Assen: Van Gorcum.
Hill, M. (1977) "Paul's Concept of 'Encrateia,' " *RTR*, 36: 70–8.
Hirsch-Luipold, R., Feldmeier, R., Hirsch, B., Koch, L., and Nesselrath, H.-G. (2005) *Die Bildtafel des Kebes: Allegorie des Lebens*, Darmstadt: Wissenschaftliche Buchgesellschaft.
Hock, R.F. (2005) "The Educational Curriculum in Chariton's *Callirhoe*," in Brant, Hedrick, and Shea 2005: 15–36.
Höistad, R. (1948) *Cynic Hero and Cynic King: Studies in the Cynic Conception of Man*, Uppsala: Blom.
Holmes, P. (trans.) (1885) "On Marriage and Concupiscence," in *The Anti-Pelagian Works*, vol. 15 of M. Dods (ed.) (1872–1934) *The Works of Aurelius Augustine: A New Translation*, 15 vols, Edinburgh: T&T Clark; reprinted (1980) P. Shaff (ed.) *A Select Library of the Nicene and Post-Nicene Fathers of the Christian Church*, vol. 5, Grand Rapids: Eerdmans, 257–308.
Hornsby, H.M. (1933) "The Cynicism of Peregrinus Proteus," *Hermathena*, 48: 65–84.
Hubert, K. (1938) "Zur indirekten Überlieferung der Tischgespräche Plutarchs," *Hermes*, 1938: 321–5.
Hudson-Williams, A. and Winterbottom, M. (1996) "Eumenius," *OCD*, 568.
Indelli, G. (ed. and trans.) (1978) *Polistrato, Sul disprezzo irrazionale delle opinioni popolari*, Naples: Bibliopolis.
——. (ed. and trans.) (1988) *Filodemo: L'Ira*, Naples: Bibliopolis.
Ingenkamp, H.G. (1971) *Plutarchs Schriften über die Heilung der Seele*, Göttingen: Vandenhoeck & Ruprecht.
Inwood, B. (1985) *Ethics and Human Action in Early Stoicism*, Oxford: Clarendon.
——. (1993) "Seneca and Psychological Dualism," in Brunschwig and Nussbaum 1993: 150–83.
——. (1996) "Sextius, Quintus," *OCD*, 1398.
——. (1997) "Why Do Fools Fall in Love?" in Sorabji 1997a: 57–69.

——. (ed.) (2003) *The Cambridge Companion to the Stoics*, Cambridge: Cambridge University Press.
——. (2005) "Seneca on Freedom and Autonomy," in Salles 2005: 489–505.
Inwood, B. and Donini, P. (1999) "Stoic Ethics," in K. Algra, J. Barnes, J. Mansfeld, and M. Schofield (eds), *The Cambridge History of Hellenistic Philosophy*, Cambridge: Cambridge University Press, 675–738.
Ioppolo, A.M. (1980) "Carneade e il terzo libro delle 'Tusculanae,' " *Elenchos*, 1: 76–91.
——. (1986) *Opinione e scienza: Il dibattito tra Stoici e Accademici nel III e nel II secolo a.C.*, Naples: Bibliopolis.
Jacquette, D. (1995) "Zeno of Citium on the Divinity of the Cosmos," *SR*, 24: 415–31.
Jaeger, W. (1948) *Aristotle: Fundamentals of the History of His Development*, trans. by R. Robinson, 2nd edn, Oxford: Oxford University Press.
Janko, R. (1984) *Aristotle on Comedy: Towards a Reconstruction of Poetics II*, Berkeley: University of California Press.
——. (1987) *Aristotle: Poetics I, with the Tractatus Coislinianus, a Hypothetical Reconstruction of Poetics II, the Fragments of the On Poets*, Indianapolis: Hackett.
——. (ed. and trans.) (2000) *Philodemus: On Poems, Book 1*, Oxford: Oxford University Press.
Jewett, R. (1971) *Paul's Anthropological Terms: A Study of Their Use in Conflict Settings*, Leiden: Brill.
Johann, H.-T. (1968) *Trauer und Trost: Eine quellen- und strukturanalytische Untersuchung der philosophischen Trostschriften über den Tod*, Munich: Fink.
Johanson, B.C. (1987) *To All the Brethren: A Text-Linguistic and Rhetorical Approach to 1 Thessalonians*, Stockholm: Almqvist & Wiksell.
John, H. (1962) "Das musikerzieherische Wirken Pythagoras' und Damon," *Das Altertum*, 8: 67–72.
Johnson, L.T. (1978) "2 Timothy and the Polemic Against False Teachers: A Re-examination," *JRelS*, 6: 1–26.
——. (1990) "Taciturnity and True Religion: James 1: 26–27," in Balch, Ferguson, and Meeks 1990: 329–39.
Johnston, P.A. (1980) *Vergil's Agricultural Golden Age*, Leiden: Brill.
Jones, C.P. (1970) "Sura and Senecio," *JRS*, 60: 98–104.
——. (1971) *Plutarch and Rome*, Oxford: Clarendon.
——. (1978) *The Roman World of Dio Chrysostom*, Cambridge: Harvard University Press.
——. (1993) "Cynisme et sagesse barbare: Le cas de Peregrinus Proteus," in Goulet-Cazé and Goulet 1993: 305–17.
Kalbfleisch, K. (ed.) (1907) *Simplicii in Aristotelis Categorias commentarium*, Berlin: G. Reimer.
Käsemann, E. (1971) *Perspectives on Paul*, trans. M. Kohl, Philadelphia: Fortress.
Kassel, R. (1958) *Untersuchungen zur griechischen und römischen Konsolationsliteratur*, Munich: Beck.
Kaster, R.A. (2005) *Emotion, Restraint, and Community in Ancient Rome*, New York: Oxford University Press.
Katula, R.A. (2003) "Emotion in the Courtroom: Quintilian's Judge – Then and Now," in Tellegen-Couperus 2003: 145–56.

Keaney, J.J. (1963) "Two Notes on the Tradition of Aristotle's Writings," *AJP*, 84: 52–63.
Keck, L. (2001) "*Pathos* in Romans? Mostly Preliminary Remarks," in Olbricht and Sumney 2001: 71–96.
Kee, H.C. (1983) *Miracle in the Early Christian World*, New Haven: Yale University Press.
Keil, B. (ed.) (1898) *Aelii Aristidis Smyrnaei quae supersunt omnia*, vol. 2: *Orationes XVII–LIII*, Berlin: Weidmann.
Keller, A.C. (1951) "Lucretius and the Idea of Progress," *CJ*, 46: 185–8.
Kendeffy, G. (2000) "Lactantius on the Passions," *Acta Classica Universitatis Scientiarum Debreceniensis*, 26: 113–29.
Kennedy, G.A. (1963) *The Art of Persuasion in Greece*, Princeton: Princeton University Press.
——. (1972) *The Art of Rhetoric in the Roman World, 300 B.C.–A.D. 300*, Princeton: Princeton University Press.
——. (trans.) (1991) *Aristotle on Rhetoric: A Theory of Civic Discourse*, Oxford: Oxford University Press.
Kenney, E.J. (1982) "Ovid," in E.J. Kenney (ed.) *The Cambridge History of Classical Literature*, vol. II: *Latin Literature*, Cambridge: Cambridge University Press, 420–57.
Kenny, A.J.P. (1978) *The Aristotelian Ethics*, Oxford: Clarendon.
Kerferd, G.B. (1978) "What Does the Wise Man Know?" in Rist 1978: 125–36.
Kidd, I.G. (1955) "The Relation of Stoic Intermediaries to the Summum Bonum, With Reference to Change in the Stoa," *CQ*, n.s., 5: 181–94.
——. (1971) "Posidonius on the Emotions," in Long 1971: 200–15.
——. (1978) "Moral Action and Rules in Stoic Ethics," in Rist 1978: 247–58.
King, J.E. (trans.) (1927) *Cicero: Tusculan Disputations*, London: Heinemann.
Kingsley, P. (1995) *Ancient Philosophy, Mystery, and Magic: Empedocles and Pythagorean Tradition*, Oxford: Clarendon Press.
Klaerr, R., Philippon, A., and Sirinelli, J. (eds and trans) (1989) *Plutarque, Oeuveres morales*, vol. 1, part 2: *Traités*, Paris: Belles lettres.
Klassen, W. (1962) "Coals of Fire: Sign of Repentance or Revenge?" *NTS*, 9: 337–50.
——. (1984) *Love of Enemies: The Way to Peace*, Philadelphia: Fortress.
Knuuttila, S. (2004) *Emotions in Ancient and Medieval Philosophy*, Oxford: Clarendon.
Knuuttila, S. and Sihvola, J. (1998) "How the Philosophical Analysis of the Emotions Was Introduced," in Sihvola and Engberg-Pedersen 1998: 1–19.
Koch, K. (2005) *Daniel: Kapitel 1, 1–4, 34*, Neukirchenen-Vluyn: Neukirchener.
Konstan, D. (1994) *Sexual Symmetry: Love in the Ancient Novel and Related Genres*, Princeton: Princeton University Press.
——. (2001) *Pity Transformed*, London: Duckworth.
——. (2003) "Before Jealousy," in Konstan and Rutter 2003: 7–28.
——. (2006) *The Emotions of the Ancient Greeks: Studies in Aristotle and Classical Literature*, Toronto: University of Toronto Press.
——. (2007) "Rhetoric and Emotion," in I. Worthington (ed.) *A Companion to Greek Rhetoric*, Oxford: Blackwell, 411–25.
Konstan, D. and Rutter, N.K. (eds) (2003) *Envy, Spite and Jealousy: The Rivalrous Emotions in Ancient Greece*, Edinburgh: Edinburgh University Press.

Konstan, D., Clay, D., Glad, C.E., Thom, J.C., and Ware, J. (eds and trans) (1998) *Philodemus: On Frank Criticism*, Atlanta: Scholars Press.
Körte, A. (ed.) (1890) *Metrodori Epicurei Fragmenta*, Leipzig: Teubner.
Koster, W.J.W. (ed.) (1975) *Scholia in Aristophanem, Pars I, Prolegomena de comoedia*, Groningen: Wolters-Noordhoff.
Krämer, H.J. (1983) "Die Ältere Akademie," in Flashar 1983b: 1–174.
Kraftchick, S.J. (2001) "Πάθη in Paul: The Emotional Logic of 'Original Argument,' " in Olbricht and Sumney 2001: 39–68.
Krentz, E. (2000) "1 Thessalonians: Rhetorical Flourishes and Formal Constraints," in K.P. Donfried and J. Beutler (eds) *The Thessalonians Debate: Methodological Discord or Methodological Synthesis?* Grand Rapids: Eerdmans, 287–318.
Kühn, C.G. (ed.) (1821–33) *Galeni Opera Omnia*, 20 vols in 22, Leipzig: Cnobloch; reprinted (1964–5) Hildesheim: Olms.
Kuiper, T. (1925) *Philodemus over den Dood*, Amsterdam: H.J. Paris.
Kümmel, W.G. (1948) *Das Bild des Menschen im Neuen Testament*, Zürich: Zwingli.
Kumaniecki, K. (1969) "A propos de la Consolatio perdue de Cicéron," *AFLA*, 46: 369–402.
Lapidge, M. (1978) "Stoic Cosmology," in Rist 1978: 161–85.
Lattimore, R.A. (1942) *Themes in Greek and Latin Epitaphs*, Urbana: University of Illinois Press.
——. (trans.) (1951) *The Iliad of Homer*, Chicago: University of Chicago Press.
——. (ed.) (1955) *Euripides*, vol. 1, Chicago: University of Chicago Press.
Lauffer, S. (1953) "Der antike Fortschrittsgedanke," *Actes du XIème Congrès internationale de philosophie*, 14 vols, Amsterdam: North-Holland, 12.37–44.
Ledbetter, G.M. (1993–4) "The Propositional Content of Stoic Passions," in K.I. Voudoures (ed.) *Hellenistic Philosophy*, 2 vols, Athens: International Center for Greek Philosophy and Culture, 2.107–13.
Leighton, S.R. (1984) "Eudemian Ethics 1220b11–13," *CQ*, 34: 135–8.
——. (1987) "Aristotle's Courageous Passions," *Phronesis*, 33: 76–99.
——. (1996) "Aristotle and the Emotions," in Rorty 1996: 206–37.
Lesher, J.H. (1991) "Xenophanes on Inquiry and Discovery: An Alternative to the 'Hymn to Progress' Reading of Fr. 18," *Ancient Philosophy*, 11: 229–48.
Lévy, C. (1993) "Le concept de *doxa* des Stoïciens à Philon d'Alexandrie: essai d'étude diachronique," in Brunschwig and Nussbaum 1993: 250–84.
Lewis, C.S. (1936) *The Allegory of Love: A Study in Medieval Tradition*, Oxford: Oxford University Press.
Leyerle, B. (1995) "Clement of Alexandria and the Importance of Table Etiquette," *JECS*, 3: 123–41.
Liddell, H.G., Scott, R., and Jones, H.S. (1996) *A Greek-English Lexicon*, 9th edn with revised supplement, Oxford: Clarendon.
Lilla, S.R.C. (1971) *Clement of Alexandria: A Study of Christian Platonism and Gnosticism*, Oxford: Oxford University Press.
Lincoln, A.T. (1989) "The Promise and the Failure: Mark 16:7, 8," *JBL*, 108: 261–87.
Lloyd, A.C. (1978) "Emotion and Decision in Stoic Psychology," in Rist 1978: 233–46.
Long, A.A. (ed.) (1971) *Problems in Stoicism*, London: Athlone.
——. (1980) *Soul and Body in Stoicism: Protocol of the Thirty-Sixth Colloquy, 3 June*

SELECTED BIBLIOGRAPHY

1979, Berkeley: Center for Hermeneutical Studies in Hellenistic and Modern Culture; rev. version in Long 1996d.

——. (1986) *Hellenistic Philosophy: Stoics, Epicureans, Sceptics*, 2nd edn, Berkeley: University of California Press.

——. (1996a) "Arius Didymus and the Exposition of Stoic Ethics," in Long 1996b: 107–33.

——. (1996b) *Stoic Studies*, Cambridge: Cambridge University Press.

——. (1996c) "The Socratic Tradition: Diogenes, Crates, and Hellenistic Ethics," in R.B. Branham and M.-O. Goulet-Cazé (eds) *The Cynics: The Cynic Movement in Antiquity and Its Legacy*, Berkeley: University of California Press, 28–46.

——. (1996d) "Soul and Body in Stoicism," in Long 1996b: 224–49.

——. (1996e) "Stoic Eudaimonism," in Long 1996b: 179–201.

——. (2002) *Epictetus: A Stoic and Socratic Guide to Life*, Oxford: Clarendon.

——. (2006a) *From Epicurus to Epictetus: Studies in Hellenistic and Roman Philosophy*, Oxford: Clarendon.

——. (2006b) "Hellenistic Ethics and Philosophical Power," in Long 2006a: 3–22.

——. (2006c) "Stoic Philosophers on Persons, Property-Ownership, and Community," in Long 2006a: 335–59.

——. (2006d) "Epictetus on Understanding and Managing Emotions," in Long 2006a: 377–94.

Long, A.A. and Sedley, D.N. (1987) *The Hellenistic Philosophers*, 2 vols, Cambridge: Cambridge University Press.

Long, H.S. (ed.) (1964) *Diogenis Laertii Vitae Philosophorum*, Oxford: Clarendon.

Longo Auricchio, F. and Tepedino Guerra, A. (1981) "Aspetti e problemi della dissidenza epicurea," *CErc*, 11: 25–40.

Lord, C. (1986) "On the Early History of the Aristotelian Corpus," *AJP*, 107: 137–61.

Lovejoy, A.O. and Boas, G. (1935) *Primitivism and Related Ideas in Antiquity*, vol. 1 of *A Documentary History of Primitivism and Related Ideas*, Baltimore: Johns Hopkins Press.

Luschnat, O. (1958) "Das Problem des ethischen Fortschritts in der alten Stoa," *Philologus*, 102: 178–214.

——. (1959) "Fortschrittsdenken und Vollendungsstreben im Hellenismus," *Theologia viatorum: Jahrbuch der kirchlichen Hochschule Berlin*, 88–110.

Lutz, C.E. (trans.) (1947) *Musonius Rufus, "The Roman Socrates,"* New Haven: Yale University Press.

Lyonnet, S. (1962) "'Tu ne convoiteras pas' (Rom 7:7)," in *Neotestamentica et Patristica*, Leiden: Brill, 157–65.

MacInnes, H. (1955) *Pray for a Brave Heart*, New York: Dell.

Maguinness, W.S. and Winterbottom, M. (1996) "Panegyric," *OCD*, 1105.

Malherbe, A.J. (ed.) (1977) *The Cynic Epistles: A Study Edition*, Missoula: Scholars Press; reprinted (2006) Atlanta: Society of Biblical Literature.

——. (1978) "Pseudo Heraclitus, Epistle 4: The Divinization of the Wise Man," *JAC*, 21: 42–64.

——. (1982) "Self-Definition among Epicureans and Cynics," in Sanders and Meyer 1982: 46–59.

——. (1983) "Exhortation in 1 Thessalonians," *NovT*, 25: 238–56; reprinted in Malherbe 1989b: 49–66.

——. (1986) *Moral Exhortation: A Greco-Roman Sourcebook*, Philadelphia: Westminster.
——. (1987) *Paul and the Thessalonians: The Philosophic Tradition of Pastoral Care*, Philadelphia: Fortress.
——. (ed. and trans.) (1988) *Ancient Epistolary Theorists*, Atlanta: Scholars Press.
——. (1989a) "Medical Imagery in the Pastoral Epistles," in Malherbe 1989b: 121–36.
——. (1989b) *Paul and the Popular Philosophers*, Minneapolis: Fortress.
——. (1992) "Hellenistic Moralists and the New Testament," *ANRW*, 2.26.1: 267–333.
——. (1998) "Conversion to Paul's Gospel," in A.J. Malherbe, F.W. Norris, and J.W. Thompson (eds) *The Early Church in Its Context: Essays in Honor of Everett Ferguson*, Leiden: Brill, 230–44.
——. (2000) *The Letters to the Thessalonians: A New Translation with Introduction and Commentary*, New York: Doubleday.
Manning, C.E. (1974) "The Consolatory Tradition and Seneca's Attitude to the Emotions," *GR*, 21: 71–81.
——. (1996) "Seneca and Roman Religious Practice," in M. Dillon (ed.) *Religion in the Ancient World: New Themes and Approaches*, Amsterdam: Hakkert, 311–19.
Manuli, P. (1988) "La passione nel *De placitis Hippocratis et Platonis*," in Manuli and Vegetti 1988: 185–214.
Manuli, P. and Vegetti, M. (eds) (1988) *Le opera psicologiche di Galeno*, Naples: Bibliopolis.
Marcovich, M. (ed.) (1999) *Diogenis Laerti Vitae philosophorum*, vol. 1: *Libri I–X*, Stuttgart: Teubner.
Marcus, J. (1982) "The Evil Inclination in the Epistle of James," *CBQ*, 44: 606–21.
——. (1986) "The Evil Inclination in the Letters of Paul," *IBS*, 8: 8–21.
Marcus, R. (trans.) (1953a) *Philo: Supplement I: Questions and Answers on Exodus*, Cambridge: Harvard University Press.
——. (trans.) (1953b) *Philo: Supplement I: Questions and Answers on Genesis*, Cambridge: Harvard University Press.
Marg, W. (ed. and trans.) (1972) *Timaei Locri De natura mundi et animae*, Leiden: Brill.
Marks, J. and Ames, R.T. (eds) (1995) *Emotions in Asian Thought: A Dialogue in Comparative Philosophy*, with a discussion by R.C. Solomon, Albany: State University of New York Press.
Marquardt, J., Mueller, I. von, and Helmreich, G. (eds) (1884) *Claudii Galeni Pergameni: Scripta minora*, vol. 1, Leipzig: Teubner.
——. (eds) (1891) *Claudii Galeni Pergameni: Scripta minora*, vol. 2, Leipzig: Teubner.
Marti, B.M. (1945) "The Meaning of the *Pharsalia*," *AJP*, 66: 352–76.
Martin, C. (trans.) (2004) *Ovid: Metamorphoses*, New York: Norton.
Martin, D. (1995a) *The Corinthian Body*, New Haven: Yale University Press.
——. (1995b) "Heterosexism and the Interpretation of Romans 1:18–32," *BibInt*, 3: 332–55.
——. (1997) "Paul without Passion: On Paul's Rejection of Desire and Sex in Marriage," in H. Moxnes (ed.) *Constructing Early Christian Families: Family as Social Reality and Metaphor*, London: Routledge, 201–15.

Martin, H. and Phillips, J. (1978) "Consolatio ad Uxorem," in Betz 1978: 394–441.
Martin, T.W. (2001) "The Voice of Emotion: Paul's Pathetic Persuasion (Gal 4:12–20)," in Olbricht and Sumney 2001: 181–202.
Martyn, J.L. (2002) "De-apocalypticizing Paul: An Essay Focused on *Paul and the Stoics* by Troels Engberg-Pedersen," *JSNT*, 24: 61–102.
Mathiopoulos, M. (1989) *History and Progress: In Search of the European and American Mind*, with a foreword by G.A. Craig, New York: Praeger.
Mattern-Parkes, S. (2001) "Seneca's Treatise *On Anger* and the Aristocratic Competition for Honor," in E.I. Tylawsky and C.G. Weiss (eds) *Essays in Honor of Gordon Williams*, New Haven: H.R. Schwab, 177–88.
Mayer, C. (ed.) (1986) *Augustinus-Lexikon*, vol. 1: *Aaron–Conuersio*, Basel: Schwabe.
McLelland, J.C. (1976) *God the Anonymous: A Study in Alexandrian Philosophical Theology*, Cambridge: Philadelphia Patristic Foundation.
Meeks, W. (1982) " 'And Rose Up to Play': Midrash and Paraenesis in 1 Corinthians 10:1–22," *JSNT*, 16: 64–77.
——. (1993) *The Origins of Christian Morality: The First Two Centuries*, New Haven: Yale University Press.
Méhat, A. (1966) *Étude sur les "Stromates" de Clément d'Alexandrie*, Paris: Seuil.
Meineke, A. (1859) "Zu Stobaeus," *Sokrates: Zeitschrift für das Gymnasialwesen*, 13: 563–5.
Mekler, S. (ed.) (1886) *Philodemos Peri Thanatou IV*, Vienna: C. Gerold's Sohn.
Merlan, P. (1950) "Lucretius – Primitivist or Progressivist? *JHI*, 11: 364–8.
Mette, H.J. (1984) "Zwei Akademiker heute: Krantor von Soli und Arkesilaos von Pitane," *Lustrum*, 26: 7–94.
Michaelis, W. (1968) "πάσχω," *TDNT*, 5: 904–39.
Miller, W. (trans.) (1913) *Cicero: De Officiis*, London: Heinemann.
Mills, M.J. (1985) "Φθόνος and its Related πάθη in Plato and Aristotle," *Phronesis*, 30: 1–13.
Milobenski, E. (1964) *Der Neid in der griechischen Philosophie*, Wiesbaden: Harrassowitz.
Mitsis, P. (1988) *Epicurus' Ethical Theory: The Pleasures of Invulnerability*, Ithaca: Cornell University Press.
——. (1993) "Seneca on Reason, Rules, and Moral Development," in Brunschwig and Nussbaum 1993: 285–312.
Moles, J.L. (1996) "Diatribe," *OCD*, 463–4.
Moraux, P. (1951) *Les listes anciennes des ouvrages d'Aristote*, Louvain: Éditions universitaires de Louvain.
——. (1984) *Der Aristotelismus bei den Griechen: Von Andronikos bis Alexander von Aphrodisias*, vol. 2, *Der Aristotelismus im I. und II. Jh. n. Chr.*, Berlin: de Gruyter.
Morgan, J.R. and Stoneman, R. (eds) (1994) *Greek Fiction: The Greek Novel in Context*, London: Routledge.
Most, G.W. (ed.) (1997) *Collecting Fragments = Fragmente Sammeln*, Göttingen: Vandenhoeck & Ruprecht.
——. (2003) "Philosophy and Religion," in Sedley 2003: 300–22.
Motto, A.L. (1954–5) "Seneca on Theology," *CJ*, 50: 181–2.
Moxnes, H. (1988) "Honor, Shame, and the Outside World in Romans," in J. Neusner

et al. (eds) *The Social World of Formative Christianity and Judaism*, Philadelphia: Fortress.

Mühlenberg, E. (1966) *Die Unendlichkeit Gottes bei Gregor von Nyssa*, Göttingen: Vandenhoeck & Ruprecht.

Mulvany, C.M. (1926) "Notes on the Legend of Aristotle," *CQ*, 20: 155–67.

Murphy-O'Connor, J. (1982) *Becoming Human Together: The Pastoral Anthropology of St. Paul*, Wilmington: Michael Glazier.

Mynors, R.A.B. (ed.) (1964) *XII Panegyrici Latini*, Oxford: Clarendon.

Nehamas, A. (1994) "Pity and Fear in the *Rhetoric* and the *Poetics*," in D. Furley and A. Nehamas (eds) *Aristotle's Rhetoric: Philosophical Essays*, Princeton: Princeton University Press, 257–82.

Neyrey, J.H. (1980) "The Absence of Emotions – the Lucan Redaction of Lk 22, 39–46," *Bib*, 61: 153–71.

Nilsson, M.P. (1961) *Geschichte der griechischen Religion*, 2 vols, 2nd edn, Munich: Beck.

Nisbet, R. (1980) *History of the Idea of Progress*, New York: Basic.

Nisbet, R.G.M. and Hubbard, M. (1970) *A Commentary on Horace: Odes, Book I*, Oxford: Clarendon.

Nock, A.D. (1933) *Conversion: The Old and the New in Religion from Alexander the Great to Augustine of Hippo*, Oxford: Clarendon.

Nussbaum, M.C. (1986) "Therapeutic Arguments: Epicurus and Aristotle," in Schofield and Striker 1986: 31–74.

——. (1987) "The Stoics on the Extirpation of the Passions," *Apeiron*, 20: 129–75.

——. (1989) "Beyond Obsession and Disgust: Lucretius on the Genealogy of Love," *Apeiron*, 22: 1–59; rev. version in Nussbaum 1994a.

——. (ed.) (1990) *The Poetics of Therapy: Hellenistic Ethics in its Rhetorical and Literary Context*, Edmonton: Academic.

——. (1993) "Poetry and the Passions: Two Stoic Views," in Brunschwig and Nussbaum 1993: 97–149.

——. (1994a) "Beyond Obsession and Disgust: Lucretius on the Therapy of Love," in Nussbaum 1994b: 140–91.

——. (1994b) *The Therapy of Desire: Theory and Practice in Hellenistic Ethics*, Princeton: Princeton University Press.

——. (1996) "Aristotle on Emotions and Rational Persuasion," in Rorty 1996: 303–23.

——. (2001) *Upheavals of Thought: The Intelligence of Emotions*, Cambridge: Cambridge University Press.

——. (2003) "Philosophy and Literature," in Sedley 2003: 211–41.

Obbink, D. (ed.) (1996) *Philodemus: On Piety; Part 1*, Oxford: Clarendon.

Oberhelman, S.M. (1993) "Dreams in Greco-Roman Medicine," *ANRW*, 2.37.1: 121–56.

O'Connor, J.J. and Robertson, E.F. (1999) "Zeno of Sidon," available HTTP: http://www-history.mcs.st-andrews.ac.uk/Mathematicians/Zeno_of_Sidon.html (last accessed 13 December 2006).

O'Daly, G.J.P. and Zumkeller, A. (1986) "*Affectus (passio, perturbatio)*," in Mayer 1986: 166–80.

Olbricht, T.H. (1990) "An Aristotelian Rhetorical Analysis of 1 Thessalonians," in Balch, Ferguson, and Meeks 1990: 216–36.

——. (2001) "*Pathos* as Proof in Greco-Roman Rhetoric," in Olbricht and Sumney 2001: 7–22.
Olbricht, T.H. and Sumney, J.L. (eds) (2001) *Paul and Pathos*, Atlanta: Society of Biblical Literature.
Oldfather, W.A. (trans.) (1925–8) *Epictetus: The Discourses as Reported by Arrian, the Manual, and Fragments*, 2 vols, London: Heinemann.
Oliver, J.H. (1953) *The Ruling Power: A Study of the Roman Empire in the Second Century after Christ through the Roman Oration of Aelius Aristides*, Philadelphia: American Philosophical Society.
Olivieri, A. (ed.) (1914) *Philodemi ΠΕΡΙ ΠΑΡΡΗΣΙΑΣ libellus*, Leipzig: Teubner.
O'Neil, E. (trans.) (1977) *Teles (The Cynic Teacher)*, Missoula: Scholars Press.
Ortiz Garcia, P. (trans.) (1995) *Tabla de Cebes, Musonio Rufo: Disertaciones fragmentos menores, Epicteto: Manual fragmentos*, Madrid: Gredos.
Ortkemper, F.J. (1980) *Leben aus dem Glauben: Christliche Grundhaltungen nach Römer 12–13*, Münster: Aschendorff.
Osborne, E. (1981) *The Beginning of Christian Philosophy*, Cambridge: Cambridge University Press.
Ostwald, M. and Lynch, J.P. (1994) "The Growth of Schools and the Advance of Knowledge," in D.M. Lewis, J. Boardman, S. Hornblower, and M. Ostwald (eds), *The Fourth Century B.C.*, vol. 6 of *The Cambridge Ancient History*, 2nd edn, Cambridge: Cambridge University Press, 592–633.
Paquet, L. (1988) *Les cyniques grecs: Fragments et témoinages*, 2nd edn, Ottawa: Presses de l'Université d'Ottawa.
Parker, C.P. (1901) "Musonius in Clement," *HSCP*, 12: 191–200.
——. (1906) "Sacer Intra Nos Spiritus," *HSCP*, 17: 149–60.
Pauw, D.A. (1995) "The Influence of Emotions upon Events in the Acts of the Apostles," *EkklPhar*, 77: 39–56.
——. (1997) "The Influence of Emotions upon Events in the Gospel of Mark," *EkklPhar*, 79: 47–61.
Penella, R.J. (1979) *The Letters of Apollonius of Tyana*, Leiden: Brill.
Perrot, C. (1983) "Les exemples du desert (1 Cor 10: 6–11)," *NTS*, 29: 437–52.
Pesce, D. (1982) *La Tavola di Cebete*, Brescia: Paideia Editrice.
Petit, F. (ed. and trans.) (1978) *Quaestiones in Genesim et in Exodum: Fragmenta Graeca*, Paris: Cerf.
Pfitzner, V.C. (1967) *Paul and the Agon Motif: Traditional Athletic Imagery in the Pauline Literature*, Leiden: Brill.
Piccaluga, G. (1996) "Ius e Vera Iustitia (Lact.Div.Inst. VI 9.7): Rielaborazione cristiana di un valore assoluto della religione romana arcaica," *L'Etica Cristiana nei secoli 3. e 4.: eredità e confronti*, Rome: Institutum patristicum Augustinianum, 257–69.
Piper, J. (1979) *Love Your Enemies: Jesus' Love Command in the Synoptic Gospels and in the Early Christian Paraenesis*, Cambridge: Cambridge University Press.
Pistelli, H. (ed.) (1888) *Iamblichi Protrepticus*, Stuttgart: Teubner.
Plezia, M. (1975) "De Ptüolemaeo Pinacographo," *Eos*, 63: 37–42.
——. (1985) "De Ptolemaei Vita Aristotelis," in J. Wiesner (ed.) *Aristoteles: Werk und Wirkung*, Berlin: de Gruyter, 1–11.
——. (1986) "Encore sur la Vie d'Aristote de Ptolémée," *LEC*, 54: 383–5.

Pohlenz, M. (1896) "Über Plutarchs Schrift περὶ ἀοργησίας," *Hermes*, 31: 321–38.
——. (1898) "De Posidonii libris Περὶ παθῶν," *Jahrbücher für classische Philologie*, supp. vol. 24: 535–634.
——. (1909) "Das zweite Buch der Tusculanen," *Hermes*, 44: 23–40.
——. (1916) review of *Antike Schriften über Seelenheilung und Seelenleitung auf ihre Quellen untersucht*, by P. Rabbow, *GGA*, 178: 533–59.
——. (1949) "Paulus und die Stoa," *ZNW*, 42: 69–104; reprinted in K. Rengsdorf (ed.) (1969) *Das Paulusbild in der neueren deutschen Forschung*, Darmstadt: Wissenschaftliche Buchgesellschaft, 522–64.
——. (1964) *Die Stoa: Geschichte einer geistigen Bewegung*, 3rd edn, Göttingen: Vandenhoeck & Ruprecht.
——. (1965) *Kleine Schriften*, ed. H. Dörrie, 2 vols, Hildesheim: Olms.
Pomeroy, A.J. (trans.) (1999) *Arius Didymus: Epitome of Stoic Ethics*, Atlanta: Society of Biblical Literature.
Porter, F.C. (1902) "The Yeçer Hara: A Study in the Jewish Doctrine of Sin," in *Biblical and Semitic Studies*, New York: Scribner's, 93–156.
Porter, J. (2003) "Epicurean Attachments: Life, Pleasure, Beauty, Friendship, and Piety," *CErc*, 33: 205–28.
Poster, C. (2001) "The Affections of the Soul: *Pathos*, Protreptic and Preaching in Hellenistic Thought," in Olbricht and Sumney 2001: 23–37.
Price, A.W. (2005) "Were Zeno and Chrysippus at Odds in Analyzing Emotion?" in Salles 2005: 471–88.
Procopé, J. (1993) "Epicureans on Anger," in G.W. Most, H. Petersmann, and A.M. Ritter (eds) *Philanthropia kai eusebeia: Festschrift für Albrecht Dihle zum 70. Geburtstag*, Göttingen: Vandenhoeck & Ruprecht, 363–86.
Puglia, E. (ed. and trans.) (1988) *Demetrio Lacone, Aporie testuali ed esegetiche in Epicuro (PHerc. 1012)*, Naples: Bibliopolis.
Quasten, J. (1962–75) *Patrology*, 3 vols, Utrecht: Spectrum.
Rabbow, P. (1914) *Antike Schriften über Seelenheilung und Seelenleitung auf ihre Quellen untersucht*, vol. 1: *Die Therapie des Zorns*, Leipzig: Teubner.
Rabel, R.J. (1975) "Theories of Emotion in the Old Stoa," unpublished Ph.D. dissertation, University of Michigan.
——. (1977) "The Stoic Doctrine of Generic and Specific *Pathē*," *Apeiron*, 11: 40–2.
——. (1981) "Diseases of the Soul in Stoic Psychology," *GRBS*, 22: 385–93.
Rackham, H. (trans.) (1934) *Aristotle: The Nicomachean Ethics*, rev. edn, London: Heinemann.
Ramelli, I. (2003) *Anneo Cornuto: Compendio di teologia greca*, Milan: Bompiani.
Ramelli, I. and Lucchetta, G.A. (2004) *Allegoria*, vol. 1: *L'età classica*, Milan: V&P Università.
Reale, G. (1990) *A History of Ancient Philosophy*, vol. 4, *The Schools of the Imperial Age*, ed. and trans. J.R. Catan, Albany: State University of New York Press.
Reardon, B.P. (trans.) (1989a) "Chariton, *Chaereas and Callirhoe*," in Reardon 1989b: 17–124.
——. (ed.) (1989b) *Collected Ancient Greek Novels*, Berkeley: University of California Press.
Reggiani, C.K. and Radice, R. (1987) *La filosofia mosaica: La creazione del mondo secondo Mos*, Milan: Rusconi.

Rich, A.N.M. (1956) "The Cynic Conception of AUTARKEIA," *Mnemosyne*, 4th ser., 9: 23–9.
Riedweg, C. (2002) *Pythagoras: Leben, Lehre, Nachwirkung: Eine Einführung*, Munich: Beck.
Rieks, R. (1989) *Affekte und Strukturen: Pathos als ein Form- und Wirkprinzip von Vergils Aeneis*, Munich: Beck.
Riesco, J. (1966) "Dios en la Moral de Seneca," *Helmantica*, 17: 49–75.
Ringeltaube, H. (1914) "Quaestiones ad veterum philosophorum de affectibus doctrinam pertinentes," inaugural dissertation, University of Göttingen.
Rist, J.M. (1969) *Stoic Philosophy*, London: Cambridge University Press.
——. (ed.) (1978) *The Stoics*, Berkeley: University of California Press.
——. (1982) "Are You a Stoic? The Case of Marcus Aurelius," in Sanders and Meyer 1982: 23–45.
——. (1989) *The Mind of Aristotle: A Study in Philosophical Growth*, Toronto: University of Toronto Press.
——. (2002) *Real Ethics: Reconsidering the Foundations of Morality*, Cambridge: Cambridge University Press.
Robbins, F.E. (ed. and trans.) (1940) *Ptolemy: Tetrabiblos*, London: Heinemann.
Robin, L. (1916) "Sur la conception Épicurienne au progrès," *Revue de Métaphysique et de Morale*, 23: 697–719.
Rodríguez Martín, J.-D. (2003) "Moving the Judge: A Legal Commentary on Book VI of Quintilian's *Institutio oratoria*," in Tellegen-Couperus 2003: 157–68.
Rolfe, J.C. (trans.) (1946) *The Attic Nights of Aulus Gellius*, vol. 1, rev. edn, London: Heinemann.
——. (trans.) (1952) *The Attic Nights of Aulus Gellius*, vol. 3, rev. edn, London: Heinemann.
Rollin, B. (2000) *First, You Cry*, 2nd edn, New York: Quill.
Rorty, A.O. (1984) "Aristotle on the Metaphysical Status of *Pathē*," *Review of Metaphysics*, 38: 521–46.
——. (ed.) (1996) *Essays on Aristotle's Rhetoric*, Berkeley: University of California Press.
Rose, V. (ed.) (1863) *Aristoteles pseudepigraphus*, Leipzig: Teubner.
——. (ed.) (1870) "Aristotelis qui ferebantur librorum fragmenta," in vol. 5 of I. Bekker *et al.* (eds) (1831–70) *Aristotelis opera*, Berlin: G. Reimer.
——. (ed.) (1886) *Aristotelis qui ferebantur librorum fragmenta*, Leipzig: Teubner; reprinted (1967) Stuttgart: Teubner.
Roskam, G. (2004) "A Note on the Relation between εὐφυία and προκοπή in Ancient Stoicism and (Middle-) Platonism," *Hermes*, 132: 232–6.
Rouse, W.H.D. (trans.) (1992) *Lucretius: On the Nature of Things*, rev. M.F. Smith, rev. 2nd edn, Cambridge: Harvard University Press.
Rousselle, A. (1988) *Porneia: On Desire and the Body in Antiquity*, Oxford: Blackwell.
Royse, J.R. (1991) *The Spurious Texts of Philo of Alexandria*, Leiden: Brill.
Rubin, S. (1901) *Die Ethik Senecas in ihrem Verhältnis zur älteren und mittleren Stoa*, Munich: Beck.
Ruiz Gito, J.M. (1993) "Olvido y actualidad de un texto griego en España: *La Tabla de Cebes*," *Estudios clásicos*, 35: 49–63.

SELECTED BIBLIOGRAPHY

——. (1997) *La Tabla de Cebes: Historia de un texto griego en el Humanismo y la Educación europea*, Madrid: Cláscias.
Runia, D.T. (1986) *Philo of Alexandria and the Timaeus of Plato*, Leiden: Brill.
——. (1993) *Philo in Early Christian Literature: A Survey*, Assen: Van Gorcum.
——. (1998) "Hippobotos," *DNP*, 5: 580–1; English trans. (2005) in *BNP*, 6: 348.
Russell, D.A. (1973) *Plutarch*, London: Duckworth.
Rüther, T. (1949) *Die sittliche Forderung der Apatheia in den beiden ersten christlichen Jahrhunderten und bei Klemens von Alexandrien*, Freiburg: Herder.
Salles, R. (ed.) (2005) *Metaphysics, Soul, and Ethics in Ancient Thought: Themes from the Work of Richard Sorabji*, Oxford: Clarendon.
Sampley, J.P. (2002) "The First Letter to the Corinthians: Introduction, Commentary, and Reflections," *NIB*, 10: 771–1003.
Sand, A. (1967) *Der Begriff "Fleisch" in den paulinischen Hauptbriefen*, Regensburg: Pustet.
Sandbach, F.H. (ed. and trans.) (1969) *Plutarch's Moralia*, vol. 15, Cambridge: Harvard University Press.
——. (1975) *The Stoics*, New York: Norton.
Sanders, E.P. (1977) *Paul and Palestinian Judaism*, Philadelphia: Fortress.
Sanders, E.P. and Meyer, B.F. (eds) (1982) *Jewish and Christian Self-Definition*, vol. 3: *Self-Definition in the Graeco-Roman World*, Philadelphia: Fortress.
Schenkeveld, D.M. (1998) "The Idea of Progress and the Art of Grammar: Charisius *Ars Grammatica* 1.15," *AJP*, 119: 443–59.
Schenkl, H. (1965) *Epicteti Dissertationes ab Arriani Digestae*, 2nd edn, Stuttgart: Teubner.
Schiesaro, A. (1997) "Passion, Reason and Knowledge in Seneca's Tragedies," in Braund and Gill 1997: 89–111.
Schimmel, A. (1975) *Mystical Dimensions of Islam*, Chapel Hill: University of North Carolina Press.
Schimmel, S. (1979) "Anger and Its Control in Graeco-Roman and Modern Psychology," *Psychiatry*, 43: 320–37.
Schmeling, G.L. (ed.) (1996) *The Novel in the Ancient World*, Leiden: Brill.
Schmeller, T. (1992) "Stoics, Stoicism," *ABD*, 6: 210–14.
Schoedel, W.R. (2000) "Same-Sex Eros: Paul and the Greco-Roman Tradition," in Balch 2000: 43–72.
Schofield, M. (1991) *The Stoic Idea of the City*, Cambridge: Cambridge University Press.
Schofield, M. and Striker, G. (eds) (1986) *The Norms of Nature: Studies in Hellenistic Ethics*, Cambridge: Cambridge University Press.
Schowalter, D.N. (1993) *The Emperor and the Gods: Images from the Time of Trajan*, Minneapolis: Fortress.
Schrage, W. (1988) *The Ethics of the New Testament*, Philadelphia: Fortress.
Schwartz, E. (1903) "Zu Clemens ΤΙΣ Ο ΣΩΖΟΜΕΝΟΣ ΠΛΟΥΣΙΟΣ," *Hermes*, 38: 75–100.
Schweitzer, A. (1930) *Die Mystik des Apostels Paulus*, Tübingen: Mohr.
Scourfield, J.H.D. (1993) *Consoling Heliodorus: A Commentary on Jerome, Letter 60*, Oxford: Clarendon.
——. (2003) "Anger and Gender in Chariton's *Chaereas and Callirhoe*," in Braund and Most 2003: 163–84.

Seddon, K. (2005) *Epictetus' Handbook and the Tablet of Cebes: Guides to Stoic Living*, London: Routledge.

Sedley, D. (1977) "Diodorus Cronus and Hellenistic Philosophy," *Proceedings of the Cambridge Philological Society*, n.s., 23: 74–120.

——. (1989) "Philosophical Allegiance in the Greco-Roman World," in M. Griffin and J. Barnes (eds) *Philosophia Togata: Essays on Philosophy and Roman Society*, Oxford: Clarendon, 97–119.

——. (1993) "Chrysippus on Psychophysical Causality," in Brunschwig and Nussbaum 1993: 313–31.

——. (1996) "Crantor," *OCD*, 405.

——. (1997) "Metrodorus of Lampsacus," in Zeyl 1997: 342–3.

——. (ed.) (2003) *The Cambridge Companion to Greek and Roman Philosophy*, Cambridge: Cambridge University Press.

Segal, C. (1969) *Landscape in Ovid's Metamorphoses: A Study in the Transformations of a Literary Symbol*, Wiesbaden: Steiner.

——. (1990) *Lucretius on Death and Anxiety: Poetry and Philosophy in De Rerum Natura*, Princeton: Princeton University Press.

Sellars, J. (2006) *Stoicism*, Berkeley: University of California Press.

Sevenster, J.N. (1961) *Paul and Seneca*, Leiden: Brill.

Shackleton Bailey, D.R. (ed. and trans.) (2002) *Cicero: Letters to Quintus and Brutus, Letter Fragments, Letter to Octavian, Invectives, Handbook of Electioneering*, Cambridge: Harvard University Press.

Sharples, R.W. (1996a) "Andronicus," *OCD*, 88–9.

——. (1996b) "Hieronymus (1)," *OCD*, 706.

Shaw, T. (1998) *The Burden of the Flesh: Fasting and Sexuality in Early Christianity*, Minneapolis: Fortress.

Sider, D. (ed. and trans.) (1997) *The Epigrams of Philodemos*, Oxford: Oxford University Press.

Sihvola, J. (1989) *Decay, Progress, the Good Life? Hesiod and Protagoras on the Development of Culture*, Helsinki: The Finnish Society of Sciences and Letters.

——. (1996) "Emotional Animals: Do Aristotelian Emotions Require Beliefs?" *Apeiron*, 29: 105–44.

Sihvola, J. and Engberg-Pedersen, T. (eds) (1998) *The Emotions in Hellenistic Philosophy*, Dordrecht: Kluwer.

Siker, J. (1994) "How to Decide: Homosexual Christians, the Bible and Gentile Inclusion," *ThTo*, 51: 219–34.

Simon, B. (1988) *Tragic Drama and the Family: Psychoanalytic Studies from Aeschylus to Beckett*, New Haven: Yale University Press.

Singleton, D. (1972) "Juvenal 6.1–20 and Some Ancient Attitudes to the Golden Age," *GR*, 19: 151–64.

Smith, A. (1996) "Character and Intellect in Aristotle's Ethics," *Phronesis*, 41: 56–74.

Smith, J.W. (2004) *Passion and Paradise: Human and Divine Emotion in the Thought of Gregory of Nyssa*, New York: Herder and Herder.

Smith, J.Z. (1990) *Drudgery Divine: On the Comparison of Early Christianities and the Religions of Late Antiquity*, Chicago: University of Chicago Press.

Smith, P.C. (1998) *The Hermeneutics of Original Argument: Demonstration, Dialectic, Rhetoric*, Evanston: Northwestern University Press.

SELECTED BIBLIOGRAPHY

Snyman, A.H. (1993) "Persuasion in Philippians 4.1–20," in S.E. Porter and T.H. Olbricht (eds) *Rhetoric and the New Testament: Essays from the 1992 Heidelberg Conference*, Sheffield: Sheffield Academic Press, 325–37.

Sollenberger, M.G. (1992) "The Lives of the Peripatetics: An Analysis of the Contents and Structure of Diogenes Laertius' 'Vitae philosophorum' Book 5," *ANRW*, 2.36.6: 3793–879.

Sorabji, R. (ed.) (1997a) *Aristotle and After*, London: Institute of Classical Studies, School of Advanced Study, University of London.

——. (1997b) "Is Stoic Philosophy Helpful as Psychotherapy?" in Sorabji 1997a: 197–209.

——. (1998) "Chrysippus-Posidonius-Seneca: A High-Level Debate on Emotion," in Sihvola and Engberg-Pedersen 1998: 149–70.

——. (1999) "Aspasius on Emotion," in A.M. Alberti and R.W. Sharples (eds) *Aspasius: The Earliest Extant Commentary on Aristotle's Ethics*, Berlin: de Gruyter, 96–106.

——. (2000) *Emotion and Peace of Mind: From Stoic Agitation to Christian Temptation*, Oxford: Oxford University Press.

——. (2002) "Zeno of Citium on Emotions," in T. Scaltsas and A.S. Mason (eds) *The Philosophy of Zeno: Zeno of Citium and His Legacy*, Larnaca, Cyprus: Municipality of Larnaca, 221–38.

——. (2004) "Stoic First Movements in Christianity," in Strange and Zupko 2004: 95–107.

Sorel, G. (1969) *The Ilusions of Progress*, trans. by J. and C. Stanley, Berkeley: University of California Press.

Spanneut, M. (1957) *Le stoïcisme des pères de l'église: De Clément de Rome à Clément d'Alexandrie*, rev. edn, Paris: Seuil.

——. (1994) "*Apatheia* ancienne, *apatheia* chrétienne. Ière partie: L'*apatheia* ancienne," *ANRW*, 2.36.7: 4641–717.

——. (2002) "L' '*apatheia*' divine: des Anciens aux Pères de l'Église," in M. Maritano (ed.) "*Historiam perscrutari*": *Miscellanea di studi offerti al prof. Ottorino Pasquato*, Rome: IAS, 637–52.

Spengel, L. von (ed.) (1854–85) *Rhetores Graeci*, 3 vols in 2, Leipzig: Teubner.

Stacey, W.D. (1956) *The Pauline View of Man in Relation to Its Judaic and Hellenistic Background*, London: Macmillan.

Städele, A. (1980) *Die Briefe des Pythagoras und der Pythagoreer*, Meisenheim am Glan: Hain.

Stählin, O. (ed.) (1906) *Clemens Alexandrinus*, vol. 2, *Stromata, Buch I–VI*, Leipzig: Hinrichs.

——. (ed.) (1909) *Clemens Alexandrinus*, vol. 3, *Stromata, Buch VII und VIII; Excerpta ex Theodoto; Eclogae propheticae; Quis dives salvetur; Fragmente*, Leipzig: Hinrichs.

Steinmetz, P. (1994) "Die Stoa," in Flashar 1994: 491–716.

Stendahl, K. (1962) "Hate, Non-Retaliation and Love: 1QS X, 17–20 and Romans 12:19–21," *HTR*, 55: 343–55.

Stevens, J.A. (1993) "Posidonian Polemic and Academic Dialectic: The Impact of Carneades upon Posidonius' *Peri pathōn*," *GRBS*, 34: 229–323.

Stowers, S. (1990) "Paul on the Use and Abuse of Reason," in Balch, Ferguson, and Meeks 1990: 253–86.

——. (1994) *A Rereading of Romans: Justice, Jews and Gentiles*, New Haven: Yale University Press.
——. (1995) "Romans 7.7-25 as a Speech-in-Character (προσωποποιία)," in T. Engberg-Pedersen (ed.) *Paul in His Hellenistic Context*, Minneapolis: Fortress, 180–202.
Straaten, M. van (ed.) (1962) *Panaetii Rhodii Fragmenta*, 3rd edn, Leiden: Brill.
Strange, S.K. (2004) "The Stoics on the Voluntariness of the Passions," in Strange and Zupko 2004: 32–51.
Strange, S.K. and Zupko, J. (eds) (2004) *Stoicism: Traditions and Transformations*, Cambridge: Cambridge University Press.
Striker, G. (1996a) "Emotions in Context: Aristotle's Treatment of the Passions in the *Rhetoric* and His Moral Psychology," in Rorty 1996: 286–302.
——. (1996b) *Essays on Hellenistic Epistemology and Ethics*, Cambridge: Cambridge University Press.
Sumney, J.L. (2001) "Paul's Use of Πάθος in His Argument against the Opponents of 2 Corinthians," in Olbricht and Sumney 2001: 147–60.
Swain, S. (ed.) (1999) *Oxford Readings in the Greek Novel*, Oxford: Oxford University Press.
Swancutt, D.M. (2004) "Paraenesis in Light of Protrepsis: Troubling the Typical Dichotomy," in J. Starr and T. Engberg-Pedersen (eds) *Early Christian Paraenesis in Context*, Berlin: de Gruyter, 113–53.
Tannehill, R.C. (2007) "Participation in Christ: A Central Theme in Pauline Soteriology," in *The Shape of the Gospel*, Eugene: Wipf & Stock, 225–39.
Tarán, L. (1981) *Speusippus of Athens*, Leiden: Brill.
Tatum, J. (ed.) (1994) *The Search for the Ancient Novel*, Baltimore: Johns Hopkins University Press.
Taylor, M. (1947) "Progress and Primitivism in Lucretius," *AJP*, 68: 180–94.
Teggart, F.J. (1949) *The Idea of Progress*, rev. edn with an introduction by G.H. Hildebrand, Berkeley: University of California Press.
Tellegen-Couperus, O. (ed.) (2003) *Quintilian and the Law: The Art of Persuasion in Law and Politics*, Leuven: Leuven University Press.
Temkin, O. (1973) *Galenism: Rise and Decline of a Medical Philosophy*, Ithaca: Cornell University Press.
Tepedino Guerra, A. (1977) "Filodemo sulla gratitudine," *CErc*, 7: 96–113.
Theissen, G. (1987) *Psychological Aspects of Pauline Theology*, trans. J. Galvin, Philadelphia: Fortress.
Thesleff, H. (1961) *An Introduction to the Pythagorean Writings of the Hellenistic Period*, Åbo: Åbo Akademi.
——. (1965a) *The Pythagorean Texts of the Hellenistic Period*, Åbo: Åbo Akademi.
——. (1965b) review of *Nigidio Figulo*, by Adriana Della Casa, *Gnomon*, 37: 44–8.
Thom, J.C. (1994) " 'Don't Walk on the Highways': The Pythagorean *Akousmata* and Early Christian Literature," *JBL*, 113: 93–112.
——. (1995) *The Pythagorean Golden Verses: With Introduction and Commentary*, Leiden: Brill.
——. (1997) " 'Harmonious Equality': The Topos of Friendship in Neopythagorean Writings," in Fitzgerald 1997: 77–103.

——. (2001) "Cleanthes, Chrysippus and the Pythagorean *Golden Verses*," *AClass*, 44: 197–219.
——. (2005) *Cleanthes' Hymn to Zeus: Text, Translation, and Commentary*, Tübingen: Mohr Siebeck.
Thompson, J.W. (2001) "Paul's Argument from *Pathos* in 2 Corinthians," in Olbricht and Sumney 2001: 127–45.
Thornley, G., Edmonds, J.M., and Gaselee, S. (eds and trans.) (1916) *Daphnis & Chloe by Longus, with The Love Romances of Parthenius and Other Fragments*, London: Heinemann.
Thraede, K. (1972) "Fortschritt," *RAC*, 8: 141–82.
Thurén, L. (1999) "Was Paul Angry? Derhetorizing Galatians," in S.E. Porter and D.L. Stamps (eds) *The Rhetorical Interpretation of Scripture: Essays from the 1996 Malibu Conference*, Sheffield: Sheffield Academic Press, 302–20.
——. (2000) *Derhetorizing Paul: A Dynamic Perspective on Pauline Theology and the Law*, Tübingen: Mohr Siebeck.
Tieleman, T. (1996) *Galen and Chrysippus: Argument and Refutation in the De Placitis, Books II-III*, Leiden: Brill.
——. (2003) *Chrysippus' On Affections: Reconstructions and Interpretations*, Leiden: Brill.
Tissol, G. (1997) *The Face of Nature: Wit, Narrative, and Cosmic Origins in Ovid's Metamorphoses*, Princeton: Princeton University Press.
Todd, R. (1978) "Monism and Immanence: The Foundations of Stoic Physics," in Rist 1978: 137–60.
Toohey, P. (2004) *Melancholy, Love, and Time: Boundaries of the Self in Ancient Literature*, Ann Arbor: University of Michigan Press.
Trapp, M.B. (ed.) (1994) *Maximus Tyrius Dissertationes*, Stuttgart: Teubner.
——. (trans.) (1997a) *Maximus of Tyre: The Philosophical Orations*, Oxford: Clarendon.
——. (1997b) "On the Tablet of Cebes," in Sorabji 1997a: 159–79.
Tsouna, V. (1998) *The Epistemology of the Cyrenaic School*, Cambridge: Cambridge University Press.
——. (2001) "Philodemus on the Therapy of Vice," *OSAPh*, 21: 233–58.
——. (2003) " 'Portare davanti agli occhi': Una tecnica retorica nelle opere 'morali' di Filodemo," *CErc*, 33: 243–8.
Tulin, A. (1993) "Xenophanes Fr. 18 D.-K. and the Origins of the Idea of Progress," *Hermes*, 121: 129–38.
Usener, H. (ed.) (1887) *Epicurea*, Leipzig: Teubner.
Valantasis, R. (1999) "Musonius Rufus and Roman Ascetical Theory," *GRBS*, 40: 207–31.
Van Doren, C. (1967) *The Idea of Progress*, New York: Praeger.
van Geytenbeek, A.C. (1963) *Musonius Rufus and Greek Diatribe*, Assen: Van Gorcum.
Vander Waerdt, P.A. (1985) "Peripatetic Soul-Division, Posidonius, and Middle Platonic Moral Psychology," *GRBS*, 26: 373–94.
Verbeke, G. (1991) "Ethics and Logic in Stoicism," in M.J. Osler (ed.) *Atoms, Pneuma and Tranquility: Epicurean and Stoic Themes in European Thought*, Cambridge: Cambridge University Press, 11–24.

Viano, C. (2003) "Aristotle on Emotions and *Thumos* in Aristotle's *Rhetoric,"* in Konstan and Rutter 2003: 85–97.
Vitelli, C. (ed.) (1979) *M. Tulli Ciceronis Consolationis fragmenta*, Florence: A. Mondadori.
Vlastos, G. (1966) "Zeno of Sidon as a Critic of Euclid," in L. Wallach (ed.) *The Classical Tradition: Literary and Historical Studies in Honor of Harry Caplan*, Ithaca: Cornell University Press, 148–59; reprinted in G. Vlastos (1995) *Studies in Greek Philosophy*, vol. 2, D.W. Graham (ed.), Princeton: Princeton University Press, 315–24.
Vögtle, A. (1936) *Die Tugend- und Lasterkataloge im Neuen Testament: Exegetische, religions- und formgeschichtlich Untersucht*, Münster: Aschendorff.
Voelke, A.J. (1969) "Les origines stoïcennes de la notion de volonté," *RTP*, 19: 1–22.
Völker, W. (1938) *Fortschritt und Vollendung bei Philo von Alexandrien: Eine Studie zur Geschichte der Frömmigkeit*, Leipzig: J.C. Hinrichs.
von Staden, H. (1982) "Hairesis and Heresy: The Case of the *haireseis iatrikai*," in Sanders and Meyer 1982: 76–100.
Wachsmuth, C. and Hense, O. (eds) (1884–1912) *Ioannis Stobaei Anthologium*, 5 vols, Berlin: Weidmann.
Walbank, F.W. (1972) *Polybius*, Berkeley: University of California Press.
Walcot, P. (1978) *Envy and the Greeks: A Study of Human Behaviour*, Warminster: Aris & Phillips.
Walzer, R. (1947) *Galen on Jews and Christians*, Oxford: Oxford University Press.
Warner, R. (trans.) (1955) "The Medea," in Lattimore 1955: 55–108.
Warren, J. (2004) *Facing Death: Epicurus and His Critics*, Oxford: Clarendon.
Webb, R. (1997) "Imagination and the Arousal of the Emotions in Greco-Roman Rhetoric," in Braund and Gill 1997: 112–27.
Wehrli, F. (ed.) (1967) *Aristoxenus*, vol. 2 of *Die Schule des Aristoteles: Texte und Kommentar*, 2nd edn, Basel: Schwabe.
——. (ed.) (1969) *Hieronymos von Rhodos, Kritolaos und seine Schüler*, vol. 10 of *Die Schule des Aristoteles: Texte und Kommentar*, 2nd edn, Basel: Schwabe.
——. (1974) *Hermippos der Kallimacheer*, supplementary vol. 1 of *Die Schule des Aristoteles: Texte und Kommentar*, 2nd edn, Basel: Schwabe.
——. (1983) "Der Peripatos bis zum Beginn der römischen Kaiserzeit," in Flashar 1983b: 459–599.
——. (ed.) (1974) *Hermippos der Kallimacheer*, supplementary vol. 1 of *Die Schule des Aristoteles: Texte und Kommentar*, 2nd edn, Basel: Schwabe.
Weiss, H.D. (1989) "A Schema of 'The Road" in Philo and Lucan," *SPhilo*, 1: 43–57.
Welborn, L.L. (2001) "Paul's Appeal to the Emotions in 2 Corinthians 1.1–2.13; 7.5–16," *JSNT*, 82: 31–60.
Wendland, P. (1886) *Quaestiones Musonianae: De Musonio stoico Clementis Alexandrini aliorumque auctore*, Berlin: Mayer & Mueller.
——. (1895) *Philo und die kynisch-stoische Diatribe*, part 1 of P. Wendland and O. Kern (1895) *Beiträge zur Geschichte der griechischen Philosophie und Religion*, Berlin: Reimer.
West, M.L. (ed.) (1978) *Hesiod: Works & Days*, Oxford: Clarendon.
White, L.M. (1981) "Scholars and Patrons: Christianity and High Society in

Alexandria," in E. Ferguson (ed.) *Christian Teaching: Studies in Honor of LeMoine G. Lewis*, Abilene, TX: Abilene Christian University Press, 328–42.

——. (2003) "Rhetoric and Reality in Galatians: Framing the Social Demands of Friendship," in Fitzgerald, Olbricht, and White 2003: 307–49.

——. (2004) "A Measure of *Parrhēsia*: The State of the Manuscript of PHerc. 1471," in Fitzgerald, Obbink, and Holland 2004: 103–30.

White, L.M. and Fitzgerald, J.T. (2003) "*Quod est comparandum*: The Problem of Parallels," in Fitzgerald, Olbricht, and White 2003: 13–39.

White, N.P. (1978) "Two Notes on Stoic Terminology," *AJP*, 99: 111–19.

White, S.A. (1997) "Hieronymus," in Zeyl 1997: 271.

Wiesen, D.S. (trans.) (1968) *Saint Augustine: The City of God against the Pagans*, vol. 3, Cambridge: Harvard University Press.

Wilke, K. (ed.) (1914) *Philodemi: De Ira liber*, Leipzig: Teubner.

Wilken, Robert (1995) *Remembering the Christian Past*, Grand Rapids: Eerdmans.

Williams, B. (1994) "Do Not Disturb," review of M. Nussbaum, *The Therapy of Desire*, in *London Review of Books* (20 October), 25–6.

——. (1997) "Stoic Philosophy and the Emotions: Reply to Richard Sorabji," in Sorabji 1997a: 211–13.

Willis, W.L. (1985) *Idol Meat in Corinth: The Pauline Argument in 1 Corinthians 8 and 10*, Chico: Scholars Press.

Wilson, E.O. (ed.) (2006) *From So Simple a Beginning: The Four Great Books of Charles Darwin*, New York: Norton.

Wilson, M. (1997) "The Subjugation of Grief in Seneca's *Epistles*," in Braund and Gill 1997: 48–67.

Wilson, W. (trans.) (1888) *The Writings of Clement of Alexandria*, vol. 2, in A. Roberts and J. Donaldson (eds) and A.C. Coxe (rev.) *Ante-Nicene Christian Library: Translations of the Writings of the Fathers Down to A.D. 325*, vol. 12, Edinburgh: T&T Clark; reprinted (1971) *The Ante-Nicene Fathers: Translations of the Writings of the Fathers Down to A.D. 325*, vol. 2, Grand Rapids: Eerdmans.

Wimbush, V. (1987) *Paul the Worldly Ascetic: Response to the World and Self-Understanding according to 1 Corinthians 7*, Macon: Mercer University Press.

Wimmer, A. (1955) "Trostworte des Apostels Paulus und Hinterbliebene in Thessalonich (1 Th 4, 13–17)," *Bib*, 36: 273–86.

Winkler, J.J. (trans.) (1989) "Achilles Tatius, *Leucippe and Clitophon*," in Reardon 1989b: 170–284.

Winston, D. (1984) "Philo's Ethical Theory," *ANRW*, 2.21.1: 372–416.

——. (1992) "Philo's Conception of the Divine Nature," in L.E. Goodman (ed.) *Neoplatonism and Jewish Thought*, Albany: State University of New York Press, 21–42.

——. (1995) "Sage and Super-sage in Philo of Alexandria," in D.P. Wright, D.N. Freedman, and A. Hurvitz (eds) *Pomegranates and Golden Bells: Studies in Biblical, Jewish, and Near Eastern Ritual, Law, and Literature in Honor of Jacob Milgrom*, Winona Lake: Eisenbrauns, 815–24.

Winston, D. and Dillon, J. (1983) *Two Treatises of Philo of Alexandria*, Chico: Scholars Press.

Wisse, J. (1989) *Ethos and Pathos: From Aristotle to Cicero*, Amsterdam: Hakkert.

Witherington, B. (1995) *Conflict and Community in Corinth: A Socio-Rhetorical Commentary on 1 and 2 Corinthians*, Grand Rapids: Eerdmans.

Withington, E.T. (trans.) (1927) *Hippocrtes*, vol. 3, London: Heinemann.

Wolfson, H.A. (1948) *Philo: Foundations of Religious Philosophy in Judaism, Christianity, and Islam*, rev. 2nd printing, 2 vols, Cambridge: Harvard University Press.

Woods, M. (ed. and trans.) (1982) *Aristotle's Eudemian Ethics: Books I, II, and VIII*, Oxford: Clarendon.

Wormell, D.E.W. (1935) "Hermias of Atarneus," *YCS*, 5: 57–92.

——. (1996) "Hermias (1)," *OCD*, 691.

Wright, M.R. (1997) "*Ferox uirtus*: Anger in Virgil's *Aeneid*," in Braund and Gill 1997: 169–84.

Xenakis, J. (1969) *Epictetus: Philosopher-Therapist*, The Hague: Martinus Nijhoff.

Yarbrough, O.L. (1985) *Not Like the Gentiles: Marriage Rules in the Letters of Paul*, Atlanta: Scholars Press.

Young-Bruehl, E. (2003) *Where Do We Fall When We Fall in Love?* New York: Other Press.

Zeller, E. (1889–1903) *Die Philosophie der Griechen in ihrer geschichtlichen Entwicklung*, 6 vols, 4th edn, Leipzig: Reisland.

——. (1919–23) *Die Philosophie der Griechen in ihrer geschichtlichen Entwicklung*, W. Nestle and E. Wellmann (ed.), 3 vols in 6, 5th–7th edn, Leipzig: Reisland.

Zerbe, G. (1992) "Paul's Ethic of Nonretaliation and Peace," in W. Swartley (ed.) *The Love of Enemy and Nonretaliation in the New Testament*, Louisville: Westminster/John Knox, 177–222.

Zeyl, D.J. (ed.) (1997) *Encyclopedia of Classical Philosophy*, Westport: Greenwood.

INDEX OF ANCIENT AUTHORS AND TEXTS

1. Hebrew Bible

Gen	237n	11:9	13
1–11	13	15:13	204
3:1	206		
3:1–6	13	Exod	
3:14 LXX	208, 210	15:23	213
3:21	13	21:30	208
4:1–8	13	24:28	209
4:8	14		
4:12 LXX	205	Lev	
4:13–15	205	8:21	210, 211
4:17	13, 14	8:29	210, 211
4:20	13	9:14	209, 211
4:21	13		
4:22	13	Ps	
4:23–4	13	4:4	115n
6:11	13	4:5 LXX	80
9:20	13		
9:20–7	13	Prov	
11:2	13	10:21	300
11:3–4	13		

2. Apocryphal/Deuterocanonical Books

4 Macc			
2:6	237n	14:8–14	319n
		14:15–31	319n
Wis			
13:1–9	319n		

3. Old Testament Pseudepigrapha

Ps.-Phocylides			
193	233n		
		T.Reu.	
T.Jos.		2.9	205
7.8	233n		

4. Josephus and Philo

Josephus, *A.J.*		*Deus*	
4.328–9	218n	35	312n
		52	207
Philo	12, 15, 88,	59	207
	93, 201–20,	75	203
	292	162–5	203
Abr.		*Ebr.*	
29	202	6	218n
32	217n	53	219n
73	219n		
170	220n	*Fug.*	
202	207	157	203
220–3	292, 313n	158	213
223	313n	202	212
243–4	220n	213	212
257	203		
		Gig.	217n
Agr.			
30	202, 214n	*Her.*	
59	216n	46	219n
73	205	121	203
76	205	167	202
103	204, 216n	185	202
160–1	147n	232	202
		269	204
Cher.		272–3	213
14	312n	285–6	203
50	212	307	202
86	203		
		Leg.	
Conf.		1.28	214n
24–5	220n	1.40	203
		1.72–3	205
Congr.		1.73	205
26	202	2.6	219n
55	213	2.8	212, 216n
		2.10	220n
Decal.		2.11	205
142	206	2.12	212
142–53	237n	2.74–5	206
145	217n, 218n	2.86	212
146	206, 217n	2.99	202
		2.100	217n
Det.		2.100–2	212
6–9	203	2.107	206
46	220n	3.22	312n
110	292	3.65–8	206
119	218n	3.86–7	217n
161–2	203		

3.107–10	206	*Plant.*	
3.113	206, 209, 217	35	207
3.114–28	208	*Post.*	
3.115–18	202	25	219n
3.116	209	30–1	212
3.118	205, 219n	71	213
3.128–40	209	79	217n
3.129	208	83	217n
3.129–59	208, 211	101	203
3.131	212	155–9	213
3.136	205, 212		
3.139	201, 206	*Praem.*	
3.140	212	68–73	205
3.140–1	209	161	217n
3.141	210		
3.141–2	210	*Prob.*	
3.147	210, 211, 220n	159	204
3.160	213		
3.161	210	*Prov.*	
3.210	312n	1.56	212
3.219	212	1.66	212
3.248	213		
		QG	
Migr.		1.79	216n
67	208, 210, 211, 220n	2.12	220n
		2.33	202
84	203	2.57	217n
		2.59	214n
Mos.		4.73	215n, 216n
1.21–2	207		
1.297	204	*Sacr.*	
2.139	216n	8	207
2.147	203	9	203
2.165	219n	95–6	207
2.280	205		
		Somn.	
Mut.		1.36	209
19	203	1.152	219n
30	220n	1.173	212
50	202	2.13	206, 220n
111	202	2.14	218n
160	204	2.25	212
161–3	205	2.146	203
181–5	203	2.161	205
211	202	2.200	205
225	202	2.234–6	212
		2.266–7	212
Opif.		2.276	205
75	220n		
162	206	*Spec.*	
117	202	1.148	205

INDEX OF ANCIENT AUTHORS AND TEXTS

1.252	203	4.102	203
4.79	205	4.113	213, 216n
4.79–105	218n		
4.83	213	*Virt.*	
4.84	237n	14	220n
4.92–4	202	177	203
4.94	205		

5. New Testament

		1–7	230
Matt		1–8	252, 255
7:14	310n	1:5	243, 264n
19:21	290	1:18	223, 236n
19:28	309n	1:18–25	283n
		1:18–32	230, 231, 265n, 319n
Mark			
4:7	314n	1:20	264n
4:19	313n	1:20–3	272
10:17–31	309n	1:22	265n
10:25	284, 287, 309n	1:23	265n
		1:24	236n
Luke		1:24–5	229
8:14	314n	1:24–7	231, 237n
11:13	280n	1:26	222, 236n
14:33	290	1:26–7	228, 229, 231
18:25	309n	1:27	236n
		2	264n
John		2:1	264n
7:39	280n	2:5	236n
		2:17	254
Acts		2:17–24	254
2:38	280n	3:21–3	265n
4:31	280n	3:21–6	273
5:32	280n	3:24	265n
6:3	280n	3:27–31	275
6:5	280n	4–5	264n
8:15–19	280n	4:4–5	264n
10:47	280n	4:17	272
11:24	280n	4:17–25	283n
15:8	280n	4:19–25	273
19:2–6	280n	4:24	282n
		5:5	272, 280n
Paul	12, 15, 25n, 81, 98, 114, 221–37, 238–66, 267–83, 290, 292	5:8	262n, 264n
		5:12–21	265n
		6	262n
		6–8	266n
		6:1–11	273, 281n
		6:1–14	252
		6:3	282n
Rom	230, 232	6:4	282n
1	264n	6:11	282n

359

6:12	236n, 264n	1 Cor	226, 229, 232, 259, 262n
6:16–17	264n		
7	229, 230	1–3	257, 259
7:5	222, 223, 236n	1:4	249
7:7–8	229, 236n	1:4–9	249
7:23	237n	1:4–10	249
8:1–2	282n	1:5	249
8:1–4	272	1:6	249
8:1–17	274, 281n	1:8	249
8:3–4	276	1:9	249
8:5	248	1:10	249, 264n
8:5–13	248	1:13–17	266n
8:6–7	248	1:18–2:16	273
8:6–9	269	1:26–31	275
8:8	248	1:26–2:5	266n
8:9	248, 280n, 282n	1:29	255, 265n
		1:30	282n
8:9a	248	1:31	255, 265n
8:9–11	248	2:1	258
8:9–17	272, 274	2:1–5	257
8:12–13	248	2:2	258
8:13	248	2:4	257
8:18	233n, 282n	2:5	257
8:39	282n	2:6–16	257, 266n
9	262n	2:7	258
9:10–23	252	2:10	258
9:14–23	265n	2:12	280n
9:20	265n	3:1	258
9:22	236n, 263n	3:1–3	257, 266n
10:6–13	273	3:3	258
10:14–15	250	3:11	259
10:14–16	250	3:11–15	259
10:16	250	3:15	259
10:18	250	3:16	272, 280n
10:19	250	3:21	255
11:1	280n	4:14–21	236n
11:33–6	272	5–6	229, 236n
12	228	5–7	246
12:1–2	274, 275, 283n	5:1–5	257
		5:6–7	246
12:19–21	227	5:7	281n
13:4	236n	5:8	246
13:13–14	236n	6:1–11	257
14:7–8	282n	6:7–8	246
14:21	290	6:8	257
14:23	247	6:9	246, 257
15:7–13	275, 283n	6:9–10	263n
15:18	264n	6:9–11	263n, 269, 274, 276
15:30	235n		
15:30–3	277	6:11	246, 257
16:19	264n	6:13–14	276
16:26	264n	6:14	282n

6:15	281n	7:11	236n
6:19–20	263n, 272, 275,	8:6	256
	281n, 282n	8:10–11	256
7	227, 230	10	237n
7:1–5	237n	10–13	225
7:5	246	10:6	263n
7:9	232	11	236n
7:32–5	227	11:28	235n
8	237n	11:29	236n
8:1–13	246	12:7–8	282n
8:2	264n	12:9–10	282n
8:2–3	264n	12:10–12	235n
8:4–6	272, 275	12:20	236n
9:24–7	235n	13:1–10	236n
10	262n	13:5	263n
10:1–12	246	13:11	264n
10:5	246		
10:6	229, 236n, 246	Gal	223, 225,
10:6–10	236n, 237n		226
10:9	246	1	251
10:10	246	1:6	257
10:12	246	1:12	251
10:13	249	1:12–16	243
10:19–20	247	1:13–14	251
10:23	114	1:16	251
11:29	263n	1:16c	251
11:32	263n	2:5	251
12–14	266n	2:14	251
12:3	266n	2:16	282n
12:26	233n	2:16–21	273
13:12	244, 264n	2:19	255
15:12	282n	2:19–20	256
15:23	282n	2:19–21	274
		2:20	273, 274
2 Cor	225, 226, 232	2:21	265n
1–7	225	3:1–2	273
1:5–7	233n	3:2	280n
1:6	233n	3:3	256, 266n
1:8	282n	3:4	233n
1:22	280n	3:5	280n
2:3–11	228	3:13–14	276
2:6–7	236n	3:14	266n
3:17–18	274	3:25–8	257
4:6–10	269, 275, 276	3:26	282n
4:7	276	3:27	282n
4:14	282n	4:4–6	272, 273,
5:17	282n		276
5:19–20	243	4:6	266n, 272,
5:21	282n		274, 276, 280n
6:10	235n	4:6–7	257
7:8–13	228	4:9	250, 251
7:9–11	236n	4:12–20	225

5:5	258	4:6–7	283n
5:13–26	262n	4:7	277
5:13–6:10	235n		
5:16	234n	Col	
5:17–24	257	1:24	233n
5:18–24	269	1:29–2:1	235n
5:19–21	223	3:5	222, 236n
5:20	236n		
5:22	257	1 Thess	223, 224–5, 227
5:23	232		
5:24	222, 257, 236n, 282n	1:6	234n
		1:8	282n
5:25	273	1:9–10	272, 275
5:25–6	257	2–3	227
6:1	257	2:13	269, 272
6:14	257	2:14	233n, 235n
6:14–16	275	2:15–16	224
		2:16	236n
Eph	80, 81	2:17	235n, 236n
4:26–7	79–80	2:17–20	234n
		3:5	234n
Phil	262n	3:9–10	283n
1:6	256, 266n	3:10	263n, 266n
1:9–10	262n		
1:9–11	269, 277	3:11–13	277
1:12	256	4	235n
1:19	280n	4:3–5	229, 237n
1:23	236n, 282n	4:3–8	237n
1:25	256	4:5	4, 222, 236n
1:27–30	235n	4:7–9	274
1:29	233n, 282n	4:8	272, 280n
2:6–11	272, 275	4:9–12	225
2:12	263n, 264n	4:13–18	282n
2:12–13	249, 274	4:13–18	227
2:13	269, 263n	4:13–5:11	234n
2:15–16	263n	4:17	282n
2:16	265n	5:16–18	283n
3:2–3	283n	5:23–4	282n
3:2–16	275		
3:8	282n	2 Thess	
3:9–10	273	2:14	233n
3:10	233n, 244, 262n		
3:10–11	282n	2 Tim	
3:11	244, 262n	1:12	233n
3:12	244, 245, 257, 262n, 264n	1:14	280n
		3:11	233n
3:12–14	244, 257		
3:12–16	262n	Phlm	
3:14	244	6	282n
3:20	244		
3:20–1	282n	Jas	
3:21	244	1:19–20	81

1 Pet		1 John	
1:12	276	3:24	280n
		4:13	280n

6. Non-canonical Early Christian Literature

Athenagoras, *Suppl.*		1.4	286
22	280n	2.2	309n
		3.1	308n, 319n
Augustine		3.2	311n
Civ.		3.3–4	311n
8.17	3, 4	3.3–6	291
9.4	4	4.4–9	309n
19.1.2–3	52	5.1	309n
		11	313n
Nupt.	17n	11.2	290, 308n
2.55	4, 5	11.4	310n
		12.2	287, 296
Clement of Alexandria	12, 23n, 284–321	12.3–5	310n
		14.5–6	290
		20.6	293
Paed.	288, 298, 301, 305–6	25.4	293
		26.8	310n
1.1	311n, 318n, 319n, 320n	29.2–3	318n
		34.3	319n
		35.1–2	319n
1.2	319n	40.5–6	318n
1.6	319n	41	288
1.9	311n, 319n, 320n, 321n	41.1	287, 303, 308n, 319n
2	288	42	306, 317n
2.1	290, 292, 300, 314n, 317n, 318n	42.5	321n
		42.6–7	321n
		42.13, 15	321n
2.1–7	311n		
2.2	300	*Strom.*	
2–3	301	1.3	320n
2.4	311n	2.2	319n
2.7	311n	2.5	287, 309n, 310n, 321n
3	288		
3.2.5	317n	2.6	319n
3.11	318n	2.11	318n
		2.13	294
Protr.	288, 293	2.20	301
1	293, 297	2.22	18n
2	311n	3.3	310n, 312n
11	315n	3.7	314n
12	318n	4.1	310n
		4.23	314n
Quis div.	284, 287–8	4.5	295, 296
1.1–3	285	4.6	319n, 321n
1.3	308n		

5.5.27.8	77n	Justin Martyr	288
5.8	292, 318n		
7.5	309n	Lactantius	
7.6	314n	*Div. Inst*	14
7.10	312n	5.12.1	14
		6.9.4	14
Eusebius	288		
Hist. eccl.		Malalas, J.	310n
6.11.6	310n		
6.14.1	310n	Maximus the Confessor	122, 131
Praep. ev.	132n	Origen	104, 288, 292
11.38	313n	*Cels.*	
		5.7	280n
Gregory of Nyssa	21n, 25n	8.51	104

7. Classical, Hellenistic, Roman, and Late Antique Works

Achilles Tatius	196	Antiochus of Ascalon	203, 214n
4.7	193		
5.19.1	197n	Antipater of Tarsus	11, 235n
5.26.2	197n		
		Antisthenes	48, 50, 52, 54, 57, 59, 61, 64, 206
Aelius Aristides	304		
Or			
26	285–6		
26.1–5	307n	Antonius the Epicurean	83, 110
Aetius		*AP*	
4.13.6	121n	5.112	95
		11.41	95
Alcinous [Albinus]	15, 214n	Apollodorus of Seleuceia	52
Did.			
17	214n	Apollonius of Tyana	68, 70, 72, 77n, 289
24	214n		
24.2	218n		
30.1	25n		
30.5–6	218n	*Ep. Apoll.*	
32	217n	1	70
32.4	212	86	70
		87	70
Anacreon	44n	88	70
Anaximander the Younger of Miletus	77n	Apollonius the Paradoxographer *Mirabilia* 46	312
Androcides the Pythagorean	77n	Apuleius	218n
		Archytas	73
Andronicus of Rhodes	9–10, 19n	*De educ.* 41.9–18	68 76n

364

INDEX OF ANCIENT AUTHORS AND TEXTS

41.13–14	76n	1.9.1–4, 1099b9–20	240
41.16–18	76n	2.2 1104b1–3	43
De leg.	68	2.2.1104b4–24	76n
33.14–18	75n	2.3 1104b11–13	42
33.17	76n	2.3 1104b13–14	47n
33.17–18	76n	2.4.5–6 1105b	65n
		2.4 1105b21	19n
Aresas		2.5.1–2	148n
De nat. hom.		2.5.2	148n
49.3–8	75n	2.5.2 1105b	54, 55
		2.6 1106b24–5	47n
Aristippus	66n	2.9 1109b	206
		3.1	240
Ariston of		3.1 1109b30	47n
Ceos	19n, 213n	3.1 1111a24–b4	207
		3.5	240
Aristophanes		3.5.2 1113b6–7	240
Clouds 1481–509	44n	3.5.5 1113b18–19	240
		3.5.20 1114b22–3	240
Aristotle	6–7, 8, 9, 10,	3.5.22 114b31–32	240
	18n, 19n, 20n,	3.7 1115b11	43
	22n, 24n,	3.7 1115b12, 23	43
	29–47, 45n, 54,	3.7 1116a11, b31	43
	55, 59, 67, 69,	3.8 1117a17–20	43
	80, 82, 105,140,	4.9 1128b13–14	39
	155, 156, 224,	6.13 1145a4–6	43
	234n, 240, 242,	7	155
	260, 312n	7,1–10	155
		7.2.1–10	155
An. post.		7.3.6	156
2.2 90a15–16	32	7.3.7	157
2.8 93b5–6	45n	7.3.8	157
		8	35
De an.		8.1 1155b18–21	36
1.1	37	8.1 1155b27–1156a5	36
1.1 403a	55	8.3 1156a9–14	46n
1.1 403a19–24	38		
1.1 403a26–7	37	*Gen. an.*	
1.1 403a27	45n	2.736b28	218n
1.1 403a31–b1	38		
3.10–11	65n	*On Emotions: Anger*	7–8, 19n, 20n, 35
Divisions	7, 35		
		On the Statesman	20n
Eth. eud.	40–1		
2.2 1220b	55	*Poet.*	
2.2 1220b12–14	41	14. 1453b5	46n
6	8		
		Pol.	
Eth. nic. [= *EN*]	87, 46n, 240	3.4 1277a28	44
1.1098b	203	3.4 1277b17	44

365

Rhet.	31–2, 33, 35, 42, 46n	*Top.*	31
		4	31
		4.6 127b26–32	31
1.1 1354a24–6	35	4.6 127b31	45n
1.1360b	203	6	31
1.11 1370b13	36	6.13 150b27–151a19	31
2	31, 33–5, 93	8	31, 32
2.1	33	8.1 156a30–3	31
2.1 1377b24	33, 34		
2.1 1377b26–7	35	Aristoxenus of	
2.1 1377b28–9	34	Tarentum	67, 68
2.1 1377b31–1378a1	34		
2.1 1378a	55	Arius Didymus	122, 123, 124–6, 130, 131, 132n, 147n, 202, 205
2.1 1378a8	35		
2.1 1378a18–19	35		
2.1 1378a20–2	33		
2.1 1378a22–3	33		
2.2 1377a31–3	32		
2.2 1378a30–2	32	*Epitome of Stoic Ethics*	10, 148n
2.2 1378a32–3	41	5a	124
2.2 1378b5–7	45n	5b1–6f	124
2.2 1379b11–12	41	7–7g	124
2.2–3	33	8–9b	124
2.2–11	35	10–10a	125
2.3 1380b16–18	41	10–10e	22n
2.4	80, 87, 91–2		
		Arrian	126
2.4 1382a12–13	33		
2.5	33	*Epict. diss.* (see also Epictetus, *Diss.*)	
2.5 1382a21–2	32	3.22	60
2.5 1382a35–b2	43	3.22.13	60
2.5 1382b3–4	42	3.22.20	60
2.5 1383a5–8	36	3.22.42	60
2.6	97, 98		
2.6 1383b12–13	32	*Introductory Letter*	
2.6 1383b12–14	46n	2	126
2.7 1358a23,	25, 33–4		
2.7 1385a16	34	Aspasius	10, 76n, 214n
2.7 1385a18	45n		
2.7 1385a18–19	34, 45n	Athenaeus	301
2.7 1385a19	45n	*Deipn.*	
2.7 1385a20–34	34	6.79 261D–E	38
2.7 1385a.26	45n	10.77	77n
2.7 1385a26–7	45n	14.643F	11
2.7 1385a29–30	45n		
2.7 1385a34–b10	34	Attalus	53
2.8–9	33		
2.8 1385b13–14	42	Atticus	114
2.9	92, 97		
2.9 1386b9–14	42	Aulus Gellius	
2.9 1386b12–14	42	*Noct. att.*	
2.9 1386b15–16	42	1.26.7	11

INDEX OF ANCIENT AUTHORS AND TEXTS

1.26.11	3, 218n	1.1.7	191
9.5	54	1.1.7–8	192
9.5.3	57	1.1.8	191, 197n
19.12.3	3	1.1.10	191
		1.3.3–5	183
Bion of Borysthenes	11, 58, 103, 104, 110, 111	1.4.12–5.1	183
		1.7	185
		1.8.2–4	183
Calcidius		1.9.3	182
Comm. Tim.		1.12.6	187
293	280n	1.12.7	187
		1.14.1	197n
Callicratidas		2.1.1	182
De dom. felic.		2.2.8	197n
103.5–10	75n	2.3.5–8	197n
		2.3.8	187, 197n
Callimachus	23n	2.4.1	187, 193, 197n
		2.4.2–3	187
Calvenus Taurus	11	2.4.3	197
		2.4.4	188, 193
Carneades	9, 20n	2.4.4–5	188
		2.4.5	194
Ceb. Tab.	15–16, 75n, 288, 292, 296–9, 302	2.4.7	192
		2.5.3	197n
		2.7.4	182
4.2	313n	2.8.1	188, 194
5.2	313n	2.8.2–4	189
5.2–6.3	31n	2.10.7–8	189
8.1	320n	3.1.3	182
9	292	3.2.6	188
9.1	317n	3.2.17	197n
9.2–3	317n	5	197n
9.3	317n	5.5.5	197n
10.4–11.1	317n	5.8.2–3	182
12–13	319n	6.3.2	194
19.1–2	313n	6.3.3	197
19–21	317n	6.3–4	184
21	313n	6.3.7	193
22.1–2	297	6.3.8	194
23.1–2	297	6.3.8–9	194
26	317n	6.4.5–7	195
26.3	317n	6.4.10	184
28.1	317n	6.5	184
30–2	316n	6.5.8–10	184
32.3	317n	6.6.1	183
33–5	319n	6.7.1	197n
33.3	316n, 317n	8.1.3	185, 190, 191
Chariton	12, 175, 181–5, 187–97	Chrysippus	10, 21n, 24n, 65n, 81, 91, 92, 103, 104, 111, 114, 123, 125,
1.1.2	190		
1.1.4	194		

INDEX OF ANCIENT AUTHORS AND TEXTS

	128, 129, 132n, 147n, 201, 208, 212, 217n, 219n, 220n, 270, 271, 279n, 280n, 288, 294, 295, 315n	*Off.* 1.18.60	149n
		Or. Brut. 128	17n
		Pro Caelio	94
Therapeutikos Logos	10, 102–3, 104, 110, 119n	*Quint. fratr.* 1.1.37	11
Cicero	3, 8, 9, 65n, 118n–119n, 147n, 214n–215n, 218n, 234n, 315n	*Tim.* 1.1	67–8
		Tusc. 2 3.7 3.12	9, 21n 21n 3 216n
Acad.		3.15	17n
1.22	203	3.18	17n
1.38–9	17n	3.18–21	21n
2.8	121n	3.19	21n
2.22	203	3.20	3
2.131	218n	3.21	20n
2.134	203	3.25.61	316n
2.135	9, 212, 214n	3.54	20n
		3.59–60	20n
Acad. post.		3.82	215n
135	21n	4.4	21n
		4.10	3
Att.		4.10–11	202
1.17.4	116n	4.10.23	315n
		4.11	218n
Brut.		4.14	3
117	21n	4.43	212, 214n
		4.44	213
De or.		4.54	17n
1.214	17n	5.38–9	281n, 282n
		Claudius Ptolemy	
Fin.		*Tetrabiblos*	
3.14.48	147n	3.11–14	23n
3.16–76	131n	3.12	12
3.35	3	3.13	12
4.23	21n	3.14	12
4.56	202, 220n		
		Cleanthes of Assos	10, 21n, 81, 202, 271
Inv.			
1.36	3		
1.41	3		
		Clitarchus	
Leg.		*Sent. Clit.*	71
1.22–5	281n		

INDEX OF ANCIENT AUTHORS AND TEXTS

85	71	Diodorus of Sicily	72, 75n
86	71		
		Diogenes Laertius	7, 8, 18n, 19n, 25n, 49
Crantor	9, 10		
On Grief	20n	1.15	53
		1.19	51, 57
Crates	49, 53, 54, 58	1.20	51
(*see also* Ps.-Crates)		2.88	51
		3.92–102	65n
Cynic Letters	48, 54	4.1	19n
(*see also*		4.12	6
Ps.-Crates,		4.27	9
Ps.-Diogenes,		5.1	20n
Ps.-Heraclitus,		5.22–7	7
Ps.-Socrates)		5.24	7
		5.44	9
Demetrius the Cynic	53	5.45	9
		6	51
Demetrius Laco	94, 101–2, 109	6.3	57, 206
		6.19	53
		6.20–81	57
On Textual and Exegetical Problems in Epicurus		6.28	57
		6.31	57
cols 67–8	83	6.37	57
		6.44	57
Democritus	90	6.48	57
		6.54	57
Demonax	53	6.64	57
		6.66	57
Dio Chrysostom	48, 53, 61, 286, 293	6.67	57
		6.70–1	58
		6.71	57, 58, 63
Or.		6.103	51, 52
4	61	6.103–4	52
4.114–15	317n	6.104	52, 53, 66n
6	61	6.105	62
8–10	61	6.117	55
8.12–19	61	6.127	62
8.12–35	61–2, 64	7.4	10
8.15	61	7.84–131	131n
8.16	61	7.85	217n
8.20–6	61	7.85–6	56
8.20–35	61	7.110	10, 55, 123, 132n, 315n
8.21	62, 206	7.111	10, 55, 56, 208, 132n, 316n
8.27–35	61		
9.2	317n		
11	286	7.111–14	65n
33	286	7.116	56
33.2–8	308n	7.120	147n
38	308n	7.121	52, 56
38.1	308n	7.127	137
77/78.45	314n		

7.134	280n		260, 261, 288,
7.143	281n		295, 298, 304,
7.166	10		312n
7.167	10		
7.175	10	*Diss.*	122, 133n
7.178	10	1.1	127
7.189–202	133n	1.1.4	126
7.198	24n	1.1.5–6	126
8.17	77n	1.1.7	126
8.18	77n	1.1.12	133n
8.30	75n	1.2	126, 127
8.46	75n	1.2.1	127
10.27–8	149n	1.2.5	127
10.28	9	1.2.6	127, 133n
10.117	91, 108	1.2.7	127
		1.3.1–6	281n
Diogenes of Babylon		1.4	24n, 127
(Seleucia)	10, 24n, 81	1.4.1	127
		1.4.3	128
Diogenes of Oenoanda	9, 20n, 312n	1.4.5	128
		1.4.5–12	128
Diogenes of Sinope	48, 49, 51,	1.4.13	133n
(*see also* Ps.-Diogenes)	52, 53, 54,	1.4.14	128
	57, 58, 61,	1.4.16	149n
	62, 64	1.4.18	134n
		1.4.19	134n
		1.4.23–4	128
Dio of Prusa *see* Dio		1.4.26	128
Chrysostom		1.4.27	135n
		1.4.28	134n
Dionysius of Heracles	10	1.5.2	202
Peri apatheias	10, 21n	1.6.15	126
		1.6.19	129
Ep. Pyth.		1.6.40	239
1.2.9–12	70	1.11.5	129
5	70	1.14.2	129
5.2.11–15	70	1.14.6	281n
6	70	1.14.11–17	281n
6.2.19–20	70	1.18	11
6.6.47–8	70	1.20.15–16	133n
6.7.62–4	70	1.22.18	196
6.7.66–7	70	1.27	130
		1.27.3	130
Diotogenes, *De regn.*		1.27.9	130
73.9–15	75n	1.27.10	135n
74.9–11	76n	1.28	10
		2.1	135n
Epictetus	15, 22n, 60–1,	2.5.2	135n
	64, 91, 122,	2.5.4–5	126
	123, 126–31,	2.8	281n
	218n, 222,	2.8.13–14	282n
	235n, 239, 242,	2.8.23	130

INDEX OF ANCIENT AUTHORS AND TEXTS

2.8.9–17	281n	*Ep. Men.*	
2.8.27–9	281n	128	90
2.10	126	135	150n
2.17.18	130		
2.17.19–22	130	*Epistle to Herodotus*	96
2.17.24	130		
2.17.29–34	133n	*On Nature*	96
2.17.31	130		
2.17.34	128	*Rat. sent.*	
2.18.5	307n	149	219n
2.18.5	289		
2.18.8	131	*SV*	
2.18.8–10	289	65	278n
2.18.26–9	313n	74	120n
2.18.29	135n		
2.21	129	Eudemus of	
3.1.25	127	Rhodes	20n
3.2.2	133n		
3.2.3–5	131	Eumenius	14, 23n
3.2.4	130		
3.18	129	Euphrates of Tyre	93
3.18.6	129		
3.19.1	129	Euripides	157
3.19.2	129	*Medea*	44n, 155
3.19.3	129, 133n	1078–80	157
3.19.5	129		
3.22.9–10	50	Galen	10, 22n,
3.22.13	129		76n, 110,
3.22.51–2	312n		170, 175–80,
3.22.73	308n		183, 185,
4.2	220n		189, 191–2,
4.6.9	135n		194–7, 208,
4.7	10		212, 217n,
4.8.20	130		292, 293,
4.10.1	129		294, 295,
4.10.6	129		296, 301,
4.12	320n		303–4, 312n,
			318n
Ench.			
1.5	148n	*De affect. dig.*	
29.2	313n	(= *Passions*)	10–11, 175–80,
48	209		196n, 293
		1.1	197n
Epicurus	9, 79, 80, 81,	1.2	176, 177
	82, 83, 85,	1.3	176
	87–90, 91,	1.4	177, 178, 180,
	93–4, 95–7, 99,		196n
	105, 106, 108,	1.5	178, 196n
	109, 112, 113,	1.6	179, 189, 190,
	114, 115, 116n,		192
	117n–8n, 209,	1.7	177, 179, 185,
	240		191, 192

371

1.8	178	Gorgias	
2.5	320n	*Helen*	
3.1	293–4	15–19	44n
5.1–2	83		
7.7–9.21	320n	Hecato	10
9.11	320n		
9.13–15	320n	Heraclitus	318n
9.15	320n	*All.*	
10.2–4	303, 318n, 320n	33.8	217n
		Herillus	10
De loc. affect.			
1.3	294	Hermippus of Smyrna	19n
3.9–10	315n		
		Herodes Atticus	3
De nat. facul.			
3.7	315n	Herodotus	
		Histories	
De peccatorum dignotione	12	7.35	44n
		Hesiod	23n
De sanit. tuen.		*Op.*	
1.1, 5	315n	106–201	13
1.8	295, 318n	Hesychius	7, 8, 19n
4.11	315n	*Vita Aristotelis*	19n
PHP	21n, 213n		
4.2	217n, 315n	Hierocles	236n
4.5	315n		
4.6.35	218n	Hieronymus of Rhodes	11
4.7.28	213		
5.5	214n, 216n	*On Not Being Angry*	22n
5.5.6	219n		
5.5.29	212	Hippobotus	51
5.6	201, 208		
5.6.1	5	Hippocrates	312n
5.7.29	217n		
44.2.43	205	*On Head Injuries*	17n
Quod an mor.		*Vict.*	145–6
5	318n	4.88	146
9	295		
		Hippothous	197n
Golden Verses (GV)	71, 72, 95, 148n	Homer	96, 286
9–11	71		29–30
17–19	71	*Il.*	
18–19	78n	1.599	44n
33–4	71	2.270	44n
38	71	3.30–7	44n

INDEX OF ANCIENT AUTHORS AND TEXTS

18.104–11	105	223	73
18.108–9	45n	224	74
18.109–10	45n	225	73
22.59	44n	228	73
22.136–7	44n	230	74
24.516	44n	233	74
24.743–5	96	234	73
24.745	96	251	75n

Od.	61	Isocrates, *Antid.*	
22.347	207	22	45n

Horace	85, 95, 98, 106, 114, 118n, 120n	Julian, *Or.*	
		6.181D	52
		6.182C	52
		6.189B	52
Carm.		6.186B	51
1.24	97	6.187C–D	52
		6.187D	52
Ep.		6.189A	52
1.14.36	95	6.190D	50
1.20.25	85	6.193D	56
		6.201A	50, 52
Sat.	97		
1.3	116n	Juvenal, *Sat.*	131
		10.356–66	135n

Iamblichus	292		
Protr.		Longinus	
107.7	77n	*Subl.*	
107.20	77n	15	320n
112.24–13.7	77n		
113.8–18	77n	Lucan	16
121.9–25	77n		
		Lucian	76n, 292, 304, 307n
VP	72, 77n		
64	73, 74	*Bis. acc.*	
78	73	3	278n
94	73	20	278n
110	74		
110–11	74	*Demon.*	
111–13	74	6–9	320n
112–13	78n		
114	74	*Nigr.*	
131	73	35–6	305
154	77n		
180	74	*Tim.*	
181–2	74	36	292, 314n
196	73		
197	73	Lucretius	87, 94, 95, 105, 107, 109, 114–15, 120n
204	73		
205–6	73		
218	72		

373

INDEX OF ANCIENT AUTHORS AND TEXTS

De rerum nat.	155	Nicasicrates	89, 110, 112–14, 115
3	114		
3.1–93	278n		
3.294–319	115	Nicomachus of Gerasa	68, 72
3.320–2	115	*Harmonicum*	
4	94	*enchiridion*	78n
4.823–57	278n		
4.1190	117n	Nigidius Figulus	67, 68
4.1191	117n		
4.1278–87	95	Numenius of Apamea	68
4.1282–7	94		
5	23n	Oenomaus of Gadara	53, 62
5.110–234	278n		
6.1–95	268n	Ovid	12
		Ars	
Marcus Aurelius	91, 261, 304	3.667	174n
Med.			
2.1	281n	*Metam.*	153–74
2.10	39	1.618–19	173n
5.27	281n	1.237	173n
8.54	281n	7	159
12.26	281n	7.10–11	174n
		7.11	158
Maximus of Tyre	23n	7.12	158
Diss.		7.17	158
7	12	7.18–21	157
14.7–8	279n	7.19	158
		7.47–8	158
Metopus		7.55–6	159
De virt.	68	7.70–1	159
118.1–6	75n	7.73	158
119.8–10	76n	7.76	158
119.28–20.1	76n	7.87	159
120.1–2	76n	7.88	159
120.4–5	76n	7.92–3	158
120.23–5	76n	7.146	173n
120.25–21.1	76n	8	159
121.2–5	76n	8.35–6	174n
121.7–8	76n	8.38–42	160
121.10–12	76n	8.39	160
		8.44–5	160
Metrodorus	9, 87, 108, 111, 118n	8.51–2	160
		8.72	160
		8.75	160
Moderatus of Gades	68	8.76–7	160
		8.97–8	171
Musonius Rufus	53, 123, 288, 295, 296, 298–300, 301	8.450	161
		8.462–3	161
		8.463–4	161
frg. 6	298–9	8.470–4	162
frg. 18A	300	8.474	162
		8.475	161

8.486–7	163	P.Herc.	81, 83, 88, 92
8.491–2	163	1005, col. 14.8–9	87
8.497–8	163		
8.506	163	Panaetius	9, 10, 21n,
8.508	162		24n, 81, 89,
8.511–12	164		95, 218n,
8.532	164		288
9.451	174n		
9.454	164	Parthenius	181, 192
9.466–7	165		
9.473	174n	Peregrinus	53
9.487	165		
9.487–94	174n	Persaeus	147n
9.491	174n		
9.494	165	P.Mil.Vogl.	24n
9.509	165		
9.514	165	Phaedrus	116n, 120n
9.514–17	165		
9.515	165	Philodemus	8, 9, 15,
9.518	166		79–115, 116n,
9.521	166		118n
9.523–5	166	*De dis*	121n
9.527	166, 173n		
9.543	166	*Epigrams*	
9.544	166	4	95
9.546	166	5	95
9.562	166		
9.571–2	166	*On Anger (Ira)*	11, 79, 80,
9.581–2	167		82, 84, 89,
9.616–17	167		100–5,
9.630	174n		106, 110–15,
9.635–9	174n		116n, 118n,
9.638–40	167		119n, 120n,
9.670–82	174n		178
9.673	174n	col. I	110
9.786–7	168	col. I.7–27	103
10.298–9	169	col. I.15–19	110
10.300–3	169	col. I.16–17	110
10.314–15	169	col. I.20–26	110
10.320	169, 174n	col. I.20–27	196n
		cols II–VIII.8	110
10.338	169	cols II.6–VIII.8	103
10.371–2	170	col. III.13–18	196n
10.372	170	col. IV.4–19	196n
10.372–7	170	col. V.16–25	110
10.420–1	170	col. VI.6–9	111
10.452	170	col. VII.19–20	101
10.473	170	cols VII.26–XXXI.24	101
10.473–4	170	cols VIII.16–XXXI.23	102
10.475	170	col. XIII.22–30	111
10.477	170	cols XVIII.34–XXI	111
10.485–7	171	col. XIX.14–16	101

cols XIX–XXI	101	frgs. 6–13	110
col. XX.24–5	101	frgs. 7	110
col. XXXI.11–24	103	frgs. 14–17	110
col. XXXI.18–21	111		
col. XXXI.24–27	113	*On Death*	79, 82, 88, 89,
cols XXXI.			97, 100, 102,
24–XXXIV.6	104		103, 105–9,
col. XXXI.24–6	111		114, 115n,
col. XXXI.			118n, 119n,
24–XXXIV.7	111		120n
col. XXXIV.16–24	111	12	106
cols XXXIV.		13.37	107, 109
16–XXXV.5	85	14.5–10	107
cols. XXXIV.		17.33	108
16–XLVI.15	105	17.35–6	107
col. XXXIV.21	111	17.36–18.16	107
cols XXXIV.		17.38	108
24–XXXV.6	84	19.1–2	107
cols XXXIV.		19.3–11	107
24–XXXVI.30	112	19.30–3	107
col. XXXIV.31–8	84	20.1–3	106
cols XXXV.		20.3–22.9	107
5–XXXVI.21	85	20.7–8	107
col. XXXV.17	120n	22.9–25.2	107
col. XXXV.18–20	85	23.7–8	108
col. XXXV.28	119n	25.2–10	107
col. XXXVI.13–21	86	25.38	108
col. XXXVI.20	101	26.1–7	108
col. XXXVI.22–6	101	29.10–11	108
col. XXXVII.4–6	112	32.30–1	106
col. XXXVII.19	102	33.37–35.34	82
col. XXXVII.		38.14–39.25	108
20–XXXVIII.34	102	38.25	109
col. XXXVIII.6	101		
col. XXXVIII.9–10	119n	*On Frank*	
col. XXXVIII.		*Criticism (Lib.)*	79, 82, 86, 88,
34–XXXIX.8	112		89, 97–100,
col. XXXVIII.36	101		101, 106, 108,
col. XXXIX.19–25	113		112, 118n, 150n
col. XXXIX.26	101	col. IIb.8	100
col. XXXIX.30	101	col. VIIIa7–9	120n
cols XXXIX.39–XL.2	115	col. VIIIb.11–13	100
col. XL.16–22	101	col. XIIb	150n
col. XL.20–1	82	col. XIIIa.7–13	98
col. XL.21–5	113	col. XVIIa	100
col. XLI.8	102	col. XIXb	99
cols XLI.31–XLVI.13	113	col. XXIb	150n
col. XLIV.19–20	100	cols XXIIa–XXIIb.	
col. XLVI.17–35	86	1–9	99
col. XLVIII.3–16	86	frg. 3	98
col. XLVIII.17–32	86	frg. 7.10	100
frgs. 1–4	110	frgs. 10–11	99

INDEX OF ANCIENT AUTHORS AND TEXTS

frg. 12	100	*Phaed.*	
frg. 12.4–6	100	81A	314n
frg. 26.9–10	100	112–13	292
frg. 39	98	113D	313n
frg. 45.1–10	99		
frg. 61.1	236n	*Phaedr.*	
frgs. 63–5	100	232A–233D	314n
		240D	216n
On Piety	110, 280n	246A–D	296
		246–7	205
On Poems		253C–254E	313n
1	110	271D–E	304
On the Good King		*Phileb.*	6, 18n,
According To Homer	82		30, 31,
			38, 45n
On the Stoics		36C6–D2	31
col. III	9	37E10	31
		37E12–38A2	31
Philostratus	304,	38B9	31
	312n	40D8–E4	31
		42A7–9	31
Vit. Apoll.		46A8–47C3	30
1.8	289	46A10	45n
		47C2	45n
Vit. soph.		47C3–D4	30
479–84	320n	47D5–50A9	30
561	320n	47D8	30, 45n
Plato	18n, 55, 56,	47E	55
	59, 69, 78n,		
	140, 145,	*Resp.*	84, 94
	155, 157, 208,	4.429C	214n
	213, 214n,	4.430B–C	214n
	287, 292, 293,	4.435–442	313n
	294	4.436A	218n
Apol.		4.440A	218n
23B	61	8.561C	218n
24B	46n	9.571C	217n
		10.617C	220n
Ep.	45n	240D	216n
6	18n	329C	314n
6.322E–323A	18n	406A	312n
		439B	216n
Lach.		439D	216n
191D	214n	439E–40	44n
		571D	150n
Leg.		588C–590A	217n
1.644C–D	54	589A	216n
5.736E	310n		
5.742E	310n	*Symp.*	
808D–E	316n, 317n	207E	214n

377

INDEX OF ANCIENT AUTHORS AND TEXTS

Theat.
156B — 214n

Tim.
33A — 218n
42A–B — 54
42D — 220n
44A — 218n
47B–C — 219n
69B–72D — 313n
69C D — 54
69D — 216n
69–70 — 202
70E — 217n
86B–90E — 220n
90A–D — 219n

Pliny the Younger — 93
Pan. — 286

Plotinus — 292

Plutarch
(see also Ps.-Plutarch) — 10, 11, 20n, 76n, 96, 136–50, 147n, 148n, 149n, 229, 242, 293, 301, 302

Adol. poet. aud.
15F–16A — 149n

Adul. amic. — 97, 148n
29 — 305
55C — 236n
61A — 285
66B — 236n
70D–E — 236n
73D–E — 236n

Alc.
23.5 — 236n

An. corp.
2 — 302
500C — 314n
501D–E — 321n

Ant.
80 — 122

Comm. Not. — 147n
1062B–1063C — 147n
1062E–1063B — 147n
1063A — 147n

De esu
1.6 — 300

De gen. Soc.
588C–594A — 279n

Exil.
599A–C — 236n

Is. Os.
73 — 319n

Mor.
48E–74E — 307n
69E–F — 305
75A–86A — 15
105E — 314n
380C — 319n
452F–464D — 11
500B–502A — 12
500D–F — 302
707B — 318n
995F–996A — 300

On Anger — 11

On Praising Oneself Inoffensively
543E — 147n

On the Absence of Anger — 11

On the Cleverness of Animals
962A — 147n

Parallel Lives — 11, 144

Praecept. ger. rei publ.
814D — 122

Quaest. conv.
612E — 150n

631A	147n	76A	137, 148n
636B	138, 147n	76D	142
666D	150n	76E	142
727C	77n	77A–B	138
728B	77n	77B	141
734E	150n	77C	140, 141
		77E	141
Sera		78A	142
549F–550B	145	78C	143
550D–F	149n	78E–F	142
551D	145	79B	142
551D E	145	79D	142
555A	150n	79F	144
		80A	143
Stoic. abs.		80B–C	142
1058B	147n	80E	143
		81A	142
Stoic. rep.		82A	144, 145
1042E–1043A	147n	82C	144
		82F	141
Suav. viv.		82F–83A	145
1088F–1089C	97	83A	145
1097E	88, 96	83C	141
1101A	88	83D	141
1101A–B	96	83E	148n
		84A	139, 148n
Tranq. an.		84B	143
467B–C	314n	84B–85D	144
471D	314n	84D	143
473B	314n	84E	140, 143
476F	236n	85B	144
		85C	144
Virt. mor.	140	86A	139
440D	140		
441C	134n	*Virt. vit.*	148n, 150n
443C	141, 218n		
443C–D	141	Polybios	123
443D	140		
444B	218n	Polystratus	
446E	209, 218n	*On Irrational Contempt*	
451C	218n	19.3–8	92
451D	140		
451D–452A	140	Porphyry	
452C	236n		
		VP	72
Virt. prof.	15, 136–50,	42	77n
	147n, 148n,	112–13	78n
	150n, 242, 298		
75A–B	137	Posidonius	10, 11, 21n,
75B–C	139		22n, 24n, 89,
75B–D	137		201, 202, 208,
75E–F	137		212, 214n,

	216n, 217n, 218n, 295, 316n	Ps.-Plutarch *Apophth. Lac.* 207A–B	122
Propertius 1.14.19–25	95	*Cons. Apoll.* 102D 104C	9 216n 20n
Ps.-Anacharsis	53	*De fato*	
Ps.-Aristotle		572F–574D	279n
Mund. 398B	214n	*De lib. ed.* 12A 12E	147n 77n
Problems 2.26	46n	Ptolemy-al-Garib *Life of Aristotle*	7 19n
Ps.-Crates, *Ep.* 3 15 16 19 21 34.4	63, 64 63 63 52 63 52 63	Pythagoras, Pythagoreans *Pythagorean akousmata* *Pythagorean Sentences*	67–78, 155, 289, 290, 300 71, 72 71
Ps.-Demetrius *Typ. epist.* 3–9 6	320n 320n	2b 2c 21 23 71 88 116	72 72 71 71 71 72 72
Ps.-Diogenes *Ep.* 5 7 10.2 12 21 27 28.5 33.4 37.6 42 47 50	62–3, 64 62, 66n 56 56 52, 63 63 62 63, 314n 66n 63 56, 64 63 63	Quintilian *Inst.* 6.2 6.2.8 6.2.9 6.2.20 6.2.29–32 10.1.88 Quintus Sextius Seneca	118n, 234n, 304 17n 17n 4 17n 4 320n 155 11 8, 15, 22n, 39, 53, 98, 242, 261, 267–83
Ps.-Heraclitus	53		
Ps.-Libanius *Epist. char.* 4	320n	*Ben.* 2.1.4 4.4.1–2 4.7.1	283n 283n 281n

380

Ep.
5.1 270, 280n
6.1 270, 271
6.1–6 270
6.5 149n
7.8 270
8.2 270, 271
10.4 283n
11.9–10 149n
13.15 270, 281n, 282n
16.1 270
16.2 280n
20.4 279n
20.6 270, 280n
23.1–2 279n
25.5–7 270
26.5–7 270
27.1 271
28.6–7 271
31.8 282n, 283n
31.8–11 273, 282n
31.9 282n
31.11 272, 276, 282n
32.1–2 280n
34 270
34.1–2 280n
34.3 270
35 270
37.1 279n
37.3–4 281n
41 267, 269, 270, 271, 273, 275–7, 279n
41.1 271, 278, 280n, 282n, 283n
41.1–4 269, 306
41.2 271, 273, 274, 275
41.3–4 275
41.4 273, 275, 276, 277
41.4–5 282n
41.5 273, 276
41.6–7 282n
41.6–9 281n
41.7 282n
42.1 279n
44.2 279n
48.11 282n
50.8 279n
53.8 282n

53.11 282n
65.12 281n
65.16 282n
65.16–17 282n
65.20 282n
65.21 282n
65.16–22 282n
65.24 281n
66.12–13 281n
66.12 272, 276
68.8–9 271
71.16 282n
71.28 270
71.34 279n
71.35 279n
72.6 271, 279n
72.9 279n, 280n
72.10 279n
72.11 279n
73 274
73.11 282n
73.12 282n
73.12–16 273
73.16 274, 276, 279n, 281n, 282n
75 270
75.6–7 286, 320n
75.8 270, 280n
75.8–14 280n
75.9 279n
75.10–12 279n
75.13 270, 279n
75.13–15 203
75.14 270
76.19 279n
81.11 87
82.7 282n
87.19 282n
87.21 282n
90.46 274
90.28 282n
90.29 281n
92.1 281n
92.27 281n
92.29 282n
92.29–30 282n
92.29–31 273
92.30 280n, 282n
92.32 282n
92.33–4 282n
92.33–5 282n
92.34 281n

381

94.31	202	*Nat.*	
95.36	207	2.45	272, 280n
98.2	282n		
98.9	118n	*Polyb.*	
99.15–21	216n	18.5–6	216n
102.21	281n		
102.21–30	281n, 282n	Sextus	77n
102.22	281n	*Sent. Sext.*	71, 72
104.22–3	281n, 282n	70	77n
104.23	281n	71b	77n
108.3	280n	72	77n
108.8	281n	75a	71
108.35–7	65n	75b	71
109.15	279n	204	72
115.3–5	282n	205	72
116.4–5	95	206	72
116.5	24n, 270	207	72
117.12	279n	209	72
117.15	279n	435	71
120.14	281n		
120.14–16	282n	Sextus Empiricus	
120.15	282n	*Math.*	
121.14	281n	9.90	202
124.8	281n		
124.14	281n, 282n	Simplicius	
124.21	282n	*On Aristotle's*	
124.21–2	282n	*Categories*	
124.21–4	281n, 282n	253.7–8	40
124.23	274, 281n, 282n	253.8–13	40
124.24	282n	*On Aristotle's Physics*	
		965.1	39
Helv.			
6.7	281n, 282n	Socrates	46n, 66n
8.3	281n		
13.3	279n	*Socratic Epistles*	
16.1	216n	30–32	19n
17.5	282n		
		Sophocles	174n
Ira	10, 19n, 22n, 104		
		Speusippus	6, 18n–19n
1.12.3	39, 43		
1.14.1	43		
2.10.6	203	*On Pleasure*	18n
2.36.1	11		
3.3.1	212, 214n	Sphaerus	10
Marc.		Stobaeus	58, 122
7.1	216n	*Ecl.*	
21.6	283n	2.7.5–12	122
24.5	282n	2.7.9	205

2.7.11	147n	1.1.6	40
2.7.20	148n	2.6.6–11	46n
2.38–9	202		
2.57–79	124	*On Comedy*	38
2.59	124		
2.79–85	124	*On Emotions*	9, 39
2.85–8	124		
2.88	132n	*On Grief*	9
2.88.8 90.6	125		
3.18	219n	*On Sweat*	
		36.226–30F	39
Flor.			
2.7.20	44	Timaeus	
3.19.12	39, 47	*De univ. nat.*	213n
4.20.64	40	217–18	75n
4.35.34	93	224.7	78n
103.22	312n		
		Timasagoras	111, 112, 113–14

Tabula of Cebes see Ceb. Tab.

Strabo	19n	*Tractatus Coislinianus*	
Geogr. 13.1.57	18n	10–11	46n
		13–20	47n
Teles the Cynic	48, 64		
frg. 2	58–9	Trypho	
frg. 5	58	*Rhetores Graeci*	
frg. 7	10, 59	3.194.7	77n
Theages, *De virt.*	68	*XII Panegyrici*	
190–3	75n	*Latini*	14, 23n
191.28–9	76n		
192.6	76n	Varro	52
192.7–8	76n		
192.11	76n	Virgil (Vergil)	12, 23n, 95, 97, 114
192.24–193.7	76n		
192.30–193.7	76n	Xenocrates	6, 18n, 19n, 214n
193.15	76n		
		On Emotions	19n
Theano	70		
		Xenophon of Athens	
Theodorus	58	*Mem.*	
		1.2.14	61
Theophrastus	9, 18n, 20n, 25n, 29, 30, 38–44	1.3.5	61
		1.6.10	66n
Caus. plant.		Xenophon (Novelist)	12, 175, 182, 185–7, 190–97
5.15.1	312n		
		1.1–2	191
Hist. plant.		1.3.4	197n
1.1.2	41		

INDEX OF ANCIENT AUTHORS AND TEXTS

1.4.1–3	194	5.13	197n
1.5.5–9	192	5.13.3	197n
1.6.2	191, 193		
1.9.9–10.1	195	Xenophanes	23n
2.3.1–3	186		
2.3.4–8	186	Zeno of Citium	10, 21n, 24n, 81, 122, 123, 129, 132n, 141, 145, 147n, 202, 271, 294, 315n
2.5.5	186		
3.2	191, 197n		
3.7.1	197n		
3.11.3–5	187		
3.12	186		
3.12.3	186	Zeno of Sidon	81–2, 83, 87, 89, 110, 111, 114, 115, 116n, 120n
5.1	191		
5.4	187		
5.7	187		
5.9.13	197n		

8. Secondary Sources

BDAG	2	SM	
		1	176, 177, 178, 179, 180, 185, 189–90, 191, 192
FHSG			
271.3	39		
436.5	9		
436.15	9		
438	9	SVF	
438.6–8	40	1.41	10
438.8–12	40	1.66	279n
438–48	9	1.111	280n
441.3–4	39	1.120	271
446.1	39	1.154	271
446.1, 6–7	43	1.158	280n
449		1.163	280n
A.35	44	1.187	62
526.4	39	1.197	217n
557.1–2	40	1.205	55
709.1.10	38	1.205	10
		1.206	55, 217n
GP		1.211	10, 214n
17	95	1.216	279n
18	95	1.234	141
		1.370	214n
LSJ	85, 113	1.409	10
		1.422	10
851	85	1.481	10
1069	95	1.570–5	10
		2.54	216n
OLD	4	2.310	280n
		2.473	271
PL		2.644	271
44:469	4, 5	2.1100	280n

3.49	62	3.392	216n
3.65	11	3.394	206
3.169	205	3.409	217n
3.173	205	3.429	315n
3.178	56	3.432	220n
3.223	282n	3.456	10, 56
3.225	282n	3.461	56
3.261	52	3.474	104
3.378	125, 201–2, 214n	3.476	217n
		3.478	104
3.389	125	3.510	220n, 312n
3.391	216n	3.552	279n

INDEX OF MODERN SCHOLARS

Adler, M. 213n, 218n, 219n, 220n
Akinpelu, J. A. 281n
Alesse, F. 24n, 147n
Alexander, L. C. A. 22n, 23n, 175, 197n
Alexiou, E. 11
Allen, W. C. 233n
Ames, R. T. 16n
Amir, Y. 217n
Anderson, G. 196n
Anderson, R. D. 225, 235n
Anderson, W. S. 17n, 174n
Angeli, A. 87, 115n, 117n
Annas, J. 17n, 20n, 24n, 52, 84, 85, 86, 87, 89, 94, 102, 123, 130, 132n, 133n, 215n, 217n, 219n, 313n
Armstrong, D. 22n, 25n, 79, 106, 108, 116n
Arnim, H. F. A., von 21n
Arnold, E. V. 131n
Asmis, E. 9, 113, 117n
Atkins, E. M. 24n
Aune, D. C. 23n, 220n, 221, 233n, 237n
Aune, D. E. 21n, 22n, 48

Babbitt, F. C. 147n, 149n
Babut, D. 147n, 148n
Bailey, C. 219n
Baillie, J. 23n
Balch, D. 227, 235n, 236n
Ballester, L. G. 22n
Baltes, M. 214n
Banchich, T. 25n
Bardy, G. 311n
Barlow, C. W. 24n
Barnard, P. M. 307n, 308n
Barth, P. 131n
Barton, C. A. 2, 17n
Bauer, W. 263n

Becchi, F. 22n, 69, 70, 75n, 76n
Becker, L. 21n, 90-1
Behr, J. 311n
Bekker, I. 20n
Ben Ze'ev, A. 20n
Berger, K. 229, 233n
Bernays, J. 65n
Bett, R. 9
Betz, H. D. 319n
Beye, C. R. 23n
Bignone, E. 117n, 118n
Billerbeck, M. 50, 53, 60, 61, 65n
Billig, L. 45n
Blank, D. L. 10, 18n, 24n
Blowers, P. M. 25n, 122
Blundell, S. 23n
Boas, G. 23n
Bollack, J. 92
Bonhöffer, A. 25n, 222, 233n, 234n
Bonner, G. 17n
Bons, J. A. E. 17n
Börger, H. 280n
Borle, J. P. 23n
Bormann, K. 220n
Boswell, J. 228, 236n, 237n
Bouché-Leclercq, A. 23n
Boughton, J. S. 23n
Bowen, A. 23n, 24n
Bowersock, G. W. 320n
Bowie, E. L. 196n
Boyancé, P. 119n
Boyarin, D. 230, 237n
Bracher, K. D. 23n
Bradley, K. 311n
Brandenburger, E. 234n
Brandwood, L. 45n
Brant, J. A. 196n
Braund, S. 2, 4, 11, 17n, 279n

INDEX OF MODERN SCHOLARS

Bréhier, É. 21n, 210, 216n, 218n, 220n
Brennan, T. 21n, 88, 132n, 135n, 219n
Brinton, A. 20n
Brooten, B. 231, 237n
Brown, P. 313n
Brown, R. D., 94–5, 117n
Brunschwig, J. 17n, 45n
Bultmann, R. 223, 234n, 241, 257, 261n
Buresch, K. 20n, 103, 119n
Burkert, W. 75n
Burton, H. F. 280n
Bury, J. B. 23n
Bury, R. G. 316n
Butterworth, G. W. 307n, 308n, 313n, 314n, 317n, 321n

Cairns, D. L. 17n
Campbell, G. L. 23n
Campbell, J. S. 23n
Cancik-Lindemaier, H. 279n, 282n
Cancik, H. 277, 279n, 282n
Capasso, M. 97, 117n, 118n
Celentano, M. S. 17n
Centrone, B. 75n, 77n
Chadwick, H. 77n
Chaplin, M. 25n
Choufrine, A. 311n, 314n
Clark, F. L. 310n
Clay, D. 9, 149
Code, A. D. 18n
Cohn, L. 213n, 218n, 219n, 220n
Colaizzo, M. 115n
Colardeau, T. 131n
Colish, M. L. 234n
Collier, G. 237n
Colombo, A. M. 24n
Colson, F. H. 213, 216n, 217n
Cooper, J. M. 20n, 21n, 212, 219n
Countryman, L. W. 229, 237n
Crönert, W. 104, 113
Cruse, P. 16n
Curran, L. C. 173n
Curti, C. 310n, 316n

Dalmeyda, G. 196n
Dancy, R. M. 18n, 19n
Daniélou, J. 25n
Darwin, C. 1, 16n
Davies, W. D. 223–4
Dawson, D. 311n
de Faye, E. 310n
de Jonge, M. 313n

De Lacy, P. H. 96, 126, 133n, 150n, 201, 205, 208, 212, 213, 214n, 216n, 218n
Decleva Caizzi, F. 24n
Deming, W. 197n
den Boer, W. 23n, 320n
Des Places, E. 214n
deSilva, D. 281n
Destro, A. 273
DeYoung, J. B. 236n
Dibelius, M. 241
DiCicco, M. 4, 225, 235n
Diels, H. 39, 132n
Dihle, A. 7, 23n
Dill, S. 279n, 280n
Dillon, J. 22n, 25n, 75n, 77n, 149n, 214n, 218n, 220n, 279n
Dindorf, W. 307n
Dion, J. 23n
Dobbin, R. F. 127, 132n
Dodds, E. R. 23n, 54
Doi, T. 16n
Donini, P. 21n, 24n
Dorandi, T. 9
Downing, F. G. 226–7, 235n
Dudley, D. R. 65n
Duff, T. 150n
Düring, I. 7, 18n, 19n

Ebner, M. 23Jn
Edelstein, L. 11, 21n, 22n, 24n, 56, 131n, 201, 208, 209, 212, 213n, 216n, 217n, 218n, 219n
Edwards, R. A. 77n
Einarson, B. 96
Ekman, P. 16n
Elsner, J. 25n
Emeljanow, V. E. 52
Emilsson, E. K. 23n
Engberg-Pedersen, T. 2, 23n, 25n, 150n, 235n, 238, 262n, 263n, 264n, 266n, 268, 273, 281n, 307n
Erler, M. 9, 22n, 89, 113, 115n, 116n, 117n
Erskine, A. 20n, 131n
Etheridge, S. G. 148n
Evans, D. 16n

Fantham, E. 279n
Favez, C. 20n
Fedler 21n
Feher, M. 313n
Fell, J. 308n

INDEX OF MODERN SCHOLARS

Ferguson, E. 25n
Ferguson, J. 311n
Field, G. C. 6, 19n
Fillion-Lahille, J. 22n, 104, 119n
Fiore, B. 149n, 229, 236n
Fish, J. 105, 115, 116n, 118n, 120n
Fitzgerald, J. T. ix, 1, 18n, 22n, 23n, 24n, 25n, 75n, 79n, 120n, 175n, 226, 233n, 235n, 239, 282n, 307n, 311n, 313n, 316n, 317n
Flashar, H. 18n
Flusser, D. 234n
Fortenbaugh, W. W. 6, 17n, 18n, 20n, 29, 41, 45n, 46n, 47n
Fowler, D. P. 22n
Francis, J. A. 311n
Frede, M. 3, 93, 131n
Fredrickson, D. 231
Freud, S. 90
Fritz, K., von 75n
Furley, D. 23n
Furnish, V. P. 281n

Galinsky, K. 116n, 131n, 173
Gardiner, H. N. 135n
Garnsey, P. 23n, 24n
Garrett, S. 226, 235n
Garver, E. 25n
Gaselee, S. 181
Gass, M. 281n
Gastaldi, S. 20n
Gatz, B. 23n
Gawlick, G. 17n, 20n
Giani, S. 76n
Gibson, R. J. 279n
Gigante, M. 24n, 97, 118n
Gigon, O. 15, 19n, 25n
Gill, C. 2, 4, 17n, 21n, 22n, 23n, 117n, 219n, 279n
Girard, R. 229
Glad, C. E. 98, 228, 235n, 236n, 307n, 316n
Glibert-Thirry, A. 9, 22n
Glover, T. R. 279n
Godwin, J. 94
Gomoll, H. 10
Gomperz, T. 278n
Goold, G. P. 184, 185, 196n
Gordon, P. 20n
Görler, W. 17n, 20n
Gosling, J. C. B. 54, 56
Gottschalk, H. B. 19n

Gould, J. B. 21n
Gould, T. 21n, 54
Goulet-Cazé, M. -O. 51, 52, 58, 62, 278n
Grant, M. 18n, 318n
Grant, R. 311n
Graver, M. 2, 4, 17n, 20n, 21n, 117n, 215n, 220n
Green, A. 218n
Gregg, R. C. 20n
Grese, W. C. 146n
Griffin, M. T. 24n
Gross, D. M. 16n
Grosseteste, R. 9
Gummere, R. M. 149n
Gussen, P. J. 318n
Gutbrod, W. 234n
Guthrie, W. K. C. 23n

Haber, L. L. 24n
Hadot, P. 15
Hadzsits, G. D. 149n
Hägg, T. 196n
Hamerton-Kelly, R. G. 229
Hamlyn, D. W. 65n
Hammerstaedt, J. 65n
Hani, J. 9, 20n
Hankinson, R. J. 22n, 294, 315n
Harder, A. 23n
Harkins, P. W. 22n
Harms, W. 16
Harris, B. F. 53
Harris, W. V. 2, 22n, 116n, 148n, 236n
Hays, R. B. 236n, 281n
Hedrick, C. W. 196n
Hegel, G. W. F. 48
Heine, R. E. 25n
Heinemann, Y. 208, 213n, 218n, 219n, 220n
Heitz, J. H. E. 8
Helmbold, W. C. 148n
Helmreich, G. 196n, 315n, 316n, 318n, 319n
Helms, J. 196n, 197n
Henrichs, A. 280n
Henry, B. 120n
Hense, O. 10, 39, 66n, 122, 132n, 147n, 148n, 217n, 219n
Hershbell, J. P. 77n, 141, 147n, 148n
Heylbut, G. 10
Hicks, R. D. 7, 18n, 91, 117n, 132n, 150n
Hijmans, B. L. 288, 312n, 315n

388

Hill, M. 232
Hirsch-Luipold, R. 25n
Hobbes, T. 88
Hock, R. F. 182
Höistad, R. 61, 66n
Holland, G. S. ix
Holmes, P. 17n
Hornblower, S. 6, 19n
Hornsby, H. M. 65n, 278n
Hubbard, M. 118n
Hubert, K. 318n
Hudson-Williams, A. 23n

Indelli, G. 11, 85, 87, 92, 103, 104, 105, 111, 116n, 117n
Ingenkamp, H. G. 148n, 149n
Inman, J. 118n
Inwood, B. 3, 4, 11, 20n, 22n, 24n, 54, 55, 56, 94, 95, 132n, 202, 205, 217n, 218n
Ioppolo, A. M. 20n

Jacquette, D. 280n
Jaeger, W. 6, 18n
Janko, R. 46n, 47n, 110, 120n
Jewett, R. 223, 234n
Johann, H.-T. 20n
Johanson, B. 224, 234n
John, H. 78n
Johnson, L. T. 233n
Johnston, P. A. 23n
Jones, C. P. 61, 278n

Kalbfleisch, K. 40
Käsemann, E. 234n
Kassel, R. 20n
Kaster, R. A. 2
Katula, R. A. 17n
Keaney, J. J. 19n
Keck, L. 234n
Kee, H. C. 312n
Keil, B. 307n
Keller, A. C. 23n
Kendeffy, G. 23n
Kennedy, G. A. 46n, 234n
Kenney, E. J. 154
Kenny, A. J. P. 8
Kerferd, G. B. 279n
Kidd, I. G. 11, 21n, 22n, 24n, 56, 201, 208, 209, 212, 213n, 216n, 217n, 218n, 219n, 280n
King, J. E. 218n

Kingsley, P. 75n
Klaerr, R. 146n
Klassen, W. 228
Knuuttila, S. 2, 18n, 55, 117n
Koch, K. 23n
Konstan, D. ix, 2, 10, 17n, 20n, 21n, 98, 118n, 150n, 197n, 307n
Körte, A. 118n
Koster, W. J. W. 46n, 47n
Kraftchick, S. 225
Krämer, H. J. 9, 18n, 19n
Krentz, E. M. 22n, 24n, 122, 225
Kühn, C. G. 315n, 319n
Kuiper, T. 115n
Kumaniecki, K. 20n
Kümmel, W. G. 234n

Lane, R. T. 17n
Lapidge, M. 280n
Lattimore, R. A. 20n, 29, 157
Lauffer, S. 23n
Ledbetter, G. M. 20n
Leighton, S. R. 20n, 41, 55
Lesher, J. H. 23n
Lévy, C. 214n
Lewis, C. S. 196
Leyerle, B. 311n
Lilla, S. R. C. 218n, 311n, 315n, 318n
Lincoln, A. T. 233n
Lindner, G. B. 308n
Lloyd, A. C. 20n, 117n
Long, A. A. 4, 21n, 22n, 48–9, 55, 56, 123, 124, 126, 131n, 132n, 133n, 149, 201, 205, 214n, 280n, 281n, 292, 313n, 316n
Long, H. S. 132n
Longo Auricchio, F. 116n, 121n
Lord, C. 19n, 20n
Lovejoy, A. O. 23n
Lucchetta, G. A. 25n
Luschnat, O. 23n, 24n, 147n, 148n
Lutz, C. E. 317n
Lynch, J. P. 18n, 19n
Lyonnet, S. 237n

Machiavelli, N. 88
MacInnes, H. 135n
Maguinness, W. S. 23n
Malherbe, A. J. 19n, 50, 53, 147n, 148n, 221, 227, 233n, 235n, 238, 241, 261, 269, 278n, 313n, 314n, 320n
Manning, C. E. 22n

INDEX OF MODERN SCHOLARS

Manuli, P. 22n
Marcovich, M. 117n
Marcus, J. 224
Marcus, R. 215n
Marg, W. 77n, 213n
Marks, J. 16n
Marquardt, J. 196n, 315n, 316n, 318n, 319n
Marti, B. M. 16
Martin, C. 174n
Martin, D. 230, 232, 237n, 238, 241, 261, 262n, 263n
Martin, H. 235n
Martin, T. 225
Martyn, J. L. 263n
Mathiopoulos, M. 23n
Mattern-Parkes, S. 22n
McLelland, J. C. 314n
Meeks, W. 232, 237n
Méhat, A. 310n
Meineke, A. 122
Mekler, S. 119n
Ménage, G. 19n
Merlan, P. 23n
Mette, H. J. 20n
Michaelis, W. 2, 234n
Miller, W. 147n
Mills, M. J. 20n
Milobenski, E. 17n
Mitsis, P. 88, 280n
Moles, J.L. 119n
Moraux, P. 7, 8, 19n, 75n, 76n
Morgan, J. R. 196n
Most, G. W. 2, 11, 16, 21n
Motto, A. L. 283n
Moxnes, H. 236
Mueller, I., von 196n, 315n, 316n, 318n, 319n
Mühlenberg, E. 25n
Mulvany, C. M. 19n
Murphy-O'Connor, J. 237n
Mynors, R. A. B. 23n

Naddaff, R. 313n
Nehamas, A. 46n
Neyrey, J. H. 233n
Nilsson, M. P. 278n
Nisbet, R. 23n
Nisbet, R. G. M. 118n
Nock, A. D. 311n
Nugent, S. G. 23n, 153
Nussbaum, M. 2, 5, 16n–17n, 20n, 49, 94, 114, 117n, 132n, 138, 139, 155, 235n, 313n, 316n, 320n

O'Connor, J. J. 115n
O'Daly, G. J. P. 17n
O'Neil, E. 21n, 59
Obbink, D. ix, 110, 117n, 118n
Oberhelman, S. M. 150n
Olbricht, T. H. ix, 2, 224
Oldfather, W. A. 130, 196, 218n, 239
Oliver, J. H. 307n
Olivieri, A. 118n, 307n
Ortiz Garcia, P. 25n
Ortkemper, F. J. 228
Osborne, E. 311n
Ostwald, M. 18n, 19n

Paquet, L. 57
Parker, C. P. 318n
Pauw, D. A. 233n
Penella, R. J. 77n
Perrot, C. 237n
Pesce, D. 25n
Pesce, M. 273
Petit, F. 215n, 216n
Pfitzner, V. 226, 235n
Philippson, R. 118n
Phillips, J. 235n
Piccaluga, G. 14
Piper, J. 228
Pistelli, H. 77n
Plezia, M. 7, 19n
Pohlenz, M. 21n, 22n, 131n, 213n, 215n, 223, 233n, 234n
Pomeroy, A. J. 22n, 131n, 132n, 147n, 217n
Porter, F. C. 234n
Porter, J. 88
Poster, C. 234n
Price, A. W. 21n, 117n
Procopé, J. 22n, 111, 113, 114, 116n, 117n, 121n
Puglia, E. 83

Quasten, J. 309n, 310n

Rabbow, P. 22n
Rabel, R. J. 20n, 22n
Rackham, H. 148n
Radice, R. 210, 213n, 216n
Ramelli, I. 25n
Reale, G. 75n

Reardon, B. P. 184, 196n
Reggiani, C. K. 210, 213n, 216n
Rich, A. N. M. 65n
Riedweg, C. 75n, 77n
Rieks, R. 23n
Riesco, J. 280n
Ringeltaube, H. 111, 113, 114, 121n
Rist, J. M. 45n, 56, 88, 131n, 280n, 313n
Robbins, F. E. 23n
Robertson, E. F. 115n
Robin, L. 23n
Rodríguez Martín, J.-D. 17n
Rolfe, J. C. 17n
Rollin, B. 108
Rorty, A. O. 20n
Rose, V. 7, 8, 19n, 20n
Roskam, G. 24n, 147n, 148n
Rouse, W. H. D. 115
Rousselle, A. 315n
Royse, J. R. 215n
Rubin, S. 279n, 283n
Ruiz Gito, J. M. 25n
Runia, D. T. 51, 214n, 311n
Russell, D. A. 149n
Rüther, T. 314n
Rutter, N. K. 2, 21n

Sampley, J. P. 282n
Sand, A. 234n
Sandbach, F. H. 11, 219n
Sanders, E. P. 281n, 282n
Schenkeveld, D. M. 23n
Schenkl, H. 133n
Schiesaro, A. 24n, 148n, 279n
Schimmel, A. 214n
Schimmel, S. 22n
Schmeling, G. L. 196n
Schmeller, T. 268, 276
Schoedel, W. R. 237n
Schofield, M. 94
Schowalter, D. N. 308n
Schrage, W. 281n
Schwartz, E. 308n
Schweitzer, A. 241
Scourfield, J. H. D. 20n
Seddon, K. 25n
Sedley, D. N. 4, 9, 21n, 24n, 49, 55, 56, 115n, 116n, 132n, 149n, 205, 214n
Segal, C. 120n
Sellars, J. 21n
Sevenster, J. N. 234n, 280n, 283n
Shackleton Bailey, D. R. 11

Sharples, R. W. 11, 19n, 22n
Shaw, T. 313n, 316n
Shea, C. 196n
Sider, D. 95
Sihvola, J. 2, 18n, 20n, 23n, 55, 235n
Siker, J. 236n
Simon, B. 172, 173
Singleton, D. 23n
Skinner, B. F. 52
Smith, A. 47n
Smith, J. W. 21n
Smith, J. Z. 233n
Smith, P. C. 235n
Snyman, A. H. 234n
Sollenberger, M. G. 18n, 19n
Sorabji, R. 2, 3, 10, 15, 20n, 21n, 24n, 25n, 75n, 88-95, 97, 100, 102, 104, 106, 107, 117n, 219n, 233n, 313n, 316n
Sorel, G. 23n
Spanneut, M. 21n, 313n
Spengel L., von 77n
Spinoza, B., de 213
Stacey, W. D. 234n
Städele, A. 77n
Stählin, O. 307n, 309n, 314n, 317n, 321n
Steinmetz, P. 10, 21n, 22n, 24n
Stendahl, K. 227
Stevens, J. A. 21n, 55, 56
Stoneman, R. 196n
Stowers, S. 13, 25n, 230, 232, 237n, 254, 265n
Straaten, M., van 9, 10
Strange, S. K. 21n, 90
Striker, G. 20n, 126
Sumney, J. L. 2, 225, 235n
Swancutt, D. M. 311n

Tannehill, R. C. 281n
Tarán, L. 18n
Tatum, J. 196n
Taylor, C. C. W. 54, 56
Taylor, M. 23n
Tazi, N. 313n
Teggart, F. J. 23n
Temkin, O. 315n
Tepedino Guerra, A. 116n, 121n
Terian, A. 215n
Theissen, G. 229
Thesleff, H. 68, 75n, 77n, 78n
Thom, J. C. 15, 22n, 67, 75n, 77n, 78n, 148n, 280n

Thompson, J. W. 235n
Thraede, K. 23n
Thurén, L. 225, 235n
Tieleman, T. 2, 3, 10, 20n, 21n, 104, 119n
Tissol, G. 158, 160, 174n
Todd, R. 280n
Toohey, P. 2
Trapp, M. B. 12, 15n, 23n
Tsouna, V. 54, 88, 117n, 119n, 120n
Tulin, A. 23n

Usener, H. 87, 92, 96, 109, 209

Valantasis, R. 311n
Van Doren, C. 23n
van Geytenbeek, A. C. 318n
Vander Waerdt, P. A. 214n
Verbeke, G. 280n
Vernant, J.-P. 313n
Viano, C. 20n
Vitelli, C. 20n
Vlastos, G. 115n
Voelke, A. J. 280n
Vögtle, A. 222, 223, 233n, 234n
Völker, W. 23n, 25n
von Staden, H. 319n

Wachsmuth, C. 122, 132n, 147n, 148n, 205, 217n
Walbank, F. W. 123
Walcot, P. 17n
Walzer, R. 195
Ware, J. 23n, 24n, 25n, 267
Warner, R. 157
Warren, J. 106
Webb, R. 320n
Wehrli, F. 11, 19n, 22n, 75n
Weiss, H. D. 16
Welborn, L. 225
Wendland, P. 318n

West, M. L. 23n
Whitaker, G. H. 212, 216n, 217n, 220n
White, L. M. ix, 22n, 23n, 25n, 75n, 284, 307n, 308n, 311n, 313n, 316n, 317n
White, N. P. 21n
White, S. A. 22n
Wiesen, D. S. 4
Wigodsky, M. 96, 120n
Wild, R. A. 77n
Wilke, K. 102, 103, 104, 113, 116n, 117n
Wilken, R. 135n
Williams, B. 90
Willis, W. L. 237
Wilson, E. O. 16n
Wilson, M. 279n
Wilson, W. 307n
Wimbush, V. 227, 236n
Wimmer, A. 235n
Winkler, J. J. 193, 197n
Winston, D. 23n, 25n, 201, 215n, 218n, 219n, 220n
Winterbottom, M. 23n
Wisse, J. 4, 17n, 234n
Witherington, B. 235n
Withington, E. T. 17n
Wolfson, H. A. 207
Woods, M. 46n
Wormell, D. E. W. 18n
Wright, M. R. 23n
Wright, R. A. 25n, 136

Xenakis, J. 135n

Yarbrough, O. L. 237n
Young-Bruehl, E. 16n

Zeller, E. 65n, 278n
Zerbe, G. 228, 236n
Zumkeller, A. 17n
Zupko, J. 90